IN THE TIME OF HARVEST

IN THE
TIME OF HARVEST

ESSAYS IN HONOR OF
Abba Hillel Silver
ON THE OCCASION OF HIS
70TH
BIRTHDAY

Editor

DANIEL JEREMY SILVER

Board of Editors

SOLOMON B. FREEHOF	EMANUEL NEUMANN
DANIEL JEREMY SILVER	SOLOMON ZEITLIN

THE MACMILLAN COMPANY   NEW YORK
COLLIER–MACMILLAN LTD., LONDON

"A Highway of Nations" by Dr. Moshe Davis will appear in a
forthcoming book entitled *The Emergence of Conservative Judaism,* to be published by The Jewish Publication Society of America,
and is here included by the kind permission of that publisher.

FIRST PRINTING

THE MACMILLAN COMPANY, NEW YORK
COLLIER-MACMILLAN CANADA, LTD., GALT, ONTARIO
DIVISION OF THE CROWELL-COLLIER PUBLISHING COMPANY

PRINTED IN THE UNITED STATES OF AMERICA

LIBRARY OF CONGRESS CATALOG CARD NUMBER: 62-21613

CONTENTS

Introduction vii

Abba Hillel Silver—An Appreciation HAROLD P. MANSON 1

Gleanings of an Abundant Harvest 28
 Edited by DANIEL JEREMY SILVER

Bibliography *Edited by* MIRIAM LEIKIND 99

The Ingathering of the Exiles and an Exemplary Nation 121
 DAVID BEN-GURION

The Levites Among Arabian Tribes IZHAK BEN-ZVI 129

"A Highway of Nations" 136
 (*A Chapter in Nineteenth Century America-Eretz
 Yisrael Activities*) MOSHE DAVIS

Israel in the World of Ideas ABBA EBAN 146

Paul—What Manner of Jew? MORTON S. ENSLIN 153

A Hitherto Unknown Jewish Traveler to India 170
 The Travels of Rabbi David D'Beth Hillel to India
 WALTER J. FISCHEL

The Chuppah SOLOMON B. FREEHOF 186

Biblical Archaeology and Reform Judaism 194
 NELSON GLUECK

Religion and the Free Society ROBERT GORDIS 200

Israel—*A Pilot Project for Total Development of* 215
 Water Resources WALTER CLAY LOWDERMILK

The Oldest Known Synagogue Record Book of Continental   227
    North America 1720–1721   JACOB R. MARCUS

David's Reign in Hebron and the Conquest of Jerusalem   235
    BENJAMIN MAZAR

Israel and the Diaspora   EMANUEL NEUMANN   245

On Toynbee's Use of the Term *Syriac* for One of His   255
    Societies   HARRY M. ORLINSKY

American Cultural Influence on Israel   RAPHAEL PATAI   270

A Jewish State in Midian—*The English Sources on*   284
    Paul Friedmann's Scheme of 1891–2
    OSKAR K. RABINOWICZ

Ben Sira and the Nonexistence of the Synagogue   320
    A Study in Historical Method   ELLIS RIVKIN

"Son of Man"   SAMUEL SANDMEL   355

"The Sprouting of the Horn of the Son of David,"   368
    A New Source from the Beginnings of the Doenme
    Sect in Salonica   GERSHOM SCHOLEM

The Future of the Zionist Movement   MOSHE SHARETT   387

The Idea of Redemption in Hassidic Thought   401
    ZALMAN SHAZAR

Monarchy   DANIEL JEREMY SILVER   421

On Some Obscure Passages in the Book of Psalms I-XXXV   433
    NAPHTALI H. TUR-SINAI

The Origin of the Idea of the Messiah   SOLOMON ZEITLIN   447

The Contributors   461

INTRODUCTION

RABBI ABBA HILLEL SILVER came to the Temple in August of 1917. A young man, only two years past his ordination, he took over one of the leading congregations in America and has served it faithfully and led it courageously ever since.

Looking forward to his seventieth birthday, and mindful of forty-five years of consecrated ministry, the congregation was eager to dignify the occasion in a way which would express their abiding friendship and admiration. It was decided that the most appropriate tribute would be a publication of a Jubilee Volume which would set out Dr. Silver's own activities, list his writings, briefly indicate his concerns, and contain contributions by rabbis, scholars, and world leaders who have shared his interests and worked with him in common cause. It was felt Dr. Silver would appreciate this contribution to scholarship more than any personal token. It was known that many of his friends and fellow workers were eager to add their well-wishes to those of the congregation. It was anticipated that the community at large would benefit by such a delineation of his life and accomplishments. The publication of such a work was undertaken and made possible through the generosity of many of his Temple friends and is intended as a statement of their respect.

We are grateful to Rabbi Daniel Jeremy Silver, who undertook the many-sided responsibilities of editing this volume, and to Drs. Solomon B. Freehof, Emanuel Neumann, and Solomon Zeitlin who, in addition to Rabbi Daniel Silver, lent their advice as a Board of Editors. As is usual in the case of such a *Festschrift*, no attempt was made to circumscribe the subject matter of the individual contributors. Their essays represent their expression of personal and scholarly homage. However, it will be noted that by and large the articles center on Dr. Silver's primary areas of concern: Judaism and Jewish survival, the Bible and Rabbinic scholarship, the common weal and mankind's betterment.

What needs to be added is only a word of loving respect on behalf of those whom Dr. Silver has helped to educate in their faith, consecrate in their marriage, find rootage in their community, support in their grief, and establish in their civic undertakings by the quality and example of his person and by the challenge and force of his intellect and his preaching.

EDGAR A. HAHN   A. M. LUNTZ
CO-CHAIRMEN, *The Abba Hillel Silver Jubilee Committee*
BERTRAM J. KROHNGOLD
PRESIDENT, *The Temple*

As the cold of snow in the time of harvest,
So is a faithful messenger to him that sendeth him;
For he refresheth the soul of his master.
                                    PROVERBS 25:13

IN THE TIME OF HARVEST

Abba Hillel Silver—An Appreciation

HAROLD P. MANSON

*

A REMARKABLE UNITY pervades the still-incomplete lifework of Abba Hillel Silver. His entire career runs in a straight line toward an almost inevitable meeting with an exacting assignment from history.

The nature of that assignment was decreed by "the inescapable logic of events" (a phrase that would figure prominently in his public utterances). His historic task was to realize the revolutionary program which had been set in motion by Theodore Herzl in 1897—to secure international recognition for the reconstitution of an independent Jewish State.

An American rabbi, preeminent as a leader of Reform Judaism, but nurtured by East European Jewish traditions and folkways, and bound in love to the masses of his people; undeviatingly committed from early childhood to the Herzlian concept of political Zionism; schooled in the processes of political action in a democratic society; endowed with a powerful intellect, a commanding personality, and oratorical skills that could persuade masses and move them to action, Dr. Silver was perfectly cast for his role by life itself.

*

The S. S. *Kœln,* out of Bremen, reached New York harbor on a June day in 1902. Among the new immigrants whom it brought to Ellis Island was a thin, dark, curly-haired, nine-year-old boy, decked out in a sailor suit for the occasion. Abba Silver, held in tow by his mother, Dinah, had arrived together with his older brother and a sister to rejoin their father, Rabbi Moses Silver, in the new home which he had established in America. Behind them was the Lithuanian town of Neinstadt-Schirwindt where the six Silver children were born—and also a tradition of learning and scholarship which they would transplant in the exciting new land that welcomed them.

One of the dominant themes of Abba Hillel Silver's later life and action was born on that day: belief in America as a force for good in the world. He would come to know America intimately—her vastness and diversity, but mostly her power to achieve a better life—and would eagerly make his own contribution to her civilization.

The America he first encountered was New York's lower East Side. His childhood in the family's tenement on Madison Street was altogether happy. The drabness of tenement life at the turn of the century seems to have been shut out. Here, as in Neinstadt, his home was a place of scholarship, tolerantly administered by Rabbi Moses Silver.

The third in a succession of ordained rabbis, Moses Silver did not make the rabbinate his profession. In Neinstadt he had earned a modest livelihood in the soap business, but learning was the essence of his life. In New York he taught in a Hebrew school and also gave free instruction to many gifted youngsters. He remained dedicated to scholarship until his death at the age of eighty-seven at his home in Jerusalem, where he and his wife settled in 1924. Shortly before his eightieth birthday Moses Silver published two volumes of a Biblical commentary, *Hishukei Kessef* (*Filigree of Silver*), which were well received by both scholars and laymen and which reflect his learning and his piety. The range of his intellectual interests was wide and included not only traditional Biblical and Talmudic studies, but modern Hebrew literature and the secular humanities as well.

There were not many Jewish homes at the turn of the century in which such coexistence was actively encouraged or even acceptable. Traditional Jewish learning and "secularism" were generally in conflict, giving rise to fanaticism and intolerance on both sides. Moses Silver taught his children to view Judaism in its entirety and to reconcile, rather than accentuate, apparent diversities.

Zionist thought was, inevitably, a central influence in such a home. Heroic Biblical figures inspired visions of a reborn Jewish nation. The essays of Ahad Ha-Am, the philosopher of cultural Zionism, were read and discussed in Hebrew. The lifework of Theodore Herzl, the founder of modern political Zionism, was followed avidly by the entire family.

In 1904, the year of Herzl's untimely death, the two Silver boys formed the Dr. Herzl Zion Club. It was the very first Zionist Hebrew-speaking group in America and was to serve as a training ground for the future leadership of the movement. Its first president was thirteen-year-old Maxwell Silver, who was succeeded two years later by Abba Hillel Silver. The club held debates and performed plays in the

Hebrew language. A half-century later one of the group reminisced: "Abba always played the young hero, with flashing eyes and swordplay. He was built for the role. He looked the part."

The club's membership included Emanuel Neumann, who would later head the Zionist Organization of America and be Silver's closest associate in the political leadership of United States Zionism; the future Hebrew educator Israel Chipkin; a number of subsequent leaders of the rabbinate, including Barnett R. Brickner, Abraham Feldman, Benjamin Friedman, Jesse Schwartz, as well as many others who were destined to make significant contributions to American Jewish life. Of this élite group and its meetings on the lower East Side, Neumann wrote in 1953: "I joined . . . on a wintry Saturday evening, when the club was celebrating the Bar Mitzvah of the president. Its president then and its natural leader for years thereafter was Abba Hillel Silver. His was a firm rule, tempered always with a saving sense of humor. He was loved, admired and obeyed. His word at the end of a long debate had the ring of finality and was accepted without demur. The very quality of his voice brought conviction."

One of the recorded incidents in the history of the Dr. Herzl Zion Club is prophetic. The club had been plunged into ideological controversy almost from its inception. At first, the anti-Zionist views of the rigidly Orthodox left it without a meeting place, but for the home of Rabbi Moses Silver, to whom the boys turned for guidance and support. Finally, the group received permission to meet in the nonsectarian Educational Alliance. With the advent of a new director of that institution, the club was again facing homelessness. Its name was considered too "political." One day the director was making the rounds with one of the benefactresses of the Educational Alliance. On entering the room where the Dr. Herzl Zion Club boys met, they were astonished to find the meeting being conducted in Hebrew. The director and the good lady lectured the group severely on their poor display of "Americanism" in choosing to speak an alien tongue. When they finished, a tall boy in his early teens stood up and announced calmly that the Dr. Herzl Zion Club identified itself with the Zionist movement, that it would continue to use the language which David had found suitable for the composition of the Psalms, and through which Isaiah had expressed his vision of universal peace and justice. Quite speechless, the director and the lady withdrew. The Dr. Herzl Zion Club continued to conduct meetings in Hebrew at the Educational Alliance—and Abba Hillel Silver had won his first ideological battle against an attitude which he would encounter and best time and again in his career.

In 1911, after graduating from Townsend Harris High School, where he was one of the top students, Abba Hillel Silver took a step which must have been anathema to some of his neighbors and also worried a number of his young Zionist comrades. Like Maxwell a few years earlier, he decided to enter the Hebrew Union College in Cincinnati—the center and stronghold of Reform Judaism. To the ultra-Orthodox this was a few steps short of apostasy. To some of the Herzl Zion boys, mindful of the anti-Zionist attitude which then permeated Reform Jewry, it represented a threat that their leader might be taken over by the "enemy." He, however, was certain that he and other friends who were to accompany or follow him to Cincinnati would ultimately occupy and dominate the citadel of Liberal Judaism. Interestingly enough—perhaps typically—the Silver boys' decision received warm encouragement and support from their father.

Accepted by the Hebrew Union College, he also enrolled in the University of Cincinnati with the intention of completing his rabbinical studies simultaneously with his general college education. He carried this off with resounding success, accomplishing nine years' work at the College in four years and graduating from both institutions in 1915.

The motif of leadership runs throughout his college years and is fresh in the memory of fellow students.

Young Rabbi Silver's first pulpit was in Wheeling, West Virginia, at the Eoff Street Temple. Wheeling was chiefly significant in his life for the presence of Virginia Horkheimer, daughter of a leader of the community, and the product of five generations on American soil. The courtship outlasted his stay in that city and was continued from Cleveland until their marriage in 1923.

This wonderfully happy union must occupy a central place in any evaluation of Rabbi Silver's career. Virginia Silver, a personality in her own right, has been content to realize herself as wife to a remarkable man and mother to two fine sons. Living in the atmosphere of love and support which she created, Rabbi Silver received an added measure of confidence and strength for his career. He also received valuable counsel—for Virginia Silver proved to be very astute in taking the measure of a person.

Silver was all of twenty-four when, after two years in Wheeling, he received a call to one of the most important pulpits in America—Cleveland's Tifereth Israel (The Temple). From 1917, the year of his arrival in Cleveland, it has been his beloved spiritual home and the workshop of his creative spiritual life.

There were, of course, doubts about his maturity. He was, after all, succeeding the venerable Rabbi Moses J. Gries, and skeptics anticipated a fiasco. His first sermon, which has become something of a legend, swept away all reservations. An electrified congregation came away with the proud knowledge that they had chosen as their spiritual leader a most extraordinary man.

Not that it was all smooth sailing thereafter. The words which rang out from Rabbi Silver's pulpit were not designed to please, but to summon to moral and social action. His uncompromising Zionism, his internationalism in a Midwest stronghold of isolationism, his espousal of the cause of organized labor long before labor became a major force in American society, his attacks against some of the most powerful economic and political interests in the state and nation— these and other views were extremely distasteful to some leaders of the city. Conflict and controversy were inevitable, as were victory and vindication for the unyielding rabbi who had won the hearts and minds of the congregation and large sections of the community. It became clear at the very outset that Abba Hillel Silver could be held only on his own terms.

The beginnings of his work in Cleveland were interrupted by the First World War. He served in France where his ministry to the Allied troops won him the Academic Palms as Officier de l'Instruction Publique.

Upon his return he plunged into the work of making The Temple not only the largest, but perhaps the most progressive and educationally creative Liberal Jewish congregation in America. Two years after his arrival the membership had risen from 725 families to 916. Five years later, in 1922, Rabbi Silver laid the cornerstone for the inspiring edifice where the congregation has worshiped since 1924. In 1959 a great new wing was added to The Temple, which today boasts a large school, a fine library, and an exceptional museum of Jewish religious and ceremonial art, among the many other educational and cultural facilities available to its membership of 2,400 families. This many-faceted institution is now jointly administered by Rabbi Abba Hillel Silver and his son, Daniel Jeremy Silver, the fifth in the family's unbroken chain of rabbis and scholars—a moving and poetic culmination of one of the senior rabbi's most cherished dreams.

An achievement like The Temple would for most men represent total fulfillment, leaving little time or inclination for other endeavors. The very process of building and physical expansion can become an all-absorbing occupation. Spiritual and moral purposes have too often been trapped and entombed in the cornerstones of magnificent edifices. Their size and complexity impose heavy administrative demands on the spiritual leader, who is in constant danger of being transformed into a corporation executive or professional fund raiser. But Rabbi Silver has kept the emphasis where it belongs: on Jewish teaching and worship.

Moreover, the daily tasks of the rabbinate, however significant and rewarding in themselves, could not contain his searching mind. He heard other voices. The love of scholarship could not be stilled and he somehow found time to study and to write—though never to the extent that he wished.

In 1925 he received the degree of Doctor of Divinity from Hebrew Union College. His thesis was later expanded into his first published book, *Messianic Speculations in Israel* (1927)—regarded by scholars as a classic contribution to the study of Messianic concepts. The subject matter is highly illuminating in relation to Silver's total personality. Superficially it would appear that nothing could be more alien to the spirit of one who is so totally committed to action in the modern world than the mystical quest for the Messianic era and its meaning. Nevertheless, it is precisely this subject which absorbed him as a young scholar and which has recurred frequently in his writings. He applied his keen intelligence to gain a fuller understanding of the Messianic motif which is unmistakable in Jewish experience over the centuries. The qualities of Jewish mystical thought—its fervor and scope—appealed to him, though he firmly rejected mystical solutions to man's problems. He brought these qualities to his work in the rabbinate and the Zionist movement.

In attempting to define the unique nature of Silver's leadership of the Zionist movement, the author wrote in 1949: "No real understanding of Dr. Silver—the man and the leader—is possible without an appreciation of the fact that he is first and foremost *Rabbi* Silver, a person of deep spiritual convictions and a profound scholar. . . . He regards his pulpit in Cleveland, Ohio, with the reverence and devotion of one for whom there can be no greater calling in life. If we bear this fact in mind, many things which at first glance appear mystifying become crystal clear: why he underwent the physical discomfort of spending many days of each week on trains and planes, commuting between New York and Cleveland or Washington and Cleveland—this over a period of six years—in order to be back in his pulpit on the Sabbath; why, even in the midst of the most severe crises in his political life, he could be found at The Temple happily engaged in teaching a class of children; why, surrounded by admiring multitudes in New York, he would confide to his friends that he yearned for the peace of his study; why he always spoke so wistfully of the days when he could devote himself to Jewish scholarship—the days when he wrote the profound *Messianic Speculations in Israel*.

"When we view Dr. Silver in the light of his dedication to the spiritual essence of Judaism, we are better able to understand his unshakable faith that the Zionist cause would triumph, no matter what the obstacles, as well as the quality akin to mysticism which is present even in his most 'political' utterances—a quality which some regarded as a contradiction of his basic character, but which those close to him understood to be the true expression of that character."

Two decades of intermittent but impressive scholarly activity were abruptly halted when Silver was called to the leadership of the American Zionist movement—though this phase of his creative life was energetically resumed following his withdrawal from Zionist politics. He wrote three more books prior to his assumption of active political leadership. *The Democratic Impulse in Jewish History* (1928) is a compact presentation of his view of Judaism as essentially a people's religion and of Jewish creativity as people-based. The primary role occupied by the Jewish people in his concept of Jewish history would determine his approach to all aspects of Jewish life—including, of course, the Zionist program which, to his mind, required a strong popular foundation. The interaction between people and leader—each drawing inspiration from the other, with the former always paramount—would be a fascinating subject of inquiry throughout his life. He would also have the opportunity, given to few scholars, of translating his concepts into living history.

Silver foresaw the vast economic changes that would sweep over America in the 1930's. In *Religion in a Changing World* (1930) he outlined a program toward a just social order and described the role that a vigorous religion would have to assume. It was in the prophetic tradition. The volume was for many months a nonfiction best-seller.

In *World Crisis and Jewish Survival* (1941), a collection of essays (including his 1940 Dudleian Lecture at Harvard), the scholar is embattled against the then-triumphant Nazi tyranny, and there are signs of the emerging political leader. There is also a ringing confidence in the Jewish people's ability to survive the holocaust and to go forward toward the fulfillment of its role in history.

With his passionate devotion to social justice, Rabbi Silver was impelled to take stands on vital issues in the life of his city, state, and country. His Sunday morning sermons, which supplement the regular Temple services on the Jewish Sabbath, quickly became events of community-wide importance, attracting huge audiences of both Jews and non-Jews. One of the most civic-minded cities of

America, Cleveland responded warmly to Abba Hillel Silver, and forward-looking citizens turned to him for guidance and leadership. His unabated popularity has been phenomenal, not merely because he managed to remain a "prophet with honor" in his own community for so many years, but because he has achieved this without aiming at popularity. Never concerned with his professional career as an end in itself, he sought no favors and did not tailor his opinions and actions to conform to prevailing attitudes. Indeed, his words and actions were frequently disturbing to the comfortable and socially unconcerned.

After the First World War, when Cleveland, like so many other American cities, fell prey to the Palmer anti-Red hysteria, Rabbi Silver took the lead in restoring civic sanity. In 1921 he engaged in a running debate with no less formidable an opponent than Newton D. Baker, the former Secretary of War in Wilson's cabinet and one-time Mayor of Cleveland. The issue was the open shop versus the closed shop, with Silver arguing vigorously in support of the labor unions. He resigned from the Chamber of Commerce, of which Baker was then president. But vindication was not long in coming and Cleveland's unions achieved the closed shop.

In 1928 he initiated an enterprise in social pioneering which had tremendous effects. It was due to his vision and energy that The Temple became the birthplace of the unemployment insurance movement in Ohio and perhaps also in the United States. Eight years of unremitting effort on the part of Rabbi Silver and his associates resulted in the passage by the Ohio State Legislature of an unemployment insurance bill which he helped to frame.

During the depression years he was a militant champion of organized labor and an unrelenting foe of the "wreckers" among Ohio's industrialists and financiers. With the intensity of a Biblical prophet he denounced by name the prominent citizens who qualified as "financial jugglers" and "pirates." His zeal stimulated public protests and reform movements which made decency and social responsibility prevail.

The importance and scope of Rabbi Silver's contributions to his community may be gathered from the section on Cleveland in John Gunther's *Inside U.S.A.* (1947) where he is described as "probably its most distinguished citizen."

All of these works, however, were prologue and preparation for the chief task which was still to come. Silver had retained his intimate association with the Zionist movement from the days of the

Dr. Herzl Zion Club. By 1920 he was well known in Zionist circles as a brilliant young orator and was invited to address the international Zionist conference in London that year, sharing the platform with such eminent personalities as Lord Balfour, Lord Cecil, Dr. Chaim Weizmann, and Max Nordau. In the rift that developed between Dr. Weizmann and Louis D. Brandeis, the leader of American Zionism, Silver strongly supported Brandeis. The conflict, which was ideological in part, involved the control and administration of philanthropic funds raised in the United States for work in Palestine through the efforts of American Zionists. Silver was a loyal member of the group headed by Brandeis and Judge Julian W. Mack, and when Brandeis and Mack withdrew from leadership of the Zionist Organization of America, he went with them. He returned to active service in the movement in the late twenties, accepting Dr. Weizmann's leadership. But his early differences with the head of the World Zionist Organization would recur periodically and, at one critical moment, decisively.

With the rise of Nazism in Germany, Silver reacted with characteristic militancy. He was not content merely with denunciation of Nazi persecutions. Together with Samuel Untermeyer he organized the anti-Nazi boycott in the United States. This brought him into sharp conflict with those American Jewish leaders who objected to "provocative" actions which, they held, might worsen the plight of the Jews in Germany. His dire predictions, based on a keen awareness of the evil forces which had been unleashed in the world, were borne out by subsequent horrors.

The immediate importance of Palestine became increasingly apparent with the growing acuteness of the Jewish refugee problem. Huge sums of money were required for the rescue and rehabilitation of the largest possible number of European Jewish refugees—and the greater holocaust was still to come. Regarding this task as the solemn responsibility of American Jewry, Silver undertook a leading role in fund raising, becoming chairman of the United Palestine Appeal in 1938 and also co-chairman of the United Jewish Appeal. The years of his leadership in this sphere were marked by greatly intensified activity and by the establishment and attainment of ever higher fund-raising goals. It is well worth noting that some of the highest peaks in the history of American Jewish fund raising were reached under the leadership of a Zionist rabbi. It would appear—later organizational mythology notwithstanding—that the Zionist label was not a liability in the raising of "big money" and that successful leadership is not necessarily confined to successful businessmen.

In the midst of his fund-raising efforts Dr. Silver was primarily concerned with Zionist statesmanship, rather than mere philanthropy. He made the United Palestine Appeal an instrument of education, which served to prepare American Jewry for the decisive political role that it was to play some years later. He had remained true to the Herzlian vision.

When the Zionist Revolution entered its climactic phase during the Second World War, no cause seemed more hopeless than the goal of a Jewish State in Palestine. The phenomenal progress of the *Yishuv,* the courageous Jewish community of Palestine, and its significant contributions to the war effort were rewarded by the White Paper policy barring Jewish refugees from the country. While the slaughter of European Jewry was being carried out with methodical efficiency by the Nazis, Great Britain left no doubt about her determination to scuttle her international obligation to assist the development of a Jewish National Home. Nevertheless, World Zionist diplomacy, based in London, clung resolutely to the hope that the partnership with Britain, which had begun so promisingly in 1917 with the issuance of the Balfour Declaration, would be resumed. In such circumstances the very idea of an independent Jewish State was fading fast from the world of political reality, even as this idea became the sustaining hope of the Jewish people, even as the *Yishuv* was readying itself for the decisive struggle, and even as the Zionist movement was confronted by a never-to-be-repeated opportunity to place its case high on the international agenda and to press for Jewish statehood as an act of world restitution and justice.

Only the entry of a powerful new force in support of the Zionist cause could avert a political disaster and infuse new strength and confidence for the major battles that lay ahead. That force was—had to be—the United States of America. The pivotal fact of the political struggle for Jewish statehood was that its center was shifting—at first slowly, almost imperceptibly, and later with tradtion-shattering velocity—from London to Washington, as the center of world leadership generally was moving to an America which had neither sought nor prepared itself for such a role.

To anticipate this major trend and bring the Zionist cause into the mainstream of a historic process, and then to accelerate that process to win international approval of a Jewish State—this was the challenge to Zionist statesmanship. A new type of leadership, closely attuned to the American scene but motivated by classic Zionist concepts, was required. This became the monumental task of Abba Hillel Silver.

He had perceived the trend even before the beginning of the Second World War. A conversation, which took place between Emanuel Neumann and himself at the Twenty-first World Zionist Congress, held in 1939 in Geneva under the shadows of impending war and the recently issued British White Paper, is highly significant in the light of later developments. Neumann urged him to aspire to active political leadership of the Zionist movement in America. He replied that a world war would surely break out soon, that one of its probable results would be a shift of the center of gravity in world affairs to America, and that this would be the appropriate moment for his entry into the political arena. Neumann, then returning to America from a seven-year stay in Palestine, resolved to prepare the ground.

The American Emergency Committee for Zionist Affairs, representing all major parties in the United States, was established in New York in 1940. In the three years that followed Neumann struggled to create a foundation for Zionist political action. Hampered by the inadequate commitment of Zionist colleagues to such a course, as well as by budgetary problems, he nevertheless managed to bring about the formation of the American Palestine Committee, numbering hundreds of members of both Houses of Congress, cabinet members, governors, and many other influential figures in public life. Subsequently he also fostered the formation of a special national committee of Christian clergy, the Christian Council on Palestine, and initiated other important activities in the field of public relations. Official contacts between the Zionist movement and the State Department in Washington were developed and cultivated. However, Neumann was the first to decry the inadequacy of Zionist efforts against the background of slaughter in Europe, perfidy in London, and silence in Washington. He voiced his protest by resigning his post. The ways of personal diplomacy had brought Zionist polity to a dead end. The old methods of *shtadlanut,* the approaches to governmental leaders by eminent Jews reinforced by nothing more than personal prominence and charm, had been thoroughly discredited.

The new voice and new approach were sounded on May 2, 1943, at the National Conference of the United Palestine Appeal in Philadelphia. Dr. Silver unfolded the Jewish people's condition in all its shocking reality. Then he took the offensive. He attacked not only British policy—criticism of which had been frequently voiced by other Zionist orators—but challenged the attitude of President Franklin Delano Roosevelt himself. ("The tragic problems of the Jewish people in the world today cannot be solved by chiefs of government or promi-

nent officials sending us Rosh Hashanah greetings!") He next summoned the Zionist movement to carry out a program of political
action, prophetically describing the outcome:

"We are confident that the inescapable logic of events will in due
time make Palestine a Jewish State. For a shorter or longer time this
may be halted or retarded, but the rebirth of Israel as a nation in its
historic home is as sure to come to pass as God's word never returns
empty until it has accomplished that for which it was sent.

"The inescapable logic of events! When all the doors of the
world will be closed to our people, then the hand of destiny will force
open the door of Palestine. And that hour is rapidly approaching."

His assumption of active political leadership was now an inevitable—and for his opponents, an unavoidable—development. Dr. Weizmann had suggested it in 1942 during a visit to America. He had
developed a high appreciation of Silver's talents during the latter's
1942 visit to war-torn London. But Weizmann's proposal had been
blocked by some Zionist leaders who feared Silver's militancy and
resented his none-too-gentle criticism. Now a group of American
Zionists headed by Neumann earnestly requested Silver to head a
reorganized Emergency Committee. It was to be called the American
Zionist Emergency Council and it would create an imperishable
record.

From August, 1943, onward Silver's biography and the history
of Israel's establishment become inseparable—for any review of the
momentous years that followed his acceptance of the chairmanship
of the American Zionist Emergency Council brings into bold relief
the decisive influence he exercised in determining the character, policies, and program of Zionism in its most crucial period.

He made a careful—and, as it turned out, accurate—estimate of
the many fronts on which he would have to fight. He would have to
contend with the British and with Arab propaganda (in those years
largely a creation of British policy); with the United States Administration, headed by the most popular of world leaders, Franklin D.
Roosevelt, and guided by an anti-Zionist State Department; with the
oil interests and with the confusion-spreading anti-Zionist minority
in American Jewry—and others as well. His confidence that this array
of powerful forces could be—and would be—subdued was not motivated by foolhardy courage, though courage he had in full measure.
It was a combination of iron logic and iron nerve which dictated his
every action and which he sought to instill in the movement he led.
Had he not succeeded in this, had the Zionist movement remained

embedded in conventional methods and attitudes, the outcome would surely have been different. Recognizing this at the very outset, he set about to transform the whole character of American Zionism—to convert a club of well intentioned and highly motivated, but politically passive, Zionist personalities into the nerve center of a revolutionary program with a mass following. And since time was short and his own temperament rebelled against procrastination and clever rationalizations, he was often impatient and "difficult" with those who would not or could not meet what he regarded as the clear and unmistakable challenge of the hour.

There was ample evidence that an overwhelming majority of American Jewry was prepared to support the full Zionist program. The opportunity for an impressive demonstration of this fact was at hand at the inaugural gathering of the American Jewish Conference in New York in the late summer of 1943. The resolution favoring a Jewish Commonwealth was violently opposed by the non-Zionist minority and was all but abandoned by prominent Zionist spokesmen in the name of "unity" and in return for non-Zionist support of unlimited Jewish immigration into Palestine. It was saved by Silver's powerful plea to the delegates to reject such compromises. "If we surrender our national and historic claim to Palestine," he warned, "and rely solely on the refugee philanthropic appeal, we shall lose our case as well as do violence to the historic hopes of our people."

The Jewish Commonwealth resolution was adopted by a vote of 502–4.

American Jewish opinion had been crystallized and confirmed. Now the task was to make that opinion a potent force in influencing American policy. This was the responsibility of the American Zionist Emergency Council which within a year became the most effective instrument of public relations and organized action in the history of the Zionist movement and probably in the history of American Jewry. Indeed, in the melancholy and perhaps exaggerated opinion of some targets of the Emergency Council—British Foreign Office spokesmen, United States State Department officials, and Arab propagandists—it was for a time the most successful activity of its kind on the American scene. In its final form it was the handiwork of Dr. Silver—a highly efficient and sensitive instrument, completely responsive to his technique and style.

A Washington Bureau was established and superbly conducted by Rabbi Leon I. Feuer, the many-talented spiritual leader of Toledo, Ohio, who had served as Rabbi Silver's close associate at The Temple in Cleveland for many years. An intensive program of education on the Palestine problem had to be carried out in Washington. Friends were won in Congress and other areas of government.

The Emergency Council's policies were hammered out in an executive committee composed of representatives of all Zionist parties. This in itself was a formidable task in view of historical differences in ideology and methodology between the parties and their leaders. Inevitably, too, there were clashes of personality which sometimes overshadowed issues; old grudges which intruded into discussions of vital questions and made objective evaluations difficult. Nevertheless, this group was the power center of the organized Zionist movement. It had to be held together and made to function effectively—often against the wishes of some of its own members. Silver achieved this by a combination of reason and power. In political debate his arguments were usually irrefutable. But this alone would not have persuaded the opponents of his militant policy of exerting pressure on the Administration in Washington. His policy had to be backed by the force of public opinion. A mobilized mass movement, dedicated to the realization of his program, would not only be the chief factor in the main struggle for a Jewish State, but would prove vital on the internal front as well. It would enable him to push through his policies and frustrate those of his opponents who were bent on scuttling his program. In any case, his philosophy of Jewish life determined that the leader must seek and obtain his mandate from the people. This he did—and the masses of American Jewry, led by the Zionist rank and file, responded with unprecedented enthusiasm. It soon became clear to the British Foreign Office, the American State Department, and to the leaders of Zionism in the United States and abroad that the overwhelming majority of American Jews strongly supported Abba Hillel Silver.

The Emergency Council's program was carried out by a staff personally directed by Silver, and this was a main factor in its success—apart from the dedication of its members. Many observers of the American Jewish scene have said that never before or since was there a staff performance to approximate that of the Emergency Council team which functioned from late 1943 through 1948. It was not a very large group by present organizational standards, though the allegations of its anti-Zionist enemies created the flattering impression of a heavily financed army of propagandists. The anonymity of many of its most important members is a deficiency in the recorded history of Zionism which will, one day, be corrected. For example, the name of Harry L. Shapiro, the devoted and profoundly human executive director of the Emergency Council, surely belongs in any record of Israel's emergence. The Silver method excluded any dichotomy between the leader and the professional executive. Key executives of the Emergency Council became his close and loyal friends and, when occasion required, fighters for his policies and program.

The history of the Palestine Resolution which was introduced in both Houses of Congress early in 1944 is an object lesson in political action within the American democracy. The sponsorship was impressive—in the Senate it was called the Wagner-Taft Resolution; in the House, the Wright-Compton Resolution. The primary purpose of the bipartisan measure was later explained by Silver in an address to the convention of the Zionist Organization of America: "If our cause was to be placed on the national and international agenda, if the attention of the American people and of the world was ever to be drawn forcibly to our problem on the eve of the effective date of the White Paper, and if the official silence in Washington was ever to be broken, the most effective, perhaps the only way in which it could be done, was by producing the discussion of our problem in the world's greatest forum of opinion—the Congress of the United States. What happens there is news, national and international. In fact, the very discussion of a problem before such a forum is a political event.

"Our investigation indicated beyond any reasonable doubt that sentiment among the members of Congress was highly favorable. Our nationwide poll, taken by our three hundred community contact groups all over the country before we introduced the resolutions, made it clear that when and if the resolutions came to a vote they would pass by very large majorities."

But the resolutions did not come to a vote. The Administration brought about a postponement of action through the intervention of the War Department, which argued for delay on military grounds. In response to the strong public resentment which this evoked, President Roosevelt, after a meeting with Dr. Silver and Dr. Stephen S. Wise, authorized the two Zionist leaders to issue a public statement in his name to the effect that "the American Government has never given its approval to the White Paper of 1939 . . . and that when future decisions are reached full justice will be done to those who seek a Jewish National Home."

Only later was it learned that immediately after the issuance of this and subsequent pro-Zionist pronouncements by the President of the United States, the State Department sent reassuring messages to Arab governments, advising them that there had actually been no change in American policy.

Silver refused to let the matter rest with Roosevelt's statement. He felt that the President's declaration should not be considered a substitute for Congressional action, but a powerful argument for speedy passage of the Palestine Resolution. He was, moreover, convinced that the "military" objections to the resolution would be withdrawn if sufficient public pressure was exerted on the Administration. The Emergency Council therefore held a great rally in New York's Madison Square Garden—the first of many huge mass demonstrations that would take place at critical moments of the struggle.

Silver then shifted the Zionist political front to Chicago, where the national conventions of the Republican and Democratic parties were to take place. Intensive efforts by the Zionist representatives at the conventions brought about the adoption of unequivocal Jewish Commonwealth planks in the platforms of both parties.

There is a wirespread tendency to write off the platforms of our major parties as pronouncements dictated exclusively by expediency, designed solely for vote-catching purposes, and therefore not really binding on the winning party. If this cynical view has any validity, the fault lies chiefly with some of the best elements in American society. Their own attitude is what, in the end, determines the seriousness and the binding character of party declarations. If they choose to regard the platform of the party in power as a solemn commitment and insist on action to redeem the party's pledge, they may be astonished to find that platforms are highly meaningful. The author was one of those engaged in the effort to secure the 1944 pro-Zionist planks in Chicago and the 1948 pro-Israel planks in Philadelphia, and can assure the cynics that they were not lightly or easily adopted. Moreover, their subsequent significance on the highest political level was unquestionable—simply because the organized Zionist movement chose to view them as serious declarations of policy and proceeded accordingly.

The wisdom of Silver's policy of seeking support from *both* of the major parties (a political truism today, but an unsettling concept for some Zionist leaders during the Roosevelt era) was strongly illustrated when President Roosevelt was induced to affirm his support of the Palestine plank in the Democratic platform. His memorable message to the convention of the Zionist Organization of America in October, 1944, had been immediately preceded by the pro-Zionist declaration of the Republican candidate for the Presidency, Governor Thomas E. Dewey. The "military" objections to passage of the Palestine Resolution were removed in a letter from Secretary of War Stimson to Senator Robert A. Taft, co-sponsor of the measure, and it was decided that the matter be reopened in Congress. Clearance was sought from President Roosevelt and Secretary of State Stettinius; but notwithstanding the Democratic Party's declaration and Roosevelt's own statement, the Administration opposed action. On December 11, 1944, Stettinius appeared personally before the Senate Foreign Relations Committee and argued against the Palestine Resolution in the name of the Administration. Such pressure from the Executive Branch made it impossible to pass the measure and it was tabled by a bare majority.

Within the American Zionist Emergency Council the situation was even more discouraging. When the Administration's opposition was encountered, a violent dispute developed. Those Zionist leaders who preferred to rely on Roosevelt's promise that he would, at some future date, support Zionist aspirations opposed further action which might prove embarrassing to the just-reelected President or incur his hostility. Silver, on the other hand, felt that every effort should be made to induce the Administration to withdraw its opposition. Unfortunately, the proponents of these two views adopted separate and conflicting procedures in Washington. Thus, while Silver was pressing for a change in the Administration's attitude toward the resolution, other Zionist leaders were assuring public officials that they would not seek action against Roosevelt's wishes. The tabling of the resolution was, in these circumstances, inevitable, and Silver was forced to resign from leadership of the American Zionist Emergency Council.

The heated controversy in American Zionism which followed these developments proved to be an essential phase in the political education of the movement and of American Jewry. Silver's supporters sprang to the defense of his policies. Led by Neumann and organized by executives of the Emergency Council who had resigned in protest following Silver's removal from leadership, they formed the American Zionist Policy Committee which conducted a whirlwind campaign for the recall of Dr. Silver. In six months of debate between the "Silver activists" and the "Wise moderates" the central issue was crystallized: "The most effective representation (to leaders of government) in a democracy is through organized public opinion . . . Zionist leaders who cannot whole-heartedly join in such an effort, or who are too entangled in party politics to appraise situations objectively and to follow an independent Zionist line should step aside. We have nothing to lose now but our illusions. We have a new life to build for our people!" This was the essence of Silver's challenge.

It was taken up by the vast majority of American Zionists. After President Roosevelt's death and the disclosure of his secret correspondence with King Ibn Saud, the demand for Silver's return to political leadership became ever more insistent. In July, 1945, he was recalled to head the American Zionist Emergency Council and shortly thereafter he was also elected President of the Zionist Organization of America.

The Palestine Resolution was reintroduced in Congress, with Dr. Neumann representing the Zionist position in Washington. Opposition on the part of the State Department under President Truman was no less vigorous than it had been under President Roosevelt. But this time the Zionist ranks could not be split. After a full debate in the Senate, the resolution was overwhelmingly adopted on December 19, 1945.

The lessons taught by Dr. Silver during this period were to be applied definitively during the next three years. The rank and file, if not all Zionist leaders, now understood that a Jewish State could not be won by appeals to vague humanitarianism and that the tragic plight of European Jewry was not, in itself, a persuasive argument for action by the world's leaders. The Zionist case had to be backed by political force—and the movement had come to realize that it was not without real political bargaining power. It had the increasingly strong and determined *Yishuv* in Palestine, and it had the growing support of American Jewry, the largest Jewish community in history. Now it had, too, the full endorsement of the Legislative Branch of the United States Government and the backing of millions of non-Jewish American citizens. It could no longer be put off or ignored and would henceforth address itself to the Executive Branch with greater confidence and far better results.

Silver's clashes with the Roosevelt Administration had led some of his opponents to attribute partisan political motives to his actions. In certain instances their own involvement in the affairs of the Democratic Party caused them to think in such partisan terms. Silver was a Republican, hence bent on embarrassing and defeating Democrats. For them it was as simple—and crude—as that. His friendship with his fellow-Ohioan, Senator Taft, was, moreover, proof that he was a "reactionary" to boot.

He never bothered to reply to these insinuations. He was disdainful of labels like "liberal" and "reactionary." In Ohio he had supported both Democrats and Republicans for high public office, always seeking the better man. In national affairs he had strongly supported the New Deal during Roosevelt's first two terms. He had opposed a third term for Roosevelt and had announced his support of Wendell Willkie (whom many liberals belatedly recognized as one of their own). He had awakened Robert A. Taft's interest in the Zionist cause early in the latter's political career and had carefully nurtured the Senator's Zionist sympathies which, in the end, became a powerful factor in determining the course of American policy on Israel. As for his political views, he was quite content to let the record speak for itself. A review of that record—of the positions he has taken on both national and international issues—makes it clear that neither of our great political parties fully encompasses his political and social philosophy. If there were those who preferred to regard his program of political action as pro-Republican in purpose, he merely shrugged and went on with his work. His attitude proved advantageous to the Zionist cause during the Roosevelt and Truman Administrations, in view of their concern about the way in which "that Republican rabbi" might exploit the shortcomings of their Palestine policies.

Silver's initial assessment of President Truman was hopeful where Zionist aspirations were concerned. As a good Missourian the new President would "have to be shown." He would have to be convinced that American public opinion truly supported the establishment of a Jewish State, but once so convinced he would move forward. This analysis proved to be amazingly correct—though it was Silver's sometimes unpleasant duty to create the kind of public pressure which, while serving to persuade the President, also irritated him. Such a relationship may not cement personal friendships, but it can make for good politics, American style. In this instance, it helped to bring about the establishment of the State of Israel.

Silver was not similarly hopeful about the new Labor Government which had come to power in Britain at war's end. He urged restraint and a wait-and-see attitude on his Zionist colleagues, some of whom were prepared for dancing in the streets in view of the Labor Party's official position on Palestine—a policy declaration that was more "maximal" than the World Zionist program. The rude awakening was not long in coming. The White Paper policy was to be continued, and by one who would prove to be a bitter and vengeful foe—Ernest Bevin.

In August, 1945, President Truman sent his famous letter to Prime Minister Attlee requesting that 100,000 certificates be granted for the immigration of Jews into Palestine. The British Government countered with the suggestion that an Anglo-American Committee of Inquiry be set up to investigate the position of the Jews of Europe, as well as the situation in Palestine. Silver refused to cooperate with the Committee, correctly appraising it as a delaying device and an excuse for inaction.

The Anglo-American Committee completed its report at the end of April, 1946. Silver immediately initiated representations in Washington, and President Truman, in releasing the text of the report, issued a statement which drew an important distinction between the positive recommendation that 100,000 homeless Jews be transferred to Palestine *immediately,* and the long-term recommendations which were opposed to Zionist aspirations.

However, there was no action on the 100,000 certificates. Instead, a Cabinet Committee was appointed on June 11, 1946. The product of the discussions between the deputy members of this committee and a corresponding British group was the "Morrison-Grady Report," which was actually Foreign Secretary Bevin's favorite scheme for the federalization of Palestine. This plan would have put an end to the idea of an independent Jewish State. Silver called for the full mobilization of American Jewry against it and, under pressure of an aroused and indignant public opinion, President Truman was persuaded to reject it. Bevin's fury against the "New York Jews" and the rabbi who led them was echoed in large sections of the British press which sought, without success, to discredit Dr. Silver.

Meanwhile, a carefully designed trap was being laid. With their guns pointing at the heart of the *Yishuv,* the British were projecting a round-table conference with the Jews and the Arabs. It was reported that the British would be willing to entertain a proposal for the partition of Palestine if such a proposal were to emanate *from the Jewish Agency.* The Executive of the Jewish Agency, meeting in Paris in August, 1946, responded that "it is prepared to discuss a proposal for the establishment of a viable Jewish State in an adequate area of Palestine." Silver, who had not been present at the Paris meeting, denounced this action as an enormous tactical blunder, declaring: "If it is true that the present Government of Great Britain is unwilling to grant us statehood in even part of Palestine, and the record of the present British Government is very clear on this subject, what point is there in making one grand gesture of renunciation after another and in publicly proclaiming our readiness for supreme sacrifices when our gestures are disdained and our sacrifices are contemned?"

He demanded a reaffirmation of the Biltmore Program calling for the reconstitution of *all* of Palestine as a Jewish Commonwealth, adding: "When proposals will be made *to us* by governments, which we will find truly reasonable and which will meet our fundamental needs and satisfy our national aspirations and our sense of justice, the whole movement will be prepared, I am sure, to give them every serious consideration. . . . Sound and just proposals are bound to be made to us sooner or later if we do not lose our nerve and our perspective." He resigned from the Jewish Agency Executive, determined to bring about a decisive disavowal of its action at the World Zionist Congress.

The fateful Twenty-second World Zionist Congress—the first since the beginning of the war in 1939—opened at Basle, Switzerland, on December 9, 1946. It was to make one of the most momentous decisions in modern Jewish history. The underlying issue was clear from the very outset: would the Zionist movement persist in its efforts to achieve its goals through Great Britain, or would the Congress terminate a relationship which had become tragically unhappy and which foretold political disaster for the movement? The lines were drawn on the specific question of the London conference announced by the British Government for January, 1947, with the participation of representatives of the Arab states and of the Jewish Agency. Was the Jewish Agency to go to London in order to propose partition as its solution of the Palestine question, or would the Congress reaffirm the Biltmore Program?

Dr. Chaim Weizmann, President of the Jewish Agency and of the World Zionist Organization, was emphatically in favor of participation in the London conference on the basis of the partition proposal which the Jewish Agency Executive had put forward the preceding summer—and he made it clear that his future leadership of the World Zionist Organization depended on whether the Congress would support his stand. Dr. Silver was the chief spokesman against the course of action proposed by Dr. Weizmann. Declaring that it was bad tactics for *Zionists* to have proposed partition, he categorically opposed any proposal which would establish partition as the maximal Zionist position in international discussions of Palestine's future. He contended that this would inevitably result in the further whittling down of Jewish rights in order to arrive at a new compromise solution. Underlying his position was the confident expectation that a reasonable partition proposal would be offered to the Zionists (as indeed it was in 1947 by the United Nations Special Committee on Palestine) if only the movement would stand firm.

In the final vote, a winning bloc, extending from left to right, upheld Dr. Silver's position.

Another major issue at the Congress was the Jewish resistance movement in Palestine. On this question, too, there was a sharp difference between Weizmann and Silver. Weizmann deprecated physical resistance to the British regime in Palestine and deplored "the heroics of suicidal violence" on the part of Jewish youth. He urged instead

"the courage of endurance, the heroism of superhuman restraint."
Silver, on the other hand, hailed the resistance movement as one of
the chief factors in the creation of a Jewish State and pledged his
help to it.

Soon after the Congress a frustrated British Government, in its
meetings with Zionist leaders, revealed the plan for Palestine which
it had hoped would emerge as a compromise between the White
Paper policy and a Jewish Agency partition formula. The British solution turned out to be an inferior edition of the Morrison-Grady federalization plan. The soundness of the "Silver line" which the Congress
had adopted was further demonstrated when Bevin, having been
defeated in his attempts to impose a Palestine solution unilaterally,
had no alternative but to announce that the British Government would
refer the Palestine question to the United Nations—though some Zionists were alarmed by the British move. Many observers anticipated
that the Jews would suffer a crushing defeat in the United Nations;
not without reason, for the balance of forces did not, in the beginning, seem to favor the Zionist cause.

As head of the newly established American Section of the Jewish
Agency, Dr. Silver was now charged with the enormous responsibility
of directing the preparation and presentation of the Jewish case before the United Nations. He proved to be no less skilled in the arts of
diplomacy than in the techniques of political action. He and his colleagues sought and won the understanding and, ultimately, the support of members of widely divergent blocs and groupings of nations.

Two years earlier he had boldly declared that the Zionist movement should seek support not only in Britain and the United States,
but from the nations of the world generally—including the Soviet
Union. This struck many as incredibly naïve, in view of the Soviet
Union's consistent record of violent hostility to Zionism. Others applied stronger epithets to his proposal, though finding it difficult to
reconcile "radical" with "reactionary." The appropriate word, of course,
should have been "statesmanlike," as was shown when the Soviet
Union—motivated by self-interest, to be sure—supported the establishment of a Jewish State in the United Nations debate.

Convinced that the results of the United Nations deliberations
would depend largely on the position that would be taken by the
United States, Silver once again mobilized American Jewry and the
non-Jewish supporters of the Zionist cause. The case for a Jewish
State became a burning issue throughout America.

On April 28, 1947, the United Nations General Assembly opened
its first session on Palestine. After prolonged debate an invitation to

present its case was extended to the Jewish Agency. On May 8th a unique event took place. A spokesman of the Jewish people sat in a council chamber together with the official representatives of the nations of the world and formally voiced the demands of his people for national recognition and for the right to reestablish a national state in their ancestral home. It was a moment rich in drama and in historic significance. Dr. Silver's persuasive address, as well as his subsequent appearances before the United Nations, brought a new sense of pride and dignity to Jews the world over.

Silver's strategy proved to be decisive in the achievement of the United Nations Partition Resolution. During the last nerve-wracking days of the General Assembly's session it was by no means certain that the necessary two-thirds majority would be obtained for the resolution. The outcome depended entirely on whether the United States would use its great influence with the nations which normally follow its lead and urge them to vote in favor of the plan. Some representatives of the State Department were not at all helpful. As the time for the vote approached, the issue was very much in doubt. A last-minute respite was afforded by the Thanksgiving holiday, and during those critical twenty-four hours the Jewish Agency delegation exerted the most strenuous efforts to avert defeat. Silver, Moshe Shertok (Sharett), Neumann, and all their colleagues of the Jewish Agency Executive were indefatigable, as were the members of the Jewish Agency staff, including Abba Eban, Eliahu Epstein (Elath), Moshe Toff, to name only a few. The cooperation of many other Jewish leaders and friends of the cause was quickly enlisted. The results of this concerted effort were discernible when the United States delegation warmly urged other nations to follow its lead in support of the partition plan. On November 29, 1947, by a vote of 33–13, the General Assembly gave international sanction to the establishment of a Jewish State.

In a moving description of that memorable day, Neumann writes: "One by one we left the hall and drifted into the lobby. We were all overcome by emotion. I glanced at Silver and saw what I had never seen before—he wept."

While a Jewish State had been voted by the United Nations, it was far from established. The British now devised a series of schemes to frustrate the will of the United Nations and upset its decision. By systematically disarming the Jews and arming the Arabs, they anticipated that the Jewish State would be unable to defend itself against the Arab onslaught and that, consequently, British forces would be in a position again to take over control in Palestine. In order to carry out this plan the British Government had to ensure that the United Nations Security Council would do nothing to halt the Arabs' attacks or to implement the Partition Resolution. However, the British miscalculated two vital factors. They underestimated the determination of the *Yishuv* to stand firm even against the most discouraging odds, and they believed that, in cooperation with their friends in the United States Department of State, they would be able to win—and hold—American support.

For a time they were remarkably successful. A shocking reversal of United States policy took place on March 19, 1948. The American Government argued in favor of an international trusteeship over Palestine in place of partition. For almost two months the United States delegation worked to reverse the November 29th decision and to substitute its trusteeship plan. During this period Silver devoted himself chiefly to the activities of the American Zionist Emergency Council, which gave massive expression to public indignation over the Administration's reversal. On April 4, 1948, an estimated 50,000 Jewish war veterans paraded down New York's Fifth Avenue in protest against the State Department's betrayal, while 250,000 demonstrators denounced the Administration at a rally in Madison Square Park.

Silver and his colleagues conducted a simultaneous offensive in the United Nations against the United States trusteeship scheme. In the Security Council and in the Political Committee of the General Assembly he presented effective refutations of the arguments which had been employed to justify the United States proposal.

The Jewish Agency's representatives had succeeded in defeating every attempt of the British and American delegates to bring about a repudiation of the Partition Resolution. As the May 15th deadline for the proclamation of the Jewish State approached, representatives of the State Department tried a last-minute gambit to avert the proclamation. They sought to engage the Jewish Agency in a round-table conference and proposed a temporary trusteeship arrangement. They implied that this proposal was supported by the President and coupled the offer with threats of dire consequences if it were rejected. Some Jewish leaders—including men who were soon to become high dignitaries of the new Government of Israel and of the World Zionist Organization—were ensnared by this maneuver and were prepared to accept the State Department's plan. They had been persuaded that the alternative might be the physical destruction of the *Yishuv*. Silver, however, insisted that the sole purpose of the proposal was to postpone indefinitely the establishment of the Jewish State. He believed that David Ben-Gurion was determined to proceed with the proclamation and, moreover, that only the Jews of Palestine could make the final decision, since it would have to be underwritten with their blood. All that he and his colleagues could do was to offer a political judgment, leaving the ultimate decision up to the *Yishuv*. At the same time, Silver felt, the action that would be taken by the American Section of the Jewish Agency could either fortify Ben-Gurion's position or weaken it. This was, therefore, the most crucial action ever to be taken by the American Section. Fortunately, a bare majority voted with Silver to inform Ben-Gurion that they had rejected the State Department's offer.

On May 14, 1948, the State of Israel was proclaimed, and the President of the United States announced *de facto* recognition—even as American delegates to the United Nations were still busily engaged in trying to block the establishment of the State.

On that day, too, Abba Hillel Silver, in the last of his appearances before the United Nations, said: "At ten o'clock this morning the Jewish State was proclaimed in Palestine. . . . Thus, there has been consummated the age-old dream of Israel to be reestablished as a free and independent people in its ancient homeland.

"The Jewish State is grateful to the United Nations for having placed the stamp of its approval, and the stamp of the approval of the world community, upon the historic claims of Israel, and for the efforts which it made in the face of opposition to achieve that which the Jewish people have accomplished. The Jewish State, in setting out upon its career, is conscious of the many grave problems, foreseen or unanticipated, which confront it. It prayerfully appeals, therefore, to all freedom-loving peoples, and especially to those who gave their fullest endorsement to the establishment of the Jewish State a few months ago, to give a full measure of their support and of their strengthening to this newest republic established by this, the most ancient of peoples. The Jewish State will strive to be worthy of the confidence which has been placed in it by the nations of the world, and will endeavor to realize, as far as it is humanly possible, those prophetic ideas of justice, brotherhood, peace and democracy which were first proclaimed by the people of Israel in that very land."

He had completed his greatest work.

The leaders of the new Government of Israel lost no time in showing their appreciation. There is irony—and, for the Zionist movement, tragedy—in the fact that almost immediately after he had achieved this triumph, Dr. Silver was compelled to resign from leadership of the movement. The internal conflict which precipitated his resignation was presumably over the management of fund raising for Israel in the United States. It is now generally understood that this was a false issue, and that the real question was the negative attitude of Israel's leaders toward the post-State Zionist movement. Silver's philosophy of Zionism—all-encompassing in its view of Jewish history and the Jewish people in their entirety—could never be reconciled with Ben-Gurion's negation of all Zionist activity that is not Israel-centered or State-based.

Realizing that a prolonged controversy with the Government of Israel on the question of the funds could destroy the campaign of the United Jewish Appeal, which was indispensable for Israel's survival, Silver preferred to resign his chairmanship of the American Section of the Jewish Agency. The underlying issues of that conflict are, thirteen years later, still being debated. Validation of Silver's position has been amply provided, particularly by those Zionist leaders who had opposed and succeeded him in 1949, but who adopted his views when they were confronted by Ben-Gurion's unabated ideological warfare against the movement.

Silver's withdrawal from active Zionist leadership did not, of course, affect his profound commitment to Israel's growth and development. His frequent, though for the most part unpublicized, interventions in Washington at crucial moments of Israel's recent history; his distinguished services as Chairman of the Board of Governors of the Israel Bond organization, and especially his incisive analyses of major political developments—these have kept him at the center of affairs. For the masses of American Jewry he is the living symbol of their own greatest moment.

Once again he found time for scholarship and for writing. His *Where Judaism Differed* appeared in 1956. It is an extraordinary blending of painstaking research with a strong reaffirmation of Judaism's distinctiveness and of its rational character. Existentialist faddists or those interested in jet flights to salvation will derive no comfort from this book, but it has all the qualities of a permanent contribution to the literature on Judaism.

Moses and the Original Torah (1961) is a scholarly quest for the pure faith of Moses imbedded in the Pentateuch. Rabbi Silver finds the classic impulses of Judaism in that original Torah and in the moral revolution wrought by Moses, "throneless monarch of a spiritual kingdom."

That he himself has been motivated by these same impulses and by the prophetic tradition is manifestly clear from his life and work.

The public image of Dr. Silver differs considerably from the man. His overpowering personality on the platform, his forcefulness in debate, and his fighting spirit have obscured other qualities. The first word that comes to mind is simplicity—a directness of approach, a quick arrival at the heart of the matter—a quality which one tends to associate with great artists. With friends he is hearty and warm. His enjoyment of life is huge and without ambivalence.

Abba Hillel Silver, Jewish statesman, taught a generation and trained it for the privilege of experiencing Israel's rebirth. He poured his gifts—his very soul—into this generation, and it became strong and proud. He has ennobled his time.

Gleanings of an Abundant Harvest

EDITED BY
DANIEL JEREMY SILVER

*

O N NINE HUNDRED AND EIGHTY Sunday mornings over the past
forty-five years, Dr. Silver has risen in the pulpit of The Temple
to speak his mind. These sermons had been patiently thought out
and written out. Most were committed to memory. All were delivered
with the rare oratorical skill which he uniquely possesses.

Fortunately, each of these lectures was taken down stenograph-
ically as it was being given. All the colors of four and a half decades
of world history are represented here. All the important moods and
adjustments of this period are assessed and judged. Dr. Silver never
scrupled to tackle the most difficult and emotion-packed problems of
the day.

I have, in this collection, tried to indicate briefly some of the
major positions he took and the emphases he gave to his teaching. I
have largely omitted those lectures dealing with the politics of the
establishment of the State of Israel; these have been published elsewhere. Also, I have largely omitted the many scholarly lectures which
sprang from his pen and his wisdom. His basic philosophy and religious outlook can be assessed by reviewing his published work. These
lectures and their spiritual and personal counterparts require a fuller
treatment than was here possible. They are profound and suggestive,
and display a wealth of knowledge, but they are essentially variations
on a theme, an age-old theme.

What is unavailable in print is a touchstone to Dr. Silver's social
philosophy. From 1917 to the present, he has projected himself into
the major debates of the day and has made his pulpit a firm and
forceful vehicle for the prophetic tradition which is his model. Never
one to torture himself whether or not the pulpit should engage in such
discussion, Dr. Silver took the bull by the horns and spoke his piece
without cant, without posturing, and with remarkable consistency.

I would make only this one further remark. I have sought to indicate his interests and his principles rather than the reasoning which

led to these positions. Sunday morning lectures usually lasted some thirty to forty-five minutes. They required in reproduction some fourteen or fifteen typewritten pages. The quality, the power of these lectures is the close reasoning and the breadth of factual information which the preacher brought to bear. Dr. Silver takes you step by step, with inexorable logic, from a statement of the problem to the statement of his conclusion. One misses entirely the quality of fulmination and unreasoning emotion which is the hallmark of some popular preachers. If Dr. Silver's mood is prophetic, his technique is professorial, his logic precise.

Finally, these lectures made their impact. They were not words hurled vainly into an empty hall. Each Sunday fourteen, fifteen, sixteen hundred people thronged to worship. Each Monday the newspapers reproduced a précis. Each week what was said was debated by Cleveland citizenry. His was a voice that was heard.

INSTALLATION PRAYER

At this sacred hour I would pray to Him who is my strength and my fortress and my refuge, that I might prove worthy of the service to which I have been called, and deserving of the faith which men have placed in me; that His spirit might descend upon me, granting to my work and my ministry an abiding value and an enkindling enthusiasm and a power which will enable me to touch the lives of some of you, win some soul to higher aspirations, and guide some hand in its outreachings for the higher gifts of God. I would pray for the men and women of this congregation, and for their earnest efforts to rise and to raise to ever higher altitudes, to widen the circle of their life's interests so as to include a segment of the infinite. I would pray that their loyalties and sincerities may reveal unto them the purposefulness of life and the glory of service, that they may drink deep of the waters of contentment at the fountains of spiritual salvation; and I would pray that Tifereth Israel, rededicated and reconsecrated, may in a still larger measure serve the cause of Israel and of Israel's faith, that it may continue to be a blessing unto men, reaching out into their lives, mellowing their higher ambitions and inspiring their finer motives; that the young men and women who shall be reared under its influence may grow into splendid manhood and womanhood, and into a supreme and transcendent devotion to their people and to its great, imperishable mission.

October 14, 1917

IS THE TREATY OF PEACE A "PEACE" TREATY

The treaty of peace as we have it cannot, by any stretch of the imagination, be called a peace treaty. There is no promise of peace in it. It has many of the earmarks of the Peace of Vienna of 1815 and the Treaty of 1871. It is imperialistic to a degree and vindictive in a frightful measure. The spirit of *vae victis* (woe unto the vanquished) is written large in it. One looks in vain for that spacious generosity, that spirit of forgiveness and reconciliation, that healing sympathy which one was led to anticipate from the words of our leaders and our spokesmen. . . .

Immediately after my return from France, where I had more than one occasion to witness the horrible imprints of the heel of the Hun, yet knowing that peace can never be based upon hate, I said, in addressing a large body of citizens here in the city: "After the war, during the terrible months of peace discussion, and during the coming years of universal reconstruction, we shall need a type of patriotism which soars higher, is more universal, more encompassing and one more hard to achieve. For remember, friends, it is much easier to sacrifice one's life than to sacrifice one's prejudices. If the peace which we shall establish is to be established on the abiding rock of permanence and not upon the shifting sands, then it must be a peace based upon universal justice, on reconciliation, on mutual helpfulness among all the peoples of the earth. . . ." If this war is not to be the beginning of a chain of terrible catastrophes, if this is not to be an open sesame to a universal calamity, then we must take into our lives and into our souls the large, all-embracing spirit of our land, which is "with malice toward none and with charity for all."

I thought of it then; I hoped for this spirit throughout the months of peace discussion, not because I loved Germany, but because I loved humanity and I loved peace; because I knew, because every student of history knows full well that any beaten nation that feels embittered and abused thinks not of peace but of war and plans vengeance, and history is always ready to supply such a nation with such an opportunity. No nation is so utterly beaten and so thoroughly broken but that time and change will strengthen it and give it the desired opportunity. . . .

The treaty of peace, to my mind, is fatally weak in two essential regards. First of all, in its relation to Germany, and, secondly, in its relation to the rest of the world. By the treaty of peace Germany is deprived of close onto forty-five thousand square miles of Europe.

Much of it justly. Alsace-Lorraine is not German, and Schleswig is not German. There is very little that we ought to regret in this rectification of an ancient wrong. But I venture to say that the Saar Valley and Danzig, and the segregation of East Prussia, and the surrender of Upper Silesia and West Prussia will be a bone of contention for generations to come, a festering wound in the very body of Europe. . . .

How far have the fourteen principles been realized in this treaty? How far has the treaty gone to solve the perplexing problems of Europe, Africa, and Asia? I say very little. The treaty of peace has deliberately taken a large tract of territory belonging to a peace-loving people that fought in this war (China), a tract of land holding millions of people (Shantung), and surrendered it entirely to Japan. Japan, in many respects, is the Prussia of the Pacific. Why was this done? Because Japan "permitted" China to enter into this war, and because of that Japan is to be paid.

What has become of the principle of self-determination of peoples? What is happening to it in Korea? What has the treaty of peace to say concerning Ireland, a people struggling to be free and live its own life? Nothing. What has the treaty of peace to say concerning Russia? Nothing. Its policy has been the same policy of watchful waiting, of blundering, as it has been since the days of the Russian Revolution. They failed with the Kerensky government; they supported the Korniloff uprising and they failed; they failed to come to an understanding with the Soviet government, thereby prolonging the war another bloody year, and now they are endeavoring to back up Kolchak. Will they have greater success than they have had heretofore?

What have the framers of the treaty of peace to say concerning religious freedom and toleration in the world? Have they spoken a word? Have they had the courage to announce for all time the right of peoples to enjoy their own religious convictions, unmolested? They have not. They are now seeking by subterfuge to introduce this principle in individual treaties, which have not the binding power, nor the authority, nor the grandeur of a declaration from a peace conference.

The prospect to me seems rather unpromising. Our hopes have not been realized. Our spokesman and leader, the man who for two years was the arbiter of the destinies of the world, is coming back a sadder and a smaller man. Perhaps a league of nations may rectify some of these errors. It is rather doubtful. The league of nations would have been a strong binding institution if the rights of all peoples had first been established, and the desires of all had first been satisfied, but as long as questions of life and death, questions which are close to the very life of a people, remain unsolved, this mechanism of a league of nations can little avail. It might prove to be a house of cards for all we know.

June 1, 1919

THE RED TERROR AND THE WHITE

. . . Why do I speak of this? Because I believe that we are today being stampeded into a psychology of intolerance, of bigotry; because I believe that we are losing that gracious quality of being able to listen patiently to another man's opinion, even if that opinion differs radically from ours; because we have lost the capacity for looking at truth when the truth is ugly and unattractive; because men are terrifying us into a veritable intellectual stupidity; because we are being victimized by a systematic propaganda to keep us from thoroughgoing reforms, by waving before our eyes the specter of revolution, the danger of radicalism. . . .

The sure way of establishing peace and order is not the way of Ole Hansenism; the sure way is not the way of Guy Empeism; the sure way is not the way of self-appointed leagues for the protection of American democracy. The surest way is to remove every barrier, every dike that confines the free expression of ideas in this land. Let ideas clash, let there be an exchange and conflict of opinion, out of which truth will come. This is the philosophy of democracy.

Let us set about making our economic organization attractive to men; let us set about honestly to destroy that cancer of the human society, that corrosive disease—poverty, that destroys not only the physical life of man, but the moral and the spiritual life. Let us set about to destroy the slums, the ghettos, and the filth, and the ugliness of our large cities.

We dare not assume a philosophy of indifference and say these things must always be. They need not always be. They are because you and I are indifferent to them. Let us set about protecting childhood and womanhood, saving them from the destructive strain of industrial life. Let us set about giving the working man a sense of independence, and a sense of pride by identifying him closely with the industry in which he works, so that he will feel himself not merely a tool but a fellow creator.

Let us try honestly to distribute a little more equitably the social goods, a little less to those who have too much and a little more to those who have too little. Let us set about honestly to extend and increase opportunities for education, for self-culture, for healthy entertainment. Let us democratize as far as possible the advantages of art and culture and learning to all. Let us kill revolution by establishing happy homes, by building in this spacious land of ours millions and millions of happy firesides. . . .

Lastly, the sure way of avoiding danger and unhappiness in our land is the way, long, it is true, but sure—of education; education through an honest press. It is heartbreaking to see how little of truth men receive today from their newspapers. Somehow our press has become, consciously or unconsciously, willingly or unwillingly, an instrument in the hands of men who are interested in stifling every new idea just because it is new, and every new reform just because it is a reform. . . .

We are today in a period of transition; we are growing and changing daily. Our leaders of tomorrow, our educated youth coming from our colleges and our universities, must be inspired with the conviction that democracy is not a ready-made thing, to be accepted or rejected, but that it is a philosophy of life that is progressive, creative, dynamic, constantly changing, constantly adjusting itself to new conditions as new situations present themselves. . . .

Let us not at this late date, when all of us have worked so much for it and prayed so devoutly for it, be frightened into an attitude of mind that is intolerant of new ideas. Let us not institute a white terror of oppression in this land of freedom. The danger of the red terror is that it leads to anarchy; the danger of the white terror is that it leads to the red terror. We are great. We are strong. We are sound. Our institutions are sound, our political organization has stood the test of one hundred and thirty-five years and more; our people are politically educated; they are sane, they are deliberate. Do not, in the name of all that is sacred in American life, establish a new reign of terror in this land where terror need never, never reign.

November 30, 1919

ZIONISM

I don't know that I have ever asked myself just why I am a Zionist. I don't know that I have ever stopped to analyze my feelings toward the movement.

I know that colleagues and friends in the movement—many of them—have done so. When I ask them what brought them into the movement, one will say that he is anxious for the restoration of Palestine because Israel has need of a haven of refuge for the denied and oppressed of our brothers.

Another will say: "We needs must have Palestine because the creative spirit of the Jew—the genius of the Jew—must have a congenial atmosphere and environment. Hebrew culture and literature must be given an opportunity to develop in an atmosphere and environment helpful instead of hurtful."

I suppose a third one would say that he is in favor of the restoration of Palestine because he is desirous of having the faith of his people—Judaism—live in an environment which is congenial and inspirational and not unfriendly and undermining.

A fourth one would say he is in favor of it because he would like to see the economic ideals of the prophets of Israel, the ideals of justice and the sanctities of human life, given a chance to be tried out, given a local habitation and a name in the land of the Prophets.

I suppose that each one of these reasons is valid and cogent. But I came to the movement years ago through none of these reasons. I am in the movement today not because of any or all of these reasons, but simply—just simply—because I am a Jew!

This might sound strange. Not that a Reform Rabbi should be a Jew, but that a Rabbi should not have a logical reason for joining the movement—which I do not profess to have.

But, the truth of the matter is that we do the important things in life, not because we ought to do them on the strength of logic, but because we have to do them. It is not our fine logic that determines our major attitudes. It is our background, our emotions and our sentiments. We are moved by onrushing waves that are almost irresistible, passions and longings. We then call in our minds to justify us.

I am a Zionist because I belong to a people for whom the hope of a return to Zion has been a sustaining and inspiring influence for two thousand years: because it was the unspoken hope and the oft-spoken prayer of generations and generations; because the prayers of my forefathers were saturated with that hope; because in my ears there still resounds their sweet, sad echo; because the poets of my people, throughout the darkness and the gloom of the centuries sang not of war and the delights of men, but of Zion. I am a Zionist because the past has a charm for me that is irresistible, and the future has a call that is undeniable. . . .

Some hesitate to join our movement today because they fear

that they will be accused of a double allegiance, that men will suspect their patriotism. No one—I say, no one—has accused us of disloyalty except a few timid, cowardly, so-called Jews. The American knows full well that the Jew loves America, and that the Zionist loves America. He knows that loyalty to one's kinsmen, who may not be as fortunately situated as he is, does not imply disloyalty to one's own country. Rather does it imply generosity of spirit and a liberality of outlook. . . .

There are some who hesitate to join our cause because their minds have been confused by certain religious or theological notions —certain academic questions: Are we a race? Are we a people? Are we a nation? Are we a religion? Are we anything?

You know that when a man starts to ask himself such questions he is on the verge of morbidity. The healthy man does not need to analyze himself or question himself as to why he lives. Life itself is its own justification.

The question of what we are has always seemed to me to be so pathetically futile. Do you think that the Jew in Ukrainia, who is being massacred, is first being consulted as to whether he is a people or a religion or a race or a nation? Do you think that the anti-Semites in Germany ask themselves before they denounce a Jew whether that Jew is Reform or Orthodox?

Let's face facts. We are a people. We are recognized as such by the world. We are a religion. Our people has always been completely identified with its faith. We are a race insofar as there are any races in the world. We are more than that. We are a unique blending of all of these things. I recall the statement of the Rabbis: "Israel and his faith and his God are one." . . .

Some of my practical friends do not want to come to our movement because they say that we are dreamers. If the restoration of Palestine were only a dream that could never come true, I would still be for it.

But it is more than a dream. It is a growing reality. It is an experiment which is actually being tried out—an experiment in rehabilitating not only broken lives, but also broken spirits.

I tell you frankly that the real tragedy of the *galut* (exile) is not to be found in massacres, in suffering, in disabilities and anti-Semitism, in expulsions, in ghettos. The real tragedy of the *galut* is to be found in the yellow streak which your children are compelled to carry within their souls.

To me the ghastliest phase of it all is to see the men and women— more especially the women of our people—the descendants of the

Maccabees—the children of a race which was bent but never broken—fawning their way into places where they are not wanted, apologizing, currying favors, like spiritual paupers, begging tidbits of the world.

Lastly, there are those who say: "It is a very fine thing, but it is so hard. It is such a tremendous undertaking. It is too difficult." . . .

Nothing that is worthwhile in life is ever achieved without suffering. Nothing that we get without suffering is worthwhile. We do not want Palestine given unto us. We are not a race of beggars. We want to acquire it—to purchase it—with our efforts, our toil, and our sacrifices. We want the children of Palestine, in the days to come, to say with a spirit of pride: "This is my land, because my fathers died for it." When our forefathers were about to enter the Promised Land in the days of Moses, did God give it to them as a free gift? God said: "Go into the land and conquer it." Let your bones whiten the hills and plains of Palestine, and then the land will be dear to you.

"When God looks with favor upon the works of a man even his enemies make friends with him." Now God has looked with favor upon our labors. Great powers have given their plighted word that they would help in the restoration of Palestine as a Homeland for the Jewish people. England has spoken. France has spoken. Italy has spoken. America, through its great leader, has spoken.

Shall we, now, in this critical moment, fail? Shall we confess to the world that we really never meant seriously the things for which we prayed?

We are going to say to the world: This is the moment for which we have waited, and this will be the moment when the heart and soul and the hand of our people will come into action.

April 19, 1920

WHY BOLSHEVISM WILL FAIL

. . . I believe that Bolshevism in theory is fundamentally primitive and naïve, and in practice wicked and destructive. I believe that it does not and will not make for greater human freedom or greater human happiness; and I believe that industrial democracy and industrial progress must be sought along other lines than those of class struggle and the dictatorship of the proletariat.

I believe in industrial democracy, and I believe in progressive economic development. I am all too familiar with the shortcomings, the injustices, and the glaring inequalities in wealth and power in our present economic organization. But all these facts, to my mind, do not justify a system which, in the name of absolute perfection, justice, and freedom, is perpetuating the very abuses which we are decrying in the capitalistic system.

You will recall that I was among the first—perhaps the very first in the city of Cleveland—who denounced the Russian blockade; that I was among the very first who demanded the withdrawal of American troops from Russia. I did it on principle, the very reverse of the principles of Bolshevism; for on the ground of Bolshevism, on the ground of class struggle, on the ground that force is the only means for achieving a goal, the Allies were absolutely justified in establishing a blockade of Russia. If you preach class struggle you must not raise a cry when the other fellow begins the struggle. If you preach the unity of workingmen throughout the world you must not raise a cry if the same doctrine is adopted by the capitalists of the whole world. If you preach force and justify force you must not criticize your antagonist if he too uses force.

But I constantly attacked the blockade of Russia on a principle which, to the Bolshevik, would appear frightfully bourgeoise; not on the principle of economic determinism, and not on the principle of a materialistic conception of history, but I attacked it and denounced it and demanded its revocation on the ground of an absolute principle of human justice and the right of every nation to determine its own life, its own form of organization, its own political scheme and its own destiny.

But just as I do not believe in a British blockade of Russia, I do not believe in a Bolshevik blockade of Russia; and my reading—and I assure you that it has been unprejudiced—and my study have led me to the conclusion that Bolshevism has established in Russia a blockade under methods of suppression and ruthlessness such as no autocratic capitalistic government in our generation has attempted. . . .

I shall not qualify this sentence one bit when I say that the government of Russia today is absolute and despotic. That is due, of course, in large measure, to civil war, to the danger of counterrevolution, to the external pressure by foreign powers; but it is also due, I believe, to the philosophy of the men in control of affairs. When men preach dictatorship of the proletariat, it means exactly what the word implies—dictatorship. A dictatorship makes no allowance for individual freedom and the expression of individual opinion, for the free exchange of ideas. Dictatorship is dictatorship—czarism, and nothing else. . . .

Bolshevism preaches universal revolution as a means of attaining its great goal. I tell you that universal revolution today would not only not achieve that desired goal of Bolshevism, but would throw humanity into the bloody slime of a new medievalism, a new Dark Age, because world revolution means war; and war means hatred and the unleashing of passions and the throwing open of the dikes of all that is cruel and hateful and ugly in human life.

Universal revolution today would mean infinitely more than what the war of the past few years has meant. It would mean the absolute destruction of those things in civilization which we have achieved through centuries of building. Revolution would dissipate the spirit of human kindliness and love in the hearts of men; revolution would make us beastly. And in the name of no theory and no ideal, however exalted and however tantalizing and however perfect, in the name of no creed and no metaphysical speculation should humanity be hurled into revolution, struggle, suffering, hunger and starvation, and the vulgarization and the brutalization of human life. These things can be accomplished too readily, but corrected, if at all, with enormous difficulty.

Am I justifying the status quo and conditions as they are? Am I condoning the inequalities and patent abuses and suffering and poverty and the denial of rights of human beings? No! No! But I say that all these things can be and will be corrected by means and agencies less cruel, less stringent, less destructive, less dangerous than the means preached by Bolshevism.

So long as we have democracies and so long as we have education, we can, by dint of constant effort and labor, so change the minds of men that ultimately the structure of human society will be revamped. What this world needs more than it needs all else—what this tired and tortured world of ours needs more than it needs food is a little bit of human love, of human kindliness, the healing balm of reconciliation. . . . What America needs today, my friends, is not the preachment of any doctrinaire, not the theory of any fanatic. What it needs today is the inculcation of a spirit of broad kindliness and tolerance, so that we can all get together and work together to solve each difficulty as we see it; to experiment with new ideas as they are presented to us; remembering at all times that love is more potent than hate, and more permanent. . . .

Three years ago, when I spoke on "Bolshevism—How to Meet It," I said: "Kill Bolshevism with love." I repeat it again after three years of study and observation—Kill Bolshevism with love.

November 28, 1920

THE COMING INDUSTRIAL STRUGGLE—
THE OPEN VS. THE CLOSED SHOP

. . . I want at the very outset to scotch an idea which, to my mind, is pernicious—an idea which is being injected into this controversy. Some protagonists of the open shop have appropriated for their particular form of organization the name "American." Theirs is the American plan—implying that any other plan is un-American. I want to say at the outset that all this talk of one form of shop organization being American and Christian and patriotic, while another is the very reverse of it, is unmitigated balderdash and bunk, and particularly pernicious at this time.

A breed of professional, self-ordained saviors of America has sprung up in recent years, composed mostly of jobless and discredited newspaper men and magazine writers, who believe in saving America daily at so much per, and who believe in shaking down the employer of labor for all sorts of contributions to all sorts of antilabor, anti-Bolshevik, anti-Socialist funds. . . .

The question ought not at all be confused and rendered ugly and passionate by the injection of the question of patriotism and Americanism. America will endure a thousand years from today when half a dozen industrial systems will have come and gone. Furthermore, if the policy of an organization like the Bethlehem Company, in refusing to sell structural steel to a contractor who employs union labor exclusively, is American, then I, for one, am at a loss to understand what "American" stands for.

I believe that the issue of the open versus the closed shop is not the real issue. I believe that the employer who is in this crusade is interested less in the problem of the open shop than he is in the real question at the bottom of it; the question of collective bargaining, and the right of representation of labor in the management of industry.

My belief is that this campaign for the open shop is an attempt to destroy trade unionism in the United States. While it is true that the open shop does not discriminate in theory against the union workingman, in practice the union man is always subject to a blacklist, which the employer may call into being at any time.

If the struggle is, as I conceive it to be, an attempt to destroy trade unionism in the United States, there are a few fundamental propositions which, to my mind, are incontrovertible.

The first is that trade unionism in some form or other is here to

stay. After all is said and done, the workingman sees in his union his
one safeguard against exploitation, his one protection against selfish-
ness on the part of organized capital. The workingman knows that all
his gains of yesterday—higher wages, shorter working hours, elimination of child labor, factory inspection—that all these gains have been
won by the united efforts of organized labor against the continuous
hostility of capital, with few, very few exceptions.

With the idea of the union goes the idea of collective bargaining,
and that is the second fundamental proposition. Without the right of
collective bargaining, the union is ineffectual. The workingman cannot expect to sell his labor at an advantage if he is compelled to compete with his fellow workingmen in the labor market. For the con-
tract between capital and labor to be a fair one, there must be an
equality of some sort established between capital and labor, and that
equality can be established only when labor is organized.

December 19, 1920

JEW AND CHRISTIAN—WHEN WILL THEY MEET?

There is room upon earth for Jew and Christian, for Mussulman and
Buddhist, and there is room in Heaven for them, too. It is strange
how every sect takes an option on Heaven, and refuses to have space
sold to people whom it does not like as neighbors. Now, really, there
is no crowding in Heaven. Judging by the conduct of men and nations
in the last few years, the "Standing Room Only" sign will not be found
up there but in another place altogether.

Life was meant to be diversified and manifold. I wish people
would realize this fundamental truth. The task of civilization is to
unite these diversified elements into one, voluntary, cooperative effort
for the mutual benefit of all. Civilization means the recognition on
the part of each group of the fundamental needs common to all and
of ways to satisfy these needs. Civilization is not a whitewashing of
all peoples; it is not the forcing of all peoples into one preconceived
mold, so that they will all speak alike and look alike and act alike.

Civilization is the recognition of the needs that are common to
all of them, which justify a united effort on the part of all. When the
man from India recognizes that disease is his enemy, and the man
from Norway recognizes that disease is also his enemy, and that their
task is to apply themselves to medical research, in order to eradicate,
as far as possible, disease, then the man from India and the man

from Norway have met; they have met and are united as to tasks and purposes.

When the man from Moscow recognizes that education is his greatest need, and that the future of his children and of his people depends upon the spread of education, and the man from Vermont, or Massachusetts, or Cleveland recognizes the very same truth, and applies himself to the same problem, then the man from Vermont, or Massachusetts, or Cleveland has met the man from Moscow and can work with him cooperatively.

The man from Moscow may continue to drink tea and the other may continue to drink whatever the law will permit him; one may like one style of dress and the other a different one; one may use one language and the other another, but they have met on the basis of a fundamental need and they can work together.

When the man from Germany will realize that a beaten France means an imperialistic Germany, and when the Frenchman will realize that a bankrupt Germany means an impoverished France, the Frenchman and the German will have met in one common understanding. Their backgrounds may be different and their temperaments may be different. One may like one form of art and the other another, but they have found a common meeting ground, and they have met.

It is like the rain of heaven that falls upon the mountains; some runs east down the slopes, and some runs west. Their courses are different, but their source is one and their ultimate meeting place is one—the great sea. And that is what I mean when I speak of Christian and Jew meeting.

When Christianity and Judaism will realize that their source is one—God, that their destiny is one—to make love and justice triumphant in life; then they will have met completely and perfectly.

February 6, 1921

AMERICAN JUDAISM

For American Judaism, like America itself, is still a thing in the making; and herein lies the promise—and the challenge. We have not yet evolved an American Judaism which is native to the soil, having the touch and the hue and the personality of American life. We have two rather confused types of Judaism here, both European formulations, both transplanted here, both serviceable for a time but sufficiently foreign and irresponsive as not to be able to serve as the ultimate religious program of American Israel. American Orthodox Judaism is East European Judaism, narrowed by centuries of isolation and disabilities into a rigid discipline and a rather circumscribed group loyalty; a system highly elaborated but not highly developed, whose dynamics are not the onsweeping social and universal vision of the Prophets. American Reform Judaism is still a copy in content and form of that Western European Judaism which was born under the rationalistic incantation of the early nineteenth century, which was more of an intellectual criticism than a religious revival, and which laid Judaism to rest on a pillow of vague humanitarianism. The one is rather narrow, the other is rather dry. The one lacks the reach and sweep of the prophetic zeal which gives to our sacred literature its unique grandeur. The other lacks spiritual intensity, the religious fervor which gives a sacramental character even to ceremony, and the tradition which fostered learning and placed the study of the Torah above the ritual of the Temple.

There is today a most earnest outreaching everywhere in our land for a synthesis of these two types of Judaism, which holds great promise. We need the one as we need the other. We need the broad universalism and fine humanitarianism of the one even as we need the warmth, the color, the depth and the discipline of the other.

American Israel may well achieve this helpful synthesis. American Judaism is far removed from the shadow of the ghetto walls which isolate spiritually even more than physically. It may breathe the free air of a universal and prophetic faith. It may seek contacts with all other religions in the fellowship of common service. Because American Israel is not burdened with the necessity of catering to the prejudices of people in order to win political equality, because it enjoys the privileges of citizenship not as a gift bestowed but as a right won by labor and loyalty, it need not feel obligated to deny itself, to efface itself, to denude its cultural life nor whittle its faith down to the bone of an ethical formalism or a set of moral proprieties. American Judaism may be richly and intensely Jewish, full of content and possessed of a strong cultural individuality.

To be sure, American Judaism will stress the social program of our faith. The war has vindicated our social program and has underscored in blood the code of national and international morality first proclaimed by Judaism. Judaism because of its freedom from excessive eschatological concerns, and because of its insistence upon national as well as upon personal righteousness is today perhaps the one religion that has a program of political salvation for the Western world. When Poincaré and Mussolini and Lenin may fail, Isaiah, Micah, and Amos may yet triumph!

But American Judaism will not forget that "the march of progress is within us," that the goal of perfection lies within the human soul. Our faith is concerned as much with man's soul as with man's institutions. Judaism is an inner faith and an inner pilgrimage—a religion of piety and prayer and communion. It is our hope that American Judaism will react to the mystic faith of American democracy by reemphasizing the mystic elements of our faith. Democracy is the religion of man's transfiguration and is the most mystic concept in politics. A religion nurtured in such an atmosphere will be more than a system of sociology. It will be profoundly personal, inward, a religion of glow and fervor and ecstacy, a religion of song, light, and freedom, a religion that holds forth promises of revelation and divine intimacies to those who seek the dwelling place of God.

Some such vision and hope we have for American Judaism, and this, I take it, is our supreme task. The pioneers in American Israel were faced with a tremendous task and bravely did they perform it. Theirs was the task of organization. They organized our first communities, built our first schools and synagogues, established our first rabbinical college, planted our first philanthropic institutions to care for the needy and the distressed. Ours is yet another task. It is to evolve an American Judaism, to readjust our faith to our greater spiritual needs, to integrate Jewish life, to inform, organize, and direct Jewish purpose. Our task is to raise the standard of Jewish learning, to heighten the pitch and accelerate the tempo of our cultural life. A mighty task this and a mighty challenge to stalwart hearts!

Ours is the task of bringing God back into our lives and the lives of our children—the God of our fathers—the God of our children—the God whom we need, and whom they need.

January 22, 1923

THE ORGANIZED CONSPIRACY
AGAINST THE PUBLIC SCHOOL

The avowed reason for the movement to introduce the teaching of religion in our public schools is that this generation is utterly Godless, that it is utterly bad, and that only the teaching of religion in the public schools can save the youth of America from the dire consequences which are sure to follow.

Now, in the first place, I am not at all convinced that this pessimistic view of the moral quality of this generation is a true one. I do not believe that this generation is morally more lax than the generation which preceded it. I am not at all convinced that the child who is a graduate of the parochial school is any more moral than the child who is a graduate of the public school. Nor am I convinced that the child who is a graduate of the schools in those European countries where religious instruction is compulsory, is morally superior to the American child who is a graduate of the public school.

But assuming that the contention is true; assuming that this is a Godless generation, and that its only salvation lies in the teaching of religion, the question still remains: Why should it be taught in the public schools? There are other agencies which can, which ought to assume this responsibility. Millions of dollars have been spent by churches upon their Sabbath schools. Why have these Sabbath schools failed to do their duty? And if they have failed, why should the public school now be saddled with their failure? If the churches have failed to establish proper schools for the training of religious teachers, if they have failed to build the required physical facilities, if they have failed to attract children to the church schools, why should the public school, with its already heavy program, be required to make good where the church has failed?

The child may be taught religion on Sunday, morning and afternoon. He may be taught religion on Saturday morning and afternoon. He may be taught religion after school hours any day of the week. There are thousands of Jewish children, here and elsewhere, who receive daily instruction in Hebrew and religion after school hours. Why cannot the church copy this practice instead of injecting religion into the public school curriculum, with all the attendant dangers which are involved? . . .

Think of what it would mean in practice! The public school has been the great melting pot of American life, the great leveler. The public school has hitherto been the great unifying force in American life. Here boys and girls meet and are given the same instruction in the same classroom, by the same teacher. No lines are drawn, no religious or racial discriminations are introduced. But now, under the proposed plan, children in each school and in each classroom will be separated and grouped on religious grounds. One child will attend a class marked Protestant; another child will attend a class marked Catholic; and still another child will attend a class marked Jewish. How many more classifications will there have to be? The public school will become a theologic battleground. . . .

You might think that I am stressing the point too much. You might think that I am anticipating trouble which in reality will never come to be. Let me tell you that I know exactly whereof I speak. I know where religious bigotry leads, once given a chance to assert itself. When the immigration bill was introduced a few years ago, and the quota idea was projected, I said then that this is the beginning of a movement to restrict as far as possible the immigration of Catholics and Jews to the United States. People doubted my word. But already we have accepted as a basis of quota immigration the census of 1890. I suppose within a few years a bill will be introduced in Congress to restrict quota immigration to the census of 1840 or 1820. Or perhaps to 1776! Who knows? . . .

April 13, 1924

MY TEN YEARS OF MINISTRY IN CLEVELAND

I tried to keep constantly before me in the past ten years the sanctities of human life which my profession was charged to safeguard. Thus during the war I worked for peace. I did not belong to that small band of much abused and much persecuted men called pacifists. I was not a pacifist. I gave to my government, in common with the millions of other fellow citizens, my unstinted and loyal service. At the behest of my government I crossed the high seas during the war and served in the capacity which was assigned to me, and upon my return I traveled through the length and breadth of this land in an effort to stimulate the purchase of Liberty Bonds. One of the Allied governments bestowed a decoration upon me for distinguished services. But all through that time I was mindful of my specific mission as a Rabbi, which was not the prosecution of a war but the establishment of peace. I was the servant of One who is called "the King of Peace."

So that in the midst of the war, in the midst of the rampant war spirit, in the very midst of a propaganda which called for hate, for war to the hilt, for a war of extermination, I called for peace. I called for the decencies of international relationship; I called for a peace which should be based on justice and not on revenge. I called for a speedy peace. I was misunderstood. Frequently during the war I was subjected to spying and to criticism; but I saw my duty and I tried to follow it. Since the termination of the war I have made the preachment of peace one of the major themes of my ministry.

I believe that it is the specific duty and the supreme opportunity of the church in modern society to work aggressively for the establishment of machinery which will make war less likely and peace more permanent. I am convinced that the church today is confronted with a choice of roles: either the role of aggressive and affirmative leadership, or the role of pious irrelevancy. The church must decide—and when I speak of the church I mean church and temple and synagogue, and any and every organized religious institution—the church must decide whether it means to vindicate its historic claim of being the peacemaker of mankind, and affirmatively to set out organizing the religious conscience of mankind in the cause of peace, or whether it means to continue along as heretofore, more cautious than courageous, more shrewd than wise, and be content to repeat mechanically its ancient phrases about peace and goodwill.

Ten years ago there set in an economic upheaval which has, in a sense, continued to this day. In some countries the existing economic order was torn up by its very roots; in other lands where no such radical economic changes took place, the war nevertheless unleashed a pack of economic problems, strikes and lockouts, many of them of menacing proportions. Because of these upheavals men became extreme in their views and intolerant. Class struggles appeared and class dictatorship—the most brutal in the history of civilization. Here again, in the midst of these economic struggles, I tried to safeguard the sanctities of human life. I spoke for sanity, for social justice, for the rights of labor. I spoke for greater security for the toiling masses of the world, for their right to enjoy a greater share in the profits of industry. I championed their inalienable rights of organization and collective action. I championed their cause when I believed that justice was on their side, but I criticized it when I believed that justice was not on their side.

A few days ago a chauvinistic organization known as the National Society of Scabbard and Blade did me the honor of including my name among three American Jews in a list of fifty-six public men and women in this country, whom they charged with patriotic heresy, who were un-American, and somehow tainted with Bolshevism. Among the fifty-six were the names of Senator Borah, Professor John Dewey, Jane Addams, Mrs. Carrie Chapman Catt, Sherwin Eddy of the Y.M.C.A., and many others—a very fine company to be in.

I am afraid that I shall continue to be misunderstood as long as God will help me to remain faithful to the prophetic mission of a minister. Here again I believe that the church has a definite role to play in the world. I do not believe that the church ought to identify itself with a propaganda for one economic system as against another. I do not believe that the church ought to involve itself in economic dogmatism; but I do believe that it is not enough for the church to speak of social justice in the abstract. After all, the church is not an academy for abstract sciences; the church is an agency for social reconstruction. It has a mission, a purpose, and an ideal to serve. I believe that in a world which is still so sadly disfigured by want and poverty, where so many lives are still starved by poverty, and drained by exploitation, it is the sacred obligation of the church to speak out fearlessly for the rights of the laboring masses of the world, for the rights of the denied and the dispossessed of the earth.

During the last ten years, as a result of the war, a wave of intolerance swept over our world. Groups appeared, amply financed and physically well organized, to spread the gospel of hate—hate between Jew and non-Jew, between Catholic and Protestant, between the Nordic and the Mediterranean—hate based on pseudo-scientific theories of race; hate which turned brother against brother, and people against people.

So during the past ten years I devoted myself to the cause of tolerance and understanding between peoples and races and religions. I joined with my fellow clergymen of other denominations in this city and elsewhere—and Cleveland is particularly fortunate in having a large number of Christian clergymen who have remained true to the spirit of their Master in an effort to counteract these movements of hate, to foster goodwill and to provide opportunities for cooperative work among all groups and religions within our community. For that reason, too, I devoted myself so fully to our great Community Chest—not merely because it was an instrument of beneficence, intelligent and rational in its administration, but because it was a mighty instrument for uniting the souls and minds of our people into common tasks, because it made possible for our citizens to get acquainted with one another, to understand one another better, to lose that sense of estrangement which makes for suspicion, which ultimately makes for hatred.

The last ten years were trying and tragic years for our people. In Eastern Europe millions of Jews were crushed by the war and by the horrors which followed the war. Millions were left homeless, a prey to every disaster and misfortune. They stretched out their hands to seek help of their brothers across the sea, to their more fortunate brothers in America. Great programs of relief were launched by the Jews of the United States who did not abandon their brothers in distress. American Jews engaged in a mighty effort to save the lives of millions of Jews overseas. I was privileged to lend my services to that great effort.

The last ten years saw an achievement in Jewish life which two thousand years waited for in vain. The Balfour Declaration, which ushered in a new epoch in Jewish history, was issued, and I gave of myself unstintingly to make real this dream of our people to reestablish on the sacred soil of Palestine, so rich in memories, a Jewish homeland and a civilization which would, in the days to come, bless mankind with spiritual gifts, even as it did in the years long ago.

In America Jewish life during the last ten years enjoyed a renaissance. This was due to the war, to the rise of anti-Semitism, perhaps to the number of leaders who came to us from across the sea. Jewish life became more active, alert, and enterprising than at any time in its past history. Many new synagogues were built, new schools, and new community centers. In this expanding program of American Jewish life, I believe that our Temple played a not insignificant role. In this work, I endeavored to stress two things, which I hope to continue to stress in the years to come. First, Jewish unity. I endeavored to serve Israel, not a fraction of Israel. I endeavored to serve "the whole community of Israel." I did not identify myself with one wing or with one sect or with one group. I love my people, all of them, of whatever wing or sect or group they may be.

I believe that Israel is and will continue to be a variegated, many-faceted people, like every creative people. To that end I sought to bring all Jewish groups closer together in mutual understanding and cooperation. I worked for that which alone will ensure the immortality of our people—education. Israel cannot survive unless its mind is enlightened and its soul invigorated. Israel cannot continue unless the roots of its life are sent down deep into the rich soil of its past cultural creations and achievements. No Jew will be able to face the onslaught of circumstances, the undermining and assimilative influences about him, unless from earliest childhood his being is surcharged with Jewish learning and Jewish enthusiasm. All of our institutions, here and elsewhere, must have for their foundations Jewish loyalty based upon Jewish education. Once these foundations are destroyed the whole of Jewish life will crumble into the dust.

May 22, 1927

THE FAITH OF AN UNTIRED LIBERAL

. . . There is a creed to which the liberals of all ages have subscribed, and I submit it to you as a guide to the city of God.

We believe in man, in his slow ascendant progress; in the autonomy of his spirit and in the primacy of his claims over all other claims of social organization or interests. We believe in the fullest measure of freedom compatible with the fullest measure of responsibility.

We believe in authority, but only the authority which is sanctioned by consent and reason.

We believe in social progress, but progress achieved through education, through experimentation, through toil.

We believe that good government is not as important as self-government, and that values bestowed are not as desirable as values achieved, and therefore we reject any millenniums proffered to us on the spearpoint of hate.

We believe that all truth is made manifest through the clash and the conflict of diverse and opposing opinion, and that at the very heart of liberalism and human progress is the free exchange of ideas and the exercised privilege of nonconformity.

We believe in tolerance but not in indifference; in enthusiasm but not in fanaticism; in convictions but not in dogmatism; in independence of thought but not in isolation; in conflict for great ideas, but never in hate.

October 21, 1928

THE DEMOCRATIC IMPULSE IN JEWISH HISTORY

. . . The patient, sober Pharisees among us, who have not forgotten the lessons of their history, will not be stampeded. They will bear in mind that many a sad cycle of frustration and defeat is yet in store for mankind before the Kingdom will be consummated. Conscious that Israel has still as great a role to play in the future as it had in the past, they will continue to pay scrupulous heed to the discipline and the morale of the group. They will fan the flames of enthusiasm and loyalty not only for the ideals of Israel but for the people of Israel as well. They will think in terms of the people of Israel and not merely in terms of an abstract theology and a moral code. They will be reverent not only of prophecy but of the people which gave birth to prophecy and to prophets and which may yet vouchsafe many a startling revelation to mankind. They will remember the profound observation of the Rabbis: "Elijah said: Once as I was walking about a man came to me and questioned me in matters of the Law. He said: Rabbi, I have two things in my heart and I love them both dearly, the Torah and Israel, but I do not know which of the two comes first. I said to him: Most men would say that the Torah comes first. I say unto you that the holy people Israel comes first." The modern Pharisees will proceed to enrich and beautify and vitalize Jewish group life. They will hold fast to all the agencies which in the past preserved the integrity of the people—Israel's language, Israel's lore, Israel's hope of national rehabilitation, Israel's memory-laden customs and habits of life adjusted to modern needs.

Above all, they will proceed to reeducate the Jew. Herein Liberal Judaism has been most culpable. It has quite unconsciously but nevertheless quite effectively prepared the way for an appalling and devastating analphabetism in our ranks. Jewish learning is the rarest of phenomena among Liberal Jews. We have relegated the priceless heritage of our people—of the entire people—to the ordained and the professional few. We are thereby in danger of destroying the democratic character of our faith. If Judaism is to remain a democratic religion, if it is not to degenerate into a Rabbinic hierarchy, it must be on the basis of Jewish learning broadly disseminated through all the classes of our people. There is one inexorable law in our history. Without learning and study Judaism cannot survive. Wherever a Jewish community failed to kindle the lamp of learning and relied solely upon worship, observance, and philanthropy, it ultimately disappeared.

January 5, 1928

THE NATIONAL GET-RICH-QUICK DEBACLE

. . . Seemingly a thorough investigation is in order, a thorough investigation of our entire financial setup in this country, of our banks and banking systems, of our mergers, of our investment trusts, of our holding companies. Clearly an economic system, which in normal times makes possible such a wild pyramiding of fictitious values, altogether unrelated to the real available capital of a company, an economic system which makes possible the exploitation of the gambling proclivities of a people, and which makes possible, as this does, the utter collapse and ruin of the fortunes of men, is not a sound system.

For one thing, it makes for its own destruction. I do not know of anything that is more likely to make of a man a Red and a Bolshevik, an enemy of the present economic system, than just this which took place in Wall Street during the last few years. When the men who are compelled to labor hard to earn a scanty living, and see themselves denied in many instances the necessities of life, not to speak of the comforts of life, and their wives and children go without many of the things which they believe their wives and children are entitled to—and that holds true of millions in our country—when they see through the columns of their newspapers how wealth is made—without work, without the sweat of the brow, they would have to be very objective, to say the least, not to resent such a system. . . .

Not so very long ago speculation in the stock exchange was limited to a few; nowadays the whole country seems to have become stock conscious, and something quite drastic must be done to protect ourselves from ourselves. We must warn our people that this tendency to get rich quick through manipulation and speculation finds its saddest result not in the loss of money—that is sad enough—but in the ultimate undermining of our national character, in the ultimate cheapening of the dignity of work and labor, in the ultimate holding in contempt those homespun virtues of thrift and savings which once upon a time were looked upon as of the very essence of a strong, robust national life. . . .

This brings me to a few quotations which I would like particularly to give to the younger men and women. There is one quotation which is found in the Book of Proverbs, "Wealth gotten by vanity will in the end be diminished." We have all learned that lesson. "But he who gathers little by little from the work of his own hands, he shall increase." That sounds like a platitude, doesn't it? It sounds like a truism; but it is one of those dynamic truisms that people overlook so frequently, bringing disaster upon themselves. All truth is platitudinous, when you come to think of it.

I have another quotation from the Rabbis which I would like to have placed in the front of the desk of every businessman: "Choose thou life, that is, work." For when all is said and done, life is labor, and labor is life. Life is not the accumulation of wealth, and life is not the swelling of the bank account. Life is expressing ourselves through work which is congenial to us. The happiest moments are those in which we achieve through our own efforts something we love to do.

And another quotation from our ancient sages: "Great is labor, for it brings honor upon those who honor it." Only that wealth is honorable which is the result of your labor, your thinking, and your planning. Now do not misunderstand me. There is no virtue in poverty, and there is no vice in wealth. I am not one of those who look upon wealth as intrinsically evil. It is not. I believe that every man ought to strive for a measure of wealth which will give him a sense of independence, and which will make possible for him and his dear ones a decent standard of living. I have no particular criticism to make of the man who has accumulated a great deal of wealth.

I have a great criticism to make of wealth which is gotten in such a way that it makes honest, human toil undignified and cheap and contemptible, because that wealth earned, used, and enjoyed is not the result of one's planning, building, and working. The businessman who goes into Wall Street to speculate and makes a lot of money, I may call shrewd and clever and bright, but all of his achievements there bring absolutely no dignity with them, no honor, no credit; for he has contributed nothing to the social assets of this country or to its moral assets.

This country was explored, and built up by men who were not contemptuous of wealth, who wanted wealth, but who were ready to pay the price for wealth in hard work and the sweat of body and soul. They plunged through the wilderness, they carved a highway through the mountains, they dug the mines, they cleared the forests, they harnessed the waterpower—by work! As a result of this tireless labor, wealth and prosperity came to them and to their descendants.

We must turn the minds of men back from Wall Street to Main Street, back from paper profits to real values, back to production, building, achievement, back to adding something to the wealth of the nation. . . .

November 17, 1929

THE FUTURE OF CAPITALISM

Capitalism will survive if it will make the necessary adjustments to changed conditions. The highly centralized, technologically speeded-up, mass-producing, industrial capitalism of our day is a totally different thing from the capitalism of a generation or two ago. It has created new and serious problems, not the least of which are the tremendous power over the political life of a people which inevitably accompanies huge concentration of capital and control of industry; the progressive reduction of the middle class, which has been the backbone of our country; the lack of coordination between production and consumption; and technological unemployment alternately attracting and repelling workingmen and consequently depriving these men of economic security and protection.

The incitement to war by economic imperialism is still another problem which modern capitalism will have to solve.

If it cannot or does not wish to solve these problems it will be superseded by socialism. There is no particular calamity involved in that. Some things will be gained under a new economic setup and some things will be lost. Life will go on just the same. The worst that can happen is that some of us will have to go to work or forego some of our creature comforts. This may not be bad at all either for ourselves or for our children.

I refuse to be stampeded, however, in my social or economic thinking by the threat of a proletarian dictatorship. I refuse to see "red" every time a man voices a radical opinion or advances a measure of progressive legislation. Also I refuse to go into ecstasy every time a six-weeks' expert on Russia tells me that the Soviets have built another dam or another railroad or that their exports in 1930 are above those of 1929. I always knew that they could do just that if only given time and a chance, for economic production does not necessarily depend upon private competitive enterprises or upon private ownership.

Large-scale economic production is possible under state socialism as well as under private ownership. Which is more desirable is another question. Which system will in the long run yield the greatest good to the greatest number, remains to be seen. But that a people of 160,000,000, possessing one-sixth of the earth and untold potential wealth, could produce mightily, given any form of government or economic setup which is not outrightly stupid and medieval, is to me no miracle and I refuse to get excited about it.

It is my guess that America will choose the way of *regulating* capitalism rather than destroying it, of helping the workingman and the farmer to a greater measure of social goods rather than driving them to measures of despair; of improving our democratic institutions rather than scrapping them and resorting to class dictatorship even for the sake of Kingdom Come; of preserving personal freedom and liberty of thought even at the cost of a measure of economic in-equality.

February 23, 1931

WHY CLEVELAND IS NOT TAKING
CARE OF ITS OWN

. . . What is the way out? Well, first and foremost, there must be forthcoming adequate relief for the unemployed. The Federal Government must supplement the relief extended by state and municipality. The Federal Government found it necessary to assist railroads and bankers, perhaps it will find it necessary to assist poor working-men who need food, raiment, and shelter.

Such a bill was introduced, the LaFollette Bill. It was defeated. It is bound to come up again. It is altogether fair and proper that the Federal Government should carry some of the burden of the unemployment situation. It is not fair that the state should carry the entire burden because in most instances the revenues of the state are derived from taxes on real estate which fall heavily on the small home-owner and tenant. The revenue of the Federal Government is obtained largely from income taxes which are fair and just because every man pays only on the basis of his income. If the income is less, the contribution is less. If the income is more, the contribution is more. As long as there are millions of poor in these United States, the millions of the rich must be taxed to the maximum.

The United States does not need five hundred, nor four hundred nor three hundred nor fifty nor ten nor five multimillionaires. It can do without them. The United States does need and require for its existence a satisfied and provided-for working class. When there are over forty millions of people in the United State belonging to these families of unemployed who are suffering, that suffering, that want constitutes a menace to the stability of our government, to the rich and the poor alike. . . .

Then there must be an extensive program of work. Relief is no substitute for work. These people do not want relief. They want work. They are entitled to work. Our local municipalities, our counties can do a great deal in setting in operation a work program immediately, putting people to work on farms, paving and resurfacing streets, constructing necessary new public buildings, improving the parks. Put them to work, if only part time! Let a man feel that what he gets, he gets because he worked for it, not as charity. . . .

I believe that we will have to come sooner or later, the sooner the better, to a system where intelligent planning will have to be resorted to and there will have to be some form of central control to cope with the lack of coordination between production and consumption. Something must be done whereby these peaks and slumps will be straightened out, so that we will not run headlong for a few years in crazy and artificially created prosperity and then in a short time be compelled to disgorge all the profits which we made in the prosperous years. . . .

We should look upon unemployment as a risk, just like fire or like accident and we should insure a man against periods of enforced unemployment so that he will not be forced to eat up the little savings of his which he had accumulated in the hope of improving his living conditions a bit. He must not be forced into the dolorous role of tramping the streets day after day and week after week looking for work, dragged down and down to the depths of despair and, finally, compelled to come to the doors of the charities begging for alms for himself and his family. That is indecent! That is morally wrong! Someday we may see the light. Perhaps these hard desperate years of depression will help us to see the light.

April 3, 1932

THUNDER OVER EUROPE

Every opportunity that I have to talk to Jewish groups, I tell them that the Jewish people throughout the world must align themselves affirmatively and vigorously with the liberal forces in the world. Fascism is a great menace to the Jewish group. If Fascism wins, we are lost, as every minority group is lost. The French Revolution opened the doors for the Jewish people to become free human beings. For the first time in nearly two thousand years they were given a chance to live as human beings. If Fascism wins, these doors will again be shut. They will be shut in Austria if the Nazis get in. We owe it not merely to the interest of humanity, we owe it to our own self-interest here and elsewhere to destroy Fascism.

The Jewish problem in Germany and Austria is not a problem of material relief. The Jewish problem is a political problem and must be fought with political weapons. I should like to see millions poured into a fund for the purpose of undermining Fascism and Fascist propaganda throughout the world.

February 18, 1934

MUST THERE BE A SECOND WORLD WAR?

This sounds fantastic, and hardly believable. But if you read Hitler's *Mein Kampf,* you will be able to see that the Nazis are obsessed with the dream of creating in Europe a vast racial empire. They are not so much concerned with persecuting the five hundred thousand Jews in Germany. They are concerned, through the utilization of an aroused race idolatry, to build a new German empire and subdue many peoples.

It is clear that their undisclosed plan is known to every chancellery in Europe and is contributing to the mad rush toward military alliances and preparedness which is going on today. It is also clear that as long as the Nazi regime remains in power and as long as the industrial magnates support it, the prospect of war in Europe draws nearer every day.

There is no way of satisfying these madmen. Any concession to them simply whets their appetites. They are determined to build a new empire in the twentieth century. It cannot be done. It is too late for empire building in Europe.

There is only one other nation in the world which is still trying to build an empire and that is Japan. Japan is hoping to do it in Eastern Asia and at the expense of China which is unorganized and which is itself split fifty ways by rival groups and parties. Japan, too, will come to grief.

March 11, 1934

IS PROSPERITY RETURNING?

A year ago businessmen asked for more and more government funds to assist business projects of all kinds. Now that big business feels that it can navigate alone, it wants the full freedom of exploitation which it enjoyed in the days of prosperity. It has recovered its old slogans. Again you hear the cry for complete freedom for private enterprise.

The New Deal as I see it is not a matter of choice. It is a matter of necessity. Our traditional system can no longer operate. There must be central planning and coordination. In the past we produced for the sake of profit. We must now begin to produce for the sake of use, keeping in mind the well-being and the security of our people. . . .

The New Deal, as I see it, is coming to be. If it does not come to be, one of the two things will happen. One will be Fascism. But Fascism does not solve the economic problems of a people. Mussolini and Hitler are examples. The other will be Communism. All its achievements in the past fifteen years do not show that it brings prosperity to its people.

The New Deal is the American way of solving the economic problem. It is experimental and courageous. The businessman who has vision and understanding of what is going on in the world will not rally to the banner of the reactionaries, but will stand by and uphold the hand of the President and those men who are trying not merely to lift us out of the depression, but to correct the evils which brought it about so that our children will have a more secure and happier world in which to live.

April 22, 1934

THE CRISIS IN SOCIAL WORK

Charity cannot deal with the problem of poverty in modern society. Organized philanthropy is a survival of an individualistic society which assumed little or no corporate responsibility for its handicapped. But a new type of society is now in the making. Society in the future will not wait upon voluntary individual aid and private sporadic generosity to care for the disabled, the sick, the aged, and the unemployed. That which is socially necessary will become socially mandatory. There will always be room for private initiative in social service to supplement the basic social institutions of the state, to experiment in new types of service, and to point the way of progress. But the elementary and indispensable tasks of safeguarding the health of its people, of protecting childhood, of caring for the weak, the aged, the widow and the orphan, and of giving relief to the workless are the direct, fixed, and continuing obligations of organized society, and must be so met.

Certainly the care of the unemployed is not within the province of charity. Unemployment is industry's problem and industry's burden, not charity's. Industry must not be permitted to lay its myriad casualties periodically at the door of philanthropy. This is a grotesque, not to say a criminal, procedure. The most highly developed industrial system in the world employs millions of men in the production of huge wealth which largely goes into the hands of the relatively few owners of industry, pays its men in normal times wages which fall short of the requirements of a decent standard of living, and as soon as the opportunities for profit-making cease, throws these men into discard, advising them to go to the charitable agencies, to which the workers themselves had previously been asked to contribute, to beg for famine rations for themselves and their families. Such is the cynicism and brutality of our economic order! It has even failed to give to its workers the security of servitude which Feudalism once gave its serfs. So that a new terror has now come into the world. Every generation has its own overshadowing dread—pestilence, famine, invasion, the devil or the catastrophic end of the world, and the lives of that generation are darkened because of it. Into the twentieth century has come the dread terror of unemployment which hangs like a pall over the homes of the toiling masses.

The state must compel industry to lay aside adequate reserves out of which benefits can be paid to the worker whenever he is forced into involuntary unemployment. These benefits will be his as a matter of right, not of charity. Labor is not a commodity which may be purchased and disposed of at will. The worker is more than a partner in industry. His interests are primary and paramount. Industry exists to provide a livelihood for the working masses of the world and to supply them with the necessities of life. Capital's share is secondary. First must come the adequate wage, security, protection against the disabilities of accident, sickness, old age and unemployment, and then may come the profits to investor and stockholder. . . .

October 25, 1934

INTELLECTUAL PINKS AND CONSERVATIVE
BLUES

In its report of the "Secret Seven," the Cleveland Chamber of Commerce was not out to expose the Communists who do not menace it. They were out to expose all liberals and progressives and all folks who are advocates of peace or who are looking for a better and juster economic order, which may benefit the average American at the expense of the plutocrat.

Most of its printed report is a bitter and shameless attack upon these people—not upon the Communists. It is an attack which is cunningly devised to paint all liberals and progressives with the red brush of Lenin and to cast suspicion on every piece of social legislation which aims to alter the status quo. That, of course, has been the favorite device of all reactionaries. Instead of teaching people how to judge proposals on their merits, the reactionary sets out to arouse an emotional resistance to these measures so as to keep people from thinking rationally about them. . . .

So it isn't the Reds, really, who upset the sensitive stomachs of the well-fed Reactionaries. Their numbers and activities are not at all important. It is the "eloquent prophets of the Better Day, these naïve folk who so readily accept fantastic formulas," who believe in "the coming of the bright and shining better world that can be a reality the day after tomorrow, or just next week, or the week after that." The members of the Chamber of Commerce are not troubled by the financial bandits who wrecked the banks in Cleveland. Some of these gentlemen are undoubtedly still members of the Cleveland Chamber of Commerce because none of them has as yet been sent to Atlanta. They are not troubled by those who in high places helped to wreck this fair town. But it is the schoolteachers and professors and social workers and priests and ministers and rabbis and liberals generally, the men who are heartsick at the debauch of our economic life by financial racketeers and big business racketeers, heartsick at the sight of ten to fifteen millions of people out of work, degraded to the indignity of the dole—it is these people who upset the sensitive stomachs of the members of the Chamber of Commerce.

Strangely enough, the gentlemen who up to 1929 dangled before the eyes of the American people the prospect of the abolition of all poverty, of a chicken in every workingman's pot and two cars in his garage, were not rabbis or social workers or educators, but the high-pressure salesmen of American capitalism and big business. In 1928, a few months before the financial debacle of '29, Mr. Herbert Hoover, certainly the prime spokesman of the great tradition of rugged individualism, had this to say to the American people: "We in America today are nearer to the final triumph over poverty than ever before in the history of any land. The poorhouse is vanishing from among us. We have not yet reached the goal, but given a chance to go forward with the policies of the last eight years, and we shall soon, with the help of God, be within sight of the day when poverty shall be banished from the land."

This report of the Cleveland "Secret Seven" indulges in much humor at the expense of the pink reformers who would like to bring about the "Better Day" by taking away the power of the wicked capitalist and by establishing the power of the virtuous state. It is as if the reformer, the liberal is anxious to build up the power of the state at the expense of the individual while the defenders of the old order, whose citadel is the Chamber of Commerce, are leery of state power and intervention. But who turned to the state when the present system seemed to be breaking down? Who ran to Washington for hand-outs? Who dipped into the public till? Did the rabbis and social workers? Bankers, railroads, shipping industries, aeroplane companies—everyone who had a run-down business or thought he needed a subsidy—everyone ran to Washington and asked for help. The state evidently is all right when you want to milk it. When industry has ten to fifteen million people whom it can no longer employ, then it is all right to take these people and lay them at the doorstep of government and ask the state to help them. When the state wants to step in to supervise big business so as to avert such disasters—then that is to be condemned as encroachment upon private enterprise. . . .

February 17, 1935

MY TWENTY YEARS IN THE MINISTRY

Among the things which I learned, things which I suppose all thinking men learn, is that the task of reforming the world, shaping it a little nearer to one's heart's desire is not as easy as I thought it was. My devotion and enthusiasm to social reconstruction is quite as ardent as it ever was. I believe that I have lost something of that impatience, something of that urgency which fills all youthful idealism and aspiration. Whereas as a young man I was inclined to attribute all social evils to sheer human perversity, wickedness, and the malice of individuals, I have come through the years to understand the vast impersonal forces which operate in the life of society. I have come to understand something about systems in which good men, well intentioned men, quite unconsciously, often against their own will, are made to work iniquity. I have come to look for solutions not only in the ethical improvement of the individual, in the spiritual regeneration of man himself, but in the reorganization of the social and economic setup so that the individual will have a better chance to work for a better personal life.

I have come to understand during these years something about the imperfections which are inevitable, which are inescapable in all social organizations. I have come to understand that public morality can never reach those summits which private morality can reach. Bearing this in mind, one is spared many heartaches which would otherwise be his when he looks about him and regards the many retrogressions and throwbacks in society. This does not mean that a leader, a rabbi, or a social reformer must compromise with social imperfections and evils. But he must learn to attack them with greater deliberateness and with longer-ranged plans, realizing that there are no quick roads to social salvation.

Thus, for example, I was wrong about Prohibition. I was outraged by the manifest evils of drunkenness, and the miseries which it brought about. I believed, as millions of other people believed, that these evils could be done away with by prohibiting the sale of liquor. But the years have taught me as they have taught many other people that that is not the way to do it. There is no quick method of changing the habits of a people. The more patient, painstaking, laborious methods of education, control, and guidance are the ways which may yield steady gain in the solution of this problem.

I was wrong on the subject of the World War. I was twenty-four years old when our country entered the World War. As a young man I was caught up by the messianic dream that this would be a war to end war, a war that would make the world safe for democracy, and firmly believed that it would make the world safe for democracy and that this war would end all wars, but I was wrong. War can never end war. Democracy can never be made safe through bloodshed.

Today, when I think of peace, I try to keep myself from thinking of it along romantic lines. I try not to pin my hopes on some impossible technique such as pacifism, having realized that pacifism is possible only to the aristocrats of the human race. But the masses are not that kind of people. And so my hopes for ultimate peace lie today in those step-by-step constructive efforts to strengthen international agencies for peace such as the League of Nations, such as the World Court, and on worldwide propaganda for peace and the lowering of international tensions which will make war less and less likely and armament less and less necessary.

Through these years I have also become less and less enthusiastic about the promise and performance of both political and economic radicalism, now that I have seen radicalism in action. I have seen in

Italy, Germany, and Russia and other parts of the world, movements which sought to bring about Kingdom Come overnight. I have had occasion to observe their ruthlessness, impatience, and intolerance and their readiness to sacrifice means to ends. In an effort to pour new wine into old bottles, they have not only poured out much precious old wine but they frequently have destroyed the bottles themselves. I have seen some of the most sacred human values, for which men have struggled through the ages, trampled under foot because of the radicals' stampede to Kingdom Come.

I have, of course, far greater sympathy for the motives of the radical left than for the radical right, but I have no sympathy for the method of sacrificing means to ends which both employ. I have become through the years a much more convinced liberal than ever before.

The years have taught me to know the evils in the present-day economic system. I know and understand and I have frequently had occasion to point out, sometimes at great cost, these evils of our individualistic society. On the other hand, I know also the evils of state absolutism. While I am convinced that a measure of social ownership in our country will have to come, while I am convinced that the wealth of our nation should be more equitably distributed, while I am persuaded that the highly concentrated wealth of the nation in the hands of the few ought to be wiped out, I am not persuaded that Communism is the only other alternative. Radical and necessary changes can be brought about through democratic processes. I am not persuaded that all private ownership is morally wrong, that all private ownership should be destroyed, that all private agriculture should be collectivized, that all economic functions should come under central bureaucratic control. I have lost my veneration for absolutes, for counsels of perfection, for extremism. They ask too high a price for their millennial promises.

My twenty years, too, have given me a heightened sense of movement in history. I have come to understand the poet who said, "For each age is a dream that is dying and one that is coming to birth." I have lived through wars and revolutions and depressions. I have heard men talk and I have talked myself about the collapse of civilization in the world. But civilization has not collapsed. The world has not come to an end. I have come to feel more and more the undefeated vitality of human life, the amazing capacity which it has for recuperation and survival. While in one part of the world there is reaction, in another there is progress. Across a broken field of many obstacles, the human race is moving forward, checking up year by year some additional gain, some precious value which is then added to the sum total of mankind's treasures which we call civilization. I am more persuaded now than ever of the reality of human progress.

April 28, 1935

IT CAN'T HAPPEN HERE

Can all these things happen here? Given a long depression, given a spineless government unwilling or unable to make drastic reforms for the people, given a clever and unscrupulous demagogue—and Big Business, hoping to check reform, to curb organized labor and reduce taxes by helping to finance such a demagogue, and you can have a dictatorship in these United States, perhaps not as ruthless and brutal as in Italy and in Germany, but you can have it.

How can we prevent it? How can we guard ourselves against it? There are three ways of guarding ourselves against the blight which has fallen upon tens of millions of people abroad. First to defend every basic American liberty, every constitutional guarantee, every tradition of American liberty—not to beguile ourselves into thinking that these liberties can be sacrificed, even temporarily, with impunity. Once we accustom ourselves to treat lightly the ancient liberties for which man shed his blood—the right of free speech, of free assembly, of a free press, of free worship—it is but one step from surrendering our government to gangsters. These liberties are your dearest heritage. You will be the people who will suffer most when these liberties are destroyed, not the ones who destroy them.

Secondly, the way to defend ourselves against Fascism is to expose the forces that are subtly and secretively imposing Fascist ideology upon us. The Hearsts, who, day by day, terrify the American people with a trumped-up Red Scare—the ideological hucksters who seek to persuade the American people that they are being menaced by Communism—these are the masked enemies of America. This is how the Nazis came into power in Germany. They incited people with their wild and furious attacks on Communism and so frightened and confused them that they were ready to sacrifice all their liberties.

Lastly, the way to protect ourselves against Fascism and Communism is to reform our economic life in such a way that there will never be millions of distressed people in our midst who will pray for some radical change.

The answer to dictatorship is liberalism, not communism, liberalism! Unfortunately liberalism is almost discredited today.

May 10, 1936

TAKING STOCK

. . . From 1932, when England wrecked the League of Nations by obstructing international action against Japan, from the moment when England refused to allow the League to proceed against Japan, thereby destroying the authority and the prestige of the League and encouraging Mussolini and Hitler to carry on their political adventures, from the time that Great Britain made private naval arrangements with Germany without the knowledge of the Allies and gave prestige and backing to Hitler, right through to the time that Great Britain refused to back up France when Hitler marched into the Rhineland and remilitarized it, right through the Ethiopian fiasco, up to the present double-dealing in Spain, England has been a dangerously blundering and confusing factor in the international situation. It made possible the present invasion of China by Japan just as it has made possible the increasing strength of the Fascist regimes in Europe. Apologists and propagandists call this uncertain, inept, and improvised diplomacy of England, "muddling through," and they rationalize it into a cardinal virtue. But it is hard upon the world, this "muddling through," and it will ultimately be hard on Great Britain herself. . . .

December 26, 1937

THE RIGHTS OF THE MINORITIES AND
THE NEXT WAR

The genius of America, except in one instance where it failed disastrously, has evidenced itself in resisting the hard concretion of minority groups. Europe is concerned with the rights of minorities; America with the rights of men. The allegiance of an American citizen to his country is direct and immediate, not through a group. Whatever other supplementary loyalties American citizens may have to their religions, or to the memories or cultures of their former homelands—

and few men are without such subsidiary loyalties—their transcendent and basic loyalty is to America.

The American tradition confirmed the individual in his inalienable rights. It proclaimed that the right to life, liberty, and the pursuit of happiness belonged to the individual not because he was a citizen of a state or a member of any particular group or community, but because he was a human being. These rights were given to him by his Creator.

In only one instance did the genius of America falter and fail. It permitted the existence in its midst of one legally disfranchised and socially and economically exploited minority—the Negro. And this one failure embittered our national life from its very inception, snarled and tangled our political processes for three-quarters of a century, and finally led to a tragic Civil War in which five hundred thousand men laid down their lives on the bloody altar of minority persecution. And that problem, as you know, is even now far from being liquidated.

Those people therefore who would break up American life into hostile racial and religious groups and would teach their fellowmen to judge American citizens not on the basis of individual worth, character, or achievement but on the basis of the race to which they belong, or the religion to which they subscribe, are the deadliest foes of the spirit and genius and peace of the American people.

If we wish no minority problems to plague us in this country as they have plagued the nations abroad, let us be careful not to create them. They are easily created—just as Germany created a Jewish minority problem where none existed—but they are damnably hard to end.

Such attempts have not infrequently been made in our country by men who never quite caught the spirit which is America.

Lincoln witnessed such an attempt in his own day. The "Know-Nothing Party" sought to disfranchise and reduce to the status of a disfavored minority the newly arrived Irish and German immigrants and Catholics. Lincoln clearly saw in it a threat to America and denounced it:

"I am not a Know-Nothing; that is certain. How could I be? How can any one who abhors the oppression of Negroes be in favor of degrading classes of white people? Our progress in degeneracy appears to me to be pretty rapid. As a nation we began by declaring that 'all men are created equal.' We now practically read it 'all men are created equal, except Negroes.' When the Know-Nothings get control, it will read 'all men are created equal, except Negroes and foreigners and Catholics.' When it comes to this, I shall prefer emigrating to some country where they make no pretense of loving liberty—to Russia, for instance, where despotism can be taken pure, and without the base alloy of hypocrisy."

A similar attempt was made not long ago in the Klan movement. The American tradition again resisted it.

It is cropping up again today—as a result largely of the propaganda of subsidized alien Nazi agents, representing a government which is the sworn enemy of all democracy but proposing in the United States to save our democratic form of government for us by preaching hate against Jews, or labor organizations whom Fascists do not like. Americans will have to resist it again. Not for the sake of the Jews who are the targets at this particular moment—but for the sake of the spirit, the unity and the peace of mind of America!

February 26, 1938

THE "NEW REALISM" IN INTERNATIONAL AFFAIRS

This is the story of the last few years and of the part which Great Britain has played in bringing chaos into the world.

Her excuses are well known. First of all it was claimed that the policy of Britain was aimed to avert war. But it is clear to every thoughtful observer that it does not avert war, but postpones war, while enabling nations to prepare for a bigger and better war to come. The appetites of the aggressors are not to be appeased. Yesterday it was Austria, today it is Czechoslovakia, tomorrow it may be Hungary and Romania. Every forward step made by the imperialistic countries is clearly and unmistakably a step nearer to the next world war. All this talk about appeasement, this giving in to dictators for the sake of appeasement is a hoax.

This appeasement is to be had at the expense of other nations, not Great Britain. Up to this time you have read of no appeasement at the expense of Great Britain. England is always ready to offer sacrifices but not at her expense but at the expense of Austria, Czechoslovakia, etc. However, there will soon come a time when this perverted altruism will be played out and the smaller and weaker nations will refuse to be offered up on the altar of British altruism. When that time comes there will be a war which will suck the whole of Europe into it. . . .

It is clear to every thoughtful observer that only the breakup of Russia will satisfy the Fuehrer of the Third Reich. He has said it over and over again. He means it. He has now organized an anti-Communist front of Germany, Italy, and Japan. He would like to see Russia smashed and ultimately destroyed. That means war. And it will not be an isolated war but a war which will entangle every nation on the face of the earth. . . .

May 8, 1938

WHAT IS BEHIND THE EFFORT TO LINK
JEWS WITH COMMUNISM?

. . . This you may pass on to your friends, Jewish and non-Jewish. The Jewish people of the United States will not be blackmailed into joining any reactionary movement or any "Red Hunt" or anti-Communist crusade because of any threat of reprisal such as the intensification of an anti-Semitic campaign or broadcasting still further the accusation that Jews are sympathetic with Communism. We have too wide a perspective of history to be tricked into such a position. We are going to denounce Communism and Fascism and Nazism for their unsound principles, for their reliance upon what we regard as immoral methods—for their heartless disregard of the rights of the individual. We are going to speak in defense of democracy, liberalism, justice, equality, and brotherhood, and we will take our chances with the rest of mankind. Just at the moment we are the most hard pressed. Just now we are on the anvil being beaten by the hammer. This is not a novel experience for us. We will endure. We will suffer. We will endure and we will carry on, faithful to the classic teachings of our faith. Freedom, justice, liberty, tolerance, brotherhood, goodwill —these are the things we shall labor for, work for, and suffer for.

December 11, 1938

CHRISTIAN–JEW

. . . I do not want any human being to sacrifice his convictions, but I do not want anyone to make any demands of me to sacrifice mine. That is a very simple but seemingly difficult thought for most people to grasp. I am not even averse to men who are inclined to extol their nation or race or religion, who are inclined to claim for them superior virtues or excellencies, or exclusive salvation. All I ask is that they should not use their particular conceits to victimize me or to crush me or to victimize others.

If a people thinks that it is the leaven of the earth, if a people thinks that it is the original *Urvolk,* the original stock which alone possesses those gifts and energies which are required to regenerate a world, as Fichte told the German people to believe—I have no objection to that. But I want to know at whose expense that is to be achieved. And how? At their own expense, or at mine? Through their own sacrifice, or through the sacrifice of us or of others? By improving themselves or by the subjection of others. . . .

The essential ties of the world are not the ties of uniformity, but the ties of goodwill, the kindly disposition to meet on the basis of our common humanity and to explore opportunities for cooperation in tasks advantageous to all.

Our world is held together not by the overzealous, impatient, and intolerant would-be saviors of mankind, but by the hierarchy of men of goodwill whose wisdom and kindness of heart are the oil which lubricates the machine of human progress.

Goodwill is much more than tolerance. Goodwill is much more than amiable garrulity about brotherhood in the abstract. Goodwill is an active principle. The emphasis is on "will," the determination to destroy prejudice within one's self, to discover ways of working together with other people. . . .

December 24, 1939

A THIRD TERM FOR PRESIDENT ROOSEVELT

. . . In my judgment, Mr. Roosevelt's successor, be he Republican or Democrat, will have to face these problems realistically and honestly. He will, in the main, be compelled to follow the same line that Mr. Roosevelt followed. He, too, will have to think in terms of the masses and not of the classes. He, too, will have to think in terms of relief and reconstruction, from the bottom up, and not from the top down, in terms of the laborer, the farmer, the young boy seeking a job, and not in terms of the corporation and the banker. . . .

Nevertheless, because of the very admiration of his friends for Mr. Roosevelt, and the recognition of all that he has achieved, many of his friends, among whom I am one, would urge him not to stand for reelection. The third term is not a law, but a tradition, a tradition which reflects the political wisdom of the American people, a custom which is even more powerful than a law. It is a custom which has not been violated in one hundred and fifty years. During these one hundred and fifty years there have been critical times, some of them more critical than the present. . . .

With this tradition the American people has come through a century and a half unscathed. The question which now arises is whether the times in which we live require a break with this tradition. To that question, I for one, answer, "No!" particularly at this time when popular governments are receding all over the globe, when the trend is definitely in the direction of dictatorship and greater concentration in the hands of the one indispensable man, it is desirable that the President of the greatest free nation of the earth should reaffirm his faith in democracy by refusing the tempting offer of a third term, to indicate that free government is not dependent on any one man, however good and able he may be. To insist on the reelection of Roosevelt this year on the ground that he is the sole leader to whom the American people can turn, the one man among one hundred and fifty million citizens who can lead them, is to acknowledge publicly the bankruptcy of democracy.

March 31, 1940

PROPHETIC PREACHING

Religion has not always been faithful to its informing purpose. After the first great impulse which creates a religion embodies itself into an institution, it loses much of its daring and courage. All religions at the first moment of their revelation, when they leap hot and frenzied from the soul of some God-intoxicated seer, are purging fires, consuming flames. They speak in thunder and sweep life with a "besom of destruction." They are "set over nations and over kingdoms, to root out and to pull down, to destroy and to overthrow, to build anew and to plant." The world stands aghast and frightened. It turns upon the prophets of the new revelation and destroys them, only to kneel a moment later and worship them.

But soon the hot coals of religious passion cool off. The heroic mood vanishes. Loyalties lose their sacrificial quality. The voice crying in the wilderness becomes an echo, faint and timid. Enthusiasm is quenched in habit. Religion becomes institutionalized. Hierarchy and vested interests appear. The church becomes an end in itself. When its interests are at stake it will compromise and yield and betray men in their direst needs.

This danger, of course, is inherent in all organization. Whatever moral pioneering has been done in the world has been largely the work, not of groups, but of individual spiritual rebels and nonconformists. Revelations never come to groups. There were schools of prophets in ancient Israel, but they were merely the monitors of ancient superstitions. It was only after the individual separated himself from the school and the group and pursued his own solitary quest of truth, that prophecy discovered its authentic voice and mood.

The church, therefore, freighted down with organization, must constantly war against itself to save its soul. The church must protect itself against the downward drag of institutionalism and the paralysis of will which result from overorganization and prosperity. The church triumphant often spells the faith defeated. How often has the church been a flunkey to the rich! How often has its revolutionary passion for justice and social righteousness been held in leash by worldliness and sycophancy! The church set out to admonish men to put away the evil of their doings, to "cease to do evil, learn to do well, seek justice, relieve the oppressed, judge the fatherless, plead for the widow," but it ended by truckling to the powerful and the rich, and by sharing in the spoils of the marauders and exploiters of society.

In the Temple at Jerusalem, there was a flute fashioned out of reeds, an old flute, having come down from the days of Moses. The sound of the flute was sweet and beautiful, ravishing the souls of worshipers. One day the priests at the sanctuary decided to decorate the flute, and they covered it with gold. The flute was never the same again. Its sweet, clear, cool tones were now harsh, metallic, and jarring. Gold has coarsened its melody. . . .

April 7, 1940

1941—THE YEAR OF CRISIS AND INDECISION

The closing days of 1941 found our country for the first time since the last world war a united people, a patriotically aroused people, a people ready to make whatever sacrifice it may be called upon to make willingly, to save America. All forms of intolerance went underground for the duration. Anti-Semitism went underground for the duration. The American people understand clearly now what it should have understood long ago—that anti-Semitism is a form of Nazi attack, part of the total war program, a branch of fifth column activity. We are a united people today. And we are girding ourselves for the great struggle ahead. . . .

Not only was our country not prepared for the war in a military sense. It was also not prepared for it in a spiritual sense. President Roosevelt understood as did Churchill that it was necessary to set clearly before the fighting forces of free men the objectives of the war. What are they fighting for? What can they look forward to at the end of the war? A charter which men would underwrite with blood, if necessary! You will recall that dramatic meeting in mid-Atlantic which resulted in the drafting of the eight-point statement of peace. We are fighting for a free world, for a free life. We are fighting to make possible four basic freedoms for human beings—freedom of speech, freedom of thought, freedom of worship, freedom of the press. We are fighting to put an end to unbridled brutality, to international anarchy, to the suppression of racial minorities or religious minorities. We are fighting to create the kind of a world in which every individual belongs and has his rights—which rights may not be abrogated by dictators and tyrants. We are fighting for a world of peace, international justice.

While the war itself will not achieve it, while the armistice itself will not automatically bring about that kind of world, the defeat of Hitler and what he stands for—the recrudescent barbarism, the twentieth century barbarism, the racialism and chauvinism—will be destroyed, and the ground will be cleared for another earnest effort to build a world in which free men will live in dignity and security.

It is good that we have now a united free world fighting this desperate foe. It is good that we have agreed not to make a separate peace with any or all the defeated governments. It is good to know that a billion people are today banded together to put an end to that which has afflicted the world now for all too long.

January 4, 1942

A FREE WORLD FOR FREE MEN

May I point out that America should not assume the role of Lord Bountiful for the whole war-torn world. We should not be made to play the role of a global, good-natured philanthropist. It is a pleasant role to assume. It makes you feel good, but it is a dangerous role to assume. It is a role which we cannot carry through. Our own burden will be terrific after the war. Our own people will have to work much harder for a long time for a lower standard of living until the crushing burden of war debt will be lifted from their shoulders. For decades to come we shall be paying staggering taxes. We will therefore not be able to take upon our own shoulders the whole load of reconstruction. We do not possess the strength to do that.

Following the last war we were persuaded that we had to lend billions of dollars to our erstwhile enemies so that they could become lucrative customers again of our manufactured goods. We did just that. Then we were told that we could not get our own money back except in goods, and we did not want their goods to flood our own markets and close down our own factories. The billions which we loaned Germany and other nations did help them. It helped them to build up their industrial plants and to become our competitors and to undersell us in the markets of the world. Many millions of our loans were used to beautify the cities of Germany, to build stadiums and sport palaces and to equip its military establishment.

The billions which we loaned did not restore either Europe or the United States to economic stability. When the orgy of building and undergirding could not be carried on any longer, the whole economic structure collapsed in '29.

These same generous economists are again trying to sell us the same set of ideas for the end of this war. Again they are abetted by Nazi sympathizers and Fascists, and again they are playing upon the motive of forgiveness. As soon as Hitler and Mussolini are out of the way, the American people should turn to the German and Italian people and say to them: "Too bad you wrecked the world and brought untold misery on mankind. Too bad you perpetrated the bestialities which you did. It really was not your fault. It was the fault of Hitler and Mussolini. You were just innocent victims. Now you are real democrats. We are delighted with you. From now on we will pour out our money and make you strong again. One hundred and thirty millions of Americans will work to make you strong enough to wreck the world again as you did in 1939 and 1914." . . .

I say this not in any spirit of vindictiveness. I base it exclusively on what happened after the last war. The American people should not assume the sole responsibility for footing the entire bill. Nor should it give the impression that it is prepared to launch a global Lend-Lease which after the war will drop "manna" in every backyard of the world. Whatever relief we will be able to give in concert with our Allies, without subjecting our own people to severe privations, we will, of course, in all conscience give. But other nations likewise must assume responsibility to feed the masses of the world. Whatever we can do to help restore law and order, to set up stable governments, we must, of course, do. Whatever we can do by agreement with other nations to facilitate international trade by removing trade barriers, high tariffs, quota systems, preferences, and controls, we should, of course, do. . . .

November 29, 1942

THE CONSPIRACY OF SILENCE

What is really driving us toward Palestine, and why is our movement irresistible? Our sages say that two Arks led the Children of Israel through the wilderness on to the Promised Land: the Ark wherein lay the body of Joseph, and the Ark of the Covenant. Two Arks! An Ark of death and an Ark of faith!

Two million dead are leading us on today through a dread wilderness to Palestine! The martyred hosts in this last and greatest tragedy of our dispersion—they are leading us on. The horror and pathos of their needless deaths—they are leading us on. Their bodies lie in unknown mass graves, but the Ark which enshrines their imperishable memories moves on before us. The vast ghostly company from the slaughter-pens of Warsaw, Cracow, and Lemberg now joins the older companies of the First World War, and the tortured hosts of all the foregoing generations, back to the holocaust in the days of Chmielnicki, and the still earlier martyrs from every century and from all parts of Europe. It is their spirits which give us no rest, which warn us against all vain illusions and false hopes. It is their innocent blood which will not be covered up, until out of their martyrdom a new life will be born for their homeless people.

The legendary hero of the brave Czechs, Zizka, the avenger of Huss, on dying, asked his followers to remove his skin and to make of it a drum with which to lead the Taborites into battle! That is how a great people employs even death to lead it on to victory and to life!

Along with the Ark of Death there moves before us also the Ark of the Covenant—the Ark of Faith—our covenant with the future, our faith in our destiny, in ourselves and in the God of our Fathers who sleepeth not, nor slumbereth. "Exiles are never terminated and peoples are never made free except through faith."

The hammer of destiny is even now fashioning a new world, and Israel is again the anvil which bears the strokes of humanity. It is a noble role, but we are a little tired of this role. We have been noble and beaten for so long. We now wish to be noble and free and, as a free people in its own land, to work with all other free peoples for a just and peaceful world.

May 2, 1943

ON THE EVE OF INVASION

We are invading Europe to destroy a root evil, to cut away a cancerous growth which has kept Europe and the rest of the world from settling down to those peaceful pursuits which alone can give mankind a better and juster world order—industry, trade, and cultural and spiritual activities.

We are invading Europe to destroy the spirit of militarism, the spirit of national aggression, the lust for domination. We are invading Europe to create permanent forms, instrumentalities, and opportunities for international cooperation which will render a resort to war and violence every twenty or twenty-five years unnecessary. We are invading Europe to build a new society in a shattered and chaotic world.

We ought to ask ourselves at this moment: "Are we really moving in that direction? Is mankind moving toward unity, toward the creation of permanent forms of international cooperation, toward the uprooting of the spirit of militarism and aggression in the world?" It is hard to say. We are not at all sure. On the one hand there is every indication that we are actually moving in that direction. A few months ago, in the city of Moscow, representatives of four great nations, the Soviet Union, Great Britain, the United States, and China met and issued a declaration which, if adhered to, will be a decisive turning point in human history. They agreed that "the united action which they pledged for war will be continued after the war for the organization and maintenance of peace and security." "They recognized the necessity of establishing at the earliest practicable date a general international organization, based on the principle of the sovereign equality of all peace-loving states, and open to membership by all such states, large and small, for the maintenance of international peace and security." They agreed that "pending the reestablishment of law and order and the inauguration of a system of general security, they will consult with one another and with other nations with a view to joint action on behalf of the community of nations."

This is vision. This is promise and hope. This is heartening prophecy for the future of the world. This makes all sacrifices worthwhile. They are resolved, first of all, to wage war together to the end.

They have agreed to destroy Nazism, and not to return the sword to the scabbard until that is done. They agreed to bring to punishment those unspeakable human beasts who were responsible for the appalling atrocities. They also agreed to collaborate after the war for peace, to work together during the transition period, for the creation of a permanent international organization. This opens up new and wonderful vistas for mankind.

On the other hand, one has heard disconcerting talk in recent months, and has observed disconcerting acts which do not reflect the spirit of this Moscow Declaration. We have witnessed, for example, unilateral action on the part of the Soviet Union with regard to Poland. If powerful nations permit themselves to act unilaterally without consulting their Allies, the world will fast revert to bitter rivalry and competition. . . .

One hears talk about the absorption of this or that small state with the Soviet Union. One hears talk about dividing Europe into two large spheres of influence—Eastern Europe, Southeastern and Central Europe into the Soviet Union sphere and Western Europe into the British sphere of influence, the one sphere to be communistically dominated and the other capitalistically. Such a division of Europe into two rival and ideologically competitive systems is simply the prelude to a third world war.

All such arrangements carry in them the seeds of future wars, civil war, and revolution. The organization of mankind after the war can be either a worldwide, overall organization, or it can be nothing. It can be either a system of collective security for all or it will be the old system where groups of nations which possess real or fancied interests in common try to make themselves secure by means of costly and never quite adequate armaments against rival groups of nations. Such a system has always led and must always lead to war. . . .

February 27, 1944

THE ATLANTIC CHARTER—
ANOTHER SCRAP OF PAPER?

So it appears that an agreement has been made between the Soviet Union and England to divide Europe and other parts of the world into two great spheres of influence, a Soviet sphere, the East, Finland, Poland, Bulgaria, Romania, Yugoslavia, Hungary, Czechoslovakia, Austria—a congeries of satellite states under the aegis of the Soviet

Union, and another a British sphere in the Mediterranean and in Western Europe—Italy, Greece, Portugal, Spain, Belgium, Holland.

Germany, of course, remains unaccounted for in this new balance of power. Germany, therefore, remains a focus of intrigue between these two masters of Europe. In which sphere will Germany finally find its place? . . .

In the light of all that has happened, the decisions, permanent or tentative, which were taken at Dumbarton Oaks take on a rather sinister significance. It becomes apparent that what was planned there was the sanction of military alliances of a few great powers to dominate the many. In the light of this, it is crystal clear why the great powers will reserve for themselves the veto power against the many, so that they can never be declared aggressors. They have consented to the creation of a world force which may be used by the Security Council of the new world organization to enforce its decisions, but they have at the same time made sure that any one of the big Powers can veto a decision without itself being declared an aggressor and that force will not be employed against it. . . .

It is high time that America should begin to assert its moral authority in this situation and publicly refuse to sanction or condone by silence any deals which are made at the expense of the smaller nations. We must return to the fundamentals of the Atlantic Charter, the Four Freedoms, the ideals for which we entered the war: no territorial changes while the war goes on; peoples must be permitted to choose their own governments; a real world organization created not to freeze the status quo for French, Dutch, English, or Russian imperialism; but one created to protect every people in its sovereign rights regardless of size or strength. A statement should be issued by our government that we are not in favor of a new balance of power, that we are opposed to new military alliances. I think that this is greatly needed at this time. I am not so sure that we will make such a statement or that we will make the effort to live up to the principles of the Atlantic Charter. But it should be made or we shall lose the peace before we have won the war.

December 24, 1944

WHAT IS REFORM JUDAISM?

Those who run to Reform Judaism as to an easy sort of religion, one which makes few demands and can be easily tucked away in a corner of one's life—for example, observing Yahrzeit, coming to Temple on

Rosh Hashanah and Yom Kippur, and paying dues to a Temple—those Jews are simply missing the whole spirit of this great spiritual forward-looking movement in Jewish life and thought.

Those who would use Reform Judaism as a way of escape from spiritual commitments and disciplines, as a sort of back door to religious indifferentism, as a vehicle to become amateur gentiles, are abusing the genius and the spirit of this great religious movement in Jewish life.

Reform Judaism is Judaism, a religion which makes demands upon its devotee of the highest ethical conduct and of study, worship and observance. It is a way of life, or it is nothing.

A Reform Judaism without a Jewish home, without fixed habits of prayer and worship, without the observance in some form of the Sabbath and the festivals, without Jewish knowledge and study, without the deep emotional content of life which is stirred by ceremonies and observances, without eager and joyous identification with all that is fine and noble in Jewish communal life, and in all that contributes to the preservation of our people's life and faith in the world, is no Judaism at all.

There is but one Judaism. It is a covenant. It is a covenant with God and with Jewish destiny. It is a conviction and a commitment. It is a way of life whether it be Reform, Conservative, or Orthodox Judaism. I assume that in the life of our people there is room for all three forms of Judaism. What is essential is dedication to the essential spirit of Judaism and to its preservation. If there is love in your heart for Judaism you will be a good Jew. The beautiful temples, the beautiful organ, the beautiful ritual will mean nothing to you unless you put yourself into your faith.

March 26, 1946

LIBERAL JUDAISM AND ISRAEL

If history is any guide, the Jews of today who will continue to live in other lands will, by and large, maintain the same attitude toward the State of Israel as their forefathers did. Theirs will be a most sympathetic relationship toward that land. They will materially help it to absorb as many Jews as will wish to go there or may have to go there. They will help to build up its cultural, scientific, and spiritual institutions, as well as its economic life so that it may become a land of which Jews everywhere can be proud.

Israel will again come to be the nonpolitical center of world Jewry. Pilgrims will go there as of old—and not merely the pious. There will be a free flow of manifold communications, of mutual stimulation, of give and take. Israel will again come to exercise a unifying and sustaining influence in Jewish life everywhere.

We shall remain one people, one historic community, as of old. But the Jews of Israel will be Israeli citizens and the Jews of the United States will be citizens of the United States, and similarly with Jews in other lands.

They will owe undivided allegiance to their respective countries and they will discharge loyally their full duties as citizens, as Jews have always done. But they will retain a special attachment to the land of Israel which will in no way interfere with their duties and obligations as citizens of their respective countries. . . .

Israel will not be a theocratic state, but for all Jews—that is, for all those who wish to remain Jews—Israel will continue to be the land of the treasured memories as well as of unfolding social and cultural realities which, if nobly conceived and achieved, will be eagerly welcomed as stimulating influences in their lives. Is not this expressed in the ancient prayer of our people: "Oh, cause Thou a new light to shine over Zion, and may we all be worthy to enjoy its light speedily."

Some ten years ago I had occasion to write:

"To the thoughtful Jews it is becoming increasingly clear that there are no substitutes in Jewish life for religion. Neither philanthropy nor culture nor nationalism is adequate for the stress and challenge of our lives. All these interests can and must find their rightful place within the general pattern of Judaism. But the pattern must be of Judaism, the Judaism of the prophet, the saint, the mystic and the rabbi; the Judaism which speaks of God, and the worship of God, and the commandments of God and the quest of God."

There have been many false prophets of "ersatz" Judaism in our midst who have frequently misled our people. There were professional social workers, for example, who announced that a full complement of scientifically administered hospitals and orphanages and other social agencies was a sufficient *vade mecum* for the Jewish people, and that the synagogue and religious schools were quite unnecessary. At best, they were to be tolerated only as a concession to those who still take such things seriously, and in order not to create unpleasant friction in the community.

There were certain educators who resented the intrusion of religion in their ultrascientific curricula. Judaism, they said, was not a religion, but a way of life—that is to say, their way of life, which, of course, was nonreligious or antireligious. Jewish education should, according to them, not be religious at all, only nationalistic and linguistic. At best, the religious note might be smuggled in, but only as a concession to old-timers and cranks who do not know any better.

There were those Jewish spokesmen who offered Jewish nationalism as a substitute for Judaism, forgetting that nationalism as such, unredeemed by a moral vision and responsibility, had sadly fragmentized our world, provincialized its peoples, and is driving nations madly from one disaster to another; forgetting, further, that there is a widely felt and widely answered need for religion and religious institutions even among peoples whose national life is already fully established, who are in their own lands, and who are possessed of a rich national culture.

The upbuilding of a Jewish national home in Palestine is one great, urgent, and historically inescapable task of Jewry. The upbuilding of Jewish religious life in America and elsewhere throughout the world, inclusive of Israel, is another. One is no substitute for the other. One is not opposed to the other.

November 17, 1948

HOW FAR CAN A DOLLAR GO?

How far will the dollar go? We are trying to do two things with the power of our money. We are trying to extend economic aid to European and other countries, and we are trying to use the power of our money to bring them into an alliance with us against the Soviet Union. We are trying to counteract Communist ideology with money. There are not enough dollars to do that! We tried to do it in China. We sent hundreds of millions of dollars into that country, but China went steadily into the ranks of the Communists. The dollar cannot go that far.

We are being driven to rebuild Germany with our money and we will soon help Franco in Spain with our money in pursuit of this very policy of encircling the Soviet Union.

We are by way of launching a bold new project called Point 4. . . .

Behind this bold new project is the thought that with the power of our money and our financial aid, we can organize and keep organized the free world against an aggressive Soviet bloc. We are engaged in a new crusade, just as we were in the First World War, to make the world safe for democracy, which ended in Hitler and Mussolini, and in the Second World War.

I am inclined to believe that this is the way of national bank-ruptcy. I am inclined to believe that however powerful the dollar is, it is not that powerful—not powerful enough to run the world. I do not believe that any single nation, even as great and rich as our be-loved country, is by itself able with the power of its wealth to control the political life of the world. I am afraid that by pouring out our resources as we have begun to do, by increasing our terrifying na-tional debt by four, five, and six billion dollars annually, as we have been doing, we are undermining the stability of our own economic life and by so doing, the stability of the economic life of the world. We might make a greater contribution through our statesmanship, through our spiritual leadership in the world, by throwing the weight of our authority and prestige to the United Nations to enable this body to assume the responsibility for doing what needs to be done, to keep the world economically stable and to keep the nations of the world that are free, free.

There has been too much of a tendency to go it alone, to do it alone, because we have been enchanted by the power of our own wealth. It is not wise to divide the world into two parts and to under-take to arm one half of the world against the other. We haven't the strength and the ability to do it, even if it were morally justified.

The dollar can go very far in helping peoples economically. The dollar by itself cannot go far enough to ensure the freedom of peoples who do not wish to be free and the peace of the world. Some day we will wake up to the limitations of the potency of the dollar. We will then perhaps go back to a basic idea that "not by strength and not by might, but by My spirit, saith the Lord."

January 29, 1949

ARE YOU RELIGIOUS—ARE YOU A JEW?

To be sure, The Temple—our Temple, any Temple—is for fellowship, and the element of sociability should not be ignored, but a synagogue is not a social club. Some people really think that the Temple should not only be a social club, but an exclusive club, forgetting that the purpose of a church, a temple, or a synagogue is to make men aware of their common humanity, rich and poor alike, young and old. Sinners all, we all share a common need of repentance and improvement.

The synagogue is commissioned to do what no other agencies in the community are obligated to do, to give spiritual guidance, ethical inspiration, education to young and old in the tenets and practices of Judaism, in the life, history, and culture of the Jewish people, and to be a sanctuary for public worship. The synagogue should arouse a hunger for these things, and then try to satisfy that hunger.

Being a member in a synagogue is quite a different thing from being a member, say, in a society to maintain an orphanage or a home for the aged or any other philanthropic institution. Such institutions we support for others, for the less fortunate whom we wish to help. A synagogue we join for ourselves, and unless we use it, it cannot serve us. We have to be receptive vessels for the influence which a religious institution can give.

It is quite fantastic to say: "I love music, but I never go to a symphony. I never go to an opera. I never listen to music but I love music." I am not intolerant of Jews who have only a checkbook relationship to the synagogue and not a prayer-book relationship. I do not judge them harshly, and I certainly do not read any Jew out of the fold unless he wishes to read himself out. "A Jew even if he sins is a Jew." There is always the hope that such a Jew may become a *baal teshuvah,* may repent and return. The sheer affiliation with a synagogue is evidence of a vague loyalty to the central institution of the Jewish faith. I do not quarrel with such Jews, but I am sorry that they miss in their lives the strength and the beauty which the message of the synagogue can bring to them—the uplift, the deepening and the enrichment of spirit.

April 16, 1950

FREEDOM IN THE UNITED STATES

I recall that my first appearances before the City Club or under its auspices were during the Red Scare of 1919–1921, the witch-hunting days of the A. Mitchell Palmer era during the intolerant backwash of the First World War when our community, along with other communities in the country, was shut tight against free speech under the scare of Communism, and when the City Club, in an effort to reassert basic Americanism, established open forums on our Public Square and in other parts of the city to give men a chance to participate in free discussions. . . .

We are moving, I am afraid, into another such period today,

induced by the same scare of Communism. It is more serious today, for Communism has became a greater menace than it was thirty years ago, and democracies have lost a good deal of their confidence.

In fighting Communism we must make doubly sure that we are fighting Communists, not citizens whose views we do not happen to like. It is so easy to permit our prejudices and our dislike for the unlike to run away with us. It is so easy to brand and to excommunicate a man who does not happen at the moment to agree with a policy which is favored by our Government or by the majority of our people, but whose disagreement may be grounded in a profound patriotic devotion and loyalty to our country. We must ask ourselves what it is that we want to suppress and why we want to suppress it and whether the suppression will ultimately serve the best interests of our free and democratic America.

In our zeal to fight Communists, we must not forget to fight Fascists, and there are plenty of them in our midst though they go by different and less revealing names. Sometimes they arrogate to themselves a monopoly of American patriotism. They are as dangerous to American democracy as are the Communists. The Nazi-Fascists in Germany rode into power on the pretext of fighting Communism, and proceeded to destroy the German republic; and in so doing they established one of the most vicious and contemptible, and to their own people most disastrous, dictatorships in history.

In the days to come, there will be many political adventurers and unscrupulous demagogues who may wish to ride into power, like Hitler, on the issue of "fighting Communism." They will stop at nothing. They will not limit themselves to routing out Communists from government. They will try to rout out everybody whom they do not like from our educational system, from our universities and colleges, from our churches, from the press. These people will rally around themselves, as Hitler did, all the reactionaries, all the enemies of social liberalism in this country. Ultimately they will exploit racial and religious animosities to serve their political ends. Let us learn from history. The time to speak out against all this is now. . . .

October 27, 1950

A LETTER TO MR. TRUMAN

I pass on to the second and more serious matter about which I should like to write to President Truman. In his address to the country the other evening, he summoned the American people to unity and self-sacrifice because of the grave danger in which our country finds itself. "Those of us who work in the government," he stated, "will do our best, but the outcome depends, as it has always depended, on the spirit and energy of our people."

In my humble judgment there has been very little wrong with the spirit and energy of the American people. They did not fail, either in unity or in the spirit of sacrifice, either in the First World War or in the Second World War. Whatever was asked of them they performed, competently and patriotically. They gave their sons to the war, and their daughters—as many as the government demanded. On the battlefields our fighting men gave an excellent account of themselves, and withdrew from no sacrifice in life or blood. Our shops, our mines, our mills were adequately manned. Whatever taxes our government imposed upon our people they paid. Whatever restrictions and rationings were imposed upon them were complied with. There never was and there is not now any reason to doubt the loyalty, the patriotism, and the readiness to sacrifice on the part of the American people in defense of their country or their freedom. I doubt whether the proclamation of a state of national emergency was really required to make the American people aware of how serious the present situation is.

The American people are not illiterate. They read their newspapers, they listen to their radio, they know what is going on in Korea; they know what is going on in the United Nations. Their sons are even at this moment fighting and some of them dying in Korea.

But they, the American people, do not make our foreign policy. They did not send our armies unprepared into Korea. They were not consulted as to whether we should go into Korea. According to our Constitution, Congress, and Congress alone, has the power to declare war and make peace. The Congress of the United States was not consulted about sending our troops into Korea. President Truman alone decided this grave issue by the simple device of calling this intervention not a war, but a police action. This police action has already cost our people 40,000 casualties.

Our allies likewise were not consulted. In his speech last Friday evening, the President said that we must work with a sense of real partnership and common purpose with the other free nations who need our help as we need theirs. These partners were ignored when President Truman ordered our troops into Korea. The question is, why?

The United Nations, too, was not consulted. It is the prime responsibility of the United Nations, not of the United States, to resist aggression in the world. It was only after President Truman launched our military effort in Korea that the United States asked for the approval of the United Nations. This is not the procedure outlined in the Charter of the United Nations.

There is in my judgment need for a reexamination of our entire foreign policy which has been going from bad to worse ever since President Truman, on his own responsibility, announced the so-called Truman Doctrine and pledged our country to resist Communism all over the world, a commitment on which we are simply not able to make good and one which our allies are unwilling to back up. A reexamination of our entire foreign policy is called for. . . .

In his address the other evening the President announced four things which the American people must do and will do in this crisis. I am in perfect agreement with all these four things. First, he said, we will continue to uphold and, if necessary, to defend with arms the principles of the United Nations, the principles of freedom and justice. Fine! But please, let the United Nations decide when the principles of freedom and justice are endangered, and what should be done about it! That is its business. Let the deliberations and decisions and actions be collective—not unilateral! Let us not act first and then get the approval of the United Nations for our actions. The United Nations has assumed the responsibility of keeping law and order in the world. Please, let us not have a private Truman Doctrine of our own. Let us not do our own private policing. Let us not jump into Formosa or Indo-China or Korea or elsewhere—and there are a hundred potential danger spots in the world—until the United Nations directs us, along with all other nations, to act. We must avoid not only aggression, which we are not likely to indulge in, but aggressiveness as well. Let us strengthen the United Nations. Let us channel whatever help we can give to the world through the United Nations. Let us strengthen this international organization, which is the sole hope of a stable world to come.

Secondly, the President said he would continue to work with the other nations to strengthen our combined defenses. Excellent! But let us be practical about it! Let us make sure how far the other nations are prepared to go along, and how much they are prepared to pay out of their own resources to strengthen their own defenses. Of course, they will permit us to help finance their military establishments, but they may not be willing to use them every time we think they should. Let us not drain our own resources too far to equip other nations militarily. Let us think first and foremost and always of our own defenses. Again, in our eagerness to organize the world against the Soviet Union and line up the free nations of the world against Communistic dictatorship, let us not undermine our moral position in the world by allying ourselves with Francos and Fascists and Titos and Nazis in Europe and reactionaries in Asia. It makes the Voice of America sound hollow in the ears of the world. In the long run that will undo everything that we are trying to do.

The President urged us further to build up our army, navy, and air force and to make more weapons for ourselves and our allies. By all means, let us build up to full strength, but let us not bankrupt ourselves by trying to arm half the world against the other half. Our resources are not limitless. Our government is already 257 billion dollars in debt. It is the hope of the Soviet Union that we will destroy ourselves through bankruptcy and sink our military strength into the great Serbonian bog of Asia.

The President finally urged that we expand our economy and keep it on an even keel. Nothing is more important than that. We must guard against inflation through greater production, higher taxes, and through price and wage control. In this connection, an American has the right to ask why the President of the United States did not use up till now the powers which were clearly his to control prices and wages, and why he permitted our country to move into the dangerous inflation spiral in which we already find ourselves.

These are some of the things about which I should like to write to Mr. Truman. I should also like to draw his attention to some words which he himself uttered the other evening, and suggest that in those words lies the right direction of statesmanship in these dire days. He said, "There is no conflict between the legitimate interests of the free world and those of the Soviet Union that cannot be settled by peaceful means, and we will continue to take every honorable step we can to avoid general war." This is quite different from the dogmatism, the rantings and the war-mongering of so many others, which are so frequently heard these days. . . .

December 17, 1950

A GREAT AGE

I believe that the age in which we live is a great age and that we are moving toward an even greater age. I believe that our present age is one of the greatest in human history. We are too near our times properly to appraise them. . . .

In characterizing our age as great, I am thinking in terms of social progress and welfare, in terms of human advancement and civilization. More is being done in our day for the improvement of the conditions of the common man, for the raising of his standard of living, his health, his education, and for his protection against the disabilities of sickness, unemployment, and old age, than in any generation, than any five generations in the past. Never were more determined efforts made to bring about a fairer sharing of the wealth that is produced and a better way of life for all.

Never have the submerged races and peoples of the earth risen as they have risen in our day to demand and to achieve, as they have to a large measure achieved, freedom and self-determination. Within the last eight years one-fourth of the earth's population—more than five hundred million non-self-governing people—have obtained their political freedom. Imperialism and colonialism are in their death throes. Backward peoples are pressing forward into the light of a new day, and the exploitation of the dark races of the earth is rapidly drawing to a close.

What we are witnessing in our day, if we have eyes not only to see things, but also to see into the heart of things, is not social disintegration, but a radical new reintegration of humanity, a profound change in the social evolution of man, a change not free, of course, from dangers—for there is no progress without danger—but one of boundless and immeasurable potentialities.

I do not wish to overdraw the picture. I am not suggesting that our age is approaching idyllic perfection, or that the millennium is just around the corner.

The important thing to consider is not whether we are on the eve of the millennium, but whether the major trends of our age are in the direction of the hoped-for good society, or away from it. Is our age trying to eradicate poverty and illiteracy and to raise the standard of living of people, regardless of race or color or creed? Is it trying to satisfy the legitimate aspirations of peoples to national freedom and independence? Is it trying to organize the world for peace and for international cooperation? I believe that, in all these major trends, our age has given welcome evidence of great determination and considerable progress. It is moving purposefully in the right direction— the abolition of war, the reduction of poverty, and the elimination of racial inequality. These are the three major trends of our century, and they are the major trends both in the East and the West, in the Communist as well as in the non-Communist world. What is tearing these worlds apart is a difference not of ideology or objective, but of method.

Ours is a great age, and I believe that we are entering into an even greater age. The wave of the future, the true direction of man's pilgrimage and destiny may be, from time to time, thwarted and opposed, dammed up, as it were, and obstructed, drawn off and retarded, but it cannot be permanently stopped.

In our day this forward thrust of man has encountered the stubborn and insolent resistance of materialism, of Nazism, of Fascism, and as regards method, of Communist dictatorship. These have violently resisted the spiritual aspirations which constitute mankind's wave of the future. They put shackles on man, even when they promised him larger freedoms. They divided and stratified men, even when they prated about a classless society. They fomented war even when they preached peace. But the onmoving tides of man's spirit, fathoms deep and irresistible, have now swept over the shattered ruins of some of these sinister aberrations and dark conspiracies of the rebels against light—though they have not as yet entirely obliterated them. The tides are now swirling around the bastions of the remaining dictatorships of the earth. They will surely succumb. They cannot, in the long run, win in the contest for man's heart and man's loyalties. Man has struggled through the long, weary centuries to free himself from the bondage of nature. He will not voluntarily and for long submit to the bondage of man. Neither dictatorship nor racialism nor statism nor militarism can or will command the future of the human race. They represent the sunk wreckage of the past which the storms of our day have dredged up again from the bottom of their buried depths and have set afloat again dangerously upon the ship lanes of the world.

November 21, 1953

ON THE THRESHOLD OF THE FOURTH CENTURY

What may endanger our Jewish future here is not conscious escapism or deliberate assimilationist tendencies such as characterized Jewish communities elsewhere and at other times: rather, a too facile adaptability, an unconscious drift and a carefree relaxation of all disciplines—not out of conviction but out of sheer indifference—such as belonging to synagogues but not attending them, or emptying our homes of all Jewish content, or sending children to schools which are so limited as to time that they cannot really give them an adequate

Jewish education, or in very many instances, in all too many, in fact in the majority of instances, not giving them any education at all. This last fact represents our major failure on the American scene, and our most menacing problem.

No religion is worth its salt which does not make great demands upon its adherents. The greatest enthusiasm was always engendered by faiths which called for the greatest sacrifices on the part of their devotees who received in return great compensation and satisfactions which their souls desired. According to our tradition, increased merit and worth were bestowed upon Israel through the very abundance of the commandments which were given to it. Too many of our people want an easygoing religion, one which does not interfere with their leisure, their sleep, or their television, which calls for no study and no observance, which does not challenge or disturb them, a religion without any spiritual travail, without any stab of thought or conscience, without any sacrifices, the religion of self-pampering people. No religion has ever survived in that kind of an emotional and intellectual vacuum, Judaism least of all.

It is a great virtue in our people that they are generous in heart— charitable and responsive to all human need and suffering. It is a noble tradition of Israel and a by-product of a religion which, foremost among all the religions of mankind, made charity and loving-kindness central in its code of human conduct. But Judaism is much more than charity, and the charitable impulse alone will not preserve our faith and our people. "This Book of the Law shall not depart out of your mouth, but you shall meditate on it day and night, that you may be careful to do according to all that is written in it; for then you shall make your way prosperous, and then you shall have good success." No Jewish community ever survived for long which did not cultivate Jewish learning and study and which did not cultivate the prescribed way of Jewish life, at least in its essentials.

What we should fear most is the rise of a generation of prosperous Jews who have no spiritual anchorage, or a generation of clever, restless Jews of quick ferment and high voltage, rooted in no religious tradition, reverent of no moral code, ignorant of all Jewish learning and held to social responsibility by no inner spiritual restraint, who will range and bluster all over the American scene from literature and art to politics and government and will commit their fellow Jews in the eyes of the American people. Such floating mines are a danger to any people, but especially to a minority group. Some of these mines are already exploding.

If American Jewry of tomorrow will restore what has become

peripheral in our life to the center again—the synagogue, the school, the academy, and the religious disciplines of Judaism—if it will recapture the wisdom of our ancient teachers who admonished us that the study of the Torah outweighs all other commandments for it leads directly to them all—then American Jewry is destined to enjoy a resplendent century of spiritual growth in this gracious land.

November 21, 1953

AMERICA'S STAKE IN HUMAN FREEDOM

Regardless of how powerful we become militarily, we shall still have to settle in time all our differences with Russia in one of two ways: war—atomic war, which is unthinkable, which everyone agrees would result only in civilization being destroyed altogether; or negotiation—the way of give-and-take, the way of statesmanship in which skillful and inspired diplomacy is perhaps more effective than any assumed preponderance of power which can only be established in actual combat. . . .

In order to build up to strength and checkmate the aggression of the Soviet Union, we have been attracting to our democratic front dictators of the type of Franco and Tito. This has not strengthened our position with the free peoples of the earth. It has seriously brought into question our role as the defender of human freedom against all types of dictatorship. We have also made a rearmed Western Germany the keystone of our entire scheme of European defense.

We, who had denounced and fought the Germans for being aggressively militaristic, are now insisting that they should rearm. Because of our absorption in the building up of a front against Russia, we have invited Western Germany to rearm and to join the defense forces of the North Atlantic Treaty Organization. This, of course, can only come about if Germany remains divided; but the German people want to be united far more than they want to fight on the side of the Allies against Russia. They have had their stomach full of fighting Russia in the last world war. They do not want their country to become the battleground for a war between the United States and Russia; nor do they want a civil war to rend their people apart. Stalin, you will recall, countered our move by putting forward his program for a united, disarmed, but neutral Germany. Stalin, too, as a result of the disastrous cold war between Russia and the United States, was forced to retreat from the position which he and we and the Allied heads took at Potsdam in August, 1945, where they agreed that "all war potentials of Germany were to be destroyed—war plants, warships, aircraft and arms—so that Germany would never again be able to make war." From this sound, statesmanlike position, Russia too, under pressure of the cold war, has retreated.

The entire arch of our foreign policy in Europe, with a cooperating Western Germany as its capstone, is, I fear, doomed to collapse. We are not willing or ready to face the issue of a united, disarmed, and neutral Germany. A divided Germany will be the signal for a third world war. In this war Germany will again be fighting only for Germany, not for democracy or for any alliance. . . .

December 12, 1958

ZIONISM AND AMERICAN JEWRY

I am persuaded that the synagogue will be the institution primarily responsible for the survival of the American Jewish community, as it has been responsible for our survival throughout our Dispersion. To fulfill this task, the synagogue must become much more a place of religious education than it has been heretofore. An essential feature of this Jewish religious education is the teaching of the Hebrew language, in which our religious culture has most fully expressed itself. No Jewish community ever survived for long which ignored Hebrew. No Jewish community ever contributed culturally to Jewish life which did not foster the Hebrew language and literature. The Hebrew language is not only the repository of our most glorious cultural trophies. It has been a powerful instrument for progress and renewal in Jewish life, the bond of union, and the chain of continuity. The Hebrew language served our people as the weapon with which to batter down the spiritual and intellectual walls of of the ghetto. It was the highway along which our people moved into the modern world. One cannot, of course, think of our national renaissance movement from the early Hibbat Zion days to the recent crowning days of struggle and victory without thinking of the brilliant galaxy of Hebrew writers, poets, and essayists who inspired and sustained it.

If we are thinking of any cultural link in the future between Israel and the Jews of the Diaspora, then we must be thinking in terms of the Hebrew language. We must raise generations of Jews who will be able to read the language in which the future cultural creations of Israel will be cast.

February 21, 1955

BRIDGES AND WALLS

Our world is divided today by political walls and iron curtains. There are those who would build these walls still higher, who resent those who suggest ways for razing those walls and leveling them off. In every age there have been the wall-building doctrinaires, the exponents of the irreconcilable. Either I or you can survive! No middle road—no meeting ground—no compromise! This, of course, is the fateful road to war, and wars only serve to erect new walls on the ruined foundations of the old.

There are nations which put their trust and security in strong walls, in impregnable Maginot Lines, in Chinese walls. But they all crumble sooner or later. "The Lord God hath a day upon every lofty tower and upon every fortified wall." A nation must not put its sole trust in armament, even as formidable as atomic bombs. The very strength of a nation often brings about its downfall. It becomes overconfident and precipitate; it drains off its strength in endless military adventure; its domestic economy breaks down, and unrest and revolution finally weaken it and prepare it for ultimate defeat.

A nation should put its trust in the strength of its moral and intellectual life, the justice and fairness of its laws and institutions, the well-being and contentment of its citizens, the moral training of its youth, and the stability of its homes.

Our classic religions urged men to be builders of bridges rather than of walls. Life abounds in tragic chasms which separate men, in deep rivers and their swift, dark currents. Men should learn to build bridges across them, but bridges are more difficult to build than walls. Charity, compassion, sympathy, magnanimity, open-mindedness are such bridges. So is friendship; so is tolerance; so is brotherhood. "Love thy neighbor as thyself" is perhaps the noblest and most enduring of all bridges ever devised. "With malice toward none; with charity for all," is another bridge which an immortal American built across a river of blood and civil war.

Every earnest effort at international understanding and cooperation is a bridge leading to the Kingdom of God, to the good society.

The League of Nations was such a bridge. It collapsed. Bridges often collapse and must be rebuilt. The United Nations is such a bridge. It is in danger of collapse. We must see to it that it does not collapse. War is never a bridge. At best it is a Bridge of Sighs leading men from doom to death.

April 4, 1955

THE RIGHT TO WORK

Perhaps the various groups who have become so concerned about a free citizen's right to work . . . could tell us how to ensure the right to work for the over five million unemployed who are able-bodied, competent, and who wish to earn a living for themselves and their families, and who are denied their right to work during recessionary periods in our economy.

The same group of people now clamoring for the theoretic right to work, fought bitterly in 1930 against the enactment of unemployment insurance which has proven such a lifesaver in successive periods of recession and which today many responsible people, including the President of the United States, are urging that its benefits be extended.

Even in those desperate years when 16,000,000 of our people were unemployed and heads of familes were selling apples on the street corners in order to earn a few pennies for bread for their families, our unemployment insurance proposal was fought bitterly by the powerful business organizations in Ohio on the grounds that it was un-American, radical, socialistic, and that it rewarded idleness.

Every man in a free society should have the right to work. But every man, once he finds employment, also has the moral duty to join an organization of fellow workers which achieved for him through its organized efforts the favorable conditions he enjoys in his employment and affords him protection for the future. Everyone is morally obligated to share in the responsibilities if they wish to avail themselves of the rewards of collective effort. The theoretic "right to work" —which no one questions—is qualified by man's moral responsibility to assume the obligations which assure him the very things which he seeks in his employment.

Organized labor, of course, is not without its shortcomings. At times they are most unreasonable. But so is management. It has been gratifying to note the courageous and statesmanlike action which responsible leaders of labor have taken in an attempt to clean the house of labor of its grafters and corruptionists.

It has been my conviction for many years that no free society and no free economy can long endure in the modern world without a strong organization of its working people. A strong labor movement not only protects workers against exploitation but, at the same time, will save capitalism and free enterprise from those very abuses which ultimately destroy it.

October 8, 1958

A CATHOLIC PRESIDENT IN THE WHITE HOUSE?

It occurs to me that the simplest answer to the question "Should a Catholic be elected to the Presidency of the United States" might well be "Why not?" There is nothing in the Constitution of the United States which prohibits it. The Constitution of the United States is quite clear on this point. The framers of our Constitution—many of them keen legal minds as well as great patriots—wanted to be very clear and specific on this point. And so they wrote into the Constitution the following: "No religious test shall ever be required as a qualification to any office or public trust under the United States." Words could not be more precise or clearer. Our Constitution also has as its First Amendment—the first article in the so-called Bill of Rights—the following: "Congress shall make no law respecting an establishment of religion or prohibiting the free exercise thereof."

It is clear that the framers of our Constitution did not wish the United States to be either a Protestant country, or a Catholic country, or a Christian country. They did not wish to give preference to any one religious body or to prevent the free exercise of any religion. They wanted the new state which they were setting up to be a secular state. They were not unfriendly to religion. Many of them were church members and belonged to various denominations. They believed in God and they sought to build their new state upon the highest ethical and moral ideals of religion. But they also wanted to keep church and state separate and distinct—each free from the interference of the other in its own legitimate sphere. They knew very well, because they were not far removed from the events, the evils, the strife, and the bloodshed which were visited upon the Old World—its governments and its peoples—when a specific church was officially recognized by government and received privileges denied to others and when the free exercise of religion was either denied or curtailed. . . .

Their profound wisdom has stood the test of time—170 years—the most turbulent and revolutionary years in the history of mankind. Because of that wisdom, our country has prospered—and no religion has suffered because of it. On the contrary, all religious bodies, from the extreme liberal to the extreme orthodox, have thrived. What is equally important is that they have learned to live together and at times to work together for the common good.

A man should be elected to office because of his character, his ability, and the issues which he represents—not because of his religion, and no man should be defeated for office because of his religion.

May 17, 1959

MY VISIT TO THE SOVIET UNION

I have always believed in coexistence and have for years advocated it. The Russians have adopted a new way of life which is theirs. I would not choose it for myself or for America. It has basic serious defects which we cannot ignore even as it has merits, which we should not underestimate. But their way of life is theirs, and whatever is wrong with it they themselves will have to correct in the future.

It has not been demonstrated that the two systems cannot exist side by side. There is much that each can learn from the other, though neither at the moment seems to be inclined to acknowledge it. Neither system has said the last word. Both have undergone change in the past, and undoubtedly will do so in the future. Life may bring them much closer together, even though their dogmas and ideologies seem to be worlds apart and irreconcilable.

Certainly their differences cannot be resolved by the sword. The problem before the world today is not which system is the better, but how the two can keep from destroying each other—and mankind. Both are strongly entrenched and sufficiently powerful that one cannot destroy the other without destroying itself. The question is then not which will bury the other, but whether a war, once unleashed between the East and West, will not bury them both.

We must learn to live on the same globe with the Soviet people and they with us. Neither they nor we are always in the right. The leaders of both countries must try to reduce tensions. The peoples of the world are waiting for signs of a new and inspired statesmanship both in the Kremlin and the White House. The old is leading us nowhere, only from one crisis to another. Let us not be afraid to trade with each other in goods or in ideas. Let us compete in only one way —which system can do more for its people.

October 22, 1961

BUILDING SHELTERS

. . . As I look about me and see what is happening to our proud and lofty civilization, how we are being driven underground by fears which have resulted from the evil work of our own hands, I wonder whether the terror and judgment of God have not finally came upon this generation. The idols which we have worshiped, the idols of silver and gold, of power and greed, of pride and prestige, of weapons and armaments, are finally driving us, cowering, into the holes of the earth, like primitive man into his cave.

I have no advice to give on the subject of underground dugouts, and no blueprints on how to construct the most comfortable fallout shelter with the latest improvements. There are already quite a few samples in the market, and there will be many more, as international tensions continue to mount and manufacturers rush in to capitalize on the increasing apprehension of our people. There will be a steadily growing demand for local, state, and national shelter-building programs which may cost tens of billions of dollars, and no one will be able to argue successfully against them. After all, Europe built shelters during the Second World War, though we did not have to.

What alternative, then, is there to the building of shelters? None! It seems logical, too, that if shelters must be built, they should be built for everyone, rich and poor alike. Why should only the more affluent be spared? I see where people are already discussing the pros and cons of hanging up signs on their private shelters—"Keep Out, Or Else!"—as a clear gesture of neighborly love in the day of the thermonuclear holocaust.

To such a sorry pass has our civilization come! Such is the bankruptcy of the statesmanship and leadership of the powerful men who have been directing the affairs of our world.

And let it never be said that the fault is theirs and not ours. It is theirs and ours. Let us not add the sin of self-righteousness and sanctimoniousness to the desperate crisis which engulfs us all, and for which we are all responsible.

What must be done, especially when our government tells us to do it, must be done, but need we have come to this pass? And shall we now be improving the situation one iota by concentrating on a crash shelter-building program and by focusing the attention of our people on ways of finding security—a false security in all probability—in a world which will be incinerated in atomic fires, as our Western world surely will be in another war. Should we not rather rouse the spirits and passionate indignation of our citizens and of people throughout the world, before it is too late, and direct them in one great popular outcry and in an insistent and clamorous demand upon political leaders everywhere to make every reasonable concession and compromise—not surrender, but compromise—in order to banish nuclear war? No people on earth wants it and no government should be allowed to retain the nuclear bomb as a threat, deterrent, or diplomatic pawn against any other government.

Last Tuesday the Political Committee of the United Nations voted overwhelmingly to outlaw the use of nuclear weapons in war. The United States and Great Britain voted against it. Why? Because, they claimed, the threat of Soviet aggression is such that they could not give a blanket pledge never to use atomic weapons. Is that a sufficient reason? Was not another precious opportunity missed right there and then by the free world? The Soviet Union, which had but recently resumed nuclear testing, in total disregard of the world's entreaties, voted for the resolution. Its cynicism was underscored by the statement of its spokesman that the Soviet Union was ready to deal a crushing blow to any aggressor. Can their vote be taken seriously? Thus, the two major powers, which really control the situation, and which have maintained right along that they must retain the nuclear bomb, not only for their own security, but to protect the world which looks to them for protection, have been told by their ward nations: "No, thank you, we do not want that kind of protection." The whole world wants to banish the threat of nuclear war and all the resultant tensions and fears which drive men and nations to build underground shelters. Russia and the United States stand in the way, each blaming the other for not doing that which both agree must be done, if the world is to be saved from catastrophe. We seem to have entered an era of calculated semantic befuddlement where both sides say the same thing and agree to the same thing, but neither means a word of what it says. . . .

Perhaps the next meeting of the chiefs of state and their foreign ministers should be held, not in marble halls, but in a fallout shelter, somewhere in the bowels of the earth, where they will be kept day and night, and, if necessary, until all food and drink is gone and the air becomes foul, and their confinement stifling and unbearable. They should not be permitted to leave until a treaty outlawing all nuclear war and the banning of the manufacture and testing of nuclear weapons is finally signed by them, and all existing nuclear bombs are turned over to international control. This is not a serious suggestion but do you know of a better one?

November 19, 1961

LOOKING FOR SECURITY IN AN INSECURE WORLD

The world which is being so drastically recast before our very eyes will not permit anyone to withdraw to some carefree island of private security where he will be safe from all its rifts, twists, and dislocations. No generation is free to decline its encounter with destiny.

It is one thing to recognize the besetting dangers and resolve to go on in spite of them. It is quite another thing to fiddle while Rome is burning. In the former case, one may try to check the danger, to overcome the evils, and to try to make the world secure by removing the causes of its insecurity. In the latter case, one will play until the flames engulf and consume him.

If our world is ever to be made secure—in a sense no age was ever entirely secure, though none has been threatened with such total destruction—it will not be achieved by men who have little spirit of adventure in them, who do not wish to involve themselves in any crusade, who like all things as they are. Such people are likely to bring about the fall of their own world. The dynamics will then remain with the hungry peoples of the earth, those who are not satisfied and unambitious, who want many things because they have so few, who do *not* like things as they are, who are willing to take every risk —for what have they to lose? There is a terrific drive, a pent-up resentfulness and rebelliousness in the souls of the masses of the earth, the masses who have now begun to clamor for their human birthright. How will the more favored peoples of the world confront them? With what? Will a pampered, soft, spiritless, goal-less generation be able to meet their furious challenge with blandness and indifference, or simply by ignoring them? . . .

It should be clear to everyone that for many years to come our world will be profoundly disturbed and unsettled. The prophet Zachariah spoke of such a time as "not day and not night." The coming days will be full of frustrations, confusions, and alarums. The waves will run high and the tides will be treacherous. Those who will have no stamina, no fighting spirit, and no compass will go under. There will be very few smug and safe cubicles of refuge indeed for men who like themselves the way they are, and who like all things *as* they are.

But, while insecure and uncertain, it will by no means be a hopeless world. Abounding in great risks, it will be rich in even greater rewards. There will be new horizons and new frontiers to challenge the adventuresome spirit of youth. In science and industry, in invention and discovery, in the arts and the humanities, progress will be unlimited. We are far from having reached the ultimate stage in the evolution of mankind. The twentieth century is building a better and ampler world for man, and the twenty-first century will advance and improve upon it. There will be more of the good things of life for everyone. A society will emerge which will be free from the dark heritage of the past, the age-old curse of poverty, misery, and exploitation, of inequality, racialism, and intolerance. It will be an exciting world, and for the man of courage and faith, a welcome and challenging world. Throughout the ages men of faith and courage have never been afraid to build their homes and plant their vineyards on the very slopes of volcanoes.

January 14, 1962

A Bibliography of the Writings of
Abba Hillel Silver

MIRIAM LEIKIND

*

A SELECTED LISTING of books, articles, and addresses, which may be found in many libraries.

The bibliography is arranged chronologically: title, source, and date. Books appear first, followed by articles and addresses.

ABBREVIATIONS USED

AH	*American Hebrew*
AI	*American Israelite*
AJ Conf.	*American Jewish Conference*
ALLR	*American Labor Legislation Review*
AZ	*American Zionist*, formerly *New Palestine*
AZR	*American Zionist Reporter*
B'B'	*B'nai B'rith Monthly*
Bus. & Com.	*Business and Commerce*
Can. Zion.	*Canadian Zionist*
CCAR	*Central Conference of American Rabbis Yearbook*
Chris. Cent.	*Christian Century*
CJFWF	*Council of Jewish Federations and Welfare Funds*
CPD	*Cleveland Plain Dealer*
CSW	*Conference of Social Work Annual*
CW	*Congress Weekly*
EC	*Economic Bulletin*
HN	*Hadassah Newsletter*
HUC	*Hebrew Union College*
Jch	*Jewish Chronicle*
Jcr	*Jewish Criterion*
JDB	*Jewish Daily Bulletin*
Jew. Ed.	*Jewish Education*
JNFNB	*Jewish National Fund News Bulletin*
JSSQ	*Jewish Social Service Quarterly*
JS	*Jewish Standard*
JT	*Jewish Tribune*
LP	*Labor Palestine*
LJ	*Liberal Judaism*
Mich. Ed. Jr.	*Michigan Education Journal*
NCCJ	*National Conference of Christians and Jews*

NCJSS   *National Conference of Jewish Social Service*
NEA Jr   *National Education Association Journal*
NJM   *National Jewish Monthly, formerly B'nai B'rith Magazine*
NJ   *New Judea*
NJCSW   *New Jersey Conference of Social Work*
NP   *New Palestine*
NY State Ed.
Bull.   *New York State Education Bulletin*
NYT   *New York Times*
PY   *Palestine Yearbook*
PW   *Pioneer Woman*
Rec.   *Recreation*
Rel. Ed.   *Religious Education*
TB   *The Temple Bulletin*
TY   *The Temple Yearbook*
UAHC   *Union of American Hebrew Congregations*
UPA   *United Palestine Appeal*
U.S. Bur.
Labor Bull. *United States Bureau of Labor Bulletin*
U.S. Dept.
State Bull. *United States Department of State Bulletin*
ZOA   *Zionist Organization of America*

1915   Am Ha-Arez in Soferic and Tannaitic Times   HUC
        Monthly. Cincinnati, 1914–1915, vol. 1, Dec. 1914,
        pp. 9–14; Jan. 1915, pp. 24–27; Feb. 1915, pp. 19–27

1916   Religion and the Jewish Child; Symposium   CCAR, vol.
        26, pp. 232–237

1917   Religion of Youth   AI, Cincinnati, vol. 64, no. 7, Aug.
        16, p. 1
        Prayer   TY, vol. 19, p. 29

1919   Judaism and Christian Science   The Temple, 15 pp.
        Some Problems of Human Life Propounded in the Bible;
        a series of three popular lectures: "Job" Why is there
        suffering?; "Ecclesiastes" Is life worth living?; "The
        Psalms" How can man find God? The Temple, 30 pp.

1920   Blazing a Trail Through Life   The Temple, 7 pp.
        Prejudice: How to Meet It   The Temple, 10 pp.

The Spiritual Legacy of the Pilgrim Fathers   The Temple, 12 pp.

1921   The Heritage   The Temple, 15 pp.
              How to Be Happy in an Imperfect World   The Temple, 12 pp.
              Facing the Future   The National Pipe and Supplies Association, separate, 15 pp.
              Is God a Superstition?   The Temple, 9 pp.
              The Fable of the Tired Businessman   The Temple, 9 pp.

1922   What Is Culture?   The Temple, 10 pp.
              Friends I Have Made and Lost   The Temple, 9 pp.
              What Has Become of the Melting Pot?   The Temple, 8 pp.

1923   Rising Tide of Choler   The Temple, 15 pp.
              Our New Task; address, Golden Jubilee Convention UAHC   UAHC Convention Report, 8 pp.   The Temple, 8 pp.
              America; poem   NYT, Aug. 17, p. 10:5
              Discussion; Social Justice   CCAR, vol. 33, pp. 264–267, 273–275
              Discussion; Devotional Literature in the Vernacular   CCAR, vol. 33, pp. 422–423

1924   Dedication Sermon; On the Occasion of the Dedication of the New Temple of Congregation Tifereth Israel, Cleveland, Ohio   The Temple, 8 pp.
              Woodrow Wilson's Contribution to Civilization   The Temple, 14 pp.
              On Establishing a Homeland in Palestine   NYT, May 28, p. 26:3
              Views on Third Party   NYT, Oct. 29, p. 2:7

1925   Discussion; Church and State   CCAR, vol. 35, pp. 74–75
              A Threefold Benison   CCAR Holiday Sermons, pp. 5–10
              Renewal   The Temple, 8 pp.

Organized Religion and World Peace   Adin Ballou Foundation, separate, 5 pp. The Temple, 6 pp.

Ingathering of the Spirit   NP, Mar. 27, p. 335

Correspondence; Louis Marshall and Rabbi Silver on the Question of Palestine and Russian Jewish Colonization NP, Nov. 6, pp. 370–371

1926   The Development of Human Personality Through Religious Experience   csw, vol. 53, pp. 272–276 jssq, vol. 3:1, pp. 1–5

Discussion; External Relations of Federation   csw, vol. 53, pp. 29–37

Memorial Day Address   csw, vol. 53, pp. 61–62

Why Do the Heathen Rage?   The Temple, 37 pp.   jt, July 23, pp. 1–2, 16; July 30, p. 2; Aug. 6, p. 4; Aug. 13, pp. 4, 9

Why Europe Misunderstands America   The Temple, 8 pp.

A Consummation: Palestine and the Jewish Spirit   NP, Jan. 22, pp. 78–89

Jews' Hope in Zionism; address, Karen Hayesod Women's League   NYT, Apr. 27, p. 8:2

Statement Before Departure for London on July 14 . . . Commenting on Russian Colonization Scheme   NP, July 23, p. 65

We Hand You the Torch: Confirmation Address   jt, May 7, p. 1

1927   History of Messianic Speculation in Israel from the First Through the Seventeenth Centuries   New York: Macmillan Co., 268 pp.

History of Messianic Speculation in Israel . . . with a new preface by the author   Boston: Beacon Press paperback, 1959, 268 pp.

A Saint of Democracy   *Abraham Lincoln: the Tribute of the Synagogue.* J. H. Hertz, ed., New York: Bloch Publishing Co., pp. 643–649

The Vision Splendid   *Best Sermons.* J. F. Newton, ed., New York: Harcourt, Brace & Co., pp. 205–216

Concluding Remarks UAHC, 30th Council, pp. 100–103

Leisure and the Church *Playground,* Jan., pp. 539–543
Homiletic Review, Aug., pp. 153–154

The Church and Social Justice CSW, vol. 54, pp. 45–50
The Temple, 7 pp.

Education and the Good Life; Baccalaureate address University of Cincinnati, separate, 12 pp.

Summer's Impressions of Palestine NP, Sept. 16, p. 218

1928 The Democratic Impulse in Jewish History New York: Bloch Publishing Co., 43 pp. CCAR, vol. 38, pp. 199–216 3rd Annual Institute of Judaism, HUC separate, pp. 1–6

What Is Happening to the American Home Today Child Welfare Com. of America, Pub. No. 68, Series 1928, 8 pp.

The Synagogue, the Church and Social Justice *Reflex,* vol. 2, June, pp. 1–8

How Shall We Measure Life? The Temple, 8 pp.

Liberalism at the Crossroads The Temple, 7 pp. *The Ohio Teacher,* Jan. 1929, pp. 203–206

Letters to the Editor: Answer to Mr. Herbert Salow's article in *Menorah Journal,* Sept., p. 259 NP, Sept. 28, p. 225 NP, Nov. 2, p. 351

The One and the Many *World Unity,* Nov., pp. 81–88

Eleventh Anniversary of the Balfour Declaration NP, Nov. 9, pp. 373–374

Jewish Education B'B', Dec., p. 103

1929 The Faith of an Untired Liberal NJCSW, vol. 28, pp. 12–18

Herzl and Jewish Messianism *Theodor Herzl, A Memorial.* M. W. Weisgal, ed., New York, pp. 254–257 *Political World of American Zionism.* Samuel Halperin, ed., Detroit: Wayne State University Press, 1961, pp. 13–14

Relationship of the Church to the Public Employment Service U.S. Bur. Labor Bull., vol. 501: pp. 70–78

Discussion; Revision of the Union Prayer Book CCAR, vol. 39, pp. 137–139

1930   Religion in a Changing World   New York: R. R. Smith, 204 pp.

The Role of Religion in a Changing World   Rel. Ed., vol. 25, June, pp. 516–522 *Reflex,* July, pp. 3–11

The Things Men Live For   *Cleveland Anchor,* Mar., pp. 7–10

Pulpit Freedom   *Christian World,* May 17, pp. 2, 3, 19

Zionist Convention: 33rd Annual   NP, July 25, p. 19

Conference of the Allied Jewish Campaign, Washington, D.C.   NP, Mar. 14, pp. 162–163

Religion Firm Despite Detractors   NYT, Dec. 22, p. 22:8

1931   Our National Debt to the Unemployed   ALIR, Sept., pp. 313–314

Recreation and Living in the Modern World   Rec., Jan., pp. 531–535, 578–579

The Need for Reconsecration   NP, Jan. 16, pp. 11–12

Is Civilization Outracing Man?   *Cleveland Musician,* Nov., p. 7

Secular Education Called Insufficient   NYT, Mar. 19, p. 47:2

1932   Crises in Social Work   CSW–Report 59th Annual Meeting, pp. 53–64   NYT, May 18, p. 11:1; May 22, p. 2:1

Prophetic Preaching   *Varieties of Present-Day Preaching.* G. B. Oxnam, ed., New York: Abingdon Press, pp. 104–117

Step into the Study   *If I Had Only One Sermon to Prepare.* J. F. Newton, ed., New York: Harper & Bros., pp. 125–133

Rabbi Silver Answers a Zionist Carpetbagger   AH, Mar. 18, pp. 457, 462, 467

Letters to the Editor on Dr. Herbert L. Willett's "The Jews and Christians" *Christian Union Quarterly,* Apr., pp. 364–365

Job Insurance   *Cleveland Musician,* July, p. 7

Depression and American Jewish Life   AH, July 22, pp. 205–212, 216

The Relation of the Depression to the Cultural and Spiritual Values of American Jewry   Jew. Ed., Oct./Dec., pp. 148–149

1933   League's Manchurian Debate   CPD, Jan. 8

Address given to Brith Sholom   *Brith Sholomite,* July/
        Aug., pp. 12–16, 23

Still Blundering   JDB, Oct. 22, p. 6

League of Nations and the Jews of Germany   JBD, Oct.
        20, p. 6   TB, Oct. 29

Chicanery   JDB, Oct. 29, p. 3   TB, Nov. 5

Touring for Good Will   JDB, Nov. 5, p. 3   TB, Nov. 12

A Pyrrhic Victory   JDB, Nov. 12, p. 5   TB, Nov. 19

In Time of Crisis   JDB, Nov. 19, p. 5   TB, Nov. 26

National Planning   JDB, Nov. 26, p. 5   TB, Dec. 3

A Little More Resistance, Please!   JDB, Dec. 3, p. 9   TB,
        Dec. 10

Nazism vs. Civilization   Chicago Commission for the
        Defense of Human Rights Against Nazism, separate,
        pp. 21–25

Housecleaning   JDB, Dec. 10, p. 5   TB, Dec. 17

A Church of Laodiceans?   JDB, Dec. 17, p. 5   TB, Dec. 24

Prescribing for Israel   JDB, Dec. 24, p. 5   TB, Jan. 7,
        1934

Hollywood—A Jewish Liability   JDB, Dec. 31, p. 5

1934   The Decline of the Individual   *Oberlin Alumni Maga-
        zine,* Nov., pp. 39–43 *Friends Intelligencer,* July, pp.
        471–474 Rel. Ed., July 1937, pp. 211–216 Mich. Ed.
        Jr., Dec. 1937, pp. 173–174 *Youth Leader,* Dec. 1938,
        pp. 161–163

Enlarge the Place of Thy Tent!   JDB, Jan. 4, p. 5

A Great Lonely Soul   JDB, Jan. 14, p. 5   TB, Jan. 21

An Emergent Community   JDB, Jan. 21, p. 6   TB, Jan.
        28

Statesmen in Duodecimo   JDB, Jan. 28, p. 6   TB, Feb. 4

A People Acts   EC, Jan., p. 4

Social *Gleichschaltung*   JDB, Feb. 4, p. 7

Relief Is Not Enough   JDB, Feb. 11, p. 6   TB, Feb. 18

Labor's Stake in the Struggle; address, testimonal dinner
        to Mr. William Green   AFL, separate, Feb. 14, pp. 38–
        40 JDB, Feb. 18, p. 7   TB, Feb. 25

Anti-German Boycott   JDB, Feb. 25, p. 7

Educating Children for the New Deal   NEA Jr, Feb. 26,
        pp. 97–99 NYT, Feb. 27, p. 17:2

Reply to Mr. McAfee   Chris. Cent., Feb. 28, p. 293

Boycott Bites In   EC, Feb., p. 4

Labor's Great Role in Palestine   LP, Feb., pp. 3–6

The Bible and the Book of the Dead   JDB, Mar. 4, p. 7
TB, Mar. 11

"This Thing of Giving"   JDB, Mar. 11, p. 6 TB, Mar. 18

Bearing Gifts   JDB, Mar. 18, p. 7 TB, Mar. 24

The Full Orbit of Our Responsibility   JDB, Mar. 25, p.
12 TB, Apr. 1

On the Alert   EC, Mar./Apr., p. 4 TB, Apr. 15 JDB, Apr.
8, p. 6

L'Hitraot   JDB, Apr. 1, p. 6 TB, Apr. 8

A Charonic Enterprise   JDB, Apr. 15, p. 7 TB, Apr. 22

The Line of Confusion and the Plummet of Happiness
JDB, Apr. 22, p. 6 TB, Apr. 29

The International Jew   JDB, Apr. 29, p. 6 TB, May 6

Less Armament   *Wharton News of Finance and Commerce,* Apr., p. 9

Address   Chicago Committee for the Defense of Human
Rights Against Nazism, separate, May 2, 8 p.

Father Coughlin   JDB, May 6, p. 6 TB, May 13

To a Confirmand in the Year 1934   JDB, May 13, p. 6

Hostages   JDB, May 20, p. 6

Why We Boycott Germany   EC, May, p. 4

Keep Up the Boycott   EC, June, p. 4

Twilight of the Nordic Gods   EC, July, p. 4

No Loans to Hitler's Bloody Regime   EC, Aug. p. 4

A Universal Boycott   EC, Sept., p. 4

A Happier New Year   JDB, Sept. 9, p. 2

Al Chet   JDB, Sept. 16, p. 3

Weasel Words   JDB, Sept. 23, p. 5 TB, Oct. 14

Boom Days in Zion and After   JDB, Sept. 30, p. 5

Vivisection   JDB, Oct. 14, p. 5 TB, Oct. 21

Pogroms Are Not Such Simple Matters   JDB, Oct. 21,
p. 16 TB, Oct. 28

Yorkville Is Not Yet America   JDB, Oct. 28, p. 5 TB,
Nov. 4

Not Revenge   EC, Nov., p. 4

Orange Juice   JDB, Nov. 4, p. 7 TB, Nov. 11

Red Messiah   JDB, Nov. 11, p. 7 TB, Nov. 18

Beginning of Wisdom   JDB, Nov. 18, p. 5 TB, Nov. 25

State Control   JDB, Nov. 25, p. 7 TB, Dec. 2

Chanukah 5695   JDB, Dec. 2, p. 6 TB, Dec. 9 *Every Friday,* Dec. 7

A Letter to Twelve Jewish Students   JDB, Dec. 9, p. 7 TB, Dec. 9

The End of the Matter, All Having Been Heard   JDB, Dec. 16, p. 7 TB, Dec. 23

Sabotage   JDB, Dec. 23, p. 7 TB, Dec. 30

Discussion; On Including Service Which Does Not Agree with Present Theology of Prayer Book   CCAR, vol. 44, pp. 78–79

Incontinent-Al Congress   JDB, Dec. 30, p. 6 TB, Jan. 5, 1935

1935   Israel: a paper on the Declaration of Principles Adopted by the Pittsburgh Rabbinical Conference in 1885 CCAR, vol. 45, pp. 312–354 also a separate

Jews and Christians in the New Era   *World Fellowship.* C. F. Weller, ed., New York: Liveright Publishing Co., pp. 851–860

Ersatz   JDB, Jan. 6, p. 7 TB, Jan. 13

Where Our Security Lies   JDB, Jan. 13, p. 7 TB, Jan. 20

Land Hunger   JDB, Jan. 27, p. 7 TB, Feb. 3

Towards a "Total" Jewish Program   JDB, Feb. 3, p. 3 TB, Feb. 10 *Every Friday,* Feb. 8, p. 1

The Lesson   JDB, Feb. 10, p. 3 TB, Feb. 17

The Radicalism of the Jew   JDB, Feb. 17, p. 5 TB, Feb. 24

Brotherhood Day   JDB, Feb. 24, p. 5 TB, Mar. 3

We Cannot Be Bartered With   EC, Mar., p. 4

Speaking the Truth in Love   JDB, Mar. 3, p. 5 TB, Mar. 10

What One Should Learn on the Road of Ages   JDB, Mar. 24, p. 5 TB, Mar. 31

About Dr. Zhitlowsky   JDB, Mar. 31, p. 7

Nazism Must Lead to War   EC, Apr., p. 4

Siraj   JDB, Apr. 7, p. 5

Eternal Loveliness of Passover   JDB, Apr. 21, p. 5

How Youth Faces the New World   NY State Ed. Bull., May, pp. 616–619

Right of the Individual   *Living Church,* May 11, p. 588

Achilles' Heel of Nazidom   EC, Oct., p. 4

New Position of the Jew   *Brooklyn Jewish Center Review,* Oct. 31, pp. 5–6, 18

Sportsmanship EC, Nov., p. 4
"Transvaluating Jewish Values" *Reflex*, Nov., pp. 5–10
The Townsend Plan and Social Security The Temple,
  11 p.
Keep Away from Berlin EC, Dec., p. 4

1936   Marching Toward Brotherhood *Youth's Work in the
              New World*, T. O. Nall, ed., New York: Associated
              Press, pp. 69–75
            From National Tragedy to National Salvation NP, Feb.
              7, pp. 10–11 TB, Mar. 1
            Evaluation from the Standpoint of the Layman NEA Jr.
              Feb. 22–27
            Ancient Paths; Baccalaurate address HUC, separate,
              10 p.
            Should the Church and Synagogue Fight Communism
              TB, Nov. 22

1937   Address B'B', 85th Annual Convention Report, pp. 122–
              127
            Rededication to Zionism NP, May 28, pp. 1, 6
            Are American Jews Communists? AH, July 2, p. 4
            Jewish People Cannot Be Intimidated NP, July 12, p. 11
            Some Fundamental Needs of Human Life *Christian
              Register*, Nov. 11, pp. 668–670
            Discussion; Guiding Principles of Reform Judaism
              CCAR, vol. 47, pp. 105, 112, 113
            Discussion; Spanish Revolt CCAR, vol. 47, pp. 157, 158–
              159

1938   Status of Palestine CJFWF Convention Report, pp. 62–
              69
            The Rights of Minorities and the Next War; address given
              to Cleveland City Club Cleveland, City Club, sep-
              arate, 7 p. TB, Oct. 15, 1939
            With Courage and Faith NP, Feb. 28, p. 6
            A Time of Affliction NP, Mar. 25, p. 5
            Religion in a Troubled World *War Cry*, Apr. 23, p. 5

On Being Jewish; address B'B', 86th Annual Convention Report, n.p.

Jews Do Not Despair NYT, Mar. 24, p. 8:5

Rededication to United Palestine Appeal NP, Sept. 23, pp. 1, 10

A New Year's Message to the Jews of America NP, Sept. 23, p. 3

Some Aberrations of Our Day; address *Youth Leader*, Dec., pp. 161–163

World Crisis and Jewish Survival; address CCAR, vol. 49, pp. 309–330 CCAR, separate, 22 pp. AH, Sept. 8, p. 50

David Alroy *Universal Jewish Encyclopedia*, I. Landman, ed., New York: Universal Jewish Encyclopedia, Inc., 1939–1943, 10 vols., vol. 1, pp. 206–207

Nehemiah Hayyun *Universal Jewish Encyclopedia*, I. Landman, ed., New York: Universal Jewish Encyclopedia, Inc., 1939–1943, 10 vols., vol. 5, pp. 258–259

Out of the Darkness NP, Jan. 20, pp. 1, 3, 7 TB, Jan. 29

Religion in Present-Day Jewish Life UAHC Convention Report also UAHC, separate, 11 pp. TB, Feb. 26

The Refugees—Four Talks UJA, separate, 20 pp. TB, Mar. 19, 26

How Can Schools and Colleges Foster Democracy in Students Nat'l Assoc. of Dean of Women Jr., Mar., pp. 99–100

Is Fascism a "Domestic Affair" NJM, Apr., pp. 256–258

Crisis of World Affairs *National Elementary Principals*, Apr., pp. 144–151

Keep America Free, Just, Tolerant and United; address, American Legion National Convention Separate, Sept. 17 TB, Oct. 8 *Jewish Veteran*, Sept./Oct., p. 3

The Nazarene TB, Nov. 12

American Way of Life *Youth Leader Digest*, Dec., pp. 154–156

Zionists Advised to Shun Conflict NYT, Aug. 20, p. 15

1940   Prophetic Conception of the Ministry Dudleian Lecture for the Academic Year 1939–1940. Harvard University, 33 pp.

Challenge to Civilization NP, Jan. 12, p. 5

Outlook for America   csw, 67th Annual Report, pp. 38–
49 Separate, 12 pp. NYT, May 31, p. 15:1 TB, Jan. 19,
1941

Social Justice   *Survey Midmonthly,* June, p. 190

National Day of Prayer; NBC Radio address Separate,
mimeographed

Spiritual Foundations of Democracy   TB, Nov. 24

Palestine and the World Jewish Crisis   UPA Yrbk, p.
19–24

Palestine Drive   NYT, Dec. 27, p. 15:3

1941   World Crisis and Jewish Survival; a Group of Essays
New York: R. R. Smith, 221 pp.

A Call to American Jewry   NP, Jan. 3, p. 5

Building a New Citadel   UPA Yrbk., p. 10

The Cause of Zionism Must Not Be Minimized   NP, Jan.
31, p. 5

Preserving the Genius of Americanism   *Current Religious Thought,* Mar., pp. 20–23

Social and Religious Tolerance as Related to National Defense   *Southern Assoc. Quarterly,* May, pp. 1–10

Significance of This Conference to Ohio's Children
Ohio Welfare Conference Report, pp. 11–14

I Count My Blessings   TB, Nov. 23

1942   Vision Splendid   *Best Sermons, Bk. 4.* J. F. Newton, ed.,
New York: Harcourt, Brace & Co., pp. 26–27

Introduction   *Why a Jewish State,* by L. I. Feuer. New
York: R. R. Smith, 94 pp.

Spiritual Return and National Redemption   CCAR, vol.
52, pp. 239–253 CCAR, separate, 15 pp. TB, Apr. 12

The Shape of Things to Come; address given to the City
Club of Cleveland TB, Jan. 11

In War and Peace, The Role of Jewish Palestine; CBS
address UPA separate TB, Jan. 25 NP, Jan. 23, pp. 6–9

Palestine—End of Jewish Homelessness   UPA Yrbk., pp.
5–6

Morale Building in America   *Amer. Assoc. of School
Administrators Jr.,* pp. 82–90 *The Nation's Schools,*
vol. 29, p. 47 TB, Mar. 8

A Century in Retrospect   cw, Mar. 20, pp. 5–7

Jews and the Allied Cause   NP, May 15

Alarm, Remembrance and Rebirth   TB, Oct. 11

Tribute to Our Men in the Service Honor Roll   TB, Nov. 8

America's Minority Groups in War and Peace   Foreign Missions Conference of North America Convention Report, pp. 48–50 Federal Council of Churches of Christ of America, separate, 12 pp. *Social Action,* Jan. 15, 1943, pp. 30–37

The Religious Basis of a Just and Enduring Peace   HUC separate, 8 pp. TB, Dec. 27

1943   Toward American Jewish Unity   *The Zionist Idea* by Arthur Hertzberg, ed., New York: Doubleday, pp. 592–600

Symposium on Palestine   American Jewish Conference, First Session, New York AJ Conf. Proceedings, pp. 98–103

Prayer   American Jewish Conference, First Session, New York AJ Conf. Proceedings, pp. 301–302

The Answer Today Must Be Judaism   Jew. Ed., Jan. Mar., pp. 130–133

Soil for National Rebirth   JNF NB, Feb., pp. 6–8, 16, 24

When Freedom Comes   JCR, Apr. 16, pp. 4, 91

Advance on All Fronts   UPA, 16 pp. NP, May 7, pp. 5–8

Freedom for All or Freedom for None   *Highroad,* June, pp. 18–20

National Idea   NP, Sept. 10, p. 6–8

World's Attitude   NP, Sept. 24, p. 10

Zionism—What It Is—What It Is Not   The Temple, 32 pp.

1944   Jewish National Home in Palestine   Hearings before the Committee on Foreign Affairs, House of Rep. 78th Congress, 2nd Session H.R. 418, 419, pp. 24–30, 168–170

What Alone Can Save Our Democratic Way of Life   *Best Sermons* G. P. Butler, ed., New York: Ziff-David Publishing Co., pp. 275–282

Dreamer and Builder of Zion   *Chaim Weizmann* . . .
M. W. Weisgal, ed., New York: Dial Press, pp. 209–
216

Reform Judaism and CCAR   *Political World of American
Judaism* by Samuel Halperin, Detroit: Wayne State
University Press, 1961, pp. 243–244

Letter to Chaim Weizmann   *Political World of American Judaism* by Samuel Halperin, Detroit: Wayne
State University Press, 1961, p. 271

Political Leadership   *Political World of American Judaism* by Samuel Halperin, Detroit: Wayne State University Press, 1961, pp. 293–294

The American Jewish Community in Wartime and After
The Zionist Idea by Arthur Hertzberg, ed., New York:
Doubleday, 1959, pp. 600–602 JSSQ, Sept., pp. 16–27
NP, June 9, pp. 422–424, 446–447

Address: American Jewish Conference, 2nd Session,
New York AJ Conf. Proceedings, 390 pp., pp. 57–67
NP, Dec. 15

An Exchange of Correspondence Between Arthur Hays
Sulzberger, publisher of *The New York Times,* and Dr.
Silver   NP, Jan. 7, pp. 187–189

Thoughts on Freedom   TB, Oct. 22

No Compromise Short of Palestine Commonwealth   NP,
Oct. 27

Chaim Weizmann on His 70th Birthday   TB, Nov. 19

Statement of Resignation as Co-Chairman of American
Zionist Emergency Council   NP, Dec. 29, pp. 1–2

1945   Messiah   *An Encyclopedia of Religion,* Vergilius Ferm,
ed., New York Philosophical Library, pp. 485–486

Pseudo-Messiahs   *An Encyclopedia of Religion.* Vergilius Ferm, ed., New York Philosophical Library, pp.
619–620

Presidential Acceptance Address   CCAR, vol. 55, pp. 173–
174

Political Situation in Zionism   PY, Washington: ZOA,
vol. 2, pp. 3–17

For Human Rights; testimony before the Senate Committee on Foreign Affairs on behalf of the CCAR   LJ,
vol. 13, No. 6, pp. 52–54

Three Tasks for American Jewry   TB, Jan. 21

Moral and Psychological Basis of a Lasting Peace   *Social Education*, Feb., pp. 55–59 TB, Feb. 25, Mar. 4

How the American Palestine Resolution Was Sabotaged   JS, Mar. 9, p. 3

What Is Zionism?   JCh, Mar. 18, pp. 128–131

A Jewish State   AH, Mar. 30, p. 7

"Nothing to Lose But Our Illusions"   American Zionist Policy Committee separate, 14 pp.

Jewish People Must Not Remain Without Status   Can. Zion., May 4, p. 4

London Conference   NP, Sept. 28, p. 11

On the Record; excerpts from public statements of national leaders on Palestine   NP, Oct. 31, p. 13

Statement on Memorandum to Secretary Byrnes   NP, Oct. 31, p. 6

We Were Slaughtered by Our Enemies; We Were Betrayed by Our Friends; address, 48th convention of Zionist Organization of America   NP, Nov. 30, pp. 14–15

America and the Yishuv; Radio Jerusalem address   NP, Dec. 31, pp. 1, 4

Spearhead for a New Civilization   PW, Dec., p. 3

1946   President's Message   CCAR, vol. 56, pp. 217–230

Address; American Jewish Conference   New York AJ Conf. Proceedings, pp. 130–145 NP, May 23, 1947, p. 5 TB, Feb. 24

What We Can Expect of the Anglo-American Committee of Inquiry   NP, Jan. 28, p. 3

Zionism Is Nationhood Not Refugee Problem   NP, Jan. 28, pp. 1–2

We Shall Live at Last as Free Men on Our Own Soil   NP, Feb. 28, p. 8

The Mobilization of American Jews   NP, Feb., pp. 1, 3

The Synagogue in the World Today   UAHC, 39th Biennial Report, Cincinnati TB, Mar. 17

To the Jews of America: A Declaration   NP, Apr. 19, p. 1

Power Politics with Jewish Lives   NP, May 24, p. 3

At Destiny's Crossroads   *Land and Life,* May, p. 1–6

Why the Congress Should Be Held in America   NP, June 3, p. 2

Denounces Anti-Labor Charges   NP, June 10, p. 5

Zionist Congress and Zionist Organization of America Statement   *Zionist Review* (new series), June 28, p. 5

Worthless Pledges   NP, July 12, p. 7

Against Spiritual Demobilization   LJ, July, p. 5–10

A Reply and Indictment   NP, Aug. 28, pp. 2, 8

Deportation and Death   *Menorah* (S. A. Zionist Youth Council), Sept., pp. 13, 28

Rosh Hashanah Message   NP, Sept. 20, p. 15

Those Who Love Freedom and Justice   NP, Sept. 20, p. 4

Rosh Hashanah Evening Sermon   TB, Oct. 20

American Zionists on President Truman's Pronouncement NP, Oct. 21, p. 3

Our Battle for Jewish Statehood; address before the 49th Annual Convention of the ZOA   Separate, 18 pp.

"The Jewish State"   NP, Nov. 15, pp. 12–14

Exchange of Cables: to Dr. Chaim Weizmann from Dr. Silver   NP, Nov. 15, p. 9

Address; given before Fourth Session of World Zionist Congress   NJ, Dec. 1946/Jan. 1947, pp. 39–41

1947   Jewish State in Palestine; statement to the Political Committee of the General Assembly of the United Nations on May 8   Abba Hillel Silver, Moshe Shertok, David Ben-Gurion before the UN, American Zionist Emergency Council separate, pp. 3–10 NJ, May, pp. 151–153 TB, May 18 *United Nations Weekly Bulletin,* May 20, pp. 548–551 *Congressional Record,* May 16, pp. 2–8 (vol. 93, part ii A2327–2329) NP, May 9, p. 1 *Vital Speeches,* May 15, pp. 453–456 NYT, May 9, p. 4

The Jewish People to the United Nations; statement made on Oct. 2 to the Ad Hoc Committee on Palestine of the United Nations General Assembly Abba Hillel Silver, Moshe Shertok, Chaim Weizmann before the UN, American Zionist Emergency Council separate, pp. 3–10 *Palestine,* vol. 4 pp. 81–89 NJ, Oct/Nov., p. 7–11 NYT, Oct. 3, p. 20

Hails Congress Results   NP, Jan. 3, p. 1

We Stand to Lose More Than Gain by London Conference
  NP, Jan. 3, p. 7

Pleads for Palestine Truce to Give Executive Chance to
  Work   NP, Jan. 24, p. 2

Assails British Ultimatum   NYT, Feb. 6, p. 3:1

Who Has the Right to Decide   NP, Feb. 14, p. 9

A Personal Message to You   NP, Feb. 28, p. 12

An End to Injustice   NP, Feb. 28, p. 7

Bevin Trying to Split Yishuv   NP, Apr. 14, p. 3

Assails U.S. Position in U.N.   NP, May 9, p. 2

Test Case for United Nations   Palestine and Middle
  East, May, pp. 78–81

U.S. Stand—Uncommunicative   NP, June 13, p. 5

The Jewish People   *Furrows*, June, pp. 10–13

An Unbeaten and an Unbeatable People   NP, July 22,
  pp. 10–11

Cause and Effect in Palestine   *Palestine*, Sept., pp. 65–
  68

We Extend a Hand of Amity to the Arabs   NP, Sept. 30,
  p. 2

Palestine Partition Acceptable   *Vital Speeches*, Oct. 15,
  pp. 10–15

A Sovereign Jewish State Will Redound to the Everlasting Glory of the U.S.   NP, Oct. 17, pp. 6–8

Hadassah Expansion   HN, Dec., p. 8

Jewish Agency Accepts Partition Proposals   *United Nations Weekly Bulletin*, Oct. 14, pp. 477–478

Goals and Outlook for Jewish Life in America   CJFWF,
  separate, 10 pp.

1948   President's Message   CCAR, vol. 57, pp. 237–256

Israel and the United States   PY and *Israeli Annual*, vol.
  4 Washington: ZOA, pp. 3–20

Statement for the Jewish Agency to the UN Security
  Council   NYT, Mar. 20, p. 2

Jewish Agency for Palestine Before the Security Council
  of the UN   Jewish Agency, separate, 62 pp.

Review at the Security Council   NJ, Mar./Apr., pp. 95–
  99

We Must Stand on Guard   NP, Jan. 9, pp. 3, 5

Assails Malevolent Neutrality   NP, Feb. 18, p. 3

For the Healing of Nations   NP, Mar. 17, pp. 6–7

Exhorts U.S. to Back Partition   NYT, Apr. 1

We Will Win the Final Battle   NP, Apr. 14, pp. 6, 11

Trusteeship, a Futile Move; CBS radio address   NP, Apr. 14, p. 3

Jewish State Will Strive for Peace and Cooperation   NP, May 18, p. 2

Jews of America Did Not Let Us Down   NP, May 28, p. 10

Arab Aggression   NJ, May, pp. 130–131

What of the Future?   NP, June 25, p. 8

World Jewry Will Not Let Israel Down   NP, July 23, p. 7

Rebirth of a Nation   UPA Yrbk., pp. 16, 76, 79

1949   Vision And Victory: A Collection of Addresses, 1942–48: The Conspiracy of Silence; Toward American Jewish Unity; at the Congressional Hearings; as the Deadline Approached; a Year's Advance; Nothing to Lose but Illusions; After the Anglo-American Inquiry; To the World Zionist Congress; The Vital Role of Tactics; Before the World Tribunal; We Will Make This Sacrifice; The Month of Exaltation; The Test of the U.N.'s Authority; The American Reversal; Trusteeship or Independence?; The Jewish State Is Born; The Changing and the Changeless; American Jewry in War and After; Liberal Judaism and Israel.   New York: ZOA, 232 pp.

Centennial Reconsecration Sermon   TB, Dec. 25

Statement to UPA Board of Directors   NP, Mar. 11, p. 2

Declines Nomination to ZOA Presidency   NP, Mar. 31, p. 10

State and Zionist Organization   JS, June 10, p. 3; July 1, p. 4

A Tribute to Emanuel Neumann   NP, June 14, pp. 16–17

Time for Expansion Is Now   NP, June 14, p. 7

The Case for Zionism   Reader's Digest, Sept., pp. 54–58

Israel Must Be Made Secure   NP, Dec. 13, p. 6

Discussion; On the Nature of Man   CCAR, vol. 58, pp. 278–284

1950 The Future of the American Jewish Community CCAR, vol. 60, pp. 358–373 CCAR, separate, 12 pp.

An Open Letter to Mr. Truman The Temple, 12 pp.

What Is Greatness? TB, Jan. 15

Fountain of Youth TB, Feb. 19

Founders' Day Address HUC seperate, 16 pp. TB, Apr. 9, 16 pp.

Let Us Build with Eager Hearts and Willing Hands NP, July, p. 9

On Raising Our Sights—Rosh Hashanah Sermon TB, Sept. 11

For a Creative Jewish Community in the U.S. Amer. Assoc. for Jew. Ed. separate *Jew. Ed. Newsletter*— Amer. Assoc. for Jew. Ed., Feb. 19, 1951, p. 15

1951 Prophetic Religion and World Culture *Religious Faith and World Culture*. A. W. Loos, ed., New York: Prentice-Hall, 294 pp., pp. 125–141

Shall We Rearm Germany? The Temple, 12 pp.

Address: Jewish War Veterans TB, Apr. 22

Dr. Silver, Mrs. Myerson Clash on U.S. Zionist Stand AZ, Sept., p. 6

Achievements and Failure of Zionist Congress AZ, Sept., 15

House of Living Judaism: dedication address UAHC separate, 10 pp. TB, Nov. 4

Message of Israel Broadcast The Old and the New, TB, Dec. 16; The One and the Many, TB, Dec. 23; The Wall and the Bridge, TB, Dec. 30

1952 There Is Yet Room for Vision; ordination address HUC separate, 10 pp.

American Leadership in the World Today; address before the American College of Physicians TB, May 4, May 11

What We Set Our Hand to Do . . . We Shall Complete *Westralian Judaean*, May 4–5

Address: UPA Conference TB, Jan. 20

Relationship Between the American Jewish Community and Israel NCJSS, Fall, pp. 66–67

Invocation: Republican National Convention   NYT, July 8 CPD, July 9

Pouring It Back; statement defending Eisenhower on the McCarran-Walter Immigration Bill *Time*, Oct. 27, p. 23

General Debate   23rd Zionist Congress Proceedings, Jerusalem, pp. 80–84

1953   Introduction *History of the Jews*, rev. & enl., Paul Goodman, New York. E. P. Dutton & Co., pp. 7–11

Prayer: Presidential Inauguration   NYT, Jan. 21, p. 19

Jewish Life and Destiny   AZ, Feb. 5, pp. 12–13

Address; 60th Birthday Testimonial   TB, Feb. 22, AZ. Feb. 20, p. 2

On the Threshold of the Fourth Century; address before the Biennial of the UAHC   UAHC separate, 14 pp. TB, May 17

Religion, Bulwark of a Free Society *Independent Woman*, July, inside cover

Israel Under Attack   CW, Nov. 2, pp. 5–7 JS, Dec. 1, p. 16

Five Tests of a Good Book   *Canadian Jewish Chronicle*, Nov. 27 TB, Dec. 13

1954   America's Stake in Human Freedom; address before the City Club of Cleveland   TB, Jan. 3

Warning by ZOA on Arab Arming   AZR, Mar. 1, pp. 1–2

Crisis of Religion in Education   Rel. Ed., Mar./Apr. p. 67–68

Anti-Israel Elements in the U.S. Dept. of State   AZR, July, pp. 4–5

Broken Home   Golden Anniversary of Religious Education Association   TB, May 2

1955   Exchange of Correspondence: President Eisenhower and Rabbi Silver U.S. Dept. State Bull., Nov. 28, pp. 894–895   AZ, Nov., p. 6

Need for Peaceful Settlement of Near East Problems U.S. Dept. State Bull., Nov. 28, p. 895

Zionism and American Jewry   zoa Program and Education Bulletin (Tercentenary issue), pp. 3–6

Role of American Jews   az, Mar., p. 3

Security Pact in Mutual Interest   az, July, pp. 1–2

A Mistaken Mid-East Policy   az, Nov., p. 1

Israel Wants to Live   tb, Dec. 11

1956   Where Judaism Differed: An Inquiry into the Distinctiveness of Judaism   New York: Macmillan, 318 pp., also jps 1957

Address: Board of Governors, Israel Bond Organization tb, Jan. 22

Address: Launching the 1956 Campaign of Israel Bonds tb, Feb. 12

Unflagging Persistence–Now As Then–An Answer to Ex-President Truman's *Memoirs*   az, Feb., p. 5

What Brotherhood Means to Me   nccj separate, 16 pp.

U.S. Cannot Shirk Arms Responsibility   az, Apr., pp. 1–2

B'nai B'rith Has Built More Than Buildings   njm, June, p. 10

Appeasement; statement issued on the Israel-Egypt situation   az, Oct./Nov., p. 3

Fires in the Middle East   Amer. Zion. Council separate, 14 pp.

Real Testing of the U.N.   tb, Dec. 23

1957   The Parting of the Ways; address before the 50th Anniversary Convocation of the Dropsie College   tb, May 5

Forward   *A Jewish Family Bible*. Chicago: Menorah Press

1958   American Zionism's Role in the Establishment of Israel az, Apr./May, pp. 6–7

What Is the Future of Judaism in Israel   az, Sept., p. 6

Right to Work   AFL-CIO separate, 2 pp.

What Makes and Breaks a Family   tb, Dec. 14

1959   How Can American Education Be Improved *Encyclo-pedia Year Book.* New York: Grolier Society, p. 325

1960   Tribute to Spencer Irwin   Cleveland, Rowfant Club, n.p., published privately

Dilution of Zionism Means Self-Defeat   AZ, May, pp. 1, 8

Dr. Theodor Herzl; address given to National Assembly of American Zionists   Amer. Zionist Council separate, 9 pp.

1961   *Moses and the Original Torah:* the real character of Moses and the essential message of the Torah   New York: Macmillan Company, 188 pp.

במה נבדלת היהדות, a translation of *Where Judaism Differed,* by Baruch Karo   Tel Aviv: Massadah, 270 pp.

How Do You Feel About Man's Attempt to Conquer Outer Space? *Encyclopedia Yearbook.* New York: Grolier Society, p. 40

Building Walls and Shelters   TB, Dec. 17

The Ingathering of the Exiles
and an Exemplary Nation

DAVID BEN GURION

*

NOT ALL JEWS in Israel, perhaps, acknowledge that their country's two fundamental tasks are the ingathering of the exiles and the making of a model state. Some negate the possibility of the ingathering of the exiles, others deny the need to be a model state; while some see a contradiction in terms between these two goals.

Jews outside of Israel regard the matter differently. With the exception of two small hostile factions on the right and the left—the American Council for Judaism and the Communists respectively—who deny the existence of the Jewish people, it can safely be said that the general body of world Jewry, and the Zionists foremost, wish to see these two aims realized.

The Jews of the Diaspora ardently wish to see in Israel an unblemished, perfect State, one that exemplifies in its conduct and regimen the very best of Jewish and universal ideals and aspirations. It is world Jewry's desire—a perfectly legitimate desire—that the State of Israel prove worthy of the great heritage of Israel's prophets; and its citizens, institutions and undertakings bring honor upon the Jewish people, so that every Jew, wherever he lives, may take pride in Israel's status and good name.

No Israeli should make light of this desire on the ground that the Jews of the Diaspora—physically so far removed from Israel and her everyday life and problems—have no moral right to demand of Israeli Jewry what they themselves do not do; and that the demand that the Israelis be a superior nation, crowned with the highest virtues and renowned for their exemplary way of life, is a very easy demand to make of someone else.

While this argument may be technically correct, it is not justifiable from a moral point of view. Jewry's attachment to the homeland of the Hebrew nation has been a bedrock of our tradition throughout the ages. Only by virtue of this attachment were we able to return to our land and do what we have done; it was this attachment that brought us volunteers from over fifty countries to fight in the War of Liberation; nothing else could have called forth the continuing and large-scale assistance of our brothers abroad in the absorption of the new immigrants and the building of the land. There is not a Jew in the world who has no part in Israel, even if he has done nothing for her. The State of Israel is the creation of the Jewish people, not only of this generation but of every generation, and everyone who considers himself a Jew shares in all aspects of the Jewish heritage. In our time the Bible and the State of Israel are the greatest heritages of our people wherever they may be. Therefore, Jews outside the State, including those who have no intention of coming here, have the moral right—and perhaps duty—to state their mind on its way of life and the development of its national character.

Of course, the Jews of the Diaspora do not have the authority to force their will upon us. They may not *oblige* us to do what we do not wish to do or see no need of doing, nor may they prevent us from doing that which we would do; even as we cannot compel the Jews of the Diaspora to act or refrain from action in accordance with our will rather than theirs. Bonds of obligation must be mutual; no one has more authority over his fellowman than his fellowman has over him. Every Jew in the world, then, has the right to state how he feels Israel ought to be run, and such opinions and feelings have *moral* weight, if lacking in *legal force*.

The desire of Diaspora Jewry to have Israel be an exemplary state is both justified and profoundly rational. Jews the world over have a common destiny over and above all other national and international bonds. This community of fate, which is expressed in an ancient saying, "All Jews are responsible for one another," served as an elixir of life to our scattered and persecuted people through the ages. Today, according to international law, as well as the laws of the individual nations, there is no difference in status between the Jews of America, England, or any other country, and their fellow citizens; the Jews of the Diaspora have no formal, political ties with Israel, nor are they represented by her. Nonetheless, all nations realize that Israel is both the creation and the mirror of world Jewry. They know that only in Israel are the Jews truly free to do as they wish and therefore more responsible for what they do; and that only in Israel will the unique characteristics of the Jewish people be fully revealed, be they good or bad. Moreover, every intelligent and honest statesman knows full well—although not every one would say so publicly—that it is perfectly natural for the Jews of his country to show a deep interest in Israeli affairs and regard her with intimate affection, rather than simply as another foreign nation.

The Jews of the Diaspora, even if they do not plan to settle in Israel, realize that their status and prestige among their non-Jewish neighbors depends in large measure upon the status and prestige of the State of Israel. It was not only the miracle of Israel's rebirth in 1948 that sent a great wave of enthusiasm sweeping through the Diaspora. The miraculous victories of the Haganah during the War of Liberation and the Sinai campaign; the absorption of more than a million immigrants from the four corners of the earth; Israel's democratic regime; her rapid advances in education, health, science, and the development of her natural resources; the aid that she has extended to the new nations of Asia and Africa—all these achievements have enhanced the prestige of every Jew throughout the world in his own and his neighbor's eyes.

A Diaspora Jew therefore *may* demand of an Israeli Jew what he does not demand of himself, because he knows that only in Israel are Jews truly and fully masters of their own fate, that there they are able to accomplish much more than Diaspora Jews can—and *"noblesse oblige."* World Jewry, then, rightly expects that Israel be not "just" a state like all other states. And while they may not be clear as to what Israel must do in order to become a model state, as Herzl and many others before him envisioned, they have the desire, rooted in the age-old heritage, to see Israel be a beacon to the nations.

*

As to the ingathering of the exiles, the Jews of the Diaspora certainly have no doubts with regard to its importance, and although it is precisely in Israel that there is a divergence of opinion about the scope of the ingathering and the feasibility of creating a model state—for it is in Israel that these goals must be realized, and it is one thing to express a noble desire, but quite another to put it into effect—yet the State of Israel itself has stated its official position in unequivocal terms.

In the historic document that proclaimed the creation of the state, Israel's two great goals were clearly set forth. "The State of Israel will be open to Jewish immigration and the Ingathering of the Exiles"—this was the first responsibility that the new nation took upon itself at its very birth. And the declaration goes on to say: [The State of Israel] "will rest upon foundations of liberty, justice and peace as envisioned by the prophets of Israel." This second obligation is no easier to fulfill and no less significant than the first.

It is not certain—and not crucially important—whether the Declaration of Independence of May 14, 1948, is legally binding or not. What does matter is that the Jewish people, at that momentous and crucial point in its history, gave utterance in this Declaration to its age-old hope and desire, and all the parties in Israel, from Agudat Israel to the Communists, signed that historic document.

However, Israel was not satisfied with a mere declaration. In order to give it legal force, she soon thereafter passed two enactments which are actually the primary and basic laws of the State: the Law of Return, which opens the gates of Israel to all Jews who wish to come and settle in her, and awards them the right of citizenship immediately upon their immigration; and the State Education Law, which determines what character will be imprinted upon the people ingathering in their country, and how to educate the young generation in order to enable it to achieve that character. These two laws indicate the aim, the way and the historic destiny of the State of Israel.

The Law of Return establishes that this country does not belong solely to its inhabitants, but is the State of the Jewish people wherever they may be; and that the right of immigration does not derive from or depend on Israel's consent, as is the case in all other countries; the mere fact that an immigrant is a member of the Jewish people bestows this right upon him, for this is his promised land. The right of any Jew to settle in Israel does not depend on the consent of the citizens of the State, but is a fundamental promise, embedded in the very fact of his being a Jew. Indeed, the State of Israel exists to uphold and guarantee this right.

The State Education Law, which applies to every child in Israel, sets forth the image of the nation that Israel seeks to create, and declares by what means the goal shall be attained. The Law states: "It is the goal of State education to base Israeli primary education on the values of Jewish culture and the achievements of science; on love of the homeland and devotion to the State and the Jewish people; on training in agricultural labor and in crafts; on fulfillment of *pioneering principles; on the aspiration for a society built on liberty, equality, tolerance, mutual aid and love of mankind.*"

Israel did not content herself with establishing the knowledge and qualities with which the younger generation should be endowed, but stated explicitly the historic goal toward which the country aims, and defined the structure of the society that is to be brought into being.

The major and central goals of Israel are implied by these two laws; neither has as yet been reached, nor will they be attained easily or in the near future. This does not mean to say, however, that they are merely pious wishes or goals for some distant future; rather, they are a *process* rooted in the factors responsible for the establishment, development, survival and future of the State. Both the dream of the ingathering of the exiles and the vision of the creation of a new society are beginning realized before our very eyes.

The Third Commonwealth, unlike the First and Second, is entirely the product of an ingathering of exiles. Truly, it is amazing: for thousands of years our prophets and seers have awaited the ingathering of the exiles, and only in our generation has it come to pass.

As far back as the Book of Deuteronomy we are told: "Then the Lord thy God will turn thy captivity, and have compassion upon thee, and will return and gather thee from all the peoples, whither the Lord thy God hath scattered thee. If any of thine that are dispersed be in the uttermost parts of heaven, from thence will the Lord thy God gather thee, and from thence will He fetch thee. And the Lord thy God will bring thee into the land which thy fathers possessed, and thou shalt possess it; and He will do thee good, and multiply thee above thy fathers" (30:3–5).

Isaiah, the prophet of consolation, declared: "Fear not, for I am with thee; I will bring thy seed from the east, and gather thee from the west; and I will say to the north: 'Give up', and to the south: 'Keep not back. Bring My sons from far, and My daughters from the ends of the earth'" (43:5–6).

Even Jeremiah, the prophet of wrath and destruction, foretold in pity: "I will turn your captivity, and gather you from all the nations, and from all the places whither I have driven you, saith the Lord; and I will bring you back unto the place whence I caused you to be carried away captive" (29:14). However, the ingathering of our scattered people in the land possessed by our forefathers began only during the past few generations.

The exodus from Egypt marked, in a way, the beginning of Jewish history. We know very little of this event shrouded in wonder and legend, but there is no doubt as to its verity or its prime importance in the history of the Jewish people. We find it mentioned not only in the Pentateuch and the Early Prophets (Joshua, Judges, Samuel, and Kings), but also in the utterances of the great literary prophets, Isaiah, Hosea, Micah, Jeremiah, and Ezekiel, as well as in several Psalms and elsewhere. Wherever it is mentioned it is spoken of as a central and primary event, and we can trust the memory of the people and the testimony of its prophets.

However, the exodus from Egypt did not constitute an ingathering of exiles. Rather, it constituted a passing from the house of bondage in which, according to the Torah, the people was born, to the promised land.

Likewise, the first return to Zion in the days of Zerubbabel was not an ingathering of exiles, even though a Jewish Diaspora had come into existence prior to the destruction of the First Temple. Isaiah spoke of "the captives of Egypt, and the exiles of Ethiopia" (present-day Sudan) and of "the remnant of His people, that shall remain from Assyria, and from Egypt, and from Pathros, and from Cush, and from Elam, and from Shinar, and from Hamath, and from the islands of the sea" (20:4 and 11:11); and a later prophet, Joel the son of Pethuel, made explicit mention of the sale of Judeans to "the sons of the Jevanim" (the Greeks) by Tyre, Zidon and Philistia (4:6, 4). However, only the Jews of Babylonia returned to the land of Israel 2,500 years ago, after the declaration of Cyrus, and the returning exiles numbered less than 50,000 souls. The Jews of Egypt and Cush and the islands of the sea did not return. Only in our time has there been a true ingathering of exiles—from Europe, Asia, Africa, America and Australia, and in much greater proportions than in the days of Zerubbabel. During the thirty-year period of the British Mandate nine times the number of the Babylonian immigrants entered Israel's gates; and in the fourteen years since the establishment of the State, over twenty-five times that number have settled in the homeland. From Babylonia alone (present-day Iraq) almost three times the number of Zerubbabel's immigrants have come to Israel. Yet in spite of all this, only slightly more than one-sixth of present-day world Jewry is to be found within Israel's borders.

No one can predict with any degree of certainty the tempo or ultimate scope of the ingathering of exiles still to be witnessed in Israel. Guesses, wishful thinking and cut-and-dried formulae are useless. On the other hand, this historic process—and the ingathering of the exiles *is* a primary historic process in the life of Israel and the Jewish people—should not be regarded as something that will come to pass automatically, in accordance with "natural laws" over which we have no control, even as we have no control over the movements of the stars and planets. Historic processes depend upon the wills of human beings, and human wills are activated by human needs and by the values men hold dear. Man is no blind and helpless tool in the hands of "history." On the contrary: history is made by men. Man can channel and control a historic process if he knows how to recognize the true needs of his fellows and base those needs on the values that enrich and ennoble human existence. A historic process is accelerated or held back according to the scope and force of the deliberate and conscious efforts of groups and individuals. Clashes of will take place in the realm of history, and the will that does not yield is destined to win the victory. The process of the ingathering of the exiles depends upon the will of the Jewish people, both in Israel and the Diaspora; and particularly upon the steps taken by the State and its emissaries, and the pioneer spirit of its citizenry.

The same considerations apply to the molding of the new society in Israel. Like the ingathering of the exiles, this process, too, is unfolding before our eyes and has only just begun. It is not happening of or by itself; it is being brought to pass by the impetus of a pioneering effort and the people's needs; and pioneering achievement, linked with the people's needs, will carry the process onward. At the same time, what Israel is doing for herself in education, in raising the status of the worker, in the integration of the immigrants, in the labor settlements, and in the cooperative and workers' movements—serves as a working example for the new nations of Asia and Africa.

In her fourteenth year of independence, Israel cannot boast that she is near her historic goal. Many more Jews than have already entered Israel long to reach her shores, and shall do so—unless external forces shut the doors of exit in their faces. Only one-fourth of the small territory belonging to Israel is settled; an important sector in the north and a much larger area in the south are still empty. The scores of new towns set up since the establishment of the state are only a beginning, though a promising beginning, to be sure. The Lachish region, Dimona, Kfar Yeroham, Eilat, Mizpeh-Ramon in the south; Beit-Shean, Kiryat-Shmoneh, rejuvenated Safad and other cities in the north—all have been built mainly by new immigrants. In addition, new immigrants have founded some five hundred agricultural settlements in all parts of the country. Still more new towns will be built in the near future: Arad and Besor in the Negev, and Carmiel in Galilee.

The more than threefold growth of Israel's population during the fourteen years since the establishment of the state, and the growing immigration today—from Europe, Africa, Asia and the Western Hemisphere—show that the task of ingathering the exiles is being fulfilled at this very moment.

In addition, Israel's activities among the new countries of Asia and Africa, some of whom won their independence at the same time as she, but most of whom became autonomous only during the last few years, show that her role as a model to other nations is certainly not a matter of wishful thinking. Over 2,000 young Asians and Africans have come to Israel to complete their studies in agriculture, in the creation of regional development areas, the organization of pioneer youth, of cooperative movements in general and cooperative agricultural settlements in particular, and other matters. Scores of students from these new nations are studying in Israeli institutions of higher education: the Hebrew University in Jerusalem, the Technion in Haifa, the Faculty of Agriculture in Rehovot, and the Medical Faculty. Israeli experts in agriculture, irrigation, aeronautics, navigation, secondary and higher education, and construction and road-building, are engaged in fruitful work in a number of African and Asian countries.

The new social patterns in Israel, founded upon mutual aid and cooperation on a fully voluntary basis; the enhancement of the values of labor for the elevation of the worker as a creative and progressive force in society; the training of Israeli youth in *Nahal* and *Gadna* for pioneer work in the absorption of new immigrants and the fructification of the desert; the cultivation of science both for the broadening of the scope of human knowledge and for practical application in the realms of health, agriculture and defense—all these things serve as an example for younger nations, and acquire loyal friends for Israel in Asia and Africa, in addition to the friends she has in Europe and America.

The achievements of our reborn country during these past fourteen years have demonstrated conclusively that Israel is indeed equal to the task of ingathering and integrating the exiles, and serving as an example to new nations.

The Levites Among Arabian Tribes

IZHAK BEN-ZVI

*

IN A STIMULATING ARTICLE, published in the *Junker-Festschrift*,[1] Père R. de Vaux deals with a topic which I myself have discussed elsewhere,[2] namely the antiquity of the settlement of Israelites in northern and southern Arabia. On the basis of Biblical and Arabic sources as well as recently published Babylonian documents, Père de Vaux concludes that the term *lawi'u* in Minaean and other early Arabic documents, which designates a certain group of people, is related to Hebrew *Léwî*,[3] either they are derived from a common stem or—as it seems more probable—the Arabic word had been borrowed from Hebrew. The second alternative, which might never have left the realm of speculation, has been substantiated by recent documents supporting the theory that Israelites settled in Arabia as far back as the period preceding the return to Zion.

In the present article I intend to adduce evidence in support of de Vaux's contention that the term *lawi'u* was indeed borrowed by the Arabs from the ancient Israelites.

The fact that Hebrew tribes did penetrate into the Arabian peninsula at such an early date and came into contact with nomadic and settled Arab tribes lends support to the contention that the term *léwî* was brought along by those same Hebrew tribes and passed on to the Arab tribes, among them primarily to the Minaeans. From his study of the Nabonidus inscriptions of Harran, published by Professor Gadd,[4] Père de Vaux has discovered the connection between the conquests of Nabonidus and the beginnings of the colonization of the Judean exiles who had come with the Babylonians to the northern

---

1 "Levites Mineens et Levites Israelites," *Festschrift für H. Junker*
(Trier, 1961).

2 "On the Antiquity of the Settlement of Israelite Tribes in Arabia,"
Eretz Israel (Jerusalem: The Society for the Exploration of Palestine and Its Antiquities, 1959),
VI, 130–149.

3 In the Talmud the term *bar Leway*
(בר לואי) appears in a few places,
e.g., "Rabbi Joshua *bar Leway* (the
Levite)" Babyl. Talmud, (Sabbath
156).

4 C. J. Gadd, "The Harran Inscription," *Anatolian Studies* (1958),
pp. 35–93.

part of Hejaz, to the desert oases: Teimā, Dadanu, Padakku, Khibrâ, Ladikhu, and Yatribu.

Professor de Vaux calls attention to the Minaean inscriptions from al-'Ulā, an important oasis in northern Arabia and the site of ancient Dedan. Dedan, of course, is listed among the sons of Abraham and Keturah, and is also mentioned by Isaiah, Ezekiel, and Jeremiah. It may be assumed that from those early times onwards, Hebrew tribes spread out in the Arabian peninsula, as far south as Yemen; and that in the days of the Hebrew monarchy they were in contact with the Minaeans and other Arab tribes, either through trade ("the caravans of Tema") [5] or through warfare. Even though it is difficult to show when this penetration of Arabian territory began, a reference to it seems to be contained in the account of the territorial conquests of "the Sons of Simeon" and "the Sons of Reuben" in Arabia recorded in the Book of Chronicles. The first (the Sons of Simeon) are described as follows: "And they went to the entrance of Gedor ("Gerar" in the Septuagint), even unto the east side of the valley, to seek pasture for their flocks. And they found fat pasture and good, and the land was wide and quiet, and peaceable; for they that dwelt there aforetime were of Ham. And these written by name came in the days of Hezekiah king of Judah, and smote their tents, and the Me'unīm (Minaeans) that were found there, and destroyed them utterly, unto this day, and dwelt in their stead; because there was pasture there for their flocks. And some of them, even of the sons of Simeon, five hundred men, went to mount Seir, having for their captains Pelatiah, and Neariah, and Rephaiah, and Uzziel, the sons of Ishi. And they smote the remnant of the Amalekites that escaped, and dwelt there unto this day" (I Chronicles 4:39–43). [6]

Further on, in the section concerning the sons of Reuben, we are told: "and eastward he dwelt even unto the entrance of the wilderness from the river Euphrates; because their cattle were multiplied in the land of Gilead. And in the days of Saul they made war with the Hagrites, who fell by their hands; and they dwelt in their tents throughout all the land east of Gilead" (I Chronicles 5:9–10). Further on the text says of the sons of Reuben and Gad and the half tribe of Manasseh: "The sons of Reuben, and the Gadites, and the half-tribe of Manasseh, as many as were valiant men, men able to bear buckler and sword, and to shoot with bow, and skillful in war, were forty and

---

5   Job 6:19.
6   According to this account I assume that "the valley" and "unto the east side of the valley" refer to Wadi Sirhan—see *Eretz Israel*, VI, 133.

Moreover, Glaser is of the opinion that the children of Jetur originally lived in the environs of Teima, Wadi Sirhan, and Jauf. Additional support is provided by the prox-

four thousand and seven hundred and threescore, that were able to go forth to war. And they made war with the Hagrites, with Jetur, and Naphish, and Nodab. And they were helped against them, and the Hagrites were delivered into their hand, and all that were with them; for they cried to God in the battle, and He was entreated of them, because they put their trust in Him. And they took away their cattle: of their camels fifty thousand, and of sheep two hundred and fifty thousand, and of asses two thousand; and of souls of men a hundred thousand. For there fell many slain, because the war was of God. And they dwelt in their stead until the captivity" (1 Chronicles 5:18–23).

These are merely faint echoes of wars waged in ancient times by the Israelite tribes—the Reubenites and Simeonites in particular—against the Ishmaelites, the sons of Hagar, and even the sons of Keturah, Abraham's concubine. To the Reubenites and Simeonites we may add the tribe of Judah, all of whom were regarded as descended from Leah. The foregoing may be deduced from David's account to Achish, king of Gath, on his alleged raids " 'against the South of Judah, and against the South of the Jerahmeelites, and against the South of the Kenites' " (I Samuel 27:10; see also 30:29). From this episode and from what is recorded in Judges 4:11—"Now Heber the Kenite had severed himself from the Kenites, even from the children of Hobab, the father-in-law of Moses"—we learn that Kenite tribes, descended from Hobab-Jethro, dwelt alongside of Israel and intermarried with them, and that only Heber the Kenite set himself apart and went over to the side of Jabin, king of Hazor. The end of the story is found in a passage in II Chronicles concerning Uzziah, king of Judah: "And God helped him against the Philistines, and against the Arabians that dwelt in Gur-baal, and the Me'unim" (26:7).

Dr. H. Tadmor has been kind enough to point out to me that the land of the Me'unim (mât-Mu-'ne-a-a) is mentioned at an earlier date in an Assyrian inscription of Tiglath-Pileser III, which describes that ruler's conquests in the southern part of the coastal plain (734 B.C.E.) as well as the location of the country: south or southeast of the city of Nahal-Mizraim (El-Arish). It follows, therefore, that the account in II Chronicles is not anachronistic but actually pertains to the period of the divided monarchy. Therefore, we shall date the episodes in Chronicles II not later than the eighth century B.C.E.[7]

imity of the names in the Bible: "Hadad, and Tema, Jetur, Naphish, and Kedem" (Genesis 25:15).

7   In a letter to me, Professor B. Mazar writes: "It is becoming more and more apparent that during the monarchic period there were strong links between Israel and Arabia, these being primarily trade links with Arabia Felix (the land of

It is clear, then, that the Meìnim or Me'unīm (המעינים : המעונים)
of I Chronicles 4:41 refers to the Μιναῖοι as the Septuagint correctly
translated (and as the other versions did not). The conclusion of the
episode is especially interesting: "and [they] smote their tents . . .
and destroyed them utterly, unto this day, and dwelt in their stead;
because there was pasture there for their flocks . . . unto this day"
(I Chronicles 4:41–43); "unto this day," which is to say, until the
writing of this account.

When did the Me'unīm-Minaeans first enter Israelite territory?

To begin with, we must consider the discovery of Professor
Nelson Glueck in his excavations at Ezion-Geber (Tell-el-Kheleifeh);
this find supports the contention that the Minaeans were in Ezion-
Geber and Elath as early as the eighth century B.C.E. In his book *The
Other Side of the Jordan*,[8] Professor Glueck tells of sherds of a large
urn discovered in Ezion-Geber; on both sherds there were letters
identified by Professor G. Ryckmans as Minaean. Professor Glueck
goes on to say: "It has been possible since the discovery of these fragments to put them together and thus to restore most of the shape of
the jar." The period to which the inscription on the jar found in Tell
Kheleifa belongs is apparent, the more so in light of the signet ring
bearing the name of Jotham, found in one of the rooms. Here is clear
evidence of the presence of Minaeans in Elath and the surrounding
area under Judean rule (Uzziah and Jotham).

Professor B. Mazar rightly takes note of the latest sources, which
show that in the eighth century there were Minaean settlements in
the Negev too. This fact, of course, in no way denies the existence of
Meunite settlements in Transjordan at the same time. Also, even if
we accept the Septuagint reading of "Gerar" instead of "Gedor"—and
I am not yet convinced that this is the correct version—this would all
the more corroborate the fact that there were Minaean settlements in
Transjordan in the eighth century B.C.E. It is a fact that the Simeonites, who originally inhabited the Negev, also spread out in Transjordan. There they conquered Mount Seir and the adjacent territory
lying to the south and to the east. In the same source it is recorded
that they also "smote the remnant of the Amalekites . . . and dwelt
there." This in no way contradicts the fact of Israel's battle with

spices) via the caravan routes
(Dedan–Jathrib–Meon, toward Hazarmaveth) or via the sea route
from Elath. It is worthwhile to
mention a South Arabian seal impression, apparently from the
eighth century B.C.E. which was
recently discovered in Bethel." Still
more conclusive evidence is being
provided by ever-increasing archeological finds in southern Arabia;
see G. W. Van Beek, BASOR, 143
(1956); Albright, *Eretz Israel*, V,
(1958) pp. 7ˣ–8ˣ.

Amalek at Rephidim near Mount Sinai during Moses' lifetime (Exodus 17:8), and Saul's and David's wars with the Amalekites in the Negev (I Samuel 30) and it is my opinion that the Meunite tribes, just like the Amalekite tribes and their neighbors, spread out on both sides of the Arabah and about the bay of the Red Sea; and that Israelite tribes—the Reubenites and Simeonites—fought with them on both these fronts.

There can be no doubt, therefore, that Israelite tribes came into close contact with Arabian tribes, particularly the Minaeans; nor is it at all surprising that Arab tribes (who were, according to the Bible, descendants of Hagar and Ishmael or of Keturah) were influenced in their religious thinking and practices by Jewish monotheism, and that some of them were assimilated into Israelite tribes.

We have conclusive evidence of the religious influence of the Israelites upon the Minaeans during a later period, that of the return to Zion under Zerubbabel; and here I refer to the detailed list of groups who returned to Judea following the proclamation of Cyrus. The various groups are clearly designated and include priests and Levites, singers, porters, Nethinim, and servants of Solomon.[9]

The Bible explains to us in a few places who these Nethinim were. Thus, in the book of Joshua there is the incident of the Gibeonites, where Joshua and the princes of the congregation promise to let the Gibeonites live after their surrender (Joshua 9:21). "And Joshua made them that day hewers of wood and drawers of water for the congregation, and for the altar of the Lord, unto this day, in the place which He should choose" (Joshua 9:27). The last words prove that the Nethinim had this status at least as far back as the period of the First Temple and perhaps even earlier.[10]

From what is written in Ezra and Nehemiah (see below) it is clear that the Nethinim who served in the Temple went into captivity with the rest of the exiles; and many Nethinim returned together with the Jews upon the proclamation of Cyrus in 539 B.C.E. and resumed their functions in the service of the Second Temple. Their names are listed in I Chronicles, chap. 9.

The figures in Ezra and Nehemiah are especially important, in that it seems that they are original lists compiled during that very

8 Glueck, N., *The Other Side of the Jordan.* New Haven: American School of Oriental Research, 1940, pp. 107 ff.

9 Ezra 2:36–58.

10 Elsewhere the Bible tells us of "All the people that were left of the Amorites, the Hittites [etc.], who were not of the children of Israel; even their children that were left after them in the land, whom the children of Israel were not able utterly to destroy, of them did Solomon raise a levy of bondservants, unto this day" (I Kings 9:20–21).

period. Of course, the lists might not be complete, but even from that
portion which has survived it is clear that the Nethinim were absorbed into the body of returning exiles and of all those who ministered in the Temple, and were thus assimilated into the Jewish
community. In all, the Nethinim and the children of the servants of
Solomon numbered 392 persons (Ezra 2:59; Nehemiah 7:60).

It is of primary significance that in each of the above-mentioned
sources both Meunim and Mephusim are included in the category of
Nethinim. Thus, we read in Ezra, 2:50: "The children of Asnah, the
children of Meunim, the children of Nephusim" [Kethib: Nephisim],
and in Nehemiah (7:52): "The children of Besai, the children of
Meunim, the children of Nephishesim" (Kethib: Nephushesim). The
children of Nephusim in Ezra and the Nephishesim in Nehemiah are
to be identified with Naphish (נפיש) in Genesis (25:15), one of the
sons of Ishmael mentioned alongside of Teima and Jetur. We have
already mentioned that in Glaser's opinion the children of Jetur originally lived in the neighborhood of Teima, Wadi Sirḥān, and al-
Jauf.

Here, then, are clear indications of Jewish influence upon the
religion and worship of the Minaeans and the sons of Naphish, who
were of Ishmaelite descent. These facts all serve to confirm Professor
Gadd's position on the penetration of Israelite tribes into Arabia.[11]

In conclusion let us point out the strong bonds uniting the
Levites and the Simeonites. We may deduce this from the blessing of
Jacob: "Simeon and Levi are brethren; weapons of violence their kinship . . ." (Genesis, 49:5). According to the Biblical account, Jacob's
rebuke refers to the slaying of the men of Shechem by Simeon and
Levi, Dinah's brothers (Genesis 34:25), but we can assume that the
bonds linking the Levites to the Simeonites remained firm with the
passing of time, and that the Levites participated with the sons of
Simeon, Reuben, and even Judah, all of them sons of Leah, in the
conquest of the lands of Meʿunīm and the Hagrites, as was mentioned
above.

Through the influence of the Israelite tribes, including the Levites, Monotheism, the religion of Abraham, Moses, and Israel,
reached the Minaeans, the Nephusim and other Arab tribes; it is only
natural that those Israelite tribes who came into Arabia during the
period of the First Temple should have brought with them, among

11 Professor H. Rabin by letter observes that this identification is
probably correct.
In Ryckman's study the name נפש
(Naphish) appears only once, as
the name of a resident of Zaphai,
but this does not mean that there
never was a tribe bearing this
name.

other original Jewish concepts and institutions, the function of the Levite and the term *Léwî*.

APPENDIX

The stamp, made of clay, that was discovered in 1957 in the excavation of Beth-El, on which was inscribed South Arabic script coming from the eighth or ninth centuries B.C.E., is worth investigating. (G. W. Van Beek—A. Jamme, BASOR 151 [1958] pp. 9 ff.)

The surprising thing is that a squeeze of this writing matches a stamp found in the collection of Glaser which was already published in 1900. According to its notice it was discovered in El Mishad at Hazarmaveth, and is also a stamp made of clay. Furthermore, a comparison between these stamps shows that not only are the letters and the size of the stamps similar, but also that the writings are broken in the same corner. (Cf. A. Jamme—G. W. Van Beek BASOR 163 [1961] pp. 15 ff.)

This fact forces certain questions which are difficult of solution. Were both these stamps, one of which was found in Hazarmaveth in South Arabia and the second in Beth-El, by a single craftsman, and did the second one reach Beth-El following the usual trade route established between Israel and Southern Arabia? In any case, we have reliable evidence of the connection between the land of Israel and Southern Arabia in the time of the First Temple.

"A Highway of Nations"

A CHAPTER IN NINETEENTH CENTURY AMERICA-ERETZ YISRAEL ACTIVITIES*

MOSHE DAVIS

*

D URING THE NINETEENTH CENTURY, the American Jewish community was more the beneficiary than the benefactor of world Jewry. The rapidly developing Jewish community in America was fully occupied with the problems of its own growth, and the urgent local needs were given first consideration. Overseas aid was therefore limited. To the extent that the Jews of America felt an obligation to their brethren, this sense of responsibility embraced primarily those who had emigrated to the United States.

The appeals from Eretz Yisrael fell into another category entirely. The love and dedication of generations had its effect even upon people who were culturally and geographically far removed from Palestine. Printed circulars in Hebrew had found their way to responsive Jews in Colonial times, and direct contact with the Holy Land increased as the Jews in America grew in numbers and strength.[1] Already in the formative years of the contemporary American Jewish community, activities for the benefit of Eretz Yisrael stemmed from a variety of spiritual and practical reasons.[2] Some people were motivated by the traditional belief in the coming of the Messiah, while others were moved by the desire to provide a place of refuge for those

* In tribute to Abba Hillel Silver who, in addition to all he means for American Jewry, exemplifies the totality of its love for Eretz Yisrael. I am grateful to the Jewish Publication Society of America for permission to publish this material from my forthcoming book *The Emergence of Conservative Judaism.*

1 Maxwell Whiteman records that a number of items relating to Palestine are found in the papers of the Philadelphia Land Grants, 1684–1772, Penna. Mss., VII, 39. The oldest reference dating back to 1763, is a response to an appeal by the Jews of Hebron. "Zionism Comes to Philadelphia," in *Early History of Zionism in America*, Isidore S.

leaving Europe. Some thought in international political terms, beginning to hope for the resettlement of Jews in Palestine as a result of the changing political events in Europe, while still others began to dream of the realization of the Return as a fulfillment of Jewish aspirations for the redemption of the Jews and mankind. These views, which cut across the Jewish community as a whole in the United States in the past century, came to the fore in the Historical School of Judaism—the School out of which there emerged the Conservative Movement in the twentieth century. In this chapter we confine ourselves to the Eretz Yisrael activities as conceived and undertaken by that sector in American Jewish life.

During the middle decades of the nineteenth century questions connected with the transmission and distribution of money to Eretz Yisrael rather than those with social and political connotations for the restoration of the Jews in the Holy Land aroused the greatest interest. Mordecai Noah's political formulation of America's role in any possible Restoration was still in the nature of a "discourse." The problem at hand was practical aid to the residents in Zion. The Jews of the Diaspora, whether religious or not, felt it incumbent to give financial support to the communities in Jerusalem. Whoever appealed on their behalf was not turned away. And such appeals were not lacking.

The settlements in Jerusalem had sent representatives to the United States as far back as the eighteenth century. Among the first of these were Moses Malki (1758) and Hayyim Isaac Carigal (1771). Their success stimulated others. In their wake came many frauds and swindlers who proceeded to appropriate for themselves the money they had collected. Furthermore, echoes of the disputes about the division of the sums reached America. Sephardim quarreled with Ashkenazim and Ashkenazim among themselves. In addition, Jews in America began to realize that the salaries of the solicitors and the expenses of their journeys were deducted from the contributions, resulting in losses to the inhabitants of Jerusalem. American Jews, not wishing to see their money squandered, and attempting to secure transfer of the collected money *in toto*, organized the *Hebrah Terumat ha-Kodesh* (Society for Offerings to the Sanctuary) in 1833 under the presidency of Israel B. Kursheedt, one of the outstanding

Meyer, ed. (New York, 1958), pp. 191, 207.

2 From the study of Professor and Mrs. Salo W. Baron on messengers sent from Israel to the United States, we can gather a clear picture, based on records and periodicals, of the development of the relationship between the leaders of the communities in Israel and America in that period. See Salo and Jeannette Baron: "Palestinian Messengers in America, 1849–79," *Jewish Social Studies*, V (April, 1943), pp. 115–162; (July), pp. 225–292.

figures of Congregation B'nai Jeshurun in New York City. The purpose of this society was to make annual collections from its members and to transfer the money directly to the inhabitants of the "four holy cities"–Jerusalem, Hebron, Safed, and Tiberias. In this way they hoped to put an end to the unnecessary expenditures of various solicitors. When a sizable sum had been collected it was transmitted directly to Rabbi Hirsch Lehren–the original founder of *Hebrah Terumat ha-Kodesh* in Amsterdam–who was to transfer and allocate the monies at his discretion.

In time of peace it might have been possible to supply all needs from European sources, without resort to aid from the United States. But, when revolutionary disturbances engulfed European Jewry, collections failed. The revolutionary wars of 1848–1849 in Europe reduced substantially the contributions of European Jews for Eretz Yisrael. Once again, the Jews in Eretz Yisrael turned to their coreligionists in free and peaceful America. Two messengers, Joseph Schwarz and Zadok Levy, were dispatched in 1849. Joseph Schwarz was the first modern scholar of Palestinography whose works are still studied. Isaac Leeser translated his first volume into English in 1850 and called it *Descriptive Geography and Brief Historical Sketch of Palestine*. The two distinguished emissaries were welcomed by the eager American leaders. Their mission, according to Isaac Leeser's testimony, was to help to set up a society which would collect annual contributions. Leeser explained that, unlike the situation of 1833 when the *Hebrah Terumat ha-Kodesh* had been organized, "communication by steam-packets has made every country easily accessible, and commercial connexions have now been formed all over the world, so that remittance can be made promptly from here to Palestine, in a manner formerly impossible."[3] The two messengers issued proclamations in the name of the inhabitants of Jerusalem. Leeser calculated that, if each of the forty organized congregations in the country were to contribute from ten to twenty-five dollars annually, it be possible "to protect the poor of Palestine, and to snatch them from the necessity of receiving aid from the missionaries, those inveterate foes of our religion." [4] He announced the formation of a committee of eight that would receive donations.[5] But the proposal by Leeser and his friends was not realized for two reasons. First, the Jews of America were not yet experienced in the collection of funds. They therefore responded to immediate needs rather than

---

3   *Occident*, VII, (Oct., 1849), p. 344.
4   *Ibid.*, p. 345.
5   The members of the committee

were Dr. Max Lilienthal, Samuel Isaacs, N. M. Noah, Jacob J. M. Falkenau, Simeon Abrahams (who

to plans for the future. Secondly, each faction in Eretz Yisrael felt it necessary to protect its own interests by sending its own messengers.

Also in 1849, Rabbi Aaron Selig Ashkenazi, a representative of the chief Ashkenazi group who called themselves the *Perushim* of Jerusalem, arrived in America. Rabbi Ashkenazi, systematic and enterprising, succeeded in rallying wide support even though many forces on the American Jewish scene were opposed to his method of operation. One of his main achievements was to attract Samuel Myer Isaacs to his project. Leeser, who was generally opposed to the system of messengers, agreed to aid Ashkenazi's mission only on the condition that all the money collected would be transferred to Sir Moses Montefiore in London, while Ashkenazi himself would receive limited funds for his own expenses.

In the course of time, Isaacs became the mainstay of all efforts on behalf of Eretz Yisrael and was held responsible for his work by the American Jewish congregations. He was in constant correspondence with Moses Montefiore, with whom, as an English Jew, Isaacs felt a special sense of kinship. He transferred the funds to him for distribution. Before long, Isaacs began to investigate carefully the private affairs of the messengers, a step which Ashkenazi did not like at all. Isaacs complained about the disproportionate expenses of the messengers, and in the *Asmonean* of the 26th of April, 1850, he announced:

> Notice is hereby given. To the Presidents and Members of the various Societies organized throughout the United States, in support of the mission of Rabbi Aaron Selig for the Poor of the Holy Land, *not* to pay any *monies* whatever either to Messengers or through any channel except through the only accredited agents (Isaacs, Noah, and Micholl).[6]

But Rabbi Ashkenazi did not rest, either. Instead of opposing Isaacs publicly, he sought a device to win power from the hands of his opponents, while at the same time benefiting his mission. He transferred the presidency of the committee that was to receive funds from Isaacs to Morris Raphall, the rabbi of congregation B'nai Jeshurun, who had just arrived from London, and whom he had known there as a person active in such overseas matters. Raphall, being a newcomer, did not understand the motives behind this scheme and accepted the presidency.

had just returned from Palestine), Henry Moses (President of Anshay Chesed congregation of New York),

6 L. Bomeisler, and I. Leeser. Salo & Jeannette Baron, *op. cit.*, pp. 136–137.

Isaacs, however, did see through these machinations and his anger was aroused. He felt himself responsible neither to Rabbi Ashkenazi nor to any messenger, but to the Jews of Eretz Yisrael, the beneficiaries of the aid, and to the Jews of America, its donors. In order to make sure that not a trace of misunderstanding was left, he announced his intentions in public:

> The system of encouraging messengers from the East has, for years, been productive of evil; it has fostered mendicancy, it has destroyed harmony, and robbed the poor pilgrims of hope, located on Holy Ground, of a portion of the liberal means the Jews of America contribute towards their support. It cannot be too generally known, nor too widely disseminated, that a fourth part of the sums collected by messengers, swells the pockets of the employed, exclusive of his travelling expenses and what he gathers on his own private account. . . . Urged thereto by some valued friends in Europe, I have devoted my time to the subject, and have transmitted large sums to the houses of Montefiore and Lehren. In all cases requiring the amount to be distributed amongst *all* the poor, instead of fostering sectional feelings, the result has been highly advantageous to the recipients, no expense is incurred in the transmission, and the poor man obtains the whole of his due. Let us then urge congregations to *discountenance all messengers*.[7]

Isaacs' firm stand and strong statement brought about an improvement in the situation. A majority of the congregations in New York and in Philadelphia, members of the Historical School, participated in a meeting in New York, the purpose of which was to decide the division of the money in the future.[8] The main spokesmen were Isaacs and Leeser. In charitable matters for Eretz Yisrael, to adapt a Talmudic saying, they deemed direct work preferable to work through intermediaries. It was therefore clear from the outset that the inhabitants of Israel would gain if the expense of the messengers were eliminated.

The plans for systematization had little effect. Somehow the Jewish public could not be made to fulfill its obligations to the indigent of Eretz Yisrael without hearing the pathetic and heart-rending accounts of the messengers as they described the poverty and suffer-

7 *Ibid.*, pp. 137–138.
8 Among the participants were Isaacs of Shaarey Tefila; Noah and Abra- hams of Shearith Israel; Jacob M. Falkenau and Amsel Leo of B'nai Jeshurun, Henry Moses of Anshei

ing. Nevertheless, in 1854, Isaacs succeeded in collecting a fund of $5,000 for the relief of famine-stricken areas in Eretz Yisrael. One year earlier he had organized the North American Relief Society for Indigent Jews in Jerusalem and Palestine of which he became treasurer. The Society benefited from bequests by Judah Touro to the sum of $10,000 which, when invested, yielded an annual income of $700. This sum was sent directly to Jerusalem. A contribution by Moses Montefiore was added to the income from Touro's legacy. With this money a row of houses for the poor was built in 1860 outside the old city's wall, and thus was created the first residential quarter of the new Jerusalem, Yemin Moshe.

It is therefore no surprise that the various settlements of Eretz Yisrael continued to send messengers in the attempt to stimulate the generosity of American Jews. In 1861, Abraham Nissan Ashkenazi was dispatched. Isaacs and Raphall, the old and loyal friends of the cause of Eretz Yisrael, though pained by the failure of their ideas for better organization, could not, as faithful supporters of the Jewish settlement, withhold their help. Despite the economic depression which hit America on the eve of the Civil War, many rallied to the cause. Isaacs' weekly publication, *The Jewish Messenger,* was an important vehicle for bringing the mission of Ashkenazi to public attention. But when Isaacs saw that Ashkenazi was conducting himself as others had previously, he pleaded with him to leave America and once more tried to establish a central organization. Again his effort was unsuccessful.

In 1867, the Jews of America witnessed a significant development in Palestine requests. A group of twelve persons, former American Jews who had settled in Eretz Yisrael, complained that neither the German nor the Russian Jews wanted to appropriate to them a single cent of the money that had been received from America. They further complained that the Jews of the United States had no knowledge of the existence of an American Jewish settlement in Jerusalem. The American Consul in Jerusalem, Victor Beauboucher, sent separate letters to Rabbi Max Lilienthal in Cincinnati and to Samuel Isaacs in New York:

> The number of American Jews residing in Jerusalem is very limited, a dozen altogether; but these unfortunates are the most miserable of all and do not receive pecuniary succor from any

Chesed; Jacob Weinschenck of Rodeph Shalom; Isidore Raphael of Shaarey Zedek; Abraham Schwartz of Shaarey Hashamaim; Max Lilienthal; Isaac Leeser and Abraham Hart of Philadelphia.

one, the German committees never having given a cent, and those of America perhaps do no know them at all.

I have done all I could to relieve these poor people ever since two years that I am in Palestine: and seeing their increasing misery, I this day address myself to you, in order that something may be done in their favor by the Committee of which you are a member.

One of them, Benjamin Lilienthal, whom I know as an honest man, left yesterday for the States, and will be able orally to make to you the lamentable narration of the position of his co-religionists and fellow-citizens in Palestine. I have remitted to him the necessary recommendations for the success of his travel, and beg you to receive him with the attention due to a good and honest father of a family. . . .[9]

Every new source of America-Eretz Yisrael relations reveals how deeply involved the Historical School was in the fate of Jerusalem. Not only the rabbis, but also the members of their congregations aided each new enterprise and were among its organizers. In addition to their endeavors to supply the perennial needs of the inhabitants of Jerusalem, they were concerned with the long-range development of the Jewish settlement in Eretz Yisrael. In many of the appeals of Leeser and Isaacs they expressed the hope that the day would come when Jerusalem would be so firmly established as to be able to care for its own needs and redeem itself by its own efforts. The members of the Historical School did not believe that Eretz Yisrael could be rebuilt without hard and exhausting labor. In the eleventh volume of the *Occident* (1853–1854), Leeser wrote three basic articles about Eretz Yisrael, in which he discussed the possibility of agricultural development of the land. He wished to see the inhabitants of Jerusalem as farmers, vinegrowers and workers of the soil. He was therefore very happy when Gershom Kursheedt, president of the Society for Offerings of the Sanctuary and the executor of Touro's will in matters connected with Eretz Yisrael, returned from the Holy Land and gave an account of the position of manual labor there. The widespread opinion, he said, that manual labor was not acceptable to the

9   Salo and Jeannette Baron, *op. cit.*, p. 241. For a brief description of the first American society in Israel, see Frank E. Manuel, *The Realities of American-Palestine Relations* (Washington, 1949), pp. 34–35. For additional material on Benja-min Lilienthal, see Judah Aaron Segal Weiss, *Bi-Shearaikh, Yerushalayim* (In Thy Gates, O Jerusalem) (Jerusalem, 1949), pp. 60–61, 71, 265–275.

10 "Palestine and its Prospects," *Occident*, XIII (Feb., 1856), p. 523.

Palestine Jews, was basically erroneous. On the basis of this information, Leeser proposed that the workers in Israel begin to build their own institutions: libraries, hospitals, and the like. From the profit thus made, they could conceivably expand their building activities. He wrote:

> Let it not be imagined that Palestine even now is what it was twenty years ago; on the contrary, many changes for the better have taken place already, and the arts of European civilization, and the requirements, luxuries and comforts attending them, are gradually making their way, at least in Jerusalem.[10]

Leeser wanted to see the establishment of agricultural settlements in Eretz Yisrael. The Jews of the Diaspora ought not go to Israel to die in the Holy Land or to live on charity. The aged and the sick should not be sent, but rather those who were able to work. At the time Isaacs and Raphall were attempting, in the face of apathy, to collect money to help the needy in the Holy Land, Leeser began to work in other directions. In 1853 he supported the effort of Moses Sachs to organize an agricultural settlement in Jaffa. He served as president of the central committee in America, the aim of which was to collect a fund for the support of this undertaking. Isaacs followed his colleague and presently he, too, in various articles, began to demand that those who were active in work for the support of Eretz Yisrael should be more interested in contributions to agricultural funds than in charitable aid. He appeared before the Board of Delegates with such a proposal. He was also largely responsible for convincing the Board of Delegates to apportion a fund for an agricultural school in Jaffa.[11]

What moved the builders of the Historical School in the United States to such continuing efforts on behalf of the Jewish settlement in Eretz Yisrael? The foundation of their belief in the Restoration is, of course, expressed in the Tradition which they taught to their generation. Certainly ample consideration had been given to the prospects of such a "Return," not only in Jewish circles, but in Christian religious groups. A characteristic volume was Ethan Smith's *View of the Hebrews:* "exhibiting the destruction of Jerusalem; the certain res-

See also G. Kressel's article on Leeser's interest in agricultural settlements in Eretz Yisrael, *Davar* (Jan. 8, 1954).

11 *Jewish Messenger*, XXIII (May 22, 1868), pp. 4–5. See also Max J.

Kohler, "The Board of Delegates of American Israelites, 1859–1878," *Publications of the American Jewish Historical Society*, 29 (1925), p. 99.

toration of Judah and Israel. . . ." Published in 1823 in Poultney, Vermont, it answered with an unqualified affirmative the question whether the Jews are literally to be restored to Palestine.

Echoes of the same practical hopes from a geopolitical viewpoint also were heard in those days. G. W. F. Lynch, U.S.N., Commander of a United States Expedition to the River Jordan and the Dead Sea in 1847–1848, included a political prognosis in his naval report:

> The Muhammedan rule, that political sirocco, which withers all before it is fast losing the fierce energy which was its peculiar characteristic, and the world is being gradually prepared for the final dismemberment of the Ottoman Empire.
>
> It needs but the destruction of that power which, for so many centuries, has rested like an incubus upon the eastern world, to ensure the restoration of the Jews in Palestine.[12]

In this context, one can better understand Mordecai Noah's famous *Discourse on the Restoration of the Jews,* which he delivered in 1844 before an audience diverse in background and religious faith. Having suffered a stunning defeat in his effort in 1825 to found a city of refuge for the Jews on Grand Island, near Buffalo, New York, Noah came to understand, as did Theodor Herzl almost a half century later, that only Eretz Yisrael would be acceptable as the Homeland of the Jewish people. There they could gather once again to fulfill the ancient prophecy of the Return.

Leeser, too, slowly embraced the conviction that the dream of the Return might be a practical reality. Beginning as a practitioner of charity for the needy in the Holy Land, he moved on to a constructive program. He began to consider the twofold goal which was much later to be defined as Zionism: the practical building of Eretz Yisrael as the home of the Jews, and the dedication of the Land to the spiritual and cultural regeneration of the entire Jewish people, in the Diaspora as well as in Eretz Yisrael. His words, haltingly but surely, point the direction which the Historical School took in later decades:

> Will this dream be speedily realized? We cannot tell indeed; events occasionally creep slowly over the face of the world; but at other times they rush rapidly forward, and one great development follows closely on the heels of the other. The same may be the case with the now apparently distant restoration of Israelites

12 W. F. Lynch, *Narrative of the United States' Expedition to the* *River Jordan and the Dead Sea* (Philadelphia, 1849), p. 415.

to Palestine. . . . Is it then so unlikely that an effort will be made to place in Palestine and the countries immediately north, south, and east of it an enterprising race, which shall keep it as a highway of all nations, and thus prevent the occupation of it by any great power, to become a clog to the commerce of the world? . . . whereas, possessed by Israelites, feeble as they would be politically, disinclined to control others if they even could, it would be a highway of nations, and men could meet there to exchange the products of all climates in perfect security, and without injury to any other land or government. . . . One thing is certain, whether our views be realized or not, whether speedily or tardily, that it is no silly wish for us to pray for a national restoration, if we have any love for the triumphant though peaceful rule of our religion over our people, and to free them from the moral and physical yoke which will necessarily rest upon us, while we have a permanent home nowhere.[13]

As we review the thoughts and actions of the members of the Historical School regarding Eretz Yisrael, we learn more about their understanding of Judaism than their Zionism, for the Return to Zion was integral to historical Judaism. Moreover, they had unusual insight into the American spiritual tradition with respect to Zion. They knew that every American regarded himself as possessing a portion in Zion, and that the dream of the Restoration was part of the thought pattern of America. As America was a highway of peoples, so the Holy Land, in the age of a third Jewish Commonwealth, could become, to use Leeser's phrase again, a "highway of nations."

13 *Occident,* XXII (April, 1864), p. 13.

Israel in the World of Ideas

ABBA EBAN

*

> 'Where I belong and what I am
> living for I first learned in the
> mirror of history"—KARL JASPERS,
> Origin and Goal of History.

A SENSE OF SPIRITUAL and intellectual vocation has accompanied Israel since the earliest days of her national revival. Many schools of Zionism regarded this, rather than political sovereignty or economic progress, as the aim of the whole enterprise. In the days of the ancient Hebrew kingdoms Israel had developed a vitality of spirit out of all proportion to her physical size. Might not the Jewish people, reunited to the land and language of its original creativity, again renew its primacy in the spiritual life of mankind?

The driving force of Israel's history is the impulse to overcome her geographical and physical limitations. Her principal destiny lies in those domains in which matter and quantity are transcended by mind and quality. The reestablishment of the homeland was primarily sought and pusued on behalf of Jewish survival. But it was never an egocentric or parochial concern. In the messianic idea the concept of Israel's redemption is closely linked with a vision of total human salvation. Modern Zionism, too, aspires to the creation of a society which, while fulfilling central Jewish interests, will also in some measure, be a portent for all mankind.

II

There is thus nothing particularist in the Zionist purpose. The aim is not to create "a people that dwells alone." On the contrary, the founders of Zionism aspired to take Jewish history out of its isolation and cause it to flow into the mainstream of world history. Sovereignty was cherished, not for its external emblems, but for the possibilities which it opened up for a normal political discourse with other members of the international community. Similarly, Zionist thought has moved in unison with the prevailing forward winds of intellectual history. Herzl and Nordau linked Zionism with the liberalism of nineteenth century Europe. Ahad Ha-am related it to the positivism and intellectual empiricism of Spencer, Hume, Locke, and John Stuart Mill. Borochov and Syrkin adapted its spirit and ethos to the growth of socialism. Weizmann portrayed it in terms of Wilsonian self-determination; and later introduced it to the new world of the scientific revolution.

All these movements in Jewish nationalism took ancient Hebrew thought as their major premise. The Biblical past was the source of nationhood, and its living waters would fertilize the Jewish inheritance once again. But Israel would also garner the riches of mediaeval and modern Jewish thought, of European humanism and of twentieth century science.

It is too early in Israel's career to estimate how far these ends are being approached. Of the present population of two million only a third were in the country when its independence was proclaimed fourteen years ago.

The pre-State population was in many ways an *elite* community. It was part of the cultural history of Europe. Mass immigration from countries of less advanced culture threatens, in the short run, to dilute the nation's intellectual standards. In the longer term the variety and vigor of immigrant strains can be expected to have an effervescent effect. Meanwhile, the primary aim of the educational movement is to ensure that the blessings of increased quantity are not too drastically offset by a corresponding lapse of quality.

III

Israel came to birth in the blinding dawn of nuclear power, and the scientific revolution has dominated her intellectual life. Indeed, scientific research is the first field in which Israel has risen to the highest international levels. The achievements of scientific inquiry in our age overshadow even those of the seventeenth century, which historians called "the century of genius." Vast conceptual innovations, new terms for the understanding and description of nature, have gone hand in hand with dramatic technological results. Man is clothed with a power, which he never previously held, to generate and control energy; to fructify land; to conserve and utilize water; to combat disease; to multiply and diversify agricultural and industrial production; to draw mankind together in close and constant accessibility— and to associate all parts of the human family in exploring the growing universe of knowledge. Jewish thinkers have been prominent in this great eruption of intellectual energy. Not all of them would admit their Jewish backgrounds or environments to have contributed anything to their intellectual histories. But in the intensely Jewish environment of Israel the passion for abstract truth has burned fiercely. The Hebrew mind has been obsessed for centuries with the search for a unified pattern of knowledge, drawing all aspects of experience together into a web of common understanding. And modern scientific research with its emphasis on sweeping, comprehensive, transcendent systems of explanation is congruous with this trait of Jewish thought.

Nor is there any contradiction between a culture based on faith and ideas formulated by scientific method. The more a man learns about nature, the deeper becomes his reverence for the inscrutable perfection and order of the universal design. There is no mystery of the physical world which does not point to a mystery beyond itself.

Emphasis on the technological consequences of science have tended to overshadow its intrinsic educative function. When governments support scientific education and research in the hope of practical results, they are doing the right things for the wrong reasons. Science should be taught for its qualities of precision, truth, skepticism, disciplines. "The critical temper, the confidently constructive rationality, the manly intellectual humility that are essential for the practice of scientific method are not simply adornments of a well balanced mind; they are of its essence." [1]

IV

There is one special domain in which Israel's scientific development has had a strong influence on her position in the world. The newly emerging nations of Asia and Africa see Israel as their closest and most congenial arena of contact with the world of technology and science. They correctly regard their exclusion from this world as the primary source of their weakness. In political and juridical terms they have secured equality with the advanced countries of the west. But behind the stamps and coins, the constitutions, flags, parliaments, and other outward symbols of institutional freedom the old squalor, illiteracy, social exploitation, and disease linger on, unaffected by the transition from colonial rule to sovereignty, and sometimes even aggravated by it.

In this poignant situation the leaders of new nations, overwhelmed by a sudden weight of social and economic concern, look

1   Ernest Nagel, writing in *Education in the Age of Science,* ed. Blanshard. New York: Basic Books, 1958, p. 189.

around for a means of accelerated progress. The plain fact is that their peoples have been excluded from the sources of knowledge which have given the Western world the chief elements of its power. The two decisive movements of our time—the movement of scientific progress and the movement of national liberation—have so far flowed in separated channels.

Israel alone amongst the nations belongs to each of these movements. She stands at a crossroad not only in geography but in the world of ideas. She is one of the new states in the international community. But she is also an acknowledged member of the family of modern technology and science. She, and perhaps she alone, stands in simultaneous kinship to both of these worlds. And her position as the interpreter of Western science to modern nationalism is recognized by both movements.[2]

Thus, the pilgrimage of young men from new nations to Israel in quest of knowledge responds to an essential truth about Israel's dual nature. It also augurs an impressive fulfillment of ancient vision: "And nations shall flow unto the mountain of the Lord."

V

But when Zionist thinkers spoke of a spiritual center they thought mainly of a new emanation of humane ideas. The scientific revolution does not in any way justify a neglect of this vision. On the contrary it has increased man's peril at least as much as it has enlarged his welfare. For good or ill, but in any case with complete irrevocability, atomic science has set us on a crossroad from which two paths branch forth—the one leading to immeasurable abundance, the other toward disaster beyond comprehension by heart or mind. Leaders of the scientific movement are fully aware of the dangers of a scientific rationalism uninhibited by ethical and moral restraint.

Science has created problems which only the humanites can solve. The issue before mankind is not a further mastery of natural forces. The need is for a corporate existence, inspired by those elements of reverence and order, without which civilization may end in chaos. It is the humanites, after all, which remind man of his distinctively human endowments, which multiply and refine his moments of vision, which set before him embodied visions of human virtue and human destiny. And in the history of humanistic ideas Israel has an incomparable lineage. In revolt against deterministic philosophies she evolved the revolutionary ideas of personal conscience (מאוס ברע ובחור בטוב) (Isaiah 7:15), of social solidarity (ואהבת לרעך כמוך) (Le-

2 *Science and the New Nations*, Basic Books: New York. 1961.

viticus 19:18), and of international peace (לא ישא גוי אל גוי חרב ולא ילמדו עוד מלחמה) (Isaiah 2:4).

The nobility of this heritage obligates Israel's future. It fully justifies the intense concentration on the Biblical legacy which is the distinguishing mark of Israel's cultural life. The Hebrew language is not merely an instrument of expression. It is a repository of associations and memories. Its very cadence takes modern Israel back to its ancient roots. The coins, and stamps of the Israel state evoke the golden age. And archaeology, which has had a remarkable florescence in the fourteen years of Israel's sovereignty, has intensified the movement of ideas toward the Biblical past.

This is not a new Esperanto nation writing its history on a clean slate. The sense of derivation from ancient roots saves Israel from the perils of superficiality. Provincialism can exist in time as well as in space. And whosoever lives only in the present is doomed to provincialism.

The Biblical emphasis in Israel's education curriculum and cultural life does not go without challenge. There are some who question its relevance to the age of high-energy physics and ballistic missiles. On the other side it can be urged that Israel's scientific dynamism has not been curbed either by the content of Biblical studies or by the time devoted to their pursuit.

Moreover, Israel cannot ignore her central place in Jewish history. Hebrew and Jewish studies represent the legacy which Israel is commanded by history to conserve, galvanize, and reanimate in her own experience.

For many centuries European and, later, American education were dominated by the study of two ancient literatures, containing an array of masterpieces which gave full play to the imaginative, emotional, aesthetic and critical faculties and embraced the principles of ethics, metaphysics, history, politics, and economics. The Hebrew literary heritage is less versatile in some respects, but more profound in others. It has an equal capacity to inculcate a flair for symmetry and literary grace. And it gives what a leading Hellenist has called "a vision of a single, undivided universe, a sense of invisible forces at work in the familiar scene, of unreleased potentialities in the human mind and heart, of an ideal order lurking behind the manifold appearances of things." [3] Above all, the Hebrew classics have a superior dimension of time. They have the precious attribute of continuity and renewal. In a word, they are alive. Access to a classical tradition which is, at the same time, an intimate family posses-

3   C. M. Bowra, *The Greek Experience* (1957), p. 21.

sion, suffused with a nation's pride, is an opportunity which Israel's educational system cannot, in sheer sanity, ignore.

VI

Betweeen the old inheritance and the new potentiality, between religion and science, faith and reason, memory and ambition, the Hebrew mind is now free to move. The new impulse given in Israel to Hebrew literature and scientific research is further enriched by promising achievements in musical execution and plastic art. It is not possible to guarantee that Israel will again achieve the primacy which made her unfading in the memory of man. It is not for us to command the inscrutable sources of revelation. But, at least, we have restored to this people the conditions and opportunities for a creative epoch in her spiritual life: pride of soil, deep roots in a rich and revered cultural tradition; an imposingly eloquent medium of literary expression—and the special dynamism which attends a people in the early formative period of its national rebirth. Ancient examples, including her own, teach her that small peoples need not be negligible in the domains of history which lie beyond physical size and resources. She has broad constituencies for her intellectual strivings— the Jewish Diaspora for her humanistic speculation, and the society of new nations for her scientific and technological quest. And all this potentiality comes to her in the age when men are more conscious than ever before of the paramount role of knowledge in the guidance and control of human destiny.

An intense preoccupation with ideas is especially necessary for a small state striving for identity and purpose in a world dominated by great aggregates of power. Arnold Toynbee, in a part of his *Study of History* published ten years ago, predicted the eclipse of the nation state in favor of large supranational groupings in which sovereignty would be set aside. There was a certain logic in this prediction. Technology, strategy, and economic processes all transcend national frontiers. No state—least of all a small state—can aspire to autarchy in defense or economic organization. The power of international organizations is more pervasive than before; and the world is studded with the occult initials of regional pacts and common markets.

And yet Toynbee's prediction has been strangely frustrated. The past decade has been the golden age of small sovereignties. There are now twenty members of the United Nations with populations smaller than that of Israel. There are fifty states with a population of five million or less. At a time when technology makes for the unification of mankind, a new fragmentation has taken place in the political map. The small state is now a more potent factor in international life than could have been envisaged a decade ago.

Amongst the small states Israel has a special status arising from her intermediate position—poised between the advanced technological societies of the West and the newly emergent societies of Asia and Africa. Moreover, her history contains an ideological basis for a national pride and sense of mission capable of compensating for physical limitations. The cultural record of ancient Israel, Athens, Elizabethan England, and revolutionary America indicates a special potentiality of intellectual creativeness in small, compact, coherent societies in which the individual citizen has a high worth and in which communication of ideas and spiritual movements is not encumbered by vast distance and demographic mass. The small state may be an irrelevance in global strategy and economics. But it has an imposing lineage in cultural history. This consideration argues strongly for a cultural emphasis in the policies of small communities.

There are dangers to be overcome—principally those of inert ideas. A new struggling society is not always sympathetic to "egghead" priorities. Pioneering Zionism had an anti-intellectual bias. Its aim was to convert an excessively academic people into a nation in touch with the primary sources of production and creativity. Every professor or student lured away from library or laboratory to the vegetable farm or cow shed represented a victory for this much needed task of social redistribution. There was a lofty and compelling logic in this impulse. If it were not obeyed there would be no Israeli nation today; no pyramid with a base broad enough to sustain its apex. But this pastoral romanticism, with its suspicious attitude to formalized knowledge, has no place in the intellectual life—or even in the economic system—of our times. There is no escape from the power of knowledge. Its accumulated resources lie at our feet—from the dim roots of man's past to the shining possibilities of his future.

And the quest is endless. No sooner is one horizon reached than another opens up, pointing to the far limits

"Of that untravell'd land whose margin fades
    Forever and forever as we move . . ."

Paul—What Manner of Jew?

MORTON S. ENSLIN

*

THERE ARE MANY PROBLEMS still unsolved, and likely always to
remain such, incident to what may be styled "the parting of the
ways," that is, the emergence of a new and and distinct religion,
Christianity, in contrast to and in conflict with the older Judaism. Just
when did it occur? Was it due to exclusion from the Synagogue that
the Church arose? Was it voluntary departure of the latter from the
former? Was it neither, but instead a confidence that once again the
faithful remnant was continuing in the path of God from which so
many had strayed?

The very fact that these queries can arise and call forth such
different answers makes one point the clearer and more certain.
Christianity started as a movement in Judaism. All attempts to deny
this patent fact, to try to disassociate the two hyphenated adjectives
in the common phrase "Judaeo-Christian heritage," are not only wrong
but wrongheaded. If ever there were truth to the warning, "What
God hath joined together, let no man put asunder," it is here.

All attempts—and there have been many—seeking to envisage
Jesus as the conscious founder of a new religion, distinct from, not
to say, hostile to, the Synagogue, must be adjudged failures. He lived
and died a Jew. His one concern was the proclamation, as he believed
God had revealed the all-important secret to him, that at long last
God's promise, long delayed because the uniquely loved nation had
not proved itself ready, was about to be realized: the time of preparation was over, the triumph was at hand, the kingdom was to appear.
He died in despair. What was so certain had not been realized. His
was not the easy fate of one who knew that through the activity and
devotion of his followers, and of the many more whom they were to
recruit, the seeming defeat was destined to be turned into triumph
and the movement made possible by his devotion to what he knew
was God's commission was in sober reality to overcome the world. All
attempts to endow him with the ability to see what was later to be

achieved, and which came eventually to be read back as his God-given endowment—the speedy resurrection triumph, the emergence of a Christian church, distinct from the Jewish synagogue—all these are now seen to be a sad misreading of the evidence, despite the fact that once again today there is an attempt by those who are seeking to engage in a "new quest of the historic Jesus" to read back into his thinking and teaching the blueprint—if not the finished product—of what they are styling the early kerygma.

Coincident with this appraisal of Jesus and his dedication to what he believed his God-given task, to announce the speedy advent of the long awaited "kingdom of God," I think I am correct in saying that antipathies to the one earlier depicted as alone concerned with the foundation of a rival faith—and so, not unnaturally, regarded as blind and indifferent, if not actually hostile, to his own heritage—have definitely lessened. Instead Judaism is coming to see in the prophet from Nazareth a figure to be honored and prized as one of her greatest sons and proudest possessions.

Actually, as a result of critical study of the Christian gospels and of the years that produced them, it has become increasingly probable, in the eyes of many, that the picture of the attitude of Jesus in Matthew, heightened but not in essential contrast to that in the earlier Mark, as completely devoted to sounding his word to the "lost sheep of the house of Israel," with resultant unconcern for gentiles or even Samaritans, is essentially correct. The definite shift in tone and emphasis in Luke, with the conspicuous emphasis upon Samaritans, would seem a reading back into the ministry and outlook of Jesus of a concern for and endorsement of what at the time this gospel was composed was so patently present and flourishing, namely, the gentile mission. Since God never changes and since he was so signally blessing this advance, it must always have been his purpose; nay more, it must have been crystal-clear to the one who so uniquely shared his counsels. That this emphasis was understandable, even though in distinct opposition to the actual facts, will not seem passing strange to both those in the Synagogue and Church who recognize the implications of what must in both cases be styled "religions of revelation."

Here once again is but another indication of a common heritage and surely only to be explained as due to the origin of the younger as a true child of the older mother. In this connection it should also be repeated again that even as Judaism is coming to see in Jesus a figure to be revered as in the truest sense one of her greatest assets; so Christians can never be blind to the fact that among their greatest assets is the rock-ribbed ethical heritage which is theirs. On the hard anvil of adversity the mother had forged that chain—a chain whose binding is freedom—that morals and religion are inseparable. It was this heritage in no small part which enabled the daughter religion, once the ways had parted, to triumph over the many other cults with which she soon found herself in competition and to become, for better or for worse, in the course of three centuries the state religion of the Roman world. The word read back as an utterance of Jesus, "I have overcome the world," spelled precisely what his followers were destined to achieve. It is not too much to say that this success would not have been theirs save for this heritage of which she has never ceased to be proud, this heritage of homely morality which saw in the word, "Ye shall be holy even as I the Lord your God am holy," its eternal obligation. It is here that the Christian sees, and with deep gratitude, Christianity's greatest debt to Torah.

The situation changes, and materially, when mention is made of the Apostle Paul. A generation ago saw a flood of writings under such captions, as "Jesus and Paul," more commonly, "Jesus *or* Paul." For some, he was the one who "muddied the waters of the Galilean Lake," and their slogan became: "Back to Jesus." For others, he was the greatest and most original theologian, the one who gave body to the Christian gospel, and the real founder of the religion. In Jewish eyes, insofar as I am competent to venture a modest appraisal, he has rarely been an admired man. Some years ago I was talking with a Jewish scholar, widely read in this period of history and singularly free from prejudice. He had spoken at length and appreciatively of Jesus. Then came a chance mention of Paul, and his mood changed: "It would have been all right if it had not been for that damned Paul!" I smiled, but I thought I knew full well the reason for the change of tone.

This essay, called forth by the desire to have a part in honoring Dr. Silver, whose scholarly contributions in this particular period of history have been so significant, is far from an attempt to make an apologia for Paul. This is neither the time nor place for such an attempt, even were I to conclude that the controversial figure, both hated and revered in his own day, as well as in most succeeding centuries, stood in need of such. Actually, in my own case, it was not until I was well advanced in my graduate work that I would have found an occasion even to differ with the later succinct summation by my Jewish friend. During my undergraduate days I had made Paul's acquaintance, but only to dislike him intensely as an arrogant and muddle-headed theologian.

For many—I am sure it is true of Christians; I would assume it would be even truer for Jews—the most easily remembered word—at least the hardest to forget (with the possible exception of the lyrical I Corinthians 13)—is the word to his church at Philippi:

". . . though I myself might have confidence even in the flesh: if any other man thinketh to have confidence in the flesh, I yet more: circumcised the eighth day, of the stock of Israel, of the tribe of Benjamin, a Hebrew of Hebrews; as touching the law, a Pharisee; as touching zeal, persecuting the church; as touching the righteousness which is in the law, found blameless. Howbeit what things were gain to me, those have I counted less for Christ. Yea verily, and I count all things to be loss for the excellency of the knowledge of Christ Jesus my Lord: for whom I suffered the loss of all things, and do count them but refuse. . . ."

Taken out of context, not only the context of this particular letter, but of his whole thinking, I can well see how unforgiveable they may seem. The apparent minimizing of values beyond price and his seeming characterization of them not only as "loss" but "refuse," together with what must seem an almost contemptuous dismissal of the Law, God's greatest gift, and of circumcision, the proud badge of God's covenant, make talk easy about Paul having been at best a very poor Jew, spoiled by his contacts in the Diaspora, where like the earlier Esau, he had despised his birthright.

Loose talk of a "diaspora Jew" and sweeping conclusions as to the effects an upbringing in the "university town of Tarsus"—quite unmentioned, it may be observed, by Paul in any of his extant letters —are easy and dangerous. Actually, in lieu of any direct evidence— there is a marked and often disregarded difference between external tradition, which any historian is bound to weigh and ponder, and internal inference, which he has as much right to draw as those who first read the letters—it is just as plausible to reverse the argument. Precisely because he was brought up in a land well outside the direct influence of Zion, there could well have been an even greater zeal shown by pious parents, aware at every turn of the dangers, to make fragrantly vital a heritage beyond compare and to safeguard it against the allures of the fleshpots of Egypt—greater even than might have been normal to those hedged about with the security of Zion.

In the perplexing story in Acts of the difficulties which arose in Jerusalem in consequence of the appointment and activity of the seven men, among whom Stephen was prominent, there is one note which is often overlooked. The opposition which Stephen encountered was apparently not from native Jerusalemite Jews—to use the convenient phrase, representative of "normative Judaism"—but from those who were members of the "synagogue called [the synagogue?] of the Libertines, and of the Cyrenians, and of the Alexandrians, and of those of Cilicia and Asia." [1] When one is indulging in the framing of hypotheses—and glittering generalities about the nature and outlook of "diaspora Jews" in general and of Saul of Tarsus in particular are most certainly of that sort—he should realize the possibility that those in Jerusalem who took offense at the activity of Stephen and his fellows were apparently "diaspora Jews" who had settled in Zion for the precise purpose of getting free from the contaminating danger of the larger world. In a word, if we are free to frame hypotheses, we are free to wonder if these synagogues of "hellenistic Jews" were not of the most ultraorthodoxy, composed of those who had at last been enabled to return to Zion, and that their reason for disputing with Stephen was due to a feeling of outrage that some of their own members had become infected with a sorry heresy. Certainly it would not be the first—or last—occasion when a local church (and I should surmise synagogue), which had been placidly unconcerned about such matters as heresy and the ill effects upon simple piety incident to a college education, suddenly awoke to the fact that one of their own young members had contracted this same disease. What had been a matter of little concern suddenly took on real meaning.

I am not arguing that this is the case of these groups in Jerusalem. I am, however, insisting that in lieu of any definite evidence to the contrary, it is as plausible an hypothesis regarding the outlook and actions of some hellenistic ("diaspora") Jews as is the one so easily noised about today that all Jews of the Diaspora must of necessity have been far less Jewish than their fellows in Judea. Easy generalities are, and always have been, dangerous, as is evidenced by the recent charge by Ben Gurion that of necessity all Jews today who are content to live outside Israel must be atheists.

Thus, to me, easy characterizing of Paul as a poor Jew, to whom the proud inheritance into which he had entered had lost value due to his upbringing in the Diaspora, are without warrant and utterly mischievous. That Paul wrote the words in Philippians which I have quoted I do not question. That the picture of Judaism in Galatians, with its utter neglect of repentance as a cardinal principle, is grossly unfair—and was dictated by him—is perfectly clear. But neither of these, and the same is true for other utterances which we now have

1 Acts 6:9. It should not be forgotten that Tarsus was a city of Cilicia.

in black and white, throws any light whatever on how Paul felt before his shattering experience in Damascus. The reasons why he subsequently came to a position in which he could so express himself we may for the moment reserve. But we should do it with eyes wide open to the fact that these words were penned years afterward; they throw absolutely no light on his days before he changed to champion the one he had zealously sought to destroy.

This distinction, too often overlooked, appears to me central in any attempt to understand this stormy petrel of the past. To see his conversion—to use the term normal for a Christian approaching the story—as due to a deep-seated dissatisfaction with the Law of Moses, to a desire to escape from its bondage into a greater freedom made possible by a God whom he now saw in the face of Jesus, appears to me utterly unwarranted, although it has been often asserted. To see the oft-quoted passage in Romans 7, in which the contrast is made between "the good which I would do but cannot, and the evil which I would not do but do," and culminating in the tragic outburst:

> Wretched man that I am! who shall deliver me out of the body of this death? I thank God through Jesus Christ our Lord. So then I of myself with the mind, indeed, serve the law of God; but with the flesh the law of sin [2]

as autobiographical and a haunting nightmare memory of his pre-Damascus days is surely unsound. This is not autobiography at all. Rather it is a paradigm of the condition in which Paul (many years later) now sees every man to be standing, while apart from God and his gracious gift. Surely we have learned enough of that contemporary style of parenetic address dubbed the "diatribe" to remember that it was common practice to throw the argument into the first person in a far from autobiographical intent. It throws no light whatever on Paul's pre-Damascus days, and to use it as evidence of Paul's indifference or long-developing hostility to the Law of Moses is simply perverse.

It should not be forgotten that we do have a clear-cut paragraph in which Paul describes what his attitude in those days had been. It may be well to quote it:

> For ye have heard of my manner of life in times past in the Jews' religion, how that beyond measure I persecuted the church

---

2 Romans 7:24–25.   5 Acts 7:58–8:1.
3 Galatians 1:13–14.   6 Acts 9:1 f.
4 Cf. Romans 9:1–5.

of God, and made havoc of it; and I advanced in the Jews' religion beyond many of my own age among my countrymen, being more exceedingly zealous for the tradition of my fathers.[3]

To see these as the words of a "diaspora" Jew who really was not a Jew at all but had been alienated from the tradition of his fathers through contacts in a "hellenistic university town" requires a degree of (un)historical imagination which is quite beyond me. Nor is there, as I read the epistles, a hint of any pre-Damascus coolness or lack of confidence or pride in his race and its unique behests from God. On the contrary, it may be remarked, there are plenty of passages, some of which we shall later see, that indicate that though he had later reached a position where—at least in moments of passionate exaggeration; Galatians is not cool and weighed deliberation!—he could speak of having been "in times past in the Jews' religion," he never gave up his pride in being a Jew or his passionate regard for his fellow countrymen, blind though they seemed to him to be, for whom he would gladly give up his own prized salvation, would that bring them to a recognition of God's will.[4] Saul had a shattering experience—probably more exactly said, a series of them—which led him to reappraise values drastically, but the cause of them was not a lukewarm attitude to the religion of his fathers which, as a "diaspora" Jew, he could easily cast aside.

At some time in the early years Paul makes his appearance. His introduction in the confused story of the stoning of Stephen [5] and the subsequent trip to Damascus with letters from the high priest [6]—both incidents bristling with difficulties and of a sort to make me highly skeptical of their historical foundations—would seem to suggest a comparatively early date. Some have even toyed with the possibility that he had himself seen and heard Jesus, perhaps during the days he is reported to have sat at the feet of Gamaliel—this latter bit of reported biography appearing solely in a speech in Acts, entirely unmentioned in his letters, and seemingly of a sort to be used with extreme caution as a building stone.[7] Thus a date of A.D. 30–32 for his appearance in the Christian story has often been suggested. I incline to a rather later date, with A.D. 40 the most probable. I still feel that we will wisely consider the incident mentioned in II Cor. 12:1–6 a very possible clue. That this traumatic experience, in which the man was "caught up even to the third heaven" and heard "unspeakable words, which it is not lawful for a man to utter," was his

7 For the whole problem see my article, "Paul and Gamaliel," *Journal* *of Religion*, 7, 4 (July, 1927), pp. 360–375.

own needs no argument and has long been conceded by almost all scholars. That this shattering experience, so vivid before his eyes that he remembers the precise date, "fourteen years ago," was his conversion experience has occasionally been suggested, but more frequently denied. To me it seems highly probable. That Paul may well have had other moments of ecstasy, made possible by a malady to which he refers as a "thorn in his flesh" and from its mention in Galatians[8] not improbably to be diagnosed as epilepsy, would seem to me highly likely. That any of these was of a sort to eclipse his first encounter, when God saw fit to reveal his son and to endow him with his message[9] I should seriously question. If this be sound reasoning, we have here a very definite indication of date. On quite other grounds the date of the so-called "severe letter" (II Corinthians 10–13), in which the experience is graphically recalled, may be set with reasonable confidence as A.D. 54. "Fourteen years ago" would suggest 40.

The chronology in Galatian is much less clear-cut, at least it is of a nature to permit of many variations. The statement, "Then after the space of fourteen years I went up again to Jerusalem," [10] would not seem easily fitted into the chronology suggested in my preceding paragraph, especially if the "fourteen years" is to be added to the previous "after three years," [11] mentioned a few verses before. It is largely because of this seeming impasse that so early a date for Paul's conversion has been suggested. The difficulty, however, is not impassable, as has been occasionally suggested. Presumably "fourteen" as written by his scribe, would not be spelled out but indicated by the letters ΙΔ. When the whole phrase (ΔΙΑΙΔΕΤΩΝ) is examined, it is seen that everything hinges on the single-stroke letter (Ι) in the easily confused unspaced combination ΔΙΑΙΔ. Were that second iota to be regarded as an accidental dittograph, "fourteen" would be reduced to "four." And it is to be remarked that even were the numeral to be spelled out, a similar possibility of primitive scribal error is to be seen, for ΔΙΑΔΕΚΑΤΕΣΣΑΡΩΝ would easily allow the initial ΔΕΚΑ to be a careless dittograph for ΔΙΑ. It must be frankly recognized that this is conjecture. There is no manuscript known to me giving this reading. Nonetheless, though I am very cautious about employing conjectural emendations, it does not seem in this case utterly reckless. Actually, a ΤΕΣΣΑΡΩΝ (or Δ) can easily have been later changed deliberately by an early copyist to ΔΕΚΑΤΕΣΣΑΡΩΝ (or ΙΔ) to harmonize with II Corinthians 12:2.

---

8 Galatians 4:13–14.
9 Galatians 1:15; cf. I Corinthians 15:8 f.
10 Galatians 2:1.

11 Galatians 1:18.
12 Acts 11:28. For a brief but excellent discussion of the date see Jackson and Lake, *Beginnings of Chris-*

If this conjecture be allowed, many difficulties vanish. It has been felt that seventeen—even fourteen—years is a very long time of silence for his work in Syria and Cilicia. If, however, instead of fourteen years we have four years, matters would at once straighten out. The two mentioned periods, three years and four years, presumably consecutive, not both "after" the same event, would amount to seven or (allowing for a variation in the reckoning of years) even six. And such a time after A.D. 40 would bring us to approximately 46–47, which is the most natural time for dating the famine which Jerusalem suffered "in the days of Claudius," [12] at which time Paul is said to have gone to Jerusalem. Presumably the two visits of Paul to Jerusalem mentioned in Acts [13] are to be seen as variant stories—the one from the tradition of Antioch, the other from those of Jerusalem—of the one visit, namely, the one to which Paul is referring in Galatians 2. Thus I incline, although fully aware of the speculative and fragile nature, to postulate A.D. 40 as the most likely date for Paul's change of face as well as name.

Prior to his conversion he had been engaged in attempting to "persecute the church of God." Presumably this had been in Damascus. There is no slightest indication in the sober and seemingly factual account in Galations 1 of any prior activity in Jerusalem (or elsewhere) or that his shattering experience was en route to that city. Were it not for the account in Acts, it is safe to say that no one would ever have detected any lacuna in Paul's own account.

In the course of his fruitless attempt to "make havoc" of the church of God he became convinced of his folly. As I have already suggested, it seems to me most unwise to understand this change as due to dissatisfaction with the Law or his status as a loyal Jew. Rather he became convinced that his opponents were right in the contention that God was blessing them as they sought to do his will. For Paul, as for many other Jews, as he was later to his pain to discover, the cross was a stumbling block.[14] And small wonder. Did not Deuteronomy say explicitly,[15] as Paul was to paraphrase it, "Cursed is every one that hangeth on a tree"? [16] Here at base was the ground for Paul's hostility, the hostility of a passionate Jew who sought to "continue in all things that are written in the book of the law" [17]—not the whimsy of some lukewarm "diaspora Jew" who was indulging for reasons best known to himself in running amok.

What it was that convinced him that they were right—or, as it

tianity, vol. 5, pp. 452–455.
13 Acts 11:27 ff. and 15:1 ff.
14 1 Corinthians 1:23.

15 Deuteronomy 21:23.
16 Galatians 3:13.
17 Galatians 3:10.

appears to me he would have phrased it, that God was blessing their endeavors—Paul has not told us. To me the most probable explanation was the manifest success, despite persecution, of the movement. It was growing, and at a startling rate. But there is another factor to be considered. Despite himself, he found himself approving; else the easy answer: "the wicked spread themselves as the green bay tree." [18] Were I to guess, it would be because of the quality of their life and the way they met and overcame his and his fellows' attack. The real Paul, revealed in his letters, is a Paul the clear-eyed and demanding teacher of ethics, ever mindful of and insistent upon solid qualities of life, not the teacher of an at best subjective theology. Thus I am inclined to believe that it was the quality of life which he found himself forced to approve in his opponents which eventually led to his surrender. God was blessing them; only so could their success be accounted for.

The next step was inevitable, for a Jew who had drawn in with his mother's milk the confidence that God changeth not. If God was blessing the movement, he must always so have intended. How then could he have cursed Jesus, as the tragedy of the cross seemed to indicate? Manifestly this could not be. Despite Deuteronomy's ominous word, God had not cursed but blessed Jesus *despite* the fact that he had been crucified. This appears to me the first step that Paul took, and the first conviction he reached. We know him from his letters, written many years later. In them many more steps have been taken, perhaps the most important—at least, for good or for ill, it has so appeared—being the change of *despite* to *because:* God has blessed Jesus *because* he was crucified. But this was not his view in these early days. In a word, Paul was not converted to Paulinism!

From persecutor he changed overnight to champion. Paul was not a man of halfway measures. The adverb ΠΕΡΙΣΣΟΤΕΡΩΣ is one not unnaturally dear to him, for it so completely describes him: what he did, he did with might. That his change of front—from persecutor to champion—may well have had its traumatic moments appears to me most likely. His growing uncertainty, his attempts to stifle apprehension that he was wrong, his growing conviction that his opponents, not he, were actually succeeding in what he so passionately had believed he was doing, namely, God's service, may well have resulted in an experience in which he was "caught up into the third heaven," "saw Jesus," heard God's voice. What he has recorded of his ability to speak in tongues, to see visions, would certainly suggest a

18 Psalms 37:35.   19 I Corinthians 14:18.

mental balance that would permit, after a nerve-racking turmoil of indecision, a decisive, if traumatic, experience.

The point of concern is that his resultant message was in all likelihood precisely that of those he had fruitlessly sought to suppress: Jesus, as God's prophet, had sounded forth the speedy dawn of the coming kingdom; nay more, he was destined himself to inaugurate it when, in God's good time, it was to dawn. In the interim he was with God in heaven, whither God had taken him. At any moment he would descend again to consummate what he had begun. In this confidence—which, I am convinced, despite many modern efforts to change it drastically, was the earliest kerygma—it is to be noted, there was absolutely no element of hostility to the Mosaic Law, no thought of its having been a burden now to be laid aside. By God's grace he had been enabled to see that he had been wrong. God had blessed Jesus despite the sinister word anent the cross. Now that he, Paul, knew this—for God had told it to him!—of course his fellow Jews would see it too once he could speak to them. With this confidence, the confidence of every Semitic prophet, be he a Micaiah, an Amos, a Jeremiah, or a Jesus—again in this role which Paul so certainly took as a result of the shattering encounter in Damascus, we see the passionate and devoted Jew, to whom the prophetic tradition was an open book, not an indifferent "diaspora" Jew—he started his mission to his fellow Jews with perfect confidence that as the scales had fallen from his eyes, they would from his compatriots'.

That Paul believed and claimed to be in the succession of the prophets is at best uncertain, perhaps unlikely, although his self-conceded ability to "speak in tongues"—"I thank God, I speak with tongues more than you all" [19]—and his confidence that his message had been bestowed upon him supernaturally by God himself, so that when he spoke God was speaking, raise questions at this point not easily answered. Actually this confidence, often expressed, but most unmistakably in his outraged word to the Galatians:

> . . . But though we, or an angel from heaven, should preach unto you any gospel other than that which we preached unto you, let him be anathema. As we have said before, so say I now again, if any man preacheth unto you any gospel other than that which ye received, let him be anathema,[20]

is of a piece with that of all the prophets of Israel, be it a Micaiah, "As Yahweh liveth, what Yahweh saith unto me that will I speak," [21]

20 Galatians 1:8–10.   21 I Kings 22:14.

or a Jeremiah, "The words of Yahweh came unto me, saying. . . ." [22] Words which can easily seem unwarranted arrogance must be differently assessed in this setting. It is not the arrogant stating of Paul's own views; it is rather the faithful announcement of the word of the Almighty, who, in his own unfathomable judgment, has chosen him as his mouthpiece. There may well be the opportunity for pondering the mental adjustment of any man, be he a Micaiah, an Amos, a Jesus, or a Paul, which permits him to reach the conclusions so basic to the Semitic prophet; there can be no question of the "that" although a wider possibility of diagnosis may well be left open in attempting to answer the "why" and "how."

The Paul we find in his letters is a determined apostle to the gentiles, with a message in which Law and Gospel are arraigned against one another, and in which the word "Christ crucified" is central. That at the time he was writing he was convinced that in this there was no change, but that it was the compelling intent of God when he called him, is certain. Nonetheless, although Paul could not have been expected to see it, there may well have been another chapter highly important for a correct understanding of him.

That at the time of his change from opponent to champion the death of Jesus on the cross had come to be regarded as planned and ordained by God as the *mysterium tremendum theologicum*, "a ransom for many," as it was later to be phrased,[23] the way God was seeking to reconcile the world to himself,[24] is most unlikely. Rather, it was a horrid crime, but one more example of blindness on the part of these misguided fellow Jews: As your fathers killed the prophets, so do ye. This note so central in the early preaching as revealed in Acts[25] seems primitive and of a sort to raise definite questions as to the legitimacy of much modern reconstruction of the "earliest kerygma."

Presumably the "stumbling block of the cross" was as real a one to the early protagonists as it was to their opponents. In consequence of his shattering change of front Paul found himself forced over this stumbling block, as were the preachers who by their lives had forced him to see their message as blessed by God. Thus it is probable that in his new confidence Paul expected to be able to convince his fellow Jews that "despite the cross"—not "because of it"—Jesus had been blessed of God and as his agent would speedily return to consummate what he had earlier proclaimed: in a word, that his followers, Paul's erstwhile opponents, were right in their claim.

22 Jeremiah 32:6.
23 Mark 10:45; Matthew 20:28.
24 II Corinthians 5:19.

25 Acts 7:51 ff.; cf. 2:23; 3:17 ff.; 5:30.

Of course his fellow Jews would hear, would see, the truth even as did he: such has always been the first confidence of the prophet. But they did not hear, would not see. Why? Something must be holding them back, blinding their eyes. Whatever that something was, it must be evil, for otherwise they would hearken to God's word, even as had he. What was the fatal obstacle? To Jesus—in not unlike perplexity—the obstacle had been wealth and education: the wealthy and the learned were turning a deaf ear to what he *knew* was God's word; the poor eagerly were hearkening and obeying. Thus the answer seemed clear and accounts, without sociological analysis, for the crystal-clear opposition to wealth and the confidence in the "little ones" still so evident in the gospels.

For Paul the same problem "why?" was central and the answer clear. It was the death on the cross which was proving to his hearers the fatal obstacle. This proved that God's blessing could not rest on what was so signally an object of his displeasure. Seeing this problem, realizing that here was the crux, Paul refused to yield, refused to seek an easier or more defensible position. "Jesus Christ and him crucified" was his message. In the course of the years, first in fruitless attempts to batter down Jewish prejudice, later, when that had proved futile, in his turn to gentiles, his constant stress upon this one central problem led to his discovering in it ever-widening implications. In a word again to abbreviate drastically, the word "despite" came to yield to the very different "because of." But this change was not overnight, nor was it the consequence of an immediate "turning to the gentiles."

It was Jewish inability to see and not unnatural hostility to him whom they considered a turncoat and traitor—to the prophet hostility to himself always is hostility to God—that led to this radical reappraisal and resulted in the seemingly more satisfactory explanation of the cross.

Another consequence must not be overlooked in this hasty sketch. The all-important and all-tragic source of Jewish obtuseness in the eyes of Paul was not their hostility to God—they loved God as devotedly as did he. What then could be holding them back? And the answer was all too clear: it was the sinister word of Moses, which had earlier lent confidence to Paul's own opposition. Again, in a word, it was the Law. It could not be correct in its appraisal, for it was in opposition to what God himself had revealed to him. Thus in consequence of years of fruitless attempt to meet this issue, to fight the battle on this so-critical front, arose the contrast—surely never dreamed of by Paul when he first became convinced of his tragic, if innocent, alignment against God and his chosen son—Law vs.

Gospel. It was not dissatisfaction with the Law, growing restiveness under its constraints, which had gradually led an "insecure" Jew, to break away from his traditional past and easily free himself from what should have spelled freedom. Rather it was because here was to be found the fatal obstacle which deafened ears to God's so insistent demand.

Eventually Paul turned to the gentiles, not the choice by a lukewarm, hellenized Jew of a naturally more congenial clime, but, apparently, as had been the case earlier by other protagonists, because of the increasing opposition and the hopelessness of success among their fellow Jews. But how far did Paul go? To him a great way. Certainly that is a far from unique situation. To every convert, if the decision is more than skin deep, the answer is always the same: "whereas I was blind, now I see." More than that, the breaking of old ties, always a continual source of pain, and the resultant sadness and loneliness may well heighten the actual distance of departure. Did his gentile hearers feel the same? Did they see him as he now saw himself? Certainly indications in such letters as I Corinthians and Galatians would suggest quite the reverse. To many in Galatia he would seem to have appeared a Jew, who, despite his claims, was seeking to force upon them needless and unwarranted restraints. His insistence that, though freed from the requirements of the Mosaic Law, they were yet subject to precisely the same demands because such were alone "worthy of one in Christ," seemed to them, as it did to many in Corinth, and presumably in all his other gentile churches, simple casuistry. "To the Jews I became as a Jew, that I might gain Jews; to them that are under the law, as under the law . . . ,"[26] may well be pondered. He might continue, "not being myself under the law, that I might gain them that are under the law," but to gentiles—as Paul very definitely was not—this qualification may well have seemed meaningless.

If the account in Acts is correct that Paul circumcised Timothy;[27] if as is certainly possible—to my mind, even slightly probable—Titus too, gentile though he was, was circumcised, though not "under compulsion,"[28] we can see a background which made natural the charge that despite his brave words he was "preaching circumcision." Certainly, his heated denial, "But I, brethren, if I still preach circumcision, why am I still persecuted?"[29] can only be understood as an answer to those who were charging him with so doing, not to those to whom such an act must have seemed praiseworthy.

26 I Corinthians 9:20 f.   28 Galatians 2:3 ff.
27 Acts 16:3.   29 Galatians 5:11..

Nor should the patent fact be overlooked: Despite Paul's much touted "break with the Law," the fundamental place he gave to ethics, especially to sexual ethics; and the fact that precisely the qualities which he insisted were alone worthy of one who was in Christ were the qualities demanded by the Law. Here is a matter to be weighed very definitely by those who are inclined too easily to reach conclusions, in part from Philippians 3, in part from surmises about the obvious endowment—or lack of it—of a hellenized Jew who had grown up far from Zion and its devotion to the ancestral ways and beliefs.

Again it is easy—but most unwarranted, if we are to hope to view the man correctly—to overlook his obvious and sustained feeling of the superiority of Jew to gentile. His stress upon broken-down walls of separation: "There can be neither Jew nor Greek, there can be neither bond nor free, for ye are all one in Christ Jesus," [30] seems clear and unqualified. Ideally, yes—in the eyes of God. But while a path of access for all stood open, and opened at infinite cost, this is far from synonymous with complete equality in very human eyes, despite a modern attempt to turn Paul into a universalist for whom no differences or personal preferences still maintained. That Paul felt that male and female—whatever the verdict of God—were equal in dignity and status would appear to me, in view of his very definitely expressed words, a position hard to maintain.[31] The same may be said of master and slave. A bit of realism may well be exercised in our understanding of his theology and his often definitely distinct personal opinions.

"What advantage then hath the Jew? or what is the profit of circumcision?" His answer is clear and may well be pondered: "Much every way." [32] Here a Jew, not a Greek, is speaking. Nor need we limit these words to rhetorical questions. The passing, but sobering, word expressing horror at the case of flagrant immorality in the church at Corinth: ". . . there is fornication among you, and such fornication *as it not even among the gentiles*" (οὐδὲ ἐν τοῖς ἔθνεσιν)[33] reveals the man with his theological guard down. Paul had become, at least in his own eyes, primarily an "apostle to the gentiles"—and could easily read this commission back to the very moment when God had first made known his long-determined intent [34]—but not only had this been forced upon him, it was a heavy load and a constant source of horror. Reference is frequent in his letters to the murky and miasmal conditions from which gentiles had emerged into the sun-

30 Galatians 3:28.
31 Cf. I Corinthians 14:34 ff.
32 Romans 3:1.

33 I Corinthians 5:1.
34 Galatians 1:15.

shine of the gospel; it finds its completest and most revealing expression in the terrible indictment in the last half of the first chapter of Romans.[35] Here most certainly a Jew of unimpaired Jewishness is speaking, aghast as he continued year in, year out, at the laxity in sexual ethics which he found wherever he went. Certainly his years in Tarsus had not noticeably lessened his ancestral heritage in this regard.

In a word, when Philippians 3 is read—as of course, it should be —and the equally extreme statements, in part colored by the intense emotion of the moment, in the tear-blotted letter to the "foolish Galaians," are cited, they should not blind the reader's eye to the word, rich in pathos and honest pride of heritage: "Did God cast off his people? God forbid. For I also am an Israelite, of the seed of Abraham, of the tribe of Benjamin. . . ."[36] To me the never-to-be-forgotten word, when we seek rightly to appraise this stormy petrel of the yester-years, is found in the opening paragraph of Romans 9–11, a section which still bristles with difficulties and is replete with (to us) most unsatisfactory and labored argument. But this opening word is limpid clear:

I say the truth in Christ, I lie not, my conscience bearing witness with me in the Holy Spirit, that I have great sorrow and unceasing pain in my heart. *For I could wish that I myself were anathema from Christ for my brethren's sake, my kinsmen according to the flesh:* who are Israelites; whose is the adoption, and the glory, and the covenants, and the giving of the law, and the service of God, and the promises; whose are the fathers, and of whom is Christ as concerning the flesh, who is over all, God blessed forever. Amen.[37]

Here in this letter—in my judgment the last we have from his pen, most certainly his "last will and testament" to his several churches, now that he is turning to the far west—we see Paul the clearest. Many of his earlier words in other letters, written in fury and not corrected with phlegm, stand here, repeated but without the exaggerations and overemphases called forth in the heat of debate from one intent to win his case.

In the course of the years, not the years of his unbringing, but of his missionary services in the larger Mediterranean world, to men and women whose ways of life he disapproved and whom

35 Romans 1:18–32.   37 Romans 9:1–5.
36 Romans 11:1.

he constantly found repugnant in the extreme—but the hand of God was upon him, driving him to the task, for they too were "brothers for whom Christ had died"—the gospel he had received in Damascus came to be greatly changed, although, of course, he was completely unaware of the change. The task of translating it, not alone its language but its content, to make it intelligible to his hearers —this led him to changes and developments that can neither be overlooked nor minimized. To many, some of the new notes that appeared were unfortunate, many of the elements which gradually dropped from the picture, amazing if not unforgivable; nonetheless the word of Sabatier needs repetition:

> It is not the citizen of Tarsus but the Pharisee of Jerusalem . . . which explains the apostle to the gentiles.[38]

To his dying day Paul could say—and did!—with undiminished pride: "I am an Israelite, of the seed of Abraham," not, "I *was*."

---

38 A. Sabatier, *L'apôtre Paul*, p. 27. I should be inclined to omit the word "of Jerusalem," and I should question what to me is a definite overemphasis by Sabatier upon Paul's rabbinic training.

A Hitherto Unknown Jewish Traveler to India

THE TRAVELS OF RABBI DAVID D'BETH HILLEL TO INDIA
(1828–1832)

WALTER J. FISCHEL

*

I. *The Author and His Book*

IN THE ANNALS of Jewish travelers to the countries of the Near
Middle East and to India, *The Travels of David d'Beth Hillel from
Jerusalem Through Arabia, Koordistan, Part of Persia and India to
Madras,* published in English, in Madras, in 1832, occupies an excep-
tional and unusual place. Not since Benjamin of Tudela, about eight
centuries ago, the famous Jewish traveler of the twelfth century—the
Jewish Marco Polo—had there been a Jewish traveler who left such a
detailed account of the Jewish communities in Asia, in Kurdistan,
Babylonia, Persia, and India.

Very little is known about the identity of the author prior to his
journey. "Born in Europe, and established in Tsafeth near Jerusalem,
of the Seed of King David"—that is all the author permits us to know
about himself; yet from indications and allusions in his work, from
the peculiar transliterations and pronunciations of Hebrew words,
from the comparisons he made between the climatic conditions of Oriental countries with those of his country—"as in Poland" or "as in
Russia"—we can deduce that he hailed from Eastern Europe or more
exactly from Lithuania. It is, indeed, established that he was born in
Vilna, in Lithuania, as a descendant of Rabbi Hillel b. R. Naftali Herz,
the author of a book entitled *Beth Hillel*—and that he, David, left his
home town at an early age, went via Russia to Constantinople and
from there to Safed where he, together with other pupils of the Gaon
Elia of Vilna, settled down after his arrival in 1815.

1 For further details about the life
and activities of Rabbi David d'Beth
Hillel, see A. Yaari, in *Sinai*, Jerusalem, 1939, Vol. II, pp. 24–33,
1940, Vol. III, pp. 17–21; *Massaoth Erez Israel,* Tel Aviv, 1945,

In 1824 he started his long journey through Palestine and Syria, penetrated into the most obscure regions of Kurdistan, Iraq, and Persia, spent a full year in Baghdad and other communities in Mesopotamia, and sailed then from Bushir on the Persian Gulf to India. He landed in Bombay in October, 1828, but after a stay of only forty days moved on to Cochin where he remained for about four months. From Cochin, he returned to Bombay in March, 1829, for a two years' sojourn. In May, 1831, he undertook an eight-month journey through the Presidency of Bombay to Cochin and moved from there to Madras, which he reached in January, 1832.[1]

What had prompted the author to spend so many years of his life traveling through the countries of the Middle East and India? It is certain that he was not one of those many "messengers," emissaries, *shelikhim* who in those days and earlier used to leave the Holy Land to collect in the Jewish Diaspora, in remote lands, funds for the maintenance and upkeep of religious and charitable institutions and academies of Hebron, Tiberias, Safed, or Jerusalem.

There can be no doubt that David d'Beth Hillel was not such a messenger and that he undertook his journey not on behalf of any institution or organization and that certainly he did not aim to collect funds among Jews for any charitable purpose.

We are led to believe that his journey was not the result of any kind of commission but that he went on his own initiative driven by an inner call, a vehement desire and anxiety for the search of his brethren, the forgotten "Remnants of Israel" in far-off lands.

The author himself indicates that this was his real goal and that it was for this purpose that he traveled throughout the lands of Kurdistan, Babylonia, Persia, and India for eight years. In the advertisement of the *Travels*, apparently written for him by one of his English students in Madras, it is stated that the author thinks also to be able "to throw some light upon the existence and present status of the long lost Ten Tribes. . . ." The *Travels* contain also numerous references to these "forgotten remnants" in the various countries he visited. Whenever he met ancient groups, sects, or races, he sought at once to identify their beliefs, customs, languages, and manners with old Jewish or Israelite traditions, drawing somewhat hasty and mostly unfounded conclusions concerning their connections with the ten tribes. Such phrases as "therefore I conceive that they are . . . that they must be . . . some of the lost ten tribes" occur ubiquitously throughout his narrative, being applied with reckless abandon to a wide variety of

pp. 500–502; *Shelikhei Erez Israel,* Jerusalem, 1951, pp. 138, 146, and Walter J. Fischel, in *Oriens,* Leiden, 1957, Vol. X, pp. 240–242.

groups–Christians, Assyrians, Kurdish, Bucharian and Chinese Jews, the Moslim sect of the Daudiya, and even the Hindus. The innermost motive for his journey was therefore, in all probability, the search for the lost "Remnants of Israel" in Asia.

The *Travels* reflect its author's experiences, impressions, and observations during almost nine years of travel. However, as he himself states, they cover but a part of his wanderings, being in fact an English abstract of a far larger work written in Hebrew. His original Hebrew manuscript has until now not been found. The entire narrative, we are informed, "would occupy about six to seven hundred pages, particularly (the portion) about India, of which I have a great deal to say."

The book was issued in a private edition of only three hundred copies "for the author." Most of those who subscribed to it were British colonial officials and officers "of Madras and its stations" and "Bombay and its stations" who, when transferred, usually left their books behind. Consequently, it is not surprising that only a few copies of it have reached the West and that it became soon a collector's item and as rare as a manuscript. Already in the second part of the nineteenth century, the book had become so rare even in India that the editor of the Judaeo-Arabic periodical of Calcutta *Mebasser* (1872, No. 42), (urged by the editor of the *Jewish Chronicle* in London), was obliged to appeal in 1872 to his readers in India for assistance in locating a copy.

In Europe, it was just as scarce as is shown by a Hebrew letter published in the periodical, *Ha-Maggid* of 1876 (No. 23), in which the bibliophile and traveler, Ephraim Deinard of Kovno is asked by the well known Hebrew scholar Ber Goldberg, to procure for him a copy of a book by a certain Beth Hillel. In this letter, Goldberg writes: "Know, my friend, that one person from Vilna, a descendant of the author 'Beth Hillel' set his mind about forty years ago to search for the lost sheep of Israel in remote lands and he left Russia and Vilna and reached India until Calcutta. . . . What he saw and heard he put down faithfully in a book which he called *Beth Hillel* but . . . he wrote the book in the British language and the Jews did not know anything about him. . . . Therefore search for this book, perhaps you

2   D. S. Sassoon is the first Jewish scholar to have used the *Travels* as a literary source. See D. S. Sassoon: "History of the Jews in Basra," in *Jewish Quarterly Review*, Philadelphia, 1926, n.s., Vol. XVII, pp. 419–427; and his *Ohel David: Catalogue of Hebrew and Samaritan Manuscripts*, Oxford,

1932, Vol. II, p. 14, No. 897 and pp. 973–976; also *Encyclopedia Judaica*, Berlin, 1929, s.v. Baghdad, Vol. III, p. 958: s.v. Basra, Vol. III, pp. 1153–1154.
The only other earlier short references to the *Travels of David d'Beth Hillel* found thus far are in J. H. Lord: *The Jews in India and*

will find it because I do not know whether there is in Europe a copy except the one I saw in the possession of my friend, the scholar Derenbourg. It was loaned out to me but I could only glance through it. Perhaps you will be privileged to obtain a copy of it and translate it into the holy Hebrew language. . . . Your reward will be great."

It is, therefore, not surprising that David d'Beth Hillel's book has been almost completely overlooked by Jewish scholars and bibliographers and has not been mentioned in the standard works of Zunz, Steinschneider, Eisenstein, E. N. Adler, and others dealing with Jewish geographical literature.[2] The *Jewish Encyclopedia* describes it inaccurately as the first work of a Jew published in India, makes the author a "Bene Israel" and dismisses it, with equal disregard of fact, as an account of travels through India "but as otherwise of little importance."

Today, over 130 years after its first publication, his book has remained practically unknown to the scholarly world and can hardly be found in the great libraries of Europe or America. Yet, far from being "of little importance," the *Travels* are actually of the greatest significance for the reconstruction of the Jewish Diaspora in Asia [3] during the early decades of the nineteenth century and in particular for the Jews on Indian soil, those in Bombay and in Cochin.

II. *The Jews of Bombay*

Until the end of the eighteenth century the Jewish communities in India were mainly concentrated in and around Bombay in the North and in and around Cochin in the South of the West coast of India. Those two major Jewish groups were, however, not only divided geographically but also culturally and linguistically and differed fundamentally as to the traditions of their origin and historical development. The Jews in Bombay were known as the "Bene Israel," while the Jews in Cochin are divided into White and Black Jews.

Concerning the "Bene Israel" in Bombay, tradition, fiction, and legend claim for them a very early origin on Indian soil. They are said to have left Jerusalem during the time of King Solomon and, having being shipwrecked on the high seas, they landed in the Konkan terri-

the *Far East*, Kolhapur, 1907, pp. 6, 81, 117, 125; and E. Thurston, *Castes and Tribes in Southern India*, Madras, 1909, Vol. II, p. 482.

3 The chapters of his "Travels" on Kurdistan, Babylonia, and Persia have been translated into Hebrew by Walter J. Fischel in *Sinai*, Jerusalem, 1940, Vol. 3, pp. 218–254.

See also W. J. Fischel: "The Jews of Kurdistan—a hundred years ago," in *Jewish Social Studies*, New York, 1944, pp. 195–226.

The chapters on Palestine have been translated into Hebrew by A. Yaari *Sinai*, Jerusalem, 1939, Vol. 2, pp. 24–53.

tory South of Bombay, on the West coast of India. The seven surviving families settled in this region and have remained there ever since.

No historical evidence is available to substantiate the claim of such an origin. Their development is shrouded in great obscurity all through the centuries and no documents are extant concerning any aspect of their life and history after their arrival in India until they suddenly enter the arena of history a little more clearly in the eighteenth century when casual references are being made to a group of Jews in or near Bombay known as the "Bene Israel."

One of the earliest references in a European source is that of the Danish missionary Sartorius, who in a letter of 1738 to Professor A. H. Francke of Halle asserted that in Surat and Rajapore there are people who do not call themselves Jews nor understand the name, but "Bene Israel, children or descendants of Israel. They have not the books of the Old Testament nor do they understand Hebrew but Hindustani (Mahratti), the language of the country where they reside. What they know of religion is not yet ascertained except that they make use of the word "Shema" as a formula of prayer or of doctrine. . . . They are partly weavers, and partly boatmen, and supply the ships with necessaries. Others are soldiers and workmen. They practice circumcision as a part of their religion. They wear turbans and a long dress reaching to their feet, and long trowsers, just as the Mohammedans do. They do not intermarry with other Indians, but keep to their own people.

"This account I received from Indian and German Jews resident at Madras, who gained their information from other Jews who come from Cochin. One of these English Jews had seen and conversed with several of the Bene Israel in the country of Surat." [4]

In 1768 Ezekiel Rahabi, the famous Jewish merchant and agent of the Dutch East India Company in Cochin, informed the Dutch merchant Tobias Boas in The Hague that "Jews known as Bene Israel . . . are distributed all over the Maharatta province, living under the Moghuls. They live in tents, they own oil presses, some of them are

4   John Antony Sartorius: *Notices of Madras and Cuddalore in the Last Century*, from the Journals and Letters of the earlier Missionaries of the Society Promoting Christian Knowledge. London: Longman and Co., 1858, p. 162–164.

5   Because of their occupation and their observance of the Sabbath the Hindus refer to them as "Shanwar Telis" (Saturday oilmen). See in particular Ezekiel Rahabi's reply to Question number 9; his letter was written in Cochin on 25 Tishri 5528 (1768) in Hebrew and was later published by N. H. Wesseley in *Hameassef*, 1790, Königsberg–Berlin, Vol. II, pp. 129–160, 257–276.

A condensed rendering of its content in English is given by S. S. Koder in "A Hebrew Letter of 1768" in the *Journal* of Rama Varma Archaeological Society,

soldiers, they know nothing as regards their faith except to recite the Shema and rest on the Sabbath." [5]

The Dutch Commander of the Malabar Coast, Adriaan Moens (1771–1781) refers in his famous *Memorandum* to the "Bene Israel" and observes "some miles to the north of Bombay there dwell black men who call themselves Israelites and observe circumcision and also the Sabbath but no other Jewish customs or laws." [6]

M. Graham, in *Letters on India,* records at the beginning of the nineteenth century, "Bombay has several thousand useful Israelite subjects who do not refuse to communicate with the Musulmans or to bear arms." [7]

These few scattered references to the "Bene Israel" in Bombay are almost all the knowledge about the "Bene Israel" known to the West.

Considering the scarcity of information about the "Bene Israel" until the beginning of the nineteenth century, the hitherto unnoticed and unknown description of the "Bene Israel" in Bombay, as written by Rabbi David d'Beth Hillel, assumes the greatest historical relevance, enhanced by its being the first authentic eyewitness account of this still unexplored group of Jews in India.

a) THE BENE ISRAEL OF BOMBAY

The following account of the "Bene Israel" is the result of Rabbi David's observations during his two-year stay in Bombay from 1829–1831 (pp. 133–135): [8]

> There are (in Bombay) native Jews who call themselves "Bene Israel," about six hundred families who are separated from all the nations in their manners and customs, even they will not take water from another caste. They are circumcised and sanctify the day of atonement, but no other customs belonging to the Mosaical law. They were formerly very ignorant of the Hebrew language, having not a single book, but they were well acquainted with the Mahrattah books and language. But since the Arabian Jews came

1949, Vol. 15, pp. 1–6. See also F. G. C. Rutz: *Von einer hebraischen Chronik der Juden zu Cochin,* in *Allgemeine Bibliothek der biblischen Litteratur,* ed. J. C. Eichhorn, Leipzig, 1787, Vol. I, pp. 925–934, Leipzig, 1790, Vol. II, pp. 567–583; J. Winter and A. Wünsche, *Geschichte der Poetischen, Kabbalistischen, Historischen und Neuzeitlichen Litteratur der Juden,* Trier, 1896, esp. pp.

461, 459–462.

6   See *Memorandum on the Administration on the Coast of Malabar,* in Dutch records Number 13, "The Dutch in Malabar," Madras, 1911, p. 192.

7   *Letters on India,* London 1814, pp. 369–370.

8   In the following quotations from the *Travels,* we maintain as far as possible the English style and spelling of the author.

to Bombay, they commenced to learn some of the Hebrew language and purchased some of the Hebrew books. . . .

About five or six years ago the "Madras Jewish Society" [9] had established a school amongst them for the purpose of training up their children in the Hebrew language. They had no synagogue before but some years ago a fine synagogue was built by one of them named Samuel [10] who was Captain in the Honorable Company's Army.[11] He was a very rich man and childless, therefore he caused this synagogue to be built with many houses around it, the rent of which is to be appropriated for the sundry expenses of the synagogue. It is denominated in the native language "Mesgad Beney Israeyl," it is situated at Barcoot, not far from the Custom house, There is no manuscript: They are accustomed to marry their children when very young from three years and upwards, they are accustomed to marry two or three children at once.[12] Some of them are very rich, and many of them are in the Honorable Company's Army,[13] most of them are artificers: scarcely a poor man is to be found among them.

In the Mahratta countries around Bombay are around 8,000 families of them; [14] no one Levite or priest among the whole of them.[15]

I tried very much to make out from whence they came there, but it was not possible to trace it properly, because they have no

9   Under the auspices of this "Madras Jewish Society," established in 1826, a Cochin Jew, Mishael Surgun, the son of Isaac Surgun, opened Hebrew schools for the "Bene Israel" in Bombay and other places, aiming at a rejuvenation of Jewish life among this much neglected and forgotten group. Though a convert to Christianity, he devoted all his energy to the spread of Jewish and Hebrew knowledge among the "Bene Israel."

About Mishael Surgun's further activities, see H. S. Kehimkar, *The History of the Bene Israel of India*, Tel Aviv, 1937, pp. 66–67, 236–237.

10 With this Commandant Samuel b. Eliezar Ezekiel Divekar is associated the "discovery" of the "Bene Israel." He was a high-ranking officer in the British Army who was imprisoned by the Mysore ruler, Tipu Sultan, during the Anglo-Mysore Wars, and who, thanks to the intervention of some of the

leaders of the Cochin Jews, was released and brought to Cochin.

This Samuel Divekar, grateful for the help of the Cochin Jews and impressed by Jewish life in Cochin witnessed by him for the first time, vowed to build as a thanksgiving offer, a synagogue for his coreligionists in Bombay; and indeed the first "Bene Israel" synagogue in Bombay, known as "Sha'ar Ha-Rahamin" (Gate of Mercy), was established in the year 1796, and is still preserved in the Samuel Street of Bombay today. He introduced the Sephardic rite of the Cochin Jews and used their scrolls and books. Samuel Ezekiel Divekar returned to Cochin in order to bring back to Bombay Hebrew books and Torah scrolls which the Cochin Jews were ready to donate, but he died in Cochin in 1797, where his tombstone is still preserved. See Sassoon *Ohel David*, Vol. I, p. 381, Vol. II, p. 574, and Kehimkar, *loc.*

chronicle, but some traditions even these are not written, it is merely oral.[16] Some of them say that in the destruction of Jerusalem by Titus, seven vessels full of Israelites arrived on the Mahratta coast which is very near to Bombay, and when the vessels were lying anchor, a storm arose and all the vessels were lost; and from the whole of them were only saved seven families, of whom they sprung out. Some say only one family, but I cannot incline to this, as it is not mentioned in any of our histories, that in the time of Titus, Jews proceeded to India. . . .

During Rabbi David's journey from the city of Bombay through the Bombay Presidency en route to Madras, in 1831, which he reached in 1832, he registered only in one place the existence of another small community of "Bene Israel," namely in a village on the west coast known as Panoovellee (Panvel, p. 138):

There are about thirty families of Bene Israel; there is now established a school from the Jews' Society, for the purpose of teaching their children the Hebrew language.

This account on the "Bene Israel"—the earliest by a Jewish traveler from the West in the nineteenth century—was supplemented and augmented in subsequent years by Jewish and non-Jewish travelers to

cit., pp. 190 ff., 255 ff.

11 The term "Honorable Company" refers to the English East India Company in Bombay.

12 See Kehimkar, loc. cit., Chap. 6, pp. 128–150.

13 They have established for themselves a fine record as soldiers and officers in the British Army from the end of the eighteenth century on. About the martial tradition of "Bene Israel" community, see Kehimkar, loc. cit., Chap. 9, pp. 187–225. "The Bene Israel as Gallant and Faithful Soldiers"; see also India and Israel, Bombay, Vol. 1, 1949, pp. 18 ff. and Vol. 4, 1952, pp. 21–24.

   The "Bene Israel" could rise to the highest position under the British flag, since there did not exist in the early part of the nineteenth century, any distinction of caste, color, or creed. When the caste system was introduced into the Indian Army by Lord Roberts, the "Bene

Israel" could not get their desired and deserved positions under the British flag and had to give up that special occupation.

14 About the demographic changes and numerical strength in the following decades see H. G. Reissner, "Indian-Jewish Statistics 1837–1941," in Jewish Social Studies, New York, 1950, Vol. 12, pp. 349–366.

15 Rabbi David did not discuss the division of the "Bene Israel" into White, "Gora Israel," in the North and Black, "Kala Israel," in the South.

16 About their intellectual activities, the establishment of a Hebrew printing press, their liturgical books and literature as published there from the middle of the nineteenth century on, see the important study by A. Yaari, Hebrew Printing in the East: India and Baghdad, Pt. II, Jerusalem, 1940, pp. 52–82; about Poona pp. 83–89.

Bombay. Bishop Wilson,[17] who came to Bombay in 1838, greatly interested in promoting the educational level of the "Bene Israel," conveyed important information about them. The published travel accounts of J. J. Benjamin II (1848),[18] of Jacob Saphir (1859–1860)[19] and above all the *Massaoth* of S. Reinman (1884)[20] have substantially furthered our knowledge of the "Bene Israel" community. The most authentic and comprehensive account until today remains H. S. Kehimkar,[21] *The History of the Bene Israel of India,* which completed in 1897, appeared in 1937 in Tel Aviv.[22]

Recently the library of the Jewish Theological Seminary of America received from Mr. B. B. Benjamin, a leader of the "Bene Israel" in New Delhi, some legal documents pertaining to the role and function of the Kazi, the spiritual head of the community, dated 1799 and 1808 respectively.

b) THE ARABIAN JEWS IN BOMBAY

During his stay in Bombay, our traveler came in touch also with that other group of Jews, recent arrivals, the so-called Arabian or Baghdadi Jews.

At the beginning of the nineteenth century, many Jews from Baghdad, Basra, and other places of Iraq, moved to India and settled in Bombay. The central figure of the Baghdad community in Bombay became David Sassoon (1792–1864), who, in consequence of the oppression and persecution by the Ottoman Pashas in Baghdad, fled first to Bushir, on the Persian Gulf and arrived then in Bombay in 1832. His rise to influence and power, the establishment of a wide economic empire with ramifications up to Hong Kong and Shanghai, made him the pioneer of India's industrialization and, at the same time, the greatest benefactor of the Bombay Jewish community in all its shades. Most of the educational, religious, and cultural institutions in Bombay (synagogues, hospitals, libraries, museums, monuments, etc.) owe their existence to the munificence and charity of the Sassoon family.

---

17 Bishop John Wilson was the head of the Society's Mission and College in Bombay and, later, Chancellor of the University of Bombay. See his *The Lands of the Bible,* Edinburgh, 1847, Vol. II, pp. 667–668 and his "The Bene Israel of Bombay" in *The Indian Antiquary,* Bombay, 1874, Vol. 3, pp. 321–323.

18 *Eight Years in Asia and Africa,* (1846–1855), Hannover 1859, pp. 144–148.

19 Eben Saphir, Mainz, 1874, Vol. 2,

pp. 35–48.

20 *Massaoth Shlomoh,* published in Vienna, 1884, pp. 99–112. The author was a Jew from Galicia who came to Cochin and married a Cochin Jewess. He is the first to record the story of the "discovery" of the "Bene Israel" about ninety years after its actual happening. His *Massaoth,* based on hearsay and tradition, needs careful and critical analysis.

21 It was the late Dr. I. Olsvanger who

The Sassoons had, of course, not yet arrived in Bombay,[23] but Rabbi David d'Beth Hillel found there already a nucleus of Baghdadi Jews (p. 116):

> I found there few Jews and they are domineered over by Solomon Yacob,[24] a rich man and the first Arabian Jew who established himself in Bombay. He is a man of a bad disposition and notorious character, and having the means to injure those who disapprove his evil practices. On this account the Jews who speak their mind freely enough of him in his absence are careful to assent to all his saying; he is extravagant and is conciliated by flatterers even of the grossest kind. I had not been accustomed to such dishonorable subterfuges and I am a man who worship only my Creator. . . .

Rabbi David d'Beth Hillel had not one good word to say about the Arabian Jews in Bombay and, with feelings of embitterment, blamed them for the "great inconvenience" they caused him (pp. 129–130):

> I arrived at Bombay in March, 1829, and remained there for about two years, being engaged as a Hebrew teacher for some gentleman. I stayed there very discontentedly, owing to the Arabian Jews and Arabs, for on exhibiting myself with a beard and English dress, they thought that I was an Arab who had been proselyted to Christianity, and I was in consequence many times badly treated by them in the streets, and in my own dwelling.

III. *The Jews of Cochin*

Unlike the history of the "Bene Israel" the history of the Jews of Cochin is well documented. Available sources show that even before the Portuguese conquest of Cochin in 1500, a Jewish community in Cochin was in existence and continued to flourish in subsequent centuries.

was instrumental in publishing this book in Tel Aviv in 1937.

22 J. Henry Lord's book *The Jews in India and the Far East*, Kolhapur, 1907, deserves special mention. It is a highly stimulating new approach to the solution of many ethnological problems of the "Bene Israel" and the Cochin Jews. See also Solomon Moses, *Report of the First Bene Israel Conference*, Bombay, 1918; M. Ezekiel: *History and Culture of the Bene Israel in India*, Bombay, 1948; and lately, Schifra Strizower: "Jews as an Indian Caste," in the *Jewish Journal of Sociology*, London, 1959, Vol. I, pp. 43–57.

23 See D. S. Sassoon, *A History of the Jews of Baghdad*, Letchworth, 1949, for further details.

24 Solomon Yacob's full name was Soliman b. Jacob Soliman; for a different evaluation of Solomon Yacob, see D. S. Sassoon, *History*, pp. 205–206.

We learn, apart from many non-Jewish sources, that in the second half of the sixteenth century, the Jewish traveler from Yemen, Sacharia b. Saadya,[25] met Jews in Cochin and that a century later Manasse b. Israel refers to them and their four synagogues.[26]

During the Dutch rule over Cochin from 1663–1795, the Jewish community of Cochin was visited by a Jewish delegation from Amsterdam headed by Mosseh Pereyra de Paiva, in 1686, whose report, entitled *Notisias dos Judeos de Cochin, Mandadas por Mosseh Pereyra de Paiva*[27] is one of the most important historical documents and the most reliable account ever written pertaining to the Jewish community in Cochin. It is of inestimable value for the understanding of the historic and actual mode of living at that time and brought into the very light of history this ancient Jewish settlement in South India.

Rabbi David d'Beth Hillel's visit to Cochin took place under the British rule and coincided with that stage in the annals of Cochin which is marked by an economic decline of Cochin as a whole and in particular of the Jewish community. He was the first Jewish visitor to Cochin under the British rule (1795–1947) and his description conveys a static picture of the life of the Cochin Jews.

During his stay in Cochin (1828–1829) he observed very clearly the social, religious, and economic life of this oldest of all Jewish settlements on Indian soil and dealt with that threefold division of the community into White Jews, Black Jews, and Meshuhrarim which prevails in Cochin and confronts every visitor until today.

a) THE WHITE JEWS

I sailed again in a Patamar for Cochin, which keeping near the coast land, gave me an opportunity of seeing the country to ad-

25 See his *Travels, Sefer Ha-mussar,* Ms. Jewish Theological Seminary, s.v. Maqama 8.
26 See his *Humble Address,* ed. L. Wolf, p. 85.
27 Published in Amsterdam, 1687; reissued in facsimile with an introduction by M. B. Amzalak, Lisbon, 1923.
28 Goa was the capital of Portuguese India from about 1510 on, and ceased to be Portuguese territory only in our very days, December, 1961.
   About Goa's role in Jewish history and the Inquisition established there in 1560, see W. J. Fischel, "Leading Jews in the Service of Portuguese India," in *Jewish Quar-*

terly Review, Philadelphia, 1956, Vol. 47, pp. 37–45.
29 This "Jews' Town," a township with its own administration, was exclusively inhabited by Jews. At the end of the broad street stands the impressive "Paradesi" Synagogue of the White Jews, adjoining the grounds of the Palace of the Rajah of Cochin.
   All the visitors to Cochin, Jewish and non-Jewish, have described this Jews' Town in full detail. See, in particular, A. B. Salem, "Eternal Light or Cochin Jews' Town Synagogue," Ernakulam, 1929.
30 This indication of the numerical strength seems to be much too high. In the time of A. Moens

vantage. We stopped at Goa, where my fellow voyagers landed, but hearing that the inhabitants were still in darkness and the life of a Jew is not safe among them, I feared to leave the vessel. . . .[28]

Cochin is built upon an arm of the sea in Malabar coast which, extending inland, unites again with the ocean at Quilon. The view of the fort, which is now in decay, is occupied by numerous streets of handsome houses resembling a town in Europe. The English officers and respectable Dutch, Portuguese, and country-born families reside there. . . .

About a mile from the Honorable Company's custom house, at Mattancherry, is the Jews' town, consisting of a broad street about a mile long on the banks of the sea.[29] The houses are adjoining each other and are generally as good as a European street. . . .

There were here about two hundred families of White Jews when I was there.[30] They have a very fine synagogue paved with porcelain from China.[31] It is so fine perhaps not existing in any parts of Europe and Turkey which I have traveled hither.[32] The Dutch presented the synagogue with an excellent clock, for which a separate tower is built. It is richly endowed with garden lands. On festival days there is a grand display of gold and silver ornaments, some of which are placed upon the manuscripts as they are carried from the holy ark to the pulpit where the law is read and occasionally explained. . . .

In the time of the Dutch, the White Jews were great and wealthy merchants,[33] but they have since that time sunk weak, and are even in a miserable state, living chiefly by the sale of trinkets and furnitures purchased in more fortunate days. . . . They are too proud to work for their livelihood, but spend their

(1781) there were no more than 40 families of White Jews, approximately 220 souls, a number which seems to have remained static even until today.

31 This is a reference to the so-called "Paradesi" Synagogue, the only synagogue of the White Jews in Malabar which, according to tradition, was built in 1568 and after its partial destruction by the Portuguese in 1662 was renovated in 1664. The tiles with willow patterns from Canton, China, are said to have been bought by Ezekiel Rahabi, the great Jewish merchant of the Dutch East India Company, in 1762.

32 Having visited this synagogue in 1959 I can only share with Rabbi David his admiration and evaluation. It could really be called the "Taj Mahal" of the Indian Jews.

33 About the role which the Jews played in the economic prosperity of Cochin under the Dutch rule (1665–1795) see W. J. Fischel: *The Jews in India: Their Contribution to the Economic and Political Life*, Jerusalem (Ben Zvi Institute, Hebrew University), 1960, and the forthcoming study "Cochin in Jewish History" in the *Proceedings of the American Academy for Jewish Research*, New York, 1962.

time chiefly in making visits.[34] Even the reading of the Holy
Scriptures is not usual with them. But some families still retain
their landed property in value from about two thousand to ten
thousand rupees. . . .

Their marriages, like those of the Hindoos, are attended with
such considerable expense as to deter many young men from
marrying. They double the number of days of matrimonial feast-
ing customary among the Jews according to Gen. 29:27. . . .[35]

One of the privileges granted to them in their ancient charter
is the royal distinction of bridegrooms wearing a golden chain,
and the firing of guns during the fourteen days of the wedding
festivity. This charter is engraved in copper in the Malyalim languages and characters.[36] It was granted by five contemporary
kings whose signatures are affixed and from whom they are
allowed by this charter to make converts. . . .[37]

Another privilege is the holding of their paternal lands from
the crown at the half the annual acknowledged value which
would be due from the same lands. If any other Jew or foreign

34 This statement by Rabbi David
would most likely be resented by
the leaders of the White Jews. It
stands, indeed, in contrast to statements of others two generations
prior to his visit.

See the protest launched in a
letter to T. H. Baker, Judge and
Collector Magistrate of Cochin at
the time, of March 2, 1836, by the
Elders of the White Jews' Society
of Cochin, against similar derog-
atory statements made by Joseph
Wolff in his *Researches and Missionary Labours*, London, 1835, p.
477. See: *The Oriental Christian
Spectator*, Bombay, September,
1839.

35 About their marriage customs see
the above-mentioned works of J.
Saphir, Reinman, and the recent
book of Shemtob Gaguin, *The Jews
of Cochin* (Hebrew), London, 1956.

36 These famous copperplates written
in the archaic and now obsolete
Vettelutta script and in the Tamil
language, in which right and privileges are set forth, granted to a certain Joseph Rabban (Isuppu Irap-
pan) and his descendants by a ruler
of Malabar, with the name of Bhas-
kara Ravi Varma and whose title
was Cherman Perumal, have been

the subject of many investigations.
These copperplates, now in the
hands of the White Jews of Cochin,
could provide a confirmation of
their oral tradition concerning their
early migration and settlement, did
they not suffer from some serious
defects. This inscription is capable
of being calculated and interpreted
in so many ways that the suggested dates range from the fourth
century (A.D. 379) to the tenth
century and even later and until
now it proved impossible to establish their definite date. The many
discrepancies and divergencies in
the understanding of the inscription and many other details as well,
preclude its use—authentic and
genuine as they undoubtedly are—
and defy its utilization for exact
historical dating and as a reliable
historical source.

37 There is no reference whatsoever
in the copperplates to this permission "to make converts."

38 This view of the late arrival of the
White Jews to Cochin does not
represent the "official" opinion of
the White Jews. It is shared, however, by a number of scholars who
dealt with this question, foremost,
J. Henry Lord, *The Jews in India,*

White Jew may purchase these lands, they may retain the privilege which would be lost if the property should pass to another class of people. . . .

I do not know the date of this copper charter, but have reason to suppose that the White Jews arrived there some little time before the Portuguese,[38] for I have met in parts of Europe with persons of the same family names with those in Cochin, as for instance, the Rotenboorgs, Tserfates, Ashkenazim, and Sargons,[39] etc. They have no manuscripts more than two or three centuries old. . . . (pp. 116–121)

b) THE BLACK JEWS OF COCHIN

The Black Jews in Cochin and the surrounding villages, viz., Arnalata, Shynoth, and Malla, consist of about one thousand five hundred families.[40] They have six synagogues, two in Cochin, two in Arnalata,[41] in Shynoth one, in Malla one.[42] They are neat buildings. The ornaments for the manuscripts are few but handsome. The Black Jews are good people and most of them are engaged in mechanical employments. There are no agriculturists among

loc. cit., and the Rev. T. Whitehouse, *Some Historical Notices of Cochin on the Malabar Coast*, 1859.

39 The Rotenboorgs (Rotenburg) are known to have arrived in Cochin from Germany, possibly from Frankfurt am Main. The Dutch sources of the eighteenth century refer to a Samson, Joseph, and Naftali Rotenburg, all of whom played quite a role in the economic life of Cochin. The Tserfates are the Sarfatis, one of whom is the author of a *History of the Jews in Cochin*, still in manuscript. Ashkenazim refer to the well known Ashkenazy family, also of German origin, with whom Ezekiel Rahabi was related by marriage.

Sargon stands most likely for Isaac Surgun, hailing from Constantinople, the great merchant and diplomat of Calicut, who rose to great influence during the Mysore-Dutch wars (1766–1790). About him see W. J. Fischel "Cochin and Some Prominent Jewish Personalities," in *The Joshua Bloch Memorial Volume*, New York, 1960, pp. 151–164.

The places of origin of the leading families of the White Jews in Cochin have been listed by N. E. Rahabi in his *Chronicle of the Jews of Cochin*, still in manuscript; see Sassoon *Ohel David*, l.c., Vol. I, p. 370.

40 The Black Jews were always more numerous than the White Jews, but even here Rabbi David's numbers seem to be too high.

For the demographic picture of the Jews of India, in Bombay and Cochin, during the period from 1837–1941, see H. G. Reissner, *Indian-Jewish Statistics*, loc. cit.

41 Arnalata stands for Ernakulam; our traveler omits the mention of Parur as a community of Black Jews.

This community is only now in the process of liquidation, due to their immigration into Israel. During my visit to Parur I witnessed the departure of eleven Black Jewish families for Israel.

42 For the dates of the founding of these synagogues see the synagogue inscriptions of Cochin as reproduced in Sassoon, *Ohel David*, Vol. II, pp. 577–578, and in particular the comprehensive study by N. Bar-Giora in *Sefunot*, Jerusalem, 1959, Vol. II, pp. 214–215.

them. Even their garden grounds are cultivated by the Hindoos.
Many are in easy circumstances; scarcely a poor man is to be
found among them. Yesoonee, a shipbuilder,[43] is reputed to be a
very rich and is in every point, a respectable man. The Black Jews
are much more respectable for moral character and conduct than
the White Jews. They are, in general, well acquainted with the
Hebrew scriptures, which they readily translate into Malyalim
and, as far as circumstances allow them, they walk according to
the Law. They have not among them a single priest or Levite.
The White Jews say of them that they are descendants of numerous slaves who were purchased and converted to Judaism, set
free, and carefully instructed by a rich White Jew some centuries
ago; [44] at his cost they say were all their old synagogues erected.
The Black Jews believe themselves to be the descendants of the
Israelites of the first captivity who were brought to India and did
not return with the Israelites who built the second temple. This
account I am inclined to believe correct. Though called Black
Jews, they are of somewhat darker complexion than the White
Jews, yet they are not of the color of the natives of the country
or of persons descended from Indian slaves.[45] (pp. 121–122)

c) OTHER JEWS IN COCHIN

Besides, the White Jews are of two other classes, one called in
Hebrew *Meshooh'rorym,* the other *Aavodim.*[46] Both classes were
formerly slaves; the *Meshooh'rorym* are those who have been
emancipated. When one of the *Aavodim* obtains his freedom from

---

43 This Yesoonee could not be identified.
44 It is of interest to quote here the
view of Ezekiel Rahabi (d. 1771),
the leader of the White Jewish
community in Cochin, about the relationship between the Black and
White Jews as expressed in his
third query to Simon Boas: "The
Black Jews were the converts from
the natives and had been manu-
mitted. Their laws, regulations, and
prayers are the same as ours, but
there is no intermarriage amongst
these two groups, and we keep ourselves apart from them. All the
slaves we bought joined them after
manumission, as a result of which
they now form the majority. By
the grace of God they are under our
control, recognizing our lead and
submitting all their religious con-

troversies to us for a settlement.
There are, however, some differences in observing our religion and
traditions. They dress like the people
of the country, and the majority do
not pay heed to the laws of Phylac-
teries, the Mezuza, and the redemption of the first-born." (Quoted
from "A Hebrew Letter," see above,
Note 5.)
45 The very vexed question of the
"color" of both the "Bene Israel"
and Cochin Jews has been the topic
of discussions by many visitors,
anthropologists, and ethnologists.
    A rather independent and origi-
nal view, very worthy of consideration in this matter, has been expressed by J. Henry Lord in his
"The Black Jews of Malabar" in
the *Malabar Quarterly Review,*
Ernakulam, 1902, now incorpo-

his master a written document in testimony thereof is granted to him under the seal of the synagogue, for which the Master or emancipated person pays forty-one rupees. I have remonstrated against the existence of slavery in a place under the British government which has declared slavery to be unlawful, and the precept regarding the articles of property is according to the Jewish Talmud, *Deena De Malkhoota Deena,* meaning, "the law of the state is law."

My remonstrance, however, excited only displeasure. I was asked, "Why do you wish to deprive us of our property?" Persons of one class have intermarried with families of the three other classes, although fornications are by no means uncommon.[47] (pp. 122–123)

rated in his rare book called *The Jews in India and The Far East,* Kolhapur, 1907. See also, J. C. Visscher, *Letters from Malabar* (1723), trans. from the Dutch by H. Drury, Madras, 1862, esp. letter 18, "Of the Jews Black and White."

46 About the question of slavery among the Jews of Cochin see N. Bar-Giora's illuminating studies in *Sefunot,* Jerusalem, 1957, Vol. I, pp. 242–278.

47 In his *Travels* Rabbi David d'Beth Hillel continues with a polemic against Claude Buchanan's *Christian Researches in Asia* (London, 1812). He visited the Jews of Cochin between 1806 and 1807 and was the first non-Jewish visitor to Cochin under the British rule. This polemic does not interest us here.

Among the important visitors to Cochin after Rabbi David ought to be mentioned Bishop Wilson, J. Wolff, J. J. Benjamin II, and J. Saphir.

For a more recent description of Jewish life in Cochin see D. G. Mandelbaum, "The Jewish Way of Life in Cochin," in *Jewish Social Studies,* New York, 1939, pp. 423–460.

After the conclusion of this study I received a copy of a Hebrew book entitled *Bene Israel,* edited by the Chief Rabbinate in Jerusalem, 1962, in which all the Halakhic questions of the "Bene Israel" community are presented. This highly important volume is of great relevance for present-day discussions in Israel on this matter.

The Chuppah

SOLOMON B. FREEHOF

*

TO MY REVERED COLLEAGUE, Abba Hillel Silver, in homage to his great leadership and in happy recollection of an unbroken friendship since our college days, this article in the mood of our beloved teacher, Jacob Zallel Lauterbach, is, on the occasion of Dr. Silver's seventieth birthday, affectionately dedicated.

Our teacher, Dr. Lauterbach, in his later years became absorbed with the question of the relationship between Halacha and folklore. It was a favorite idea of his that many of the customs in Jewish religious life, from whatever extraneous sources they may have been picked up, were always modified, given logical explanation, and often spiritualized. Thus they were effectively naturalized into Jewish religious life. To this thesis, amply supported in many of his folkloristic articles, I wish to add that often the relationship of the Halacha to folk custom went in the opposite direction. It was not merely that the Rabbis accepted and then modified a custom coming from some extraneous source, but that often they themselves may well have helped in the actual creation of a custom in order to solve or meet some legal difficulty. In other words, Jewish religious customs were not merely borrowed folklore, but at times, though vaguely resembling folklore, were actually sophisticated creations.

In this regard, Jewish folklore is rather unique among the world folklore. Generally it is not an anonymous custom breathed in from the environmental air but actually is often the conscious product of intellectuals. This should not be surprising. There never was a people in the history of culture which had achieved so complete a suffusion of intellectuality. Jewish learning existed in a more complete saturation in the life of our people than any other culture, at least in the Middle Ages. Jewish folklore was therefore rarely merely naïve, but would often be intellectual or sophisticated.

That this is so can more easily be seen in the Aggadic folklore. When young Jacob, on leaving home, gathered the stones in the desert to lie down upon and sleep, each of the stones, we are told, quarreled with others for the privilege of being the one upon whom the righteous man should rest his head. Then God, to allay the quarrel among these, His inanimate servants, merged the stones into one single stone and Jacob rested his head upon them all (Rashi from b. Chullin 91b). If one read such a legend in any other literature, he would conclude that it is an ancient folk tale. But with us there is no such anonymous and untraceable origin for the story. Some scholar had noticed that when Jacob lay down to sleep, Scripture uses the plural, "he took the stones, etc." When he awoke, Scripture uses the singular, "he took the stone upon which he had lain." Therefore the scholar concluded that in the evening there were many stones, in the morning it was one stone. God must have merged them. This sophisticated type of legend, folklore by scholars, is found through the entire Aggadic literature.

The suggestion of this paper is that a similar process occurred frequently with popular customs. Sometimes, indeed, they were derived from some anonymous environmental source and then needed, as Dr. Lauterbach said, to be modified or spiritualized to fit into Halachic life. But sometimes there was a Halachic difficulty which required another type of observance, and then what came to look like mere folk custom was actually a sophisticated construct created by the learned, or at least rising from among the learned Jewish people.

I suggest, therefore, that this was the origin of the wedding canopy, a tapestry on four poles whose use seems so widespread among our people that it has the air of very ancient custom. It will be clear that this wedding canopy arose in a specific time (perhaps the sixteenth century). Also, some attempt will be made to explain the reason for its development in the place of its development.

It is obvious from the note of Moses Isserles to Even Hoezer, 55:1, that the canopy (the *chuppah*) as we know it now was a novelty in his day. In this note, Isserles describes the various possible meanings of the word *chuppah*. It means, he says, according to some, the retiring of the couple to privacy. According to others (Isserles continues) the mere bringing of the bride into the groom's house for the purpose of marriage was called *chuppah* (that is, even if there is no privacy and there are many people present). There are other opinions, he says, that *chuppah* means "the spreading of the cloth (the *tallis*) over her head" during the reciting of the blessing. And some say it means when she leaves her father's house with the *henuma* (either "veil" or "hymns of praise") (cf. Chekkas M'chokek to Even Hoezer 55:1, who quotes the Jerushalmi to this effect). And then he concludes as follows: "But the custom is widespread *by now* that we use the word *chuppah* for the place where we put a cloth over four poles, and then we lead them to his house where they eat together in a private place, and that (that is, the canopy *and* the privacy) is the *chuppah* which is *now* customary."

It is interesting to note that the very phrasing used by Isserles in the Tur, Yore Deah 391, indicated that the canopy was not known to his predecessors. The law discussed deals with whether a mourner may participate in a wedding. It is generally agreed that he may not participate in the wedding *festivities,* but that he may participate in the religious ceremony. In this discussion, Jacob b. Asher and all the authorities whom he cites say that the mourner may *enter* the *chuppah* (that is, it is a room); but Isserles says he may go *under* the *chuppah* (that is, it is a canopy).

Thus Isserles gives his official approval to the canopy on the four poles which he indicates is a new custom in his day. It certainly *was* new. In the detailed description of the marriage ceremony by Jacob Moellin of Mainz in *Minhage Maharil* (fourteenth century) there is no mention at all of any such canopy for the marriage ceremony. The marriage took place in the synagogue proper, and part of the garment of the groom is raised to cover the head of the bride. In none of the earlier sources, as for example in *Ha Manhig* (Abraham Ibn Yarchi, second half of the twelfth century) who speaks of the ceremonies in France, is a canopy mentioned. On page 91b, #109, he says that the word *chuppah* refers to the covering of the bride's head with the groom's *tallis* (from the verb *chofeh*). He adds that it is the custom in France and Provence to put a colored cloth on the heads of both during the ceremony. In none of the earlier Sephardic sources is there any mention of the type of canopy on four poles which we call the *chuppah*.

There is some vague possibility of a precedent for the *chuppah* (canopy) dating from Germany a century earlier. Moses Halevi Minz (fifteenth century) in his responsa "Maharam Minz," #109, gives the order and the arrangement of the marriage ceremony in his time in Germany. His description of the ceremony is very much the same as that of his teacher, Jacob Moellin of Mainz (Maharil) in *Maharil's Minhagim*. Both describe how the young couple is brought to the courtyard of the synagogue for the folk celebration called *Mayen,* at which lighted torches are carried and wheat kernels are thrown at the couple as a sign of fruitfulness. Then the couple is asked to sit down together for a short time. After that, they are brought into the synagogue itself where the ceremony takes place. Moses Minz, in his description of these preliminary folk customs, adds one element to the description given by his teacher Maharil. He says that some congregations provide a *kipah* or a vault or canopy for the couple to sit under outside the synagogue. And he adds, "This is our *chuppah* in these lands, for we do not have a *chuppah* at the recital of the blessing." Asher b. Jehiel, in the thirteenth-fourteenth century, also says that the custom in Germany is to provide a pavilion in which the bride and groom sit down together, and that this pavilion is called *chuppah* (cf. his compendium to the Talmud to Succah 25b, #8). But he adds that this pavilion cannot properly be termed *chuppah*. The term must be used for the relatively permanent dwelling of bride and groom and not for such a temporary pavilion.

Whether this *kipah* or pavilion is the antecedent of the East European *chuppah* is not more than possible. The *chuppah* as described by Isserles and used by all East European Jews and later by all Jews, was the actual place in which the blessings were recited and the religious ceremony performed. We do not know whether the *kipah* mentioned by Minz was on four poles, but the differences are clear enough. The couple sat down under it and no ceremony took place. The religious ceremony was without a canopy and in the synagogue itself.

The East European *chuppah* can therefore be considered as a new ceremony. How did such a new custom arise? We assume that it was not a mere anonymous bit of folk borrowing. In matters of marriage the Rabbis were very careful to scrutinize every variant custom. See, for example, the series of responsa of the Gaonim in "Kesubot," of Levin's *Ozar Ha Gaonim*, from Number 60 following. If, then, this new wedding custom arose and soon became a widespread custom in the sixteenth century, it was certainly with approval of the rabbinical authorities or even with their encouragement, and surely not as a mere decorative addition, but for serious legal reasons based perhaps on special social conditions. Let us trace, as far as we can, the reason for this innovation in the strictly guarded procedures of marriage.

What was it that *chuppah* meant originally? It is evident from the Bible itself that the *chuppah* was a tent or a room belonging to the bridegroom. The Psalm (19:6) speaks of "the bridegroom coming forth from his *chuppah*," and so too in Joel (2:16): "Let the bridegroom come forth from his chamber and the bride from her *chuppah*." The room or *chuppah* had to be *his* (and then theirs) because until she came under his protection or into his premises, she was still *arusah*, betrothed, and not yet *nesuah*, the very word meaning "taken by him." (Cf. also Deuteronomy 20:7: "He who has betrothed a woman and has not yet taken her.") This *chuppah*, or marriage room, was often built by the groom's father in honor of his son's marriage. The Midrash and the Talmud give many references of such loving generosity on the part of the groom's father in building a decorative *chuppah* for his son (Gen. Rabba 28:6 b. Sanhedrin 108a). (For the various forms of marriage chamber in ancient times, cf. Buechler in Poznanski's *Festschrift*, page 82 following.)

It is an unsettled question in the Law whether or not entering the *chuppah* is in itself sufficient to constitute marriage. That is, whether or not privacy is indispensable to her becoming his wife, or whether if the couple enters the *chuppah* in the company of wedding guests (without the isolation required) the mere entrance into the *chuppah* be deemed sufficient. Generally the conclusion is that not until they are in the *chuppah in privacy*, so that sexual relationship may be possible, is she actually "acquired" to him as wife.

While the groom's private chamber, therefore his premises, was the indispensable symbol of his "taking" her, i.e., *nissuim*, nevertheless there grew up many symbolic substitutes for this "taking" of the bride by the groom into his *chuppah*. For example, there arose the custom that the bride was brought to the groom in a curtained litter or sedan chair. Once she was taken into this enclosed sedan, she was deemed to have been "taken" by the groom and was his wife. Further, the custom was that the bride went forth veiled (with a *henumah;* the word may also mean "hymn") and this going forth veiled was a symbol of the privacy, which was sufficient. Also, whether she was carried in the sedan or merely led with her face veiled, the very fact that she was led toward the groom with singing and dancing, that very procession was deemed to be symbolic of *chuppah* and sufficient (cf. especially Tosfos to b. Yoma 13b, s.v. u'lechada). Sometimes the veiling of the bride was to be specifically done by the groom, thus it was more clearly symbolic of their isolation under *his chuppah*. Hence the custom arose of having the bride under the groom's *tallis* at the marriage ceremony.

All these variations indicate that the original meaning of *chuppah* as the groom's chamber expanded into various symbolic substitutes so that the word *chuppah* ceased to mean any object, such as a room, but a process, the "covering" in general. Thus *chuppah* as an abstract noun is used chiefly in the Jewish law as the symbolic act or situation or object by which the groom may be said to have "taken" (*nissuin*) the bride and she is now legally his.

As social conditions changed, some of the older variants, veiling or covering the head of the bride under the *tallis* or the setting up of a groom's special room, the *chuppah,* tended to disappear, but the general question always remained, namely, which mode of *chuppah* was actually indispensable.

The validity of these various forms of the process of *chuppah* ("taking in possession") was a serious question. It was not merely a question of decorative ceremonialism, for it was a vital matter to decide at which point the woman actually becomes the man's wife. Questions of inheritance or adultery, etc., etc., were involved in the question of just which specific action makes her formally his wife.

The legal importance of the various symbolic actions is indicated in the motivation of the statement of Joel Sirkes (the next generation after Isserles) in his commentary to the Tur, Even Hoezer, 61. He lists all the various interpretations of the process of *chuppah*, namely, that he is isolated with her (which is the Rambam's opinion, *Yad Ishus*, Chapter 10); or that it is sufficient if she comes to his house (that is, even in company, according to Rabbenu Nissim); or that the cloth is put over the head of both of them during the blessings; or merely that the father gives the girl over to the husband, etc. Then he says, "It seems that our custom, what we call *chuppah*, follows all of these various definitions, because of doubt" (that is, because "we are in doubt as to which of the various types of *chuppah* is the crucial one"). Then he gives the detail of the custom in Russia, namely, that the groom himself in the morning, in company of the Rabbi, goes to the bride's house formally to cover her face with the veil (known popularly as *bedecken die Kalle*). This ceremony accords with the opinion of the Tosfos (b. Yoma 13b) that if the bride goes forth with the *henumah*, that is, "the veil," that is considered *chuppah*. "Then we have the custom that toward evening we spread a cloth over poles and we stand the bride and groom under it and the blessings are pronounced. After that, we lead them to their house and they eat together in an isolated place, etc."

We wish that Sirkes would have been a little more explicit as to exactly why it was necessary to develop this new custom of the cloth over the four poles. Possibly it was because all the older law spoke of the bridegroom's marriage tent; therefore the various symbolic substitutes (covering the couple with a *tallis*, etc.) seemed insufficient. The Schulchan Aruch, Even Hoezer 61:1, says that if one brings his bride into the *chuppah*, she becomes his wife in the fullest sense. But this refers to the older, private groom's *chuppah*, which implied privacy. Of course such a private room would generally be available if the groom had a home of his own, and thus the original and basic meaning of *chuppah* would be fulfilled. However, the situation in Poland by the time of Isserles and in the next century made it less probable that such a private *chuppah* chamber would be available. The population grew and poverty increased. Besides, there were now tens of thousands of yeshiva students who were sought in marriage for the daughters of well-to-do parents. The description at the end of Nathan Hanover, "Yeven M'zula," describes how many thousands of marriages were arranged for these poor and homeless students. How could such a student have his own *chuppah* room which would fulfill the basic purpose of the law? Sometimes, indeed, the father of the bride would provide a room for the young groom. See the Pische Teshuva to Even Hoezer 55, where one authority says that if the father lends the prospective son-in-law a room, it virtually belongs to the groom. But clearly this was an evasion. Some substitute for the groom's private *chuppah* had to be provided. Therefore they made this tentlike arrangement of a cloth on four poles. However, if they had made it a complete tent, they would be faced with another set of legal perplexities as to whether by her entering into such a tent the bride was "acquired." To avoid such questions, they made the tent definitely public by avoiding the use of any cloth walls (Isserles carefully says *borabim*, "in the presence of the public") and, furthermore, this made it possible for the guests to be present. In other words, this was not a legal "acquiring tent," but only a tentlike symbol of it.

Yet the fact that the canopy was now reminiscent of the older tent-*chuppah*, which actually "acquired" the bride, a change in an older custom resulted. Maharil clearly describes the wedding as taking place in the synagogue. He led the couple there, and there on the *bema*, he recited the blessings. He, of course, knew of no wedding canopy. But now that there was this tentlike canopy which carried associations of the old marriage tent, it was felt improper that such a tent with its intimate associations be set up in the synagogue. Hence, undoubtedly, it was moved to the synagogue courtyard. Isserles does not give this explanation, but offers a relatively modest one. He says that the *chuppah* should be held in the open air as a mark of blessing (Even Hoezer 61:1) although in Yore Deah 391 he still speaks of the *chuppah in* the synagogue. But, clearly, sentiment must have recoiled against any sort of a wedding tent, even a symbolic one and even with open sides, in the synagogue proper.

But why have it on the synagogue premises altogether? Since it is a symbol of the special bridal bedchamber belonging to the groom, would it not be more appropriate to set up this *chuppah* in private premises, which would be closer to the old custom of the father building a *chuppah* for his son on his premises? Why was the *chuppah* set up in the courtyard of the synagogue?

Elijah of Vilna hints at an explanation which is revealing of the social situation in Russia and in Poland in past centuries referred to above. He says that often the *chuppah* would be set up in the house of the bride's father. This practice is, however, open to question because the father must bring the bride to the premises belonging to the groom. Therefore Elijah of Vilna says, "We set it up on the synagogue premises which belong to everybody" (see Biurey Hagra to Even Hoezer 55).

It might be added that the synagogue courtyard, especially in Vilna, was relatively protected premises. It was safer to have a large assembly there than elsewhere in the city.

At all events, the evolution of the wedding canopy is fairly clear. It was unknown before the sixteenth century. It was developed to fulfill certain legal requirements or, rather, to allay certain legal doubts which arose under the special conditions of life in eastern Europe. The special, decorated chamber which in the earlier law was called the *chuppah* was hardly possible on the premises of the groom, where it properly belonged. Many of the grooms were poor Talmudic students who married the daughters of relatively well-to-do merchants. It would be easy to set up the *chuppah* in the house of the bride, as Elijah of Vilna indicates. This would raise legal objections because one definition of the process of *chuppah* was that the bride should be handed over to the premises of the groom. Therefore it was held on the premises of the synagogue which were everybody's property. It was kept open-sided so that it should not be mistaken for the actual chamber of "acquiring." Since, however, the new symbolic canopy did somewhat resemble the old private wedding tent, the older custom of the Rhineland to conduct the wedding in the synagogue itself seemed no longer appropriate. Hence the ceremony was moved to the courtyard.

Biblical Archaeology and Reform Judaism

NELSON GLUECK

*

ALL OF US ARE ROOTED in the soil of our origins. Archaeological explorations and excavations in Near Eastern lands in general and in Biblical lands in particular enable us to grasp the complexity of the component parts of our background and to understand an increasing number of them. Our lives have been shaped to an important degree by the nature of our cultural and spiritual patrimony. The events which transpired on the shores and in the lands adjacent to the Tigris and the Euphrates, the Nile and Jordan rivers in ancient times exercise an amazingly powerful influence upon our lives today. Particularly strong are the impacts upon us of the religious developments which centered in the Holy Land. They bear a direct relationship to us in particular as Jews, as well as to all of those who have a stake in the welfare and future of what is called the Judaeo-Christian civilization.

The consideration of the past in general and of archaeological discoveries in Bible Lands in particular underscores a central tenet of Reform Judaism, that God is to be found and His commandment understood through an endless process of seeking and testing, of discarding and discovering, of deepening of understanding and reinterpretation in modernly significant manner of previous affirmations and customs, and of acquiring greater knowledge and adopting new practices in harmony both with ancient tradition and the advances of scientific inquiry. To seek for ourselves and our children a sure path or direction out of the baffling maze of our present, it is natural for us to examine and regularly reevaluate the ways of our fathers, the conditions of their lives, the countries of their origins, the leitmotifs of their religious philosophy, the entire miracle of our history, which reaches back now continuously for some four thousand years. The consideration of that miracle is important not only for us as Jews, but for all those who find in the Bible the unfailing guideposts of the forward march of civilization in accordance with the Biblical ideal of the universal brotherhood of man under the fatherhood of God.

The Bible is a repository of basic religious truth which retains enduring validity for us and for all mankind. We believe that the moral and spiritual values of the Bible transcend the changes of time or the vagaries of human affairs. These values are inseparably connected with our fathers' perceptions of the will of God eternal, who established the changing universe in accordance with changeless, natural law, and who subjected mankind within it to unchanging statutes of brotherly love, humanitarian justice, humility and mercy, and who gave man the freedom to choose between life and death and enjoined him to choose life.

In this sense, therefore, the tradition of the Bible is not temporary but timeless, not changeable but forever challenging. The truths of the Bible expressed in commandments and prophecy, in legend and law, in history and myth, in unvarnished biographical sketches and compressed geneological tables, and some of them repeated in different versions not only in different books but in the same chapters, are not susceptible to proof of any kind. They can neither be buttressed nor invalidated archaeologically. New discovery may perhaps modify or fill out or make clear a particular account in the Biblical annals, but it can never replace or refute or corroborate its religious worths. The discoveries by archaeological exploration and excavations in Bible Lands have a relevancy to historical events in the Bible, but in no wise affect its religious propositions or ethical decrees, which are applicable to all peoples in all lands at all times.

From this point of view, there is no relationship between archaeological discoveries in Bible Lands and the Bible itself, or between the finds of archaeology and the teachings of Judaism. Archaeology helps us understand better the lands in which the Bible and Judaism evolved. It gives us more information than is otherwise available either in the pages of the Bible or elsewhere about the historical situations, which evoked revolutionary religious doctrines, in harmony with the genius of unfolding Judaism. It was the calamitous event of the Babylonian exile, e.g., which created the setting for Jeremiah's teaching of a "new covenant," or for Ezekiel's full exposition of "individualism" and "repentance" and "restoration." There was soul searching and spiritual travail which preceded these prophecies. There was radical departure from the popular conceptions of the day. There was singularly brave opposition to political authority. What archaeology does for us is to add greatly to our knowledge about the Assyrians and Babylonians, the Persians and Greeks and others—and all the evanescent conquerors of Israel and Judah. It reveals more than we might otherwise even guess from the pages of the Bible about the Israelites and the Judaeans or their immediate neighbors.

Archaeology helps us to understand the better the likenesses and differences between, e.g., the Edomites and Judaeans of the period of the classical prophets. They spoke the same language with minor differences of pronunciation, used the same script, wore the same kind of clothes, engaged in much the same economic pursuits, fashioned and baked the same kinds of pottery, lived in the same kinds of houses—and yet the Edomites and their like have disappeared into the limbo of history, with their physical belongings becoming archaeological artifacts, while the Jewish people, the physical and spiritual descendants of their Judaean contemporaries, persist as the transmitters of the vital tradition of Judaism. What then was the difference between them?

The question becomes even more difficult, in view of the fact that the results of every excavation of every Judaean site before the Babylonian exile demonstrate that the majority of the Judaeans engaged in the worship of pagan gods. The constant fulminations of the prophets against the backslidings of the people of Israel and Judah, against their adoption of Canaanite fertility practices, become all the more significant when one finds Astarte figurines in every excavation. The general population, in circles high and low, indulged to a greater or lesser degree in idolatry, yet it was from among this very population that the prophets and priests sprang.

The findings of Biblical archaeology thus enhance the miracle of the development of Judaism. It took hundreds of years, before the God-inspired handful of people who perceived the ways and words of God were able to infuse into the spiritual tissue and substance of an entire people the acceptance of the authority of the God of Abraham and Isaac and Jacob, the complete belief in the God of History and Humanity, the unquestioning willingness to worship Him in accordance with His commandments. It is largely through the help of archaeology, as well as through the careful study of the pages of the Bible, that we know now what distinguished some of our forefathers from the time of Abraham on, and gradually distinguished the totality of Israel from their neighbors, however often many individuals may have departed from the tenets of their faith. Our fathers drew near to God and developed a religion which winnowed out magic and paganism from religious performance and understanding, and which continually deepened itself in spiritual penetration. Not an idol nor a tree nor a human being was God, but only God himself was God. And they were not content for a vague sense of communion with God to be the essence of religion. They insisted that there be substance to it. There were ceremonies and rituals, to be sure, but, above all, norms of conduct. Justice and righteousness and warm human sympathies—all these incumbent upon man in his daily living—were and have remained the very essence of Judaism.

The faith of the Biblical writers was formidable, and archaeology underscores the magnitude of that faith, because it lays bare the hard realities of the world, above which that faith soared and which no untoward happening could weaken or destroy. In their finest expressions, the Biblical writers did not present the worship of God as being a rewarding exercise that would preclude the fragility of fortune, the pains of existence, the suffering of the righteous, the abuse of the weak, the disasters visited upon the people of Israel. For them, God was the source of all being, whose ways were beyond comprehension, whose word was law, whose love somehow or other spelled survival. It was in and through the Bible that they expounded their understanding of the existence of God, the meaning of His imperatives, the nature of His relationship to individuals, to Israel, to all mankind.

Many source materials were incorporated by the Biblical writers into their texts, after having been severely edited by them in either substance or scope or form. Among these materials were large numbers of historical, topographical, and geographical allusions, some of considerable length, and others hauntingly abbreviated. The criterion for inclusion derived from their usefulness in underscoring or defining religious principles, although in some instances the underlying reasoning is obscure. Nevertheless, despite the Bible's self-imposed limitations, it furnishes us with our main body of knowledge about the ancient history of Israel and of the Holy Land and the forces that affected them both.

All too often, however, matters of obviously great importance can barely be gleaned from the Biblical records and frequently are lost in their bias or silence. There are, for instance, some glancing references to the Hittites in the Bible, and thereafter they disappear into the limbo whence its editors dredged them. Had they not had some particular connection with persons and places or periods of consequence for the primary theological or religious purposes of the Bible, they never would have appeared at all in the Biblical writings.

They figure, for instance, in the story of Abraham's purchase of the Cave of Machpelah at Hebron from Ephron the Hittite for a family sepulcher (Genesis 23). Abraham was one of the greatest of the Biblical heroes, and therefore anything pertaining to his biography stood a chance of being included in the Biblical record. There are several other references to the Hittites, one in connection with the House of Joseph, and another in connection with Solomon, and a startling one in Ezekiel 16 in the name of the Lord about Jerusalem: "Thine origin and thy nativity is of the land of the Canaanite; the Amorite was thy father, and thy mother was a Hittite." But the Bible fails to tell us who the Hittites were, and anything at all about their civilization, language, race, or land. We would have liked to have known when they penetrated into Canaan and reached as far south as Hebron to settle and become landowners there. Here again, it becomes necessary to resort to archaeology to attempt to discover more information about them. Archaeology becomes thus the servant of history, by making the ground reveal the secrets of buried civilizations.

The Biblical writers were, however, not primarily interested in giving us the details of history in the objective fashion that we judge historical writing today. This is not to assert that the historical statements in the Bible are incorrect, but it is to maintain that the Bible was primarily a religious book, a book of theology, and only secondarily a book of history, making use of historical and geographical and topographical materials. Indeed, the Biblical editors frequently refer us to the records whence they culled their materials. They mention "the book of the kings of Judah and Israel" (II Chronicles 16:11) or "the book of Yashar" (I Kings 11:41), and by implication seem to say that if the reader wants to get the full details, he should go to the library and get the pertinent volumes or scrolls off the shelves and read up the relevant materials himself. Unfortunately, none of these documents has ever yet been recovered. If they were written on perishable materials, they have long ago vanished into thin air, unless they were placed in sealed pottery containers and buried in damp-proof places, as were the Dead Sea Scrolls at Qumran and the Scrolls and Bar Kochba documents of the Nahal Hever. The chances of finding them, particularly in places like Jerusalem, are very remote indeed for many reasons.

It must be emphasized, therefore, that the full value of Biblical archaeology can be achieved only when it is pursued for the objective, historical information which it almost always so richly yields when scientifically undertaken. The depth and authority of the spiritual insights and instruction of the Bible cannot be affected positively or negatively by whether or not an archaeological discovery confirms one or more of its historical statements. The possibility indeed always remains that some archaeological discovery may someday demonstrably controvert a historical statement in the Bible. That, to be sure, has not yet occurred. All that it would prove would be that some historical fact had been wrongly recorded or some historical memory transmitted incorrectly. Nevertheless, I know of no archaeological discovery that has ever disproved a properly understood historical statement in the Bible. Many statements and stories simply do not lend themselves to the criteria of historicity, and others, notably the one dealing with the fall of Jericho, are too obscure to come as yet within the scope of archaeological relevance. It is thus, or ought to be, obvious, that the purpose of Biblical archaeology is not to "prove" the correctness of the teachings of the Bible. Indeed, I regard those people as of little faith who seek through archaeological corroboration of historical source materials in the Bible to validate the Biblical concept of God and of everything that flows from it.

For me as an archaeologist and as a Reform Jew, the full beauty and wonder of the Bible appear when it is revealed as the story of human beings developing in history, whose forefathers broke through the barriers of paganism to perceive the glory of God and to accept the moral imperatives of His revelations. The Bible portrays its heroes as all too weak human beings who rise, however, above the imperfections of their characters to the strengths derived from their vision of the nature of God. David, for instance, one of the most, if not the most beloved hero in the Bible, was portrayed with all the rawness of his passions, the violence of his misdeeds, the ruthlessness of his ambitions, but in addition also with his wisdom and courage, his sweetness and strength, his humility and devotion to his people and to God. It is with that Biblical philosophy of continuous development and understanding, of growth of wisdom, of adaptation and change in accordance with continuity of unchanging moral law and belief in God, that Reform, or Liberal, or Progressive Judaism is most happily in accord.

Religion and the Free Society

ROBERT GORDIS*

*

IN THIS HOUR of grave challenge for the free world, it is a frequently repeated truism that the Bible has served as a pillar of the democratic way of life. It is true that the Founding Fathers of the United States were very conscious of their roots in the Biblical tradition. The Declaration of Independence is deeply suffused by the spirit of Biblical faith, wedded to the rationalist liberalism of John Locke. This is strikingly exemplified in the most famous passage of this classic document: "We hold these truths to be self-evident, that all men are *created equal,* that they are endowed by their *Creator* with certain unalienable Rights, that among these are Life, Liberty and the pursuit of Happiness."

When the Continental Congress asked a committee consisting of Benjamin Franklin, John Adams, and Thomas Jefferson to propose a Great Seal for the United States, they suggested the scene of the Israelites crossing the Red Sea. To accompany the picture they proposed the Puritan apothegm, which likewise derived from the authentic Hebrew tradition, "Rebellion to tyrants means obedience to God." During the dark days of the American Revolution the sermons that were preached in American pulpits found both analogy and hope in the Biblical narrative of the enslavement in Egypt and the Exodus from bondage. George III was Pharaoh, George Washington was Moses, the American colonists were the Israelites, the Atlantic Ocean was the Red Sea, and Independence was the Promised Land.

Not all the Founding Fathers were believers in traditional religion, some of the most distinguished among them being deists. Yet even they were deeply rooted in Biblical thought. Thomas Jefferson

* It is a privilege to share in this tribute to one of the greatest leaders of American Jewry. Dr. Abba Hillel Silver is justly recognized as one of the most eloquent spokesmen for Judaism and the Jewish people in the world today. Perhaps even more significant than his great forensic gifts are the wide learning and the passionate sincerity he has brought to every phase of his rich career—his teaching of liberal Judaism, his dedication to interfaith relations based

prepared a special text of the New Testament for his own use in which he excluded miracles and other supernatural elements and preserved the ethical content of Jesus' utterances. The great pamphleteer of the American Revolution, Thomas Paine, who was called a "filthy little atheist" by Theodore Roosevelt, was neither filthy nor an atheist. On the contrary, Paine was deeply concerned with a religious faith that would not do violence to his ethical convictions.

In any summation of the spiritual sources of the American Revolution, Lecky's words are often quoted, "Hebraic mortar cemented the foundations of American democracy." Hence the frequently repeated assertion that Biblical thought, as embodied in the Judeo-Christian tradition was the source for democracy, is true. But it is not the whole truth—and that on two counts. On the one hand it fails to reckon with the full complexity of Biblical thought and on the other it ignores the varied influences that helped shape the democratic ideal. To argue for a single line of descent from the Bible to democracy is an oversimplification which becomes a distortion.

According to an old saying, the Devil can quote Scriptures for his own purpose. This is an oblique way of stating the truth that within the Bible we may find every shade of opinion, radical, moderate, and conservative, on the basic questions of life and thought. This is entirely to be expected, since the Hebrew Bible is not the work of a political sect or of a religious denomination but the distillation of the experience of an entire people.

For this reason, it has been possible for some readers to find a few passages in the Bible on the basis of which they have branded it as reactionary. The author of the statement in Proverbs: "My son, fear thou the Lord and the king, And meddle not with them that are given to change" (Proverbs 24:21), was scarcely an apostle of the revolution! The common Biblical phrase, "the Lord's anointed" (I Samuel 24:7) by which the king in Israel is described, was utilized for centuries as a basis for the doctrine of the divine right of kings, a theory which is totally rejected today by all democratic countries, monarchical and republican alike. Similarly, the existence of Biblical laws regulating slavery was used by apologists until the days of the Civil War in order to justify the institution. Passages of this type led

upon self-respect and true understanding, his significant contributions to scholarship and literature and, above all, his yoeman service to the cause of Zion and the State of Israel, which give him a place among Israel's immortals.

Because of Dr. Silver's lifelong dedication to religion and liberty, I take pleasure in presenting this study of the unique American experience in safeguarding both ideals.

a critic like Leonard Woolf to make the statement, "Democracy is essentially antireligious and anti-Christian." He might have found support for his view in the words of the first century Alexandrian Jewish philosopher, Philo, who declared: "God is one—a principle which opposes the polytheists, who are not ashamed to transfer the worst possible type of government, that of mob rule from earth to heaven."

Nonetheless, this conclusion is mistaken, being based upon an inadequate and faulty reading of the text. The Hebrew Bible, like Judaism as a whole, is a mighty river with many currents and eddies besides the mainstream, and these variations must be clearly told apart, their relative importance being carefully gauged. He who reads the Bible with understanding and sympathy will recognize that the passages which we have cited do not represent the dominant stream of thought in Biblical religion. The phrase "the anointed of God" was an old idiom, which the Hebrew thinkers of old never used to justify the doctrine that the king or the dictator can do no wrong. On the contrary, the Biblical historians and prophets were overwhelmingly convinced that the kings rarely did anything else! Samuel's scathing attack on the institution of the monarchy is well known. It may be that Hosea, who lived three centuries later, during the last days of the Northern Kingdom, also opposed the kingship in principle. So much for the theory. In practice, virtually all the Prophets found the royal rulers an affront to God and morality.

All in all, John Wyclif was not far from the mark when, in the preface to his translation of the Scriptures, he stated that the Bible believes in "government of the people, by the people, and for the people," a phrase which was destined to echo down the centuries.

Undoubtedly other factors, both theoretical and practical, played their part in the emergence of democracy. The rationalist thought of Hume and Locke gave the eighteenth century an intellectual basis for retaining the Biblical faith in the equal rights of man. The rise of individualism was a consequence of the Industrial Revolution which required the breakdown of feudal distinctions and long-established vested rights and restrictions. The growing recognition that each man counted, or, in Robert Burns's words, "A man's a man for a' that" became a dominant factor in many humanitarian movements, as the abuses of the Industrial Revolution created widespread hardship and degradation.

Yet the religious tradition of the Western world remained a significant source for the democratic vision not only for traditional believers, but also for deists, both official and unofficial. This was particularly true in the Anglo-Saxon world. Elsewhere in the West, as in France, subterranean Biblical influences may have operated, but on the conscious level there was a strong anticlerical bias, often outspokenly antireligious. The French Revolution opposed both the power and the outlook of the Catholic Church and in its early, most confident days, sought to replace it by the "religion of reason" with its own temples, festivals, and rituals. While both the American and the French revolutions produced classic statements of principles, the American Declaration of Independence was for more deeply rooted in traditional religious thought than the French Declaration of the Rights of Man.

When due allowance, however, is made for all the secular factors, it still remains true that religion is a basic element in the world view underlying democracy. It may, or may not be theoretically possible to validate democracy without a religious foundation. The writer, speaking for himself, has never found any of these proposed logical structures adequate to demonstrate the principles of democracy without a prior act of faith. Be this as it may, it is certain that these secular systems of thought rarely possess the emotional drive, the power of conviction to fire the generality of men with the passion to defend liberty and equality.

In the twentieth century, another test, tragically pragmatic, has emerged which highlights the nexus between faith and freedom. Every form of tyranny in our age has been marked by hostility to religion. All brands of totalitarianism, brown, black, and red, have made it a prime objective to destroy the church as a vital institution for worship, education, and personal ideals. The reason is obvious. Organized religion remained a citadel of resistance to totalitarianism. Thus, in the heyday of Nazism, all the institutions of a liberal society became silent and inactive and only the voice of religion was heard in protest against the new resurgence of bestiality. Einstein, surely no apologist for traditional religion, has borne testimony to this phenomenon of our day: "Only the church stood squarely across the path of Hitler's campaign for suppressing the truth. I never had any special interest in the church before, but now I feel a great affection and admiration, because the church alone has had the courage and persistence to stand for intellectual truth and moral freedom. I am forced to confess that what I once despised I now praise unreservedly."

II

It should be noted, however, that this debt of democracy to religion has, in large measure, been repaid by the beneficent influence which the democratic way of life has exerted upon the content of religion. American democracy, in particular, has contributed a significant pattern for the relationship of religion to a free society. If the American way cannot serve as a blueprint for the world community of tomorrow, it may nevertheless be useful as an ideal norm. When this new world emerges, it will necessarily be rooted in the realities of the present. It will therefore be inherently and incurably pluralist, reflecting the variety of national loyalties, racial differences, and religious divergences that mark the contemporary scene.

Moreover, in the emergent world community, there will be many more faiths that will need to be reckoned with than are comprehended in the Judeo-Christian tradition. The religions of the West, Judaism and Christianity, to which Islam may be added, have so much in common that to a Far Eastern observer they may well seem little more than variants of the same faith. There is no common background of history or outlook linking the Judeo-Christian tradition to Buddhism, Hinduism, Confucianism, or the various religions of Africa. Even more far-reaching would be the chasm separating the way of life of the religiously oriented peoples of the earth from the militantly secularist and antireligious outlook of the nations in the Communist orbit. Even if communism were ultimately to be modified or even discarded, the antireligious bias would be too deeply ingrained to disappear quickly or easily.

In the face of this bewildering plethora of religions, including atheism, there would be an ineluctable need to construct a common language of discourse for the emerging world community. A pattern would be required which would permit the free expression of divergent religious loyalties, side by side with an overarching sense of unity binding all nations together. Here the unique pattern of the separation of church and state, as it has taken shape in America, would be of the highest significance. It is true that in other democratic lands the church-state relationship takes on forms different from that prevailing in the United States. Yet I submit that the American principle of separation is bound to prove far more useful for the world than the varying forms of union or support between church and state that exist elsewhere.

It is worth recalling that the American experience in this area is unique not only in its character, but in its durability. The American Republic is the oldest continuously functioning democracy in the world. Only Great Britain is an exception and there religion occupies an altogether different position in the structure of the state. The American way is therefore far more than local in signficance.

The importance attached by the Founding Fathers of the American Republic to the status of religion in a free society is underscored by the fact that it is the subject matter of the First Amendment to the Bill of Rights: "Congress shall make no law respecting an establishment of religion, or prohibiting the free exercise thereof. . . ." A vast literature of interpretation on these sixteen words has grown up during the century and three quarters of the life of the Republic. It is embodied in Supreme Court decisions, in the discussion of legal theorists, and in the debates of the advocates of religion and of its opponents.

Like the Constitution as a whole, the First Amendment has been subjected both to a "broad" and a "narrow" construction, the detailed history of which does not concern us now. In essence, the "broad" interpretation of the Amendment understands it to prohibit all governmental aid to religion, whether preferential or nonpreferential. To be sure, there have been some contradictions in practice, but they are ignored or regarded as minor, and in any case held to be incapable of subverting the general principle. The "limited" view sees the Constitution as forbidding only preferential treatment for one religion, but not as excluding aid to all on an equal or largely equal basis.

The classic enunciation of the "broad" interpretation of the Amendment is to be found in the frequently quoted words of Justice Hugo Black in the *Everson case:* "The 'establishment of religion' clause of the First Amendment means at least this: Neither a state nor the Federal Government can set up a church. Neither can pass laws which aid one religion, or all religions, or prefer one religion over another." The "limited" construction found expression in Justice Douglas's utterance in the *Zorach case* in which he declared: "The First Amendment within the scope of its coverage permits no exception; the prohibition is absolute. The First Amendment, however, does not say that in every and all respects there shall be a separation of church and state. Rather, it studiously defines the manner, the specific ways, in which there shall be no concert or union or dependency one on the other. That is the common sense of the matter. Otherwise, the state and religion would be aliens to each other—hostile, suspicious, and even unfriendly."

In the face of such august, if divided authority, it is clear that there must be substantial legal and constitutional authority on both sides. That both Jefferson and Madison, who were leading forces in fashioning the Bill of Rights, clearly interpreted the First Amendment to mean a "wall of separation," is certain. Yet their opinion has no binding or legal force, though it is certainly significant for establishing the climate of opinion under which the Bill of Rights came into being.

Moreover, the oral tradition, to borrow a phrase from Jewish religious experience, has considerable weight in establishing the meaning of the written Constitution. Thus it is noteworthy that while the phrase "the separation of Church and State" does not occur in the Constitution, the First Amendment has always been recognized as a statement of this principle, both in popular American thought, as well as in the more precise formulation of American legal and judicial opinion.

The analysis of legal distinctions and the investigation of the original intent of the Founding Fathers are interesting enterprises. There is, however, another test, far more significant for the future of democracy, both within the confines of the United States and within the as yet unmarked territory of the world community of tomorrow. An examination of the record makes it clear that this peculiarly American doctrine of separation of church and state has been highly beneficial *to both parties*. Undoubtedly, the principle was originally adopted in order to safeguard the stability of the state and protect it against the devisiveness of sectarian strife, which is written large in the religious wars, controversies, and persecutions of Europe. This conscious purpose of the Founding Fathers has been achieved to a very high degree—America has largely been spared the ravages of a *Kulturkampf* between the religious and nonreligious elements in society. As a result, we have been free both from the clerical political parties common on the European continent and from the violent anti-clerical movements which flowered into the Nazi, Fascist, and Communist dictatorships.

Moreover, the differences among the various sects, Protestant, Catholic, and Jewish, have rarely been exacerbated to the point of violent conflict in America. The effort to raise the ghost of Catholic-Protestant antagonism in the 1960 Presidential campaign proved a failure, in large measure because it was disavowed by both parties and by their standard-bearers, so that it remained principally the province of the lunatic fringe among the bigots.

Scarcely less important has been the contribution of the First Amendment to the vitality of religion as a whole. The centrality of this principle in the development of our country has been well set forth by H. Richard Niebuhr: "What democracy and free land have meant for the political and economic development of America, the separation of church and state has meant for its religious development." [1]

1   Cf. his *Social Sources of Denominationalism*, p. 201.

Long before the present, much discussed revival of religion, or revival of interest in religion—it matters little here whether we write these phrases with or without quotation marks—the percentage of church affiliations in the United States was far higher than abroad. This phenomenon had already attracted the attention of the well known sociologist, Max Weber.[2] He sought to explain the facts on the ground that economic sanctions for church adherence have here taken the place of the political sanctions of European countries. There is some degree of truth undoubtedly inherent in his interpretation, but it is far from an adequate explanation. In Richard Niebuhr's words, "The very lack of any sort of compulsion has placed the responsibility for its maintenance upon the church itself and has invigorated it, as no reliance upon political agencies could have done." As a completely voluntary agency in American life, organized religion has attained a position of influence and prestige, outstripping by far its status in lands where the alliance of church and state is the norm.

The steadily rising percentage of the total population which is affiliated with a church, the level of development and prestige which religious education has reached, the range and extent of other church-related activities, and, by no means least, the attitude of respect, or at least of nonhostility, on the part of the nonaffiliated that religion enjoys in the United States—all these phenomena testify to a position attained by religion without parallel anywhere else in the world.

Frequently observers of religion on the current American scene criticize the current religiosity on the score of its superficiality and vagueness. Though there is substantial justice in the complaint, the criticism may be swallowed too uncritically! One often has the feeling that the critics are objecting to the fact that the masses of Americans do not seem to be interested in the niceties of the theological distinctions to which they, the critics, are committed. But the so-called "undenominational religion" of most Americans today, while undoubtedly suffering from many defects, deserves more of a defense than it has yet received. The proverbial "man in the street" would define his religion as love of God and faith in Him, though he might be unable to present a thoroughly elaborated theological position. He would insist that the love of one's fellowman expressed in decent human relations is the essence of obedience to the Divine will, no matter what other credal and ritual demands the specific tradition may make. If they possessed the requisite learning, the unsophisticated advocates of such a religion could cite chapter and verse from

2 Max Weber, *Aufsätze zur Religionssoziologie*, Vol. I, pp. 207 ff.

the Prophets and sages of Judaism and from Jesus and the saints of Christianity. Rabbinic tradition did not hesitate to declare that God himself mused, "Would that man forsook Me, but kept My law"— adding the afterthought, to be sure, "because the light within it would bring them near to Me." [3]

It is true, as one observer points out, that "classrooms filled with eager students taking courses in religion and public forums on the same subject are a far cry from betokening a sense of personal commitment to religion." But it should be noted that even this type of superficial interest in religion is rarely to be met with in Germany, France, Italy, or the Scandinavian countries, either among the youth or in the academic world. This in spite of the fact that in many of these countries the relationship of church and state is organic, and formal religious training is a compulsory element in the school system.

III

If the strict separation of church and state is as fundamental and beneficial as we have argued, how are such apparent deviations as free textbooks and bus transportation for parochial school pupils to be understood?

A study of the various instances involved suggests that the American people is unwilling to surrender its allegiance to the principle of separation of church and state, even if it does not always adhere to it in practice. In other words, the deviations are to be regarded as exceptions to the rule, not as its abrogation.

These deviations fall into several categories. Such practices as the opening of Congress with prayer, the swearing in of government officials on the Bible or its use in court oaths, and references to the Deity in Thanksgiving proclamations, are sufficiently general in character and minor in scope as not to offend either the rights or the sensibilities of the overwhelming majority of Americans.

Much more substantial acts, such as the establishment and support of chaplaincies in the armed forces and in government prisons, are also justifiable. They are based on the recognition that men who are in service or behind bars have been forcibly removed from their usual environment by the state. The government therefore may be legitimately called upon to replace such facilities as they enjoyed while at liberty or in civilian society. These include various kinds of entertainment, access to books and music, exercise, and sport. Ob-

---

3 Cf. *Jerusalem Talmud Hagigah* 1:7   for the impossible *se'or.*
   reading *ma'or*, with all authorities,

viously a very high priority among these facilities is occupied by the ministrations of religion.

Still more far-reaching is the tax exemption accorded for houses of worship and religious schools. It obviously presupposes a belief in the beneficial character of religion in the life of the citizenry and is parallel to the tax exemption granted other institutions such as museums, hospitals, universities, and other specialized schools. To be sure, each of them serves only a fraction of the population, but their functioning is regarded as beneficial to the body politic as a whole.

Because these deviations from the separation of church and state have been utilized in some quarters to justify direct government aid to religion, some high leaders in American Protestantism have called for the churches voluntarily to surrender their tax-exempt status, even though it might be theoretically defensible and is not currently being challenged. Whether such an act of voluntary self-abnegation on a large scale is likely to take place is open to doubt. The churches are finding fund-raising a painful and soul-shattering enterprise, even without the necessity of paying taxes. Besides, as we have noted, it is possible to justify a tax exemption for religious instititutions even within the framework of the doctrine of the separation of church and state.

Yet all these instances of a cooperative relationship between the state and the church—whether they be regarded as justifiable deviations or as inconsistent violations of the First Amendment—have not affected the basic pattern of separation which most Americans prefer to regard as inviolate.

IV

The penetration of organized religion into society is not limited to the area of government. Nor are the means being employed always restricted to the arts of persuasion and discussion, which religion has both a right and a duty to use in furthering its ideals. Instances are multiplying of sectarian groups seeking to impose their specific religious and ethical views on the general public by bringing pressures to bear, either overtly or subtly, on government officials and other policy-making organs. The struggle affects such areas as legislation concerning marriage, divorce, and planned parenthood, the operation of government hospitals, the censorship of books, magazines and plays, and above all, public education.

What has led to the striking change of opinion with regard to the relationship of society and religion among an articulate section of the American people during the last three decades? Many factors have played their part. Protestants have become increasingly aware of the failure of the Sunday school to transmit effectively the authentic values in Christianity, particularly in view of the growing denudation of the home of religious values. This has impelled many Protestant teachers and spokesmen of religion to look for support in their educational endeavors from the state through released time and other means. In Catholic circles, the traditional and all-but-universal view that the state is bound to support the propagation of religious "truth," which is widely held abroad, finds its attenuated expression in America in the demand for government support of parochial education. Moreover, the vast growth of Catholic education, particularly on the elementary and high school levels, but also in colleges and universities, has imposed tremendous economic burdens upon American Catholics, and given urgency to the charge of "double taxation." Finally, the alarming rise of antireligious philosophies, one of which, Communism, poses a massive threat to the democratic way of life, has led even secular-minded politicians to think of religion as offering a sorely needed ideological base for the war against Communism.

Factors such as these have led to a widespread demand that the state enter into a far closer relationship with organized religion than has been the case heretofore. This has created a constellation of tension issues—some major, others minor. Yet it should be pointed out that even issues which seem extreme and unimportant today may develop great significance as nuclei of far-reaching developments, because the situation is fluid. The advocates of government aid to religion are active in propagating their views and in moving step by step from one position to the next. The apparently insuperable obstacle of the First Amendment is met by affirming one's allegiance to the principle of the separation of church and state and then giving the Amendment a "limited construction" as forbidding only "preferential" aid to one religion.

There is, however, no dearth of illustrations in recent history to illustrate the principle that however attractive nonpreferential aid may appear in theory, it is virtually impossible to translate it fairly into practice. A sensational example was afforded recently by the School Board of New Hyde Park, Long Island, which proceeded to draw up a "nondenominational" set of Ten Commandments to be recited in the classrooms of the public schools of that community. The School Board in question was not deterred by the fact that Catholics, Protestants, and Jews differ with regard both to the contents and the sequence of the Ten Commandments. They ignored the right of nonbelievers to have their children attend the public schools as first-class American citizens. Their creative contribution, however, went further. Following the august example of an eighteenth-century poet laureate who issued a volume entitled *The Plays of William Shakespeare Revised and Improved by Colley Cibber*, they produced a revised and improved version of the Decalogue. In the First Commandment, "I am the Lord thy God, who brought thee forth out of the land of Egypt, out of the house of bondage," they eliminated the phrase, "out of the land of Egypt." Thus with one masterly stroke they eliminated the historical basis for the revelation at Sinai, the link of the Ten Commandments with the Hebrew people, and the role of Israel in Judeo-Christian religious tradition.

In the case of the New Hyde Park Decalogue, the ostensible and no doubt sincerely felt goal was the wish to achieve a "nondenominational" religion. In other cases, sectarianism is clearly avowed and defended. Thus in New York State and elsewhere, Jewish merchants who observe Saturday as their day of rest have been consistently held to be in violation of the Sabbath law and have often been fined by the courts. Efforts to pass a bill exempting them from being penalized for their religious convictions by permitting them to keep their places of business open instead on Sunday, which, incidentally, would in no sense affect the general practice of Sunday rest in America, have proved unavailing. This was due to the clear-cut open opposition of organized religious groups, who should have been eager to encourage conscientious loyalty to religion by as many of their fellow citizens as possible. Here was an excellent opportunity for the more powerful churches to demonstrate that their avowed goal of a closer relationship between religion and the state would not impugn the rights of minority groups. The opportunity has thus far not been grasped.

In recent years the religious beliefs and ethical attitudes of special groups in the field of public morals have become a subject of warm controversy. One such instance came to light in New York City, where the Commissioner of Hospitals forbade a physician to administer contraceptive therapy to a Protestant patient where it seemed indicated on medical grounds.. There is no reason to doubt the truth of the assurances which were offered that no overt pressure was brought to bear on the Commissioner by the Catholic Church to issue his decision. But it is superficial in the extreme to view the incident purely in terms of pressure exerted or pressure not resisted.

The issue goes to the heart of the democratic process. The Catholic Church, like any other religious denomination, has a right, which it may legitimately construe as a duty, to urge its standards of ethical behavior, not only upon its members, but upon all men. Morality is a categorical imperative which by its nature is binding upon all men. The Catholic Church is therefore eminently within its rights in maintaining that birth control is forbidden and in preaching this doctrine to all and sundry. But its rights are exactly of the same degree and should be governed by the same canons of procedure as is the case with those who disagree with the Church, and regard birth control as permissible or even as an ethical obligation under conditions which are far from rare in the contemporary world.

Another case in point is afforded by the practice or threat of boycott involving books, plays, or motion pictures which one religious group or another regards as objectionable on dogmatic, historical, or moral grounds. Religious leaders have a right and a duty to express their views on the culture of the day and even to urge their communicants to avoid what they regard as injurious to faith and morals. One may, of course, be permitted the hope that the canons of judgment employed will be wise and enlightened, but that is the concern of the particular church or sect which is involved. The total community becomes affected when a group imposes a boycott directed not against the offending object, but against the bookseller or theater owner who is threatened with economic ruin unless he withdraws the book from circulation or the play from production. As a result, the entire community is deprived of access to the controversial book or play. Thus the freedom of dissent, which is the heartbeat of democracy, is curtailed, and the standards of a minority are imposed upon the majority.

By far the more significant and acute of these tension areas in the field of church and state in the United States is the issue of religion in education. Because of its importance and complexity, this theme cannot be treated here.[4] But the basic conclusions that emerge on the role of religion in a free society are clear.

As any religious group gains in numbers, power, and prestige, its moral obligation to respect the democratic process becomes all the more compelling. It must be certain that in seeking to achieve its ends it is using persuasion and not pressure as its instrument.

Unless and until such free consent is achieved, all religious groups will do well to recall a truth which in the last analysis is their basic *raison d'être*—religion has an area of concern which is far

---

4   For a full discussion of this problem from various points of view, see the papers in *Religion and the Schools,* issued by the Center for the Study of Democratic Institutions. The views of the present writer are set forth in his essay "Education for a Nation of Na-

wider than the field of operation of government. In the first instance, religion is concerned with the motives and attitudes of men, what the Talmud calls *devarim hamesurim lalebh,* "matters handed over to the heart." The state necessarily can deal only with deeds, with acts adjudged beneficial or harmful to individuals or to society. Moreover, even in the area of actions, there are inherent limitations on the power of the state to enforce morality, because these are acts which the state organs are too gross to apprehend and control. The state may punish a man for beating his father; it cannot compel him to honor him. It may make public libel subject to penalty; it cannot begin to cope with private gossip and talebearing. The Talmud recognized that morality makes demands far broader than those of legal jurisprudence by establishing such categories as "free from punishment, but forbidden" or "free from punishment by human agency, but subject to divine penalty." The TV scandal of payola offered a lurid demonstration that not all that is immoral is illegal. The function of religion is to train men to live by a standard of love and justice which is beyond the power of the state to enforce.

There can be no freedom for religion unless there be freedom from religion, no liberty for any religion unless there be liberty for all religions. The stability of society, the vitality of religion, and the freedom of the human spirit all flourish best in the atmosphere of religious liberty and equality which has been created by the unique American pattern of the separation of church and state.

It is perhaps natural for leaders and devotees of religion, beset by many obstacles in their work, to be tempted to invoke the authority and power of the state to win an easy victory for their cause. The history of totalitarianism in all its colors—red, black, and brown— should help them to resist the temptation and to recall the great truth that there is no shortcut on the highway to the New Jerusalem.

In the face of mounting tensions noticeable in church-state relationships, one may wonder whether rational discussion will play a significant part in the resolution of these problems, or whether, as is so often the case elsewhere, the weight of power and the machinations of politics will not prove the decisive factors.

Yet the voice of tradition and experience is not altogether without influence in molding man's future. All the evidence suggests that the United States has been on the right path during the past century and three-quarters of its history in holding fast to the separation of

tions," *ibid.,* pp. 5–34. For the general background see the author's book, *The Root and the Branch—* *Judaism and the Free Society* (University of Chicago Press, 1962).

church and state. On this course it should persevere in the future, both for the sake of the stability of society and the vitality of religion. Moreover, America will thus be making a significant contribution to the establishment of peace, justice, and freedom as the inalienable right of all men and nations, who are citizens of the world and brothers under God.

Israel

A PILOT PROJECT FOR TOTAL DEVELOPMENT OF WATER RESOURCES

WALTER CLAY LOWDERMILK

*

Introduction: Growing Needs for Food and Water

THE WORLD'S INCREASING HUNGER for food and thirst for water must alert all nations, large and small, to face up to the urgent problems of the on-rushing "global population explosion." Peoples of the world find it difficult to believe their own population statistics. Practically all nations are doubling their numbers in 25–40 years. The human hordes who must exist, in the relatively near future, on the resources of this planet, climb to astronomical numbers as they multiply in geometric ratio. California and certain other states expect to double their numbers in fifteen years. The United States is predicted to double its population of 185 million to 370 million by the end of the century. Demographers predict the world population of 3 billion today will reach 6 to 7 billion by the year 2000, only 38 years hence. These are not abstract figures, but actual human beings who must have food, clothing, housing, jobs, education, and many services.

Freedom from hunger is a prerequisite to the enjoyment of other freedoms. Efforts to improve living standards may be drowned in this tidal wave of hungry people. This worldwide population explosion is due to a decline in death rates, resulting from increased use of medicine to cure and prevent disease, along with measures of sanitation, rather than to a new surge in birth rates. An example is the postwar antimalarial campaign in Ceylon by the World Health Organization of the United Nations which caused population to increase 40 percent in 13 years (1946–1959). Birth rates changed little, but death rates dropped 55 percent. When the French went into Morocco and introduced medicines and drained pestilential swamps, the native population doubled in 20 years. When we visited Palestine in 1939, the

Arab population was afflicted with many diseases. Today, the primitive birth rate continues, but ultramodern medical facilities of Israel have so reduced death rates among the 240,000 Arabs of the country that the United Nations recently reported that the Arabs of Israel have the highest rate of increase of any single group in the world today.

This global population explosion is the most challenging and serious problem facing leaders today. How can they initiate and carry out plans, now, to supply adequate food and obtain water supplies for domestic, industrial, and agricultural uses, when the earth's resources are taxed by a population two or three times as great as they now inadequately support. The Food and Agriculture Organization of the United Nations states that today two-thirds of mankind is underfed, poorly clothed, and inadequately housed, and has launched a worldwide campaign for Freedom from Hunger.

For years, this writer has been saying that "Civilization is running a race with famine and the outcome is in doubt." The doubt increases as 50 million additional hungry people are added each year, while food production lags behind population increase except in a few nations advanced in science and technology. We believe that the resources of this world are sufficient to support, with a higher standard of living, at least double the present numbers, if all nations would promptly change from traditional ways to full development of all resources with modern methods of scientific farming, drainage, and irrigation as Israel has demonstrated in the past few years. But lesser developed or financially poor, overcrowded countries, which are increasing in numbers most rapidly, either resist this changeover or cannot finance it. As one African minister said to me in Nigeria, "Hunger already done catch us."

Israel, out of necessity and in her own interests, has been hammering out on the anvils of adversity solutions to problems that two-thirds of mankind must face, sooner or later. These solutions are important to all emerging new nations and lesser developed countries, seeking to industrialize their subsistence agrarian economies. Increasing numbers of officials and students from other lands now come to Israel to study and ask Israel's help to put in corresponding works in their own countries. Israel is valiantly carrying out her own Point Four Program as experts by the hundred are called for by less developed Afro-Asian countries, at the same time continuing to make progress along many lines of development and research in Israel.

Israel, since Statehood, has become a pilot demonstration project of how a poor country can more than double its population in a decade, and yet increase food production to keep pace with its increasing numbers. After the first two or three desperate years of drought and influx of destitute immigrants, Israel not only grew its own food, fibers and fats, but exported surpluses to buy grains and meats. By 1957 Israel was overproducing in certain agricultural products so that surplus vegetables were fed to milk cows.

Israel has demonstrated how a people, with vision, courage, determination, and hard work, can use modern scientific methods of production, along with irrigation and full use with conservation of its lands and waters, to support a very rapid increase in population. This miracle of production was achieved on long-neglected, eroded lands, rocky hills, and scanty water resources—a veritable man-made desert.

Global Needs for Water—Dwindling Supplies and Soaring Demands

Water has been called the "key" resource in nature's storehouse. It unlocks the productivity of soils to produce all manner of growing things on earth, and also enables industry to supply man's physical needs and wants. Moreover, water is man's oldest friend and his most valuable servant, or may be a destructive foe. With it man lives, without it he dies. For water, wars have been waged, treaties signed, boundary lines set, and civilizations have developed with water or died when water supplies failed.

Early peoples settled near rivers or springs, later dug wells or made cisterns and fought for their possession and use. Canals were dug in alluvial valleys and by Roman times, great aqueducts were built to conduct water from the hills to distant cities.

An even greater fight for water is only beginning. Towns, cities, counties, states and nations will seek to get and to hold water supplies for themselves at all costs. Human welfare and the permanent economic development of an area are dependent on the abundance or degree of control and development of water resources. Southern California is an example of the extent and expense to which a region will go to provide water supplies for present and future expansion. When local supplies became insufficient, the Owen's Aqueduct was built, then the Colorado Aqueduct and now in the Feather River Project, water in the north will be conducted hundreds of miles to the thirsty southlands. For the major facilities, a Bond Issue of 1¾ billion dollars was voted by the people of California. The total project will cost its citizens much more. These are modern counterparts of the ancient Greek and Roman aqueducts that made their civilizations flourish.

Water in Our Modern Civilization

Demands for increasing water requirements for the immediate future rise with expected rapid growth in population as well as with the spread of rising standards of living for all groups in modern societies. What formerly were luxuries for the few are now considered necessities for the many—autos, television, radios, trains, buses, airplane travel, all kinds of household appliances, new materials, comforts of life in air conditioning, automatic dishwashers and home laundries, and an infinite variety of other things enjoyed in modern life.

Tremendous amounts of water are required for industries to produce from raw materials the above-mentioned benefits into useful products; for example, the requirements in water for growing one bushel of wheat are 6,570 gallons; for canning one ton of apricots 5,300 gallons; for manufacturing a ton of dry pulpwood 73,000 gallons; to produce our 5-pound Sunday newspaper, 150 gallons of water. For refining a barrel of petroleum, 18 barrels of water. (It takes 18 times as much water to run our cars as gasoline.) To manufacture a ton of fabricated steel requires 65,000 gallons of water; processing of one yard of woolen cloth, 510 gallons; for making a ton of viscose rayon, 200,000 gallons. (As reported by the United Nations in "Water for Industrial Uses," 1958) Reclamation and reuse of water for industries may in some cases reduce these amounts.

The United States now uses 290 billion gallons of water a day. This is expected to double between 1970–1980 by which time we will require 600 billion gallons each day, for making these good things we enjoy in our high standard of living. These are staggering figures. But we will pay what is necessary to have this water for our way of life, just as we do not quibble over expenditures for national defense when the life of the nation is at stake.

As lesser developed nations of the world seek to industrialize, their water needs will increase proportionally. Water development will soon become a universal problem, especially in drier regions of scarce supply.

Israel as a Demonstration for Full Development of Water Resources

Israel is a natural laboratory in which to inaugurate and demonstrate how total development of water resources can be achieved. Necessity demands that Israel use, and where possible reuse, every gallon of her scarce water potentialities. Israel's limited 7,815 square miles of land surface is a mosaic of many types of soils and land use, of temperature and rainfall. It is roughly 265 miles long and 12 to 70 miles wide. It contains three lakes. The former Lake Huleh and swamp, 230 feet above sea level has been largely drained and transformed into a small, well watered "Garden of Eden" capable of supporting some 100,000 people. The tropical valley of the Sea of Galilee is 680 feet below sea level and is irrigated by Jordan River waters. Sixty-five miles farther south is the Dead Sea, 1,290 feet below sea level and an inexhaustible mine of chemicals and minerals. More than half of Israel's territory is true or near desert.

Climatically, Israel is much like Southern California. Rains and often floods come in winter, and summers are long and dry. As in California, rainwater, as "blessings from Heaven" is more valuable to the country than gold. In Israel precipitation in the north averages 42 inches, 26 inches at Jerusalem, ranging down to 2 inches (when it rains) at Eilat on the Red Sea—Israel's back door to the Orient.

Fortunately for Israel, one geologic feature operates in favor of the conservation of rainfall; porous limestone of the landscape absorbs a high percentage of the rain and distributes water widely from the regions of heaviest rainfall through labyrinthine aquifers underground. The total discharge from springs exceeds the flow of the Jordan. A single great spring near the foothills of Judea gives rise to the Yarkon River. Another important source of moisture is heavy summer dew, which helps to grow crops in the uplands.

For the first time in history, the world is waiting for a demonstration of an ecological and a righteous relationship between Man and Nature, to show how he can maintain his increasing numbers on the limited lands and waters he controls, with the greatest possible development and satisfaction, while conserving natural resources. The Israelis have shown a love of the land that makes geology more than rocks, soil, and water; biology more than plants and animals; soils more than dirt. Rather, these are looked upon as the raw materials for building the foundation and social structure of the nation. They are to be developed, conserved, and maintained for present and future generations. To demonstrate the control of destructive forces in nature and bring land and water management into harmony with natural laws make a good basis for nations and international relations in building a better and saner world.

Israel is a natural laboratory to demonstrate, for the new nations, the ecological approach—that is, "How does man live to the greatest advantage with and in his natural environment, and maintain and improve physical and biological resources from generation to generation?" "How can he keep a thriving balance and working relationship between man and nature?"

This approach includes an inventory of the nation's lands and waters to determine its potentialities in agriculture, nutrition, forestry, and range management; various problems of flood control, impounding and storage of water in dams and underground water aquifers; various examples of methods of irrigation; plant and livestock improvement; soil maintenance and improvement; research in all land phases of the hydrologic cycle—studies of the raindrop as it strikes the earth; erosion in all its destructive forces, infiltration rates under various crops; movement of moisture in soils, problems of drainage of various types; importance of dew in Israel for summer crops and the like.

All this mass of accumulating data, with improved measures of all kinds, needs to be assembled and evaluated and made available to Israel farmers and also to students from other arid and semiarid regions of the world. This will be for Israel a great international contribution to knowledge. When all nations cooperate together and work with forces of nature for the benefit and welfare of peoples, they speak a common language which all understand. Political differences become of less importance.

Most of such studies are well under way in Israel. To begin with, Israel completed in 1953 one of the most thorough land inventories of its kind in the world. This furnished a sure foundation for formulating land-use policy and for the immense task of land reclamation and water development that has followed. This inventory showed that, given adequate water supply, about 40 percent of the country can be made suitable for irrigation by one of several methods: about 15 percent for orchard, vineyard, pasture, and other uses that will keep a permanent plant cover on the soil; 20 percent for natural pasture without irrigation, and 25 percent for forests, parks, and wasteland.

Outside the area of detailed survey, an extensive reconnaissance in the Negev has projected a program for range development and for cultivation of forage crops in those areas where the scant winter runoff can be diverted and spread over the valley floors or impounded, later to support irrigation. A major feature of the land inventory was the classification of lands according to their relative exposure to erosion by wind and water. The Soil Conservation Service uses this inventory in planning its measures to preserve the best soils for cultivation and limit "urban sprawl" to sand dunes for cities along the coast and rocky lands elsewhere. Ultimately, they plan to reclaim some areas to forests or range land, now described as unusable.

The Hydrologic Cycle

Man's manipulation of the forces of nature to control running water, and to conserve and manage it beneficially for productive uses, is much like a great chess game. Nature has made her moves; man takes staps to direct and channel these forces in accordance with his plans of control and then waits to see what responses nature makes. Then man makes the next move to take advantage of natural responses and so on until destructive forces of floods and erosion are checkmated and productive forces win. This is a fascinating game that I have watched in Isreal and certain other parts of the world.

Supplies of initially pure waters that come in the rain and snow and other condensions are the beginning of the land phase of the Hydrologic Cycle, one of the most dynamic of earth's processes. It was recognized long ago as recorded in Ecclesiastes 1:7:

> "All the rivers run into the sea,
>   Yet the sea is not full;
>   Unto the place whither the rivers go,
>   Thither they go again."

This Hydrologic Cycle was discovered again in the middle of the last century, and has become the basis of the Science of Hydrology. This has to do with the source, distribution, amounts and intensities, with disposal and work of waters on the land. The ocean as mother of waters is the source of rain on the land. "Rivers run into the sea, Yet the sea is not full." Waters of the ocean are evaporated by energy of the sun, and are blown inland and rain down on the land, and their return in rivers to the sea makes up the major Hydrologic Cycle. This is the greatest of all distillation processes. In a sense, the sun acts as a huge pump circulating water in a closed circuit—the Hydrologic Cycle.

On a worldwide basis, it is estimated that about 22.2 percent of rainfall on the land returns in the flow of rivers. The difference is accounted for by the existence of inland evaporation-precipitation subcycles and by evaporated moisture from the land being blown out to sea. It is the circulation of this small part of the earth's waters, on uplifted blocks of land, that has been the chief dynamic agency in molding the face of the earth.

For the past forty years, I have been especially interested in how peoples have failed or have succeeded in working out lasting adjustments to the dynamics of waters on lands that sustain them. Some of these experiments—as the making of artificial rainstorms, to duplicate actual storms in duration and intensity, to study erosion, infiltration, runoff and measures to prevent soil loss and damage by erosion —are now also being carried out in Israel.

In the Agricultural Engineering Building soon to be built at Technion, Israel's Institute of Technology on Mt. Carmel, Haifa, the Sam Fryer Tower will be used for studies of the dynamics of the raindrop. In heavy storms, raindrops average nearly a quarter inch in diameter. Such a drop falls with a terminal velocity of about 30 feet a second and strikes soft earth like a projectile and explodes in rain splash. Raindrops tear soil aggregates apart and put fine soil particles in suspension in unabsorbed storm water on fields. Measurements have disclosed that this churning action of raindrops may put into suspension soil particles to 20 percent and more by weight. The storm waters carry away the richest part of the soil off fields into floodwaters and both soil and water are lost to the land.

The differences of infiltration of rain are startling. Storm runoff from cultivated but bare land was measured up to 66 percent of rain of heavy storms and less than 1 percent from plots otherwise the same but covered with grass or forest, in scientific experiments. Differences in erosion were even more striking. From plots bare of vegetation, soil was eroded at a rate that would remove the seven inches of productive topsoil in 15–20 years, but from grass-covered plots, it would take 96,000 years to remove the seven important inches of topsoil. What happens to the soil surface has a far-reaching effect upon the fate of the raindrop and on the soil resource and permanence of agriculture, and the people dependent on it.

When I went to Israel to assist in the beginning of Soil Conservation work in 1951, few citizens seemed to understand soil erosion, its destructive processes, and what it is capable of doing to the land. They did not realize that soil erosion from annual floods was the villain that had washed off three feet and more of soil from the hills of Galilee and Judea and left protruding skeletonlike rocks of the limestone hills, leaving only soil between rocks and in crevasses. Fortunately roots of planted trees seek out these soil pockets and grow well even today. In a short time, the people of Israel have become soil- and water-conservation-conscious. Now, no development loans are granted for new orchards or plantations unless farmers put in soil- and water-conservation measures as prescribed by the Israel Soil Conservation Service.

It is well for Israel and other nations to take a new look at flood-waters, as well as to salt-water conversion. Newspapers generally deplore floods and their resulting inconvenience and damage. However, this damage occurs usually because lands of the country are not yet prepared to receive these "blessings" of the rain that falls. Actually, floodwaters are great supplies of fresh water available for control, storage, and supplemental supplies. While these waters have great potentialities for destruction, they also are a tremendous asset to the nation when measures are adequate to control and conserve them.

Assets of water, like financial resources, must be kept in balance. In the long run, as much of this liquid asset must be returned by nature or by man as is taken out of underground water aquifers; otherwise a deficit is created. Works of recharge and withdrawals for beneficial use make for high-level economy. Thus maximum utilization of water requires a perpetual inventory of how much has been withdrawn from underground aquifers or surface water storage basins in dry seasons and this amount must be replaced through various measures so as to maintain a balance between supply and demand. This can be done by water spreading—recharging of wells directly during winter rains, impounding of water in reservoirs, and in preparation of farmland for maximum infiltration. When a farmer used a chisel plow eight inches in depth, maximum infiltration increased 275 to 400 percent. Then when he plowed under his lush clover crop, soil absorbed water 10 to 16 times faster, wetting the soil 40 inches in two hours. As much as a fourth of all rain or snow water may get away and be lost, giving us extremes of droughts or floods. This 25 percent that gets away produces floods that carry away vital soil elements. We can hold that 25 percent to an orderly movement into the ground, down into aquifers, reviving old springs, producing clear and constant streams and storage of ground and surface water supplies for pumping. Overall water resources are large. The problem is that they are variable in amount, time and place, and quality.

Man, as yet, can do little about how much rain falls on the land, although cloud seeding continues to be investigated, but he can do an enormous amount to make better use of rains that fall.

This includes building up organic matter to increase the water-holding capacity of the soil and the use of crop litter to absorb the energy and reduce the splash erosion of the raindrop. Contour plowing and the planting of crops in strips on the contour provide another line of defense. These usually suffice against the hazards of moderate storms. Where heavy downpours occur once or more in a rainy season to overtax the first two lines of defense, more elaborate and costly measures must be designed and laid out by soil conservation engineers. Slopes must be broken by broad-base terraces to pick up and slow down storm runoff to nonerosive velocities and the terraces must be interconnected by waterways to keep the accumulated water from cutting gullies through fields. Storm waters are then available for storage in surface ponds and reservoirs or to recharge groundwaters. This requires accurate engineering in design, construction, and maintenance for running waters do not forgive a mistake or an oversight.

In this respect, research in and development of water supplies, irrigation, and drainage constitute the most significant achievement of the new nation of Israel and differentiate its agriculture most sharply from that which generally prevails in less developed countries. Drainage of the Huleh swamps alone saved enough water from evaporation losses to irrigate 17,000 to 25,000 acres of new lands, depending on the rainfall of the district to which these waters are delivered. Former agriculture in Palestine was limited to vagaries of rainfall and droughts; irrigation was confined to small areas that could be fed by gravity from perennial springs; large areas were pestilential swamps.

In the first years of statehood, Israel quadrupled the acreage under irrigation and this achievement made possible the absorption of the great influx of immigrants. Irrigation has increased yields per acre manyfold over those grown by dry farming under the same conditions. Moreover, this irrigation assures dependable yields from year to year, regardless of vagaries of rainfall. Also dry farming as carried out in Israel under modern techniques of soil and moisture conservation has increased yields manyfold over the traditional dry farming of the Arabs.

Most of the water in Israel used for irrigation comes from wells. It has been established that movable sprinkling systems are best suited to soils and local topography. Rougher, stony lands are not suited for leveling and sandy soils are not adapted to furrow or border irrigation from ditches. The grid of pumps and pipes delivers water under pressure but at low rates of flow. The high investment in pumps and piping has been more than offset by intensive year-round cultivation made possible by sprinkler irrigation. Israel adds additional irrigated lands yearly and the prospect is that this will continue until the limit of water supply is reached.

Israel is carrying on important field research in achieving the most efficient use of water. In the northern Negev, it has been found that about six inches of irrigation water, applied just before the winter rains to soak the soil to its water-holding capacity down to a depth of about four feet or more, will make the equivalent of twenty inches of rainfall, sufficient for good yields of winter crops of grain. Measures to divert and spread storm waters over lands suitable for pasture are bringing excellent results. Herds of beef and dairy cattle are beginning to multiply on restored range lands.

Ultimately, the expansion of agriculture in Israel is limited by the availability of water, for Israel, like California, has more good land suitable for irrigation than waters to irrigate them. The efficient Israel Water Planning Agency is seeking to double the 1956 water supply by 1966. A central feature of the plan derives from a proposal the writer made in 1944 in *Palestine, Land of Promise*. That proposal called for development of all possible groundwaters and the diversion of the upper Jordan waters within Israel to dry lands in the south. Also at that time, it called for the waters of the Yarmuk River to be diverted to the eastern side of the Jordan Valley for irrigation of a promising subtropical region in Transjordan.

In order to replace the flow of these rivers into the Dead Sea, salt water was to be brought in from the Mediterranean Sea and dropped 1290 feet through hydroelectric plants. This would produce electric power as well as maintain the level of the Dead Sea for extraction of its vast storehouse of minerals. All parts of the plan that do not require the collaboration of the adjoining Arab States are either completed or are now being carried out by the Israel government. The 66-inch and 72-inch pipelines are completed and in use. The 108-inch master line from the upper Jordan will be completed in 1963 and become the central stem of a grid that will supply Israel with the maximum water supplies, picked up from streams, springs, dams, floodwaters, and reservoirs.

Beyond this major undertaking, the country is conserving for use and reuse such minor flows of water as are represented by the sewage of its cities and the runoff of intermittent streams along the coast. In the Negev, where rainfall is less than 8 inches, Israel is adopting the methods of the ancient Nabataeans to impound and spread waters of flash floods for irrigation of forage crops.

This semiarid land of Israel, poorly endowed with water supplies, will, in a few years at most, have all possible sweet water developed for full use. The hopes of many peoples, including Israel, are turning to the oceans and seas as an unlimited source of water to meet the oncoming requirements of exploding populations. Israel's scientists are now preparing to tap the seawaters that lap her shores along the west and at Eilat on the Red Sea, and convert them into fresh waters. Seawaters are 96½ percent pure water. The problem and challenge to scientists and technologists everywhere is to extract this 3½ percent of dissolved solids at low costs and provide new streams and rivers of fresh waters from the abundance of the seas.

Two pilot plants, each with an output of 250,000 gallons per day, are soon to be tested for conversion of salt water into fresh. Initial costs are as yet too great to use such waters for agriculture, but regardless of cost, conversion of salt water is already a necessity for Eilat, the expanding seaport on the Red Sea, where natural supplies have been exhausted for many miles around. Success of Israel's desalinization plants would be a major victory for Israel and provide a demonstration for other arid lands.

In Israel's Negev Desert, there are considerable quantities of brackish water, where dissolved solids are usually much less than in seawater, but still not usable for domestic purposes or for growing crops. Israel has already designed and marketed a small unit for domestic purposes, reasonable in price, that converts brackish water into drinking water and other household uses on a small scale. Israel hopes to enlarge this process into economic units to convert brackish water on a large scale. We are in a technological age when men discover new ways to make lands habitable and create a better life for themselves and for others who are willing to pay the price for progress.

There are no new continents to explore and to exploit. The frontiers of today are the lands underfoot and the waters we can bring to them. Israel is working hard to make full use, with conservation of all lands and waters of her small country, to make a better way of life for her own people and is willing to share with others the results of her labors.

When we thus learn to live with the earth and cooperate with peoples around us, we may yet live to see a tomorrow when nations "shall beat their swords into plowshares, And their spears into pruning-hooks; Nations shall not lift up sword against nation, Neither shall they learn war any more. But they shall sit every man under his vine and under his fig-tree; And none shall make them afraid." (Micah 4:3-4).

The Oldest Known Synagogue Record Book of Continental North America 1720-1721

JACOB R. MARCUS

*

THE FIRST JEWISH RELIGIOUS SERVICE in North America was probably held during the High Holydays in September, 1654, in the Dutch town of New Amsterdam. A congregation was speedily organized—certainly no later than 1655—but with the decline of the Jewish community in the 1660's the congregation faded away. Within a decade or less, however, a reorganization was effected, although it was not, in all probability, until the 1690's that the new synagogal group had rented quarters of its own. By the turn of the century this Spanish and Portuguese congregation was securely established.[1]

In 1706 a new constitution was prepared—there certainly had been older ones, for Colonial Jewish congregations were constantly rising and falling and writing or modifying their organic statutes.[2] The name of the congregation in 1706—if it had one—was probably Shearith Jacob, the Remnant of Jacob. The phrase is Biblical, of course, and is taken from Micah 5:6–7:

> And the remnant of Jacob shall be in the midst of many
>   peoples,
> As dew from the Lord, as showers upon the grass. . . .
> And the remnant of Jacob shall be among the nations,
>   in the midst of many peoples,
> As a lion among the beasts of the forest.

Certainly, no later than 1720–1721, the congregation was known as

1   David de Sola Pool, *An Old Faith in the New World* . . . pp. 8 ff., 34 ff.; *American Jewish Archives (AJA)*, VII, 56; *Publications of the American Jewish Historical Society (PAJHS)*, XVIII, pp. 1 ff.

2   *PAJHS*, XXI, pp. 1 ff.

the Remnant of Jacob (*shearith yaakob*).[3] By 1728, however, when a new constitution was promulgated, the congregation referred to itself also as the Remnant of Israel (*shearith yisrael*), as it looked forward to the messianic promise of Micah 2:12: "I will surely gather the remnant of Israel."[4] Unfortunately, the constitution of 1706 has not survived; prior to the discovery of the Simson ledger, the earliest known congregational records were the minute books beginning with the year 1728. The initial entry in these minute books is the 1728 constitution, a revision of that of 1706.[5]

Among the members of the community in the first decade of the century was a man who might well have participated in preparing the lost constitution of 1706.[6] This was Nathan Simson, a German-born merchant shipper. In 1720 he was probably the *parnas*, or president, and had as such the duty of keeping the synagogue's financial accounts. Normally the *gabbai* (collector), or treasurer, was responsible for the finances of a congregation, but it is very likely that in a small Jewish group, such as the one in New York, the financial records, too, were the province of the all-powerful *parnas*. Although the word *gabbai* does occur in the Shearith Israel minute book there is no evidence that a *gabbai* functioned as such until after the Revolution of 1775–1783.[7] Within a year after his term of office had expired, Simson returned to England (1722), whence he had originally emigrated and where no doubt he had anglicized his Hebrew name of *shimshon* ("Samson") to Simson or Simpson. When he sailed back to London, he took his papers with him and inadvertently included the congregational financial records for 1720–1721 (5481). Long after his death in 1725, the papers of this childless man were deposited in the Public Record Office in London, where they are found in category 258, C. 104/13–14. Through the good offices of Daniel J. Cohen, Director of Jerusalem's Jewish Historical General Archives, the commercial papers were brought to the attention of the American Jewish Archives and were carefully examined by me. There I came across the congregational record and recognized immediately that Simson, like many of his predecessors and successors, had retained them instead of sur-

3   J. M. Corcos, *A Synopsis of the History of the Jews of Curaçao* . . . , p. 21. Data cited but not documented are taken from the unpaged Simson synagogal account book to be described below. Simson, in 1720–1721, called the congregation the Remnant of Jacob, *shearith yaakob*.

4   *PAJHS*, XXI, 3. Apparently, in 1728–1729, the congregation sometimes referred to itself as Shearith Israel and sometimes called itself Shearith Jacob. Were there two congregations then? This is very improbable.

5   These, the oldest records of the congregation hitherto known, were published in Vol. XXI of the *PAJHS*.

rendering them to the new *parnas*. And we are indeed very thankful that he did, for otherwise the account book, too, would probably have gone the way of all its precursors in Shearith Israel. None of them are extant—as far as is now known. The Simson record book enables us to push back the history of the congregation in some detail for at least eight years.[8]

This Simson ledger covers approximately the Jewish year 5481. Actually it includes the preceding month, for it began September 4, 1720, and went to September 10, 1721, stopping about twelve days before the New Year of 5482 (1721–1722). When finally posted, it was presumably to have been submitted by Simson to his successor, Jacob Franks.

Simson was very systematic in all that he did—he was a successful merchant—and his methodical approach is evident in this sixteen-page record. He identified the book by affixing to its cover a Yiddish superscription which, unfortunately, has been worn away by time. Enough has been left, however, to indicate that he was describing his ledger as the annual record of the congregational accounts. He followed the Yiddish statement with the English: "New York, September the 10, 1721." Then came, in beautifully printed Hebrew square characters, the proud legend: "I, Nathan ben Moses Samson, of blessed memory, of Bonn in the Rhine River Country." Thus he started off with three languages! All Jewish merchants of that day were at least bilingual; many were polylingual. Simson was a German who had lived in Holland and England for years; he was consequently at home in German, Yiddish, Dutch, English, and, very probably, Hebrew. His nephew, Joseph Simson, whom he had already brought to America on a trip back from London in 1718, was reputed to be a Hebraist of unusual capacity.[9]

Following the title or cover page, Simson proceeded to post the financial record of every member of the congregation—men, of course —with the debits entered on the left side and the credits on the right side. The entries of debts still owed to the congregation from the administration of the preceding president were noted in Portuguese,

6 Simson was in New York by 1703, probably even earlier. Public Record Office, London, 258, C. 104/13, p. 68a, *AJA* pagination.

7 The term *gabbai* in *PAJHS*, XXI, 30, seems to be a synonym for *parnas*. See also *PAJHS*, XXI, 142.

8 Joseph R. Rosenbloom, *A Biographical Dictionary of Early American Jews*, . . . (*BDEAJ*), under "Simson, Nathan"; *Anglo-Jewish Notabilities*, p. 217; *PAJHS*, XXV, pp. 87 ff. The account book is in C. 104/13, pp. 261–276, *AJA* pagination.

9 *PAJHS*, XXV, 89–90; Rosenbloom, *BDEAJ*, under "Simson, Joseph"; F. B. Dexter, *The Literary Diary of Ezra Stiles*, . . . , II, 553; III, 3, 32.

and all the offerings of those called to the reading of the Torah were also indicated by the usual Portuguese phrases. The Ashkenazi-born Simson, in his religious life, was an assimilated Sephardi and quite possibly understood the Spanish-Portuguese language of the Sephardic Jews with whom he associated and did business in Holland, England, and the Americas, even though his Sephardic correspondents in the West Indies seem always to have addressed him in English. On the last three pages of the ledger, the *parnas* summarized all disbursements and receipts, with ample explanatory comments, and for that, too, we are deeply grateful. His accounts balance to the penny.

Undoubtedly, Simson, as the president, had a board of *ajuntos* to consult with him, but the actual congregational religious work was carried on, in 1720, by three paid officials: the *hazzan* or cantor, Moses Lopez Da Fonseca; the *shohet* and teacher, Benjamin Wolf (Benjamin Elias, Rebbe Wolf); and the sexton, Vallentine Compenall (Campanall).[10] These three men were still living in 1728, although Wolf-Elias was then on pension. The other two were still active in their posts.[11]

The congregation then occupied a rented house on Mill Street, now South William Street; the house was owned by Jan Harpendingh.[12] They also rented from a Mr. Cooper a house which was probably used as a school or turned over to one of the congregational employees. All these expenses had to be met out of congregational funds. Their chief source in 1720–1721 was the offerings made by the generous members who were called to the reading of the Torah. In addition, freewill gifts of money were made on the Day of Atonement and on the "Pilgrimage Festivals" of Passover, Pentecost, and Tabernacles. On the eve of the New Year a number of the members—primarily the wealthy—made substantial contributions to Shearith Jacob, and those New Year gifts probably served as the core of the budget for the ensuing year. There were no fixed dues.

In addition to the rentals for the *snoga* (synagogue) and the other building, the congregation had to pay the *hazzan* £50 a year (New York currency, not sterling), the *shohet* £15, and the *smass* (*shammash*—sexton) £2.20 a year. The latter certainly secured extras in the form of wood, rent, and, possibly, cash grants. Although all

10 Moses Lopez Da Fonseca appears in the Simson Papers no later than 1714 (C. 104/13B, p. 894, AJA pagination); Vallentine Compenall, no later than 1718 (C. 104/13C, p. 68, AJA pagination).
11 *PAJHS*, XXI, 4.
12 David de Sola Pool, *The Mill Street Synagogue (1730–1817)*, . . . , pp. 16 ff.
13 The commercial transactions of Hazzan Lopez Da Fonseca and of Vallentine Compenall are documented frequently in the Simson

three were professionals, there can be no question that they also engaged in business ventures on the side to augment their incomes.[13] The salaries alone amounted to about £67, while the rent—£9 for the synagogue and £6 for the congregation's house—brought the total to a fixed expenditure of at least £82. Additional requirements were the sums needed for pensioners and the local poor, of whom there were at least three individuals or families. They received cash, beef, wood, and rent money or housing. In 1720–1721, when Simson was *parnas*, Benjamin Jacobs was a beneficiary of the congregation, receiving a grant; in 1725, Simson, back in London, was shipping goods to Jacobs! By 1728, Jacobs had so improved his lot that he was able to make a modest contribution to the reorganized Jewish community of that year when it purchased additional cemetery ground.[14] Rapid social mobility was a characteristic of Colonial America. The charity petitioner of yesterday might well become a self-sustaining householder or even a substantial citizen a decade later.

Modest sums were required also to purchase beeswax and oil for the candles and lamps, for servants to clean the synagogue and the street fronting the house of worship, for replacing window glass, for carpentry, for repairing with red silk the frayed Torah mantle or the Torah band, and for *haroset*, a Passover "salad" which was supplied gratis to every member and client of the congregation. The bill for spades was mute testimony to the fact that Shearith Jacob buried its own dead. There was at that time probably no *hebrah*, or confraternity, to perform this last act of "lovingkindness" for those who had died.

Payments of sums vowed or promised were usually in the form of cash, casually and informally handed over to the *parnas*, the *hazzan*, or the teacher, who may have served as the collector. Collection, however, was traditionally the job of the sexton. On occasion, a debtor paid his offering to one of the pillars of the synagogue—a man like the famous merchant, Rodrigo Pacheco [15]—who would meet him and dun him. The debtor, needing credit from the merchant who sold him goods wholesale, would not dare to refuse payment of what he owed. Having no ready cash, some of the debtors, including even the wealthy merchants, paid by note, and it is not improbable that such

Papers. For the former as a businessman, see also Isaac S. Emmanuel, *Precious Stones of the Jews of Curaçao*, . . . , pp. 315 ff. Benjamin Wolf, the *shohet*, was also in business. (Cf. C. 104/13B, p. 840; C. 104/13, p. 348, *AJA* pagination.)

14 Simson Papers, C. 104/13, p. 17, *PAJHS*, XXI, 8.

15 For Pacheco, see Rosenbloom, *BDEAJ*, under "Pacheco, Benjamin Mendez."

notes circulated as a form of currency. Others paid in kind or services, giving beeswax for the Yom Kippur candles or sending in a Negro domestic to clean the synagogue.

According to Simson's records—and we may be sure that they were accurate—there were thirty-seven paying or active members. Of these, fifteen were of Sephardic origin and twenty-two were Ashkenazic. Other Jews in town were beneficiaries of the community's generosity and were not included as members. The fifteen Sephardim were Abraham (Haim) de Lucena, Abraham Pinto, Abraham Burgos —formerly of Barbados and Rhode Island—Jacob Louzada, Abraham Gomez Caseres, Benjamin (Rodrigo) Pacheco—the first of the Seixas clan in town—Daniel Nunes (Da Costa)—who may already have moved to New Jersey [16]—David Angell, Isaac De Medina, (Luis, Lewis) Moses Gomez, Mordecai Gomez, Moses Lopez Da Fonseca, Abraham Gutieres, Moses Cohen Peixotto, and Samuel Coronell.

The twenty-two Ashkenazim were Abraham bar Isaac (Abraham Isaacs), Asher Myer(s), Baruch Judah, Benjamin Wolf (Elias), Nathan Simson, Eliezer bar Judah, Jacob bar Higuell (Ezekiel), Isaac Cohen,[17] Jacob Franks, Isaac Jacobs—who may already have moved to Branford, Connecticut, where he was a shopkeeper and whaler [18]—Joseph Simson, Moses Levy, Moses Michell, Moses Seby (Hart), Nehemiah Marks, Solomoh Michaell, Simon Moses, Solomon ben Mehir (Myers), Baruch Levy, Michael Asher—who was probably then living in Boston—Isaac Polack—later of Rhode Island—and Joseph bar Isgak (Isaacs).

There was one woman listed not only as having promised a contribution, but also as having paid it, thus setting an example which some of the men might well have followed. She was Rachael Levy, very probably the widow of Samuel Levy, a distinguished merchant and Jewish communal leader.[19]

Aron Levy and Isaac Emanil (Emanuel) are mentioned in the records as donors. They were probably visitors from another town or village. Emanuel was then living in Freehold, New Jersey.[20] Among the residents of New York who were charity clients of Shearith Jacob were a Mr. Silva, one of the Campanalls, and Benjamin Jacobs. Sabee

16 *PAJHS*, XXXIII, 253.
17 If this was Isaac Cohen de Lara (Larah), then he was a Sephardi (*PAJHS*, II, 85).
18 Jacob R. Marcus, *American Jewry-Documents-Eighteenth Century* pp. 317–20.
19 David de Sola Pool, *Portraits*

Etched in Stone, ... pp. 459–460.
20 *PAJHS*, XXXV, 173.
21 For the biographies of most of the thirty-seven members listed above, see Rosenbloom, *BDEAJ*.
22 Pool, *Portraits*, . . . p. 455.
23 C. 104/13B, pp. 646, 990; C. 104/

(Tzebi) Barr Ahron, who was also on the social welfare rolls, may have been an itinerant.[21]

Of the above active members, the following were not on the rolls of the congregation in 1728 when the next extant record begins: Abraham Gutieres, Samuel Coronell, Baruch Levy, Solomoh Michaell, Isaac Cohen, David Angell, Jacob bar Ezekiel, Abraham Gomez Caseres, Simon Moses, Nehemiah Marks, Isaac Jacobs, and Moses Cohen Peixotto. The last-named died in 1721.[22] Solomoh Michaell (Michaels), who may have been a brother of Moses Michaell, is documented in the Simson Papers no later than 1714.[23] David Angell appears in the Simson Papers no later than 1718.[24] Gomez Caseres, Moses, Marks, Jacobs, and Peixotto are documented in other sources and thus were already known to have been in the colonies. As far as I know, there is as yet no record of the others in the North American provinces except in this Simson ledger. The fact that eleven of the above twelve—or at least most of them—were probably still alive in 1728, but were not members of Shearith Israel, is further proof of the physical mobility of the Jewish businessmen of the eighteenth century. They hastened to leave for other, presumably greener, pastures. Some may have fled after failing in business. It is difficult for us today to appreciate the terror that the fear of imprisonment for debt struck in the hearts of bankrupt shopkeepers or merchants.

The prevailing ritual was Sephardic (Spanish-Portuguese), and the Ashkenazim or "German" Jews, although already in the majority, accepted that ritual because by 1720 it had been the only one in use in North America for over sixty years. It was traditional and common practice in Jewish life for the newcomers to accept the liturgy of the host community.[25]

On the basis of about forty male "householders" in town—not all of whom, to be sure, were married—it is safe to assume that there were anywhere from 175 to 200 Jews in the synagogal community.[26]

The total of expenditures for the year amounted to over £128, leaving a balance of almost £4, which Simson dutifully turned over to the new *parnas*. About 30 percent of the members, eleven men, made no payment on their accounts during the entire year. Either

14, p. 156, *AJA* pagination.
24 C. 104/13C, p. 68, *AJA* pagination.
25 Mishnah, *Pesahim*, IV, 1.
26 This estimate is based on the assumption that about thirty of the forty "householders," or members, in town were married and that there were about six to a family, inclusive of men, women, children, and Jewish servants. The estimate of six to a family is derived from Evarts B. Greene and Virginia D. Harrington, *American Population Before the Federal Census of 1790*, p. xxiii.

they were poor, had moved away, had died, or were indifferent to the needs of the community. One of them, Nehemiah Marks, was later to become a convert, as was his brother Mordecai.[27] Of the thirty-seven active members, twenty-four were in arrears in their payments when the accounts were closed. All told, a sum of about £88 was due the congregation in present and remote debts.[28] One man, Joseph Isaacs, a butcher who was a militiaman in 1691 during King William's War, had apparently not paid anything on his debts since 1718. Abraham (Haim) da Lucena owed over £24. This former "minister of the Jewish nation" (1710), who was also a merchant-shipper, must have fallen on evil days. By 1723 he was already bankrupt and may have been in a debtors' prison.[29]

Six men contributed about £79 of the total budget of £132. They were Benjamin Pacheco, Moses Gomez, Mordecai Gomez—who was *parnas* in 1718—Moses Levy, Jacob Franks, and Nathan Simson. The first three were Sephardim; the latter three, Ashkenazim. Moses and Mordecai Gomez were father and son; Levy and Franks were father-in-law and son-in-law, and Simson was a kinsman of the Levys—although not always friendly![30] The Simson records show that the three Ashkenazim contributed approximately as much as the three Sephardim for the support of the congregation; and one is not venturing far in suggesting that these six men constituted the "power" group, that the Levy-Franks-Simson constellation, together with the Gomezes and Pacheco, ran the congregation. If one may judge by their contributions, six of the thirty-seven members were wealthy, or at least in the upper middle class; the remaining thirty-one were in the middle or lower middle class. As has been pointed out, there were three individuals or families on the charity lists, unless—and this is a possibility—the Silvas and one of the Campanall families were retired communal servants living on their pensions.

On the whole, there were no radical differences between the community of 1720 and that of 1728, but it is a step forward (or backward!) in uncovering the past to be able to make this statement with assurance.

27 Rosenbloom, *BDEAJ*, under "Marks, Mordecai." I cannot now put my hand on the data proving that Nehemiah, the brother of Mordecai, was also a convert. This Nehemiah is not to be confused with Nehemiah, the son of Mordecai, who was born and baptized a Christian.

28 If Simson's ambiguous note that £87.18.6 were due the congregation refers only to old and remote debts, then the amount due Shearith Jacob altogether was substantially larger than the total given above.

29 Simson Papers, C. 104/14, p. 674; Jacob R. Marcus, *Early American Jewry*, . . . , I, 45–50.

30 Abstracts of Wills ("Collections of the New-York Historical Society for the Year 1893"), II, 189; *PAJHS*, XXV, 87–89.

David's Reign in Hebron and the Conquest of Jerusalem

BENJAMIN MAZAR

*

BIBLICAL LITERATURE GIVES an impressive picture of the rise of Jerusalem to the rank of metropolis of the Israelite kingdom in the days of David and Solomon. Historiographic sources, biographical tales, prophetic writings, and religious songs all give evidence of the development of this city into the political and national-religious center of the People of Israel, and of its history after the conquest of the citadel of Zion by David. Topographic and archaeological research and written documents apart from the Bible merely help to shed indirect light on this chapter.

The general view, based on Biblical evidence, is that the rise of Jerusalem to be capital of the Israelite kingdom was due to the initiative and inspired daring of King David. It is regarded as an unprecedented venture, unequalled in the previous annals of the country. It was an attempt to build a capital that would be a metropolis and a spiritual center for an entire nation.[1]

On the face of it, the historical development that led to the centralization of both cultic and political life in Jerusalem during the period of the united Israelite kingdom can be traced with considerable certainty. According to the historiographic sources of the Bible, David took the Citadel of Zion, the capital of Jebusite Jerusalem, by storm: "And David dwelt in the stronghold, and called it the city of David" (II Samuel 5:9; I Chronicles 11:5–7). David centralized all administrative and military institutions within his new capital, and promptly commenced building operations. He brought the Ark of the Covenant to the City of David and built an altar on the threshing floor of Arawna the Jebusite on Mount Zion, that Jerusalem might become the hallowed center of religious aspiration and worship. Solomon, the

---

1 See in particular A. Alt, "Jerusalem's Aufstieg," *ZDMG* 79 (1925), pp. 1 ff = *Kleine Schriften* III (1959), pp. 243 ff.

A detailed bibliography of Biblical Jerusalem is given in my article "Jerusalem" in the *Biblical Encyclopaedia*, Vol. III (1958) and in an article by Fohrer, "Sion-Jerusalem," *TWNT* VII (1961).

son of David, followed in his father's footsteps. He extended and
fortified the city and set up the new acropolis on Mount Zion. This,
including as it did the Temple and the King's palace, firmly established Jerusalem as the national-religious center of Israel and the
symbol of the unity and singularity of the nation.

This schematic and simplified review of the history of Jerusalem
during Davidic and Solomonic times is not, however, sufficient. It
fails to consider the many problems involved in this historical development and the factors that led to the choice of this particular city
and the importance attached to it. First of all, it should be pointed out
that since ancient times a certain degree of importance had attached
to Jerusalem as one of the major cities in the country, owing to its
geographic position and natural facilities for fortification. The city
lies in the center of western Palestine at the crossing of two highways;
the road along the watershed from Shechem to Hebron and Beer-
sheba, and one of the roads leading from the coastal plain to Jericho
and Trans-Jordan. The ancient city, whose beginnings go back to the
Chalcolitic period, was built on the southeastern hill, south of Mount
Zion (the Temple Hill). This hill is surrounded on three sides by deep
valleys: the brook of Kidron in the east, the Valley of Hinnom in the
south, and "the Valley" (Haggay, the Tyropoeon Valley of Josephus
Flavius) in the west, being joined to Mount Zion by a subsidiary saddle only in the north. This long and narrow hill, at present known as
Ophel or the "City of David," was highly suitable for a well fortified
and protected settlement. Water was supplied by the Gihon spring on
its eastern slope. Archaeological evidence, though extremely sparse,
suggests that it was on the top and on the slopes of this hill that the
ancient walled city was concentrated throughout all periods until its
expansion by King Solomon.[2] At the same time it is reasonable to
assume that outside the walled city—the Citadel of Zion, which after

2   On the recent excavations of Kath-
     leen Kenyon: see her short article
     "Ancient   Jerusalem,"   *Discovery*,
     April 1962, pp. 18–22.
3   Particular mention should be made
     of the Dominus Flevit cave on the
     Mount of Olives, which contained
     a collection of about twelve hun-
     dred pottery (and imported ala-
     baster) vessels dating from the
     above period (see P. Lemaire,
     *Studii Biblici Franciscani, Liber
     Annuus V*, 1954–1955, pp. 261 ff.).
        One burial site of the fourteenth
     century B.C. discovered in Nahlat

Ahim in the new city contained 56
vessels, mostly Cypriote imports
(see R. Amiran, *Eretz Israel* VI,
1961, pp. 25 ff.). To this period belongs the water cistern in the
courtyard of the Mandatory High
Commissioner's Residence (near
Talpioth) which yielded various
finds (D. C. Baramki, *QDAP* IV,
1935, pp. 165 ff.).
4   There is no satisfactory explana-
     tion for the tradition preserved in
     Judges 1:8 according to which the
     Sons of Judah conquered Jerusalem
     during the period of settlement. Did

the conquest, became David's private estate and was called the City of David—ancient Jerusalem also included various open suburbs and outlying farmsteads. It should be noted that at a considerable distance from the *Ophel* hill burial sites have been discovered, rich in archaeological finds from the Middle and Late Bronze Period, and in particular from the sixteenth–fourteenth centuries, B.C.[3]

From the Bible and from epigraphic sources it is seen that at various periods Jerusalem constituted an important city-kingdom in the central part of western Palestine. This fact emerges clearly from the Egyptian execration texts of the nineteenth century and the beginning of the eighteenth century B.C. and the El-Amarna letters of the first half of the fourteenth century B.C., while in the Book of Joshua (Chap. 10) Adoni-Zedek, king of Jerusalem, is mentioned as the head of that league of Amorite kings in the southern part of the country which conducted the war against Joshua.[4] Biblical sources, moreover, mention a place of worship on Mount Zion outside the walls of the city—the threshing floor of Arawna the Jebusite where Solomon built his temple.[5]

This holy place on top of Mount Zion is linked up with traditions connected with Abraham, stressing the great importance attached to it by the people. It is hardly by chance that the Chronicler uses the name of Mount Moriah when designating the site of Solomon's Temple: "Then Solomon began to build the house of the Lord at Jerusalem in Mount Moriah, where the Lord appeared (אשר נראה) unto David his father, in the place that David had prepared in the threshing floor of Ornan the Jebusite" (II Chronicles 3:1). He thus identifies it as the site of Isaac's sacrifice, in the land of Moriah, where Abraham had built the altar that he called יהוה יראה ; "And Abraham called the name of that place Yahweh will see as it is said to this day: 'In the mount of the Lord it shall be seen'" (Genesis 22:14).[6] This in

---

the Jebusites take hold of Jerusalem after the Judeans had destroyed the Amorite city? If the view that the Jebusites came into Palestine with the influx of Hittites after the destruction of the Hittite Empire (c. 1200 B.C.) is correct, a hint as to the mixed population of Jerusalem may be found in Ezekiel: "Thine birth and thy nativity is of the land of Canaan; an Amorite was thy father, and thy mother was a Hittite" (Ezekiel 16:3). See also *AJSL* 49 (1932–1933), pp. 248 ff.

5 Regarding the threshing floor outside the wall as a site for religious ceremonies and public worship, see J. Gray, *PEQ* 1952, pp. 111 ff.; S. Smith *PEQ* 1953, pp. 42 ff. 'Arawnah or Ha'awarnah (with the definite article, II Sam. 24:16) is apparently no more than the title of the last Jebusite king (cf. verse 23); for details see B. Mazar, *Bulletin of the Israel Exploration Society* XIII (1947), pp. 112 ff.

6 See M. D. Cassuto, *Eretz Israel*, III (1954), pp. 15 ff.

turn, of course, links up with the tradition of Melchizedek king of Salem, "the priest of the most high God," who gave his blessing and divine inspiration to Abraham: "And blessed be God the most high God, who has delivered thine enemies into thy hand. And he [Abraham] gave him tithes of all" (Genesis 14:20)—a transparent hint as to the presence of a shrine.

Obviously the figure of Melchizedek played a central part in ancient Jerusalemite traditions, and the subsequent rulers regarded themselves as his legitimate heirs bearing the twofold title of king and priest. Evidence of this may be found in Psalm 110, attributed to David, which contains the strange passage: "The Lord hath sworn, and will not repent: 'Thou art a priest for ever after the order of Melchizedek,' " representing the Davidic ruler of Jerusalem as "priest for ever"—no doubt priest to the "most high God," which became the attribute of the God of Israel.

From all the above it may be concluded that the conversion of Jerusalem into the political and religious-national center of the kingdom of Israel had a sound basis in prevailing legends and traditions and the lofty status of the city as a site of government and ancient shrine. To this should be added various features acquired during the initial period of the Israelite kingdom. The abolition of the Jebusite pocket between the Mountains of Ephraim and Benjamin in the north and those of Judah in the south made a continuous area of Israelite settlement in the center of the country. By selecting Jerusalem as the capital of the Kingdom David removed all fears as to the proprietary settlement rights of the various Israelite families, the capital being located in a neutral place. It is significant to note that after the conquest of the Jebusite Citadel of Zion, David changed its name to City of David, thus turning it into his private estate and forging a firm link between the ruling dynasty and its permanent seat.[7] This close identification between the Davidic dynasty, the City of David, and the temple on Mount Zion was to affect the fate of the kingdom for many generations to come.

In considering the conquest of Jerusalem and its choice as the capital of the kingdom of Israel, attention must be paid in the first place to the historical developments at the beginning of David's reign. The Biblical sources tell us that after having dwelt in the country of the Philistines for one year and four months (I Samuel 17:17), that

---

7   We have several examples of this in the Ancient East, cf. Tukulti-Ninurta I, king of Assyria (1235–1198 B.C.) who transferred his cap-ital from Assur to his new city of Kar Tukulti Ninurta.

8   I suggest that Gath (the Philistine capital) should be identified with

is, mainly in Ziklag on the border of the kingdom of Gath, on the fringes of the Negev,[8] David left for Hebron on receiving the news of Saul's defeat and death on Mount Gilboa: "And the men of Judah came, and there they anointed David king over the house of Judah" (II Samuel 2:4).

At the same time Abner made Eshbaal, the son of Saul, king of the major part of the Israelite kingdom, transferring his capital from Gibeah, the capital of Saul, to Mahanayim on the Jabbok River in the land of Gilead. The splitting up of the kingdom of Saul gave rise to much bloodshed between Israel and Judah, which continued throughout the reign of Eshbaal, that is, for two years (II Samuel 2:20). It is quite clear that David's reign at Hebron was preceded by military and political activity, from the time he roamed the frontier and the Judean desert as a troop commander in the service of land and cattle owners, and particularly after he became the hired swordsman of Achish king of Gath, receiving from him Ziklag as his estate. Such military and political activity consisted in the first place in the organization of a band of 600 men, headed by his thirty "mighty men," obedient to his command. This was a sufficiently strong military force to deter the nomadic tribes in the Negev from penetrating the settled areas in southern Philistine and Judea. Even while still subject to the Philistine king David exploited his status and power to forge close ties with the elders of Judea and prepare the ground for his election as king (I Samuel 30:26–31); he gave shelter too to Saul's enemies. Hebron was chosen as his capital mainly because this city of the Judean hills had always been a religious center of peculiar holiness— the city of the ancient forefathers. It was also a political center—the major city of the Celebites, with whom David had contracted ties of league and marriage.

It should be noted that there is only scanty and scattered information in the Bible on the period of David's reign in Hebron, which lasted seven years and six months (II Samuel 5:5; I Chronicles 3:4); much is said, on the other hand, of his deeds and adventures before he was anointed King of Judah.

However, by an analysis of the sources and a combination of the various pieces of evidence available, conclusions may be drawn as to the development of events during this period, which so greatly affected the character of the united kingdom and harbored the seeds of its future success. Thus we learn among other things of how David

Tell en-Najîleh in the southern part of the coastal plain, and Ziklag with Tell el-Malāḥa, south east of

Tell en-Najîleh, on the border of the Negev.

established ties with the Israelite families in Northern Gilead (Jabesh Gilead, II Samuel 2:4–7) and the Kingdom of Geshur in the Golan, by marrying the daughter of Talmai king of Geshur (II Samuel 3:3). His main attention, however, was given to the military and administrative organization of his kingdom. The historiographic sources frequently mention David's thirty "mighty men," Gibborim.[9] It appears that this was a military institution organized according to a tradition prevailing in the period of the Judges, for the sources more than once mention thirty companions or friends of certain charismatic personalities and chiefs of tribal organizations. It transpires that David set up this institution—consisting of well known military men mainly from the tribe Judah and his neighbors in the south as well as from Benjamin—while he was still roaming the land as commander of his band of 400 and then 600 men. Among these captains a group of three stood out in particular, one of them being the head of the "mighty men." Two versions of the list of thirty "mighty men" have been preserved in the Bible (II Samuel 23, and I Chronicles 11); the list no doubt relates to an early period of David's reign in Hebron, with some names added in the course of time. According to this list, Jashobeam the son of Hachmoni stood at the head of the "mighty men" (the name is misreported in II Samuel) while before, during the Ziklag period, Jishmaia the Gibeonite (I Chronicles 12:4) was chief— no doubt one of Saul's enemies who had joined him together with the group of Benjaminite archers (ibid., verses 2–3). The terminus ad quem of the list may be deduced from the fact that it includes Assael the brother of Joab (II Samuel 23:24) who was killed by Abner during the period of Eshbaal in the battle near Gibeon (II Samuel 2:18 et seq.; 3:1). It may thus be dated to the period prior to the death of Eshbaal, that is, during the first or at the latest the second year of David's reign in Hebron.

Indeed, at that time the post of king's military commander was created, according to the tradition obtaining in the country in the time of the Canaanite kingdoms and the Philistines, as well as during the reign of Saul (cf. Genesis 21:21; Judges 4:2; I Samuel 14:50, etc.). From the beginning of David's reign this post was filled by Joab son of Zarujah, one of David's relatives. We find him heading David's men in the battle of Gibeon (II Samuel 2:12–13) and at the head of David's troops on their forays, in place of David himself (II Samuel

9 For details see my article "The Mighty Men of David" to be published in the Essays in honor of David Ben-Gurion.

10 See Y. Yadin, Proceedings of the World Congress of Jewish Studies, 1947, Vol. I (1952), pp. 222 ff.

11 It seems that the Philistines did not react against the capture of the citadel of Zion and the other mili-

3:22). His role was similar to that played by Abner for Saul and Eshbaal.

It is noteworthy that Joab's rise to the rank of military commander was connected with the central event of that period, namely the conquest of Jerusalem. No more than vague and conflicting reports of this event have been preserved in II Samuel 5:6–9 and I Chronicles 11:4–7. While the garbled source in II Samuel states that the Jebusites relied on their fortifications and took certain actions connected with the blind and the lame—that is, magic and sorcery[10]— which proved of no avail against David who captured the citadel, the Chronicler in I Chronicles 11:4–6 simply says: "And David and all Israel went to Jerusalem, which is Jebus, where the Jebusites were, the inhabitants of the land. And the inhabitants of Jebus said to David: 'Thou shalt not come in hither.' Nevertheless David took the citadel of Zion; which is the city of David. And David said: 'Whosoever smiteth the Jebusites first shall be chief and commander. So Joab the son of Zeruiah went first up, and was chief.'"

According to this story the capture of the citadel of Zion was an act of supreme heroism, so that "whoever smiteth the Jebusite" was worthy to be chief and commander of David's forces. Thus Joab's rise to command was linked with his valiant deed in the capture of the citadel of Zion. But since Joab is already mentioned as chief of David's men during the time of Eshbaal, at the beginning of David's reign in Hebron, the question arises whether the capture of the Zion citadel should not be predated to the beginning of David's reign, rather than to the eighth year of his reign which is generally accepted by scholars. This would explain and shed light on a number of obscure events in the history of David and his young kingdom. It becomes clear, for instance, why the road from Hebron to Gibeon lay open to David during his war against Eshbaal, and why he was not forced to send his troops through the Jebusite pocket.[11]

In particular this would shed light on the account of David's wars against the Philistines in the surroundings of Jerusalem, for the abolition of the Jebusite pocket would serve to explain the background of the story recounted in II Samuel 5:17–25. According to this source the Philistines opend war on David as a result of his being made king of all Israel in Hebron, after Eshbaal's death: "But when the Philistines heard that they had anointed David king over Israel, all the

tary and political activities of David as long as Israel was divided, for he was formally regarded as the vassal of Achish and the enemy of Eshbaal king of Israel. They acted according to their policy *divide et impera* until David became king over reunited Israel.

Philistines went up to seek David; and David heard of it, and went down to the citadel. The Philistines also came and spread themselves in the valley of Rephaim." [12] Since Eshbaal ruled for two years it is reasonable to assume that the crowning of David as king by the elders of Israel in Hebron "before God" (II Samuel 5:3) took place during the third year of his reign, and this act served as a cause of war and a reason for the dispatch of Philistine troops to the valley of Rephaim, to cut off the connection between Judea and Israel. The citadel in which David had entrenched himself is apparently the citadel of Zion, which had been conquered previously and converted into a military base. From it David attacked the Philistines at Baal Perazim—which is indeed a strategic point overlooking the valley of Rephaim.[13]

In this connection it should nevertheless be noted that instead of "and he went down to the citadel" the parallel version in I Chronicles 14:8 says: "and he went out in front of them," that is to say, that he reached the battlefield from Hebron without any mention being made of any citadel. At any rate, however, it is clear that the Philistines started hostilities long before David transferred his capital from Hebron to Jerusalem. These hostilities continued even after David had defeated the Philistine army at Baal Perazim. Only after the serious blow they received at Bachaim "from Gibeon until thou come to Gezer" (II Samuel 5:22–25; I Chronicles 11:13–16 were the Philistines finally beaten back from the Israelite mountain settlements, and David's position grew so strong that he could start considering the conversion of Jerusalem into his capital without fear of Philistine intervention.

In view of the above, a fresh analysis should be made of the principal source recounting the history of Jerusalem during Davidic times, namely II Samuel 5–6 and the parallel version in I Chronicles. Here we must distinguish two different stories, which became joined by

12 Undoubtedly the Philistines reached the valley of Rephaim through Adullam—Beith Natîf—Husān—Veit Jallā and stationed their forces at Bethlehem (cf. II Samuel 23:13–17) and the valley of Rephaim. As regards the citadel, it is reasonable to assume that the Zion Citadel is meant (and certainly not Adullam, which lies far off and right on the Philistine route).

13 The Philistines accordingly cut off David from Hebron by stationing their forces at Bethlehem and conquering the strategic places on the way to Jerusalem. It has been sug-

gested that Baal Perazim should be identified with Mār Eliās near Ramath Rahel (G. Dalman, *Orte und Wege*, Jesu, 3d ed., p. 21). Isaiah, in speaking of the Mount of Perazim (Isaiah 28:21), apparently refers to this place.

14 While I Chronicles 11:8 says: "And he built the city round about, from Millo even round about; and Joab spared the rest of the city."

15 After the passage on the Philistine campaigns, which was put in the wrong place. This happens also in Chap. 7 of II Samuel. Since the author started talking of the war

way of association, since both speak of Jerusalem. The one tells of the conquest of Jerusalem (5:6–8) while the other deals with its conversion into David's capital under the new name of City of David: "And David built round about from Millo and inward." [14]

It goes on to tell of the king's palace built by Hiram king of Tyre, the women he married in Jerusalem and the sons that were born to him there (5:9–16) and finally of the transfer of the Ark of the Covenant from Gire'ath Qiryath Ye'arim (Deir el-Azhar in Abu-Ghosh) to Jerusalem. In fact there is no reason to assume that these events are of necessity chronologically linked to each other and that immediately after the capture of the Citadel of Zion David made Jerusalem his capital. The contrary appears to be the case. It is much more reasonable to assume that since the author started off with the story of the conquest of the Citadel of Zion, he went on describing David's activities in Jerusalem after it became the capital and the war with the Philistines had ceased.[15] An attempt to reconstruct the evolution of events in their correct chronological order would logically yield the following scheme:

Years of David's Reign	*Events in the Life of David*
First (ci. 1005 B.C.E.)	David rules over Judah at Hebron; Eshbaal rules over Israel at Mahanayim; David conquers the citadel of Zion; war between David and Eshbaal.
Second	Continuation of the war between David and Eshbaal; Abner gets in touch with David with a view to passing the kingdom on to him.

against the Philistines he immediately attached a summary of the wars conducted outside the borders of Israel (see S. Yeivin, "David," *Biblical Encylclopaedia* II, p. 6330). Likewise the author of the Book of Kings brings the story of the conquest of Gezer and its delivery as ransom to Solomon at the beginning of his reign together with the story of Solomon's building activities, which included Gezer, during a late period of his reign (I Kings 9:16), without intending to imply any chronological connection between the two events. Many addi-

tional examples of this method of narration may be found in the Bible. It should further be noted that there are differences of opinion among various scholars as to whether the Philistine campaigns preceded the conquest of Jerusalem (see, for example, J. Bright, *A History of Israel*, 1960, pp. 177 f.) or whether they occurred after the conquest of Jerusalem in the eight year of David's reign, and after he had made it his capital (see, for example, Yeivin, *ibid.*). The solution suggested herein contradicts both these hypotheses.

Third	Death of Eshbaal; David is recognized as king over the whole of Israel; the first campaign against the Philistines and their defeat at Baal Perazim.
Fourth	The battle of Bachaim and the routing of the Philistines from Gibeon till Gezer; the strengthening of David's rule over Israel.
Fifth	Beginning of the construction of the City of David; wars with the Philistines in the coastal plain (II Samuel 21:15–22).
Sixth and Seventh	Continuation of the building activities; the king's palace and the houses in the City of David (I Chronicles 15:1) and the fortification of the city.
Eighth	Jerusalem inaugurated as the capital of Israel; the transfer of the Ark to Jerusalem.

Israel and the Diaspora

DR. EMANUEL NEUMANN

*

I

EVER SINCE THE EMERGENCE of the State of Israel, the subject of Israel-Diaspora relations has been under discussion throughout the Jewish world, largely in terms of cultural and intellectual exchange. Now and then this discussion ranged more widely—and in depth—to include the question of mutual influence, and especially the propriety of any attempt by Diaspora Jews to "intervene" in Israel's domestic or foreign affairs. Generally, however, the trend in the Diaspora has been to think and speak in terms of "building bridges" of understanding; and such phrases as a "two-way bridge" and "spiritual ties" are employed to describe both purpose and process.

Though these phrases amount at times to little more than oratorical clichés, many efforts are nevertheless in progress to foster cultural and spiritual relations between Israel and the Diaspora; and these efforts, which are growing in scope, are most fruitful. They include such things as American-Jewish youth programs in Israel, exchange students at the Hebrew University and other institutions of higher learning, spreading the knowledge of modern Hebrew, organized performances in the Diaspora by the Israel Philharmonic Orchestra and the Habimah, exhibitions of Israeli art, etc. This is not an original type of activity, but one with which the whole civilized world is increasingly concerned. The United States has long been engaged in an elaborate cultural exchange and intellectual cooperation with friendly nations; and such programs are in progress even between this country and the Soviet Union. However, in our case, we are thinking not in terms of promoting international amity, but in the context of Jewish life and the problems of Jewish existence. When we speak of "building spiritual and cultural bridges" between Israel and Diaspora Jewry, the language we use is a metaphorical circumlocution for something deeper and more fundamental than the words

might seem to connote. They reflect a continuing preoccupation with
a basic problem arising from the tremendous revolutionary change in
the life of the Jewish people brought about by the rise of Israel. Now,
for the first time in many centuries, the Jews of the world have suddenly been divided into two great segments, two categories living
under fundamentally different conditions. Diaspora Jews, wherever
they are and whatever their circumstances, have this one thing in
common: They are everywhere a minority subject to the powerful
influence of a non-Jewish civilization to which they must adjust—
and to varying forms and degrees of pressure on the part of a non-
Jewish society in whose midst they dwell; while the Jews of Israel
live in a Jewish society, as the dominant majority in the land, wholly
free to fashion their life and their own civilization as they choose.

The conditions of Diaspora existence have had and will continue
to have a most important bearing on the texture and pattern of Jewish
life—even on Judaism itself. (It is today a "Diaspora Judaism.") To
the Jews in the State of Israel, the new adventure as an independent
nation offers quite another framework and a radically different basis
of development. Already signs are not lacking that these fundamental
differences of situation and circumstance may produce divergencies
so wide and significant as to foreshadow a problem of serious dimensions in the future. One need not go as far as Jacob Klatzkin, who
years ago predicted the possibility, even the likelihood, of our ultimate
division into two distinct and separate peoples: one in Zion, and the
other in Golah; but certainly, even a trend in that direction would be
serious enough. How is it to be avoided? How is the essential organic
unity of the Jewish people to be assured? This basic problem has
many facets that demand attention.

II

At the outset, a parenthetical remark would be in place. It must
be disturbing to many Jews, Zionists as well as non-Zionists, that the
triumph of Zionism and the achievement of Jewish Statehood should
present us with new problems, some of them difficult and vexatious.
Had we not claimed that the establishment of the Jewish State would
solve *the* great problem of Jewish national homelessness and nor-
malize the Jewish position in the world? Now that the solution has
been effected, whence these new problems? The answer should, of
course, be obvious: There is no "final solution" at any time, anywhere!
The solution of an existing problem must, in the nature of things,
create new problems, though of a different order; and the new problems will, in turn, call for new solutions. This is the law of life,

against which it is idle to complain. Indeed, it is the myriads of such undulating waves—problems, solutions, and new problems again—that constitute the historic process. No people and no nation, even the strongest and most stable, is immune. Complete tranquillity is the monopoly of the grave.

It is necessary, therefore, that we address ourselves thoughtfully and frankly to this question: How is the Zionist Revolution, the rise and existence of the Jewish State, affecting the Jews of the Diaspora? Is the impact invariably and universally positive? Even the most devoted Zionist, firmly rooted in Zionist ideology, would hesitate to answer unreservedly in the affirmative.

There is, of course, no room for doubt that Israel's impact has, on the whole, been of enormous positive import—quite apart from her role in receiving and absorbing masses of Diaspora Jews in quest of sanctuary and security. The effect of Israel's independence in heightened Jewish pride and self-respect, in deepening Jewish loyalties, in raising the status and esteem of Jews in most countries, and the fresh and powerful impulse given to Jewish life—all this hardly needs documentation, though volumes could be written on this theme. One might well go further and assert that the existence of the Jewish State has not only quickened the life of Diaspora Jews and enhanced their stature, but that in certain instances it can help to protect their civil rights and political status, as well. Not only are these positive and beneficent effects already visible and palpable, but there is every reason to expect ever greater results in the future, as Israel continues its growth and consolidates its position. The Jewish State is not merely a haven of refuge for multitudes of our people, as well as a center radiating vital impulses throughout the Jewish world—it is also potentially a tower of strength, a citadel of power in the more literal sense of these words.

These are tremendous facts which place the vindication of the Zionist program beyond question. Nevertheless, even a cursory review of Israel-Diaspora relations must note aspects and developments that are not wholly positive. Situations have arisen and incidents have occurred in which acts and policies of the Government of Israel have stirred serious controversy among Diaspora Jews, or are deemed to have an adverse effect on their position. To point them out does not necessarily imply criticism but it is important to realize in how many ways Israel, functioning normally within its prerogatives as a sovereign State, impinges upon the life of Diaspora Jews.

A striking case in point is the position of Russian Jewry. Whatever the beneficial and stimulating effect of Israel's existence upon

Soviet Jews—and there is increasing evidence of that—it is obvious that the unsatisfactory relations between Israel and the Soviet Union tend to aggravate the problem of Russian Jewry. Russia's hostility toward Israel is motivated by her strategic and political designs in the Middle East. Israel's position and orientation toward the West are, from the Russian standpoint, sufficient justification for its anti-Israel policy, which is apparently reflected to a degree in the attitude of the Soviet regime toward its own Jewish citizens. This is a new and purely political element in the situation, superimposed upon traditional anti-Semitism still endemic in the Soviet Empire.

The impact of Israel on the Jewish position in Moslem countries is more complicated. To hundreds of thousands of Jews in Arab lands, Israel has brought relief and redemption from centuries of insecurity and degradation, by massive repatriation from Syria, Iraq, Yemen, and North-African countries. For thousands of others, the Israel-Arab conflict has created new problems and hardships. What is more important: We do not yet know—for it is too early to surmise—to what extent in the perspective of history the Jewish position may be affected by the new legend which is being assiduously cultivated and spread throughout the Moslem world about the Jewish "conquest" of Palestine by force of arms, of the alleged heartless "expulsion" of the native population, their "expropriation," and the creation of a million Arab refugees "doomed to a wretched existence." Myths and legends so vigorously and relentlessly propagated, die hard. They can be passionately embraced in the course of time by people far removed from the scene of conflict and having no connection with the original controversy.

One of the latest incidents to be noted was Israel's vote in the General Assembly of the United Nations censuring the Union of South Africa on the issue of "Apartheid." The immediate reaction of the South African Government was not only an abrupt change of its traditional pro-Israel posture, but also a new and unfriendly attitude toward its own Jewish community. The local Jewish Board of Deputies suddenly found itself in a painfully embarrassing situation. It was moved to dissociate itself publicly from Israel's policy; and shortly thereafter the same Board issued another statement disclaiming any intention of "interfering" in Israel's conduct of her foreign affairs. One practical result of that incident has been the virtual prohibition of the remittance of philanthropic funds from South Africa to Israel. Another and more serious consequence has been a deterioration in the position of the Jewish community in its relations with the South African Government.

No doubt the price which some Jews, outside Israel, sometimes have to pay, is well worth paying; for the boon of Jewish Statehood is priceless from the standpoint of the Jewish people as a whole. Moreover, there is ample evidence that even those who may suffer adverse consequences do so, for the most part, cheerfully and without complaint. But the point to be borne in mind is the fact that if such tribulations do occur, it is because in the eyes of the world we are *one people.* The "sins" of Israel may be visited on Jews in the Diaspora (and possibly also vice versa). If that is a fact—if in the eyes of the world we are one people and not merely "coreligionists"—what bearing does it have on the question of Israel-Diaspora relations?

Other incidents that have occurred lie in the sphere of internal Jewish affairs. Such was the controversy that arose in Israel revolving on the question, "Who is a Jew?" It originated there on a purely administrative level, but it soon transpired that it was a matter of great significance not only to Israelis, but to large numbers of Jews in the Diaspora, and had wide repercussions in the Jewish world. In the end, the Prime Minister of Israel addressed himself to fifty Jewish scholars and religious leaders *in the Diaspora,* soliciting their considered opinion. By doing so, he recognized the extent to which administrative acts in Israel affected Jewish life beyond its borders, and the necessity of taking Diaspora opinion into account.

Another illustration was the sale of Israeli arms to the German Army, which also had its repercussions in the Diaspora. No doubt there was a *raison d'état* for this policy: it may have been dictated by the inexorable demands of Israel's security. On the other hand, this was a most sensitive issue which touched the Jews of the world, evoking deep emotional reactions. Only a few years previously, in 1954, Israel's Parliament had itself adopted a strongly worded resolution expressing profound anxiety over German rearmament. In that resolution the "nations of the world" were called upon "to remember and not to forget what an armed Germany had inflicted upon the world and upon the Jewish people in particular." And the nations were urged "to prevent the danger of a repetition of that catastrophe." In speaking as it did, the Knesseth undoubtedly articulated Jewish sentiment throughout the world with regard to Germany. The sale of arms a few years later was a startling reversal of attitude—a change which the Government deemed necessary in pursuit of its foreign policies. But did the change reflect a corresponding change in attitude of Diaspora Jews? And did it, in effect, commit the Jewish people as generally to a new and friendlier attitude toward the German nation? How far and how fast is world Jewry prepared to go in the direction of reconciliation with the erstwhile enemy? And it should be noted that for Germany itself, the friendship or enmity of world Jewry has been and still is a matter of political importance. This was evidenced by the Reparations Agreement which was possibly more valuable to Germany than to Israel and the Jews, for it paved the way for Germany's moral rehabilitation and her acceptance in the family of the Free World.

III

Involved in this discussion are a host of momentous questions of fundamental significance. To what extent does Israel or the *Yishuv* act as the spokesman and, as it were, the accredited representative of the whole Jewish people in matters affecting Jewish communities and Jewish life in various parts of the world? Should the Diaspora speak out? Does it have the right to voice opinions on Israel's domestic or foreign policies? And if so, when, under what circumstances, and to what extent? Is there such a thing as an overarching, all-Jewish interest? Can there be an overall, collective Jewish policy? And if so, in what areas? And how could it be crystallized and determined?

It is readily admitted that such questions are more easily asked than answered. Nor is it intended here to suggest anything remotely resembling definite answers. What is essential, however, is that the problem be fully understood, studied and faced. It would be relevant in this connection to quote the Prime Minister of Israel in a letter he addressed to an American Zionist a few years ago, "Why," says Mr. Ben-Gurion, "do you assume that I think that Jews in foreign countries do not have the right to interfere in the affairs of Israel? My opinion is just the opposite and I have frequently stated it in public. I never thought that Israel belonged only to the Jews who live there and that the Jewish State was created only for its citizens or by its citizens alone. At the session of the Actions Committee held in Jerusalem on July 18, 1957, I stated that 'I am first of all a Jew, and then an Israeli; in my judgment the State was established for the whole Jewish people and the national unity of Jews throughout the world exists due to the Jewish people. This unity is based upon a partnership of destiny, a partnership in a great historic heritage—a partnership of the future.' "

In these utterances Ben-Gurion spoke as a Zionist; and no Zionist should have difficulty in subscribing to these views. But we must ask ourselves: What are the implications of the principle thus enunciated? And how are we to create the kind of partnership which he so emphatically asserted? On other occasions Ben-Gurion has insisted that Diaspora Jews are neither "partners" nor "builders" of Israel, but only "helpers." How are these various statements to be reconciled?

In the ongoing discussion on this level, a certain amount of confusion has been caused by the introduction of a new term into our Jewish and Zionist vocabulary—the term "Israeli." It is not only a terminological confusion, but one that bears on the very essence of the Zionist idea and calls for clarification. Israel is a modern secular, democratic state. Consequently all of its inhabitants, or at least its citizens, are Israelis, including the Christians and Moslems and those of its Jews who, to the present day, are anti-Zionist, such as Communists, Neturai Karta and other fringe groups. All these are Israelis, enjoying equal rights in the political life of the State and its daily affairs. The attitudes and philosophies of all elements of the population must ultimately determine the policies of Israel. A state is a state, and its sovereignty must be respected and zealously guarded by its citizenry.

But it is essential to bear in mind that from the Zionist standpoint Israel is not simply a sovereign State but has also another character and another role to play as *the National Home of the Jewish people*. This may appear to be an artificial distinction, too subtle and metaphysical for practical purposes; yet it is a valid distinction and a necessary one. Israel, as a state, has political relationships with other states and exercises absolute sovereignty over its individual citizens, regulating and controlling their daily lives. It maintains armed forces; it makes peace, wages war, enters into alliances, has its embassies and diplomatic missions abroad, finances itself by taxation, and exerts its police powers domestically. But it is also a Zionist State —the Jewish National Home—having a unique relationship with the Jews of the world, citizens of many lands, and a moral and historic responsibility to the Jewish people as a whole; and it is on this basis that Israel can rightly claim the devotion and continued support of Diaspora Jewry in all forms. From the standpoint of Zionist ideology, Jewish Palestine was the *National Home* even before its independence was achieved. Now that the State has been established, it must necessarily function on two planes: both as a sovereign, political entity— a state among states—and as the Jewish National Home, with a special "extraterritorial" relationship with the Jews of the world, not only as the cultural and spiritual center of the Jewish people, but as the pivot of Jewish destiny.

On that level Diaspora Jewry and the Jewish community of Israel must meet as integral parts of one universal and coherent people—not a political, but a historic entity held together by common heritage, common ideals, a sense of ethnic kinship and ultimately a common destiny. Inevitably this implies mutuality of interest and collective responsibility for the Jewish future. And it should be abundantly clear that neither the Diaspora nor Israel can bear that responsibility alone. It should also be clearly recognized that what Israel (more precisely its dominant Jewish majority) does or leaves undone, both domestically and in its foreign relations, can have far-reaching and even fateful consequences for Jews beyond its borders in distant corners of the globe in the years and generations to come.

IV

One need hardly stress once more another element in the situation causing no little concern: the possibility of a widening gulf between Israeli youth and the Jewish youth of the Diaspora, both of whom are assimilating to their respective environments in wholly different ways. In Israel their tendency is to turn their backs on the Diaspora, to skip, as it were, two thousand years of exilic history, to hark back to the heroic periods of the First and Second Commonwealths, and to regard themselves primarily as Israelis, rather than as Jews. This is part of the instinctive quest for roots and "normalcy." Our Diaspora youth in the Free World are pursuing their own quest for "normalcy" through maximum integration into non-Jewish society, shedding more and more the remnants of their Jewish heritage and distinctiveness. In both cases the question arises: How "normal" can they become and remain really Jewish, considering the unique circumstances of the Jewish people, whose "normal" position has been "abnormal" and will continue to be so for generations to come.

The question cannot be dismissed unless one assumes a total ingathering of all the Jews of the world in the State of Israel, or the virtually complete disappearance of Diaspora Jewry. If in the light of such reflections we return to Ben-Gurion's words, "a partnership of destiny, a partnership in a great historic heritage, a partnership of the future," we must ask: How is such a partnership to be created and preserved? Surely not by the concept of Israel as a "foreign State" toward which Diaspora Jews regard themselves as "helpers" and philanthropic donors. The "partnership of destiny" involving the basic unity of the Jewish people, must find expression in definite and concrete forms far beyond philanthropy, if it is to be an operative spiritual reality. Nor will "cultural bridges" suffice. More effective ways must be found for ensuring not merely the nominal unity of the Jewish people and not only the capacity for concerted action in moments of great danger, but to ensure allegiance to a common Jewish heritage and common Jewish imperatives.

What is called for is constant interaction and reciprocal influence between Israel and the Diaspora. Israel can and will fulfill its role as the invigorating center of the Jewish world, but only through such a process of give and take, and only if the Diaspora makes its own contribution toward the development of that living center not only in terms of manpower and material support, but on the moral and intellectual planes, as well. In this context, the hue and cry about Diaspora "intervention" in the affairs of Israel, raised some time ago, appears absurdly irrelevant and immature. On the one hand, Diaspora Jews cannot intervene effectively, being legally and politically precluded from doing so—and sovereign Israel has ample means to legislate all necessary safeguards. On the other hand, as we have seen, it might be claimed that Israel can and does "intervene" in the Diaspora, through the impact of its actions as a sovereign State—indeed, by its very existence. If Israelis seize Eichmann in Buenos Aires, and he is tried and convicted in Jerusalem—and if that results in considerable unpleasantness for Argentinian Jewry—is that "intervention"?

Actually, of course, there has been almost no intervention on either side. If Diaspora Jews have reacted, at times, to Israeli actions or policies, it has been by voicing their approval or disapproval; and such expression of public opinion is entirely legitimate, whether in intra-Jewish relations or in the international community generally. If fault is to be found, it is rather in the opposite direction: Israelis are insufficiently concerned with most aspects of Jewish life in the Diaspora and "intervene" too little; and Diaspora Jews are too little concerned with most aspects of Israeli affairs and "intervene" not at all—unless and until a particular shoe pinches a particular foot. One of the most oft-repeated and least justified criticisms of the "non-interventionists" has been directed against Zionist organizations in the Diaspora maintaining traditional links with their ideological counterparts in Israel, even where such relationship exists within the framework of the Zionist Movement exclusively. For as matters stand today, World Zionism provides the only international framework binding the Jews of Israel and the Diaspora together in a concrete organizational form. It is the World Zionist Congress that has become the scene of repeated meaningful confrontations between Israel and the Diaspora—the quadrennial forum for the ongoing debate on Israel-Diaspora relations.

Speaking at the last Zionist Congress, the writer said: "Whatever the shortcomings of the Movement or its institutions—and there has been no lack of emphasis on shortcomings—let this at least be pointed out and underscored: there is no other great international Jewish forum even remotely approaching the Zionist Congress in importance and authority; there is no other stage for this essential and fruitful confrontation of Israel and the Diaspora; and no other anvil on which to hammer out eventually a common and a comprehensive viewpoint, an all-Jewish policy, a collective strategy for Jewish survival in this tempestuous world. It is true that the Zionist Congress, established by Herzl, is no longer the 'parliament of the Jewish State in the making.' We have a Knesseth. But the Congress remains and must continue to serve as the 'Ecumenical Council' of the whole Jewish people the world over—its most authentic voice and spokesman."

It may be added that this function alone—to serve as a vital link between Israel and the Diaspora, spiritually, ideologically and policy-wise—amply justifies the continued existence of the World Zionist Organization even if it had no other more "practical" tasks to perform and served this one purpose alone. Those who would discourage an ongoing dialogue between Israel and the Diaspora, would stifle debate and mutual criticism, are contributing unwittingly to a widening of the gulf between the two great segments of the Jewish people; while those who would dismantle or liquidate the World Zionist Movement may be destroying one really serviceable bridge linking the two in effective partnership and fraternity. Fortunately that is not likely to happen. The Zionist Movement was dedicated by its founder to the proposition that "we are a People—*one* People." As long as it is committed to that idea and its manifold implications, organized Zionism will continue to play a decisive role in contemporary Jewish life.

On Toynbee's Use of the Term "Syriac" for One of His Societies

HARRY M. ORLINSKY

*

LET IT BE STATED at the outset that this brief essay is not intended for the author of *A Study of History:* whether he takes issue with the essay or not is quite irrelevant, since a perusal of his *Reconsiderations* makes it amply clear that it is hardly worth the effort to convince him that he may well be wrong in his views and that he might care to reconsider them. Rather is this essay meant for the general reader who might not read Toynbee in some detail or who finds himself unable to acquaint himself with how specialists regard this intrepid fact-collector.

The few specialists in the Ancient Near East who have bothered to read and comment publicly on A. J. Toynbee's discussion of that area and period in world history have been less than happy with what they have read. In this respect, they have not differed appreciably from the specialists in the other areas and epochs. But then the kind of "analysis" to be found in Toynbee's ten-volume *Study of History* was hardly calculated to win friends among scholars who study the materials at the source, and who do not tend to select data that fits perfectly into a pattern that had been created for it in advance.

For apart from other considerations, a student of the Fertile Crescent of old is hardly expected to take the time to read about his special field of interest something written by one who cannot read in the original a single source dealing with that period. The scribes of the great civilizations in question wrote in Sumerian, Egyptian, Babylonian, Assyrian, Hittite, Canaanite, Aramaic, Hebrew, and the like. But Toynbee had to depend upon secondary materials throughout for his own study of the "cradle of civilization." Everyone knows how unscholarly—indeed arrogant and less than responsible—such a procedure is, and how unreliable such analysis must be. This is especially true in the study of Western Asia and Biblical Israel, because of the rapidity with which discoveries and new analyses are made and the control that one must have over archeology and the written sources, each in their own right and in relation to each other. The writer of *A Study of History* lacked this control. It is in this connection that I often recall a conversation with a well known and authoritative cuneiformist in which I asked him whether he had read Toynbee on ancient Mesopotamia—after all, the Sumeric, the Hittite, and the Babylonic constitute no less than three out of his nineteen "societies"— and receiving the laughing reply, "No, why should I read him? What does he know about it, and what can he tell me?"

In his comprehensive analysis of *The Burden of Egypt: an Interpretation of Ancient Egyptian Culture* (1951: now a Phoenix paperback, *The Culture of Egypt*), John A. Wilson, the noted Egyptologist of Chicago's Oriental Institute, wrote (p. 32, n. 12), ". . . In subsequent chapters it may be noted that we have not found some of Toynbee's concepts or principles sufficiently applicable to ancient Egypt to warrant detailed discussion. For example, we have difficulty in accepting the sequence of 'time of troubles' (First Intermediate Period), 'universal state' (Middle Kingdom), 'interregnum' (Hyksos invasion), and 'universal state reasserted' (Empire); for us, the effectively disturbing troubles which wrecked Egyptian culture grew out of the Empire and the attempt to maintain it. Even less valid seems the concept of the worship of Osiris as a kind of 'universal church created by an internal proletariat'; the Osirian religion was mortuary and could not be the genesis of a 'new society,' and it was originally created by and for Toynbee's 'dominant minority.' These criticisms

1   Wilson's note pertains to Vol. I of Toynbee's *Study* (1935), pp. 302–315 (or pp. 68–73 of D. C. Somervell's *Abridgement* of Vols. I-VI, 1947).

   In reference to ancient Egyptian culture, particularly in the matter of the Pyramids, Toynbee wrote (p. 30 of the *Abridgement*: cf. Vol. I, pp. 128 ff.), "*The Egyptiac Society.* This very notable society emerged in the lower valley of the Nile during the fourth millennium B.C. and became extinct in the fifth century of the Christian Era, after existing, from first to last, at least three times as long as our Western Society has existed so far. It was without 'parents' and without off- spring; no living society can claim it as an ancestor. All the more triumphant is the immortality that it has sought and found in stone. It seems probable that the Pyramids, which have already borne inanimate witness to the existence of their creators for nearly five thousand years, will survive for hundreds of thousands of years to come. It is not inconceivable that they may outlast man himself and that, in a world where there are no longer human minds to read their message, they will continue to testify: 'Before Abraham was, I am.'" Wilson quoted part of this statement in his *Burden of Egypt* (p. 310), but he went on immedi-

do scant justice to Toynbee's enormously refreshing influence in assailing formerly fixed ideas. The thinking of this book owes much to him, even though his societal pattern for Egypt is rejected." [1]

In the same year Ephraim A. Speiser of the University of Pennsylvania published a paper on "The Ancient Near East and Modern Philosophies of History" (in *Proceedings of the American Philosophical Society*, Vol. 95, No. 6, December, pp. 583–588). It is to the fundamental changes that have occurred the world over since World War I, he noted, that "we owe so many contemporary or recent philosophies of history: those of Spengler and Toynbee, of Sorokin, Kroeber, and Northrop, among various others." The paper sought "to address itself to one serious defect that must leave the final conclusions in serious doubt. . . . [As] to the Near East . . . that unique and enormously significant testimony is no better than a blank in the comprehensive studies just mentioned. Toynbee and Kroeber, two authorities to whom we are especially indebted for penetrating insights, are no exceptions in this regard. They and the others make brief detours to Egypt . . . but what they come out with is a fragmentary account, out of focus and out of date and hence thoroughly misleading. . . . Even less satisfactory is the vestigial recognition, if any, that these works accord to the other areas of the Ancient Near East, especially Mesopotamia. There is, for instance, no tenable definition of civilization whereby Babylonia can be isolated from Sumer, as is done by Toynbee. On the other hand, Toynbee's Syriac society is a conglomerate of loosely assorted elements." And a footnote (no. 8) to this sentence reads, ". . . Toynbee's conclusions that the civilization of the Indus Valley was very closely related to that of the Sumerians . . . has only resemblances of a very superficial nature to support it."

ately with this very (im?)pertinent query: "Of what importance to us is such a civilization, which was so long-lived and so immortal in its physical expression?"

Very curious indeed is the fact that Abraham was dragged into this eschatological picture. Why Abraham? Is it because he is, to the world at large, the first Jew? If so, what was Toynbee's motivation in mentioning the first Jew in connection with his post-mortem of all human society? On Toynbee's sort of prophetic prognostication, several billions of people the world over—to the last man—will have disappeared for ever, while the Pyramids will continue their "triumphant," inanimate existence. Why single out the Jews, the paltry few million of them, out of the hundreds and hundreds of millions of non-Jews at hand, to be the ones over whom these monuments will gloat? Why not Sargon I or II? Or Hammurabi? Sennacherib? Confucius? Cyrus? Socrates, Plato, and Aristotle? Alexander? Jesus? Mohammed? The expression "Before Abraham was, I am" has no meaning here for the historian; it is probably most revealing for those who are familiar with psychoanalysis.

In Chapter II of his book *From the Stone Age to Christianity*
(1940), in the section on "The Encyclopaedic-Analytic Tendency in
the Philosophy of History" (pp. 60 ff.), William F. Albright, after
paying the usual tribute to Toynbee's literary style and clarity of
presentation,[2] proceeds to indicate why Toynbee has so little value for
the historian of the Ancient Near East in general and for Biblical
Israel in particular: "The task of distinguishing cultural groups of
mankind is by no means a new one. . . . It is not unfair to say that
such divisions really exist, but they cross one another and change
chronologically, geographically, and culturally to such an extent that
they become rather useless as units of classification. . . . An attempt to take a common material culture (Islamic, Christian) or
even a racial background (as in dividing Islam into two separate
modern societies, the Iranic and the Arabic) in another can only
lead to confusion . . . we consider this side of Toynbee's investigation as relatively futile. Unfortunately," continues Albright (p. 62),
"The weakness of Toynbee's method does not end here. . . ."[3]

What constituted, however, a devastating criticism of Toynbee,
though apparently not intended as such, is the opening sentence on
p. 222 of his book, where Albright takes up the period of the Judges
and the United Monarchy: "Though Toynbee seems to have overlooked the case of the Israelites between 1200 and 900 B.C., it would
be difficult to find a better illustration of his principle of 'Challenge-
and-Response under the stimulus of blows.' Under this stimulus the
Israelites attained national unity in spite of the centrifugal forces

---

2   It is of interest that scholars sometimes feel impelled to pay tribute
to Toynbee as a scholar of great
insight before they proceed to reject his scholarship altogether in
their own field. The tribute is generally paid for "insight" in fields
other than those in which the
scholars have special competence.
This is known in Yiddish as *gut
far yenem* "[It is] good for someone else [but not for me]."
    As for style and clarity, Toynbee
has collected something of an autobiography on this too, in his *Reconsiderations* (II Annex, *Ad
Hominem*, pp. 587 ff.), where he—
gleefully, it would seem—flagel-
lates himself publicly with references to and quotations from many
of his critics. In reading this volume, I was reminded of A.
Werner's review (*Jewish Quarterly
Review*, 36 [1945–1946], pp. 207 ff.)

of Jacob Klatzkin's book *In Praise
of Wisdom*, where reference is
made to Spengler and the "Speng-
lers" who "work hard to hide their
simple and obvious ideas under a
mass of verbiage . . . [and] examine every expression of theirs to
make sure that it is sufficiently
blurred."
    Recently, the lamented S. F.
Bloom of Brooklyn College, in his
pungent review of *Reconsiderations* ("Toynbee on Toynbee: his
Reconsiderations of *A Study of
History*," in *Midstream* 8 [1962],
pp. 49–56)—where he hardly takes
Toynbee seriously as a historian—
described the author as one who—
inter alia—"suffers from a kind of
word-fetishism rare in educated
men, and he has a strong appetite
for provocation. . . ." Of course
no one should take Toynbee's terminology—any more than, say, his

operating to break up the confederation. . . ." Probably an even better and more dramatic example of this phenomenon is the Babylonian Exile and the subsequent Persian Restoration, when the Judeans were literally "Withdrawn" and later permitted to "Return."

But of course Toynbee did not just happen to overlook "the case of the Israelites between 1200 and 900 B.C.," or the Babylonian Exile and Restoration, or several other pertinent events in Biblical Israel's career, for example, Judah in the Persian Period, or in the Hellenistic. Indeed, it can hardly be an accident that nowhere in his *Study* did Toynbee bother to adduce anything from Israel's rich and eventful history that would, at one and the same time, illustrate one of his principles and shed some glory on Israel.

And this leads directly to the matter of terminology. Eighteen (or twenty) out of Toynbee's nineteen (or twenty-one) societies (or civilizations) were given by him names that make sense in one way or another. The last paragraph on p. 34 of the *Abridgement* has this to say: "Our researches have thus yielded us nineteen societies, most of them related as parent of offspring to one or more of the others: namely, the Western, the Orthodox, the Iranic, the Arabic (these last two being now united in the Islamic), the Hindu, the Far Eastern, the Hellenic, the Syriac, the Indic, the Sinic, the Minoan, the Sumeric, the Hittite, the Babylonic, the Egyptiac, the Andean, the Mexic, the Yucatec and the Mayan. . . . Indeed it is probably desirable to divide the Orthodox Christian Society into an Orthodox-Byzantine and an Orthodox-Russian Society, and the Far Eastern into a Chinese and a

lumping together of all kinds of data—seriously: why should he use the common term "Appendix" when "Annex" will lift eyebrows? Why resort to the clear and mundane term "Institution" when "slum" (!) can gain Toynbee so much wider publicity? (But see Bloom, pp. 50–55.)

3   I do not understand the statement by Albright (pp. 63 ff.) that in the use of the principles "Challenge-and-Response" and "Withdrawal-and-Return" Toynbee was no innovator but that he "appears in both approaches to the problem of history as an old-fashioned spirit, acquiring the reputation of a great innovator and even of a prophet because he presents old but neglected principles with elaborate logical proof of their salient reality. All honor to him for reinstating forgotten truths!" The knowing reader, who has read Toynbee's critics directly (as usual, Toynbee has made some of the materials available, in *Reconsiderations*, e.g.., pp. 573 ff., 606 ff.), will recall that those who used the term "prophet" or the like had in mind something pejorative. As for the principles in question, surely they have been neither neglected nor forgotten! Since Hegel flourished, hardly a day has gone by without a book or an article appearing by a Hegelian or a Marxist—or by an anti-Hegelian or an anti-Marxist—dealing with precisely these principles; except that the terms employed are something like "thesis, antithesis, synthesis" or "action and reaction" or "cause and effect" or "dialectic," rather than the pretentious terms that Toynbee is so fond of toying with.

Korean-Japanese Society. This would raise our numbers to twenty-one. . . ." [4]

Whether or not there is really justification for this system of societies, at least the names for them mean something to the student of history—that is, for all the societies except the Syriac.[5] This is a curious name indeed, for under it was subsumed—along with the cultures of the Canaanites, Arameans, Ammonites, Moabites, and Edomites, among others—the great and unique culture of Biblical Israel. It would never have occurred to a student of the Ancient Near East in general, or of Western Asia alone, or of the eastern coastal area of the Mediterranean specifically, to designate this society as Syriac. It is a simple fact that the very term Syriac did not come into being until after the society onto which Toynbee grafted the term had virtually gone out of existence [6]—that is, all except that rambunctious fossil of Toynbee's, Judaism.

During the Hellenistic period, the term Syria came to refer to Aram (so, for example, in the Septuagint translation) as well as to other regions of Western Asia (so the Greeks themselves). Of course no one has argued that it was the region or the culture of the Arameans proper that was chiefly responsible for the cultures that arose on both sides of the Jordan during the last two millennia B.C. Indeed, one would be hard put to describe the Aramaic culture of the second millennium B.C., for the simple reason that there is so little to discuss.[7] Contrast, on the other hand, the rightful place that Canaan and Israel hold in the civilization of Asia-on-the-Mediterranean. Both the Bible and archeology have made it abundantly—and in the case of Ugarit-Ras Shamra dramatically—clear how the culture of these two peoples dominated the central portion of the Fertile Crescent during so much of the second and first millennia B.C. Along with such lesser luminaries as the Ammonites, Moabites, and Edomites, it was Canaan (later Phoenicia) and Israel that constituted and generated a society

---

4 Despite this statement, the reader will learn from Toynbee (*Reconsiderations,* "A Re-Survey of Civilization," pp. 546–561) that "In the course of the first ten volumes . . . I arrived at a list of twenty-three full-blown civilizations, four that were arrested at an early stage in their growth, and five that were abortive. . . . We are now in a position to draw up our revised list of civilizations . . .": 28 [of which three are qualified by "?"] Full-blown and 6 Abortive. There is nothing to prevent anyone from taking the new list any more seriously than the old one. But, in the creation of Civilizations, Bloom (p. 56) may have more justification than Toynbee when he comments wryly, ". . . *Reconsiderations* adds a Thirty-Third Civilization— Arnold J. Toynbee himself. . . ."

5 Toynbee attempts to justify this term in Vol. I, p. 82, n. 2; *Reconsiderations,* p. 393 f. The wisdom

of their own, one that, with everything that it shared with—even derived from—Mesopotamia, could not possibly be confused with the other great societies to the east, north, west, and south. Surely, it is Canaan-Israel, not Syria, that deserved onomastic mention among Toynbee's nineteen (or twenty-one, or thirty-four) societies.

Even more. In dealing with two of his societies, the Orthodox Christian and the Far Eastern, Toynbee was quite willing, because "it is probably desirable," to make two societies out of each of the two: an Orthodox-Byzantine and an Orthodox-Russian out of the Orthodox-Christian, and a Chinese and a Korean-Japanese out of the Far Eastern. Regardless of whether these terms and divisions are acceptable to specialists in those complex areas, it is utterly beyond comprehension—at least to the historian—how anyone could take himself seriously and cause cultures and peoples by the score in every part of the world to come into being, to flourish (or to abort), and to vanish, with or without progeny—and persist in denying existence to an Hebraic-Jewish society in the southwestern part of Asia; and let us not quibble whether it was full-blown, or arrested, or abortive.

Confronted by some facts that refuse to disappear in the swamp of verbiage that characterizes so much of his *Study*, Toynbee will admit (*Reconsiderations*, pp. 394 f.) that "The most fateful single event in all Hellenic history was the ideological and religious collision, in Coele Syria [read: Judea] in the second century B.C., between Hellenism and Judaism. . . . The Hellenic World was eventually converted to a religion of Jewish origin that was, and remained, essentially Judaic in its inspiration and its principles. . . . And this conversion of the Hellenic World to Christianity was the end of the Hellenic Civilization. As a result of the conversion, Hellenism lost its identity." So once again a little David of little Judah conquered an Aegean Goliath; but for Toynbee neither of the two Davids was a Judean—both were but Syriac products!

What is fascinating in this connection is that while he devotes

---

of employing this term does not appear to have impressed very many scholars.

6 This statement is true regardless of how and by whom the term Syriac was first coined and applied. It has long been held that it was the Greeks who originated the term, by clipping off the first part of the well known name, Assyria. For another explanation (on which the name *Subria* became *Suria-*

Syria by way of assumed *Suwria*), see *apud* R. T. O'Callaghan, *Aram-Naharaim* (*Analecta Orientalia* 26, 1948), p. 142 and n. 1.

7 Cf., e.g., O'Callaghan's *Aram-Naharaim* (which is subtitled: *A Contribution to the History of Upper Mesopotamia in the Second Millennium* B.C.), Chapters V–VII (pp. 93 ff.), respectively: "The Aramaeo-Assyrian Period," "Israel and Aram," and "Aram Naharaim."

an entire chapter (XIII, pp. 393–461) of his *Reconsiderations* to "The Configurations of Syriac History," Toynbee squanders still another entire chapter (XV, pp. 477-517) on the Jewish people alone, under the high-falutin title: "The History and Prospects of the Jews." It is most curious that Toynbee devotes here to the Jews more space than he does to the two chapters immediately following (XVI and XVII) combined: "The History and Prospects of the West" (518–536) and "Russia's Place in History" (536–546). So much does the Jewish people "bother" Toynbee that the East and the West—in combination! —receive less attention here than a people and a culture whose existence as a civilization he denies.[8] Toynbee will grant this prestige status to the Hittite civilization (satellite of Sumero-Akkadian), to the Iranian (satellite first of Sumero-Akkadian, then of Syriac), to the Mediaeval Western City-State (abortive), to the Nestorian Christian (abortive), to the Monophysite Christian (abortive), etc., etc.— see the chart on p. 558 of *Reconsiderations*—but he will not bestow it upon a (*pace!*) civilization that not only brought an end to Hellenism but—believe it or not!—can save the whole world from destruction if only it wills: ". . . the Jewish diaspora [*sic!*] might win converts to a denationalized and defossilized Judaism among the gentile majority around them. What the Romans did on the political plane, the Jews could do on the religious. They could incorporate gentiles in a Jewish religious community by converting them to the religion of Deutero-Isaiah. The greatest of the Prophets up to date, though not necessarily the last of them, would be, not Muhammed, but a Jewish seer who inspired his fellow Jews at last to dedicate themselves to their universal mission wholeheartedly. The World has been waiting for this

8 One may add the 15 pages devoted to "Islam's Place in History" (Chapter XIV in *Reconsiderations*), and he will find that Toynbee devoted 40 pages to the Jews, as against a grand total of 43 pages to Islam, the West, and Russia combined, all within four successive chapters! How fossilized can one get?

This obsession of Toynbee's reminds the present writer of a joke that has been making the rounds. A Jewish mother was telling her friends proudly that a son of hers had achieved remarkable success in the field of his endeavor and had become so wealthy that he was paying a doctor a hundred dollars for thirty minutes, twice a week, just to listen to him talk.

This talking, she continued, had been going on for several years, so that her son was obviously in the upper brackets in income. One crony then asked the mother, "But what does he talk about? What is it that is of such importance to your son that he sets aside so much time and money to talk about?" To which the mother replied, bursting with pride, "Me!"

9 One is reminded of an address that Toynbee gave in England, one which was widely referred to in the Yiddish and Anglo-Jewish press in this country as a retraction and reconsideration of his solemn view that the Jewish people constituted a fossil. But when the complete text of this address reached this country—not without

prophet for 2,500 years" (p. 517).[9] As the Yiddish saying goes: *Halevai volt es emes geven* ("If only this were true!").

It would seem clear by now that Toynbee, first and above all, simply refused to use any and all forms of any such terms as Hebrew or Israel or Jew, contrary to every justification for it even on his own approach. This same willfulness is apparent in his refusal—colossal ignorance would not be involved here [10]—even to make mention of the significant things that the Jewish society did and created during the past nineteen hundred years in the Diaspora—on which see Maurice Samuel's brilliant polemic, *The Professor and the Fossil* (1956).[11]

Toynbee has asserted (see the references in n. 5 above) that the Greeks gave him the idea of using the term Syriac for the civilization of Asia-on-the-Mediterranean. I wonder, however, whether the idea for the term does not derive from quite another, much later source than the Greek, the Islamic.

In one of his numerous exhibitions of self-flagellation, Toynbee writes (*Reconsiderations,* pp. 596 f.), "A second dim spot, of which I am aware, is my neglect of Israel, Judah, the Jews, and Judaism. I have neglected these out of proportion to their true importance. . . . I am ignorant of the Rabbinical Jewish literature . . . I know the Pharisees . . . through the denunciations of them in the Gospels. . . . Worst of all, I have never learnt even a smattering of Hebrew. Since childhood, Hebrew has left me cold, whereas I have had a passionate desire to learn Arabic. This partiality is evidently irrational . . . I cannot account for my acquiescence in this particular dim spot, though I am none the less conscious of its being there." More recently, we may recall Toynbee's hatred for Zionism and the State

significance it was the American Council for Judaism that circulated it ("Pioneer Destiny of Judaism," 1960, 14 pp.)—the careful reader saw at once, behind the verbiage and sanctimonious sympathies, a malicious attack on world Jewry: unless the Jews outside of Israel give up all association with Israel and unless they proceed energetically to spread their Jewish religion among the peoples of the world so as to prevent the destruction of the world in the Atomic Age—the Jews will bear responsibility for having failed to help save the world! What is one to say about such monstrous and warped "reasoning"?

10 In his *Reconsiderations* (p. 596),

Toynbee writes, "I am ignorant . . . of the Jewish philosophy that flourished in an early Islamic and a medieval Western cultural environment," with the note (6), "Samuel points out . . . that I do not mention the Talmud, the Mishnah, the Midrashim, or any Jewish philosopher—not even Spinoza." But I prefer my own statement about Toynbee to Toynbee's.

11 I am in a position to appreciate Mr. Samuel's confession (pp. 18 f.) that "My [time of?] troubles began quite early . . . on page 35 of Volume I (of Toynbee's *Study*) . . ." and before too long "It began to dawn on me that, incredibly enough, the man was quite serious. . . ."

of Israel, his concern for the Arabs who left Israel in 1948 in the hope of returning shortly to a land without Jews, and the like.[12]

Let us see what role the term Syria has played in Islamic terminology. In 1950 P. K. Hitti, Professor of Arabic at Princeton University—and not known for Zionist or Israeli sympathies—published a rather large book of some 750 pages under the title *History of Syria, Including Lebanon and Palestine*. Dr. Hitti is a specialist in matters Islamic and Arabic, not Biblical or Ancient Near Eastern. In writing this book, and in choosing the title that he did, the author manifested a lamentable unconcern for matters Biblical and Jewish, so that, as a Christian reviewer noted, "To the history of the Hebrews from the Exodus to Alexander only fifty pages are devoted, and to Herod and his father only a single page." [13] Of course, Dr. Hitti was using the term "Syria" in the manner that Arabs used it, viz., the eastern coastland of the Mediterranean. For the Land of Israel, as such, was regarded as but an appendage to Syria. Such cities as Jerusalem and Hebron had special sanctity for the Moslems; but the Land as a whole did not.

Among the numerous Moslem guidebooks to the holy places in Palestine, C. D. Matthews selected as "the two most interesting and typical" *The Book of Arousing Souls to Visit Jerusalem's Holy Walls* by Ibn al-Firkah (1262–1320) and *The Book of Inciting Desire to Visit Abraham the Friend*, etc., written in 1351 by Abu 'l-Fida', and made them available in English translation under the rather startling title, *Palestine—Mohammedan Holy Land*, published in 1949 in Yale's *Oriental Series* (*Researches*, Vol. XXIV). I say startling, because the simple fact is that Palestine was not to the Mohammedans the Holy Land, any more than, say, it was to the Christians; and in these two guidebooks it is only Jerusalem and Hebron in all of Palestine that were taken up.

What Matthews did was to make the original Arabic manuscripts say what they never did! Thus, for example, whereas al-Firkah called his Chapter XII "On the Merits of Jerusalem in Summary,"

12 I wonder whether this concern (pro-Arab as against anti-Zionist) is any more genuine than his tears for the six million Jews obliterated by the Nazis and their collaborators. I note his specific assertion, "In the Jewish [to distinguish from the Christian?] Zionists I see the disciples of the Nazis" (*Reconsiderations*, p. 628). I am not aware that Toynbee has employed the expression "disciples of the Nazis" for any of the many—alas, so many! —Christians (and Moslems) who assisted, or hoped to be in a position to assist, in the fiendish Nazi holocaust. Solomon Zeitlin ("Jewish Rights in Eretz Israel [Palestine]," *Jewish Quarterly Review*, 52 [July 1961], 31), in his devastating rejoinder (pp. 12–34) to Toynbee's denial of "Jewish Rights in Palestine" (*ibid.*, pp. 1–11), commented on this intentionally provocative

Matthews arbitrarily added "(and Palestine)"—and this in spite of the fact that this chapter begins with the clear statement: "On the authority of Abu Umamah it is related: The Apostle of Allah said, The Koran was sent down unto me in three places, Mecca, Medina, and Syria—which means Jerusalem, as Walid says." Or when he mentioned (p. xxiii, note 6) al-Maqdisi's *Inciter of Desire to Visit Jerusalem and Syria* (written in 1350) as an "Arabic document of Moslem veneration of Palestine," Matthews has, without justification, not only substituted "Palestine" for "Jerusalem" (al-Quds) but even inserted after his "Jerusalem," in the English translation of the title, the words: "(or Palestine)." Again, when he commented on the term "Syria" in A. Guillaume's *Traditions of Islam* (1924), Matthews himself adds to the Traditions on the religious merits of Syria the words: "including Palestine and Jerusalem"! But Dr. Matthews—who became an employee of an oil company in the Near East—was writing in a period when Arab and Jewish claims to Palestine were in conflict, and he was moved in the twentieth century to attribute to a couple of pious Moslem pilgrims of the thirteenth-fourteenth centuries a concept that they did not themselves manifest.[14]

Again, when Sherif Hussein of Mecca and Sir Arthur McMahon of Great Britain exchanged secret letters in 1915–1916 on the distribution of the spoils of the Ottoman Empire, Palestine as such was not even mentioned in the correspondence. But then, why should that territory—for that is virtually all that it was to the Moslems—have been spelled out by name when the term Syria was understood to include it? And that is why, for example, statistics for Palestine are so difficult to come by for the period prior to the British Mandate; the statistics for Syria, the head and the body of the state of which Palestine was but the tail, automatically included and absorbed those of the region to the south of it. But it is hardly necessary to pursue the matter here.

Now let us get back to A. J. Toynbee. We had noted previously in his *Reconsiderations* [15] the "confession" to a "dim spot . . . I am

expression of Toynbee's: "*Pace*, Professor! How many Zionists put Christians into gas chambers?"

13 H. H. Rowley, in 1951 *Book List* of the British Society for Old Testament Study.

14 For additional references, see my review of Mattthews' book in *In Jewish Bookland*, March, 1950, p. 2. See also, e.g., S. Zeitlin, "Jewish Rights in Palestine," *Jewish Quarterly Review*, 38 (Oct., 1947), 119–

134.

15 This is as good a place as any to note that Toynbee's title is something of a misnomer, and Arthur Schlesinger, Jr., has driven home this point rather well in his review of the book (*New York Post*, May 14, 1961, Book Review page): ". . . For a moment, one is involuntarily impressed by the apparent openness of manner, by the eager interest in new evidence, by the

ignorant of the Rabbinical Jewish literature . . . my neglect of Israel, Judah, the Jews, and Judaism. . . . Since childhood, Hebrew has left me cold. . . . This partiality is evidently irrational. . . ." (Of course, one who is ignorant of an entire civilization and irrationally partial against it ought not write about it.) This confession comes as no surprise even to one who might have read only the "Acknowledgements and Thanks" in Vol. X of the *Study* (pp. 213–242; "large parts" of this section were reproduced in *The Saturday Review*, October 2, 1954, pp. 13–16, 52–55, under "I Owe My Thanks"). In this bit of autobiography [16] Toynbee gives thanks to such diverse people, books, etc., as: I. To Marcus (Aurelius) for teaching me to return thanks to my benefactors . . . II. To my Mother, for making me an Historian . . . IV. To People, Institutions, Landscapes, Monuments, Pictures, Languages, and Books, for exciting my curiosity . . . V. and VI. To People and Books, for teaching me Methods of Intellectual Work . . . [and] Methods of Literary Presentation . . . VII. To People, Monuments, Apparatus, Pictures, Books, and Events, for giving me Intuitions and Ideas . . . VIII. To People and Institutions [not "Slums"?], for showing Kindness to me.

In section IV Toynbee specifies, among numerous persons and books, his great-uncle, Robert Browning, Heyerdahl's *Kon-Tiki*, E. Creasy's *The Fifteen Decisive Battles of the World*, the four-volume *Story of the Nations*, Col. G. F. R. Henderson's *Stonewall Jackson*, "My Mother's account of her conversation with the disgruntled custodian of the deserted royal palace at Hanover, when she visited it

---

asserted readiness to change views when proven wrong. Yet after a time, one begins to wonder. Toynbee's very intensity of concern with his critics, his microscopic analysis of their objections, his almost compulsive turning of the other cheek—and all combined with a stubborn adherence to his original views—begin to rouse suspicion . . . one feels more than ever in his work, despite the stylistic gestures of diffidence and open-mindedness, the presence of a ruthless and gigantic intellectual imperialism deeply persuaded that all history can be subjugated to his private network of categories and generalizations. 'I have,' Dr. Toynbee writes, 'a passion for unity,' by which he means, among other things, for 'a unitary vision of human affairs and of all other phe-

nomena.' It is on this altar that he has sacrificed the writing of history. In the end, one cannot escape the conclusion that, as William James wrote of Hegel, such a passion turns its practitioner into a philosophic monster."

16 Toynbee's obsession with himself has been noted notoriously; a normal person finds himself feeling uncomfortable in the presence of this constant exhibitionism. Bloom, e.g., has commented. ". . . In Mr. Toynbee's case . . . the personality and the purpose—it is perhaps not too much to speak of his mission —all but overwhelm the interpretation and dictate to the material. This has been said before, but the chief value of the twelfth volume of *A Study* is to dramatize the role that Mr. Toynbee plays in his own 'history.'" In the section "*Ad Hom-*

during her stay in Germany in A.D. 1885, made me realize, even as a child, that all was not well under the surface in Prussia-Germany"— and, in the midst of all these and the others, "The Genealogy of the descendants of Noah's three sons in the tenth chapter of the Book of Genesis. . . ." From among the very many hundreds of books and articles that Toynbee had read and had been influenced by, one would think that the Old Testament stood somewhere at the top of the list. He was seven years old, he tells us, when he came across Genesis 10 in a lesson in school: "I was excited to find myself, as I supposed, being admitted to an inside view of the panorama of the unfolding of human history from the bud." Apart from a reference to "The Gospels and Herodotus . . ." and "The Authorized Version of the Bible, made in the reign of King James I . . ." (in Section VII) this is all the Acknowledgments and Thanks that Toynbee owes the Bible! And one may well marvel: Did not Moses, or David, or Elijah, or Hosea, or Isaiah, or Amos, or Micah, or Jeremiah, or the Psalmist, or Job, among others, arouse in him something to remember and recall thankfully? Could it really have been only the genealogy in Genesis 10, out of the entire Hebrew Bible, that he can recall with thanks? Interestingly, *The Saturday Review* (p. 54) reproduced the following paragraph under the caption, *Toynbee on History:* "What do we mean by History? The writer would reply that he meant by History a vision —dim and partial, yet (he believed) true to reality as far as it went— of God revealing Himself in action to souls that were sincerely seek-ing Him." Is not this the very essence of the Hebrew Bible? [17]

---

inem" (*Reconsiderations*, II Annex, pp. 573–657) Bloom has noted that Toynbee "presents a full self-portrait as an appendix of 84 pages supported by 266 footnotes. He himself is the subject of the longest entry in the index: 373 references to the text, many of them to passages of several pages . . . a sample of the items . . . : Toynbee, A. J., . . . as a furniture-shifter, . . . attempts the impossible, . . . birth of [five references], . . . hypocrisy, accused of, . . . insight of, . . . not anti-Semitic, . . . openness of his mental horizon, . . . the self-destructive bent of his thought, . . . stimulating effect of his work, . . ." (pp. 735–736 of the *Index*). It is not easy to suppress a smile, and more, while perusing this entry.

17 Of course theology is not yet his-tory; and while Biblical Israel was the first to produce historians (e.g., the authors of the books of Samuel and Kings), over twenty-five centuries ago, the quotation here cited from Toynbee does not mark him a historian. G. Mattingly noted this in his review of Toynbee's *Civilization on Trial* (1948; in *Journal of Modern History*, Vol. 21, No. 4 [Dec. 1949], pp. 360–361): ". . . This is not quite the same Toynbee who wrote the first six volumes of the *Study*. . . . He now stands his former thesis (the gist of which is that the higher religions are subsidiary to civiliza-tions . . .) on its head, holding that civilizations are subsidiary to religion and that the whole of history has meaning only as it has pointed to one far-off divine event, the universal triumph of Christian-

And the litany of the saints that Toynbee compiled, with which to bring the main text of his ten-volume *Study* to a close! This is an extraordinarily grotesque mishmash even for a theologian. The prayer begins (*A Study*, X, pp. 143 f.):

"*Christe, audi nos.*

Christ Tammuz, Christ Adonis, Christ Osiris, Christ Balder, hear us, by whatsoever name we bless Thee for suffering death for our salvation.

Christe, Jesu, exaudi nos.

Buddha Gautama, show us the path that will lead us out of our afflictions.

Sancta Dei Genetrix, intercede pro nobis.

Mother Mary, Mother Isis, Mother Cybele, Mother Ishtar, Mother Kwanyin, have compassion on us, by whatsoever name we bless thee for bringing Our Saviour into the World." [18]

The prayer ends:

"*Sancta Maria Magdalena, intercede pro nobis.*

Blessed Francis, who for Christ's sake didst renounce the pride of life, help us to follow Christ by following thee.

Omnes Sancti et Sanctae Dei, intercedite pro nobis;

For *ilayhi marji'ukum jami'an:* to Him return ye every one. (Qur'ān x. 4)

Finis

London, 1951, June 15, 6.25 P.M., after looking once more, this afternoon, at Fra Angelico's picture of the Beatific Vision."

Two acts are noteworthy here for us: (1) Not one specific person in the entire Old Testament is invoked, with or without an *intercede pro nobis*. Squeezed in between John the Baptist and Lucretius

ity, which will be strengthened and advanced by the sufferings consequent upon the collapse of Western civilization. . . . No new 'higher religion' will arise from the ashes of the West, because no religion higher than Christianity is possible. Even the institutional organization of its ultimate triumph is prepared. It is 'the Church in its traditional form . . . armed with the spear of the Mass, the shield of the hierarchy, and the helmet of the Papacy' . . . 'So,' he [viz. Toynbee] says at the end of his preface, 'history passes over into theology.' And one can only sigh, 'Again!' "

I don't suppose that Toynbee is any better at theology and prophecy than he is at history, since he has now given up Christianity as the source of salvation for mankind and has substituted for it—it is almost embarrassing to mention it—that good old fossil of his, no, not the Parsees, or the Monophysite Christians, or the Nestorian Christians, or the ex-Nestorians, or the Lamaistic Mahayanian Buddhists, or the Hinayanian Buddhists, or the Jains, but—the JEWS!!!

18 The prayer goes on to invoke Mi-

on the one hand and Zarathustra and Peter on the other are "the patriarchs and prophets." (2) The litany closes with a passage from the Quran, not from the Hebrew Bible, which happens to abound with sentiments of this kind.

It is clear that Toynbee is irrationally disposed against the Jewish people, ancient, medieval, and present. He was not able to overcome this irrationality and, within his scheme of things, recognize the Jewish people as a Society. Having thus precluded the use of any form of any of the terms Hebrew, Israel, and Jew, he set about finding a term that would cover over this notable Society. In all probability he hit on the term Syriac from its significance in Moslem literature. The simple fact that the Ancient Near East never knew a Syriac Society and that no competent scholar today recognizes such a Society—in short, the truth—was of secondary account. The whole concept is but the figment of the imagination of one who recognizes virtually no good in the remarkably long and varied and fruitful career of Israel.

Shushan Purim, 5722 (March 20, 1962)

This essay was completed on Purim Day. I could not go to a museum to look at a painting, say, Chagall's Rabbi of Vitebsk or one of Rembrandt's Jews; but in my mind there did run through the thought that, just as Haman is remembered on this day only by the Jewish people, it may, ironically, well be that many, many years from now the author of *A Study* will be remembered not as a historian, or even as a theologian or a prophet, but as a—confessedly "ignorant" and "irrational" disparager of the Jews—and remembered only by the Jews.

chael and Mithras ("fight at our side in our battle of Light against Darkness"), Angels and Archangels and "All ye devoted bodhisattvas," John the Baptist and "Noble Lucretius," "*Omnes Sancti Patriarchae et Prophetae*" and "Valiant Zarathustra, breathe thy spirit into the Church Militant here on Earth," St. Peter and "Tenderhearted Muhammad . . . ," St. Paul and "Blessed Francis Xavier and Blessed John Wesley," John and "Blessed Mo-ti," the Apostles and the Evangelists and "Strong Zeno . . . Pious Confucius," Ste-

phen and "Blessed Socrates," Martyrs, Gregory and "Blessed Açoka," Augustine and Jalāl-ad-Dīn Mawlānā, "singing reed," *Sancta Pater Benedicte* and Epicurus, *Sancte Antoni* and Marcus, and Monks and Hermits.

Most of this litany was reproduced in H. A. Grunwald's article, "The Mapping of a Great Mind," for *Life* (Nov. 29, 1954, pp. 87–90, 95–98). Even in this sympathetic, journalistic article, the litany is described as "a strange conglomeration."

American Cultural Influence on Israel

RAPHAEL PATAI

*

WHEN I WAS ASKED by Dr. Emanuel Neumann to contribute a paper to a volume honoring Abba Hillel Silver, it immediately struck me that, within the field of my own scholarly interest, no subject could be more suited for such a book than a discussion of the impact of American influences upon Israel. It seemed to me that an essay dealing with this topic would touch upon the very realm—that of culture—to which Abba Hillel Silver has made such an outstanding contribution in the course of several decades as a Zionist leader, an exponent of Jewish spiritual and intellectual strivings, and a mediator between Israeli and American values.

Taking the term "culture" in its broad anthropological sense, American cultural influence is so ramified in its impingements on the Israeli scene that its full analysis cannot be attempted within the limits of a brief paper. But it is feasible within these confines to block out the subject, indicating the general areas in which such influences might be present, and then to discuss two or three complexes more fully in order to illustrate concretely how all areas would have to be handled if they were to be treated exhaustively.

I

Let us begin with a brief outline of the main facets of modern Western civilization of which American culture is the most prominent exponent. This can be done under three overall headings: I) Technology; II) Social Organization; and III) Values and Doctrines.

Under TECHNOLOGY will be found: 1) The intensive use of *Energy and Power;* 2) *The Modern Factory System* and *Industrialization;* 3) The prevalence of *Scientific Food Production* including methods of improving crops and livestocks; 4) *Food Processing,* comprising canning, freezing, dehydrating, storing; 5) *Sanitation,* including

1 A similar, though by no means identical list was drawn up several Anthropologist (Vol. 48, pp. 397–406) under the title "What Is the

great emphasis on personal hygiene, medical research, preventive medicine, public health, hospitals, clinics, and general medical care; 6) *Communications,* including the press, the postal system, telephone, telegraph, radio, television, etc.; and 7) *Transportation* by mechanical means over land and water, and in the air.

SOCIAL ORGANIZATION will be found to comprise 1) *Mass Education,* or, more precisely, organized, general, compulsory and free schooling for at least eight years; 2) *Mass Recreation and Entertainment,* including organized athletics, compulsory rest days, the general availability of theaters, movies, dance and musical performances, art exhibits, and books; 3) *Social Welfare and Services,* including the protection afforded by the legal system, philanthropic foundations, social insurance, public assistance and welfare agencies and social work; 4) *Organized Finance,* including the huge network of publicly owned banking and credit institutions with functions circumscribed by law; 5) *Armed and Security Forces,* including army, navy, air force, police, etc., general recruitment and training; 6) *Universal Suffrage* through which the entire citizenry is organized into a public body represented by its elected legislative and executive organs; and 7) *Multiple Institutional Framework,* meaning that each individual is a member of several independent organized groups, such as religious, business, social. professional, etc., organizations.

Of VALUES AND DOCTRINES there are many, but the following seven seem to be the most important: 1) *The Philosophy of Democracy,* especially as formulated by Jefferson; 2) *The Philosophy of Interests,* that is, the Madisonian doctrine that society is divided into groups with clashing interests; 3) *Socialism,* based on the principle of the subordination of individual freedom to the interests of the community; 4) *Marxism* and the philosophy of Communism built upon it; 5) *The Doctrine of Freedom,* that is, the conviction that each individual has a free choice in acting, speaking, and thinking as he sees fit, within the limits of the law; 6) *The Judeo-Christian Religion,* with its ethics and morality; and 7) *The Concept of Progress,* which could also be called "ameliorism," and which is most succinctly expressed in the readiness to search for and to accept new and better things, objects, methods, ideas, in place of the old ones.[1]

It will readily be seen that each of these twenty-one complexes is present in modern Western civilization, and each, except Marxism and Communism, is found to a remarkable degree in American culture. A full treatment of our subject would require an investigation

years ago by Oscar W. Junek in the 1946 volume of the *American*

Total Pattern of Our Western Civilization?"

into the presence or absence of each one of them in the culture of modern Israel.

II

Before discussing a few examples of American influence on Israel, one or two general words of caution should be spoken. The first is that it is often difficult to distinguish in Israel between the influences of modern Western culture in general, and those of specifically American culture in particular. Were the task one of drawing a comparison between American culture on the one hand and any West European culture on the other, it could be accomplished by focusing attention on differences in emphasis, detail, elaboration, prevalence, incidence, and the like. Such variations, however, appear as minor, in fact, all but disappear, when the objective is to isolate cultural elements newly introduced, across a considerable cultural and geographical distance, into a new country, a new society, and a new culture such as those of Israel.

A related but separate problem is presented by the circumstance that Israel, or, for that matter, any other country lying outside the Western culture continent,[2] is exposed to cultural influences which, although originating in the United States, may reach it indirectly through the intermediacy of a West European country. In such a case it is doubly difficult to make valid determination as to whether the complex in question is specifically "American" or generally "Western" as it affects the Israeli cultural scene.

Considerations such as these make it necessary to limit our discussion (quite apart from the limitations of space) to a very few cultural complexes in which the "American" character is clear enough to exclude at the outset the possibility of their general "Western" origin.

Such a clearly American cultural feature, in the realm of architecture, is the skyscraper which developed in the United States, made possible by a series of American inventions (such as the method, developed in 1882 by Leroy S. Buffington in Minneapolis, of supporting multistoried buildings on a metal frame, and the elevator Elisha Graves Otis installed in 1853 at the Crystal Palace in New York). In the first decade of the twentieth century skyscrapers began to shoot up in the cities of the United States, and although subsequently they spread into Canada, Latin America, and Europe, the skyscraper as such has remained to this day a distinctly American architectural

---

2   For the definition of this concept see my *Golden River to Golden*   *in the Middle East*, Philadelphia: University of Pennsylvania Press,

achievement. When, therefore, we learn that a skyscraper capped with a restaurant and a heliport is planned for the site of the old Herzliah high school in Tel Aviv, this must be regarded as a feature of American, and not generally Western, cultural influence. The rationale of the skyscraper is to utilize to the utmost air space in congested business areas. In spite of the relatively large size of the city of Tel Aviv, circumstances do not yet necessitate the building of skyscrapers there. If it is nevertheless done, a conscious (or perhaps subconscious) intention to emulate America must be a contributory, or even the decisive, factor.

Another typically American cultural achievement, in the technological realm, is the great utilization of the *modern factory system* involving the mass production of merchandise. Although the factory system originated in England in the eighteenth century, the first complete application of all the elements of modern mass production, including the use of the famous assembly line, was introduced in 1912 at the Highland Park Plant of the Ford Motor Company. Automation, which in recent years tends to replace the conventional production lines, was also pioneered by American industry. The techniques of modern production spread rapidly from the United States to the rest of the Western world, and especially to such highly industrialized countries as Canada, England, Germany, and France. Israel, small country that it is, offers no scope for truly large-scale mass production. But within the limits imposed by its size it already has adopted (and, where necessary, adapted) the American-invented modern factory system, to a larger extent than some much more populous European countries. It is no chance that, in spite of the political and economic disadvantages of a tie-in with a country boycotted by its neighbors, certain American firms have selected Israel for the establishment of assembly plants to supply the needs of Israel herself, and to export to the Middle Eastern and South European markets. Only in Israel were they able to find, not only the requisite politico-economic security, but also the skilled (or at least easily trained) labor and management, and, above all, the general conditions and spirit of enterprise necessary for such undertakings.

The source of all technological development is *motive power*. Modern, technologically oriented cultures depend to a greater and greater extent on the availability of mechanically produced or derived motive power. In fact, a leading American anthropologist has recently come to the conclusion that *"culture advances as the amount of energy harnessed per capita per year increases, or as the efficiency or*

Road: Society Culture and Change 1962.

economy of the means of controlling energy is increased, or both." [3]
Measured by this yardstick, American culture is far advanced over all
other cultures in the world, including the other constituents of the mod-
dern Western culture continent. Whether we agree with this definition
of cultural advancement or not, the fact remains that the United States
harnesses and uses more energy per capita per year than any other
country, and that, therefore, an emphatic reliance on mechanically
produced energy can be taken as a sign of specifically American,
rather than generally Western, influence. Although data as to the per
capita per year energy consumption in Israel are not available, a general acquaintance with Israeli technological development is sufficient
to indicate the prevailing trend in this respect. Water, electricity, oil,
gas, wind, the sun and the atom are all experimented with, tapped,
put to increasing use in mechanical production as well as everyday
life in a great drive for producing more and more motive power and
harnessing more and more energy in an unmistakably American
pattern.[4]

This drive for harnessing more and more energy, characteristic of
both the United States and Israel, is merely one expression of the general trend of seeing and seeking achievement in the making of things,
and making them within the shortest span of time, which also is
shared by both countries. To illustrate the point, let me quote the
conclusions reached by a keen observer, withholding for the moment
the identity of the country be discusses:

> . . . experts often complain that it is easier to obtain public
> funds for actual new construction that may cost, say, 1 million
> money units, than it is to be voted 25,000 money units for a
> pilot plant or an exploratory survey—the latter are said to "waste
> time and delay building." When [the people] want to pay a com-
> pliment to a member of their government, they say of him that
> he is "engaged in actually *making* things," and this is supposed
> to elevate him to a platform from which he can look down conde-
> scendingly on his inferior colleagues who are merely admin-
> istrators, intellectuals and despicable eggheads. This craze for
> the "making of things" is not unconnected with the ambition to
> construct undertakings that are larger than those of one's neigh-
> bors, or the biggest of the region, or the most colossal of the con-
> tinent, and perhaps even the most spacious or modern in the
> world.

3 Cf. Leslie A. White, *The Evolution
of Culture*, New York: McGraw-
Hill, 1959, p. 56.

4 Cf. Gerald E. Tauber, *Scientific
Endeavor in Israel*, New York:
Herzl Press, 1961, pp. 65–78.

The reader's probable guess that the above was said by an observer of the American scene and mentality is mistaken. The quoted statement was made by Alex Rubner in his book *The Economy of Israel* (New York: Frederick A. Prager, 1960, pp. 233–234) in whose original text the word "Israelis" appears in place of "the people" substituted above in brackets. While the similarity, so dramatically illustrated in this passage, does not in itself indicate the presence of American influences in Israel, it clearly attests to the presence of an attitudinal climate which predisposes Israel toward American cultural complexes and values.

This, to my mind, is a much more important factor in creating in Israel a readiness to emulate American standards than the one pointed out by Rubner a few pages after the above quoted passage. In speaking of the foreign aid Israel has been receiving, he states (pp. 244–245) that "The various [political] parties differ on the form in which the aid should be expended, but none challenge the sacrosanct practice of organizing Israeli society according to such standards as are likely to attract the optimum amount of outside support." "Outside support" undoubtedly means mainly American support, but as to its effect on the organization of Israeli society one must reserve judgment until factual details become available.

III

So much for technology and the related attitudes. As far as the second great cultural realm, that of *Social Organization,* is concerned, let us pass over such obvious and oft-quoted data as the number of American books, magazines, films, and records imported into Israel, and take instead examples from the domain of the law.

It would be too lengthy and complicated to examine in detail the circumstances which brought about the reliance of Israeli courts of law on American legal precedent. However, the unanimous conclusion of those who have observed the working of Israeli courts is that their decisions are to a remarkable extent based on United States precedents, and also that arguments presented in them rely on judicial opinions from the United States.[5] In the Israeli Supreme Court, "There is a definite trend towards citing, and relying on, American precedents . . . American cases have been cited with approval in support of arguments and decisions in the fields of criminal law, contracts, and conflict of laws."[6]

5 Cf., e.g., E. David Goitein, "American Law Comes to Israel," *Congress Weekly,* New York, Dec. 3, 1956, pp. 11–12.

6 Uriel Gorney, "American Precedent in the Supreme Court of Israel," *Harvard Law Review,* Vol. 68, no. 7, May 1955, pp. 1194–1210.

As an example of American influence on the Israeli judiciary, the Zilberg judgment can be adduced, which was the basis of the value-linking of loans in Israel. Apart from the fact that the court proceedings were in Hebrew, the entire case, in both the District Court and, subsequently, in the High Court of Appeal, could have taken place in America. The case arose out of an agreement made in 1950 between two parties. The first party gave a mortgage loan to the second, at the legal 9 percent interest rate, with the proviso that should the value of the mortgaged property rise during the term of the loan, the Israeli pound value of the loan and the interest was to be regarded as having correspondingly increased. When the two-year term of the loan expired, the mortgagee refused to live up to the agreement, and was consequently sued by the lender. In court, the lender wished to base itself on the Lomax decision (Lomax [Inspector of Taxes] v. Peter Dixon Co., Ltd.; [1943] 2 All E. R. 255) and argued that the increment on the value of the loan was only compensation for the depreciation of the Israeli pound and not interest. But District Judge Lamm found for the borrower, using the Bates case (Bates v. United States 108 F. 2d. 407. CC.A. 7th. 1939) as precedent. On appeal, Judge Zilberg of the High Court of Appeal reversed judgment saying that "in his understanding of American, British and Jewish Law, it is not usurious for the lender of money to receive compensation from the borrower for the depreciation of the original money loan." [7]

Apart from, and in addition to, this intimate involvement of the Israeli courts with American precedent, the very structure of the Israeli judiciary has come to assume a certain similarity to that of its American counterpart. Thus the Supreme Court of Israel, established in 1948, was modeled after the Supreme Court of the United States, and is a court of finality. Originally it consisted of five judges, but subsequently their number was increased to nine, equalling that of the United States Supreme Court justices. [8]

In this context it should be mentioned that a few years ago a project for the formulation of a comprehensive system of laws for Israel was initiated with the participation of Harvard and Israeli jurists, at Harvard University, designated as the Harvard-Israel Cooperative Project for Israel's Legal Development. Once this system is

7 Cf. Alex Rubner, *The Economy of Israel*, pp. 253–254, quoting *Judgements of District Courts*, IX, Advocates Association, 1954 (in Hebrew); and *Judgements of Supreme Court*, XVIII, Advocates Association, 1955 (in Hebrew).

8 Cf. *Israel Government Year Book*, 1958, p. 342; Oscar Kraines, *Government and Politics in Israel*,

adopted by the Israeli judiciary, the influence of American law and legal procedure will undoubtedly increase.

At least one observer, himself a legal expert, has felt that the major contribution made by the American legal system to the Israeli is in the realm of constitutional law.[9] In 1951, for instance, the Israeli High Court had "occasion to point out that the position of the President of Israel is more similar to that of the President of the United States than of the King of England, because of the distinctions pointed out by U.S. Chief Justice Marshall" in United States v. Burr, 25 Fed. Cas. No. 14692(d) at 34 (C.C.D. Va. 1807).[10]

As to the problem of adopting a written Constitution for Israel, the argument used by Ben-Gurion and other Mapai leaders against such a procedure was that the United States took eleven years to draft and adopt its Constitution, and that England had no written constitution at all. On the other hand, those who favored a written constitution argued that the Declaration of the Establishment of the State of Israel, like the Declaration of Independence of the United States, was not legally binding.[11]

The State Comptroller of Israel, like the Comptroller General of the United States, is an agent of the legislature and is independent of the executive authority. Also "in civil rights and liberties and in the system of appeals to the Supreme Court, Israel has adopted many practices of the U.S."

Those legislators in the Knesset who opposed dual citizenship pointed to the United States as an example, arguing "that the latter's prohibition of multiple citizenship for immigrants did not retard immigration." [12]

IV

Let us now turn to the last of the three major realms of culture, that of the *Values and Doctrines*, and try to isolate within it a telling example to illustrate American influence on Israel. The last point in our list, the concept of progress, seems to offer the most promising hunting grounds. I well remember how, as early as the 1930's, the street vendors in Jerusalem, Tel Aviv, and elsewhere used to attract customers by shouting, *"Davar hadash baaretz!"* which was the somewhat clumsy Hebrew equivalent of "A novelty in the country!" The value of novelty has not ceased to be upheld and appreciated in the

Boston: Houghton Mifflin, 1961, p. 143.

9 Uriel Gorney, *loc. cit.*

10 *Op. cit.*, pp. 1206–1207.

11 Cf. Oscar Kraines, *op. cit.*, pp. 29, 31.

12 *Op. cit.*, pp. 105, 142, 168.

Yishuv to this day. Just as in America, anything "new" almost automatically carries the connotation of being "better" than the "old." This, at least, is characteristic of the mentality of that part of the *Yishuv* which either is of European extraction, or has become Westernized. The thinking of the Middle Eastern half of the population is, of course, still largely traditional, which means a valuation of the old and a repugnance to the new.

Unquestionably the most important outcome of this difference in the attitudinal position between the Western and the Middle Eastern halves of Israel's population is the former's demand of reform put to the latter. This attitude of the culturally and socially dominant Western element in Israel to the culturally and socially recessive Middle Eastern element exhibits a marked resemblance to the one that characterized the American approach to immigrant minorities. The similarity is the more striking since it is not confined to a single static situation, but covers complex processes of correlation between ideological postures and changes in the demographic picture. And since these processes took place first in America, in fact, several decades before they were reenacted in Israel, it is tempting, to say the least, to look for signs of conscious Israeli emulation of the American precedent, even though one cannot expect in this realm to find explicit statements like those in the legal field. Let us recapitulate the main points of resemblance.

The era of greatest mass immigration to the United States was the years preceding the First World War. In the dozen years from 1903 to 1914 close to twelve million immigrants arrived, or almost one-third of all the immigrants who came in the 131 years from 1820 to 1950. The great majority of those twelve million immigrants (some four-fifths of them) came from southern and eastern Europe, that is, were culturally "alien" to the majority population of the country with its predominantly Anglo-Saxon culture. The increase represented by this immigration of twelve million over the population of approximately eighty million in 1902, was 15 percent in twelve years. From 1915 on the immigration was drastically reduced, first by war conditions, and later on by legal limitations, to figures as low as twenty-three to thirty-six thousand annually in the years 1932–1936.

In comparison, the crest of the immigration wave hit Israel with a much greater intensity. In 1948, when the mass immigration began,

13 It is an interesting detail and worth pointing out in this connection, that there was one year in which tiny Israel admitted more immigrants *in absolute figures* than the United States which at the time was 150 times more populous: in 1949 239,141 immigrants ar-

Israel had 640,000 Jewish inhabitants and an undetermined number of Arabs estimated at about 60,000. From 1948 to the end of 1951, that is, in four short years, over 700,000 immigrants were admitted, thereby doubling the total population of the country.[13] Among these immigrants, about 45 percent had come from East and Central Europe, and 55 percent from the Middle East. These Middle Eastern Jewish immigrants (about 380,000 in absolute figures from 1948 to 1951 inclusive) were unquestionably more alien culturally to the established Jewish population of Israel (who were mostly of East European, and secondarily of Central European extraction) than had been the South and East European immigrants forty years earlier to the then established American stock. From 1952 on the immigration decreased suddenly and greatly. As against the approximately 174,000 who came in 1951, only 23,400 came in 1952. As against the more than 700,000 who came in the four-year period of 1948–1951, only 87,600 came in the subsequent four-year period (from 1952 to 1955) and 175,000 in the next (1956–1959). The non-European contingent among the immigrants evinced a marked relative increase: as against the 55 percent from the Middle East in 1948–1951, in the 1952–1955 period they constituted about 85 percent, and in 1956–1959 roughly 60 percent of the total immigration.

The significant thing is, however, not that in both America and Israel immigration increased to a certain peak after which a marked decrease set in, but the reaction of the established inhabitants to the obvious cultural difference between themselves and the immigrants. In America, the reaction to the mass immigration of the pre-World War I decade was a vision of the country as a vast "melting pot" (the term itself was coined and the idea given concrete expression by Israel Zangwill) which, as Max Lerner noted, "was a dangerous metaphor since it implied that all the immigrant strains must be purified by being assimilated with something more 'American.' "[14] In a completely analogous manner, it was felt in Israel during the period of the 1948–1951 mass immigration that the "fusion of the exiles" ("*mizzug haggaluyot*") was a cultural imperative for the country, that those immigrants who were ethnically and culturally different from the *Yishuv's* self-stereotype, that is, the Middle Eastern Jews in the first place, must be rapidly and completely assimilated to the Western folkways and mores established in Israel by the Ashkenazi Jews.[15]

rived in Israel as against 188,317 in the United States.

14 Max Lerner, *America as a Civilization*, New York: Simon and Schus- ter, 1957, pp. 91–92.

15 Cf. R. Patai, *Israel Between East and West*, Philadelphia: Jewish Publication Society, 1953, p. 298.

When, following World War I and the 1924 immigration law, the number of immigrants to the United States diminished to a fraction of what it had been up to 1914, second thoughts began to come to a few influential thinkers, such as Randolph Bourne[16] and Horace M. Kallen.[17] The picture of "American culture as a kind of manufacturing process which stamps out cultural diversities and turns complex human material into a monolithic Great Stone Face" was now replaced by "the idea of a 'cultural pluralism' in which the ethnic groups cherish their own traditions while refusing to isolate themselves from the larger culture." [18] Again, in precise analogy, once the great wave of immigration to Israel subsided, by the beginning of 1952, the voices claiming for the Jewish ethnic groups (the so-called 'edoth) the right to retain at least a modicum of their own cultural identity became more and more often heard and heeded.

Thus the American-Israeli correspondence is far-reaching on both the factual and the ideological side. It would, to be sure, be difficult to adduce evidence to the effect that the Israeli switch from the melting pot idea to that of cultural pluralism came about as a direct result of American influence or of the American example. Indirect indications (which, for lack of space, cannot be discussed here) are, however, strong enough to render it probable that such indeed was the case.

For our second example in the realm of *Values and Doctrines* let us turn to an area in which one would least expect American influence—that of religion. Again, as above, we shall pass such obvious manifestations of direct and intentional American influences as the introduction of reform Judaism as evidenced by the opening, in April, 1962, of an American-sponsored reform temple in Jerusalem. Instead, let us try to have a look at the—to all appearances—specifically Israeli issue of the relationship between the state and its recognized rabbinical authorities. Characteristically, one finds that even in this most particularly Israeli problem whose solution must, of course, be sought mainly along lines indicated by Jewish history and Jewish tradition, when nevertheless foreign examples or precedents are referred to,

16 "Transnational America," in *A History of a Literary Radical and Other Essays*, New York, 1920.

17 Horace M. Kallen, *Culture and Democracy in the U.S.*, New York, 1924. In fact, Horace Kallen expressed his new idea of cultural pluralism as early as 1915 in an article in *The Nation* in which he stated: ". . . As in an orchestra, every type of instrument has its specific timbre and tonality, founded in its substance and form; as every type has its appropriate theme and melody in the whole symphony. So in society each ethnic group is the natural instrument, its spirit and culture are its theme and melody, and the harmony and dissonances and dis-

they are American. American examples are pointed to occasionally by both those who wish for a complete separation between the secular state authorities and the Jewish religious institutions, and those who advocate a closer union between them. In arguing, for instance, that a religious school system supported, not by state aid, but by the religious community itself, would attain a level higher than the present, Dr. Isaiah Leibowitz "points to Catholic religious schools in America as an example of what a believing religious community can do if it wants to." [19] His opponents, on the other hand, point to the small percentage of Jews in the United States who send their children to all-day religious schools supported on a voluntary basis, and use this American example as an argument for continued government support of the religious schools in Israel.[20]

V

In conclusion, it is tempting to speculate on the causes that may have been at work in bringing about this multifaceted impact of American culture on Israel. Several factors can at once be eliminated. American cultural influence on Israel is not based on demographic circumstances: Americans form one of the smallest immigrants' groups in the country. The numerically largest population group in Israel, that of the Middle Eastern Jews, exerts an almost negligible cultural influence. Nor is it based on the prestige of early arrivals: the Second Aliya, which laid the foundations of modern Israel, was mainly Russian and Polish, yet their culture is today merely the substratum which accepts, almost as passively as the culture of the Middle Eastern immigrants, American influences. Nor can this influence be ascribed to administrative domination: America never ruled Palestine, and as to the British who did for thirty years, their cultural influence largely disappeared with their withdrawal in May, 1948. Nor can it be attributed to close diplomatic support or harmony in the international political arena: in fact, America's attitude in connection with the Sinai campaign and on other occasions has evoked a rather bitter reaction in Israel. Yet it is America, rather than consistently friendly France, which preponderates on the Israeli cultural scene. And lastly, although in internal politics Israel's major party as

cords of them all make the symphony of civilization. . . ." Similarly, and in the same year, Louis D. Brandeis said, "The new nationalism adopted by America proclaims that each race or people, like each individual, has the right and duty to develop, and that only through such differentiated development will high civilization be attained." Cf. *Brandeis on Zionism*, Washington, D.C., 1942.

18 Max Lerner, *op. cit.*, p. 93.

19 Herbert Weiner, "Church and State in Israel," *Midstream*, Vol. viii, no. 1, Winter, 1962, p. 7.

20 *Op. cit.*, p. 10.

well as some smaller ones are socialistically oriented, it is not Russia, nor any of the other "socialist republics" of East Europe, but capitalistic America whose culture exerts by far the strongest influence on Israel.

Some observers of the Israeli scene have contended that America's influence on Israel can be explained by certain similarities between the histories of the two countries. America was originally a wild, underdeveloped and underpopulated country; it was settled by pioneers who conquered it, expanded its frontiers, lived first under colonial rule, then achieved liberty, statehood, and independence. Israel's history from 1882 on can, it is true, be described in largely similar terms. Yet even though there is a possibility that these corresponding circumstances may have resulted in certain similarities in outlook and mentality, they cannot be adduced as an explanation of American cultural influence on Israel for the simple reason that most Israelis are not sufficiently familiar with American history to be at all aware of the similarities between it and the history of Israel's settlement.

We are thus left with one possibility only: to look for the causes of American cultural influence on Israel within the nature and quality of the two cultures themselves: the American, which is ready to exert it, and the Israeli, which is willing to receive it.

There seem to be two characteristics of American culture which endow it with an unmatched power to influence: its dynamism and its dimensions. Other members of the Western culture continent are, of course, similarly dynamic and aggressive, although it seems that none of them quite measures up to America. When this, in itself perhaps not too significant, difference is coupled with the much greater difference in dimensions, the result is a cultural striking force surpassing by far anything found in other Western countries. America, more than any other country, has given Israel financial, economic, and technical assistance, and aid, in whatever form, invariably means cultural influence.

From the point of view of Israel, America as the most populous, powerful, and influential country of the West represents the goals many Israelis would like to achieve. American influence in all fields of culture is, therefore, willingly, nay, eagerly accepted by the great majority of people. In other non-Western cultures the willingness to Westernize is checked and limited by a resistance to Westernization based on the fear that the local traditional culture might get completely lost in the process.[21] No such apprehension seems to bother

21 Cf. R. Patai, *Golden River to Golden Road.*

Israel. The relative scarcity of objections to the spread of American cultural influences in Israel indicates to what extent the young Israeli culture has achieved a self-assurance which even older non-Western cultures often lack. Israel is willing to absorb as many cultural features and complexes as America is able to offer, because it knows that the sum total of these influences can only embellish or augment, but never supplant, its own old-new Biblical-Hebraic-Judaic culture.

A Jewish State in Midian

THE ENGLISH SOURCES ON PAUL FRIEDMANN'S SCHEME OF
1891–1892

OSKAR K. RABINOWICZ

*

IN HIS IMPORTANT WORK *Modern Egypt* [1] Lord Cromer, onetime "Her Majesty's Agent and Consul General in Egypt, Minister Plenipotentiary" wrote:

> When the Firman[2] of 1892 was in the course of preparation, the British Ambassador at Constantinople was assured that it was identic with that of 1879. There was, however, reason to believe that this statement was incorrect. The Porte had always been sensitive as regards European interference in or near the Hedjaz. Indeed, the law allowing foreigners to acquire real property in the Ottoman dominions forbids any European to settle in the Hedjaz. More than this, the Sultan's suspicions had been aroused by two recent incidents. One was that Turkish misgovernment had produced a revolt in the province of Yemen, which was, without a shadow of foundation, attributed to British intrigue. The second was that a well intentioned German enthusiast named Friedmann, of Jewish origin, was, at the moment when

---

1 Macmillan & Co. Two Volumes. London, 1908. The quotation is in Vol. II, pp. 267–268.
2 A former royal decree in Turkey.
3 Then the Turkish Commissioner in Egypt.
4 Saul Raphael (Landau) "Midian (Zur Warnung)" in *Selbst-Emancipation* Vienna, Nr. 19, October 2, 1891, p. 4. "Midian," a letter from a participant in the expedition, *ibid.*, Nr. 5, March 4, 1892, pp. 57–58. B. (Dr. Nathan Birnbaum), "Die Friedmanniade," *ibid.*, Nr. 5, March 4, 1892, p. 52. E. F. (a par-

ticipant in the expedition) "Aus Midian," in *Die Allgemeine Zeitung des Judenthums*, Berlin, Vol. 56, Nr. 9, February 26, 1892 (Supplement), pp. 3–4. "Paul Friedmanns Expedition nach Midian," *ibid.*, Nr. 14, April 1, 1892, pp. 161–162 (letters by a participant, dated December 12, 1891, February 12, 15, and 25, 1892). *Ibid.*, Nr. 45, November 4, 1892 (Supplement), p. 1 brings without title the court decisions *in causa* Friedmann v. various newspapers. Davis Trietsch, *Bilder aus Palaestina,*

the Firman was under discussion, endeavouring to establish a settlement of some couple of dozen Jews, who had been expelled from Russia, on the eastern shore of the Gulf of Akaba. This was suspicious. Moukhtar Pasha[3] pointed out that the Jews had always been waiting for a Messiah to reconquer Jerusalem, and that, without doubt, they would think he had now appeared in the person of Mr. Friedmann. It was not difficult to convince Moukhtar Pasha that Mr. Friedmann was devoid of such pretensions. But the suspicions of the Sultan were not easily calmed. The result was that the Firman laid down the Egyptian frontier as drawn from Suez to El-Arish. The Peninsula of Sinai, which had been administered by the Khedives of Egypt for the last forty years, would thus have reverted to Turkey. When, therefore, the Firman arrived, the British Government interposed and placed a veto on its promulgation. After a short delay, the Grand Vizier telegraphed to the Khedive accepting a proposal, which had been offered to the Sultan some weeks previously, but which His Imperial Majesty had then refused to entertain. Under this arrangement, the frontier of Egypt was drawn from El-Arish to the Gulf of Akaba. The incident was thus for the time being terminated, and the Firman was promulgated with all customary pomp.

Behind these few lines lies a most interesting attempt at the creation of a Jewish state in Midian, on the northwest shore of the Arab Peninsula, and the fascinating story of a well meaning man who was caught in the web of international intrigues which brought his efforts to nought. It all began in the late 1880's when Paul Friedmann, a baptized Jew in Berlin, conceived the idea of finding a territory for the persecuted Jews in Eastern Europe who at that time were streaming westwards in search of new homes.

Friedmann's colonization attempts have not as yet been told in English. There exist some essays in German[4] and Hebrew,[5] all based

Orient-Verlag, Berlin, 1917, Chapter "Madian," pp. 123–125. Dr. N. M. Gelber, "Eine missglueckte Judenstaatsgruendung im Midjangebiete," in *Die Stimme*, Vienna, July 28, 1932, to March 30, 1933. Josef Fraenkel, "Madian," in *Die Neue Welt*, Vienna, October 14 and 21, 1932. Saul Raphael Landau, *Sturm und Drang in Zionismus*, Vienna, 1937, pp. 169–176.

5 Azriel Guenzig, correspondence from Crakow, in *Hamagid*, Berlin, No. 43, November 5, 1891, pp. 337–338. *Ibid.*, No. 5, February 4, 1892, letter from a participant from Alexandria, pp. 38–39. Jaacob Weinshall, "Midyan Pasha" in *Maariv* (Special Supplement in memory of Herzl's anniversary in 1949), Tel Aviv, 1949. Yosef Braslavsky, *Hayadata et Haaretz*, Vol. II, Jerusalem, 1946, pp. 12–22. G. Kressel, "Medinath Hayehudim Be'eretz Midyan," in *Molad'ti*, Tel Aviv, 1950, pp. 88–90. N. M. Gelber, "Nissayon Shelo Hitzliah" in *Shiv'at Zion*, Jerusalem, Vols. 2–3, 1953, pp. 251–274.

on contemporary Continental newspaper reports and on the file *Turkey XVIII* in the Vienna States Archives. During my work in the London Foreign Office Archives, I came across a few documents and entries on this scheme, and it is this collection that I now present for the first time.[6] I am grateful to the London Foreign Office for permitting me to publish these documents. I supplement them by other contemporary references to Friedmann and his plans from English and American materials, hitherto not mentioned in the literature. Thus the following constitutes a first collection of sources in English on the Midian scheme.[7]

By the time Friedmann conceived his plans he had been recognized as an accomplished historian of sixteenth century England. At the age of twenty-nine, in 1869, he had published both in French and in Italian the diplomatic correspondence of the Venetian Ambassador in England, Giovanni Michiel;[8] and in 1884 he published a biography of Anne Boleyn,[9] Henry VIII's second wife. This work is to this day regarded as "the most important contribution to the history of this subject." [10] It is in large sections based on the diplomatic documents which Friedmann consulted in various European archives pertaining to the period. It was hailed at the time by the greatest contemporary authority on the subject, James Gairdner,[11] as "an outstanding contribution to English history." Another reviewer in the London *Spectator* [12] "rejoiced at the appearance of this book," and stated that "Mr.

6 One of these documents (Baring's letter to Salisbury of February 9, 1892) was published by Dr. Jacob M. Landau in his Hebrew essay "Nissayon Hahithyashevuth Hayehudith Bemidyan" in *Shiv'at Zion*, Jerusalem, Vol. I, 1950, pp. 169–178.

7 There is a short paragraph on Friedmann in *The Jewish Encyclopedia*, Vol. 5, New York, 1903, p. 519 (written by Prof. Richard Gottheil).

8 *Les Dépêches de G. Michiel, Ambassadeur de Venise en Angleterre pendant les années de 1554 à 1557, dechifrées et publiées par Paul Friedmann.* Imprimerie du Commerce, Venise, 1869 (288 pp.). In Italian: *I Dispacci di G. Michiel . . . deciferati da Paul Friedmann, ibid.*

9 *Anne Boleyn. A Chapter of English History 1527–1536* by Paul Friedmann, two volumes, London, Macmillan & Co., 1884 (308 pp. and 383 pp. respectively). A French

edition of this book was published 19 years later; *Lady Anne Boleyn . . .* Traduit de l'anglais par Lugné-Philipon et Dauphin Meunier. Paris, A. Fontemoing, 1903. I. Vers le schisme. II. Après le schisme.

10 Congers Read, *Bibliography of British History. Tudor Period 1485–1603*, Clarendon Press, Oxford, 1959, p. 42, No. 499. The same Bibliography regards Friedmann's introduction to his edition of the Michiel Dispatches (see footnote 8) as a "valuable preface" (*ibid.*, p. 85, No. 994).

11 He was assistant keeper of the Public Record Office, London, and among others, co-editor and subsequently editor of the *Calendars of Letters and Papers of the Reign of Henry VIII* (21 volumes). Friedmann thanked Gairdner in the preface to *Anne Boleyn* for the valuable assistance in the collection of the material. Gairdner's review of *Anne Boleyn* appeared in *The Academy*, London, Vol. 26, November

Friedmann, like Ranke,[13] tells us much that is new and important
. . . and he does it, without falling into the strange mistake into
which Ranke falls about internal English matters." Reviewers in other
important periodicals were no less enthusiastic about Friedmann's
work.[14]

Some doubts have been uttered whether Friedmann, the author
of an important English historical work, and the German, formerly
Jewish, proponent of the Midian colony were one and the same person. They were. The contemporary reviewers referred to him as "a for-
eigner writing of English affairs mainly from foreign archives," [15]
and "congratulate him on his mastery of our language."[16] Gairdner,
who had met Friedmann frequently while assisting him in gathering
the material for the biography, spoke of "the author, a German, who
has resided much in this country." [17] Probably with reference to his
Jewish descent and therefore unbiased stand towards Christian
denominations, the *Edinburgh Review* [18] found "the great value of
Mr. Friedmann's book . . . that he approaches all questions without
the smallest prejudice either towards Protestantism of Catholicism."

Friedmann's literary activity was remembered by *The New York
Times* when his Midian colonization scheme was there mentioned
for the first time: [19]

Dr. Friedmann is a gentleman of Jewish descent, a native of
Berlin,[20] and at present a resident of that city, though he has

1, 1884, pp. 282–283 (4 columns).

12 Vol. 57, 1884, pp. 1735–1737 (4
columns) and Vol. 58, 1885, pp.
16–17 (4 columns).

13 A great honor indeed for Friedmann. Ranke, one of the foremost
German historians, wrote about the
struggle for the constitutional
monarchy in England and its
achievements in the revolution of
1688, in *Englishche Geschichte
vornehmlich in 17. Jahrhundert.*

14 For instance, *The Athenaeum*, London, January 17, 1885, pp. 80–81
(3½ col.): "No historian has studied this period with greater care
than Mr. Friedmann" (p. 80); or
*The Annual Register for the Year
1885*, London, 1886, pp. 71–72
". . . for a detailed account of
the period of the Reformation, in
the form of a completed history,
one must look to Mr. Friedmann
alone," p. 71. See also further below.

15 *The Spectator, op. cit.,* Vol. 58,
p. 16.

16 *Ibid.,* Vol. 57, p. 1735.

17 *The Academy, op. cit.,* p. 282.

18 or *Critical Journal for January,
1886 . . . April, 1886*, Vol. 63,
Edinburgh, 1886, p. 61 (the entire
review stretches over 17 full pages
(pp. 54–71).)

19 June 30, 1891, p. 1, col. 7.—*The
New York Times* throughout the
article wrote of "Dr." Friedmann.
In one of the dispatches published
in *The New York Herald* (May 1,
1892, p. 21, col. 4) he was referred
to as " 'Herr' or 'Doctor' or 'King'
Friedmann." However, it was not
possible to ascertain whether he
graduated.

20 He was born in Koenigsberg, Prussia, on April 26, 1840. (Letter from
the Berlin Police President to the
German Foreign Secretary of September 2, 1891. In File Turkey
XVIII (referred to above), Nr. 1884
P.J.)

spent the greater part of his life in London, where he has earned
the reputation of a litterateur. He is related to the Mendelssohns,
the bankers of Berlin and Dessau,[21] and is himself very wealthy.

Also Lord Cromer, in one of his dispatches to Lord Salisbury [22]
and later in his book [23] referred to Friedman's authorship of *Anne
Boleyn*.

From Friedmann's literary activity we can draw two conclusions,
both pertinent to our theme. The one is that he had exhibited in his
works a good understanding of the conduct of diplomatic affairs,[24]
and the second is that, thanks to his good reputation in scholarly
circles, he would encounter no difficulties in obtaining introductions
to whomever he intended to meet, as will become clear from the
description of his negotiations further below.

When, sometime in the late 1880's, Friedmann conceived the
idea of doing something for persecuted Jews by way of settling them
in an "empty" land, the situation of the Jews in Russia had considerably deteriorated. Projects for colonizing refugees in various
lands, primarily in Palestine but also in Canada, California, Australia,
the Argentine, and others, were aired in discussions in the press and
in Jewish philanthropic circles all over the world.[25] None of these
territories, however, met with Friedmann's approval. They appeared
to him complicated as colonizing areas owing to political or administrative local conditions, or owing to the pursuit of imperialistic tendencies over underdeveloped lands by the big Powers, which made
it still more difficult to find favorable conditions for a Jewish settlement as he had visualized it. For he was against settling Jews in
existing states; he strove for an autonomy which finally might lead
to statehood. None of the countries mentioned would accept this.
He was therefore looking for an "empty" land for which neither a local
population nor any sovereign state would care much. In one of his
letters to Prof. Gottheil he wrote [26] that his first idea was:

21 Gelber (*Shiv'at Zion, op. cit.,* p.
235) quoted him as a descendant
of Veitel Ephraim Heine on the
basis of Friedmann's personal introduction in Vienna. It thus appears that Friedmann had given
one descendancy in Vienna, and
another to Prof. Gottheil in New
York, quoted in the *Times*.
22 See further below.
23 *Modern Egypt, op. cit.,* Vol. II, p.
268.
24 *The Edinburgh Review,* for instance, wrote (*loc. cit.,* p. 54) that

in his book "he has given a tolerable complete account of the relations of this country with the other
Powers of Europe."
25 The contemporary Jewish press is
full of such suggestions and discussions.
26 *New York Times, loc. cit.* Friedmann's letters to Prof. Richard
Gottheil, lecturer on Syriac languages and literature at Colum-
bia University (New York), were
the basis of a long article in *The
New York Times* referred to al-

of founding a colony for the exiled Jews in Somali,[27] which is at the east coast of Africa, near the Gulf of Aden, but after a visit of inspection to that country I concluded that it would not suit.

It was only after the negative result of this first attempt that he:

turned my attention to the Land of Midian, which extends from 26° to 30° north latitude and is situated on the Gulf of Akaba, near the head of the Red Sea.

In the further course of explaining his reasons for selecting Midian, Friedmann used an interesting argumentation which, no doubt, reveals Zionistic tendencies. *The New York Times* quoted from one of his letters to Prof. Gottheil: [28]

It is worthy of note that this idea of colonizing Jews in and about Palestine is acceptable at once to the orthodox and liberal Jews; for the former on the ground that it will be a fulfillment of prophecy, for they still look forward to the reestablishment of the Jewish Nation in Palestine, and to the latter on the purely practical ground of replacing the race under the topographical and climatic conditions in which it found its first development.[29]

Commenting on this view, *The New York Times* added:

Such were the considerations, no doubt, which eventually turned the thoughts of Dr. Friedmann to Northern Arabia, regardless of the comparatively barren nature of the country. It was undoubtedly the same idea which led the Rothschilds and the late Laurence Oliphant to found colonies in Palestine. These colonies are said to be now in a tolerably flourishing condition. Hitherto the chief obstacle in the way of carrying out the scheme on any

ready. Gottheil became later the first President of the "American Zionist Federation" (1898) and represented the Federation in the Zionist Actions Committee. He was very close to Herzl. (See Herzl's *Diaries*, Herzl Press, New York, 1960, 5 volumes. Index.) In his *Zionism* (Philadelphia, 1914) Gottheil did not mention Friedmann among the "Pre-Herzlites, "but he was the author of the short note on Friedmann in the *Jewish Encyclopedia* (see footnote 7).

27 It is noteworthy that the British Government suggested to Herzl Somaliland as a colonization area, after it had become clear that a Jewish colony in East Africa would meet with great resistance from within that territory. (Leopold Greenberg's letter to Herzl of December 15, 1903, quoted in my *Fifty Years of Zionism*, London, 1952, p. 56.)
28 *Loc. cit.*
29 This is a most unusual argument.

extended scale has been the hostile attitude of the Turkish Government, but Oscar S. Straus, ex-United States Minister to Turkey, while in that country, succeeded in softening the attitude of the Porte so far as to render further colonization possible.

Dr. Friedmann, in pursuance of his plans, made a visit last winter to the land of Midian, and has given the results of his observations in a letter to Dr. Gottheil.

With this last sentence we are already ahead of the chronology, for we left Friedmann still pondering over the practical steps which were to be taken to implement his scheme.

He was aware of the fact that in order to recruit colonists from Continental Jewry, he would have to concern himself in the first place with the authorities in these countries. He did not expect any political or other difficulties in this direction. He was sure that the governments concerned would be as happy about an orderly departure of the Jews as the Jews themselves would be in finding a place of safety. It was the territory in which to settle these Jews that was to occupy his first thoughts before embarking upon the realization of his ideas. It was thus natural that once he had made up his mind that it was to be no other land than Midian, his eyes should be directed toward England, partly because of his personal knowledge of Britain and his good contacts there, and, particularly, because Midian was within the Egyptian sphere of administration while Egypt herself had come more and more under the growing influence of Britain.

He arrived, therefore, in the summer of 1890 in London to meet the "most powerful man in Egypt," Britain's representative there— Sir Evelyn Baring, subsequently Lord Cromer, then vacationing in England. Before proceeding to London he asked the British Ambassador in Berlin, Sir Louis Mallet, to introduce him. Recollecting this first encounter and describing in detail the subsequent events, Sir Evelyn wrote one and a half years later to Lord Salisbury: [30]

Mr. Friedmann's name having been mentioned in the course of the correspondence which has taken place on the subject of the delimitation of the Eastern frontier of Egypt,[31] it will perhaps be desirable that I should report to your Lordship what I know of this gentleman and his proceedings.

I first made Mr. Friedmann's acquaintance some two or three

30 Foreign Office File F.O. 78 (4450). Confidential, No. 34, dated Cairo, February 9, 1892.

31 Reference to this is made in the first quotation from Cromer's *Modern Egypt* at the beginning of this

years ago when I was in London during my summer leave. He came from Berlin on purpose to see me. The late Sir Louis Mallet had previously written to me about him. He is a man of letters and, amongst other works, has written in English a somewhat well known history of Anne Boleyn. Though not himself a Jew, he is of Jewish extraction and takes the warmest interest in everything which affects the Jewish race. He is possessed of considerable private income, a large portion of which he devotes to benevolent works. In a word, he is an intelligent and perfectly honest man, very tenacious of his opinions, eccentric, and perhaps not very judicious in the manner in which he pursues the philanthropic objects to which he devotes his time and fortune.

He told me in London that he wished to establish at his own cost a small Colony of Jewish refugees somewhere in Egyptian territory. I told him that I did not think the scheme was at all likely to succeed, but Mr. Friedmann is not easily discouraged. He announced to me that he intended to pay a visit to Egypt in the course of the following winter. He asked me whether Her Majesty's Government would object to his proceeding: I told him that it did not appear to me that the matter concerned the English Government, that he must deal with the Egyptian Government, that he must act entirely on his own responsibility, that I should stand aloof from his proceedings, and that, although I should take no action hostile to him, he must not expect any effective support.

Mr. Friedmann accordingly came to Egypt in the winter of 1890. Count Leyden [32] spoke to me about him very much in the terms which I have used above. He said that the German Government was in no way responsible for Mr. Friedmann's proceedings, and took no interests in them, that he was an honest and well-meaning enthusiast, that his enterprise was almost sure to fail, but that it was hopeless to discourage him from making it. Mr. Friedmann came to me. I sent him to Riaz Pasha.[33] I do not think I gave him any letter of introduction but my language generally to the Egyptian authorities was in harmony with what I have said above. Knowing Riaz Pasha's dislike to European colonisation in Egypt, I thought that he would certainly oppose Mr. Friedmann's projects, and to say the truth, I rather hoped that he would do so. Greatly, however, to my astonishment Mr.

article, and will again be made further on.

32 German Consul General in Egypt.

33 Then head of the Egyptian Government.

Friedmann told me that he was very much satisfied with the conversation that he had had with Riaz Pasha, who had made no objections whatever to his undertaking. My recollection is that subsequently I mentioned the matter to Riaz Pasha in the course of conversation and that the impression left on my mind was that His Excellency took no interest whatever in Mr. Friedmann or his proceedings and that he did not wish either to discourage or to encourage him.

Mr. Friedmann then stated that he intended to visit the Sinai Peninsula [34] and the land of Midian in the hope of finding a suitable spot for his colony. I did not dissuade him. In common with others I thought that when Mr. Friedmann had personally visited the inhospitable country in which he proposed to settle, he would most probably abandon his idea. Mr. Friedmann's singular enthusiasm and tenacity of purpose rendered him, however, blind to all the difficulties which he would have to encounter. On his return he told me that he was extremely pleased with all he had seen, that he had selected a very suitable spot for his colony, and that he intended to return next year with a small party of Jews.

The result of his visit to Midian, referred to in the above report, Friedmann laid down in a brochure, written in German, *Das Land Madian*,[35] for a large part of which he obviously used Sir Richard Burton's work *Midian Revisted*.[36] But apart from the description of the territory and the consideration as to its suitability for European settlers, Friedman concentrated in his brochure on the legal aspect of a colonization in Midian and laid particular stress on paragraphs 23 and 24 of the Egyptian Law of 1875:

> . . . these lands that have no owner and can become the possession of the first owner can only be acquired with the permission of the Government; but with regard to the uncultivated lands, which by law belong to the State, these can be acquired

---

34 As will be remembered, in 1902–1903 Herzl negotiated with the British Government and with Lord Cromer regarding the establishment of an autonomous Jewish settlement in the Sinai Peninsula. In the course of these talks, the Friedmann scheme was also mentioned. (See my "Herzl and England" in *Jewish Social Studies*, New York, Vol. XIII, No. 1, 1951, pp. 25–46. Herzl's view on the Friedmann scheme is there on pp. 28–29.)

35 Printed as a manuscript in Berlin, 1891, by G. Bernstein. Madian is the rendition of Midian by the Arabic geographers.

36 Two Volumes. London, 1879. Friedmann mentioned in his brochure

with permission by the State, through an "Abadie" (a kind of leasehold) in accordance with the local regulations. Whosoever has built or planted on such land becomes full owner of the built up or planted area. However, if during the first 15 years he does not make use of such land, he loses again the right of ownership.

In a great many variations, but always within the terms of his brochure, Friedmann conveyed in his correspondence his views of the country and of the legal aspect to those whom he expected to support his scheme. The English reading public was informed about his brochure and plans in a somewhat distorted form. The name of the author was omitted and the place of publication shifted from Berlin to St. Petersburg (of all places), when *The Times* (London) published a communication from its Vienna correspondent, dated May 21, 1891: [37]

> The stringent measures adopted against the Jews in Russia must inevitably lead to their wholesale emigration, as it is out of the question that a population of four-and-a-half millions, of whom the greater part are engaged in commercial pursuits, could for any length of time exist within the rural districts assigned to them. This question is exhaustively discussed in a pamphlet which has just been published in St. Petersburg, and which contains a noteworthy suggestion. The author draws attention to a tract of land on which, in his opinion, half a million Russian Jews could easily be settled. It is situated in the north-west of Arabia, and extends along the shore of the Red Sea from Fort Akabah to El Wijht. It is still, as in Biblical times, under Egyptian jurisdiction, but at present the district is entirely neglected and all but abandoned by the Khedivial Government. The Arabian population amounts now only to some 10,000, leading a nomadic life, but the soil is said to be extremely fertile, and the climate conditions are very favourable. It is proposed to estab-

that Burton had visited Midian three times and had been looking for gold there, but in vain. Referring to this he had probably in mind Sir Richard's *The Gold Mines of Midian and the Ruined Midianite Cities*, London, 1878. Gelber (*Shiv'at Zion*, op. cit., p. 252) mentions a review of Burton's *Midian Revisited* in the London *Jewish*

Chronicle of May 25, 1877. But this as well as a later article in the same paper (May 17, 1878) refers to Burton's activities in Midian, not to his book which appeared two years later.

37 May 22, 1891, p. 5, col. 4. The London *Jewish World*, May 29, 1891, quoted this item from *The Times* in an abbreviated form.

lish there an autonomous principality with the Khedive as suze-
rain. As to the necessary funds, the author thinks they might be
raised by public subscription throughout Europe. The project is
said to have been well received in influential quarters, and, according to information obtained in Vienna, the subject has
already been broached to the Egyptian Government.

A few weeks later, a fairly comprehensive outline of the geography, climate, population, and suitability for the colonization of
Midian appeared in *The New York Times* [38] in quotations from Friedmann's letters to Prof. Gottheil.

Encouraged by his success in Egypt, Friedmann spent some time
on the Continent, visiting various countries, with a view to organizing his group of colonists. These activities of his have been fully described in the German and Hebrew literature [39] from Continental
sources and do not require repetition. He succeeded in winning support there, both with regard to finding refugees willing to join his
venture and from the Governments of Austria and Germany. The moment seemed to him now opportune to enter into official communication with the British authorities in London. He arrived there at the
beginning of May, 1891, and addressed the following letter to Lord
Salisbury: [40]

> Alexandra Hotel. Hyde Park Corner.
> London.
> 8th May, 1891.

My Lord,

The emigration on a large scale of Russian and Polish Jews
has become necessary, for the Jewish question is keeping the
mind of the Russians in a state of ferment dangerous to the
state of Europe.

The only country where the Jews may go to in great numbers
is Arabia where they would meet with no race hatred, the Arabs
expressedly acknowledging them as a younger branch of their
own stock the Beni Ibrahim. [41] The religious difference would be
but small, the Bedouin is not fanatical and would not mind it
much. If in the Yemen he treats the Jews with contempt this is
simply due to the fact that they are a broken, unarmed tribe. He
treats the broken Arab tribes: the Hutaim, the Maguani etc, even

38 *Loc. cit.*
39 Referred to in footnotes 4 and 5.
40 Foreign Office File F.O. 78. Turkey.
(Egypt. Diplomatic.) Various. January to June 1891. I. 4395. (Henceforth referred to: File F.O. 78 [4395].

worse than the Jews. Armed and disciplined Jews would be respected, they would be liked better than Europeans or Turks and might finally amalgamate.

I therefore intend to go this autumn with about 80 Galician and Hungarian Jews, picked men, old soldiers and artisans to settle and prepare for a colony in the Egyptian province of Madian in Arabia probably on the coast between Mweilah and Dubbah. The colony is to rely for its subsistence on the work the artisans will find to do for the Bedouins (who have neither smiths nor silversmiths, tailors, shoemakers, boat-builders—nor any other skilled workmen); on fishing; on trade with turquoises found in the mountains and on the polishing of them; and on working and turning of mother of pearl which is dived for on the coast. Once settled I may have little gardens to grow vegetables, then a small artificial pasture well watered by a pump to feed my cows and finally when the colonists increase, Oil, Almond and fruit trees may be grown in the mountains and vines planted. For all this the climate and soil are suitable and the Bedouins if properly treated and bribed would not much object. And if once I had 300 armed men in Madian I should be so much stronger than any Bedouin tribe that their opposition would be of no avail. So the colony might grow and prosper and attract a good many Jews from Russia, Roumania and elsewhere, new industries might be started, such as shipbuilding, cotton spinning, fabrication of pumping engines, etc.

Now for all this I want no permission from anybody. I have a right to settle in Madian just as in any other part of Egypt. And I am glad to say that having this winter seen H. E. Riaz Pasha on the matter I found him most friendly provided no responsibility were incurred. I am therefore convinced that the actual Egyptian government will not throw small vexatious impediments in my way but rather facilitate my doings. I am of course fully aware that no protection can or will be afforded to me and that in all my dealings with the Bedouins I shall have to rely solely on myself.

But if the colony prospers several questions will arise; first as to who shall rule the country which is Egyptian territory but actually in the hands of the Bedouins. If I can clearly show that the Jews are able to rule the Bedouins and to keep them in order,

41 I.e., the Children of Abraham, from whom both the Jews (through his son Isaac) and the Mohammedans (through his son) Ishmael descend.

I should like to have as much autonomy granted to the colony as possible and the influx of other strangers than Jews discouraged. Otherwise all kinds of adventurers would flock in, create disorder, quarrel and bring back the fomer anarchy. This of course will have to be decided by the Egyptian government and I only mention it to make the situation clear.

2. In case I prosper very much and get a superabundant population I shall want to extend through the rest of Arabia. The Turks I am told chiefly care for their holy land the Heggaz and their pilgrim's road to it. The rest of Arabia is of no great consequence to them and they might prefer to see it Jewish rather than in European hands. I hope that if the Jews can by fair means extend through Arabia the English government will not object to it. My hope is that they may be able to settle right across the peninsula to Oman and Hadramant and then try to build a railway which would shorten the road to India by four or five days. That of course is only a dream of the future.

There is but one difficulty which is that the Jews coming from Russia and Roumania would find nobody in Madian to nationalize them. The Russian government seems averse to allow Jews to emigrate without being naturalized elsewhere as they often are sent back to Russia and are thus a dangerous element. But I hope that even this difficulty might be solved in future.

Paul Friedmann.

Friedmann did not send this letter by mail or messenger but took it himself to the Foreign Office when calling on the Under Secretary, P. W. Currie, on May 8th. It apparently caused him no difficulty to obtain access to that office, as Currie's note to Salisbury on Friedmann's visit shows: [42]

This gentleman called on me with a letter of introduction from Mr. Cyril Hower. He stated that he was himself a Protestant but he has a scheme for which he says he can obtain ample funds for colonizing a portion of the North East Coast of the Red Sea near Mt. Sinai, which belongs to Egypt, with Polish and Russian refugee Jews. The district which he has selected is uninhabited, though there is an Egyptian fort with a few soldiers. Riaz Pasha who has been consulted offered no objection and Mr. Friedmann

---

42 File F.O. 78 (4395).

43 File F.O. 78 (4395).

44 This testifies to his diplomatic skill,

obvious in his writings, as mentioned above.

45 See my "Herzl and England" in

said he wanted nothing from H. M. Government except that they should not oppose his scheme.

As the File indicates, Friedmann personally brought the letter to Lord Salisbury when calling on Currie "with a pamphlet, descriptive of the country" (meaning, of course, his brochure on Madian). Lord Salisbury initialed Currie's note, suggested that the letter and the brochure be transmitted to Sir Evelyn Baring in Cairo, and that Friedmann's letter be acknowledged. Accordingly the following letter was dispatched to Friedmann on May 11, 1891: [43]

> Sir,
>   I am directed by the Marquis of Salisbury to acknowledge receipt of your communication of the 8th inst. and accompanying pamphlet respecting the scheme for colonizing a portion of the North East Coast of the Red Sea with Jews from Russia, Roumania, etc.
>
> P. W. Currie

The letter to the Foreign Secretary shows that Friedmann had obviously bigger ideas in mind that the initial colonization of eighty or a few hundred Jewish refugees which appeared at the moment to occupy his mind. There is no doubt that he intended to establish at first in a limited area, and subsequently as Jewish immigration, with the exclusion of non-Jews, would increase, and based on military power, a larger state, embracing "the rest of Arabia," ruled by Jews and on friendly terms with the British Government, which may become interested in that State for a safe and shortened route to India and to the rest of the Empire.[44] It is worthy of note that this idea resembles the one which Herzl advanced ten years later when negotiating with the British Government regarding the Sinai Peninsula colonization scheme.[45] But Friedmann's state conception was at the moment "a dream of the future" which he, in any case, put on record for eventual future reference, but which did not require any immediate steps. The official documents are accordingly silent on the subsequent period.

While in London he wrote a letter to Prof. Gottheil in which he mentioned his intention to leave with his group for Midian and made some remarks about the assistance that might be rendered to him in America. *The New York Times*, reporting this, stated: [46]

Herzl Year Book, Vol. III. Herzl **Press**, New York, 1960, pp. 37–48.   See also above footnote 34.   46 *Loc. cit.*

In a letter written at London in May last [1891], Dr. Friedmann says that he intends to go out in the coming Autumn with a number of well-armed and disciplined Jews from Galicia, Hungary, etc., to settle. He proposes to begin by making not only clothes, saddles, ornaments, and boats for the native population, but also by working the mother of pearl found on the shores into buttons for export.

"Now," he adds, "there are so many things which might be done for me in America, and when once I am settled I shall apply for them. But even before that something might be done for me; foremost of all, some good young American Jews or Christians friendly to Jews, might join me and assist me in my work. If they take an interest in Semitic science they would in Midian find a rich and nearly virgin field of inquiry, for there are numerous inscriptions of all kinds."

Dr. Friedmann further says that he is about to go to Glasgow to buy a steam yacht to establish communication with Suez, so as to carry mails and such persons as may join him.

As we know from the description in the literature referred to above,[47] Friedmann returned from England to the Continent to make the necessary preparations for the departure of the first group of pioneers to the selected area. The first news item about his activities appeared in an English source seven months later, in a leading article in the London *Jewish Chronicle*:[48]

The pioneer work in connection with putting to a practical test the practicability of Jewish colonization in the Land of Midian has now begun in earnest. . . . Mr. Friedmann is no mere idealist or dreamer of dreams. On the contrary, he is a thoroughly practical man, anxious to avoid disaster through any precipitate action or want of reasonable precautions against failure. For many months past he has been engaged in personal consultation with the leading members of the Jewish community in England, France and Germany.[49] The scheme will be carried out entirely with his own means. He has not asked nor desired any pecuniary support from others but only moral encouragement, advice and sympathy.

47 Footnotes 4 and 5.
48 December 25, 1891, p. 11.
49 Prof. Gottheil met Friedmann in London in the summer of 1891 (*New York Times, loc. cit.*).
50 The yacht was registered with the

Lloyd Tiestino (Trieste, Austria) and sailed under the Austrian flag. (Friedmann's report to the German Chancellery of August 18, 1891, confidentially transmitted to the Austrian Government by Prince

Mr. Friedmann has carefully selected the land upon which the first settlement will be made. To save expense in transport, one of his first steps was to purchase at Glasgow a steam yacht which he named "Israel," and which left Southampton for the East [50] six weeks ago. The yacht was specially provisioned with "kosher" tinned, smoked and other meats. The pioneers on board have been carefully selected mainly from among the Russian refugees in England and Germany.[51]

We have received a communication from Mr. Friedmann dated Suez, December 10th, stating that his pioneer party were just leaving for Midian. The party consists of Mr. Friedmann, an officer, a surgeon, two *Schochetim*, and 34 men, besides a crew of nine on board of the yacht "Israel." All were in excellent spirits and everything seemed favorable.

In fact, however, the party did not leave for Midian. Nor was it Friedmann's intention to settle there right away. His plan was first to establish a camp, a pioneering settlement on the Sinai Peninsula itself, and from there to explore the areas along the Midian shore across the Red Sea, with a view to finding a suitable spot for the first colony. He was therefore looking for a spot on the Sinai Peninsula from where he could sail across the Sea to Midian on his yacht or on other vessels. He chose the vicinity of Sherm el Moyeh, a small anchorage on the southeastern extremity of the Sinai Peninsula, about one hundred miles from Midian, across the sea, for his pioneer camp.

It appears, however, that already on the voyage from Europe some dissatisfaction among the refugees was noticeable which had increased when the party arrived in Egypt, and assumed critical proportions during the establishments of the pioneer post at Sherm el Moyeh.

Reviewing the situation since leaving Europe up to that moment, Friedmann wrote to the *Jewish Chronicle*: [52]

Sherm el Moyeh
January 8th, 1892

At first the Egyptian Government regarded the Scheme with favour. A steam yacht was bought at Glasgow (named "Israel"),

---

Ratibor on October 15, 1891. In the Vienna States Archives, File Turkey XVIII, Pr. 29/10/91.)

51 The *Jewish Chronicle* corrected itself, after receiving Friedmann's letter of January 8, 1892, stating that the party consisted at first mainly of Galician Jews and that Russian Jews were later added (February 19, 1892, p. 11).

52 *Ibid.*

and several months were spent engaging a staff and providing outfit. The intention was to engage chiefly Galician Jews (about whom enquiries could be made) who would form a nucleus round which afterwards, when plans were more matured, Russian refugees could be organized. The Jewish Committee at Cracow, however, prevailed upon me to engage Russian refugees, who declared themselves willing to work and ready to serve as soldiers.

At Alexandria, at the advice of another informal Jewish Committee, eight more Russians were engaged.

In two instances the men were objected to, but they were sent off to Suez and their fares had to be paid.

Meantime distrust and half-heartedness had been created by the mistaken kindness of those who were always timid at any risk to life or limb. Lavish promises (quite unauthorized) were also made at Breslau, and the poor uneducated Russian Jews were deluded into the belief that whatever their conduct and whatever might befall them, they would still be helped. A premium was thus set upon laziness and discontent. It was not surprising, therefore,—although very annoying—that they became dissatisfied with their food and the arrangements made for them generally, and the patience of the directors of the pioneer party was sorely tried.

At Southampton a Shochet joined the party (subsequently a second Shochet was engaged also), and a liberal supply of fresh kosher meat for ten days was taken on board; there was also kosher sausages to the last day on board.

On December 1st the party arrived at Suez where the growing discontent was made worse by the mistaken kindness of the interested sympathy of the local small Jewish community. They expected great things from the enterprise both for Israel in general, and their own pockets in particular. Desertion was encouraged and vain things were told by them of the high wages and pleasant life at Cairo and Alexandria; so that the majority of the men were already discussing whether they had not better leave at once.

It was the original intention to march from Suez to Tor [53] to give the men a good training, but this was abandoned on account of the difficulties raised by the Greeks and Bedouins who asked exhorbitant prices for their camels. So fourteen men with luggage

---

53 Tor, about 140 miles from Suez, a harbor on the Gulf of Suez, is the Biblical Elim, through which the children of Israel passed on their way from Egypt to Mount Sinai (Exodus 15:27). I wonder whether Friedmann thought of emulating the Exodus from Egypt.

and supply of coal, etc, were sent off on two Arab sailing vessels, while the rest of the party left on the 10th December on board of the yacht "Israel."

Meanwhile the women and children were left at Suez until provisions could be made for their reception at Sherm Moyeh, the intended first settlement, where the party arrived on the 12th. Next day they landed; tents were brought on shore and pitched, and on the 13th. the two Arab sailing boats entered the harbour. On the 14th. the goods began to be landed and to be carried to the camp, 400 yards from the shore. At first the men considered carrying the burdens as a sport, laughing and singing as they worked. In the afternoon they already began to shirk the work, only half a dozen worked. The next day there was more decided grumbling with the labour and with the rations, although the men were neither under-fed nor over-worked.

On the Tuesday [December 15th] one of the men engaged at Alexandria, Abraham Rasnowitch, exclaimed that he was not a donkey to carry loads, and declined to take up a case to the camp. This man caused serious discontent, and was ordered to leave the camp. He departed with another man named Schwarz. There was a ship lying in the harbour which was to leave for Dubbah,[54] whence the man might easily have returned to Suez. Rasnowitch in vain begged, later on, to be readmitted to the camp, but it was feared that he might again become a centre of discontent. Subsequently sixteen men declared their intentions to leave also, and they were accordingly sent to Tor where they were joined by Schwarz who walked over from Sherm Moyeh, without any difficulty, having been assisted by the Bedouins.[55]

I then returned to Cairo, where I found Kitchener Pasha, the Chief of Police,[56] had been very disagreeably impressed by the idea that a number of destitute Jews might wander about Egypt and give trouble. Grenfell Pasha [57] advised that the enterprise be given up, but as the only reason he gave was the desertion of some discontented men, his advice was declined. At Suez the men who had now arrived from Tor clamoured loudly for compensation, and appealed to the Russian Vice-Consul to take up their case. The men declined to make formal complaint; they wanted to be sent to America and to have a round sum in hand.

I engaged eight Sudanese workmen, formerly soldiers, to re-

54 A small harbor in Midian, across the Red Sea.
55 The distance is about 50 miles.
56 The later Lord Kitchener.
57 The Sirdar, i.e., the British Commander of the Egypt army.

place the men that had left me. At Tor, the German consular agent said that Rasnowitch had died half-way between Sherm Moyeh and Tor, on December 24th. He had been found dying by the wayside by the Greek Monks at Mount Sinai.[58]

At Sherm Moyeh all was now in order, the remaining men in good spirits and well, the Arabs friendly and the provisions still sufficient. Soon, however, there was alarming news. The captain of an Arab sailing vessel brought word that a Turkish man of war had gone along the coast up to Akabah and back. At Dubbah about 50 Turkish soldiers had landed, driven out the small Egyptian garrison of six men and were now occupying the town and levying taxes.

Friedmann did not waste time. Notwithstanding the "alarming news" about the Turkish landing, he immediately left on his yacht for Midian, accompanied by the interpreter, E. Bronstein, and by three members of his party, to look for the right spot for the first colony. He found one very soon. On his return from there to Sherm Moyeh he wrote the following letter to the *Jewish Chronicle:* [59]

Sherm el Moyeh, 15th January, 1892

Yesterday evening I returned from Mweilah [60] and Dubbah. The Turks, 22 men, a lieutenant and a number of Billi Bedouins, under the command of Mahamed Bey, Turkish Governor of el Widj,[61] had landed at Dubbah on the 25th December, pretending that there had been an agreement by which the whole coast had been ceded to the Sultan. They now wanted to take possession. Happily, the commander, Saadi Bey, acted with vigour, he refused to surrender the little hut called the Tower, or the government of the town. My old friend, Sheik Alejau of the Howeitat,[62] behaved truly and faithfully, he gathered his men and stood by Saadi Bey. The Billi Bedouins had to leave the town. The Turkish soldiers were allowed to camp under tents outside the tower until order would have come from Cairo.

That was the state in which I found Mweilah and Dubbah. The arrival of the "Israel" was hailed with joy by the Egyptians, with dismay by the Turks. I was at once the most popular man in Midian, for the people hoped I would obtain the removal of the

---

58 Mount Sinai is about 30 miles inland from Tor, and 50 miles from Sherm Moyeh. The monks were probably from the Monastery of St. Catherine.

59 February 19, 1892, p. 11.

60 A harbor in Midian.

Turks whom they hate and fear, and security against the renewal of similar attempts.

I am leaving this place [Sherm Moyeh] for Cairo tomorrow morning, having arrived yesterday evening. If I succeed at Cairo, my enterprise is well nigh safe. I took with me three Jews who were much pleased with the country, and even more so with the nearly enthusiastic reception I received. As the commander told me in their presence, it was superfluous to give presents to the great men, my coming, for which they had watched day by day, had been the greatest gift I could make them, the whole country lay at my feet. The Bedouins now actually asked as a favour to settle in their part of the country, praising its fertility. I have an offer of a large track of tolerable land at Dubbah with good water, of a thousand acres or more near Mweilah, where I am to put up a flour mill; of 500 acres of very good land, plentifully watered at Beda,[63] and of nearly 1,000 acres at Makhna.[64] All this my men heard and told the rest who had remained here. They moreover saw that wherever the land was irrigated, it produced abundant crops of vegetables, such as pumpkins, cabbages, etc.; very good dates, and above all, tobacco of the kind the Arabs like and for which there would always be a very good market. They now understood that I had not deceived them, if we could settle in the land they would have their six or eight acres, on which they could grow enough to live in plenty and even lay by a good deal. A single acre of tobacco—with actual prices—gives about £30.[65] So the whole tone has been changed. One of the men, a joiner, Rosenkranz, asks for permission for his brother to come. Stern, the smith, wants his two brothers-in-law to come. Schapira writes to eight of his friends in Galicia to come and join. The Shochet I engaged in Alexandria promises to bring over six or eight Sephardim. All things look bright.

The Sudanese have also arrived [at Sherm Moyeh] and proved good men. They are most eager for a fray with the Turks, and quite ready to serve as soldiers. Seven of the eight have served in the Egyptian army.

Friedmann left, of course, as he had written in the above letter, on January 16th for Cairo where he met Sir Francis Grenfell. There is

61 The largest town in Midian, also a harbor.
62 In his *Madian* Friedmann named these Bedouins the most numerous and powerful in the area (p. 6).
63 A harbor on the Gulf of Akaba.
64 A harbor, between Beda and Akaba.
65 $150.

no doubt that he gave him a full report about the military and political situation as he had found it during his visit in Midian, and he may even have inspired a military expedition which subsequently was to become of great importance in the political crisis about to break out in all fury. At that time an influenza epidemic swept the country [66] and Friedmann fell ill. This prevented him from returning to his front post at Sherm Moyeh, as he had planned. On the way there, after losing about a week, he stopped at Suez and wrote on January 27th from there to the *Jewish Chronicle*: [67]

Things are going favourably. On my arrival here, I found that the Sirdar Sir Francis Grenfell, as the upright man he is, had at once decided that the Turks should not remain at Dubbah. Three days after I had seen him in Cairo, a government steamer, the Ouda, with Major Frith of the Egyptian army and fifty Egyptian soldiers, left for Midian to garrison the fort of Mweilah and the government homes at Dubbah, to relieve the people from their anxiety, and to see that the Turks leave the country.

I should have followed Major Frith much sooner had I not had an attack of Influenza, from which I am now well-nigh recovered. I was to sail to-night, but bad weather prevents my leaving; I shall probably leave to-morrow.

So if only a dozen or two industrious Jews will join me the thing would be done. The Arab tribes, under Hebrew protection, the presence of the Jews making a cession to Turkey impossible for ever, while a small garrison at Beda would assure the peace of northern Midian. At Beda, I shall now place about twenty Sudanese and a dozen Midianite soldiers. That will also make Makhna quite safe.

I have just received a telegram to say that E. Bronstein, the chemist and interpreter, who had finished his time at Sherm el Moyeh, and returned to Alexandria, has left for this place, to join me, and go once more with me to Midian. He re-enters my service, which shows that he has not found that I illtreated my Jews so very much. Had not the other men mostly left the country, a good many of them would probably like to follow his example. Those who remain here, I would not take back.

66 Reported in the contemporary press. See, for instance, *The Times* (London), January 10–25, 1892.
67 February 19, 1892, p. 11.
68 Militarily—the occupation of the strategic points held by Egypt; financially—the repayment of some loaned funds to the surprise of the creditors.
69 *The Annual Register for the Year 1891*, London, 1892, Part I, pp. 325–326.

Friedmann was, of course, not aware of the fact that, while he regarded the Turkish landing at Dubbah as a local event and himself the heroic savior of the Bedouins in Midian, the situation would grow behind the scenes into a larger conflict involving the powers then juggling for positions in the southeastern corner of the Mediterranean.

The matter became one of high politics once Turkish troops landed on what was Egyptian territory, almost at the same time that Friedmann and his pioneer party set out to find a suitable spot there. This coincided with a number of other events in Egypt which were favorable to Turkish designs, and encouraged the Sultan to an unprecedented strong stand in his demands. French influence at the Porte, which jealously had watched the growing Anglo-Egyptian penetration of the area, may account to no small degree for the firmness of these Turkish attempts to make use of the changing conditions.

The most significant of these changes was caused by the death on January 7, 1892, of the Khedive, Tewfik Pasha. In accordance with tradition the new Khedive, Abbas Hilmi, was to receive a Firman from the Sultan confirming his authority in the solemn customary form. The Sultan hoped, through a show of his strength [68] and through the utilization of the uncertain situation in Egypt, to force, in return for the issuance of the Firman, some alterations on the Eastern frontier of Egypt as well as the detachment of the Sinai Peninsula from Egypt and her return under Turkish rule. He had been striving for this change for a long time, but never had the right opportunity or excuse to press for it seriously. The first such opportunity occurred as a consequence of the Arab revolt in Yemen in June, 1891, which was quelled with great difficulty by the Turkish troops after several months' hard fighting.[69] As we have seen from Cromer's statement,[70] the Turks blamed British intrigue for this insurrection. Accordingly, in August, 1891, the Egyptian issue was raised by Rustem Pasha, the Turkish Ambassador in London, with Lord Salisbury, the Prime Minister and Foreign Secretary.[71] Simultaneously Kiamil Pasha was dismissed by the Sultan from the post of Grand Vizier, and was succeeded by Djaval Pasha. This incident was regarded in France and Russia as a triumph for the policy of those States, Kiamil having been a devoted adherent of England and the Triple Alliance.[72]

A few weeks later, shortly before his departure to London, the

70 Quoted from *Modern Egypt*, Vol. II, p. 268, at the beginning of this article.

71 *The Times*, January 13, 1892, p. 5, col. 1.

72 *The Annual Register, op. cit.,* p. 326. The Triple Alliance between Britain, Austria, and Italy of 1887 for the preservation of peace in lands bordering on the Mediterranean.

then British Ambassador in Constantinople, Sir William White, was given to understand by the Sultan "that an important memorandum on Egyptian affairs was in preparation." The matter was kept in abeyance owing to Sir William's death on December 28, 1891. But on January 5, 1892, the *Times* correspondent informed his readers: [73]

> I have ascertained from the most trustworthy sources that Egyptian matters have lately much occupied the Sultan's attention. Recognizing the full weight of the rights acquired by England through salutary reforms introduced in Egypt and her undesirable claim to protect her important national interests in the Suez Canal, the Mediterranean, and the African localities connected with Egypt and the Red Sea, His Majesty inclines to admit that the question is one primarily and more directly concerning the Ottoman and British Governments.

Two days later the Khedive died. Newspapers all over the world indulged in speculations about the political future. The French press, in particular, combined the ascendancy of a new Khedive with violent attacks against English rule in Egypt. British diplomacy soon recognized that it was almost immediately to be confronted by a fight on two fronts: against the designs of France and against those of the Sultan. The situation was aptly summarized in the Vienna *Neue Freie Presse:* [74]

> France will eventually have to make up her mind as to the further occupation of Egypt by the English, and so will the Sultan. But we shall witness shortly a great diplomatic campaign. There will be all sorts of intrigues at the Golden Horn, to which, perhaps, the venerable Ismail Pasha [75] himself will not be foreign. The whole diplomacy will be absorbed by Egyptian affairs, but will all lead to no war.

Almost immediately another struggle for British diplomacy developed on a third front—in Egypt herself. The new Khedive soon found himself involved in clashes with Sir Evelyn Baring. The "undisguised

73 January 5, 1892, p. 3, col. 2.
74 Quoted in *The Times*, January 11, 1892, p. 5, col. 1.
75 The ex-Khedive who was advised on June 19, 1879, by the French and British governments "to abdicate and to leave Egypt" (Cromer,

Modern Egypt, op. cit., Vol. I, p. 135). Ever since that time he fought ardently against foreign influence in Egypt until his death in 1895.
76 Lord Milner, *England in Egypt*, London, 1920, p. 369. Abbas Hilmi

hostility of the young Khedive" [76] was the result of "the influence of the Anglophobe party" which all along had claimed "that the old Khedive was a tool in my [Cromer's] hands." [77] It raised its voice now to prevent the continuation of this British hold over Egypt, and demanded complete independence. This nationalistic propaganda was then sweeping Egypt and was led by Syrian writers who had been educated in French schools and remained under strong French cultural and national influence.

In this situation Friedmann's problem became one not of finding new, more, and better suited people for his colonization scheme in Midian, but how to extricate himself from falling between the grinding stones of the growing controversy. Alas, he was either not aware of what really went on or, as is more likely, he relied too much on Turkish incompetence and Egyptian strength, supported by the British out of power-preserving necessity. This may account for some of his expressions in the letters to the *Jewish Chronicle,* written during these very same days, quoted above. ("I was at once the most popular man in Midian, for the people hoped I would obtain the removal of the Turks. . . ." He never expected that, when the situation would require it, the powers that be would not only dissociate themselves from him, but find in him and in his expedition a welcome scapegoat for their own failures.

The files in the London Foreign Office show that Sir Evelyn Baring cabled five days after the Khedive's death, on January 12, 1892, to Lord Salisbury, that the Turks claimed the right to garrison the ports of Akaba, Ziba, and Moila.[78] As was seen from Friedmann's letter (January 27, 1892), quoted above, the British Commander of the Egyptian Army, Major-General Grenfell, decided not to accede to the Turkish occupation of the various points, and dispatched about January 20, Major Frith and his soldiers to the area. The British thus demonstrated that they not only did not intend to negotiate with the Turks about Egypt's surrender of the areas claimed by the Sultan, but also were prepared to maintain the *status quo* with military support. As an additional "demonstration" maneuvers were announced to take place soon on the Egyptian frontiers by the army, 5,000 men strong, under Sirdar Grenfell's personal command.[79]

On February 5 the Turkish Ambassador in London, Rustem Pasha,

was then seventeen.

77 Cromer, *Modern Egypt, op. cit.,* Vol. II, pp. 332–333.

78 Telegram No. 26. Confidential. Egypt. Correspondence. Affairs of Egypt, Parts 38–41 and Memoranda, 1892 and 1893 (17.14). Confidential (6277). Part XXXVIII, January to June 1892. (Will be henceforth quoted: F.O. [6277].)

79 *The Times,* February 2, 1892, p. 5, col. 1.

called on Lord Salisbury complaining on behalf of his Government: [80]

> that a detachment of Egyptian troops under a British officer has been dispatched to that coast, a proceeding which, he declares to be inconsistent with the claim of Her Majesty's Government that the provisions of the Firman should be maintained without alteration.
>
> He asserts that a straight line drawn from El Arish to Suez was the limit assigned to the territory of Egypt attached to the original Firman granted to Mehmet Ali on the 1st June, 1841, which is now at Cairo.

Conveying this complaint to Sir Evelyn, the Foreign Secretary added the following request:

> I should be glad to be informed whether that is the case, and to be supplied with a copy of the Map if you can obtain it.
>
> Can you state the circumstances under which the peninsula of Sinai and the coast-line to El Wight [81] were ceded to Egypt, and by what instrument?
>
> Rustem Pasha states that the Sultan attaches great importance to this matter and is very much in earnest in assessing his rights.

On the following day (February 6) Baring replied: [82]

> The Map mentioned in your Lordship's telegram No. 17, and said to have been attached to the Firman of 1841, has never been found. I will make further inquiries into the matter and try to arrive at the past history of the case.
>
> There is no doubt that all ordinary Maps issued for many years past place the Peninsula of Sinai and the Land of Midian within Egyptian territory. I would refer your Lordship to the concluding lines of the second paragraph of the Firman issued in 1879. It cannot be disputed that the above-mentioned territories had been within the dominions of His Highness the Khedive long before the Firman of 1879.

80 Telegram No. 17 from Salisbury to Baring, dated February 5, 1892. Document No. 70 in F.O. (6277).

81 The largest town in Midian. Friedmann spelled its name El Widj. (See footnote 61.)

82 F.O. (6277). Document No. 72. Telegraphic. No. 55. Dated Cairo, February 6, 1892.

83 Ibid. Document No. 75. Telegram No. 21. Dated February 7, 1892 (Secret).

Negotiations might be opened with a view to the delimitation of the eastern frontier of Egypt, but I think it would not be advisable to allow the Porte to extend its frontier to Suez.

When I have inquired further into the matter I will let your Lordship know by telegraph. No one here has any desire to infringe on the legitimate rights of the Sublime Porte.

The Turkish Ambassador continued, however, to uphold pressure in London. He was instructed to see Salisbury again and to repeat the Sultan's demands in no unequivocal terms. After that interview Salisbury cabled to Sir Evelyn: [83]

I gather from the language used by Rustem Pasha, and from other indications, that the difficulty about the eastern frontier has excited the Sultan to an unusual extent.

The pressure was obviously on. Baring could not any more "look for maps" or "make further inquiries." He had to act right away. The one cause that had speeded up, if not provoked the Turkish intervention as telegram No. 17, quoted above, shows, Baring would not remove: to recall Major Frith and his soldiers from Midian.

At that critical moment he was to receive support from an unexpected quarter. In the course of the Anglophobe campaign, mentioned above, the French paper *Le Bosphore*, which once before had caused an Anglo-French rift of some magnitude,[84] published suddenly wild attacks against Friedmann and his expedition. These attacks were based on the stories of some of those men who had left Friedmann and had returned to Egypt. The moral standing of this paper can be evaluated from the report [85]

that Herr Friedmann was approached and informed that some such talk (with charges against him) would be printed unless he submitted to blackmail.

Be that as it may, *Le Bosphore*, enumerating a number of accusations against Friedmann and the other leaders, stressed that his venture had the unlimited support of the British civilian and military authorities in

84 Milner, *England in Egypt, op. cit.*, pp. 97–99.
85 *New York Herald*, May 1, 1892, p. 21, col. 4, where its Berlin correspondent quoted a prominent member of Friedmann's expedition on the colonization scheme and also mentioned the following *Le Bosphore* incident.

Egypt.[86] Friedmann was thus put on the political map. His own talk during his stay in Cairo, as mentioned above, and his boasting about a possible expansion into Arabia through military support, which he probably did not confine to his conversations with the British military leader, but talked about elsewhere as well, may also have contributed to the rumors that he was a British agent. This sudden appearance of Friedmann in the political picture may have influenced Baring's further steps to no small extent, He embarked almost immediately on a diplomatic pincer movement in two directions: vis-à-vis his own Government in London and toward the Turkish High Commissioner in Cairo. He intended to influence the Porte through these two channels toward a settlement. The central point of these pincers was to be neither the military adventure in Midian nor the legal aspect of the old Turkish law, but Paul Friedmann and his expedition. Baring opened his twofold steps on one and the same day, February 7, 1892, upon receipt of Salisbury's alarming message. He cabled to Salisbury, explaining the border delimitations, and added: [87]

> A small colony of Jewish refugees was permitted by Riaz Pasha to establish itself on the east coast of the Gulf of Akaba. The chief of this colony is Mr. Friedmann, a German of Jewish extraction, and it appears that the Sultan considers this as a covert attempt to exercise English authority in this part of the world. The colony has so far proved a complete failure, and I should feel obliged if your Lordship would kindly inform Rustem Pasha that we have nothing whatever to do with its establishment.

A short while later, on the same day, Baring again cabled Salisbury: [88]

> The Turkish Commissioner paid me a visit today, and I gathered from him the difficulties which have arisen with regard to the eastern frontier of Egypt are brought about by the Friedmann Settlement. His Excellency pointed out, with much truth, that no foreigner is allowed to hold land in the Hedjaz in virtue of the 1st Article of the Imperial Rescript of the 18th June, 1867.

As an additional tidbit Baring, pointing clearly at Friedmann and his Midian venture, added that Egypt would be agreeable to

86 It was in this sense that also Baron von Heidler-Egeregg, Austrian Consul General in Cairo, reported on January 25, 1892, to Count Kalnoky, Austrian Foreign Secretary, that "Mr. Friedmann is a German citizen, his philanthropic work, however, is energetically supported only by the British civilian and military authorities in Egypt." See

the land of Midian being relinquished to the Porte. This last mentioned territory is not only useless, but expensive to the Khedive's Government.

These seem extraordinary documents. For at no time previously or subsequently did the Turkish Ambassador in London mention the Friedmann expedition in his talks with Salisbury. This must therefore be regarded as what it appears, a device by Baring to find a way out of the impasse and settle the question of the Firman. He was probably able to win over Moukhtar Pasha, the Turkish Commissioner in Egypt, for his strategy. Otherwise one could not understand why Baring, when meeting the Turkish Commissioner and after the meeting advising Salisbury as to the trend of the situation, did not convey to them the facts; by that time, and at no other time, had Friedmann established a settlement on the east coast of the Gulf Akaba or anywhere else along that coast in Midian. He held, with eight Jews, a camp at Sherm el Moyeh in the Sinai Peninsula which he intended to liquidate as soon as his party could settle in Midian. But it did not come to that. Therefore one could not have said, as Baring did, that "the colony has so far proved a failure," for it had never come into existence. On the other hand, Baring knew very well that Midian was not a part of the Hedjaz and that the rule prohibiting foreign settlements did not apply to Midian. Salisbury too should have been aware of this since receiving Friedmann's letter of May 8, 1891, quoted above, where it was clearly emphasized.

However, the "new line," centered on Friedmann, came so suddenly that the Turkish authorities in Constantinople had not been informed in time of it when they instructed their London Ambassador to see Salisbury again and keep up the pressure. After that conversation, which took place the following day, February 8, Salisbury cabled to Baring: [89]

In a conversation which I had with the Turkish Ambassador today, his Excellency pressed, in very earnest language, the question of the Eastern frontier of Egypt. I have never heard him speak so strongly during the five or six years he has been in this country; and he insists that it is from the Palace and not from the Porte, that he has received his instructions in the matter.

Vienna State Archives, Turkey XVIII, No. 4E. Cabled to Constantinople on March 31, 1892.
87 Document No. 73. Telegram No. 56. Secret. In F.O. (6277). Dated February 7, 1892.
88 *Ibid.* Document No. 74. Cable No. 57. Dated Cairo, February 7, 1892.
89 *Ibid.* Document No. 78. Telegram No. 23. Dated February 8, 1892.

His Excellency allows that it would be a fair question for negotiations whether the southern end of the boundary-line ought to
be at Akaba or at Suez. What he insists on most strongly, however, is that the Egyptian Government should withdraw the garrison of regular troops from the sea coast posts in the Hedjaz,
and in particular a regiment which has recently been sent there
under the command of an English officer. His contention is that
under the powers given to the Egyptian Government, Bashi-
Bazouks only can be sent to these places.

From this cable it becomes clear that it was not the Friedmann
issue but the military expedition under the British officer Frith with
which the Turkish diplomat concerned himself. This military expedition, sent out to Midian, as the Sirdar had stated for the purpose of
driving out the Turks,[90] was the biggest stumbling block for Turkish
designs in the area. Because only this could have prevented any territorial advantage which the Sultan hoped to attain in the course of his
bargaining for a Firman for the new Khedive. Baring, of course, understood Salisbury's hint and immediately found another or better, an
additional scapegoat. In his reply on the following day (February 9)
he cabled to the Foreign Secretary: [91]

The irritation of the Khedive against Moukhtar Pasha increases,
and His Highness believes the latter, inspired by the French, to be
the cause of the whole difficulty. Moukhtar Pasha, he said, had
admitted that he had stated in a telegram to Constantinople that
the English officer was sent to Mowhila was an officer of the Army
of Occupation. This would itself fully account for the alarm exhibited by the Sultan. I have since seen Moukhtar, who denies
the statement, but to clear up any doubt on this point I have insisted on his telegraphing to Constantinople. The especial reason
for which the English officer was sent was to prevent a collision
between the Turkish and Egyptian soldiers. He returned some
time ago to Cairo. He did not take with him a regiment, but
twenty-five men, and orders of their recall have now been issued.

Thus within forty-eight hours Baring shifted his stand from blaming
(on February 7) solely Friedmann to now (February 9) accusing the

90 See Friedmann's letter to the
    Jewish Chronicle of January 27,
    1892, quoted above.
91 F.O. (6277). Document No. 81.
    Telegram No. 59. Dated February

9, 1892.
92 Ibid.
93 The first part of this letter was
    quoted above.
94 As mentioned before this was not

French and Moukhtar Pasha as "the cause of the whole difficulty." This is a very important *volte face.* It shows that what in the first place Baring did not intend to do, to recall the soldiers, he was now forced to do by circumstances beyond his control. It also disproves both Cromer's subsequent story of Friedmann's guilt, which was quoted at the beginning of this article from his *Modern Egypt,* and his report which he sent on February 9 (the same day when accusing the French and Moukhtar!) to Salisbury, part of which was quoted above and the conclusion of which will follow further below.

It is also worth noting that in his latest telegram to Salisbury (February 9) Baring for the first time mentioned the military expedition as a possible cause of friction but even so tried to minimize its importance. Yet we know that this expedition had quite different purposes. Be that as it may, having once brought Friedmann into the picture, Baring could not drop him altogether now. And so he added to the above telegram the following paragraph: [92]

> Measures are now being taken to cause Mr. Friedmann and his party to return, and the German Consul is also writing to beg him not to remain. I am told that the party consists only of eight Jews.

Significantly, this telegram did not say from where Friedmann was to return nor where he was not to remain with his eight Jews. Thus the fiction was still kept alive of their presence in Midian while, of course, this was not the case. The same line of thoughts also permeated Baring's long letter to Salisbury of February 9, the conclusion of which reads as follows: [93]

> . . . in the autumn of 1891 Mr. Friedmann returned with some 20 or 30 people of various nationalities, including one Scotch mechanic, who, after a good deal of trouble, he transported to a spot on the eastern shore of the Gulf of Akaba.[94] In a little while he returned and paid me a visit.[95] He said that so far his enterprise had been a complete failure, and that most of his men had deserted him. I gathered, indeed, from some newspaper reports, which were published a few months ago,[96] that the men were greatly dissatisfied at the treatment they had re-

correct. Friedmann's camp was on the Sinai Peninsula.

95 Probably during his stay in Cairo, mentioned in Friedmann's letter to the *Jewish Chronicle* of January 27, 1892, quoted above.

96 This should read a few weeks or days ago. The whole press campaign started only in the middle of January.

ceived at the hands of Mr. Friedmann and his principal sub-
ordinates. Indeed, Tigrane Pasha [97] tells me that Mr. Friedmann
is to be summoned before the German Consulate on a charge of
manslaughter.[98]

Mr. Friedman, however, told me that he was in no way discouraged, and that he intended to collect another party of Jews
in Cairo with whom he would return to his settlement.

Since that time I have not seen him or heard much about him.
But he has written to Tigrane Pasha complaining bitterly of the
conduct of the Turks.

I should mention that when Mr. Friedmann started on his
expedition last autumn Sir Francis Grenfell at my instance
gave him a pass, of which I enclose a copy.[99] I thought it was
well that he should have some document to prevent, so far as
was possible, his being murdered by the Bedouins, but throughout these proceedings it has been fully explained to Mr. Friedmann that he must act entirely on his own responsibility and
that the Egyptian Government could not in any way guarantee
his safety.

I now learn that Mr. Friedmann has acquired some land on
the eastern shore of the Gulf of Akaba. This, as I mentioned in
a recent telegram, is contrary to the Ottoman Law of June 18,
1867, the first article of which precludes foreigners from acquiring real property in the Hedjaz.[100]

A communication is now about to be addressed to Mr. Friedmann requesting him to return, with his party, to Egypt proper. Fr.
Becker, the acting German Consul General, will at the same time
write to Mr. Friedmann advising him to comply with this demand.

As matters have turned out it would appear that I made a
mistake in attaching so little importance to this affair in the first
instance. I confess that, in common, I think with every one here

---

97 Egyptian Foreign Minister.

98 These charges were never brought
against him. He probably was
threatened with such possibility in
case of noncompliance with the
request to abandon his plans.
Friedmann was not guilty in the
death of Rasnowitch, the member
of his party who died on December
24, 1891 (see Friedmann's letter
to the *Jewish Chronicle* of January
8, 1892, quoted above).

99 It reads: Head Quarters, Egyptian
Army. Cairo. 22 November 1891.
Notice. Let it be known to all the
Arab Sheikhs inhabiting Egyptian
territory and under the Government of Egypt that Mr. Paul Friedmann is a benevolent gentleman
proceeding to assist his fellow crea-
tures. This notice has been given
to him to make his identity known
to the Sheikhs of tribes within the
boundaries of the frontier of Egypt
and to give him a free pass. Sgnd.
Grenfell, Sirdar. (Islamic date:

who had to deal with the question, I regarded Mr. Friedmann as a crack-brained enthusiast, who was throwing away his money uselessly, and I felt confident that, if he were left to himself he would at last see that his plan was incapable of execution. I still think that, in spite of Mr. Friedmann's singular tenacity of purpose, this is what would have actually occurred.

Had I foreseen the difficulties with the Porte which have occurred I should have adopted a more active attitude in the matter and I should have advised the Egyptian Government to forbid Mr. Friedmann from attempting to form his settlement.

The Sultan is very sensitive on all matters connected with the Hedjaz and I gather from Mouhktar Pasha's language that both he and his Imperial Master attach much importance to Mr. Friedmann's project which is altogether disproportionate to its real merits.[101] Moukhtar Pasha, indeed, intimated to me gravely that Mr. Friedmann's plan was very probably a first step towards an attempted establishment of the ancient kingdom of Jews in Jerusalem.[102]

I should add that Moukhtar Pasha has complained that the Egyptian Government has sold arms to Mr. Friedmann. He may have bought some old arms in Egypt, but, having enquired into the subject, I cannot find any trace of any having been sold to him by the Egyptian Government.[103] He asked permission of the Customs officials to export a few rifles—I believe nine altogether—which belonged to him, and the permission was, as is usual in such cases, accorded him.

While these exchanges of cables and letters went on behind closed doors, the rumors started by *Le Bosphore,* as mentioned above, swept all over the world and Baring, too, mentioned them in the dispatch just quoted. British diplomacy in Egypt could not remain undisturbed by these rumors which, on the whole, have linked Fried-

---

21. Rabi Akber 1309). This copy is a translation from the Arabic.

100 It was already pointed out that Midian was not part of the Hedjaz, but under Egyptian control and not subject to these regulations.

101 There is no evidence as to that in the cables or in the *démarche* by the Turkish Ambassador in London.

102 This sounds rather like an echo from Friedmann's letter to Salisbury of May 8, 1891 (quoted above), a copy of which, as the File in the Foreign Office F.O. 78 (4395) shows, was then transmitted to Baring.

103 From the File Turkey XVIII in Vienna we know that these arms were supplied by the Austrian Government before the yacht *Israel* left Trieste for Egypt. (See the file Administration Nr. XX.)

mann's plans with British interests in Egypt. Accordingly an obviously inspired item in the London *Times* [104] was to set the record right:

> A German named Friedmann last December induced about a score of Polish Jews to come to Egypt by promise that he would provide for them as colonists in the Land of Midian, lying to the east of the Gulf of Akaba. But his behaviour in that locality, which was eccentric rather than philanthropic, excited the suspicions of the Turkish Government, and threatened to become a cause of unpleasantness between Turkey and Egypt, the frontier between the two countries being ill-defined, and more or less debatable ground. To make matters worse, this man and some of his followers have adopted military costumes and procedure. Friedmann, who has no official recognition nor credentials more important than the usual formal letters of recommendation for protection to the commanders of frontier posts from the Egyptian authorities, has been ordered to return by the latter.
>
> Arrangements are now in course of settlement between Turkey and Egypt for fixing a definite frontier line, starting from El Arish on the Mediterranean, and terminating at the head of the Gulf of Akaba.

A comparison between the wording of Baring's letter to Salisbury of February 9 and this news item from the *Times* of February 12, confirms beyond any doubt the identical source of information. The last paragraph in the *Times*, however, already points at the basis upon which British diplomacy had expected the conflict to be solved.

Meanwhile Moukhtar Pasha had informed his superiors in Constantinople about his conversations with Baring of February 7 during which the Friedmann matter had been discussed (see Baring's telegram to Salisbury of that day). The Turkish authorities at that moment rather welcomed this version to prevent the dispute from heading toward a direct clash with England. The scene now moved to the Turkish capital. Sir Edmund D. V. Fane, Chargé d'Affaires at the British Embassy, conducted the negotiations with the Turkish authorities with regard to the contents of the Firman to be issued and to the frontiers to be delineated. He was able to report to Salisbury on February 18 [105] that an understanding had been arrived at in a conversation with the Grand Vizier, Djeval Pasha, and that Midian was

---

104 February 12, 1892, p. 5, col. 3. The report from Cairo is dated February 11.

105 F.O. (6277). Document No. 108. Telegram No. 22. Constantinople, February 18, 1892.

to return to Turkish rule while the Sinai Peninsula was to continue to be administered by Egypt. He added:

> The Grand Vizier made a reservation, however, that, without the consent of the Ottoman Government, the Egyptian Government should permit no colonization of Jews on the peninsula.

Baring received the same information from Fane and cabled on the following day (February 19) to Salisbury that he was able to persuade the Egyptian Government to send to Constantinople or to the Grand Vizier or through Moukhtar Pasha, a telegram to the effect [106]

> that the garrison would be withdrawn from Akaba, and that the Egyptian Government would undertake not to permit the establishment of any Jewish colony in the Peninsula of Sinai without the previous consent of the Sultan.

The retreat was complete: the British troops, sent to Midian under Frith, had been withdrawn and the right of approval of foreign colonization was granted to the Turkish Government, significantly, not in Hedjaz or Midian, which all the time had played so prominent a part in the cables and dispatches, but on the Sinai Peninsula herself, where the Sultan previously had not had this right.

Both British officials, Fane in Constantinople and Baring in Cairo, still pretended it to be a demand somehow linked with the Friedmann attempts at settling Jews somewhere in the area. But even this very thin link had to be abandoned in the final agreement. The Turks were not interested in Friedmann or in Jews alone, but in foreigners as such, be they Englishmen, Frenchmen, or Jews. The Grand Vizier made this abundantly clear to Fane: [107]

> His Highness understood that he [the Khedive of Egypt] was not authorized to permit any "foreign colonization whatever" to take place in the Peninsula of Sinai.

In this connection it is interesting to follow the diplomatic acrobatics with which the British diplomat in Constantinople explained this metamorphosis to his Chief in London. He wrote: [108]

106 *Ibid.*, Document No. 110. Telegram No. 73. Dated February 19, 1892.

107 *Ibid.*, Document No. 124. Letter

from Fane to Salisbury, No. 62. Dated February 23, 1892 (Confidential).

108 *Ibid.*

> Here I should explain that the Friedmann scheme (now ended) for colonizing the Peninsula was one, perhaps even the principal, reason why the Sultan took up so warmly the present question. Your Lordship is aware that the Peninsula is considered by the Turks to be included in the Holy Land of the Hedjaz and it would therefore be abhorrent to the Mohammedan mind that a Jewish, or indeed a Christian, colonization should be allowed to take place there. I remembered also that by the Law of Empire (of the 18th June, 1867) granting to foreigners the right to hold real property in the Ottoman Empire, the Hedjaz is specially excepted. Therefore I gave way to the Grand Vizier's wish, that the prohibition to establish colonies in the Hedjaz should apply, not merely to Jews, but also to all other foreigners.

This was a (deliberately?) confusing letter. It shows that all of a sudden Friedmann's scheme, contrary to all previous statements, was not intended to be realized in Midian but in the Sinai Peninsula; and that, for the convenience of a political settlement, even the Sinai Peninsula was suddenly included in the Hedjaz—200 miles away across the sea. Thus it was hoped to convince Salisbury that the Grand Vizier had confined himself to prohibiting foreign colonization in the Hedjaz, a right which was his in any case and which nobody disputed. And, in fact, the Grand Vizier did not ask for what he already possessed but insisted on obtaining the right of prohibiting a foreign colonization in the Sinai Peninsula, in an area hitherto not subject to his veto. He won even on that point as the respective clause in the agreement shows: [109]

> Que le Khédive envoie un télégramme à son Altesse le Grand Vizir déclarant que le Gouvernment Egyptien évacuera sans délai Akaba, Mouelah, et Jaba, lesquels seront occupés et administrés par le Gouvernment Impérial, et que le Khédivat n'est pas autorisé a permettre une colonisation quelconque étrangère dans la Péninsule de Sinai.

After all this, Friedmann's scheme was, of course, doomed. He was recalled to Cairo, abandoned all preparations, and returned there. He lost not only all the money that he had poured into this venture from his own resources, but had to suffer under most abusive accusations as to his own moral and personal status. Almost all Jewish papers the

109 *Ibid.* Inclosure.
110 February 19, 1892 (Leading   article).   111 *Allgemeine Zeitung des Juden-*

world over turned bitterly against him, with the rare exception of the London *Jewish Chronicle* which, even at this sad hour, emphasized that [110]

> we must still gratefully acknowledge the generous, disinterested spirit in which he undertook his self-imposed mission to found a Jewish colony in the Land of Midian.

Friedmann brought actions against a number of newspapers for libel and untrue statements. He won them all after many years of litigations and the testimonies of a great number of witnesses.[111] The general press, on the whole, did not indulge in these accusations but confined itself to repeating the version of the London *Times*, which was quoted above. There was, however, one significant exception. The *New York Herald* came to Friedmann's defense in an article from its Berlin correspondent, Melzer.[112] This article completely vindicated Friedmann on the basis of the testimony of "one of the few prominent persons who accompanied the so-called colonists." It is a long article and cannot be reproduced here in full. It suffices, however, to reprint the headline which in the *Herald* occupied over half a column and is self-explanatory:

Hebrew Refugees Refused to Work
Herr Friedmann's Colonization Scheme Said to Have Collapsed
Owing to the Laziness and Ingratitude
of His Correligionists

Much Money Wanted

One Who Witnessed the Occurrences in the Red Sea District Says
That All Charges of Tyranny Are Untrue

Insubordinate Soldiers

Some Sudanese Were Whipped on Account of Disobedience, but
Exceptionally Kind Treatment Was Shown to the Insurgents

Friedmann Vindicated

Nothing more is known about this extraordinary, well meaning, courageous, and self-sacrificing man.

thums, Berlin, November 4, 1892. Supplement Nr. 45, p. 1. *Jewish*   *Chronicle*. June 21, 1895, p. 12.   112 *Op. Cit.*, May 1, 1892, p. 21, col. 4

Ben Sira and the Nonexistence
of the Synagogue:

A STUDY IN HISTORICAL METHOD

*

I. *Ben Sira as a Source*

BEN SIRA IS A precious historical source. Indeed, it is the most crucial source that we possess of the period preceding the Hasmonean Revolt. It is a sentinel source, standing guard over the structural realities of an epoch. It is a source that cannot be defied, for
its author was an alert, intelligent, and knowledgeable observer of,
and participant in, the society that he describes. He was a *sofer*, a
scholar-intellectual, primarily concerned with the contemporaneous
scene. He is not a chronicler, though he refers to the past. Neither is
he a storyteller or a polemicist. He is an advocate of wisdom, a spinner
of apothegms, a weaver of maxims, a propounder of parables. As
such, his craft is dedicated to the contemplation of the existing order;
his talent is sharpened on the realities of daily life; his effectiveness is
dependent on accurate description. Ben Sira as a source for a segment
of the historical continuum is impeccable. The author lived in the
society that he describes, he was in a position to know this society
intimately, he was prompted to communicate information about this
society because of his interest in aiding others to live wisely within it.

1   See appendix A.
2   Cf. John Bright, *A History of Israel*,
Philadelphia, 1959, pp. 422–423;
Victor Tcherikower, *Hellenistic
Civilization and the Jews*, trans.
S. Applebaum, Philadelphia-Jeru-
salem, 1959, p. 125. Martin Noth,
The History of Israel, New York,
1958, p. 340; Samuel Krauss, *Syna-
gogale Altertümer*, Berlin-Vienna,
1922, pp. 52–66; George Foote
Moore, *Judaism*, Cambridge, 1927,
I, pp. 283–284; Louis Finkelstein,
The Pharisees, Philadelphia, 1938,
II, pp. 562–569; Salo W. Baron,
The Jewish Community, Philadel-
phia, 1942, I, pp. 55–74, and re-
affirmed in *A Social and Religious
History of the Jews*, Philadelphia,
1952, I, pp. 132–133, 351, n. 30–31.
  Since the turn of the century,
only Solomon Zeitlin, "The Origin

Ben Sira is thus a crucial source. Scholarly investigation can suggest a possible historical milieu for Proverbs, Ecclesiastes, and Job; but it cannot achieve absolute certainty. Scholars are unable to pinpoint with doubt-free accuracy the dating of Ezra-Nehemiah, nor can they be certain as to the veracity of the historical events recorded there. Ben Sira, however, is immune to challenge. It cannot possibly have been written earlier than 280 B.C.E.; nor later than the eve of the Hasmonean Revolt. It therefore preserves intact an authentic description of a society in a period limited in its total extent to approximately one hundred years.[1]

Ben Sira is crucial for another reason. No other source which is contemporaneous to this epoch is extant. The sources that do exist are either undatable, or are noncontemporaneous (e.g., Josephus), or are mere fragments of limited information. Ben Sira thus stands alone. And as long as this situation exists, he protects a segment of the past from spoliation by historians.

Not that Ben Sira has been successful in preventing spoliation. Historians have freely disregarded his sentinel role. They have battered down the defenses that the verses of his book represent; they have freely plundered the segment of history that it protects; and they have substituted for the society that he described one of their own mental construction. Institutions such as the synagogue, which were unknown to Ben Sira, are described as flourishing;[2] the institution which was flourishing, the Temple, is described as losing its hold on the people.[3] The class of *soferim* (scribes) which had no authority is pictured as molding and protecting the law, while the priestly class who wielded absolute authority are represented as sharing it with the scribal class.[4] The as yet nonexistent exegetical or *midrashic* mode is taken for granted; the existing unchallenged supremacy of the literal Pentateuch is denied.[5] The historians have poached on Ben Sira's domain; for a lone keeper, dependent on the verses of a book he penned, is no match for historians armed with footnotes and bibliographies.

Ben Sira is nonetheless a stubborn sentinel. His book cannot be

of the Synagogue," *Proceedings American Academy for Jewish Research*, III, (1932), pp. 69–81, has argued for a relatively late date, but even he would make it pre-Hasmonean.

3 Cf. especially Bright, p. 422, and Tcherikower, pp. 124–126.

4 Moore, I, pp. 37–44; Bright, p. 423; Tcherikower, *loc. cit.*, 124–126;

Jacob Z. Lauterbach, *Rabbinic Essays*, Cincinnati, 1951, pp. 28–30, 95–107; Finkelstein, *The Pharisees*, II, 570–583.

5 Bright, p. 423; Tcherikower, 124–126; Lauterbach, pp. 30–39, pp. 163–166; Finkelstein, *The Pharisees*, I, pp. 261–267; Moore, I, p. 39, pp. 253–257; Noth, p. 340.

ignored. Its verses persistently communicate descriptive data. Its authenticity cannot be challenged. It emits a message that is discernible through the "noise" that makes its reception difficult.

How is such a discrimination to be achieved? How is one to determine the true communication from the false, valid information from "noise"? Such questions are not only legitimate, but underline the crucial issue: the precarious status of any historical knowledge.

A way out of the dilemma is perhaps to be found in the perfecting of methodological procedures which will be recognized by historians as not only legitimate, but necessary. The original thinking of the scientists must be tested by procedures which are universally recognized by scientists. The original historical reconstruction of the historian should also have some procedural hurdles to surmount before his reconstruction can be secure historical knowledge. The latter may not always be achieved, but in those instances it will be evident that certain necessary criteria have not been met.

I should like to approach Ben Sira with such an end in view. What criteria must Ben Sira satisfy if it is to communicate information? It has already passed the first crucial test of a universal character. It has met the requirements of authenticity, of contemporaneity with the society that it describes, of the author's extent of knowledge, of his concern for description. Only the precise date is uncertain, and even this is confined to restricted limits.

At the moment, then, Ben Sira has satisfactorily passed these tests; at some future time, these tests may have to be reapplied and Ben Sira may not fare so well. Be that as it may, the testing apparatus has a status that is distinct from the source being tested. It is in this sense an objective instrument for measuring, which must be used by all historians. The failure of a historian to utilize these measuring principles is subject to a criticism that is objective. The criticism does not stem from disagreement with his reconstruction, but from his failure to carry through a necessary procedure.

Now for step number two. What does Ben Sira communicate, if one concentrates solely on *his* communication without resort to any knowledge outside of Ben Sira? For the purposes of this paper, I need not concern myself with *all* that he communicates. It is only essential that nothing that I exclude invalidate that which I include. I will confine my analysis to   A] the system of authority,   B] the prevailing institutions,   C] the class structure, with especial concern for the role

6   Quotations from Ben Sira are cited   Standard Version, New York, 1957,
    from *The Apocrypha*, Revised   with permission of the Division of

and function of the *soferim*. In carrying through the analysis I will appeal to no data that are extrinsic to Ben Sira.

A. SYSTEM OF AUTHORITY

Ben Sira deals with every aspect of life. He speaks of the rich and the poor, the master and the slave, the parent and the child, the peasant and the artisan, the merchant and the *sofer* (scribe). Yet he is especially concerned with the religious life and the institutions that nourish it. He filters life through an ideology that gives preeminence to God's revelation on Sinai. This is strikingly illustrated in his ascription of wisdom, his very special concern, to the Most High God and the Mosaic Law:

> "*Wisdom will praise herself,*
> *and will glory in the midst of her people.*
> *In the assembly of the Most High she will open her mouth*
> *and in the presence of his host she will glory:*
> '*I came forth from the mouth of the Most High*
> *and covered the earth like a mist . . .*'"
>
> (*Sirach* 24:1–3) [6]

> "*Then the Creator of all things*
> *gave me a commandment*
> *and the one who created me*
> *assigned a place for my tent.*
> *And he said, 'Make your dwelling in Jacob*
> *and in Israel receive your inheritance! . . .*
> *In the holy tabernacle I ministered before him,*
> *and so I was established in Zion.*
> *In the beloved city likewise he gave me a resting place,*
> *and in Jerusalem was my dominion.*
> *So I took root in an honored people,*
> *in the portion of the Lord, who is their inheritance. . . .*"
>
> (Ibid. 8–12)

> "*All this is the book of the covenant of the Most High God,*
> *the law which Moses commanded us*
> *as an inheritance for the congregation of Jacob.*
> *It fills men with wisdom, like the Pishon,*
> *and like the Tigris at the time of the first fruits. . . .*"
>
> (23–25)

Ben Sira thus focuses his attention on the Most High, on the Law of Moses. Perhaps some nuance of life is untouched by his pen, but it is not likely to be of consequence for the religious sphere. Ben Sira's perspective requires the utmost sensitivity to the issue of authority. He cannot bypass the question of who determines the Law, of who wields the ultimate authority. And Ben Sira allows for no ambiguity in this sphere; the Aaronide priests are charged with the care of the Law. Indeed, the supremacy of Aaron is enunciated in the most telling manner conceivable. *He is elevated above Moses.* Moses *gave* the Law, Aaron and his sons *perpetuate* the Law. Moses as Lawgiver is assigned *five* verses; Aaron the High Priest is allotted *sixteen* verses, not to speak of an additional *two* verses for Phineas.

Let us examine Ben Sira's assessment of Moses:

> *"From his [Jacob's] descendants the Lord brought forth*
> *a man of mercy,*
> *Who found favor in the sight of all flesh*
> *and was beloved by God and man,*
> *Moses, whose memory is blessed.*
> *He made him equal in glory to the holy ones,*
> *and made him great in the fears of his enemies.*
> *By his words he caused signs to cease;*
> *the Lord glorified him in the presence of kings.*
> *He gave him commands for his people,*
> *and showed him part of his glory.*
> *He sanctified him through faithfulness and meekness;*
> *he chose him out of all mankind.*
> *He made him hear his voice,*
> *and led him into thick darkness,*
> *and gave him the commandments face to face,*
> *the law of life and knowledge,*
> *to teach Jacob the covenant,*
> *and Israel his judgments."*

(45:1–5)

Moses is highly praised. He is most definitely the man to whom God gave His commandments. He is the man responsible for promulgating the Law. And this Law is divine, it is binding.

As for Aaron:

> *"He exalted Aaron, the brother of Moses,*
> *a* holy *man* like *him,* of the tribe of Levi.*

He [God] *made an* everlasting covenant *with him,*
  and gave him the priesthood of the people.
He *blessed him with splendid vestments,*
  and put a glorious robe upon him
He *clothed him with* superb *perfection,*
  and strengthened him with the symbols of authority,
  the linen breeches, the long robe, and the ephod.
And he encircled him with pomegranates
  with very many golden bells round about,
To send forth a sound as he walked,
  To make their ringing heard in the temple
as a reminder to the sons of his people;
with a holy garment, of gold and blue and purple, the
  work of an embroiderer;
with the oracle of judgment, Urim and Thummim;
with twisted scarlet, the work of a craftsman;
with precious stones engraved like signets,
  in a setting of gold, the work of a jeweller,
for a reminder in engraved letters,
according to the number of the tribes of Israel;
with a gold crown upon his turban,
  inscribed like a signet with 'Holiness,'
a distinction to be prized, the work of an expert,
  the delight of the eyes, richly adorned.
Before his time there never were such beautiful things.
No outsider ever put them on,
but only *his sons*
and his descendants perpetually.
His sacrifices shall be wholly burned
  twice every day continually.
Moses ordained *him*
and anointed him with holy oil;
it was an everlasting covenant *with him,*
and for his descendants all *the days of heaven,*
to minister *to the Lord and serve as* priest
  and bless his people in his name.
He chose him out of all the living
  to offer sacrifice to the Lord,
incense and a pleasing odor as a memorial portion,
  to make atonement for the people
In his commandments he gave him authority *in statutes*
  and judgments,

To teach Jacob the testimonies,
  and to enlighten Israel with his law.
Outsiders conspired against him,
  and envied him in the wilderness,
Dathan and Abiram and their men
  and the company of Korah in wrath and anger.
The Lord saw it and was not pleased,
  and in the wrath of his anger they were destroyed;
He wrought wonders against them
  to consume them in flaming fire.
He added glory to Aaron
  and gave him a heritage;
he allotted to him the first of the first fruits,
  he prepared bread of his fruits in abundance;
for they eat the sacrifices of the Lord,
  which he gave to him and his descendants.
But in the land of the people he has no inheritance,
  and he has no portion among the people;
  for the Lord himself is his portion and his inheritance."
                              (45:6–22, Emphasis mine)

What abounding love and reverence! What delight in the beauty of the vestments! How Ben Sira glories in the splendor of Aaron's majesty! He devotes more verses to the *clothing* of Aaron than to the *total* person of Moses! Moses *was* the Lawgiver; Aaron *is the High Priest,* perpetually alive in his descendants! They are at the very moment filling the Temple with the luster of their vestments. The real and living High Priest, Simon the son of Onias, is the very embodiment of Aaron!

"When he put on his glorious robe
  and clothed himself in superb perfection,
and went up to the holy altar,
  he made the court of the sanctuary glorious."
                              (50:11)

But Aaron is no mere figurehead! He is no mere functionary, the chief actor in the cultic drama! He is a holy man like Moses. God made an *everlasting* covenant with him directly. He bestowed upon him symbols of authority. And lest there stir the slightest doubt in the mind of the reader that these symbols were honorific but devoid of substance, Ben Sira states the reality of the authority in words that are explicit and specific:

"In his commandments he gave him authority in statutes
  and judgments,
To teach Jacob the testimonies,
  and to enlighten Israel with his Law."

(45:17)

Aaron is charged with the administration of the law, it is he who
teaches what it is, what it means.

And if there might still linger the thought that real authority
was not involved, Ben Sira reminds his reader that God himself
wreaked fearful destruction on those who dared to challenge Aaron's
supremacy.

"Outsiders conspired against him . . . Dathan, Abiram,
  Korah . . .
The Lord saw and was not pleased
and in the wrath of his anger they were destroyed;
He wrought wonders against them to consume them in
  flaming fire."

(45:18–19)

Note the judicious care exercised by Ben Sira in his selections
from the Pentateuch. Aaron as the cherished choice of God is under-
lined; Aaron as the maker of the golden calf is ignored!

Ben Sira, however, does not remain satisfied with his exaltation
of Aaron. He is careful to establish the legitimate high priestly line
through Phineas.

"Phineas the son of Eleazar is the third in glory,
for he was zealous in the fear of the Lord
and stood fast when the people turned away,
in the ready goodness of his soul,
and made atonement for Israel.
Therefore the covenant of peace was established with him,
that he should be leader of the sanctuary and of his people,
and he and his descendants should have
the dignity of the priesthood forever."

(45:23–24)

The crucial information in these lines is hard to miss. Phineas
is ranked with Moses and Aaron. The leadership of the sanctuary is
assigned to the descendants of Phineas forever! The living descendant

was Simon the son of Onias, and it is for him that Ben Sira reserves whatever talent for poetic imagery he possesses:

"The leader of his brethren and the pride of his people
 was Simon the high priest, son of Onias,
who in his life repaired the house,
  and in his time fortified the temple.
He laid the foundations for the high double walls,
  the high retaining walls for the temple enclosure.
In his day a cistern for water was quarried out,
  a reservoir like the sea in circumference.
He considered how to save his people from ruin,
  and fortified the city to withstand a siege.
How glorious he was when the people gathered around him,
  and he came out of the inner sanctuary.
Like the morning star among the clouds,
  like the moon when it is full;
Like the sun shining upon the temple of the Most High,
  and like the rainbow gleaming in glorious clouds;
like roses in the days of the first fruits,
like lilies by a spring of water,
like a green shoot on Lebanon on a summer day;
like fire and incense in the censer,
like a vessel of hammered gold
adorned with all kinds of precious stones;
like an olive tree puting forth its fruit,
  and like a cypress towering in the clouds.
When he put on his glorious robe
  and clothed himself with superb perfection
  and went up to the holy altar,
  he made the court of the sanctuary glorious.
And when he received the portions
  from the hands of the priests,
  as he stood by the hearth of the altar
  with a garland of brethren around him,
  he was like a young cedar on the Lebanon;
  and they surrounded him like the trunks of palm trees,
  all the sons of Aaron in their splendor
  with the Lord's offerings in their hands,
  before the whole congregation of Israel.
Finishing the service at the altars,
  and arranging the offerings to the Most High, the Almighty,

he reached out his hand to the cup
    and poured a libation of the blood of the grape;
he poured it out at the foot of the altar,
a pleasing odor to the Most High, the King of all.
Then the sons of Aaron shouted,
    they sounded the trumpets of hammered work,
they made a great noise to be heard
    for remembrance before the Most High.
Then all the people together made haste
    and fell to the ground upon their faces
    to worship their Lord
    the Almighty God Most High.
And the singers praised him with their voices,
    in sweet and full-toned melody.
And the people besought the Lord Most High
    in prayer before him who is merciful,
till the worship of the Lord was ended;
so they completed his service.
Then Simon came down and lifted up his hands
    over the whole congregation of the sons of Israel,
to pronounce the blessings of the Lord with his lips,
    and to glory in his name;
and they bowed down in worship a second time,
to receive the blessing from the Most High."

(50:1–21)

These lines speak for themselves. Simon is the living Aaron. Not only does he preside over the Temple, but he fortifies the city to withstand a siege. He is the ruler.

Ben Sira is thus aware of only a single system of authority: hierocracy. Power is concentrated in the hands of the High Priest who is assumed to be a direct descendant of Aaron and Phineas. This High Priest is assisted in the sacrificial services by the Aaronides. The Levites are not even mentioned. Aaronide supremacy is everywhere manifest. And that the High Priest directed *all* affairs is evident from Ben Sira's assertion that Simon "considered how to save his people from ruin, and fortified the city to withstand a siege."

Whence this hierocratic authority? Its legitimacy is grounded in the *literal* commands of the Pentateuch. Ben Sira is describing as *operative* a system of authority that was *promulgated* in the canonized Pentateuch. Simon the son of Onias is a living proof that the Aaronide supremacy advocated in Leviticus-Numbers was concretely achieved, and that the Pentateuchal promise to Phineas—"Behold I give unto him, and to his seed after him, the covenant of an everlasting priesthood . . ." (Numbers 25:10)—was fulfilled to the letter. The source of hierocratic sovereignty is the Pentateuch, and Ben Sira makes it very clear that the Aaronides and the Aaronides *alone* had been charged by God to wield "authority in statutes and judgments," and "to teach Jacob the testimonies, and to enlighten Israel with his law." (45:17). The Levites are excluded from the ruling class; for they were involved in challenging Aaron's supremacy. Ben Sira drives this message home by referring to the conspiracy of Dathan and Abiram, and to the uprising of Korah, acts which so enraged God that He consumed them in a flaming fire.

The pertinent texts in the Pentateuch reveal that these events were the justification for the downgrading of the Levites:

"And Moses said unto Korah: 'Hear now, ye sons of Levi: is it but a small thing unto you, that the God of Israel hath separated you from the congregation of Israel, to bring you near to Himself, . . . and all thy brethren the sons of Levi with thee? *and will ye seek the priesthood also?*'" (Numbers 16:8–10. Emphasis mine).

"And the *Lord* said unto *Aaron* [*sic!*]: 'Thou and thy sons and thy fathers' house with thee shall bear the iniquity of the sanctuary. . . . And thy brethren also, the tribe of Levi . . . bring thou near with thee. . . . And they shall keep thy charge, and the charge of all the Tent; only they shall *not* come nigh unto the *holy furniture* and unto the *altar, that they die not,* neither they, nor ye'" (*ibid.,* 18:1–3. Emphasis mine).

"'And I, behold, I have taken your brethren the Levites from among the children of Israel; for you they are given as a gift unto the Lord, to do the service of the tent of meeting. And thou and thy sons with thee shall keep your priesthood in everything that pertaineth to the altar, and to that within the veil; and ye shall serve; I give you the priesthood as a service of gift; and the common man that draweth nigh shall be put to death.'" (Numbers 18:6–7) [7]

Ben Sira's allusion to Dathan, Abiram, and Korah recalls to the reader the ninety-five verses—three contiguous chapters—utilized by the Pentateuch to guarantee Aaronide supremacy. Earthquake, fire, plague, miracle, divine command—all brought to bear to settle this

---

[7] Cited from *The Holy Scriptures,* Philadelphia, 1917, with permission of Jewish Publication Society of America.

[8] Ben Sira also refers to an assembly (ecclesia), and a council (boulé), a body of elders, and to judges. Since he does not describe the functions of the assembly or of the council, nor the provisions for membership (apparently peasants and artisans were included in the

issue. And settled it was. Ben Sira describes a society that is ruled by the Aaronides under the leadership of a High Priest descended from Phineas.

Ben Sira thus confirms the triumph of the Aaronides, and, in doing so, reveals that the Pentateuchal legislation was administered through the Aaronides, and the Aaronides *only*. This is of crucial importance, for the determination of what the law was in any given instance—especially when the law was contradictory—was the prerogative of the Aaronides. The Pentateuch's meaning as applied to the functioning of a real society was whatever the Aaronides said that it meant. To challenge the Aaronides was to challenge the Pentateuch itself, for both God and Moses, according to the Pentateuch, had bestowed upon Aaron and his sons an everlasting authority. The Aaronides therefore were, at the time of Ben Sira, completely in the saddle.

And every word of Ben Sira confirms this supremacy. Everywhere that he exhorts his reader to keep the commandments, the judgments, the statutes, he is in effect admonishing the people to heed the authority of the Aaronides.[8]

It is sufficient to point out that the Pentateuch *does* refer to an ecclesia, the *kahal,* to a body of elders, and to judges. Hence there is no basis for assuming that they performed functions other than those contemplated for them by the Pentateuch, or that these functions involved any independent authority with respect to the Law. A judge's decision does not necessarily involve the making of new law, nor the resort to hermeneutical devices. A judge's decision can be confined to the act in question and not serve as a precedent. The judge as a decider rather than a precedent-maker is to be seen in the magistrates' courts of the American judical system and in most courts of law in western Europe.

B. INSTITUTIONS

The institutions that Ben Sira refers to are the very ones that the Pentateuch enjoined. And it is the sacrificial cult of the Temple that is preeminent.

> *"He who keeps the law makes many offerings,*
> *he who heeds the commandments sacrifices a peace offering.*

assembly but were paid no heed, 38:33), it is not the scholar's task to fill the lacunae with his ignorance. So too, it is pointless to speculate on the exact functions of the judges, though Ben Sira reveals that it was a position of distinction (8:14), unavailable to the peasant and artisan (38:33).

He who returns a kindness offers fine flour,
and he who gives alms sacrifices a thank offering.
To keep from wickedness is pleasing to the Lord,
and to forsake unrighteousness is an atonement.
Do not appear before the Lord empty-handed,
for all these things are to be done because of the command-
   ment.
The offering of a righteous man anoints the altar,
and its pleasing odor rises before the Most High.
The sacrifice of a righteous man is acceptable,
and the memory of it will not be forgotten.
Glorify the Lord generously,
and do not stint the first fruits of your hands.
With every gift show a cheerful face,
and dedicate your tithe with gladness.
Give to the Most High as he has given,
and as generously as your hand has found.
For the Lord is one who repays,
and he will repay you sevenfold."

(Sirach 35:1–11)

The keeping of the law and the commandments is equated with the offering of sacrifices. The virtues of kindness and almsgiving are linked to the altar. The reader is urged to shower his abundance upon the cultus, and is assured that the rewards to the open-handed, gracious giver will be given by the Lord himself.

Ben Sira sprinkles his work with variations of the same theme. Thus he binds the love and fear of God to the priests:

"With all your soul fear the Lord,
   and honor his priests.
With all your might love your Maker,
   and do not forsake his ministers.
Fear the Lord and honor the priest,
   and give him his portion, as is commanded you:
the first-fruits, the guilt offering,
   the gift of the shoulders,
the sacrifice of sanctification,
   and the first fruits of the holy things."

(7:29–31)

The good life and sacrifices go hand in hand:
"My son, treat yourself well, according to your means,
   and present worthy offerings to the Lord."

(14:11)

Divine punishment awaits the man who reneges on his payment of his vows to the Temple:

> "Let nothing hinder you from paying a vow promptly,
> and do not wait until death to be released from it.
> Before making a vow, prepare yourself;
> and do not be like a man who tempts the Lord.
> Think of his wrath on the day of death,
> and the moment of vengeance when he turns away his face."
>
> (18:22–24)

Sacrifices are efficacious for healing the sick:

> "My son, when you are sick do not be negligent,
> but pray to the Lord and he will heal you.
> Give up your faults and direct your hands aright,
> and cleanse your heart from all sin.
> Offer a sweet-smelling sacrifice,
> and a memorial portion of fine flour,
> and pour oil on your offering,
> as much as you can afford."
>
> (39:9–11)

The selection of David for kingship is made vivid by cultic imagery:

> "As the fat is selected from the peace offering,
> So David was selected from the sons of Israel."
> (47:2)

One looks in vain for the existence of any other institution dedicated to prayer or religious ritual. And this in a book written by a man who is filled with the spirit of the Lord! Surely a man might pray privately to God, but there was no institution for praying, no set time for such prayer, no liturgy. Ben Sira nowhere exhorts the reader: "Say the Shema in the morning and in the evening testify to his oneness." Nowhere does he advise: "My son, seek out the house of prayer, and offer supplication in the synagogue, for the Lord delighteth in communal prayers, they are as a sweet-smelling sacrifice to his nostrils." Rather does Ben Sira view the Temple as especially appropriate even for a private prayer.

> "While I was still young . . .
> I sought wisdom openly in my prayers.

Before the Temple I asked for her,
and I will search for her to the last."
                              (51:14)

C. CLASS STRUCTURE AND THE *Soferim*

Ben Sira had wide-ranging interests. He brings his wisdom to bear on
every facet of life. He finds no status too lowly for his concern; none
to lofty for his attention. Thus he approaches the problem of man-
aging a slave with the pragmatic intelligence of a slave owner: the
combination of strict discipline with good treatment:

> *"Fodder and a stick and burdens for an ass;*
> *bread, discipline, and work for a slave.*
> *Set your slave to work, and you will find rest;*
> *leave his hands idle and he will seek liberty.*
> *Yoke and thong will bow the neck,*
> *and for the wicked slave there are racks and tortures.*
> *Put him to work that he may not be idle,*
> *for idleness teaches much evil.*
> *Set him to work, as is fitting him,*
> *and if he does not obey, make his fetters heavy."*
>   (33:24–28)

However,

> *"Do not act immoderately toward anybody,*
> *and do nothing without discretion.*
> *If you have a slave, let him be as yourself,*
> *because you have bought him with blood.*
> *If you have a slave, treat him as a brother,*
> *for as your own soul you will need him.*
> *If you ill-treat him, and he leaves and runs away,*
> *which way will you go to seek him?"*
>   (33:29–31)

The unfree slave is on the lowest level of the economic and social
structure. The peasant and artisan enjoy a higher status; they are
necessary for the well-being of society. Yet their opinion is neither
solicited, nor does it have a forum for its expression. The peasant and
the artisan make the leisure of other classes possible, but this function precludes such an opportunity for themselves.

The hierarchical distinction between manual labor (low social status) and intellectual preoccupation (high social status) is stated by Ben Sira as self-evident:

> *"The wisdom of the scribe depends on the opportunity of leisure*
> *and he who has little business may become wise.*
> *How can he become wise who handles the plough,*
> *and who glories in the shaft of a goad,*
> *who drives oxen and is occupied with their work,*
> *and whose talk is about bulls?*
> *He sets his heart on ploughing furrows,*
> *and he is careful about fodder for heifers.*
> *So too is every craftsman and master workman*
> *who labors by night as well as by day;*
> *those who cut the signet of seals,*
> *each is diligent in making a great variety;*
> *he sets his heart on painting a life-like image,*
> *and he is careful to finish his work.*
> *So too is the smith sitting by the anvil,*
> *intent upon his handiwork in iron;*
> *the breath of the fire melts his flesh,*
> *and he wastes away in the heat of the furnace;*
> *he inclines his ear to the sound of the hammer,*
> *and his eyes are on the pattern of the object.*
> *He sets his heart on finishing his handiwork,*
> *and he is careful to complete its decoration.*
> *So too is the potter sitting at his work*
> *and turning the wheel with his feet;*
> *he is always deeply concerned over his work,*
> *and all his output is by number.*
> *He moulds the clay with his arm*
> *and makes it pliable with his feet;*
> *he sets his heart to finish its glazing,*
> *and he is careful to clean the furnace.*
> All these rely upon their hands,
> *and each is skillful in his own work.*
> *Without them a city cannot be established,*
> *and men can neither sojourn nor live there."*
>
> (38:24–32. Emphasis mine)

The consequence of their indispensability?

> *"Yet they are not sought out for the council of the people,*
> *nor do they attain eminence in the public assembly.*

They do not sit in the judge's seat,
nor do they understand the sentence of judgment,
they cannot expound discipline or judgment,
and they are not found using proverbs.
But they keep stable the fabric of the world,
and their prayer is in the practice of their trade."

(38:33–34)

The slaves, the peasants, and the artisans have a subordinate role in society, but what of the merchant? Though Ben Sira does not specifically say that they are not sought out for the council of the people, nor do they sit on the judge's seat, he leaves little doubt that the merchant would be far from welcome:

"A merchant can hardly keep from wrongdoing,
and a tradesman will not be declared innocent of sin.
Many have committed sin for a trifle,
and whoever seeks rich will avert his eyes.
As a stake is driven firmly into a fissure between stones,
so sin is wedged in between buying and selling."

(26:29; 27:1–2)

High status, elevated esteem, and public prominence are accorded by Ben Sira to individuals like himself, i.e., the *soferim,* or scribes. These were men who did not engage in manual labor, but had ample economic resources to enjoy leisure. This is stated with disarming candor:

"The wisdom of the scribe depends on the opportunity of leisure;
and he who has little business may become wise."

(38:24)

The *soferim* presumably must be those who are sought out for the council of the people; who attain eminence in the public assembly; who sit on the judge's seat and understand the sentence of judgment; who expound discipline; who use proverbs (38:33–34).

So much by implication. But Ben Sira is not content. He catalogues the characteristics of the *soferim* in loving detail. In contrast to the peasant and artisan, the *sofer* works with his mind:

"On the other hand, he who devotes himself
to the study of the law of the Most High
will seek the wisdom of all the ancients,

and will be concerned with prophecies;
he will preserve the discourses of notable men
and penetrate the subtleties of parables;
he will seek out the hidden meaning of proverbs
and be at home with the obscurity of parable.
He will serve among great men
and appear before rulers;
he will travel through the lands of foreign nations,
for he tests the good and evil among men.
He will set his heart to rise early
to seek the Lord who made him,
and will make supplication before the Most High;
he will open his mouth in prayer
and make supplication for his sins.
If the great Lord is willing,
he will be filled with the spirit of understanding;
he will put forth words of wisdom
and give thanks to the Lord in prayer.
He will direct his counsel and knowledge aright,
and meditate on his secrets.
He will reveal instruction in his teaching,
and will glory in the law of the Lord's covenant."

(39:1–8)

Such activity brings the highest reward his society can offer:

"Many will praise his understanding,
and it will never be blotted out;
his memory will not disappear,
and his name will live through all generations.
Nations will declare his wisdom,
and the congregation will proclaim his praise;
if he lives long, he will leave a name
*   greater than a thousand,*
and if he goes to rest, it is enough for him."

(39:9–12)

The *sofer,* the scribe, is a man of distinction and learning, of piety and mature responsibility. He is well versed in the Law, the prophecies, and wisdom. His understanding is valued highly and his talents are put to good use. The issue, however, is not whether the *scribe* was learned in the Law, or a repository of wisdom, nor whether he participated in the public assembly or served as a judge. The problem is a more delicate one. Did the *soferim*, the scribes, have an independent relationship to the Law, or were they the intellectual supporters of Aaronide supremacy? Did meditation in the Law mean exegetical investigation, or the mastery of its *literal* content?

The answer to these questions is rooted in the presuppositions of the historian. If he approaches Ben Sira already convinced that the *soferim* must have had an independent function; that their intellectual activity involved exegetical techniques; that they were in some way a counterpoise to the Aaronides, then he will have no difficulty reading Ben Sira's verses in this light. If, on the other hand, he comes with no such presuppositions and reads Ben Sira as the sole source extant for determining what the *soferim* were, then his conclusions will be radically different.

A major purpose of this paper is to propose that the latter approach is the only one methodologically justifiable. It is a procedure that is binding on every historian as an inescapable demand of his discipline.

The term *sofer* occurs in several books of the Bible. It does not appear, however, in either the Pentateuch or in Joshua. And as for the other biblical books, the term is used only sporadically. In no instance is the term elaborated upon. To the extent that it is used, even in Ezra and Nehemiah, its meaning is taken for granted. The reader is assumed to know the character and the nature of the function. This is perhaps best illustrated in the books of Ezra and Nehemiah where Ezra is referred to as the *sofer*, but his function is not spelled out. What being a *sofer* entailed is not anywhere stated with precision. And insofar as Ezra's role is clear, it involved a strenuous effort to undo the intermarriages and to have the Law accepted by the leaders and the people as binding. Ezra the *sofer* is the man who underwrote the commands of the Law of Moses. In view of the solicitous concern for the revenues of the priests, Ezra seems to have been devoted to the literal meaning of the Law, and to the achievement of Aaronide supremacy.

In Ezra, it is true, one can detect a function of the scribe: the steadfast advocacy of the authority of the Pentateuch. The triumph of such authority carried with it Aaronide supremacy. The duty of the *sofer* was to support the Pentateuchally ordained priesthood. He has no independent authority as a *sofer;* he was a supporter and an upholder of the authority ordained by God and Moses.

That Ezra the *sofer* was a *sofer* in the same sense that the Baruch of Jeremiah was a *sofer* can scarcely be maintained. Nor was he a *sofer* of the kind mentioned in Judges, Samuel, and Kings. He was a special kind of *sofer*, a member of a class that arose in post-exilic times, a class that was committed wholeheartedly to the Pentateuch.

The definition of *sofer* drawn from the books of Ezra and Nehemiah is derived from the acts that Ezra performs. It is impossible, however, to determine which acts of Ezra are to be assigned to his role as *sofer* and which to his role as priest. The author at no time defines a *sofer* directly, for the character of his work is historical and narrative. He assumes that the title is sufficiently well known to need no further elaboration.

Ben Sira, however, had other purposes. He wished to extol the merits of the *sofer* and to contrast the high esteem of his calling with the menial work of the peasant and artisan. He therefore makes an exhaustive listing of the *sofer*'s interests. For this reason, Ben Sira's description must be the starting point for any analysis. It is the only source that makes the *sofer* an object of description, and does not assume prior knowledge on the part of his reader. Every other usage of *sofer* takes such knowledge for granted.

If the scholar begins with Ben Sira, he does not know in advance what a *sofer* is. He must acquire this knowledge from Ben Sira. *He therefore must be especially wary of attributing to the* sofer *any authority or any activity that Ben Sira does not explicitly acknowledge.*

Ben Sira never attributes to the *sofer* authority over the Law. He is a student of the Law, but not in charge of the Law. He is the ardent supporter of the Law, but he does not determine what the Law commands. He administers the Law, he does not tamper with it. His area of freedom is in proverbs and parables.

Ben Sira recognizes throughout his work that the Aaronides control the Law. The *sofer* is not on the same level as the priest. He may serve as judge, speak in the assembly of the people, but only as a supporter of Aaronide supremacy. And how could it be otherwise, when the Law that Ben Sira praises specifically enjoins an elaborate sacrificial cult that alone could expiate the sins of the people and that was given as a monopoly to the Aaronides? The Pentateuch, however, does not assign any function whatsoever to the *sofer;* indeed, the word itself never occurs.

The *sofer* then in Ben Sira has as yet no official function. It is a name given to designate a class of individuals who were engaged in intellectual pursuits, who were attracted to wisdom, who were available for service in the interests of the hierocracy. The name does not refer to a specific and well defined function, as does the word "priest," or "judge." A *sofer* might or might not be a priest. He might or might not be a judge. His talents might or might not be called upon by the priestly rulers. He was, however, at all times a loyal adherent of the Law that underwrote Aaronide supremacy.

Any assertion that the *soferim* were in the time of Ben Sira a class with an independent approach to the Law—any such assertion is undermined by Ben Sira's own words and is based on evidence that does not exist.

Ben Sira is thus the only source that explicitly spells out what a *sofer* was. Every other source of the pre-Hasmonean period uses the term *sofer* in the same manner that it uses the word "king," or "priest." The pre-Hasmonean *sofer*—at least to that point in time when Ben Sira wrote—must have been what Ben Sira said he was, unless there is some pre-Hasmonean source that unambiguously refutes or modifies Ben Sira's description. Any definition of the *sofer* that is derived outside of Ben Sira and which is then used to determine what Ben Sira meant by *sofer* is methodologically and procedurally without warrant. Ben Sira *describes* the *sofer;* the other sources *use* the term.

How then did the *sofer* approach the Law? Did he study it literally? Meditate upon it as the clear word of God? Or did he subject it to logical scrutiny? Did he apply to it some form of *midrashic* exegesis?

What procedure is one to follow in seeking an answer to these questions? Again the starting point must be the words of Ben Sira himself. If a historian had only Ben Sira and no other source, is there any statement of Ben Sira that necessitates an assumption of a *midrashic* mode? Is there any statement in Ben Sira that must be read as implying a nonliteral approach? Ben Sira urges the study of the Law in language no different than that of the Law itself. He is no more committed to *midrashic* exegesis than the author of the book of Joshua who puts the following commands in the mouth of God: "Only be strong and very courageous, to observe to do according to all the law, which Moses My servant commanded thee. . . . This book of the law shall not depart from out of thy mouth, but thou shalt meditate therein day and night, that thou mayest observe to do according to all that is written therein. . . ." (Joshua 1:7-8).

Ben Sira utters nary a syllable necessitating the assumption of an exegetical or midrashic approach. And if we broaden our investigation and examine the other writings of the pre-Hasmonean period, we likewise find no compulsion emanating from the text itself to conclude that the Pentateuch was not understood literally as written.

Does the Psalmist, for example, mean anything but the literal meaning of the Torah when he says:

> *The law of the Lord is perfect, restoring the soul;*
> *The testimony of the Lord is sure, making wise the simple.*
> *The precepts of the Lord are right, rejoicing the heart;*
> *The commandment of the Lord is pure, enlightening the eyes."*
>
> (Psalms 19:8–9)

And if we pursue the problem a step further, we have further confirmation that a literal approach was not only possible but tenaciously affirmed. The Sadducees, at a time subsequent to Ben Sira, when literality *was* challenged by the Pharisees, held fast to the laws as written. One can hardly improve on Josephus' rendering: "[The Sadducees] hold that only those regulations should be considered valid which were written down, and those which had been handed down from former generations need not be observed" (*Antiquities* XIII: 297).

The one realm that was not explicitly covered by the Law, and which was very near to the heart of Ben Sira, was wisdom. How did he assimilate wisdom with Torah? He took the equivalence as self-evident. He identifies the two. He links God to both simultaneously. He does not, however, resort to exegesis. He does not ask: What is the meaning of this or that Pentateuchal verse? How is this contradiction to be solved?

His method is evident throughout his work:

> *"All wisdom comes from the Lord,*
> *and is with him forever . . ."*
>
> (1:1)
>
> *"The Lord himself created wisdom;*
> *he saw her and apportioned her,*
> *he poured her out on all his works. . . ."*
>
> (1:9)
>
> *"To fear the Lord is the beginning of wisdom;*
> *she is created with the faithful in the womb. . . .*
> *To fear the Lord is wisdom's full measure. . . ."*
>
> (1:16)
>
> *"The fear of the Lord is the crown of wisdom,*
> *making peace and perfect health to flourish . . ."*
>
> (1:18)
>
> *"To fear the Lord is the root of wisdom,*
> *and her branches are long life. . . .*

The man who fears the Lord will do this,
and he who holds to the law will obtain her [i.e., wisdom]"

(15:1)

"Whoever keeps the law controls his thoughts,
and wisdom is the fulfillment of the fear of the Lord."

(21:11)

There is no exegesis here. Only the affirmation of the status of wisdom as of divine origin and hence thoroughly compatible with the divine Law.

Even more revealing is Ben Sira's device of having wisdom herself proclaim her tie to God, Torah, and Israel:

"Wisdom will praise herself,
and will glory in the midst of her people.
In the assembly of the Most High
she will open her mouth,
and in the presence of his host
she will glory.
'I came from the mouth of the Most High,
and covered the earth like a mist. . . .
In the waves of the sea, in the whole earth,
and in every people and nation
I have gotten a possession.
Among all these I sought a resting place;
I sought in whose territory I might lodge.
Then the Creator of all things
gave me a commandment,
and the one who created me
assigned a place for my tent.
And he said, "Make your dwelling in Jacob,
and in Israel seek your inheritance."
From eternity, in the beginning he created me,
and for eternity I shall not cease to exist.
In the holy tabernacle I ministered before him
and so I was established in Zion.
In the beloved city likewise
he gave me a resting place,
and in Jerusalem was my dominion.
So I took root in an honored people,
in the portion of the Lord,
who is their inheritance. . . .'"

(24:1–12)

The identification of wisdom and Torah is made firmly secure in the following verses:

"All this is the book of the covenant
of the Most High God,
the law which Moses commanded us,
as an inheritance for the congregation of Jacob.
It fills men with wisdom, like the Pishon,
and like the Tigris at the time of the first fruits.
It makes them full of understanding, like the Euphrates,
and like the Jordan at harvest time . . ."

(24:23–26)

Ben Sira solves the problem of the status of wisdom, by refusing to see it as a problem. Wisdom underwrites the Law, reinforces it; it does not challenge it. The literality of the Torah is not jeopardized; the words of the Pentateuchal text are not subjected to scrutiny. The Pentateuch is assumed to be the fruit of wisdom; it need not be proved such through exegesis. It is self-evident.

And a final reminder. Ben Sira does not accord the *sofer* any authority over the Law. The *sofer's* realm of creative activity is *outside* the Law, in a domain that the Law does not restrict to itself. Here the *sofer* is free: in the discourse of notable men; in the penetration of subtle parables; in the solution of enigmatic proverbs and obscure parables; in the search for ancient wisdom; in the probing of the meaning of prophecies. He is free to utter maxims, and to teach others understanding. But as for the Law, he is to uphold it as an eternal covenant. He is to serve as a model to others in the joy with which he keeps statutes, judgments, and commandments. And at all times, he is to remember that only the descendants of Aaron can speak with authority as to what the Law meant.

"In his commandments he [God] gave
him [Aaron] authority in statutes and judgments,
to teach Jacob the testimonies,
and to enlighten Israel with his law."

(45:17)

And among the Aaronides, the High Priest was the ultimate authority:

"Therefore a covenant was established with him [Phineas],
that he should be the leader of the sanctuary and of his people,

that he and his descendants should have
the dignity of the priesthood forever."

(45:24)

In his own day, Simon, son of Onias, was the living embodiment of the promise:

"*The leader of his brethren*
and the pride of his people
was Simon the High Priest, son of Onias."
(50:1a)

The class structure in the days of Ben Sira is now clear: peasants and artisans who work, but have no say; merchants who garner money, but lack social status; the wealthy—and these are referred to in verse after verse—whose source of wealth is unclear (they seem to be city dwellers, but if they are not peasants, or artisans, or merchants, they must be either owners of landed estates or priests) who are not always wise, but whose voice is heard; the *soferim,* the hierocratic intellectuals, who are dedicated to the Temple and the laws of Moses, who turn a neat parable and phrase a wise proverb, and who are ever ready to earn a good name in the assembly of the people and in the council of the elders; and finally the ruling class itself: the Aaronides, ministering at the altar of the Lord, expiating the sins of the people through a sacrificial cult ordained by God, garnering the fruitful offerings demanded by the Law, and standing guard over the Law as Moses had commanded. And at the very pinnacle of this society was Simon the son of Onias the High Priest who, in his once yearly entry into the holy of holies, reconfirmed, before the dazzled multitude, that his authority was of God.

As for the Levites. They assuredly must have been around, but Ben Sira finds them unworthy of even one sententious maxim. By this time they must have become living witnesses to the consequences of the rebellion of Korah against Aaron's supremacy: Temple menials who labored while the Aaronides in pomp and majesty offered sweet-smelling sacrifices to the Lord who had swallowed up Korah and all his evil company.

II. *Ben Sira, the Nonexistence of the Synagogue and the Argument from Silence*

It is now time to assess the method of analysis that has been applied to Ben Sira and to draw the necessary conclusions. A simple procedural rule has been adopted: Ben Sira must take priority over all other sources, subsequent to the memoirs of Nehemiah, for the reconstruction of pre-Hasmonean Judean society. It must be consulted as a source for our knowledge of this society, and it must not be modified, altered or corrected by a priori assumptions that have no grounding in sources contemporaneous with that society. It is the only source extant that describes a definite society, a concrete segment of the historical continuum, and a very specific High Priest, Simon son of Onias. All the other sources, such as Proverbs, Psalms, Job, Ecclesiastes, are rich in ambiguity and imprecision. Indeed, these sources are dependent on Ben Sira for elucidation, since Ben Sira alone establishes some fixed point of social-ideological reference.

The priority of Ben Sira does not carry with it an elimination of problems. The date of its composition, for example, is not susceptible to absolute determination. The *exact* meaning of *all* his words may elude our techniques. Thus we are not certain what the functions of the *ecclesia* were, or how judges were chosen. The message communicated by the source may be distorted by some lack in our conceptual apparatus. All this may be true, but the method nonetheless offers a procedure for reducing the range and intensity of distortion by eliminating assumptions that are derived from sources that are demonstrably less knowledgeable than Ben Sira.

The existence of the synagogue in the period of Ben Sira is the most notorious of these assumptions. It is nowhere specifically mentioned prior to the *post*-Hasmonean period. It is not referred to in the Pentateuch. Ezekiel, Isaiah, Haggai, Zechariah, Malachi make no mention of it, though these prophets are intensely concerned with the restoration of the Temple. The memoirs of Nehemiah are unpunctuated by a single reference to it; the activities of Ezra pass it by. The Psalms never exhort the pious to pray in a synagogue, though pray they should. Proverbs, Ecclesiastes, Job, Esther, Daniel, Judith, Tobit —nary a reference. And Ben Sira, *sofer,* student of the Law, sagacious guide for the religious life—likewise is mute.

The evidence then for the pre-Hasmonean existence of the synagogue is the unbroken silence of the sources. In the face of the sources which speak of a real Temple and a real priesthood, scholars give *priority* to silence. They introduce a set of assumptions that has no warrant in any source; they justify this step by an appeal to silence; and they then modify the communication of articulate, bona fide contemporaneous sources to comport with their assumptions. The overwhelming scholarly consensus today takes for granted that Ben Sira lived in a society where there were synagogues—synagogues that had been in existence for several hundred years. The unknown has triumphed over the known, silence over articulation. And this amazing triumph is attributable to a methodological and procedural flaw, a flaw that enlarges the range and intensity of the distortion of a source's message.

The culprit is a methodological dogma: the silence of a source with respect to some element in society is in and of itself no proof that such an element did not exist. This is indeed an excellent principle. If a scholar is analyzing an account book in fourteenth century Italy and he finds no mention of monasteries, he would have no right to utilize the silence of his *specialized* document as evidence for the nonexistence of monasteries which were legitimately outside the focus of his document. However, what of a failure to utilize business machines, to allude to corporate structures, to refer to systematic banking? And what of silence in these books with respect to stocks and bonds, steamships, railroads, trucks? If silence such as this is ubiquitous, would any scholar dare to posit the existence of modern banking, modern corporate forms, or modern means of shipping by an appeal to the silence of the sources?

What, we may well ask, is the most conclusive evidence of nonexistence? Is it not silence? Does anyone argue that nuclear reactors existed in the Egypt of the Ptolemies on the grounds that no source mentions them! Would any scholar posit Christian churches in the Athens of Pericles merely because no source refers to them?

The formula thus requires rephrasing: the failure of a source to mention the existence of some element in society is no proof that it did not exist. However, the claim for the existence of an element within society must have some positive evidence. Where no such positive evidence exists, knowledge must be confined to that for which there is evidence *with the proviso that it be subject always to revision in the light of new evidence.*

What positive evidence is advanced for the existence of the synagogue in pre-Hasmonean times? None whatsoever.[9] Synagogues are mentioned in contemporary sources only *after* the Hasmonean revolt. Archeological evidence for synagogues is confined to epochs long *after* the Hasmonean revolt. Josephus never refers to synagogues as existing in pre-Hasmonean times. The decrees of Antiochus IV aimed at destroying Judaism mention the Temple and the Law, but no synagogues. It is clear that no positive source exists.

What grounds then? The existence of the synagogue in post-

9 On the relationship of the *pro-* *seuche* to the synagogue, see Appendix B.

Hasmonean times presupposes its existence prior to that time? This argument can carry no weight, for Judean society underwent violent upheavals during and after the Hasmonean revolt. The synagogue may very well have emerged in conjunction with these tumultuous events. Would any one argue that the conventicles of the Puritans antedated the historical situation that created them? Where were the Jacobin Clubs before the French Revolution? The Committees of Correspondence before the opposition to the Crown? The Soviets before the revolution of 1905?

The second argument is that the synagogue was a logical response to the exile. A logical response, however, is not necessarily a historical response. Scholars fully aware of the triumph of synagogue over the Temple may think that it was the logical outcome of the exile. The prophets, however, who lived in the exilic and postexilic periods reacted otherwise. Every one of them looked forward to the rebuilding of the Temple with a purified sacrificial cult. They did not contemplate any other mode or institution of worship. The assembling of people to listen to prophets does not imply a synagogue form. They assembled to hear about a restored Temple.

The third argument is that once the Temple was restored it could not serve adequately the religious needs of the people because many lived too far from Jerusalem. Whether the distances were so insurmountable is certainly open to question. But even if this were an obstacle, how does it follow that the people gathered in synagogues for religious worship? The obligation to the Temple could not be offset by inconvenience. Nothing could substitute for the expiation offered by the altar. A man might pray to God as an individual, but this did not free him of giving to the priest the firstborn of his cattle and of his fruits, the heave offering, the payment of his vow. Nor did it absolve him from appearing thrice yearly with full hands at the Temple. That distance stood in the way of the peasant who believed the Law to be divine is difficult to comprehend in the light of historical religious experience.

Furthermore, it must be emphasized that the Aaronides ruled society. Their functional domain was the Temple. As long as their monopoly was secure—and Ben Sira indicates that in his day it was— it is hardly likely that they would countenance any mode of worship which might in any way divert the attention of any Jew from the Temple in Jerusalem.

But why prolong the argument? The crux of the problem is not touched by such a debate. An argument of this type can always be met with a counterargument. The fundamental issue is methodological. If one begins with Ben Sira and reconstructs society through his words and his alone, if one then analyzes the other sources of the pre-Hasmonean period, and if one finally goes back to the canonization of the Pentateuch and even to the exilic and postexilic prophets, does he discover the synagogue? Where in any source will he find it unless he is convinced in advance of its existence?

If such is the situation, by what right does a scholar create the past out of nothing?

Ben Sira thus stands as a sentinel over a segment of the historical continuum. His words defend a territory of Jewish history from scholarly spoilation. These words communicate information about his society: Temple cult, Aaronide priests, a High Priest, a divinely revealed Law, a class of *soferim*, etc. This information does not contradict the demands of the Pentateuch, nor is it incompatible with information derived from other pre-Hasmonean sources. Whatever is unclear in Ben Sira cannot be clarified by nonexistent data.

Ben Sira's articulation bars the intrusion of nonexistences. The society that he knew was a hierocracy. There were no synagogues. No Pharisees. No Oral Law. No exegetical midrash. Only sacrifices and priests and the literal Law. And also the wisdom, the proverbs, and the parables of the *sofer*. That which did not as yet exist, Ben Sira does not describe; after all, prophecy had ceased before his time—as *all* scholars will freely admit.

APPENDIX A

Virtually all scholars maintain that Ben Sira was written about the year 180 B.C.E. (cf., e.g., M. S. Siegel, *Sefer ben Sira Ha-Shalem,* Jerusalem, 1953, pp. 3–6; Charles C. Torrey, *The Apocryphal Literature,* New Haven, 1945, p. 94; G. H. Box and W. O. E. Oesterly, "Sirach," in R. H. Charles, *The Apocrypha and Pseudepigrapha of the Old Testament,* Oxford, 1913, pp. 293–294; Rudolf Smend, *Die Weisheit des Jesus Sirach,* Berlin, 1906, pp. XV–XVI). The argument for an earlier dating (c. 280) advanced by J. H. A. Hart, *Ecclesiasticus in Greek,* Cambridge, 1909, pp. 249 ff., has been rejected (cf. Box and Oesterly, *ibid.,* and Robert H. Pfeifer, *History of New Testament Times,* New York, 1949, pp. 364–365: "The arguments of J. H. A. Hart . . . to prove that the book was written in the period 300–275 are utterly unconvincing.")

It is difficult to comprehend the basis for so absolute a judgment. The internal evidence for a late dating is not so conclusive as to foreclose debate on this issue. If there had been no prologue to Ben Sira in which the grandson and translator states that he came to Egypt in the thirty-eighth year of Eugertes, it is questionable whether a 180 date could be established on the basis of internal evidence alone. It is the mention of the thirty-eighth year of Eugertes that really clinches the argument for most scholars. Only Eugertes II (170–117) could have been meant, since Eugertes I did not reign long enough, while Eugertes II did if the years of his co-regency are included.

The dating thus really hinges on the meaning of a single sentence. The Greek in no way requires the rendering given it by most scholars. The sentence reads as follows: Ἐν γὰρ τῷ ὀγδόῳ καὶ τριακοστῷ ἔτει ἐπὶ τοῦ Ἐνεργέτου βασιλέως παραγενηθεὶς εἰς Αἰγυπτον καὶ συγχρονίσας, ευρον οὐ μικρας παιδείας ἀφόμοιον.
The usual rendering is "When I came to Egypt in the thirty-eighth year of the reign of Eugertes, and stayed for some time. . . ."

However, the following translation is at least as valid as the former: "When I came to Egypt in my thirty-eighth year, in the reign of Eugertes [i.e., while Eugertes was still king] and stayed for some time [i.e., Eugertes is no longer living]." This is an unassailable translation, even if it were to be shown that ἐπι is in rare instances used in conjunction with the year of a dynasty. The point is that ἐπι does not necessarily have to be used. Indeed in the entire Septuagint ἐπι is rarely, if ever, used in such a way, despite the fact that there are many passages that refer to the years of a king's reign. Would Ben Sira's grandson, who specifically refers to the already extant translation of the Law, the Prophets and other works, be *required* by his models and Greek usage to use ἐπι to express the year of a dynasty in this way? How can anyone be certain from this sentence that he did so use it, when Greek usage not only does not *require* this meaning, but rarely, if ever, uses ἐπι in this sense?

It may be that the sentence can be translated either way. If so, then its meaning is ambiguous and cannot be used as evidence for the dating, unless some clear, explicit, and unambiguous *internal* reference can settle the issue. But no such internal evidence exists. The reference in Chapter 50 to Simon's building the wall and fortifying the city does not necessarily refer to an action by Simon II. The investment of Jerusalem by Ptolemy Soter (305–283) could have afforded Simon I the opportunity for reconstruction. (Cf. Josephus, *Antiquities*, XII:1–7.)

Certain problems posed by the book would be solved, if it were to be dated about 270. It would explain Ben Sira's failure to mention Ezra, even though he refers to Nehemiah. Such an omission by a *sofer* in c. 180—decades after Ezra-Nehemiah were written—is absolutely incomprehensible; but such an omission by a *sofer* in c. 270 is perfectly understandable, since the book had either not yet been written, or its claims for Ezra were still too radical. It may even mean that Ezra, the *sofer*, was not known to Ben Sira because Ezra had not yet attained historical reality.

An early date would also make Simon the son of Onias of Chapter 50, Simon the Just. This would confirm Josephus's positive identification of the first Simon (c. 200) as the one who was called the Just (*Antiquities* XII, 157). This would spare scholars the task of correcting Josephus (cf. Ralph Marcus, *Josephus*, Loeb Classical Library, Cambridge, 1943, VII, pp. 732–736). How Josephus can be challenged with respect to so definite a statement regarding the identity of a High Priest is, in any event, something of a mystery. Even if the Simon of Ben Sira was Simon II, it does not necessarily follow that he was called the Just. He bears no such appellation in Chapter 50.

So much for the problem of dating. I should like to emphasize, however, that *this article is not concerned with the dating.* It is concerned primarily with the question: Did the synagogue exist in the society Ben Sira describes—irrespective of whether he wrote in c. 270 or in c. 180? If he wrote earlier, then the synagogue was not yet in existence in the latter part of the third century. If he wrote later, then the synagogue was not in existence even in the last quarter of the second century. It really makes little difference, for the evidence *external* to Ben Sira for the existence of the synagogue is as absent for the later date as for the earlier.

APPENDIX B

But what of the *proseuche* ($\pi\rho\sigma\epsilon\nu\chi\acute{\eta}$)? Was this not a "prayer-house," and is it not referred to in an inscription dedicating a *proseuche* to Ptolemy III Eugertes (247–221 B.C.E.) and his consort Berenice? (See Johann Oehler, "Epigraphische Beiträge zur Geschichte des Judentums," MGWJ, L III [1909], p. 451, no. 227). Modern scholars are in agreement that the *proseuche* is indeed identical with the synagogue (cf. M. Avi-Yonah, "Synagogue Architecture in the Classical Period," in *Jewish Art*, ed. Cecil Roth, New York, 1961, pp. 157–158; E. R. Goodenough, *Jewish Symbols in the Greco-Roman Period*, Vol. II, p. 84; E. L. Sukenik, *Ancient Synagogues in Palestine and Greece*,

[London, 1934], p. 1; Harry J. Leon, *The Jews of Ancient Rome,* [Philadelphia, 1960], p. 139, n. 2.

But was the *proseuche* of the dedicatory inscription identical with the synagogue? No scholar has yet found either an inscription or a literary reference to the *synagogue*—and I stress the importance of the exact name—dating from pre-Hasmonean times. The inscription does *not* describe what the *proseuche* is; it is a dedication, that is, a symbol of loyalty. The inscription reveals nothing else. The earliest sources that refer to the *proseuche* in some detail are Philo's *In Flaccum* and his *Legatio ad Gaium.* But Philo wrote at a time when there *is* abundant evidence that synagogues *were* flourishing. Thus even if the *proseuche* had been in existence prior to and distinct from the synagogue, Philo would be aware of the synagogue and might conceivably have used the word *proseuche* to refer to both the *proseuche* and the synagogue. Thus in our own day we indiscriminately call all Christian houses of worship churches, even though they differ radically architecturally and liturgically. So, too, contemporary Jews —even rabbis—refer to both Reform and Conservative houses of worship as temples, even though the mode of service radically differs. It is thus by no means excluded that Philo might have referred to two very different institutions with the same word *proseuche* because of a single element that was shared, in this instance, prayer.

Indeed, Philo seems to be talking about a single institution, the Hellenistic *proseuche,* in his *In Flaccum,* and two distinct institutions, the *proseuche* and the *proseuche*-synagogue in his *Legatio ad Gaium.* In the latter work, the *proseuchai*-synagogues are places where Jews gather to offer "first fruits" to the Temple and to participate in religious activity. These *proseuchai* are the kind that flourished in Rome and its environs. These are indeed synagogues, and are so referred to in Agrippa's letter, cited by Philo (*Legatio ad Gaium,* ed. and trans. E. M. Smallwood, Leiden, 1961, par. 40, pp. 133–135). These *proseuchai*-synagogues were legitimized by Augustus and they were distinguished from disloyal, subversive clubs. Their existence, therefore, did not involve any disloyalty to the Emperor, since they served the religious needs of Jews.

The *proseuchai* of Alexandria and other Hellenistic (that is, pre-Roman) cities are described by Philo in *In Flaccum* and only briefly referred to in the *Legatio* (*ibid.,* lines 132–139, pp. 87–89). They are not devoted to the collection of "first fruits" for the Temple, nor are they merely nonsubversive meeting houses. Rather they are symbols of loyalty to the emperors (cf. *In Flaccum,* ed. and trans. Herbert

Box, London, 1939, lines 44–52, pp. 17–21). They seem to have been buildings erected by Jews from the time of the Ptolemies as evidence of Jewish loyalty to the "divine" monarchs. The *proseuche* was offered to, and accepted by, the Ptolemies as a substitute for the erection of statues of the emperors and for the refusal to worship them as gods. It was a substitute for the sacrifice that was offered for the emperor in the Temple at Jerusalem. The *proseuche* was thus a concrete embodiment of Jewish loyalty to the emperors. The *proseuche* therefore was not a prayer-house in general, but a shrine for prayers to be offered for the reigning family. The *proseuche* represented for the Jews the solution of a delicate problem: how loyalty to a pagan regime that deified its emperors could be made compatible with the belief in a single God. The *proseuche* permitted the Jews to do both. It likewise offered a solution for the emperor's dilemma of how to legitimize Jewish rights and residence. The *proseuche* was a concrete symbol testifying to the loyalty of the Jews.

If the *proseuchai* in the Hellenistic cities were in effect loyalty shrines, then the wounded exclamation of Philo is comprehensible:

"Actually, alone among the peoples of the world, they [the Jews] were being deprived, through loss of their *proseuche,* of the means of showing their *loyalty* to their benefactors—*which [deprivation] they would have counted as ten thousand deaths.* They have no sacred precincts in which they could set forth their gratitude. Hence they could have said to their enemies: 'Without being aware of it, you have actually taken away honor from your lords, instead of conferring it on them, *because you do not know that to the Jews everywhere in the world their* proseuchai *are manifestly bases for their expression of piety toward the house of Augustus. If they are snatched away from them, what other places or manner of honoring is left?'* " (*In Flaccum, op. cit.,* lines 45–49, pp. 18–19. Italics mine. Box's translation slightly modified for clarity).

The *proseuchai* were the means of showing loyalty to the rulers. Without them the Jews would have had no concrete way of demonstrating their loyalty.

Philo's predominant concern is not that the Jews are being deprived of institutions for prayer in general, or of an institution for the collecting of "first fruits," or of an institution for the exposition of the Law. He is not defending the *proseuchai* from the charge that they are subversive assemblies. Not at all! He is passionately—a rare indulgence for Philo—reminding his readers that the *proseuchai* are loyalty houses, they are the *only* symbols available for the Jews to demonstrate their dedication to their pagan rulers. To be stripped of these symbols is equivalent to suffering ten thousand deaths! These *proseuchai* are strongholds of loyalty, "they are manifestly bases for the expression of their piety toward the house of Augustus. *If they are snatched away from us, what other place or manner of honoring is left?*" (my italics).

Surely then we are confronted with the possibility that Philo was fully aware of the existence in his day of two institutions, the classical *proseuche* that had had its origins as a symbol of loyalty in the Hellenistic period, especially in Ptolemaic Egypt, and the post-Hellenistic *synagogue* which took strongest root in Rome and its environs. This *synagogue* is described by Philo in *Legatio,* lines 152–158, as a place where Jews gathered especially on the Sabbath to receive public instruction in their national philosophy, and where the "first fruits" for the Temple was presumably collected. It is to be noted that the practice is attributed to Jews who had been brought to Rome as prisoners of war, that is, they must have come from Palestine long after the Hasmonean Revolt. Philo calls these meeting places, *proseuchai.* However, they are identical with the synagogues that Agrippa describes in his letter to Caligula:

"When he [Augustus] discovered that the sacred 'first fruits' were being neglected, he instructed the governors of the provinces of Asia to grant the Jews alone the right of meeting in the synagogues (εἰς τὰ συναγώγια). He said these were not meetings that had their origins in drunkenness and disorderliness likely to disturb the peace, but were schools of sobriety and justice for people who practiced virtue and contributed their annual 'first fruits' which they used to pay for sacrifices. . . . He did not want the Jewish assemblies, which are held for the collection of the 'first fruits' and for other religious purposes, to be swept away in the same way as the clubs were." (*Legatio,* trans. Smallwood, lines 311b–317).

Agrippa says *not* a word about the synagogues being bases of loyalty to the Augustan house. Indeed he must point out that they are not houses of disloyalty, like the clubs, but places for religious gatherings. It should likewise be noted that these synagogues flourish in Asia and Ephesus, not in Alexandria. Philo's *proseuchai* of *In Flaccum* are not the *proseuchai*-synagogues of the *Legatio!* The *proseuchai* of Philo's *In Flaccum* were a creation of Hellenistic Jews; the synagogues of the *Legatio,* that of Palestinian Jews sometime after the Hasmonean Revolt.

It is true that when Philo describes the synagogues in the *Legatio, he* calls them *proseuchai,* which in a sense they were—Agrippa refers to their serving religious purposes. But Agrippa does *not* call them *proseuchai*, but *synagogues*. Philo thus bestowed upon them a name that was appropriate for some functions of the synagogue; indeed by calling them *proseuchai* he emphasized their religious character, for the name *synagogus*, or the Hebrew *Beth ha-Kenesseth* in no way, in the name itself, communicates any information about its *religious* function. It merely means "assembly house," not prayer-house. Philo thus used *proseuche* to make clear that it was a place of prayer, even though it was not, as in Alexandria, a place of prayer dedicated to the emperor! Philo was thus bestowing upon the synagogue a more elevated and spiritual name, something which was done by synagogue Jews themselves when they began to call the synagogue a *Beth Tefillah*, a House of Prayer, that is, a *proseuche*, even though the original name was never abandoned.

That the *proseuche* in Egypt was not a synagogue is further confirmed by III Maccabees 7:17–23. Here we read that the Jews were so overjoyed at the benign decree of Ptolemy Eugertes that they held a splendid banquet and erected a *proseuche* on the spot to commenorate the event; that is, they built a prayerhouse to the emperor as a sign of their gratitude, since they could not erect a statue or offer up a sacrifice.

And finally the dedicatory inscription to Ptolemy from Schedia in Alexandria and dating from the third century B.C.E. is further confirmation. It is after all a dedication to the emperor and his consort, manifestly then a symbol of Jewish loyalty, a prayerhouse instead of a statue, a *proseuche* instead of a sacrificial shrine. This is the most that the brief line communicates; to insist that it means more is without warrant. If this *proseuche* were a synagogue, the inscription should have said so. Since it does not, we have evidence for a *proseuche*, not a synagogue; and nothing can alter the status of the evidence—unless evidence of equivalent authority is forthcoming.

"Son of Man"

SAMUEL SANDMEL

*

THE TERM SON OF MAN may be said to constitute something of a problem in early Christian writings; it is not a problem in the same way in Jewish writings. Ezekiel's use of the term (and he uses it frequently) is readily discernible as connoting simply man; it is in Daniel 7:13 that the reading, some one *in the likeness of a son of man,* brought to the phrase Son of Man the special connotation of a messianic role. IV Ezra and Enoch use the phrase, but in the light of Daniel, as is the case in at least two passages in Mark. In rabbinic literature, however, the term seems unknown as a name for the Messiah. When Lietzmann studied the term in his fine monograph *Der Menschensohn* in 1896, he came to the conclusions herein summarized.

Lietzmann makes the point validly that previous to the Gospels Son of Man was merely a phrase; in the Gospels, however, it is transformed, as it were, into a title. I see no reason to disagree with this conclusion of Lietzmann's.[1] Yet there is reason to inquire into the nature of the phrase as a title, particularly in the Gospel According to Mark, the earliest of the Gospels. Applied as it is by Jesus to himself, it is one of several titles found in the New Testament: messiah (*Christos*), *kyrios,* son of David, son of God, king of the Jews, and the like. Other terms are logos and servant. Virtually all commentators see a certain synonymity in the terms, though, of course, they have seen specific differentiation: a frequent view, for example, is that the title Son of Man was utilized by Galilean Jewish Christianity, whereas *kyrios* was utilized by Dispersion gentile Christianity.

In Lietzmann's procedure, he lumps together all occurrences of the phrase in the four Gospels, but gives us not one single word in characterization of any one of the Gospels in which the term occurs. So too his successors. Is it valid that the problem of the phrase is unchanged from Mark through Matthew, Luke, and John? That it could remain unchanged, could well be the conclusion of a scholar;

1 See, especially, pp. 93–95.

in Lietzmann, and in virtually all other scholars, however, this is a tacit a priori assumption.

It has not seemed to me that New Testament scholarship has adequately assessed the phrase "Son of Man" in what seems to me to be the prime requisite, namely its contextual use within the Gospels. In this essay I confine myself to the phrase in Mark.

Any study of the context of the phrase "Son of Man" in Mark is dependent on an antecedent question, namely, a judgment on the purpose, method, and *Tendenz* of Mark. A consensus exists among scholars, although, of course, there are deviations within that consensus. Mark was composed, perhaps 68–72, at Rome; the church tradition, with which the name Papias is associated, and according to which Mark recorded the recollections of Peter about Jesus, can hardly be taken fully at face value, yet there might well be a reflection in Mark of primitive oral tradition. Indeed, it is possible that there existed an "Ur-Mark," [2] an ancient version, much more faithful to the reminiscences of Peter than the canonical, and later, Mark turns out to be. This canonical Mark contains the repeated motif of a "secrecy" which seems to obscure Jesus' messiahship from even his disciples; a somewhat standard explanation of the motif avers that the belief in Jesus' messiahship arose only after a belief in his resurrection emerged, and that in his lifetime Jesus never made the claim to messiahship.[3]

My own approach to Mark is quite different and would appear to those who are middle-of-the-roaders quite extreme. It has seemed to me that the consensus judgment alluded to views Mark partly through its derivatives, Matthew and Luke, and partly through its clothing Mark with that understandable veneration bestowed on canonical books. I have suggested that Mark was precanonical before it became canonical, and that it ought to be viewed by scholars in its own light, without respect to its derivatives and without respect to that special status which canonicity confers, for that status can obscure the true import of a document.

When Mark is viewed in its own light, so I have written,[4] it is an unmistakable polemic against Palestinian Jewish Christianity. Mark alleges that Pharisees, Sadducees, and "chief priests" were vicious

2 Mark is not simple Gospel; it bristles with problems. The theory of an Ur-Mark, an edition prior to the canonical Mark, seems to me unmistakably correct. I believe, too, that after Ur-Mark was rewritten to yield the present Mark, it underwent some minor interpolations, such as 14:28 and 16:7.

3 This conclusion, among others, is found in Wilhelm Wrede, *Das Messiasgeheimnis in den Evangelien*, Göttingen 1901. The German title of Albert Schweitzer, *The Quest for the Historical Jesus*, is *Von Reimarus zu Wrede*. Both in

enemies of Jesus. The disciples, also Palestinian Jews, neither understand Jesus nor were able to follow his example or fulfill his mandate; at his arrest, they abandoned him. The chief culprit among the disciples was Peter, who crowned his opaqueness by three times denying Jesus. The demons and the Roman centurion alone knew who and what Jesus was. I have concluded that the motif of "secrecy," upon which was built the theory now well ramified that Jesus never claimed to be the Messiah, is in reality quite different; it is, rather, the motif of the opaqueness of the disciples. I have felt it necessary to diverge from the corollaries found in much scholarly writing of the theorem of the "Messianic secret."

When I first conceived and even published the view of Mark as a polemic against Jewish Christianity, I had not explored in any depth the Son of Man passages. On turning to them, I have found, at least to my own satisfaction, that the passages fit congruently with the view of Mark as a polemic.

Lietzmann's valid distinction between Son of Man as a phrase, and its use in the Gospels as a title, implies that before the term became a title, it had some good currency as merely a phrase. We should be prepared to find in Mark echoes of Son of Man in its more pristine usage as merely a phrase, as in Daniel, as well as in its special usage as a title. Our inquiry is this, why does Mark bend toward this particular title, and why does he use it in the way that he does? Is Mark's singular use of the term in this way to be regarded as deliberate selection, and not mere coincidence?

The first passage we advert to is Mark 13:26, a chapter often called the "little apocalypse." The verse occurs in a sequence of quotations from the Tanach, with 13:26 being largely a citation or paraphrase of Daniel 7:13. We need not here enter into the problems of Mark 13; it is sufficient for our purposes to make two comments. First, nothing in the passage makes it out of accord with the general tone of Daniel 7 or of related passages in Enoch; second, the passage only indirectly identifies Jesus as the Son of Man. To restate this last more clearly, the necessary inference from Mark 13 is that Jesus is the Son of Man, but this connection is not specifically stated. The usage of Son of Man in Mark 13:26 is momentarily to be classed with

---

its own terms but especially in its position in Schweitzer's study, Wrede's views have been of great influence in subsequent scholarship.

On whether or not Jesus was understood in his own time, see the excellent study of Enslin, "'Twixt the Dusk and the Daylight," *JBL*, (1956) LXXV, pp. 19–26.

4 See my *The Genius of Paul*, pp. 163–175, and "Genealogies and Myths and the Writing of Gospels," *HUCA*, XXVII (1956), pp. 201–211.

the pristine, rather than with the new usage we will see elsewhere in Mark.

In a second passage, 14:62, the high priest, so it is related, asked Jesus, "Have you no answer to make?" . . . But he was silent and made no answer. Again the high priest asked him. "Are you the Christ, the Son of the Blessed?" Jesus said, "I am, and you will see the Son of Man. . . ." The closing words, indicated by my dots, are a second paraphrase of Daniel 7:13. The response of the high priest to the reply of Jesus is to tear his mantle and to accuse Jesus of blasphemy. In what the alleged blasphemy consists is not told to us. Inferentially, it would seem that Jesus' identification of himself as the Son of Man is either the basis or else the point of departure for the charge. This passage is a second demonstration that Mark was quite well acquainted with Daniel 7:13. The usage here, while it has nuances of the singular, echoes the pristine use.

We turn next to 8:31. The context is the "confession" at Caesarea Philippi. We read that Jesus "began to teach them that the Son of Man must suffer many things, and be rejected by the elders, and the chief priests and the scribes and be killed, and after three days rise again." In Mark Jesus is depicted as predicting his "passion" three times; the present passage is the first of the three. In the first prediction Mark, as he continues the narration, adds that Jesus said these thinks plainly (Greek, *parresia*). The narrative continues that Peter began to "rebuke him. . . . He rebuked Peter, and said, 'Get behind me, Satan! for of God, but you are not on the side of men.' " The passage would seem to be saying that though Jesus spoke clearly, Peter at least objected to the import of what Jesus said. Whether Peter objected because he failed to understand despite Jesus' clarity, or whether Peter understood and consequently objected, is here left uncertain. That Mark implies that Peter misunderstood, or failed to understand is a possibility.

In the continuation, however, in 9:9, a fourth use, Peter, James and John are charged not to tell any one of the "transfiguration" which they have just witnessed "until the Son of Man would have risen from the dead." In the next verse, 9:10, we read that "they kept the matter to themselves, questioning what the rising from the dead meant." Here the explicit statement averts the uncertainty of the previous use alluded to above; the disciples, we are told, do not understand.

A fifth use is in 9:31, in the context of another prediction of his passion. Jesus says, "The Son of Man will be delivered into the hands of men, and they will kill him; and when he is killed, after three days he will rise." Here again Mark appends an unmistakable comment about the disciples: "They did not understand the saying, and they were afraid to ask him."

As a title Son of Man conceals, rather than reveals.

The next uses at which we look, 9:12 and 14:21, add to the puzzle of understanding the phrase. I italicize what to us are the key words in 9:12: *"It is written* of the Son of Man, that he should suffer many things." There is, of course, no Tanach passage about the Son of Man suffering; the introductory formula can be taken to allude to Isaiah 53 or Psalms 22 and 69 (the two Psalms are paraphrased in the passion narrative). It is only by equating Son of Man with other views of Jesus, such as the Suffering Servant, that the introductory formula of a citation or allusion to the Tanach is intelligible. In 14:21 the phrase occurs twice; again I italicize the key words: "The Son of Man goes, *as it is written of him,* but woe to that man by whom the Son of Man is betrayed." We are in these passages, in view of the italicized phrase, no longer in the pristine use of Son of Man as in Daniel, but well into the boundaries of advanced Christian interpretation, well into Mark's singular use of the term.

A ninth use of the term is in 14:41. At Gethsemane, the disciples fall asleep during Jesus' prayers. Three times he prays, and then comes to them: "He came the third time and said to them, Are you still sleeping and taking your rest? It is enough, the hour has come; the Son of Man is betrayed into the hands of sinners." While commentators have found various ways of exculpating the disciples (as did later Gospels), the implication in Mark is quite clear that at the height of Jesus' preparatory agony, the disciples merely slept. When Jesus is promptly betrayed and arrested "they all forsoook him and fled" (14:50). And the chief of the disciples, Peter, three times denies Jesus, even to the point of taking an oath (14:66–72). The progression from opaqueness through denial is completed.

The tenth use is again in a prediction by Jesus of his fate; there the sequel is different from what ensues at the other predictions. It retains the motif of opaqueness, but examines it from a different viewpoint. Jesus makes a prediction of the Son of Man's sufferings (10:33–34). The sons of Zebedee make the request [5] to sit "one at your right, and one at your left, in your glory." Jesus rejects the request, at which the other ten disciples had been indignant. He says, "The Son of Man . . . came not to be served but to serve" (10:45).

5 Matthew 20:28 regards the request as unseemly, and makes the mother of the two the requester.

In this passage opaqueness is still the motif; this time it is not opaqueness as to who or what Jesus is, but opaqueness about authority among the disciples.

Three passages remain. In 2:10, Jesus states that the Son of Man has authority on earth to forgive sins; in 2:28, the Son of Man is "Lord even of the Sabbath"; in 8:38, the Son of Man will be ashamed of those ashamed of him "when he comes in the glory of his father and with the holy angels." It has been proposed, and I have myself written, that in certain passages, such as the last three, Son of Man is equivalent to I. This opinion now seems to me wrong, for I hold now that the personal pronoun would necessarily lack those overtones which are necessary to Mark.

Son of Man is Mark's principal title for Jesus. Though he is addressed as Son of David and as Rabbi (10:47–51) these titles are sporadic. Notably infrequent is the term Christ; it is used seven times; perhaps though, we should number the uses as six, for Mark 1:1, "The beginning of the Gospel of Jesus Christ, the Son of God," may be a title to the document supplied by a hand later than Mark. If 1:1 is a title added later, the first use occurs at 8:29. Jesus is at Caesarea Philippi; he asks his disciples who men said he was; they answer, John the Baptist, Elijah, or one of the prophets. To his question, what do you say, Peter answers, "the Christ." He charges them to tell no one about him [6] (8:27–30).

In 9:41 a reward is promised to "whoever gives you a cup of water to drink because you bear the name of Christ." In 12:35 Jesus, in the Temple, is denying that the Christ is a "son of David." [7] In 13:21 a warning is sounded against believing any one who says, "Look here is the Christ"; the next verse speaks of "false Christs and Messiahs, and still in the same context.

The high priest (14:61) asks Jesus, "Are you the Christ, the Son of the Blessed?" The chief priests mock Jesus, on the cross: "Let the Christ, the King of Israel, come down now from the cross" [8] (15:32).

So infrequently does the word Christ appear in Mark that were

6   I am tempted to regard 8:29–30 as an interpolation from the same hand that inserted 14:28 and 6:7. We must note that Peter's so-called confession entails no sequel and apparently no consequences. It would hence appear that Peter understands what Christ means but completely fails to understand that teaching of Jesus which supposedly ensues immediately on that understanding. In my *The Genius of Paul*, pp. 146 ff. and 166 ff. I set forth some of the other peculiarities in the Gospels and Acts which relate to Peter.

7   In the usual Jewish view, the Messiah was to be of Davidic ancestry. This Jewish view is reflected a number of times in the Gospels: Mark 10:48 and 11:10 and in the genealogies in Matthew 1 and in Luke 3 and elsewhere. A Christian transformation was to

it not for 1:1 we should ordinarily make little association between Jesus and Christ in Mark. Christ is a coincidental title in Mark; the title focused on is Son of Man.

There is a device used frequently in literature wherein author and reader share information not shared by a character within the narration. Indeed the device has become so conventional in the theater as to constitute a cliché. In Noel Coward's play, *Cavalcade,* a honeymoon couple stand on the deck of a ship planning their future. The scene ends with the wife removing her wrap from the nearby life preserver, so that we read the word *Titanic.* The dramatic impact comes out of the audience's knowing something which the characters do not. The movie biographies of Edison and Pasteur have used the same kind of device; the audience knows that Edison's inventions and Pasteur's researches come to succeed, and therefore, they respond, as it were, to the beginning efforts of the two and to the obstacles the two encounter, with increased sympathy. This same device is present in very many of the Greek tragedies. In *Oedipus Rex,* for example, the plot line was thoroughly familiar to the audience; the drama consisted in their sharing in the emotional vicissitudes of the characters who do not know what the audience does know; and the foreknowledge of the outcome by the audience not only does not decrease the interest but through heightened empathy increases it.

All "disguise" plays and stories use this same device, whether it is Shakespeare, as in *Twelfth Night,* or whether it is a farce such as *Charley's Aunt.* Perhaps preeminently in the drama is Rostand's use in *Cyrano de Bergerac,* wherein Cyrano, unseen to Roxane but visible to the audience, provides Christian with the words with which to woo Roxane, and later, and most pathetically, Roxane relates to Cyrano the great ardor which she ascribes to Christian.

Preeminently among the Gospels, John employs the device unsparingly, even to the point of making sure that it is not missed. In John 2:19 Jesus says, "Destroy this temple and in three days I will raise it up"; 2:21 tells us that "he spoke of the temple of his body."

regard the Christ as "preexistent," and hence antedating even Abraham ("Before Abraham was, I am," John 8:58; but see John 7:40–43). Modern western canons of logic would find intolerable certain inconsistencies which seem not to have bothered the ancients, see my "The Haggada within Scripture," *JBL* (1961), pp. 120–121.

8 In Mark the supposed Jewish objection to Jesus is his claim to be the Christ, while the Roman objection is to his being "King of the Jews" (Mark 15:2). The mocking of Jesus on the cross in 15:32 brings the two titles together. Dangerous as it is to conclude too much from laconic passages, it would seem that Mark distinguishes in his mind between the religious and the political.

Nicodemus, in 3:4 asks how a man can enter his mother's womb for rebirth; 3:5 ff. explains that the "rebirth" is of "water and of the spirit." In 4:11-15, the Samaritan woman has "living water" explained to her; in 4:34 Jesus says that his food is to do the will of him who sent him. In these and in innumerable other passages, John's procedure is to have Jesus encounter someone who appears to misunderstand something which the reader clearly understands; the character's misunderstanding becomes the point of departure for Jesus to clarify to the character what is already perfectly clear to the reader. Such evocation of the knowledge, superior on the part of the reader to that of the character, increases the empathy in the Gospel.

Mark too employs the device. Indeed, Mark's aim is not to inform his readers of what they do not know, but rather to employ the knowledge that they already have to heighten the emotional impact. They know that Jesus was crucified; they believe that he was resurrected. They hold him to be more than a man, the Son of God. They know that Jews did not share in this belief. They already believe that the crucifixion was neither a surprise nor a defeat, for they believe that the divine Jesus knew in advance what was to happen to him; that is, Jesus is depicted as knowing in advance of the events what the readers of Mark knew after the events from Christian preaching on Jesus. Mark hence portrays Jesus as going through a preordained schedule of events; accordingly, Jesus three times predicts his crucifixion. He informs his disciples that one of them will betray him; he informs them that they will fall away; he tells Peter that Peter will three times deny him. At Gethsemane Jesus says "The hour has come."

The thesis in Mark's Gospel, the "plot" of which was known to the reader, is that Jesus was abused by Jewish opponents, misunderstood, betrayed, denied, and abandoned by his disciples, but recognized only by the demons and the Roman centurion (and the blind beggar Bartimaeus who "sees" who Jesus is). Mark had need of a title which could simultaneously mystify his characters and still be fully clear to his readers. Had Mark focused on a title such as Christ or King, he could not have portrayed his characters as mystified. But Son of Man served admirably for this purpose in that the characters in the Gospel fail to comprehend the title, but Mark's readers understand it immediately. A brief résumé of Mark's Gospel from this special viewpoint will support the contention.

Mark's first use of the phrase, 2:10, occurs after the exorcism of the demon in the synagogue at Capernaum, the healing of Simon's mother-in-law, and the cleansing of the leper. At Capernaum again Jesus heals a paralytic, through forgiving his sins. The words, especially in context, "the Son of Man has authority on earth to forgive sins," alert the reader both to Jesus' description of himself and also to the title he uses himself.

This latter is confirmed and strengthened in the controversy over the Sabbath (2:23–28), with the conclusion, "The Son of Man is Lord even of the Sabbath." Now the reader knows clearly that Son of Man is Jesus' way of referring to himself and that the title connotes his divine role.

It is men who do not understand Jesus' role; demons, though, do. In 3:11 the unclean spirits fall down and address Jesus as "Son of God"; his friends, however, believe him insane, while the scribes say he is possessed by Beelzebub (3:21–22). In Chapter 4 Jesus tell his disciples the parable of the sower; the reader understands the parable, but the disciples do not, so Jesus has to explain it (4:10–20, 33–34). He quiets the wind; his disciples still do not know who or what he is, so (4.41) they say to one another, "Who is this that even wind and sea obey him?" Promptly, in what ensues, the Gerasene demoniac (5:1–20) addresses him as "Jesus, Son of the Most High God." Jesus performs more healings (5:21–43); when he teaches in the synagogue, the Jews are astonished at him, thinking him to be only "the carpenter, the son of Mary" (6:1-6). His fame reaches even King Herod; the character of Jesus (so clear to the demons and to the reader) is unclear to Herod, for Jesus is variously identified (6:14–16) as the resurrected John the Baptist, as Elijah, or a prophet.

Jesus feeds five thousand with five loaves and two fish (6:30–44); he and his disciples embark on a boat for Bethsaida (6:45–52). Jesus walks on the water. The disciples "were utterly astounded, for they did not understand about the loaves. . . ." (6:49–51) He feeds four thousand people with seven loaves and a few small fish (8:1–10). He declines to give a sign to the Pharisees (8:11–13). In a boat with his disciples, he warns against the "leaven of the Pharisees, and of the leaven of Herod." The disciples, not understanding, say to one another thay they have no bread; Jesus thereupon reminds them of the two miraculous feedings. To the reader it is clear that Jesus is commending himself as "spiritual" bread (see John 6:35). He says to his disciples (8:17), "Do you not understand?" The question is unmistakably intended as a sharp rebuke.

At Caesarea Philippi, Jesus asks his disciples who men say he is; they answer, John the Baptist, Elijah, or one of the prophets. He asks, "But who do you say I am." Peter answers, "You are the Christ." Jesus charges them to tell no one about him (8:27–29). One might suppose that now all is clear; but it is not. Jesus "began to teach them that the Son of Man must suffer many things. . . . And he said this plainly." Peter rebukes him, and he rebukes Peter (8:31–33). Jesus then proclaims what the responsibility of a disciple is to be—a responsibility which these disciples are destined not to meet. This proclamation is made to "the multitude . . . with his disciples." He says, "Whoever is ashamed of me and of my words . . . of him also shall the Son of Man be ashamed. . . ." Clearly the passage (8:34–9:1) is an admonition against infidelity, made to those whom Mark regards as unfaithful, and whom he will presently plainly portray as unfaithful.

Next comes the transfiguration, wherein Jesus is identified by a voice from a cloud as "My beloved Son"; he charges Peter, James, and John to tell no one about the transfiguration until after the Son of Man will have risen from the dead. Even so, they do not understand what rising from the dead means (9:2–10). They inquire about Elijah as the forerunner. Jesus replies that Elijah has already come, and (with the execution of John the Baptist in Mark's mind) Jesus says, that "they did to him whatever they pleased. So to The Son of Man will suffer many things, and be treated with contempt." In both cases, we are told, the incidents conform to what "is written" (9:9–13). Next, he exorcizes a demon from a boy, this after the disciples were unable to do so (14–29). Passing through Galilee, he teaches his disciples a third time that "The Son of Man will be delivered into the hands of men, and they will kill him; and when he is killed, after three days he will arise." The disciples do not understand the saying (though the reader does), and they are afraid to ask (30–32). The disciples discuss who among them is the greatest; Jesus disparages their talk and takes a child in his arms, this to emphasize his disparagement of their wish for greatness (33–37). The disciples complain to him of a man not among them who casts out demons in his name. Jesus says, "Do not forbid him . . ." (9:38–50).

The disciples want to obstruct children from coming to Jesus; he replies, ". . . to such belongs the kingdom of God" (10:13-16). A man, told to dispose of his wealth and thus to follow Jesus, was unwilling. "Peter began to say, We have left everything and followed you." Jesus gives the double answer, that the faithful will be rewarded—and Mark does not regard the disciples as faithful—and that "many that are first [i.e., the disciples] will be last; and the last [subsequent Gentile followers] will be first" (10:17-31).

On the road to Jerusalem, Jesus again tells them that "The Son of Man will be delivered to the chief priests . . . and after three days will rise." The passage tells that, before these words, "they were amazed; . . . and afraid." The response to Jesus' words is the request of the sons of Zebedee for preferred places. In his reply, Jesus says, "Whoever would be first among you, must be your slave to all . . . For the Son of Man also came not to be served but to serve" (10:35-45).

At the Temple, Jesus is questioned about his authority (11:27-33). He speaks a parable—this time a clear one, as though Mark has forgotten that he had ascribed to parables the function of concealing. The parable about the vineyard owner is not really a parable, that is, it is not a didactic anecdote, but a symbolic story; it alleges that Jews (the tenants) had killed the prophets (the vineyard owner's servants) and his son (Jesus). God (the vineyard owner) would come and destroy the tenants and give the vineyard to others (the Gentiles; 12:-1-12). Jesus, questioned about taxes, replies that to Caesar must be rendered what is Caesar's, and to God what is God's (13-17). He debates resurrection with Sadducees (18-27). A scribe praises him for his answer on the commandments and he praises the scribe. Thereafter "none dared ask him any question" (28-34). He denies that he is descended from David (for he is a divine preexistent being; 35-37); he denounces hypocrisy, extolling a poor widow for her mite (38-44).

In the "little apocalypse," he predicts the destruction of the temple (readers knew that it had been destroyed in 70). The disciples ask when this will be, and what the sign will be (Mark 8:12 had stated that "no sign [shall] be given to this generation." Matthew 16:1-14 and 12:38-39 and Luke 11:29 amend the view; Jesus' three days in the tomb, equated with Jonah's three days in the whale, is a sign which is to be given). Jesus tells them only to "watch."

Next, we are told that it is two days before Passover. In Bethany a woman pours nard over Jesus' head. He says, "She has anointed me beforehand for burial" (14:1-9). Judas, who, as the reader knows, is to betray Jesus, goes to the high priest. In an upper room, while eating with disciples, Jesus says that one of them will betray him; "the Son of Man goes as it is written of him, but woe to that man by whom the Son of Man is betrayed." (Mark does not relate what happens to Judas; Matthew 27:5 tells that Judas hanged himself; Acts 1:18 tells that Judas, "falling headlong, he burst open in the middle, and all his bowels gushed out."

At the Mount of Olives Jesus predicts that Peter will deny him three times before cockcrow (14:26-31). At Gethsemane, Peter, James, and John fall asleep. All, however, is working out as foreordained: "The hour has come; the Son of Man is betrayed into the hands of sinners (32–41). Judas betrays Jesus with a kiss: Jesus says, ". . . Let the scriptures be fulfilled" (43–52). Jesus is brought before the high priest; Peter is at a distance, "with the guards, and himself by the fire." The high priest asks, "Are you the Christ, the Son of the Blessed?" Jesus says, "I am; and you will see the Son of Man sitting at the right hand of Power. . . ." They condemn him as deserving death; the guards rain blows on him. A maid says to Peter, "You were with the Nazarene, Jesus." He denies it; "I neither know nor understand what you mean." She tells the bystanders "This man is one of them." Peter denies it. The bystanders say, "Certainly, you are one of them." Peter swears, "I do not know this man of whom you speak." Immediately the cock crows (14:53–72).

Jesus is led before Pilate, who asks, "Are you the King of the Jews?" Mark scarcely prepares us for this question, for the only thing that has come before that has in any way associated Jesus with kingship is in the shouts of the crowd at Jesus' entry into Jerusalem. "Blessed be the kingdom of our father David that is coming" (11:10). The reply of Jesus, "You have said so," has yielded an abundance of interpretations; some assert that Jesus is acquiescing, and some that he is ignoring the question.[9] From the sequel (The chief priests accused him of many things and Pilate again asked him, "Have you No answer to make? See how many charges they bring against you?"), I am led to suppose that Mark's intent here is to suggest that Jesus was silent, a motif borrowed from Isaiah 53:7. Pilate's wish to free "the King of the Jews" is frustrated by the shouts of the crowd, "Crucify him." Jesus is first mocked and then crucified. The inscription of the charge is "King of the Jews."

When Jesus has died, the Roman centurion says, "Truly this man was the Son of God." The Gentile has seen what the Jewish disciples and the Jewish opponents were unable to see.

His death was witnessed, Mark tells us, by three Galilean women; (no Galilean men were present; they had fled). It was Joseph of Arimathea, not a disciple, who buried Jesus. The two Marys saw where Jesus was laid; Salome, the third woman, joins the two; the three buy spices and go to the tomb, but it is empty.

Had Mark chosen to put into the mouth of Jesus some phrase other than Son of Man, he would have had an inordinate difficulty in carrying through his theme that Jesus was misunderstood by his disciples and by other Jews. Any other term—Christ, or King—would have

---

9 Matthew 27:11–14 seems to suppose that Jesus is denying it as if it were a false allegation; John 18:33–37 recounts the incident with an emphasis on "my kingship is not of this world."

been too clear to permit misunderstanding, and unless Mark could convincingly portray opaqueness, misunderstanding, and infidelity, his thesis was gone. Son of Man served him in that it could be clear to his readers, but not understood by his characters.

Son of Man as a title is a literary device of Mark. While conceivably the Jesus of history in his lifetime may have been associated or identified either in his own mind or in that of his disciples with the Son of Man in Daniel, we are in the realm of conjecture. What we can be sure of is that Mark's use of the phrase as a title is a literary device, and not primarily an echo of the Jesus of history. In Mark Son of Man has only the dimmest echoes of the antecedent Jewish use. Mark is far from being a document faithful to the Jewish scene; it is a tendentious, highly theological document, coming from a Gentile Christian environment.

The phrase in Matthew, Luke, and John is a subject for another essay.

The Sprouting of the Horn of the Son of David,

A NEW SOURCE FROM THE BEGINNINGS OF THE DOENME SECT IN SALONICA

GERSHOM SCHOLEM

*

THE FOLLOWERS OF SABBATAI ZEVI in Salonica who organized themselves into a secret sect within Islam have aroused the interest of scholars in recent years. Our sources of information were extremely scarce and obscure until recently, when they were considerably expanded owing to the discovery of various manuscripts from the circles of the "Doenme" (as they were called by the Turks), which are now in Israel. As a result, mere opinions and conjectures, many of them very tenuous, have been replaced by serious study. In a lecture delivered at the Tenth International Congress for the History of Religion (1960) I summarized the state of our information at the present, as reflected in the current stage of study.[1]

Sorely lacking, however, even in these important discoveries, were documents from the time of the inception of this sect, so shrouded in obscurity. We knew that there existed a group of some two hundred families that had apostatized during the lifetime of Sabbatai Zevi[2] and whose ranks were later augmented by several hundred families in the mass apostasy of 1683. But with all the wealth of sources uncovered concerning the Sabbatian groups that remained within Judaism, we were exceptionally poor in authoritative information from the circles of the first apostates, especially in writings and documents composed in their midst. We knew that the life of the sect

---

1   *Die krypto-jüdische Sekte der Doenme (Sabbatianer) in der Türkei,* published in *Numen, International Review for the History of Religions,* Vol. VII (Amsterdam, 1960), pp. 93–122.

2   See my Hebrew work, *Sabbatai Zevi and the Sabbatian Movement in His Lifetime,* Tel Aviv, 1957, p. 711.

3   Abraham Danon, *Etudes Sabbatiennes,* Paris 1910, pp. 6–13. The first [Hebrew] edition of his article appeared in the *Sefer ha-Shanah,* edited by N. Sokolov, Vol. I, 1901, pp. 160–171. Danon's comments

rested on eighteen commandments or "ordinances" (Hebrew: *sedarim*; Spanish: *encommendanças*), which, according to the tradition, were fixed by Sabbatai Zevi himself, that is, prior to 1676. The text of these commandments was formerly known to us only in Spanish, in different versions whose variations reflect the tendency toward mitigation of the anti-Moslem tenor which is still obtrusive in the first formulation. It was clear that the Spanish text was merely a translation from Hebrew, made in successive generations, when the knowledge of the Hebrew language progressively waned among the masses of the Doenme in Salonica. Such Spanish versions were published and explained by Abraham Danon [3] and Abraham Galanté,[4] who received copies from the "Believers" (*Ma'aminim*), as the sectarians called themselves.

Recently it was my good fortune to find, among the important new collection of Sabbatian manuscripts from the bequest of Rabbi Saul Amarillo that were given to the Ben-Zvi Institute of the Hebrew University,[5] a very significant document, which is translated in full below. In a manuscript of exceptional importance, assembled and largely copied from manuscripts that came into his possession, the Salonica scholar Rabbi Abraham Miranda gathered whatever he encountered bearing on the sects of the "Believers." The transcriptions in this valuable volume were apparently made in approximately 1760. This scholar's relations with Sabbatian circles, both Jewish and apostate, were obviously very close indeed, but I shall not treat this problem here. In any case, it is a fact that many things which the apostates later concealed from every outsider—to the point where not a single one of their writings was available to scholars for many generations —were still openly revealed to Abraham Miranda (died ca. 1802). Along with other compositions of Nathan the Prophet of Gaza (called by the Sabbatians, MaHaRaN), there are preserved here two tracts whose language and content indicate that they were not written by Nathan, but were ascribed to him by the author, apparently one of the leaders of the apostates. Nathan died on January 11, 1680, before the mass apostasy in Salonica clearly alluded to in one of these texts, which will be discussed at length elsewhere. The other one (Ms. Amarillo, Ben-Zvi Institute Ms. 2262, pp. 161–165), is written in the

are valuable although not all of them are accurate.

4   Abraham Galanté, *Nouveaux Documents sur Sabbetaï Sevi*, (Istanbul 1935), pp. 40–46.

5   See the Hebrew essay of Abraham Amarillo, "Sabbatian Documents from the Archives of Rabbi Saul Amarillo," *Sefunot*, Book V (1961), p. 237, for a description of the manuscript from which the text is taken. My sincere thanks are due to Mr. Amarillo for his kindness in permitting me to publish the document.

same characteristic style and serves as a sort of preface to the text of the Eighteen Commandments, which appear here in the original Hebrew. It may be argued that the commandments were in fact drawn up during the lifetime of Sabbatai Zevi and served as the basis for the organization of the first nucleus of apostates, since all groups of the Doenme accepted them as his words, whether they were actually uttered by him or merely attributed to him. Nothing in them contradicts this assumption. On the contrary, it is clear from the text under discussion that there is a difference between the commandments themselves, with their simple and lucid formulation, and the imaginary tale which precedes them and which serves quite artificially as a kind of introduction and explanation of their promulgation. This imaginary atmosphere recurs in the other text as well, which is written in the very same style, and which also cites the Eighteen Ordinances governing the comportment of the Believers after their apostasy, but not in their entirety.

It seems, nevertheless, that this apocryphal literature, which fulfilled an important function for the first apostates, underwent editing and suffered additions and subtractions. The first treatise, judging from its subject matter, was composed some time after the death of Jacob Querido (ca. 1690), Sabbatai Zevi's brother-in-law, by one of Querido's opponents among the scholars of the sect, and it contains no obvious contradictions to historical chronology. Not so with the treatise under discussion. It ascribes to Nathan a metaphysical biography of Sabbatai Zevi which, while it is similar in some respects to the first text—especially in its characteristic terminology—still adds impossible dates, such as Nathan's presence in Gaza when the soul of Sabbatai Zevi was conceived in 1626, long before Nathan was born! All this was done without consideration for historical facts and indeed with intent to obscure them. The author knew a number of details, and it is reasonable to assume that he knew Nathan quite well and was acquainted with facts and events, but all this serves him merely as a background for a totally imaginary concoction.

The name of our treatise is "The Sprouting of the Horn of the Son of David." Its purpose is to explain why the Redemption had not yet come even though the Messiah had already revealed himself in the world. The answer is: the Princes of the Nations obstructed it. The Messiah must gain the support of the Angel-Prince of Ishmael in order to prevail in his war against the forces of darkness, especially against the Angel-Prince of Edom (Samael). To obtain his assistance

6 On this incident, see *Sabbatai Zevi*, p. 116. The tale in the new manu-   script explains the legendary recast of the event, undoubtedly out of

in this war (the entire issue of the Redemption is described here emphatically as a "war"), he is constrained to consent to enter his realm for a period of time together with his "Warriors," that is, those "Believers" who submitted to the decree of apostasy.

The special importance of the tale under discussion is that we can see from it how the historical life of Sabbatai Zevi becomes progressively obscured, starting immediately after his death: mystic legend replaces the events. Samael, the Angel-Prince of Edom, is the principal enemy; he persecutes Sabbatai Zevi and is the cause of all his tribulations. Episodes in his life, such as the event in his youth in Izmir when he nearly drowned, have become a great struggle with the power of Samael.[6] What in fact happened before Sabbatai Zevi went to Jerusalem is here placed after his return to Izmir. And hence developed, in the account of the new legendary tale, the covenant between the Angel-Prince of Ishmael and the Redeemer. The conclusion of this covenant is the central feature of the story. In the text before us a limit is specifically set for the period of validity of the covenant, viz. the time that must pass from the apostasy until the second and final "revelation" of the Redemption: 120 years. This number is an innovation that attests to the hope of the sect's members to return to their original stock and their true messianic status. In the first treatise mentioned above, which purports to have been discovered by Nathan after the "Concealment of the Master" and in fact was written some 15–20 years after the death ("concealment") of Sabbatai Zevi, a different period is set for the length of the "war": 12 *Shmittah* periods, or 84 years. Perhaps these 12 *Shmittah* periods, which ended in 1751 (84 years after the apostasy of Sabbatai Zevi), were replaced through an exegesis on the 120 years in later redactions of the treatises, toward the middle of the eighteenth century, when it was already clear that the first specified period would not suffice. Or perhaps we must assume that from the very beginning of the sect's organization, different figures for the periods of time were in currency side by side. This disparity is especially surprising since, as I have noted, both texts have the same style.

Sabbatai Zevi acceded to the suggestion of the Angel-Prince of Ishmael, after having refused at the outset, because he realized (according to the author of the treatise) that he could not vanquish him, "for the iniquity of his covetousness is not yet complete," and he would not be able to rescue the "fragments of the tablets" from him "except by entering into a firm covenant with him until that time." Nathan (that is, the imaginary Nathan) transcribes the epistle (also

the stories on Sabbatai Zevi current in the circles of his disciples.

imaginary) which Sabbatai Zevi wrote him on the day of his entrance
into the covenant, that is, his apostasy. The latter enjoined him to
undertake a mission of propaganda, to explain the secret of the apostasy to the "camp" of the "Believers," so that they might understand
this act and would "not gape with their mouths to speak against their
King." From the context it is clear that the word "camp" here refers
specifically to the corpus of apostates, whose position is particularly
lofty: "they are elect ones [bne 'aliyah] into whose realm no other man
can enter." These ideas are perfectly consonant with the words of
Rabbi Israel Ḥazzan, Nathan's *amanuensis*, in his Sabbatian commentary on the Psalms, where he is prodigious in his praise of the
apostates, "Wearers of the Turban," although he himself was not one
of them.[7] The anonymous author, writing in Nathan's spirit as well
as his name, faithfully reflects the ideas that were current among the
prophet's disciples during those years.

   "Nathan the Prophet" further transcribes another epistle which
he claims to have received from Sabbatai Zevi after having sought
guidance regarding his actions and having asked him whether he too
was to apostatize ("and enter with them—that is, with the members
of the elect group—into the war"). The text concludes with the tran-
scription of Sabbatai Zevi's answer, in which he explains why Nathan
is not required to apostatize—a question often discussed in Nathan's
circle—but on the contrary, he and his associates must stand apart
and continue diligently in their task, that of expounding the true
faith in their writings. At the same time, he is required here to call
public assemblies and explain the matters to them, and further—and
this comes as a kind of unexpected addition discordant with what
immediately precedes—to communicate to them the "Eighteen Dicta"
which they (here the reference, in an abrupt transition, is to the sect
of apostates and not to Nathan and his associates) were to keep even
in their new status. This conclusion has a completely imaginary character. For reasons which are well known to us, the historical Nathan
did not dare to call "public assemblies" for the purpose of preaching
to the apostates, and we have no reason to assume that he in fact did
so in his last years. If the Eighteen Commandments had already been
given to the first apostates, prior to 1683—which is possible but not
certain—then they were intentionally inserted extrinsically into the
pseudepigraphic epistle, to provide an added explanation for their

7 See my book, pp. 728–734, and my   salem 1952, pp. 157–211.
   essay on Hazzan's book in 'Alei   8 *Be'iqvot Mashiah*, Jerusalem, 1943,
   'Ayin (Hebrew), *Shlomoh Zalman*   pp. 69–87.
   Schocken Jubilee Volume, Jeru-   9 See *Kirjath Sepher*, vol. XXI

origin. This artificial addition would explain the lack of logic in the sentences which precede the list of the commandments. In any case, we now know the framework in which the commandments were preserved and transmitted in certain groups of the Doenme.

We also learn from this document the first and original formulation of these commandments. It is clear that the order here is to be preferred to that in the (Spanish) list which came into the possession of Danon, in which the order was already deranged, as I shall point out in the notes. The copyist had before him several manuscripts of the commandments and he noted some of the various readings.

The author of "The Sprouting of the Horn of the Son of David" was also familiar with other apocrypha from the literature of the Sabbatians. Pseudo-Nathan mentions his commentaries on the Book Raziel, or in the Book of Raziel, by which he apparently refers to a real or apocryphal composition which in these circles was attributed to Nathan and which is quoted in the above-mentioned treatise, called "What Happened During the Concealment of the Master, from a Manuscript of the MaHaRaN himself." *Zikhron ha-'Edut* ("The Record of the Testimony"), mentioned in the letter attributed to Sabbatai Zevi, was explained by the copyist Abraham Miranda as an allusion to the five chapters of *Sahadutha di-Mehemanutha* ("The Attestation of Faith") which were written in 1668. It is unlikely that he was correct; another explanation is more reasonable (see note 67). It is obvious, however, on the basis of another piece in the same manuscript, that these chapters and the ideas expressed in them were known to the author. The Hebrew text of the *Sahadutha di-Mehemanutha* was published in my book, *In the Footsteps of the Messiah*.[8] There I weighed the possibility that it may have been written by Nathan himself, a consideration that was correctly criticized by Isaiah Tishby,[9] and in my extensive study on Sabbatai Zevi [10] I left the question of the author open. But the manuscript under discussion preserves (in the margin of p. 74) an important note on the origin of the *Sahadutha* itself which is copied there. Rabbi Abraham Miranda writes: "Rabbi Abraham Ha-Yakhini wrote in his book *Ne'eman Shmuel* [11] that they [that is, the chapters of the *Sahadutha*] are [written] by the saintly *Solomon Laniado* of blessed memory." The presumption is that Ha-Yakhini, who was familiar with all the arcana of the "Believers," did not write this without good reason, although for the time being we are

(1944), p. 17.

10 Cf. my book, pp. 714–719.

11 In Sabatian circles this work was still known in the eighteenth century and was quoted in the sermons of Judah Levi Toba, one of the Doenme scholars of the late eighteenth century.

unable to state the circumstances under which this treatise was written. Laniado was one of the rabbis of Aleppo, and although he was well known as a Sabbatian,[12] we have no other information to the effect that he wrote visionary compositions in the years after the apostasy, or that in 1668 he visited Sabbatai Zevi in Adrianople.[13]

It is remarkable that in the writings of Cardozo no mention is made of these early treatises from the circles of the apostates. He does refer, in a letter from 1702, to "compositions which contain accounts of the articles of faith of the apostates in Salonica," which came into his possession about the year 1696 in Adrianople.[14] But the context there shows that the reference is to kabbalistic writings of Jacob Qerido and his disciples, while the texts in Ms. Amarillo can be shown to have originated in a group of the Doenme that was in opposition of Qerido.

[*Translation of the Hebrew document MS Ben-Zvi Institute 2262, p. 161 ff.*]

With the help of the Lord,
this was copied letter for letter from the manuscript
of MaHaRaN the Prophet himself.

The Sprouting of the Horn of the Son of David [15]

In the year 5386 [1626], on the second day of Rosh Ha-Shanah,[16] the horn of the Son of David was remembered [the Messiah was conceived], namely our Master our King the Messiah of the God of Jacob, his exalted majesty [17] Sabbatai Zevi.[18] I, his servant and his house,[19] was in Gaza, of the cities of Israel, and there came to me the *maggid*, namely Elijah (of blessed memory), joyful, and he said to me, "Have you not known of the sprouting of the horn of the Son of David in this year? [20] Know that on the Day of Judgment

---

12 Cf. my book, pp. 108–112, 179–181, 638.
13 Until now I have assumed that this text was composed in the circle surrounding Sabbatai Zevi in the wake of a new Messianic inspiration which began to stir in him. If we are to rely on the testimony of Abraham Ha-Yakhini, the possibility must be considered that they are all visionary compositions written about Sabbatai Zevi at a distance, in Aleppo, without any personal contact with him. Of a heavenly *maggid* who revealed himself to Rabbi Solomon Laniado

as early as 1665 we now have a testimony from that same year; see below, n. 32.
14 Cf. *Sefunot*, Book III–IV, p. 224.
15 The title of the document is צמיחת קרן בן דוד, which refers to the advent of the Messiah of the seed of David; cf. Jeremiah 33:15 and Ezekiel 29:21.
16 This is an imaginary date; it would be more than ten months until the birth of Sabbatai Zevi on the 9th of Av, 5386.
17 Abbr. יר"ה, "may his majesty be exalted."
18 Abbr. ש"צ, as often in this docu-

fault was found with the Seventy Princes,[21] because they put to death ten men who were free of guilt.[22] And the Lord was zealous for his people, and he commanded to bring before him the Book of Records.[23] And there was found written the righteous deed of Mordecai the Saint, that he gave bread and water, in a year of drought, to the poor of the land, even to selling the furniture of his home to buy wheat for the poor.[24] Then the Lord inquired of those standing before him [participating] in judgment what had been done to Mordecai for this. And they said, "Nothing has been done for him." Then the Blessed One summoned Michael, the Angel-Prince of Israel, and said to him, "Take this pearl [25] and deliver it into the hand of Mordecai the Saint of the stock of the Son of David, and be careful with it until it issues into the air of the world, and when it issues into the air of the world I will make known to you what you shall do." And the Seventy Princes went out in despair.[26] And I came to tell you, that you may be prepared by the time it be revealed to you, to declare to you what you shall do in the End of Days. For I have heard from behind the [celestial] veil that you shall be over his house, and according to your word all his people shall be ruled [27] in the End of Days. For you are the chief prince of the tribe of Ephraim; [28] be strong and of good courage!"

Then I rejoiced with a great joy, and guarded all the words of the *maggid* in my heart. And it came to pass when the time was come about that the *maggid* came to me at the yeshiva, and he made the announcement to me of the birth of our Master. Then he showed me his form, lustrous and pure, without any blemish. And he showed me his dwelling place, and the guardians who were rearing him in the palaces of the king, and seventeen princes [*Nesi'im*] attending on him to offer him everything he desired. At that moment I prostrated myself and made obeisance to the Lord, who had graciously allowed me to

---

ment and in Sabbatian literature.

19 עבדו וביתו; perhaps it should read, "his servant and *the faithful one* of his house."

20 As if some prior revelation had been made to Nathan regarding the year 5386 as the year of the Redemption.

21 That is, the Seventy Angel-Princes of the Nations, *savei ha-'ummoth*.

22 The reference is clearly to the Ten Martyrs (עשרה הרוגי המלכות). The transition to the next subject, the election of Mordecai Zevi to be the father of the Redeemer, is not sufficiently clear.

23 The scene is based on Esther 6:1 ff., probably owing to the name of Sabbatai Zevi's father.

24 We have no record of such an incident in any of the other sources on Sabbatai Zevi known to me.

25 The soul of Sabbatai Zevi.

26 Because they had been unable to prevent his earthly birth.

27 Cf. Genesis 41:40.

28 This is a novel item of information. When the "Twelve Tribes" were chosen in Gaza, or again later in Adrianople, was Rabbi Nathan then appointed the Head of Tribe of Ephraim?

contemplate the visage of his exalted majesty, the Messiah of the God of Jacob. And the man grew in comeliness and wisdom in a manner unlike this world, and wheresoever he turned he prospered. And it came to pass after a time that he rose up from the land of sorrows, which is Izmir,[29] to come to the cities of Israel, for there were gathered the Princes of the hosts of Israel to anoint him king over Israel. And he came to the Holy City, Jerusalem (may it be rebuilt and restored), at the end of three days,[30] and he turned to the great yeshiva, where the head of the yeshiva was Rabbi Moses Galante (preserve him, his Rock and Redeemer).[31] And there he taught mysteries of the Torah to all who drew near to him, and he was wiser than any man, and the people turned one to the other in astonishment [over him]. The head of the yeshiva, together with but a few of the most wise, discerned who he was,[32] but he was as one that held his peace.[33]

And it came to pass on a certain day [34] that all the Princes of the people of the children of Israel assembled themselves in the Academy of King Solomon (of blessed memory) which is in the Women's Court of the Temple. And they brought our Master the King and anointed him with the horn of oil that was hidden in the floor of the Court of the Priests, and they sounded the shofar and proclaimed, "May David our Master live for ever." Now when the Seventy Princes heard that they had anointed our Master, they were sore afraid, and they all assembled together to wage war before [against] our Master. And the matter was told to our Master, and he assembled all the camp of God and went forth to engage them; and they fled, hiding themselves in the four corners of the earth. And our Master rose up to make a circuit around all the land of Havilah [35] to release the captives beyond the mountains that are under the dominion of the Princes of Fear, and

29 Also in the first treatise, mentioned above, Izmir is called ארץ תלאובות. The allusion is to the persecutions by the scholars of the city, which caused his departure for "the cities of Israel" and the land of Israel.

30 A new legend about his traveling miraculously from Izmir to Jerusalem in three days.

31 Abbr. רב מ״ג בר״ו According to this source, Sabbatai Zevi was a member of his yeshiva; cf. my book, p. 200.

32 They understood that he was the Messiah. Rabbi Moses Galante in fact supported Sabbatai Zevi at the outset, but after the apostasy his participation in the movement was intentionally obscured. When I wrote my book, I had not yet seen

a document from the prewar library of the Vienna Jewish community (cf. A. Z. Schwarz, "Die Hebraeischen Handschriften in Oesterreich," 1931, nr. 1418), which is a letter from Aleppo written during the very time of these events, addressed to "a certain eminent personage of Constantinople." It contains the following statement: "Let it be known to you that in this city [Aleppo] we have twenty prophets and four prophetesses. Some of them are well known, two of whom are the eminent Rabbis Moses Galante, who went as an emissary from the land of Israel (may it be rebuilt) but a short while ago, and Isaiah Ha-Kohen, whose reputation and saint-

he passed on and came to Gaza, into the synagogue. And I came to the synagogue while it was still day, and saw him seated opposite the ark. I went near to him and asked him his name and the name of his city, and he replied, "Do you not know my name? And I, before I was formed in the belly I knew you, and before I came forth out of the womb I sanctified you, I have appointed you a prophet to this holy people,[36] and yet you ask my name?" At that moment I bowed down and said, "May our Master the Faithful Shepherd [37] live forever." And after the prayer service we came to the house, and the house was too small to contain the camp of our Master that followed at his feet,[38] going to the Land of Havilah to war [p. 162]. On the night after the Sabbath he summoned me to the roof and said to me, "Stand up on your feet and hear the words of the living God." And I heard [him] speak to me: [39] "Son of Man, go and say to this people, 'Remove the evil of your deeds from before my eyes and return to the Lord with all your heart, and profane not my name among the nations, and obstruct me not among the mountains and valleys, among the Princes of the Peoples who pursue me in the mountains and hills. I have solemnly sworn that anyone who disobeys my command, thereby profaning me, horror will overwhelm him, and he shall not behold the majesty of the Lord.' [40] As for you, go to the land of Pathros—which is Salonica [41]—and to the land of Ashkenaz, and make known to them the way in which they shall walk and the deed which they shall do, until the time of my coming to you in Custalin [42] which is Izmir." And the King went on his way, and wheresoever he turned he prospered. And he made a circuit around all the land of Arabia and all the land of the Hittites [43] and he brought all their princes, led in procession [44] under the dominion of the Angel-Prince of Ishmael,[45] to

liness we have always heard of . . . also Rabbi Solomon Laniado, of whom it has been said that he is King Solomon, and had a revelation of the *maggid* and of Elijah (of blessed memory); and also the other men of the place have had revelations of Elijah, whether in the *midrash* [synagogue] or elsewhere." What I wrote about Moses Galante in my book should now be revised in accordance with this source.

33 The syntax and context indicate fairly clearly that the reference is to Sabbatai Zevi, who had not yet revealed himself, and not to Moses Galante.

34 Here again the document relates legends and visions concerning events in the world of the angels.

35 An allusion to his descent to Egypt and his encounter with Nathan in Gaza on his way back, all in mystic-legendary tones.

36 Cf. Jeremiah 1:5.

37 *Ra'ya mehemna.*

38 The angels that escorted him, going out to war against the *kelipoth.*

39 Sabbatai Zevi charges him to preach repentance to the House of Israel; cf. Ezekiel 2:1–2.

40 Cf. Psalms 55:6 and Isaiah 26:10.

41 Salonica is so called in the first treatise as well.

42 The designation is obscure.

43 He passed through Syria and Asia Minor, "the land of the Hittites."

44 נחוגים; cf. Is. 60:11.

45 The angel-guardian of Islam.

blind his eyes at a single time. And there went forth the Angel-Prince of Esau,[46] whom the King had made to turn after the Angel-Prince of Ishmael to honor him, and Esau became jealous of Ishmael, and he gathered up all his host to destroy him.

And it came to pass after a period of time that our Master came to the Land of Izmir. And Samael[47] heard of it and he pursued and overtook him near the pool of water, at the opportune time when our Master went to wash and to plunge the Princes of Fear into the depths of the sea.[48] And Samael, coming after him, stole his raiment, on which were engraved the names of the *yiḥudim*[49] to cut off the seed of Amalek at this time, and sin caused[50] that the raiment, the garments of vengeance, was maculated by the hand of Samael, and he cast our Master to the end of the great ocean. And the horn of Israel was nearly cut down, if not for the Lord who was for us; and he said to him: "Be not affrighted, neither be dismayed. Lay hold of my Throne of Glory and I shall garb you in rich apparel, in robes of light.[51] For the missing raiment was of leather and it is injurious to Samael and his company." At that moment our Master prayed before the ark[52] of the Lord that was in the sea, "Answer me, O Lord, answer me." Immediately the right hand of the Lord was exalted and he took [him] up out of the miry clay[53] and brought him to his place at the pool,[54] where the Associates were waiting, lowing and moaning.[55] And they saw him and their spirit restored, and he recounted to them the entire event. And they brought him splendid raiment to wreak vengeance upon Samael and his company. And he ascended and said to the Associates: "Know then how much sin has brought about, for the Wicked One gained advantage over me, but he could not prevail over me. He stole my raiment, to obstruct the vengeance of his people, and he did not know that I have stained all my raiment[56] with the blood of his people. For 120 years it shall be in his power, but no longer. And so it is stated explicitly, 'Therefore shall his days be a 120

46 The angel-guardian of Christendom. (Esau and Edom are, of course, identical).

47 Abbr. ס״מ, as often in Kabbalistic literature.

48 The mystery of this bathing in the sea is thus a war of forces, between the Evil One and Sabbatai Zevi; cf. n. 6. The event is described in several poems of the Doenme.

49 Literally "unifications," that is, magical formulae through which concentration on the Holy Name would produce a desired effect.

50 גרם החטא, an expression often used

as a pious expletive.

51 מכתנות אור, a play on Genesis 3:21; note also the following phrase in our document.

52 הכל instead of היכל.

53 Cf. I Kings 18:37; Psalms 118:16 and 40:3.

54 This legend combines two separate incidents, accounts of which were communicated to Coenen (*Ydele Verwachtinge der Joden*, 1669, pp. 94–95): an episode regarding a wolf that attacked Sabbatai Zevi alongside the pool of the Santa Veneranda fountain, and the epi-

years,' [57] ruling over a land which is not his, manifesting his pride and exalting himself in the branches of the tree from which he shall not eat and the scent of which he shall not inhale." And it came to pass that when the Angel-Prince of Ishmael heard what Samael had done to our Master, he sent to have our Master brought, to make a covenant with him. But he did not listen to him, for he said, "Surely I will seize Samael and his company; I shall make no covenant." And he sent to him a second time [saying]: "I am as you, my people are as your people, my horses are as your horses. Let us pursue him until we cut him off." And our Master sent to him [saying], "Suffer me a little, until it be known [58] whether the matter has been decreed from on high and what will be at the end of the time."

On that night our Master could not sleep, and he commanded to bring the Book of Records of the Consolations. And the sons of God came to present themselves before him,[59] to hear ancient [that is, concealed] matters. And there was found written the end of the blessing with which the Angel-Prince of Ishmael was blessed, "And I will multiply him exceedingly," [60] which is an allusion to the 120 years during he would have honor over the horn of Israel and this is the secret of [the continuation] "twelve princes shall he [Ishmael] beget," and behave as one who acts magnanimously toward our Master, so that he should provide him [Sabbatai Zevi] with aid during the aforementioned 120 years and not wage war against him to wrest from him the crown: and they are the sons of the king [the Turkish rulers] that hold sway over them. And sinfulness has caused the making of a covenant with him for 120 years to support him, for the honor of our father Abraham (of blessed memory), who said, "O that Ishmael might live. . . ." [61]

And it came to pass on a certain day that our Master rose up and went to him and made a covenant with him and exalted him above the Princes. And they set a great condition between them, that

sode of his sinking in the sea. So also in the poems of the Doenme; cf. M. Attias and G. Scholem, *Poems and Paeans of the Sabbatians* (1948, Hebrew), the note to p. 136.

55 In place of "the Associates," the Doenme poems mention only "Rabbi Barzilai, the disciple of our Master," who was present at the time: "Until evening he wept his weeping, and he brought a garment from his house and rejoiced with the Son of David." This Rabbi Barzilai is the one who established

the fast on this festival eve which commemorates the deliverance of Sabbatai Zevi and is called "Purim"; cf. my book on Sabbatai Zevi, p. 116.

56 Cf. Isaiah 63:3.

57 Genesis 6:3. Here the verse is interpreted as referring to the period of time of Samael's dominion over the Messiah and his followers.

58 The text lacks "it be [made] known."

59 Cf. Esther 6:1 and Job 1:6.

60 Genesis 17:20.

61 *Ibid.*, v. 18.

at the fullness of the aforementioned time he [the Angel-Prince of Ishmael] should deliver to him all the sons of the king under his power; and if he should violate this condition, his memory would perish from above and his roots below in the midst of the camp of Samael and his company. So he passed into covenant with him [p. 163] hotly to pursue Samael and his camp.[62] And the *maggid* came and reported the entire deed that was done, and I was astonished and trembling seized me. And there came to me a letter from our Master in which was said, "Have you not known and have you heard not what Samael has done to me, that he concealed his coming from me and stole the ornament and hid it in the sand, and sin caused that I was not able to cut him off. And I rose up to do battle [together] with the Angel-Prince of Ishmael, and he entered into a covenant with me for a fixed period of time. And I knew that the war with [against] him would not succeed, for the iniquity of his covetousness is not yet complete, and I am not able to rescue the fragments of the tablets from his hand except by entering into a firm covenant with him until that time. And thus, on this day I have entered into covenant with him, together with the Associates. And behold he aids me but not out of his generosity, for he has seen that misfortune is decreed against him. And he stands apart, looking and watching what will be the judgment [destiny] of Samael. And from between his eyelashes [from his expression] it is discernible that he is transgressing [63] upon the two opinions. Perhaps he will rebel against me within the aforesaid period, and you will see wonders, how I shall set him against them.[64] But if he keeps his covenant and fulfills my wishes as we stipulated with him, no harm will come to him, only they shall become hewers of wood and drawers of water for the congregation [65] throughout their lives; and in regard to them it is stated explicitly. 'For the youngest shall die a hundred years old,' [66] and the entire blessing will be realized for him. For the time being he holds fast to my covenant, to pursue Samael and his company. As for you, son of man, be not affrighted, neither be dismayed; be strong and of good courage, and let not this

---

62 An allusion to the apostasy of Sabbatai Zevi.
63 פֹו"שע; a paranomasia, as indicated
  by the sign customarily used in
  abbreviations. The pun, based on
  I Kings 18:21, combines the sense
  of lamely vacillating (פסח) between
  two opposed loyalties with the no-
  tion of transgression or rebellion
  (פשע), possibly linked by a third
  verb meaning "to step" (פסע).

64 The text translated "I shall set him
  against them" is obscure.
65 Joshua 9:27.
66 Isaiah 65:20; perhaps the phrase
  following in the Bible is also implied, in the event that the covenant
  should be violated.
67 This is a comment of the copyist,
  Rabbi Abraham Miranda, who
  transcribed the *Dokhranei di-Sahadutha* on page 31 of the manu-

thing be ill in your eyes. For without this there would be no power to stand, seeing that the wrongdoing and sinfulness of the sons of your people [Israel] are mighty, and the enemy is mighty, and if I do battle with him I shall not succeed." And I have meditated in the Records of the Testimony (apparently the *Dokhranei di-Sahadutha* found on page 31),[67] and there all the matters are explained with utmost clarity, and I gained understanding and wisdom therein and found everything decreed from on high, including what will result and [how] healing will accrue to us through our doing this thing. For he will bring an extermination wholly determined upon Samael, and will cooperate with the Angel-Prince of Ishmael. And all this has come upon us because of our father Abraham, and further that our sins caused a delay for this additional period.

Now I will tell you what you shall do. Assemble the camp and address them persuasively, for I am aware that their mind and heart within them have grown indifferent since they have heard of this matter. And you, open their eyes and let them see and hear that this is not of my invention. And let them not gape with their mouths to speak against their King and profane him among the Enemies of Fear,[68] and let them not be upon the two opinions, wandering to and fro. Explain to them in detail the things which you have heard. And let them not be as their fathers, a stubborn and rebellious generation, [a generation] that set not their heart aright, and whose spirit was not steadfast to [with] God.[69] Therefore let them keep their faith in their hearts,[70] and this is their righteousness, for they are men of preeminence into whose company no other man can enter, and they shall behold the Salvation with their own eyes. For what need have I of this trouble, to bring in one ewe lamb among seventy wolves, if I did not know that it has been thus decreed from on high from earliest times—as you shall perceive and understand in the prophecies of the prophets who came before you—that this thing must be, in order to deliver a number of families that are ensconced in them [71] and also in the Seventy Princes of the Nations [among all nations], and at the

script. But in that text there is no mention of all that is related here, and perhaps we should understand the words "I meditated in the Records of the Testimony" as referent to the celestial book of records which he studied according to the account above, where the main features are recorded in a fashion similar to here.

68 צרי הפחד; perhaps in the sense of "terrible enemies"; above we find the expression שרי הפחד (Princes of Fear).

69 The quotation is from Psalms 78:8, with the omission of the second דור and exchanging אל for את.

70 They are to keep their true faith secret.

71 This idea is in fact expressed in the *Sahadutha di-Mehemanutha*.

time appointed they shall all come forth from Sheba [72] and proclaim the praises of the Lord, and who believes [73] shall live."

Now when I saw the script and the letter, my spirit was restored in me, and I meditated in every prophet and found the entire deed and all the wars, in truth, that the matter was decreed from on high, as you may perceive from the Book of Raziel, for there the matters are explained clearly.[74] And I sent a letter to our Master, that he should uncover my ear concerning who would be those going with him to war,[75] and whether it was his wish that I should assemble them and enter with them into war.[76] Then he sent forth his hand a second time in the script of an epistle and said to me, "Son of man, I have appointed you a watchman in the midst of the people, to tell them all that I shall announce to you. And it is unseemly for you [p. 164] to assume two crowns: leave the crown of kingship to the seed of the house of David.[77] And furthermore, because your seed came up out of Ethiopia and Egypt, and they were unsuccessful [78] because they raised their hand before my coming to them, and so it is explicitly stated in the prophets, 'Ephraim, he mixes himself with the peoples, Ephraim is become a cake not turned.' [79] Therefore, do not bring upon us wars of which we have not heard: this war is sufficient to us. And also, the priests are not warriors; sufficient to them is the war of the princes that are destined to stand up against them, as some of them stood up in the days of the Hasmonean and his sons. And if my desire were in you and your tribe, I should have uncovered your ear before making the covenant. Therefore stand apart upon your task, you and the Associates that are with you, and you will behold wonders. And I am this day weak, though anointed King,[80] until the time of revelation to you and the Associates. Now this is what you shall do for them.

---

72 Cf. Isaiah 60:6.
73 האמין instead of המאמין (the Believer).
74 His commentaries in the Book of Raziel are mentioned by our pseudo-Nathan also in the first treatise, "The Concealment of the Master." (The word for "Master" there is אמיר"ה, which combines the Arabic word *emir* with the abbreviation "Our Master and King, may his majesty be exalted.")
75 Who have been chosen for the mystic apostasy.
76 Whether he also should apostatize.
77 Cf. the taunt hurled at Alexander Yannai, B.T. *Kiddushin*, 66a.
78 An allusion to the premature departure of the Ephraimites from Egypt, according to the Midrash.

Nathan is said in our text to be a descendant of the tribe of Ephraim.
79 Hosea 7:8.
80 II Samuel 3:39.
81 According to what is written above, that the apostates are the ones called upon to go to war with the Messiah, it follows that the simple meaning of this sentence would refer to those who had not apostatized: it is they who must engage in meditation on the divine mysteries, or *Ma'aseh Merkabah*, and expound the secrets of the faith. But from the continuation here it is clear that the reference is in fact to the sect of the apostates, since the commandments set out here are binding on those who

Call public assemblies and explain to them the matters just as they are, and warn them that while I am against [engaged in] the war, they shall occupy themselves with *Ma'aseh Merkabah*.[81] And further, let them adorn themselves with these Eighteen Dicta, which they shall observe:

  i. They shall be scrupulous in the Faith of Heaven, that he is one and only, and besides him there is no god, and providence does not belong to any prince or ruler except him.[82]

  ii. They shall believe in his Messiah, who is the true Redeemer and there is no other redeemer except him, namely our Master, our King, Sabbatai Zevi [83] of the seed of the house of David (of blessed memory).

  iii. They shall not swear falsely by his blessed name or by his Messiah, for his master's name is in him [84] and they shall not profane it.

  iv. They shall honor his Blessed Name, and so also they shall honor the name of the Messiah when they make mention of it, and so also [shall each do] for any greater than he in wisdom.

  v. They shall advance from strength to strength in recounting and disclosing subtleties in the mystic messianic faith, *raza demeshiḥa;* so also, on the eighteenth [other texts: sixteenth] [85] day of Kislev they shall all of them assemble together in one house, and there they shall recount to one another what they have heard and understood of the mystic faith of the Messiah, *raza di-Mehemanutha di-Meshiḥa.*[86]

accepted Islam. The transition to the list of commandments is quite artificial, as if the writer had added here things which had already been ordained and promulgated among the "Believers" as the regimen for the apostates, "Wearers of the Turban," or "the Warriors."

82 The careful wording of this article of faith apparently contains mystic aspects: the deity according to the Sabbatian mystery of faith is solely the master of providence—but this "God" is not at all identical with the *Ensoph.* I have treated this question of the attitude of the first Sabbatians to providence in my book, pp. 779, 784.

83 צ״ק is written here in large letters.

84 Cf. B.T. *Sanhedrin* 38b on Metatron; the expression is here applied to the Messiah, in whom the power of the Lord resides.

85 ס״א וי׳; a marginal note by Abraham Miranda.

86 The sentence from "so also" is listed separately as the seventh commandment in the later Spanish version which reached Danon. The correct date is the 16th of Kislev, and so it appears in the extant lists of holidays in several manuscripts from the 1680's, as in the Sabbatian notebook of Abraham Rovigo (at the Ben-Zvi Institute) and in Ms. Adler 493 (at the Jewish Theological Seminary in New York).

vi. There shall be among them no murderers, even [of those] among the Nations, even if they detest them.[87]

vii. There shall be among them no thieves.[88]

viii. There shall be among them no adulterers. Although this is [only] a commandment of the Created World,[89] because of the thieves it is necessary to be scrupulous [in observance].

ix. They shall not bear false witness, nor shall they speak falsely to one another; and they shall not inform among themselves, even to [against] unbelievers.[90]

x. They are not permitted to come [bring] in [91] anyone under the turban,[92] even one who believes intensely.[93] For he who is of the Warriors, will come in himself with a complete heart and a desiring spirit without any trace of coercion whatever.

xi. There shall not be among them any that covet what is not theirs.[94]

xii. They shall keep the feast [other texts: the fast and the feast] in Kislev [95] with great rejoicing. [Says the copyist: it is the feast of the miracle of "He brought me up also out of the tumultuous pit, out of the miry clay," [96] which is on the sixteenth of Kislev, as is known; this is the day on which he was plunged into the great ocean by

---

87 The antecedent of "them" is the Believers, and the import is: even when gentiles are inimical to the members of the sect. This is confirmed by the Spanish version.

88 This commandment is omitted from the Spanish versions and is replaced by the second part of V.

89 It is only a commandment of the *Torah de-Beri'ah* (the evanescent law), as contrasted with the *Torah de-'Atsiluth* (the supernal law) that was revealed by Sabbatai Zevi. The prohibitions in the sphere of sexual relations are also included in the evanescent law. The warning here alludes to the secret orgiastic ceremonies in which all these "obsolete" injunctions were violated, although it was necessary to maintain them on the surface.

90 Danon's version erroneously read: "even against Believers." That of Galante was correct: אפילו קי נון סון מאמינים.

91 לחיוכנס, instead of לחכנים.

92 The Spanish version is based on a Hebrew text which read "the faith of the turban," that is, Islam.

93 See now the important evidence on Sabbatai Zevi's behavior in this regard in the detailed account of his effort to persuade a number of eminent "Believers" to take the turban in the presence of the Sultan in 1671; cf. *Sefunot*, Book V (1961), pp. 258–259. There also this point is emphasized: Sabbatai Zevi insists on the fact that there be no coercion, and in fact most of the scholars who were invited to visit him and who debated the subject with him at length did not agree to apostatize and were sent away peaceably.

94 It is clear that x and xi have been inverted: the first ten ordinances are peculiarly Sabbatian reformulations of the Biblical Ten Commandments, while the remaining eight were innovated specifically for the Sabbatians.

Samael and was delivered, as is recounted on a previous page.] [97]

    xiii.   They shall behave graciously toward one another, fulfilling his [each other's] desire.

    xiv.   They shall study privately the Book of Psalms, a daily measure every day.

    xv.   Each and every month they shall look up and behold the birth of the moon and shall pray that the moon turn its face opposite the sun, face to face.[98]

    xvi.   They shall be scrupulous in [their observance of] some of the precepts of the Ishmaelites, among whom they have come, to blind their eyes and eradicate his [their] seed.[99] And as for the fast [of Ramadan], those that keep it shall not be concerned, and similarly about their sacrifices to the demons they shall not be concerned; [100] and those things which are exposed to their [the Moslems'] view they shall observe.

    xvii.   They shall not intermarry with them, neither in their lifetime or in death, for they are an abomination and their women are creeping things, and concerning them it is said, "Cursed be he that lies with any kind of beast." [101]

    xviii.   They shall be scrupulous to circumcise their sons and remove disgrace from upon the holy people. For my desire is in these Eighteen Ordinances,[102] although some

95   The Spanish version has: "on the 16th of Kislev."

96   Psalms 40:3.

97   The two inserts are marginal comments by Abraham Miranda; cf. the account above in the text. The list itself does not refer directly to the section of the text which precedes the commandments.

98   This is the observance of the Sanctification of the (New) Moon according to the Zoharic interpretation of it as an allusion to the hope for a "holy union" between the sun and moon ("face to face"). See for example Zohar I, 64b; II, 232a.

99   ולקעקע ביצתו, undoubtedly an error for ביצתם or ביצתן; the idiom is a rabbinic expression (see for example *Vayikra Rabba* 11).

100   That is to say, they must observe them because of what the Moslems would say. The reference, of course, is to the rigidly observed Ramadan and the ceremonies connected with it, violation of which would entail great danger for the apostates. On the other hand, they are not to be anxious lest the observance of these Moslem religious practices have a deleterious effect on them. The formulation of these commandments shows how far the first apostates were from voluntarily accepting the laws and customs of Islam.

101   This extreme formulation (which is absent from the text that reached Galante!) is modeled on the words of the Talmud which refer to the daughters of the *'am ha'aretz* and which cite the verse from Deuteronomy 27:21 (cf. *Pesaḥim* 49b).

102   ח"י סדרים; this standing expression has been preserved in Hebrew even in the later Spanish translations. The speaker is, of course, Sabbatai Zevi.

of them belong [only] to the law of the Created World, [p. 165] for the Throne has not yet been made whole,[103] until the vengeance of the Children of Israel is wrought upon Samael and his company. At that time all will be equal, [there shall be] no proscribed and no permitted, no polluted and no pure, for they shall all know them [me],[104] from the least of them to the greatest of them. And caution the Associates who are Believers but have not taken the turban—which is the war—that they must be scrupulous in their observance of the law of the Created World and the Supernal World; [105] they must not omit anything until the time of the Revelation.[106] Thenceforward they will be attired in the Tree of Life, and all will be equal."

May it be his will that he [Sabbatai Zevi] soon be revealed; amen.

Thus far the copy of the communication, letter for letter.

103 An allusion to the rabbinic tradition, linked to Exodus 17:16, that the Throne of God will remain incomplete as long as the seed of Amalek (the power of evil) is not annihilated. See for example Midrash Tehillim on Psalm 97:1.

104 אותם instead of אותי (cf. Jeremiah 31:33), correctly rendered in the Spanish version.

105 Here we have significant evidence regarding the difference between the two camps of Believers in the eyes of the writer of the treatise (or of the "Ordinances"): the Believers within Judaism must keep the Law of the Created World—namely traditional Judaism—in its entirety, as well as the Law of the Supernal World, corresponding to the mystical theory and secret practices of the Believers; the apostates, on the other hand, must keep only part of the Law of the Created World, not its entirety.

106 This is the standard terminology in Nathan's writings for the Second Coming of Sabbatai Zevi.

The Future of the Zionist Movement

MOSHE SHARETT

*

THERE ARE FEW SUBJECTS in Jewish life of recent import that have given rise to so much confusion and controversy as the question of whether the Zionist Organization still has a right to exist or if it has forfeited that right. In a way, such a phenomenon of heart-searching and internal conflict is inevitable in the context of contemporary events, and we should not feel dismayed or disgruntled by it. An epoch-making transformation has occurred in the position of the Jewish people with the rise of an independent Israel. I believe it to be inherent in human nature that there should be an element of lag and inertia in the process of man's psychological adjustment to new realities. It is under the impact of these new realities that the Zionist Organization has been challenged to prove its title to continue in being.

The challenge is threefold. First, on the face of it, an organization is an instrument for attaining an end, not an end in itself. Theodor Herzl's purpose in calling into being the Zionist Organization was that it should serve as an instrument for bringing about the creation of the Jewish State. That purpose has been fulfilled. The Jewish State has been created. Israel represents the decisive, spectacular and overwhelming triumph of Zionist philosophy, of Zionist faith, and of Zionist vision and action. Once the end has been achieved there seems to be no further need for the means. The onus of proof to the contrary appears to be on the organization.

The second challenge is that Israel today is of such enormous, universal significance in Jewish life that old distinctions between Zionist and non-Zionist circles, or rather between Zionists and a-Zionists, have been obliterated. What characterizes the present situation is a most impressive, worldwide rallying of massive Jewish support for the State of Israel, regardless of former organizational barriers or ideological divergencies. What purpose then is served by the Zionist Organization as such and why keep it up? If there be need to give an organized expression to the attachment of the Jewish people to Israel, let it be something universally Jewish—a framework open to all.

There is a third challenge. It is pointed out that the Zionist Organization lacks vigor, that it has lost its capacity to attract new forces to its fold, that, in particular, it makes no appeal to the young generation in Jewry, and that, above all, it does not concentrate on practical activities of specifically Zionist nature, such as *Aliyah,* Hebrew education, and the general deepening of Jewish consciousness. This being so, what is the Zionist Organization's title to maintain its continued separate existence?

There is, of course, yet another challenge, addressed by some to every Zionist personally. It is, why does he not make Israel his home? But even those who do not hold the view that the Zionist Organization is a league of *olim,* immediate or prospective, cannot ignore the first three issues.

The conclusions drawn from these queries are obvious, and seem, at first sight, perfectly logical. Yet on deeper probing the issue turns out to be by no means so elementally simple and clear-cut.

In attempting this analysis let us exclude premises which are neither relevant nor valid. One such premise is the invocation of memories of the past—the tribute, so rightly paid, to the monumental, historic merit of the Zionist Movement in bringing about the great fulfillment. One can rest on laurels, but they are of no use as springs of action. They cannot serve as roots of a new vitality. Another premise of most doubtful validity is the fact that the Zionist Organization exists today—that it cannot be dissolved by a decree from outside. This argument again, plausible as it may seem, cannot carry the Zionist Organization very far. The problem, after all, is not one of constitutional legalities but of the facts of life. If the Zionist Organization ceases to discharge vital functions, if it is pervaded by the sense of its own futility, no force of tradition or formal status will save it from disintegration and indignity.

So the questions upon the answer to which the future of the Zionist Movement is predicated must be the following ones. First, are there specific and vital tasks for the Zionist Movement to discharge in this phase of Jewish history, the central facts of which are the existence and growth of independent Israel and the rallying of the Jewish people around it? Second, if there are such tasks, does the World Zionist Organization or do the Zionist movements in various countries actually assume and discharge them?

In trying to answer these two crucial questions, let us first consider the problem of the Zionist Movement in its worldwide aspect, and then examine the position of organized Zionism in one particular country—the United States.

What does the existence of the World Zionist Organization signify?

I believe that it signifies, in the first place, the consciousness that there is a Jewish people, united in its global dispersion and representing one entity throughout the world.

It signifies, in the second place, the conviction that this body of people is united not merely by the memories of the past or by an identity of faith and ritual, but because it possesses a central will and pursues a central purpose. In this respect the World Zionist Organization knows no rival in Jewish life. The central will and purpose which it represents are primarily to promote and participate in the growth of Israel—in numbers, strength, and creative capacity—and to ensure the fulfillment by Israel of its historic mission.

In the third place, it signifies that it is the aim of this world organization to radiate its influence throughout the Jewish people by inculcating in all parts of it the consciousness of its distinctiveness and unity, by focusing its energies upon the support of Israel and by deepening and enriching the meaningfulness of Jewish life in the Diaspora under Israel's inspiration.

Last, but not least, it signifies not only an association for some worthy common purpose but a fellowship of sons and daughters of Jewry, a living communion of men and women who share the same convictions about their people's historic substance and destiny; who are united in the consciousness of their Jewish identity as the crux of their spiritual selves; who see in Israel the culmination of Jewish history, the focal point of contemporary Jewish life, a magnet progressively evoking in the hearts of increasing numbers of Jews the urge of personal transplantation into it.

Unlike all other Jewish associations of worldwide dimension which pursue essentially static objectives, the World Zionist Organization alone deserves the distinguished and exacting title of a Movement. This is so because of the dynamic nature of its purpose and the part played in its life by its own spiritual credo. What I want to emphasize is the tremendous political and practical significance of the fact that there is a world framework—the Zionist Organization—and a world tribune—the Zionist Congress—which symbolize and give expression to the dynamic unity of the Jewish people and its concentration around Israel.

Can this inestimable asset—inestimable primarily for Israel but also for the Jewish world as a whole—be so lightly given up? Should not every conceivable effort be made to safeguard it and breathe new life into it?

The Zionist Congress and the World Zionist Organization are the creations of Theodor Herzl's genius—the first as a tribune, the second as an instrument. Herzl bequeathed these two assets to the Jewish people and thereby wrought a revolution in its life. Upon Herzl's death and for many years after, they remained facts of internal Jewish life, making little impact upon the world outside. But twenty years after the first Zionist Congress, it was given to Chaim Weizmann to secure the international recognition of the Jewish people as a worldwide political entity—not merely as a historic fact, of interest to historians and archeologists—but as a political fact of present-day international import; an entity internationally endowed with political rights in regard to the Land of Israel. Five years later, in 1922, the World Zionist Organization was internationally recognized as a body representing the entire Jewish people on that particular plane. These are positions of far-reaching importance both in the internal life of the Jewish people and on the world scene. Without at least a reasonable assurance of adequate substitutes or alternatives, it is irresponsible to assume that these assets can simply be dispensed with.

It is of course possible to argue that the Zionist Organization formally recognized by the powers of the world at that particular time was merely intended to serve as an instrumentality for the attainment of statehood, and now that statehood has been attained it clutters the scene of history gratuitously and should be discarded, the sooner the better.

But Jewish statehood, the consummation of age-long hopes and prayers and the product of a concentrated, dogged effort which lasted several decades, is in its turn not an end in itself, but merely a means to an end. It is not the crowning piece of the edifice. It is not even its top story. We do not know when the edifice we are engaged in erecting will be completed. Statehood is just a broader base and an infinitely more powerful lever for the continuation and acceleration of the great historic process of the return of multitudes of the Jewish people to its birthplace—to the source of its inspiration and the site of its glory; a process of return, the historic goal or the ultimate end of which is shrouded in the mists of the unpredictable future.

This being so, the reliance of the Jewish State upon the Jewish Dispersion on the one hand, and conversely, the attachment of the Dispersion to the State—this interdependence of the center and the perimeter—have grown and are growing more compelling and more complex, than they were in the pre-State era, and the need to give an organized expression to that singular nexus is now more imperative than ever.

In point of numbers, in the dimensions of its membership, the Zionist Organization today is but a fraction of that great, solid mass of the Jewish people who are heart and soul with Israel in her trials and struggles, who so deeply share her worries, rejoice in her successes, pin their hopes on her future. Yet in point of weight, as distinct from numbers, the special value of the Zionist Organization lies in its being the only centralized expression of the Jewish people's attachment to Israel.

If the Zionist Organization evacuates the scene of history, there is no certainty that any wider or more representative body, or any alternative body will take its place. The odds are that its place will remain vacant. An inestimable asset of Jewish life will be lost, possibly lost forever.

Those who would prefer or, to say the least, would not mind the disappearance of the Zionist Organization, would rest content with the establishment of direct and separate connections between the Government of Israel and each of the Jewish communities throughout the free world. That is to say, they envisage that in each country a Jewish organization would have to be set up for the purpose of entering into a special and direct relationship with the Government of Israel. Those who oppose this idea are convinced that the proposed arrangement, if it at all comes about, will perforce remain of a most irregular and hazardous character. Moreover, they fear that it will be fraught with international difficulties, today nonexistent. For it is one thing if the Jews of the free world, by way of exercising their elementary rights under democracy, choose to get together in each country with a view to cultivating this connection, and then join hands over state frontiers in order, of their own accord, to establish a world organization for the purpose. It is quite a different thing if that connection becomes a subject of what might look to be an interference by a certain State in the internal life of another country. Israel can evoke a certain emotional reaction to its work, to its achievements, to the problems of its future. It cannot implant such a reaction, and it must beware of appearing to try to do so by an outside intervention. The validity and legitimacy of the attachment depend on its genuineness; and the test of its genuineness is its spontaneity. To enjoy validity and command legitimacy the world organization must spring from below—it must grow out of the Jewish Diaspora as a result of its natural gravitation toward Israel, and not appear to be foisted by Israel upon the Diaspora.

The State of Israel welcomes direct contacts with any Jewish group or circle anywhere in the world. It cannot insist that all its connections with the Diaspora should necessarily be conducted through the channels of the Zionist Organization. Yet, from this natural reservation to the negation or disregard of the supreme value of a world tribune and of a world framework which would symbolize and activate the concentration of the Jewish people around Israel is, to say the least, a very far cry. Every conceivable effort seems to be worthwhile to maintain and strengthen these historic instruments.

But an effort is imperative, for, with all their transcending value, these institutions can bring about their own undoing by continuing adrift and not addressing themselves to the crucial issues that confront them.

The main organizational issue is one of a seemingly growing paradox. Here is the Zionist Organization, claiming to represent the entire Jewish people in its relation to Israel and to occupy a preeminent position in Jewish life generally. But the contemporary Jewish world is replete with organizations of all sorts which do not formally accept the Zionist program, yet they all, or nearly all, feel attached to Israel, and are anxious to maintain a most intimate relationship with it.

To avoid confusion, friction, and conflict between the Zionist Organization and these groups, between these groups and the State of Israel, between the State of Israel and the World Zionist Organization, against the background of the diversity, complexity, and yet the vital character of all these contacts, is it not indicated that the World Zionist Organization should strive to secure the association of other Jewish bodies—to group them around itself, inasfar as they are ready to cooperate, and in whatever form their cooperation may prove practical?

Authoritative pronouncements have been made in Israel by the Government and by the Central Committee of Israel's leading party, giving full recognition to the World Zionist Organization but envisaging the eventual formation of an all-embracing Jewish world association around the State of Israel. These resolutions have rejected the thesis that the starting point for such an endeavor should be the scrapping of the existing world framework, that is, of the Zionist Organization. They rather envisage an evolutionary process which, starting from the present position of the World Zionist Movement, would gradually envelop and bring together all Jewish forces which accept Israel as a central asset of world Jewish life. The attainment of this high objective must again be primarily the concern of the Zionist Organization itself.

To sum it up, the function of the World Zionist Organization is so vital that if it did not exist, it would have to be created.

Another fundamental reason why it is so important to maintain a world framework for the association of the Jewish Dispersion with the State of Israel bears upon a most vital problem of Zionist finance. I use the term "Zionist finance" not in the narrow and technical sense of the financial arrangements necessary to keep the Zionist Organization itself going, but as applying to the global effort of the Jewish people on behalf of Israel.

Now it should be clear that for decades to come—first, as long as Israel continues to be engaged in basic development work—that kind of work which does not result in the creation of assets which are commercially utilizable; and secondly, as long as Jews driven by material misery or spiritual enslavement continue to flock to Israel without any means of their own; as long as these twin processes keep on, the Jewish communities of the free world, and first and foremost the American Jewish community, will be called upon to finance absorption and development by gift monies on a considerable scale—gift monies which neither funds provided by the sale of bonds nor any private investment capital, much as both are urgently needed, can replace.

For reasons too well known to require explanations, these gift monies cannot possibly take the form of direct contributions from abroad to Israel's Treasury. So again, if the Treasury of the Jewish Agency Executive did not exist, some such central and extragovernmental receptacle for campaign funds flowing in from other countries would have to be improvised. As things stand, without that measure of common discipline which the various national campaign organizations accept in relation to the Zionist Congress as a budgetary authority—whether they are directly represented on it or not—the financial effort of world Jewry in aid of Israel would become decentralized as regards both the direction and sponsorship of the campaigns and the allocation of funds collected. The havoc which this state of things would play with any organized development work is incalculable. Countries would be left entirely to themselves as to whether to run a campaign at all, when to run it, what target to adopt for it. They would be more and more prone to decide these questions from the standpoint of local needs and interests, that is to say less Zionistically, rather than with a view to the needs and interests of Israel. The drive and the pull now supplied by Jerusalem, the motive force which stems from the dynamics of Israel, would be catastrophically reduced. To add chaos to confusion, each country might insist on its prerogative to pick and choose the purpose to which its funds should be devoted. The present advantages of central planning and central budgeting, in accordance with a scale of priorities centrally and responsibly fixed, would all go by the board. Only this central form of planning, budgeting, and disbursement can ensure to the global Jewish effort the highest measure of effectiveness, so that it should serve its purpose more rationally, more constructively, and more Zionistically, than would otherwise be the case. Even the new arrangement now in force in the United States as regards the administration and disbursement of U.J.A. funds allocated to Israel, does not impair the basic principles of central authority and control. U.J.A. funds can be applied only to purposes contained in the overall Zionist budgetary program, and their allocation is, therefore, fully coordinated and harmonized with the allocation of campaign funds coming from other countries.

Yet all this is not enough if Zionism is to remain, or rather again to become, a movement worth its name. No amount of constitutional prerogatives or of technical functions can alone prevent the spiritual deterioration of the Zionist Movement. The mere fact that the World Zionist Organization serves as a unique public platform, worldwide in its scope, that it enjoys formal status legislated upon by the parliament of Israel and that it wields important administrative authority in Israel, is no guarantee for its survival. If the Zionist Organization continues to rely only on its outward attributes and does not address itself to creative tasks, it will progressively be drained of its lifeblood and will eventually be reduced to an empty shell.

The movement can survive only if it is reinvigorated. It can be reinvigorated only if a new spirit is infused into it. What is decisive in the life of a movement is its substance, not its form, its living spirit, not its official status. In saying this, far be it from me to belittle, let alone ignore, the importance of an acknowledged formal status and of an officially assigned set of public functions. But, again, no reliance should be placed on them as sources of new life. They can act as a stimulant to the movement's spirit. They cannot generate it. The challenge to the movement's spirit can be met only by the movement itself. Either the stuff is in it or it is not.

This challenge must be met locally, in each and every country. The initiative, the drive, and the concrete performance of the central organs of the World Zionist Organization can determine a great deal, but in the final analysis it is the men and women of whom the organization consists who must bear the brunt of responsibility. It is up to them to prove their idealism, their dedication, and their practical worth and effectiveness.

Why should a non-Zionist Jew become a Zionist today? Supposing he is a good Jew and all for Israel, but he is not a member of any Zionist organization; why should he become one? Or, for that matter, why should a non-Zionist Jewish organization, which is all out to assist Israel, associate itself with the Zionist Movement? Would they thereby become more intensely Jewish in their thinking or action, or at least more Israel-minded? What is there in the program and activity of the Zionist Organization as such—apart from those components of it which engage in direct and practical work for Israel—which holds out to them a promise of deeper satisfaction or higher fulfillment in terms of their Jewish life?

The question can be put differently and perhaps more pointedly. Supposing there is not much practical chance of inducing masses of Jews to join the Zionist Organization as individuals or of securing the association with it of important extra-Zionist groups. Would that mean the end of the Zionist Movement, its gradual shrinkage, and eventual disappearance from the scene of Jewish history, as the present generation of Zionists dies out and no younger generation arises to take their place? I do not think it should. Provided there is an even limited inflow of younger members, there is still a vital task for a live and vigorous Zionist Movement to perform. It all depends on its capacity to radiate its influence outside its ranks, to permeate masses of Jews with its spirit, and to make its message theirs. To do that it need not necessarily expand, much as its numerical expansion is in itself desirable. But it can do that only if it is a living force. Is it?

To be a living force is to engage in activities that are vital to the moment.

I would limit myself to indicating three momentous tasks which are essentially Zionistic; which on the American scene have so far been attended far more by the agencies of the World Zionist Movement than by the American Zionist organizations; for the assumption of which there is no rival to the Zionist Movement and which, if undertaken and pursued vigorously by the Zionist Movement, would not only confer a tremendous boon on American Jewish life but would serve as a lever of Zionism's own revival and rally new forces to its banner.

These tasks are first, *Aliyah;* secondly, Hebrew education; thirdly, general educational work, Zionistically inspired, amongst the youth and adults.

The issue of American *Aliyah* must once for all be faced by the American Zionists themselves. It is undignified for the American Zionists always to be confronted with the problem by admonitions from Israel. I personally would deny Israel's right to address such admonitions. I would certainly question their effectiveness. Either these admonitions are self-addressed or they are futile. The matter must become the concern of the American Zionists themselves. It is up to them to adopt and put into effect their own *Aliyah* policy and practice.

I have never shared the view which insists on personal readiness and determination to migrate and settle in Israel as the basic or exclusive criterion for being a Zionist. But there is a second tenet to which I adhere at least as firmly as I do to the first, and that is that a Zionist organization which does not place the promotion of *Aliyah* in the forefront of its practical program calls in question its very title to being considered Zionist.

Two points may here perhaps be appropriately driven home, both elementarily Zionistic.

First, it is a fundamental Zionist concept that the completeness and inner poise of Jewish life is unthinkable anywhere in the Dispersion. Jewish values can be cultivated to enrich Jewish life; Jewish traditions should and can be upheld to make Jewish life distinctive and resistant to assimilation; Jewish associations can be maintained and developed in practically all countries of the free world. But a fully normal balance and integrality for a Jew as a human being and as a son of his people are attainable today only in Israel. Everywhere else, even in the freest of all societies, they are balked and thwarted by the irresistible impact of surrounding cultures, the overwhelming pressure of the non-Jewish environment. This being so, whilst one can remain in the Diaspora and be Zionist in one's thinking and public activity, he who opts for *Aliyah* chooses the road of practical Zionist fulfillment.

Let me add this. If we were to examine the manpower composition of each of the groups of *olim* to Israel from the so-called Western countries—the lands of freedom and security, of complete political emancipation, of prosperity, and contentment, such as the United States, England, Canada, South Africa, Australia and New Zealand, countries of Western Europe and of Latin America—we would find that an average member of each of these relatively small groups of immigrants is, in sheer human value, worth far more than his opposite number amongst the masses of immigrants from other countries. By the service he renders, the influence he exercises, the contribution he makes, his role in shaping Israel's life is distinct and invaluable. Yet I am confident that were we to send out a questionnaire to all these people asking them, "Why did you come over? Why did you settle?"— or, perhaps, putting it more specifically, "Did you come over because you felt that the country needed you, or did you come because you felt you needed the country?", then in 90 percent of the cases, if not in 99 percent, the answer would be, "I do hope I am useful to the country, that is, the country needs me, but that is not what decided me to come and settle. I made up my mind to come over because I reached the point where I felt that I needed the country—because it is there that I wanted to live and raise my children." This is Zionist fulfillment—my first point.

As for my second point, it is this. Diaspora Zionism should beware of involving itself in a hopeless contradiction. On the one hand, it fosters admiration for Israel's exploits and achievements. It cultivates pride in its very existence and its active record. It voices concern for its difficulties. It preaches faith in the progressive enhancement of its inspiration. On the other hand, it seems to recoil from drawing the most obvious conclusion from this frame of mind. I could cite cases in many a country where parents, old-time Zionists, faithful Zionists, do their utmost to deter or prevent their children from settling in Israel. This is an unworthy paradox. Parents who have devoted a lifetime to the preaching of a doctrine cannot resent their children's wanting to live up to it. When they decide themselves to become the heroes of that fantastic romance, the builders of that fascinating civilization, the defenders of that priceless possession, the direct beneficiaries of that renascent culture, are they then not the direct and finest product of that great historic movement which we call Zionism?

I would submit that it should be the ambition of World Zionism to turn out more and more of such *olim*. This is a question of a climate that must be created, such as would be favorable for the development and success of such a process. It is also a question of practical work by way of organizational and financial assistance. Primarily, the *halutz* youth movement should be assigned its due pride of place in the scheme of Zionist activities. It should be treated as the favored child of American Zionism, as an asset of supreme value in its life.

In case there are mental reservations to be overcome, I would suggest that the issue can also be rationalized in other terms. For example, Israel's progress is effectively assisted in a large variety of ways by the United States government and the American people. Valuable assistance flows to Israel from the U.S.A. through nongovernmental and non-Jewish channels for research and experimentation, and in support of all sorts of institutions. The overall picture is one of a large-scale, generous, purposeful, and most constructive assistance by the American Democracy to the State of Israel in the process of its growth. If that is the case, why should not such assistance also take the form of the transplantation into Israel of a small fraction of the enormous reservoir of American manpower? Zionism is in no need of such a justification, but it may be pertinent to point out that, objectively considered, *Aliyah* from America to Israel will proceed in no contradiction to the established policy of the United States, or to the general orientation of the American people, regardless of party or class.

Now for the second great task. Hebrew education among world Jewry is constantly gaining ground on many planes and in many ways. Its fullest and most effective embodiment is the Hebrew Day School. Yet what has so far been achieved in this direction may fairly be regarded as merely experimental and path-breaking. The time has passed when the preservation of Jewishness was a matter of deeply rooted routine, ensured through the automatic handing down of a religious, scholastic, and, if you are not afraid of the word, behavioristic tradition from one generation to another. The perpetuation of Jewishness, of Jewish consciousness and of a Jewish way of life, must now be the subject of a conscious, organized, concerted effort.

A modern Jew cannot resist assimilation unless he is proud of his origin and conscious of his responsibility for the Jewish future of his children. To be a vital force, such consciousness and pride must be rooted in the knowledge of the Jewish cultural heritage, accompanied by an ability to follow and comprehend the creative processes unfolding in Israel. The only solution to the problem lies in a purposeful program of positive Jewish-Hebrew education and in the general spreading of the knowledge of the Hebrew language.

The question of learning Hebrew is also one of the challenges which must be faced, first of all by Zionists. It is not beyond human ken, certainly not beyond the capacity of civilized men and women, and I can cite any number of examples to prove it, to master yet another language in addition to the national language of their country. The educated class of the Canadian French can all speak English fluently and correctly, read any English book and write any letter in English that may be necessary. The same holds good of members of the Afrikander community in South Africa; the educated among them all speak perfect English in addition to Afrikans. The entire class of the Indian intelligentsia is in full command of the English language, in addition to the national language of the province. Most educated people in Switzerland and Holland are at least bilingual. Most well educated Italians speak French. Why should it be beyond the possibility of well educated Jews to acquire the knowledge of a second language, particularly if this is the language of their own people, the instrument of its cultural creativity, the vehicle of its distinctive literary expression, ancient and modern? And why should this banner of Hebrew renaissance not be raised by the Zionist Movement?

What is essential is to impart the knowledge of Hebrew to the children and make them feel at home in it, in speech, reading, and writing. The blessings of Diaspora freedom can and should be fully utilized with this end in view. A proper Jewish and Hebrew education is perfectly consistent with the children's general education. Modern trends of liberal thought fully uphold the legitimacy and worth of cultural pluralism, not only between nations in the global scope but within each national entity.

But Jewish education cannot certainly remain confined to, and cease with, the school. The future of the young generation of Jewry in its entirety is now at stake. The role of this rising generation, not only in determining the fate of the Jewish community, but in exerting a powerful influence—constructive or destructive—on the world position of the Jewish people as well as on the future of the State of Israel, cannot be overestimated. Is this generation being brought up in the full cognizance of their tremendous Jewish responsibilities? Can one be a Zionist if his soul is not tormented by this fateful query? Can there be a Zionist organization, true to the significance and dignity of its name, if it does not actively concern itself with this challenge?

I regret that one does not see much convincing, dramatic evidence of such concern, certainly not on the part of the largest Zionist organizations. Nothing is farther from my mind than to disparage the efforts that are being made in this direction, but they are so far away, not only from the distant goal, but from what is immediately possible, that one cannot help voicing a considerable measure of disappointment.

The fate of the Zionist Movement is in its own hands. It must shed the inferiority complex which has crept into it. It can certainly regain its self-respect by becoming the State's partner in the historic enterprise, in the furthering of which it has a decisive role to play. It can impress Israel, not by invocations of its past record, nor by claims of status of the future, but by its spirit and its concrete performance. If there are facts to show—eloquent facts, tangible facts—Israel will not fail to be impressed. The Israelis have been brought up to respect facts, but they are impressed not only by material, physical facts. They are quite alert and receptive to the facts of the spirit. What they are impervious to is mere high-sounding verbiage which is not related to deeds.

It is up to the Zionist Movement to prove that it refuses to continue to vegetate as a shriveled relic of a rapidly receding past but that there is in it a potent embryo of an expanding future.

The Idea of Redemption in Hassidic Thought

ZALMAN SHAZAR

*

IT CAN HARDLY BE SAID of Hassidism that it has a special vision in regard to Redemption. It is that same ancient vision of the beatific age current in Jewry from time immemorial. The Hassidim, generally never made innovations. They accepted the Shulhan Aruch—all its paragraphs and provisions; they accepted the Written and the Oral Law, everything stated in the Zohar and everything that has become hallowed in the Jewish people; they accepted everything as it really is. Hassidim are not innovators, they are revivers. They introduce more life and content into everything that they receive. They introduce an additional measure of fresh vitality such as had hardly been sensed before. Barely had that hidden wisdom, that "internal significance of the Torah" as the Hassidim term it, touched upon the various aspects of the Torah, ancient and time-hallowed, than they become illumined by a magnanimous internal light. This applies to every one of the *mitzvot*. Not even the Kabbalah innovated precepts, but its influence upon them can hardly be overestimated. Let us take, for example, a hallowed precept which every Jew fulfills and lives through fifty times a year—that of the Sabbath. This forms a great fundamental in Judaism and the laws concerning the observance of the Sabbath, with all the thirty-nine forbidden works and their ancillaries, have been accepted among Hassidim and Mitnagdim alike. Nonetheless the image of the Sabbath in Jewry has become unrecognizable since the time of R. Isaac Lurie. Since his time a different form has been taken on by the Sabbath table, the Sabbath table hymns are different and so is the spirituality that emanates from the Sabbath atmosphere. The *kavanot* have, as it were, infused life into the *mitzvot* and the *Leshem Yihud* that is recited before their fulfillment, has, as it were, sparked off the *kavanot*. Like the Kabbalists before them, the Hassidim that followed did not invent anything but rather introduced a new form of vitality. The fire of Hassidism entered, as it were, the heart of the *mitzvot* and these have shone with a new appearance.

If this is true in regard to every *mitzvot* and to every value of

Judaism, so much the more would we have expected it to be felt keenly and enthusiastically when we speak of the essence of all precepts throughout the long generations of our exile, namely, "the yearning for redemption." Surely here one would have expected the revelation of a greater historical manifestation than had been apparent hitherto. We are now wont to apply historical terms, and to call this: Messianism—that is, not only Messianism as a principle of faith, as a beatific vision, toward which creation as a whole is striving and which is the constant heritage of the nation, but as it is conceived by every generation, as being the task of that particular generation, compelling it to certain urgent and daring tasks in order to speed up the end or to draw nigh to the end. We are permitted to differentiate between the various periods in accordance with the nature and intensity of this yearning for redemption, and in accordance with the deeds by which the people endeavored to effectuate their aspirations. The desire for redemption is general and is shared by all the faithful of the House of Israel, in all the lands of their dispersion and in all periods, but the manner of mourning for the *Galut,* for instance, by the "mourners of Zion" cannot be compared to the intense feelings expressed in the poesy of Rabbi Yehuda Halevy in his "Zionides." Nor can one compare the poetry of Rabbi Yehuda Halevy to the fire burning in the heart of that Maranno-Messianist, Rabbi Shlomo Molcho, who mounted the pyre while "fulfilling" his messianist precepts in the days of David Reubeni. Nor can one compare the expression of these two to the concepts nurtured by the age of the Kabbalists of Safad in the sixteenth century as a result of the storm that originated at Izmir and Gaza. Nor can one compare it to the flood of *aliya* to *Eretz-Israel* that broke forth, in their wake, from Poland and Italy. Indeed, from a certain point of view we should be right in saying that every generation has its messianic speculations, despite the general, constant messianic belief, both as a religious principle and as a spiritual background common to all generations.

What, therefore, was the share of Hassidism in this variegated historical complex, and why was its share as it was? Why had the fire of enthusiasm that marks the Hassidic movement in all the spheres of its religious activity waned as it were here? Why did it not burst forth into a mighty flame? How was it that modern historical science feels called upon to establish a fundamental difference between the period of the Kabbalah and that of Hassidism—between the mother and her daughter—that the mother Kabbalah was marked by an "active and dynamic Messianism," whereas the daughter Hassidism turned its Messianism into a latent and dormant feeling? In fact there were some who opined that Hassidism was "neutral" to Messianism. How is it that the flame died down at its very focus?

One may, perhaps, have recourse to two historical legends dating back to these two periods in order to bring this paradoxical change into relief.

It is related that when R. Isaac Lurie was asked why he had chosen Safad for the place where the Kabbalistic science was to be revealed, he answered: "the numerical value of the word צפת is תק"ע (570) and the wisdom of the Kabbalah has been revealed only for the purpose of fulfilling the precept תקע בשופר גדול לחרותנו 'sound the great trumpet for our liberation.' "

Again it is told that when Reb Nahman of Bratzlav—that most Messianic and most lyrical of all Admurim—was asked why he chose the town of Uman in the Ukraine as his final resting place rather than *Eretz-Israel,* he answered: It is because it is there that the martyrs of the anti-Jewish pogroms in the Ukraine of the years ת"ח and ת"ט (5408 and 5409) are buried and he wanted to lie beside them.

Do we not see here a shifting of the focus from pole to pole? What happened in the meantime, that this fire cooled off?

Did a Hassid in the days of the Baal Shem Tov experience the disaster of the *galut* to a lesser degree than did a Kabbalist of the time of the Ari? Was his faith in the certainty of redemption impaired or his yearnings for redemption weaker? Surely the sources of Hassidism are open to us. Many among us have known the Hassidic veterans of our generations, their spiritual content, the light of their thought and custom. Can we possibly believe that at the root of their soul there was a sort of "unconcern" about the desire for redemption? Why, therefore, had that enthusiasm, which is so characteristic of every true Hassid when the performance of any precept is at stake, apparently lost its dynamism in this respect, which concerns all the aspirations, the very soul of true and loyal Judaism?

It must be that something of fateful import had taken place between 5332 in Safad and 5495 at Tlust, in the wake of which these ethereal wings were cast in chains and weighted down.

Is not the reason for this change to be sought in that shattering historical event that took place in those years, which in this sensitive sphere gave birth to a whole complex of fears and impediments and cast a dreadful spell on the spiritual battle of those deeply concerned for the fate of the nation and for the fate of belief in the nation?

For in the period that separates the time of the followers of the Ari in *Eretz-Israel* and the disciples of the Baal Shem Tov in Podolia, there took place that great eruption that was brought on by the shattering of Messianic hope that was touched off at Izmir and Gaza and whose repercussions spread over many communities in the Diaspora; the aftermath of which still continued to claim victims in the same regions of Wolynia and Podolia in which the Hassidic Movement was born and from which it was to spread far and wide. No objective on-looker can remain oblivious of all that took place and pulsated deep in the soul of wakeful and stirred sons of Jewry, after the catastrophe of 1667, the great shock that came in the wake of the rise in faith, and the deep pain and shame and spiritual sorrow that resulted from the revelation of the falseness of the hopes, a bitterness the like of which the nation had not previously experienced.

Who knows to what depth the people would have sunk if the heal-ing and encouraging hand of the Baal Shem Tov and his disciples had not been held out to it. It was the hand of a believer and a healer. It was the hand of a man who professed implicit faith and was out to bring succor.

If I were able to liken the messianic flame that burned in the heart of the fathers of Hassidism and yet outwardly refrained from showing itself, I should say that it might be compared to the prayer uttered by Hannah at Shilo, where "the heart was filled to overflowing, the lips moved, but no sound was heard," as though through internal and external clamps, the moving lips were held in a vise so that no sound might be heard, as though some vow had been forced on all the lips of the faithful that no messianic voice be uttered and that they refrain from any semblance of "speeding up the end." Bitter experience was still in front of them and spread terror. These feel-ings of yearnings, cast in fetters, that the times imposed upon the fathers of Hassidism were later turned into a prototype and continued to wield influence when the circumstances that engendered it no longer obtained.

This is the great price that Hassidism paid in order to mount the breach and to rescue the messianic hope and with it the belief of the Jewish people in its future. There was a strict embargo both external and internal, on every practical expression. Every Hassid had to divert the essence of this belief and desire internally into his own soul, strictly eschewing all public and overt acts to a point of pitilessness, lest the nation fall once again into that dreadful and threatening abyss from which it had just been extricated with suffering and in-describable sacrifice and the mouth of which was still wide open to swallow alive everyone who dared to speed up the beatific end.

In other words, a change had set in in deed, but not in thought and desire.

In its very purity there burns an arduous desire for redemption, deep within this original religious-popular movement. In the days of Hassidism, as in the days of the Kabbalah; and with the rise of the leading personalities among it, this deep desire and belief rose and came to the fore in accordance with the grade and conception of each personality. Yet what was the difference between them? That tragic form of Messianism that had proven false weighted down the soul of the nation, and served as a dividing wall. The historian and research worker must wander far and wide among the historical recesses of the Jewish people until he can reach the period with which we are now dealing. But suddenly he finds a mighty upheaval in the theme of history, as though an extinct volcano of which the lava had lain amassed for generations had burst into activity, causing the institutions of national thought to topple. For the movement of Rabbi Israel Baal Shem Tov was not engendered in a period of tranquillity and of plain sailing, as in the days when the *Epistle to Yemen* was written by Maimonides, nor in days of rescue and of aspiration to great heights of holiness, as in the time of the Ari. It sprang in a period when the Jewish people had fallen into an abyss of sorrow and despair, in a period when the most precious of Jewish hopes had been shattered. It arose in a country of sorrow and suffering, among sorrowful and poverty-stricken masses in the steppes of Wolynia and Podolia, Wallachia and Reizen. This protective light broke out among the masses who had beheld the internal and external disaster with their own eyes.

We have all heard about the conditions in the Jewish communities in Podolia at the time that Rabbi Israel Baal Shem Tov first made his appearance as an infant-teacher's assistant. We must, however, call to mind the conditions of the Jewish people as a whole in that period. At the time that the Baal Shem Tov was born (5458–5460) the first Hassidim, those who preceded the Baal Shem Tov and who are known in Jewish history as members "of that holy society of Rabbi Yehuda Hehassid," lived in Shidlovcy and Kalish, Grodno and the other townlets of Poland and Lithuania. These set out to settle in *Eretz-Israel,* some on foot, others by conveyance. When they arrived in groups at Vienna they were joined by enthusiastic Hassidim from Fürth and Hanau and Frankfurt. Rich people and public workers of renown came to their assistance and raised money in order to finance their *aliya.* Great hopes were nurtured that when these God-fearing and holy men and Kabbalists would gather in Jerusalem and come "to make supplication in the courts of the Master of the Universe" their words would reach the portals of heaven and they would be able to do in the holy city that which it was impossible to bring about in the townlets of Poland and Lithuania. But hardly had three years gone by—when the Besht entered *heder* not as an infant-teacher's assistant but as a small child carried on the shoulders of another teacher's assistant—before these first Hassidim, those *olim* filled with so much yearning were driven out in disgrace and despair from Jerusalem. Rabbi Yehudah the Pious died three days after his arrival to *Eretz-Israel*. All we have left of him is the memory of "the *Hurvah* of Rabbi Yehudah Hehassid." A heavy veil of suspicion covers the firmament of the disciples of Rabbi Yehuda the Pious. They were accused of the most serious crime of the generation, that of an exaggerated desire for deliverance and of a too close clinging to the "pangs of redemption." Rabbi Yehudah's disciple and follower, Reb Gedaliah of Semiatiz, was forced to take up the staff of wandering and go out to Europe in order to bring the message of the *Yishuv* and its suffering. Some of them in their despair, perished, others went to greater extremes.

This took place during the early life of the Besht. What about his last years? Three years before the Baal Shem Tov's death there was held in his immediate environs the most shameful and painful trial that ever took place in the life of Jewish existence in the *Galut:* namely, the trial of Kaminitz-Podolsk occasioned by the fact that a group of stray and embittered members of the Jewish community, eaten by a blind and deep hatred of themselves, dared to level false and base accusations against their people, with the result that the authorities sent armed guards to the Jewish communities and forcefully confiscated copies of the Talmud and burned them in public in the squares of Jewish populated areas.

Whether Dubnow was right in assuming that the Baal Shem Tov participated in person in the defense of the Jewish people against its internal vilifiers, or whether Balaban was correct in claiming that the Besht was not included among the defenders in that he did not find his name among the signators of the protocol, or whether truth lies with Dr. Wertheim, who has just argued that the Besht only prepared the arguments and that he himself would not enter the courtroom, in that the trial was conducted in a church; there can be no doubt where his mind and heart lay at the time. The Besht was aroused together with all those who were moved by the pain suffered by their people. This explains the dream which, according to legend, he had on the eve of the Day of Atonement when he saw a great accusation against the Jewish people, in that the Oral Law had suddenly departed from them, and so he hurled himself into the Ark of the Law and shouted in a great and terrible voice: "Woe, they desire to take the Torah from us, and how can we continue to exist among the nations even for half a day. . . ." He continued that all the Tannaim and Amoraim appeared before judgment and during the closing moments he moaned and roared like an ox before slaughter and his supplication reached the final portal of justice until the decree was abrogated. Does one need superior historical imagination to gather from this legend the extent that Frankist libel worked upon him and in the repelling of which both he and all the leaders of his generation were engaged? Indeed, in that period, a Jewish hand that had emerged from the bowels of the messianic movement when, after the revelation of its falsesness, it sped quickly down the slope of decline, wrote in Poland; "Zion shall no longer be redeemed nor shall Jerusalem arise again."

In the very year of the Besht's death some hundreds of Jewish families within the very center in Podolia in which his star had risen, abandoned their Judaism.

During the sixty years of his life—from the time of the banishment of Rabbi Yehudah Hehassid's disciples from Jerusalem in his childhood until the apostasy of the Frankists at Kaminitz in the year of his death—there was a continuous tossing between two opposing poles—the pole of yearning for a full and speedy redemption and the pole of suppressed feelings and restraint and the strict vow not to do anything in public that might feed this urge.

If one were to try to find the nature of the Messianic outlook of the generation of the fathers of Hassidism, he would find it to be torn between this dramatic tension in the soul of the leaders among them, and which in various manifestations and in varying measures is characteristic of all those within that circle.

Who knows whether it is not possible within this tension of the chords of the heart, to find also an explanation of the riddle that, precisely at this time, melody broke out from the heart of the people, and became one of the fundamental assets of Hassidic expression. Even as we read in Jeremiah: "There is in my heart as it were a burning fire shut up in my bones, and I weary myself to hold it in but cannot." If one were now to open his heart and attune his ear to the original and ancient Hassidic melodies and hearken to the way they rise to the utmost heights and drop to the nethermost abyss; if one listens to the song of yearning which no words are capable of describing, and to the fall into painful despair, one would be able to sense on the one hand the eternal struggle against impediments and enemies seeking to thwart, and on the other hand, an expression of faith uplifting to the utmost heights of elation. When the soul was wrought up to this breaking point, shaken by the force of desire and fearful to give this desire expression, melody without words burst out from its depth, for there is no language that is more eloquent than the language of music. The songs expressive of such spiritual desire as those of Rabbi Israel Najarra, which had quenched the thirst of the yearners of the Kabbalistic generation, failed fully to satisfy the silent yearners of the generation of the fathers of Hassidism, and so the realm of melody spread among the people as it had never spread before or since, and it became a Hassidic heritage from generation to generation.

Only at those rare intervals when one of the Hassidic fathers clothed his song in words did he convey in these lower verbal rungs of melody something of the treasure of those wordless chants. Recall how the Habad Hassidim sang then, and continue to sing to this day, the Kabbalistic hymn: "B'nei Hehala." See what an outpouring in words there was on the part of that poet-Admur, Rabbi Aharon the Great, when he sang "Leyom shekulo Shabat." This hymn of praise continues to be sung by the remnants of his followers. One may hear it sung by the Karlin Hassidim at the *Shalosh Se'udot* in old Tiberias and in the *Shtiblach* of Meah Shearim in Jerusalem; *Ya, Achsif noam Shabbath* (O Lord, how much I yearn for the sweetness of the Sabbath). Recall how the Rebbe of Kalov sang in that mixture of Hungarian, Yiddish, and Hebrew:

> *Wald, Wald, wer aveggenummen,*
> *Well ich zu der Kalle kennen kummen.*

Essentially, however, this outpouring was not in need of words, for the word was likely to be a hindrance to expression. Only pure melody unencumbered by words or the semblance of words can give full expression to feelings and encourage and heal. Listen to the melodies ascribed to the Baal Shem Tov himself, to the melodies of the "old Admur" of Ladi and to the scores of other melodies of ancient origin and you will realize what I am trying to convey.

This spiritual conflict between longing and halting inhibitions is characteristic of the whole history of the desire for redemption of our exiled people. While still on the threshold of the messianic movements after the expulsion from Spain, the first nucleus of the legend-story about Yosef della Reina stands out in its stark somberness. Oh, how strong was his yearning and how menacing were his inhibitions and the brakes applied from within and without. Ever since, the shadow of that danger has not ceased to darken the light of feeling.

This has been an incessant and constant duel, an ever-present struggle in the soul of the nation. Hassidism which came into the world after the great and gruesome experiences of the "messianic days that did not materialize" was doomed to continence. It was decreed for it that the storm must rage silently within its soul and give no expression of its real feelings, like the Leviathan who is paralyzed by superior forces, a sort of "king held in the grip of enchantment."

The Baal Shem Tov gave a new motivation of the theory of the Messiah thereby changing the concept of the bringing of the Messiah. It was even said: Just as every Jew is possessed of a portion of Divinity, so there is within the soul of every Jew a portion of the soul of the Messiah. And he said: In order to bring the Messiah, every Jew must contribute his own portion of the Messiah within him. When every Jew prepares that Messianic portion within him that lies at the root of his soul, the whole structure of the Messiah will have been prepared and been made ready. The soul of the Redeemer dwells, therefore, deep within the souls of the nation and is inseparable from these. Everyone must bring his share of the Messiah and only then can the whole of the Messiah come.

This is by no means a condoning of nonredemption—there is nothing further removed from Hassidism than this—but rather a transposition of the center of gravity of the struggle over the bringing of the Messiah to a struggle within the soul of every individual.

This, too, is bound up with unfathomable effort. For everyone has Satan lurking within himself. In order to weaken man and to foil him and also in order to set up all the external forces against man so that he is unable to summon courage in order to withstand them, Satan is likely even to weaken within him the very desire to stand up against them.

The threatening symbol of this struggle is to be marked in all the efforts of Hassidism. Who of them did not endeavor to go to *Eretz-Israel* and against whom did not arise those stumbling blocks—internal and spiritual perhaps more than external—both imaginary and real, so as not to allow thought to be translated into action? In Hassidic terminology these stumbling blocks are known as "eclipses and disguises, restraints and inhibitions."

Legends told of ghosts risen from their graves in order to hold up and prevent the journey. All sorts of evil spirits joined hands in order not to allow the proposed *aliya* to be implemented. Supernatural forces strove against one another: and the hindering ones gained the upper hand.

The Baal Shem Tov himself decided to go to *Eretz-Israel*. His daughter Edel went with him. The initial letters of her name were interpreted א Esh ד Dat ל Lamo. This took place years after his revelation. His journey was accompanied by numerous miracles. He came as far as Constantinople and there could not summon strength to continue the journey. The fact that his brother-in-law, Reb Gershon of Kitov, joined his ranks was perhaps the first great victory of the believer from Tlust over the scholar from Brody. Nonetheless, and perhaps because of that, it was the latter who was chosen for the mission to *Eretz-Israel*. Apparently he had great ideas in mind, at any rate expectations of great things. This hope can still be heard from the *"Old Man"* of Tiberias. When he met the Baal Shem Tov's grandson, Rabbi Nahman of Bratzlav, who in many respects was the Baal Shem Tov's heir, and asked him, in an intimate conversation: "Surely, it is unlikely that the Baal Shem Tov's grandson should have come here with mediocre objectives, like all good Jews, only in order to live in the holy atmosphere of *Eretz-Israel;* most likely you had some supreme motives and a supreme mission in mind." Indeed, he went up to the Yeshiva Beth El, where he stayed in the company of Rabbi Haim ben Attar, the author of the "Or-Hahayim," who served as a master, and with the *Hida* (Rabbi Haim Yosef David Azulai) as associate. Only this year, when the remains of the latter were transferred to Israel, the story was revealed of how *Hida* and his two companions endeavored to bring down the Messiah, and of all that happened to them and how, as a result, he was doomed to remain for twenty-five years in foreign climes, in Livorno. Again the hindering forces had the upper hand.

Once again this is a new recital of the old recurring motif of Rabbi Yosef della Reina.

Between one victory and another, Rabbi Nahman of Horodenka comes to settle in *Eretz-Israel* and Reb Mendel of Premyslan, each man and his own great and lofty ideas, and there comes Reb Menahem Mendel of Vitebsk, the senior associate of the old Admur of Ladi, author of *Pri Haarez*, there comes Reb Abraham of Kalisk and with them that fiery creature, Reb Israel of Polotsk. A permanent institution for the *aliya* of Hassidim to *Eretz-Israel* is set up with emissaries and committees. Reb Manahem Mendel say: "We are here and you are there." In other words he and his disciples are in *Eretz-Israel* while the old Admur and his followers are in the *Golah* and together they will be able to carry through the settlement of the Hassidim—for great things, for the opening of the gates of heaven, for the drawing near of redemption.

One knows of that stirring story of Reb Abraham, the associate of the author of the *Tanya*, and that holy Kabbalist called the "Angel" by Hassidim. When he was still young he occupied the position of preacher at Fastov, and he decided to go to *Eretz-Israel*. From heaven, however, his intentions were foiled and he died there at an early age. The story is told of Reb Israel of Polotsk who came to *Eretz-Israel*— also after numerous vicissitudes. He succeeded in arriving, together with his master and associate, but was sent back in order to summon financial aid for *Eretz-Israel* and to bring up more Hassidim. But on his return journey to *Eretz-Israel* he called again at Fastov where he made a pilgrimage to the grave of the "Angel," but there met his death, and there was buried. There is a third story of how Reb Shneur Zalman, author of the *Tanya*, a man of deep reason, of great mind and broadness of outlook, decided to go to *Eretz-Israel*. He, too, passed by Fastov but, bearing in mind what had happened to his associate, Reb Abraham, and to his disciple, Reb Israel, the story goes that he commanded his coachman "to beat the horses into a trot," for who knows what might happen also to him. Apparently, it was a place of danger. Perhaps he, too, might be held up. He did pass unscathed but did not reach *Eretz-Israel*. In other places stumbling blocks arose to prevent him from reaching his goal.

Even Reb Nahman of Bratzlav, the man who perhaps more than anyone else could fight his internal inclinations, a man of overflowing spirituality, an ascetic saint who was wholly a torch of love and belief, knew beforehand what pangs the impediments would bring on, so he said: "Whoever wishes to have the merit of arriving in *Eretz-Israel*, which is the acme of holiness to which a Jew can aspire, . . . must know that very many impediments are strewn in his path and that it is impossible to emerge victorious from this war except by hallowed daring and great perseverance. By exerting daring and perseverance to arrive in *Eretz-Israel* and by giving no heed to the many preventive forces in his way, one is granted victory in this war in order to be able truly to arrive in *Eretz-Israel*. The thing is bound up with many struggles both internal and external. The main sufferings (by which *Eretz-Israel* is achieved) are the preventive forces that must be shattered before one arrives. The great *Zaddikim* experienced numerous hardships on their way to *Eretz-Israel*. Close to our own time there were Reb Naftali Katz (author of *Semichut Hahamin*) and the Baal Shem Tov, of blessed memory, who were prevented by force of circumstances from coming to *Eretz-Israel*.

"There are people who imagine that they are desirous of going to *Eretz-Israel* and yearn deeply to go there, but are prepared to undertake the journey only in comfortable circumstances, but not under stressful conditions. This is not a true desire, because whoever wishes truly and sincerely to go to *Eretz-Israel* must go there on foot."

And he adds; "Whoever wishes to be a Jew, that is to ascend from one degree to a higher one, cannot achieve that purpose except by *Eretz-Israel,* that is *Eretz-Israel* in all its simplicity—'mit die heiser und die stiber' " (over its houses and dwellings).

He also composed a special prayer: "Merciful and compassionate God, make me worthy in Thy great mercy that both I and the whole House of Israel may be filled with yearning and true desire to go to *Eretz-Israel,* until I be granted through Thy great mercy and loving-kindness to put that desire into practice. It is my will and desire to arise and to travel thither and to arrive in *Eretz-Israel* in peace and with utmost speed and that I, too, may be granted to hop and to prance there."

Of himself he said shortly before his departure, "I know that I will be beset by impediments and difficulties without end and without measure, but so long as my soul is within me and there is a breath of life in my nostrils, I am fully prepared to suffer and to bear with everything to the point of self-sacrifice, that I may go to *Eretz-Israel.*"

He undertook the journey and has left us a travelogue which is a lyrical document of adventure and suffering, a supreme Odyssey, expressive of the struggle against impediments that underlies the whole thirst for redemption of Hassidism. It contains everything: a description of storms at sea, of the French war, of the shattering of the ship against the breakers, a losing of the way, adventures with Arab marauders, danger to life, illness, false accusations, exile, earthquakes, floods, dangers unending and innumerable. His disciple concludes the tale by saying, "What we have related—is like a drop in the ocean of the sufferings and adventures, dangers and fears that befell our master of blessed memory, on his journey to *Eretz-Israel.* . . ."

This wondrous and awe-inspiring narrative expresses that singular desire for *aliya* of the Hassidim, the whole of which is a call for desire and faith to overcome the impediments on the way. If a Jewish artist has not yet arisen to write the music of this lofty and ethereal "journey," surely it is that our poetic muse is still latent within us.

Just as we have been able to explain the spring of melody in Hassidism as stemming from the tension of the messianic struggle, so I believe one must seek and find here the core of that optimism so characteristic of Hassidic mentality. It drew its vitality from the certainty that the world is heading toward accomplishment and redemption. Despite everything we are drawing nearer day by day to the final beatific goal.

Allow me to mention what is related of the "Seer" of Lublin. He had a special clock on the wall and the Hassidim were wont to say that the clock belonging to the Seer of Lublin had a chime that was different from the chime of any other clock. This clock found its way from place to place until it arrived at an inn where one of the leaders of the Hassidim recognized it by its chime. On being asked how he was able to recognize it, the answer that he gave explains the whole theory I am trying to explain to you. He said: "With other people whenever the clock chimes, a feeling of melancholy descends, for it announces that we are one hour nearer death, that life passes quickly and that we are one hour nearer the end. But the clock of the Seer of Lublin calls out hour by hour: Look, the journey is shorter; O how happy are we that we have drawn nearer by one hour to the coming of the Messiah." Belief that we are heading toward redemption is strong and unshakable. With such a clock on the wall it is easier to bear the sufferings of life. For that reason joy fills the recesses of the soul, and for that reason, too, there is a love for the whole House of Israel, since redemption is close at hand for every individual Jew and it is only with all Jews together that one can advance toward the Messiah. The Baal Shem Tov said that every individual Jew has his own share in the Messiah. Reb Nahman added: Every individual Jew has his own personal share in *Eretz-Israel*. There is a part of *Eretz-Israel* in the soul of every Jew. A Jew who comes to *Eretz-Israel* comes, as it were, to that part of the Divinity that lies deep within him and redeems his own share in *Eretz-Israel*. If the whole House of Israel were to come to *Eretz-Israel*, then the whole of *Eretz-Israel* would be redeemed.

Despite these struggles that enveloped the Hassidic desire and yearning for redemption and for *aliya*, a yearning that was damped and cowed, replete with horrors and held up by impediments, it resulted nonetheless also in deeds of prayer and hope, even in actual immigration, settlement, and upbuilding. Even if one's steps are fettered, they nonetheless do not cease. The Old Admur himself was a Gabbai and the Nassi of an *Eretz-Israel* Fund. The accepted and hallowed title Nassi ("president") that is current among the Habad Admurim, had its origin in the fact that they were "Presidents of the *Eretz-Israel* Fund." Even as Rabbi Yosef Delattes wrote in the year 5318 of the appearance of the Zohar, that it was published only for the purpose of bringing near the redemption, so Reb Zusya of Anopol announced in the year 5557 when the Tanya was first published, that with the Tanya in hand, the Jews will advance towards the Messiah.

When Tiberias served as the metropolis of Hassidism, emissaries were sent out every year to the Hassidim of Russia and Lithuania, Poland and Zamut in order to encourage and fire their hearts and raise regular contributions. No one wielded greater influence on Hassidic audiences than those who were able to "repeat" the sayings and teachings of the Rebbe and those emissaries who collected the regular contributions for *Eretz-Israel*.

There was not one Hassidic dynasty in the Diaspora that failed to establish a stronghold in *Eretz-Israel,* in Tiberias or Jerusalem, Hebron or Safad. There were as many *stieblech* as there were Zaddikim and as many emissaries as there were *stieblech*.

When the Habad *aliya* began and grew, it transformed Hebron into the metropolis of all the ramifications of the Habad movement. Impediments, however, did not cease. The numerous splits and constant disruptions were seen as the machinations of Satan, as the outcome of the secret and covert hand aiming at thwarting and holding the movement in check. Reb Menahem Mendel of Vitebsk, the father of the Hassidic settlement in *Eretz-Israel,* said at the time, "*Eretz-Israel* is the *Shechina* itself." The Old Admur wrote in "Igereth Hakodesh" (Tanya, Chapter 15): "This love for the Holy Land must burn like living coals, deep in the heart of a man, as though this very day, the Holy One, blessed be He, had bestowed a benign spirit upon it. From year to year the light that is constantly renewed and increased, rises ever upwards in supreme holiness."

In the history of the Hassidic *aliya* we also learn of the duty of spiritual "hachshara" for *aliya* and of the pangs of absorption in the country. The words then uttered apply also to future generations. Thus Reb Abraham of Kalisk wrote in his epistle: "This I would set my heart to answer . . . unto all those who ask for advice in their desire to settle in the Holy Land. Everyone arriving to the land of Israel must experience, day in, day out, numerous vicissitudes, tribulations, and metamorphoses, time and time again, until he is able to find his feet there . . . and comes to love its ruins and to enjoy a dry morsel of bread among them. It is not the fleet of foot that always arrive. It is not a matter of a day or two days, nor of a month or a year, for many years must pass until he becomes fully absorbed and integrated in the life of the country . . . even as it is written: 'Every man must experience a rebirth there.' In other words, he who comes to settle in the Holy Land must pass through a new period of conception and birth and suckling and swaddling clothes, just like the newborn babe who sees the country face to face and is spiritually bound up with it.

". . . He who comes . . . and brings with him his customs and habits . . . is thrown actually off his mind and is tossed about like a ship in a stormy sea and troubles others with his personal affairs . . . so far that he finds fault with the land, until the Holy One, blessed be He, turns His countenance upon him and so he finds rest and calmness. But this thing has no limits, nor is it bound by time, for it is found by everyone according to his deeds and the root of his soul. . . . Therefore everyone must prepare himself for everything that has been said here and must put himself to the test in order to see whether he has the strength to withstand all this. . . . Only then can he set out securely . . . and will rest secure and in tranquillity."

The son of the disciple of the Baal Shem Tov, Reb Moshe Shoham, writes of the difference between he who comes to *Eretz-Israel* for its own sake and he who flees to *Eretz-Israel* because he must leave his country of residence. His words are piercing in their significance and biting in style: "It is written, 'and Abraham went . . . and they set out to go to the land of Canaan.' Therefore we read, 'and they came to the land of Canaan. . . .'" On the other hand of Terah it is written: 'And they set out with them from Ur of the Chaldees in order to go to the land of Canaan.' In other words, Terah did not go to Canaan for its own sake, but only because he had set out from Ur of the Chaldees. That is why we read: 'And Terah died at Haran.' "

Yet things did not reach a state of concerted effort on the part of the Hassidim and of those engaged in the work of settlement including the non-Hassidic Kollelim, and others. Hassidic dissension in all spheres contributed its share and even the Hassidim among themselves failed to arrive at concerted and *united* effort. Each Hassidic dynasty established a niche of its own in *Eretz-Israel* and a fund of its own in its particular region in the Diaspora for the maintenance of its own *stiebel* and of its own settlement. At the inception of the split that set in at the time of the Old Admur, there came to the assistance of the Reb Abraham of Kalisk in Tiberias Reb Mordecai of Lachowitz, and it is that split that led the Kollelim of Karlin and Stolin, Slonim, and finally Koidanov to branch out. When Habad transferred its metropolis from Tiberias to Hebron, establishing their Quarter there and concentrating rich supporters and veteran settlers around it, activity for Habad interests in *Eretz-Israel* became the main concern of every Habadist *stiebel* in the Diaspora.

The House of Rizin branched out into the courts of its Admurim, every son and grandson of that family regarded it as a holy duty to establish a *stiebel* of his own in Tiberias. Thus there cropped up nooks and niches of Vishnitz, Bohush, Otinia, Boyan, and great things were done by the Kollel of Lvov.

It may now be said that in the nineteenth century things reached such a head that the whole of the Ashkenasi *Yishuv* of Tiberias, the whole *Yishuv* in Safad, half the Ashkenasi *Yishuv* in Jerusalem, as well as the whole of the Ashkenasi *Yishuv* of Hebron rested on the shoulders of the Hassidic movement, split up, as it was, into its various trends, dynasties, and courts.

At that time there were to be found among all the leaders and workers of the various Kollelim in every land of the Diaspora no force so active in the field of financial aid for *Eretz-Israel* and of bringing over people for settlement in *Eretz-Israel* as the Hassidic movement, nor was there to be found in the Hassidic movement itself any special branch, old or new, that failed to establish a stronghold of its own in the Holy Land and to devote its best forces and workers for that purpose. But every activity was carried on separately, each Hassid rallying around his own particular banner, each Admur around his own particular *stiebel*.

When the arch opponent of Hassidism raised its head and the *Haskalah* spread far and wide, the rift between Hassidim and the Maskilim growing ever deeper and ever wider, activity for *Eretz-Israel* did not cease among the Hassidim, although their withdrawal from concerted effort with other builders of *Eretz-Israel* became more pronounced. When the various branches of the Haskalah joined hands with the first workers for *Eretz-Israel* settlement, the apprehensions and the wariness of the Hassidim increased sevenfold and their attitude became fixed and established, not only for that generation but also for their sons and grandsons after them.

All the "eclipses and disguises, restraints and inhibitions" that we have traced so far received a new touch and a new color from the stress of the times. When the time came for the Hibbat Zion movement to be born and afterwards when political Zionism came to take its place, organized Hassidism already stood at the other end of the arena, ready to take up the challenge. Together with its extreme "Mitnagdic" rival, it joined hands against this new force which was suspect both of speeding up the end, and of Haskalah tendencies. As we are all aware, the struggle was hard and bitter. A few daring individuals did, it is true, stretch out a helping hand and give us their blessing, but organized Hassidism and its leadership opposed the movement.

We are aware of the details of this struggle. In summing up, however, I should like to say that "as the hart panteth after the water brooks" so the Hassidic soul throughout the generations panted for redemption and for *Eretz-Israel*. Yet only a trickle of Hassidic immigrants flowed all the time. They came singly, fighting hard against the impediments and the hindrances and restraints. But that trickle never ceased, like the waters of Shiloh that flow slowly and do not cease, bringing comfort and sustenance to the *Yishuv* in *Eretz-Israel* and to the soul of the nation throughout its dispersion. Every time something great took place in *Eretz-Israel,* or when some great wave of immigration arrived to take up the work of upbuilding, or when some new enterprise was set on foot, daring spirits in Hassidism broke their fetters and overcame the traditional opposition and inhibition. Surely all of us had suffered and had felt pangs of frustration when our Hassidic teachers and our ancestors were against us, when we broke away to come to *Eretz-Israel.* But every time something was created and arose there, some precious chord was plucked somewhere in the deep recesses of Hassidism, silently and without undue formality, and answered our call. Somewhere someone arose to take hold of the tendrils of the mighty plant that had there sprouted. The facts are numerous. I shall only recall a story which I regard as essentially fatalistic in nature.

Literature dealing with the history of Hassidism has devoted far too little attention to that singular figure of the Admur, Reb Shmuel, the son of the *Zemah Zedek,* a dominant figure in the ranks of the presidents of the Habad movement. It is of him that Hassidic tradition related that when he was a mere lad, circles closely connected with the Rabbi's court computed the following year to be the year of the beatific "end." Reb Shmuel looked forward eagerly to the impending wonders of the promised year. When the year drew to a close and the miraculous events failed to take place, he came to his father, Reb Menahem Mendel, and asked, "What about the 'end' that had been hinted at?" His father wished to encourage him and to console him and said: "It is possible to square the discrepancy. Surely the coming of the Messiah is a revelation of the internal content of the Torah and this year has seen the publication of the book *Likkutei Torah* of the Old Admur. . . ." The young Shmuel answered rather heatedly, "But what we really want is the coming of the Messiah in concrete form and to our own world of reality."

In regard to his sharp criticism of all those among the leaders of the Diaspora who remain cold and unmoved by the call of *Eretz-Israel,* we have the following saying which has remained ingrained in the memory of veteran Hassidim and which is ascribed to Reb Shmuel: "Does the atmosphere of *Eretz-Israel* really bring on wisdom? At any rate it is clear, that the atmosphere of the Diaspora makes one foolish."

Most characteristic is the story published by the late Admur Reb Yosef Yitzhak Shneerson in his biography of his grandfather, Reb Shmuel.

In the year 5641 (which was a year of excesses against Jews) the Rebbe, Reb Shmuel, said: "If I had been listened to, a lot of Jewish blood would have been spared . . . I wanted to tell them (the representatives of the Government) that unless they changed their attitude to the Jews, I intended to set out for *Eretz-Israel* taking with me a 100,000 families. And I would have carried my plans through. But then there was the affair of the Bilu (*Bnei Yisrael lekhu ven-elkha*) and I did not want to lend them authority." He continued: "If there had been also an ending of that verse: ('Be'or Adonai') 'in the light of God' I, too, would have joined them."

With every additional wave a new echo was called forth. After the Balfour Declaration, the Rabbi of Yablona came to Palestine to settle with his Hassidim. With the third *aliya,* there came to settle at Kfar Pines Reb Yeshayahu of Grodzisk. Before him had come the Zaddik of Drohobicz who erected the "Yegiah Kapayim" Quarter in Jerusalem. Some few individuals joined the arrivals, but the leaders were still frightened off by the hindering forces. When the late Reb Shlomo Aaronson, Rabbi of Kiev, a stalwart Habad Hassid, who was later to become the Rabbi of Tel Aviv, asked the Admur, Reb Shalom Dov Ber, to explain his opposition to the movement, he said, "Every motor vehicle is in need of a brake and we are the brake." That sharp-witted Rabbi and Hassid retorted, "A brake is undoubtedly an important part of every car, but a car is motivated by a motor and not by a brake, and we are enjoined to go on."

When the dividing mountain towered very high, there were always individuals possessed of a burning soul to climb to the top, but they remained lonely and unsupported.

Already in the days of the Hibbat Zion movement the Admur of Pilov tried to organize a settlement of 1,000 Hassidic families—the Association of the Thousand—in face of the opposition of the Admurim of his generation, but his plan did not come off.

Touching is the short exchange of letters, at present preserved in the Archives of the Zionist Movement, between that simple-hearted Hassid and first historian of the Hassidic Movement, Dr. Aron Markus, and the father and originator of the Zionist Movement, Dr. Theodor Herzl. As is well known, Herzl maintained contacts with the Admur of Tchortkov who had sent him his blessing, and on whom Herzl pinned great hopes. Dr. Markus had suggested that scores of Admurim who, he claimed, held sway over 3,000,000 Hassidim, be convened and he promised to bring all of them under the wings of Zionism. The plan did not come off, for just as the Rebbe Reb Shmuel had hesitated to join the Bilu movement, because of its "secular" leadership, so Herzl in the early days of the Zionist movement was hesitant of seeking Hassidic cooperation because of their "clericalism."

The dividing mountain that rose high, continued to tower.

When it towered ominously, something strange occurred. Those who openly manifested their Hassidism, God-fearing and observant Jews, stood aloof, became "Hassidim in secret." The offspring of the Hassidim, those in whose veins there flowed the blood of Hassidism and in whose soul Hassidic traditions held sway, hurled themselves body and soul, without any hindrance and without impediment, into the Zionist movement. The splendor of their yearning continued to lend fervor to the Halutzic movement and to the Labor movement, to the work of settlement and defense, to literature and to the movement of revival in *Eretz-Israel* and in the Diaspora. Nameless and label-less, the Hassidic heritage surged forward in order to fulfill its mission and brought vitality and song to the Zionist movement and to the Halutzic movement within it.

Perhaps I may be permitted to conclude my remarks with some personal reminiscences which may possibly hint at the trend of development.

The unsurpassed devotion of the late Admur of Lubavitch, Rabbi Yosef Yitzhak Shneerson, who was the father of the Jewish religious underground, beset by such great suffering and by such deep mani-festations of loyalty in Russia, is too well known to need recounting. One also knows how greatly he yearned for the speedy redemption of the Jewish people immediately after the European holocaust. To this day Habad Hassidim are wont to make use of his enthusiastic New Year greeting: "For immediate redemption." I recall that day in 1948 when I was at Lake Success as a member of the Political Com-mittee sent from Palestine to consult with the Jewish Agency delega-tion to the United Nations. It was the morning before the historic vote that the telephone rang in my room in the hotel. The man at the other end of the line was Rabbi Gur Aryeh, son-in-law of the late Rebbe, Reb Yosef Yitzhak and brother-in-law of the present Rebbe in New York. The Rebbe was dangerously ill. He said: "The Rebbe wants to know what is happening at the Committee." I was touched on hearing that question addressed to me. The state of affairs at that particular moment was difficult in the extreme. Our people were glued to their telephones in their endeavors to canvass support during the fateful vote, and it was doubtful whether we should be able to muster a majority. I said, "Please inform the Rebbe that we are badly in need of help." Rabbi Gur Aryeh transmitted the message to the Admur and then returned to say: "The Rebbe wishes me to inform you that the Holy One, blessed be He, will help." He added: "The Rebbe asks you to call on him the day after the vote."

When I presented myself on the day following the U.N. decision we had a long conversation about the *aliya* of the remnants of the Russian Hassidim to *Eretz-Israel* and the establishment of a Habad village in Israel. When, in the course of our talk, I complained bitterly about our persecution at the hands of the Hassidic leaders before we had set out for *Eretz-Israel*, the late Rebbe told me plainly in the presence of his son-in-law: "Then, no; now, yes!" Acting upon his decisive change in outlook, he cabled to Paris that his Hassidim from Russia should not emigrate to Canada, as they had originally planned, but should go to *Eretz-Israel*. So the idea of Hassidic village of Kfar Habad was implemented.

In other words, the impediments and hindrances began to scatter and the halting forces—the "brakes'"—were transformed into a motive power.

The yearning that had been pent up throughout the centuries at last began to surge forth in mighty waves to the desired goal. Those who in the days of sorrow and depression had, with all the fire in their hearts, insisted on reciting day and night in every *kaddish* prayer: "*Veyatzmach purkanei vikarev meshichei*" ("may there be a sprouting of our liberation and bring near the coming of the Messiah"), will, now that the liberation has begun to sprout, walk shoulder to shoulder with the toilers and builders so as to bring near the hoped-for day.

Monarchy

DANIEL JEREMY SILVER

*

JUDAISM NEVER REFINED political theory as a dogmatic discipline; however, until late in the Middle Ages monarchic idiom permeated political discussion. "The sceptre shall not depart from Judah" (Genesis 49:10), so ran the cherished promise.

Tradition held the appointment of a sovereign as one of the commands imposed upon the children of Israel on their entry into the Promised Land (Sanhedrin 20b). The practice of cataloguing all Torah Law, whether current or in abeyance, led to a continuing relisting of the Deuteronomic stipulation, "Thou shalt in any wise set him king over thee" (Deuteronomy 17:15). Messianic hopes blazed with the vision of a reestablished autonomous Israel under a royal descendant of the House of David. "And there shall come forth a shoot out of the stock of Jesse" (Isaiah 11:1). To establish this dream it was assumed that God's covenant with the Davidic house was irrevocable: "If you can break My covenant with the day, and My covenant with the night, So that there should not be day or night in their season; Then may also My covenant be broken with David My servant, that he should not have a son to reign upon his throne" (Jeremiah 33:20-21). Caught up in the drama of the king-messiah, and duty bound to the text of the Deuteronomic law and to the context of pre-exilic history many an apologete attempted a philosophic rationale of monarchic forms. Typically, Aaron ha Levi (13 c.) wrote in his *Sefer Ha Hinuch:* "No settlement can be established unless an individual is made head whose power and authority will be obeyed. This is made necessary because men's opinions vary. No group can ever agree on any single program. Lacking some sovereign authority men would frustrate their every purpose. In order that these may succeed and be effective a society must accept the opinion of one man whether it be good or bad. Sometimes a group will find great profit in the sovereign's counsel, at other times the opposite. In any case authority is better than division of opinion, for the latter makes frustration and futility inevitable" (Comm. #71). Isaac Abarbanel (15-16 c.) was among the first, if not the first, to abandon the piety of monarchic idiom. In his *Commentary to Deuteronomy* he asked rhetorically, "Is the king essential to the state or can it exist without him?" and answered categorically, "Common sense dictates that one man in the position of a monarch is more liable to be wrong than many people acting together." Furthermore, "If the king is just it is still better to have a government of many just men" (*Comm.* to Deuteronomy 17:14, I Samuel 8:4).

Were Abarbanel's views *sui generis* or heretic? Not at all; among the rabbis monarchy (as an assumption of Jewish political life) was more a delightful end-of-days piety than a determined theological principle. The king of rabbinic political theory was in effect not a king at all. Law allowed him personal privilege but little power. A summary statement on the sovereign's authority is found in Mishnah Sanhedrin. The royal office is here dismissed in four brief paragraphs. The entire discussion is ancillary to the more detailed and extensive statement on the judiciary, into which it was subsumed. No one may ride the king's horse, sit on his throne, compel him to act as a litigant or witness in court, marry his widow, view him while he is having his hair cut, and so forth. The king enjoys certain claims over the spoils of battle. He is enjoined to lead the troops in war. He has broad rights of eminent domain for his armies, but he may not declare war. This authority is vested with the High Court of Seventy-One. There is no indication of any legislative authority.

In the Talmud we find individuals who questioned whether Deuteronomy 17:15 did in fact sanctify the throne. Basing themselves on I Samuel 8, both R. Nehorai and R. Judah read this text as a statute of limitations set down against the establishment by the people (*sic*) of sovereign authority not as a divine ordering of the monarchist position (Sanhedrin 20b). Stray antimonarchist theories can also be found in the literature: "God hath given unto all as heritage—the kingdom, the priesthood, and the sanctuary" (II Maccabees 2:17), and also the formula: "All Israel are the sons of kings" (Sabbath 67a). The king of rabbinic theory emerges largely as an idyllic figure who personifies in his character the attitude of the Torah Law and who thus performs a necessary role of social reordering in the eschatological drama.

The rabbinic treatment of monarchy was an ambivalent one, largely because the Biblical source was itself inconsistent. The anointing of Saul as the first king was seen by Biblical historians as a political change of critical significance. Two versions of the event, both historically suspect, were retained, one which sees the king as divinely chosen (I Samuel 9–10:24) while the other views the popular outcry for a king as evidence of a lack of faith in God. "They have rejected Me, that I should not be king over them" (I Samuel 8:1–22, 10:17–24). Similarly, though Deuteronomy 17:14 ff. states unequivocally, "One from among thy brethren shalt thou set king over thee" (v. 15), the context is one of resigned acceptance to circumstance. "When thou art come into the land which the Lord thy God giveth thee, and shalt possess it, and shalt dwell therein; and shalt say: 'I will set a king over me, like all the nations that are round about me'" (v. 14). The text dilates not on royal prerogatives but on what the king may not do: conflate his army, exaggerate his harem, overtax the populace, and so on (v. 16 ff.). The most generous interpretation which can be made sees this document as a *mishpat hamelucha*, a Biblical Magna Carta of national rights vis à vis the king, sealed and effected by an act of royal submission to the entirety of Torah Law. "And it shall be, when he sitteth upon the throne of his kingdom, that he shall write him a copy of this law in a book, out of that which is before the priests the Levites. And it shall be with him, and he shall read therein all the days of his life; that he may learn to fear the Lord his God, to keep all the words of this law and these statutes, to do them; that his heart be not lifted up above his brethren, and that he turn not aside from the commandment to the right hand or to the left; to the end that he may prolong his days in his kingdom, he and his children in the midst of Israel" (vv. 18–20).

A case can be made—and many have done so—for a preexilic theology which not only authorizes monarchy but makes the royal person sacrosanct. Nathan's prophecy seems on this point quite explicit: "Now therefore thus shalt thou say unto My servant David: Thus saith the Lord of hosts: I took thee from the sheepcote, from following the sheep, that thou shouldest be prince over My people, over Israel. And I have been with thee whithersoever thou didst go, and have cut off all thine enemies from before thee; and I will make thee a great name, like unto the name of the great ones that are in the earth. And I will appoint a place for My people Israel, and will plant them, that they may dwell in their own place and be disquieted no more; neither shall the children of wickedness afflict them any more, as at the first, even from the day that I commanded judges to be over My people Israel; and I will cause thee to rest from all thine enemies. Moreover the Lord telleth thee that the Lord will make thee a house. When thy days are fulfilled, and thou shalt sleep with thy fathers, I will set up thy seed after thee, that shall proceed out of thy body, and I will establish his kingdom. He shall build a house for

My name, and I will establish the throne of his kingdom for ever. I will be to him for a father, and he shall be to Me for a son; if he commit iniquity, I will chasten him with the rod of men, and with the stripes of the children of men; but My mercy shall not depart from him, as I took it from Saul, whom I put away before thee. And thy house and thy kingdom shall be made sure for ever before thee; thy throne shall be established for ever" (II Samuel 7:8–16). Psalm 72 clearly echoes this spirit. The impression gained from these sources is that God willed into being, supported, and will perpetuate the monarchy. Supporters of this evaluation add that the prophets who complained against so many other fallings away from earlier, more pristine practices (with but one exception, Hosea) do not hold the institution of monarchy suspect per se, however much they delight to chronicle the sins of the present incumbent. Furthermore, the dream of return and rebuilding is heavily drenched with the hope for a reestablished royal authority (Amos 9:1 ff., Jeremiah 23:5, Isaiah 11:1 ff., Ezekiel 45:1 ff.); and the stuff of this dream of reestablishment became the substance of the later vision of the royal messiah.

Some modern scholars go further and find in various crannies of the Bible allusions to a theology involving the sacred character of the king's person, his divine adoption upon coronation, his crucial role in cultic practice, and even a glimpse of the king as the god incarnate. Such a view has no support in the historical or legal material, but relies heavily on a literal interpretation of some scattered and not always pertinent phrases such as that in Psalm 2, "The Lord said unto me: 'Thou art My son. This day I have begotten thee'" (v. 7) and in Psalm 110, " 'Thou art a priest forever after the manner of Melchizedek' " (v. 4) or again, from I Samuel 10, "And the spirit of the Lord will come mightily upon thee, and thou shalt prophesy with them, and shalt be turned into another man" (v. 6). Such exegesis is sophisticated, but neglects the metaphoric force of language. Further, it insists on the one fact which cannot be granted in reviewing Hebrew history; that it is best studied as an ordinary phenomenon of Near Eastern cultural history and not with a view to its own uniqueness. One has only to recall the prophetic finger-pointing at royal guilt and the character of the historical material which amply chronicled the private sins and foibles of the greatest of the kings to recognize that in Israel the king was at most a personage, never a personification.

Historically, what is certain is that after several centuries of loose tribal confederation monarchy became established, that this monarchy lasted until the Assyrian and Babylonian exiles respectively, and that there was little popular and no religious enthusiasm for its reestablishment after the exile. While monarchy was in effect there were no built-in institutional checks save the occasional rebelliousness of "all Israel" and a continuing tradition of communal self-government. The want of an effective institutional check and balance system such as we enjoy today must not be taken to imply a religious justification of any conceit of royal power. The historical books do not contain a single instance wherein the king established fundamental law by fiat, nor do they contain a single commendation of unfettered power. Royal authority implies always a covenant between God and the king, a covenant by whose moral terms the king must abide to be assured of God's continuing favor. Samuel quickly pulled the rug from under Saul when he overstepped these bounds. Prophet after prophet hammered the theme of royal submission to the Torah. There is even some indication of a written constitution of stipulated power: "Then Samuel told to the people the terms of authority (*mishpat hamelucha*) and wrote it in a book and placed it before the Lord" (I Samuel 10:25 [author's translation]).

The kings held effective power in the fields of military activity, foreign relations, and taxation. They were ceremoniously enthroned. All had dynastic expectations. They had appointive control of the chapel clergy, hired a personal bodyguard, managed royal monopolies and royal lands, controlled a household including senior state advisors, the harem, and servants. Some may indeed have pretended to other glories more common among neighboring despots. Yet it is clear that even those most friendly to the monarchic principle insisted the king was under the Law and not a law unto himself. The Judean editors of the Book of Kings did not whitewash the Davidic heirs. Nathan was a royalist, yet he pointedly levels charges against David (II Samuel 12). From Nathan's day at the beginning of the monarchic period to Jeremiah's at the end the spokesmen of God made it unmistakably clear that the king's powers were in no way absolute.

"*Woe unto him that buildeth his house by unrighteousness,*
  And his chambers by injustice;
  That useth his neighbour's service without wages,
  And giveth him not his hire;
  That saith: 'I will build me a wide house
  And spacious chambers,'
  And cutteth him out windows,
  And it is ceiled with cedar, and painted with vermilion.

Shalt thou reign, because thou strivest to excel in cedar?
Did not thy father eat and drink, and do justice and righteousness?
Then it was well with him.
He judged the cause of the poor and needy;
Then it was well.
Is not this to know Me? saith the Lord.
But thine eyes and thy heart
Are not but for thy covetousness,
And for shedding innocent blood,
And for oppression, and for violence, to do it.

Therefore thus saith the Lord concerning Jehoiakim the son of Josiah, son of Judah:

They shall not lament for him:
'Ah my brother!' or: 'Ah sister!'
They shall not lament for him:
'Ah lord!' or: 'Ah his glory!'
He shall be buried with the burial of an ass,
Drawn and cast forth beyond the gates of Jerusalem."

(Jeremiah 22:13–19).

If one must broaden this into a theology, the theory seems to have been that God's support of the throne—His covenant with the king—was a contingent one, dependent upon the quality of that worthy's person. "And Samuel said unto Saul: 'I will not return with thee; for thou hast rejected the word of the Lord, and the Lord hath rejected thee from being king over Israel.' " (I Samuel 15:26). David is made to repeat this divine admonition to Solomon: "If thy children take heed to their way, to walk before Me in truth with all their heart and with all their soul, there shall not fail thee . . . a man on the throne of Israel" (I Kings 2:4). The spirit of these admonitions never changed, thus Jeremiah: "Hear the word of the Lord, O king of Judah, that sittest upon the throne of David, thou, and thy servants, and thy people that enter in by these gates. Thus saith the Lord: Execute ye justice and righteousness, and deliver the spoiled out of the hand of the oppressor; and do no wrong, do no violence, to the stranger, the fatherless, nor the widow, neither shed innocent blood in this place. For if ye do this thing indeed, then shall there enter in by the gates of this house kings sitting upon the throne of David, riding in chariots and on horses, he, and his servants, and his people. But if ye will not hear these words, I swear by Myself, saith the Lord, that this house shall become a desolation" (Jeremiah 22:2 ff.). To justify a message of confirmation and hope some of the later prophets mitigated the pristine polarity of this doctrine and made God's withdrawal of His backing less ultimate; but this was soothing balm, not basic teaching.

Given these facts, one is tempted to make the following reconstruction: monarchy was a latecomer on the Hebrew scene; tribal autonomy was tenaciously held during three centuries of Palestinian life, lived entirely among petty nations and city-states where the concept of kingship or tyranny was well established. Monarchy was not universally welcomed. It came into being under the duress of external political pressure. I Samuel 8, the rejection by Gideon of the proffered throne (Judges 8:22 ff.), Jotham's mocking parable of the bramble in derision of Abimelech's ambitions may all be late (Judges 9:6 ff.), but they certainly reflect the spirit of the period of changeover. Judgeship, that is, occasional federation under an acclaimed general with a limited brevet, went as far as the tribes would trust human authority. Such distrust was elemental with the ancient Hebrews. Judge after judge set down his commission without pretense to dynasty. Blood played no part in the selection of the judge. They came from the most ordinary families in Israel. One is even mentioned to have been the son of a harlot (Judges 11:1).

"In those days there was no king in Israel" (Judges 17:6). Monarchy was never projected back beyond Saul. Abraham lived among kings, yet none of the Patriarchs held that title. Moses had power which came close to being absolute, but never any pretense to title. His authority was charismatic. He established no dynasty. Joshua held military, but never legislative, power. He established no dynasty even in his own tribe. He needed the consent of the several tribes to his strategy (Joshua 7). He assumed his lands not by aggrandizement but by the decision of the tribal assembly (Joshua 9:49 f). His commission expired, and with the end of the emergency it was returned to the elders (Joshua 24:31 f.).

How came kingship, then, into being? The traditional explanation has been that under the pressure of external attack, especially after the success of the Philistine invasion, centralized military and economic authority became imperative. This is certainly the explanation of I Samuel 8.

One may well ask where lay the power which needed to be organized if the tribes west of the Jordan suffered Philistine domination. Guerrilla bands and city plotters seldom inaugurate exotic political forms. The suggestion intrudes that there is a parallel between Saul's Israel and De Gaulle's France. Without any actual grant of power, during the Nazi occupation General De Gaulle came to personify the hope of the French people. A past hero and accurate prophet of events, a prostrate France invested its hopes in him. He became its *de facto* head. It would seem that Saul also fell into grace. He was called to be a judge, the plowman summoned to the defense of the confederation, in this case against the Ammonite (I Samuel 11). He had success east of the Jordan. He was given lands there. In the meantime the Philistine advance gained momentum. The once chosen Saul came to be the absentee hope of those who fell before the Philistines.

Saul's first brevet, his captaincy in the Ammonite war, certainly was typical of a judge. Even later, when he was legitimatized with broader powers for the Philistine campaign, Samuel named him not king but *Nagid* (I Samuel 9:16), a term which Albright and others equate with "military commander" (cf. *Samuel and the Beginning of the Prophetic Movement*, p. 8). Saul and/or his sons, like Abimelech in an earlier age, may have had larger expectations but in these they were frustrated. "Now there was long war between the house of Saul and the house of David; and David waxed stronger and stronger, but the house of Saul waxed weaker and weaker" (II Samuel 3:1). It is really doubtful whether there was a "house of Saul." Abner and those who rallied to Ishbaal seem to have been motivated by the intransigence of the northern tribes toward Judean hegemony rather than by any conceit of hereditary legitimacy (II Samuel 2). Certainly no subsequent attempt was made in Israel to reestablish the fortunes of the house of Kish. No pretender to the throne ever intimated such a cause. The Bible never speaks of the throne of Saul as it does of the throne of David, nor does it mention a royal chronicle of his acts as it does of the subsequent reigns.

The conceit intrudes that kingship in an operative sense began with David rather than with Saul, that Saul was in reality, if not the last of the judges, certainly a transitional figure, not the first of the kings. His story is most reminiscent of Gideon's. His sons had similar hopes but as little chance. The tribal assembly continued to image itself as the ultimate source of power. Samuel selected him as *Nagid*.

David was the first in Israel successfully to establish a dynasty. David initiated a new concept of power. Saul lacked the distinguishing hallmark of all later kings, their employment of a mercenary force. His command, as that of the judges before him, was of the free men of Israel. David from the first was not an elected captain of tribal volunteers but chief of a hired band (I Samuel 22). David seems to have grabbed power rather than to have been selected for it. This chief of Hessians introduced a revolutionary new power structure—the heavy hand of professional troops financed by the proceeds of a royal domain, first and always booty then the perquisites of the territory allotted him by the Philistines, in time the taxes and tariffs of the royal city of Jerusalem. It is not known why mercenaries were not a feature of political life before David. It is possible that the small-ness of tribal landholdings and the lack of commercial wealth pre-cluded their hire. What is clear is that no conscript army, fighting between harvests, could withstand the discipline and training of these bands.

It would appear that David sought power rather than being selected for it. True, the Bible tells us that he was anointed by Samuel, but again this was as *Nagid*. Samuel may only have been selecting the most likely commander in chief of the forces, or he may have been legitimatizing an unusual emergency extension of powers for this commander. David was accepted by the "men of Judah," but a tribal assembly of Israel delayed acceptance for seven years (II Samuel 2:11) and Israel seems to have come under his authority un-willingly and largely by force of his military power and military suc-cess. "All Israel" is active throughout David's reign in challenging his authority. Absalom appealed to the dissatisfaction of the tribes of Israel (II Samuel 15:2). There is no indication that Israel willingly accepted the existence of Jerusalem as a national capital, or the posi-tion of the royal sanctuary as central cultic shrine, or Solomon's re-districting of territory for administrative purposes. The older tribal denominations reappear in the later history of the Northern Kingdom.

David certainly viewed himself as a king. He was eager to cen-tralize power and the symbols of authority. This alone would explain his radical deployment of the Ark to Jerusalem and his figuratively cementing it to the royal sanctuary's floor. Solomon continued build-ing the paraphernalia of royalty (I Kings 5:15 ff.). He was ceremoni-ously anointed (I Kings 1:32 ff.). He sought to break down tribal autonomy by imposing administrative districts (I Kings 4:7 ff.). He built great fortress cities for his governors and his chariots (I Kings 9:15 ff.). Pomp and circumstance, power and pageantry become in-separable from power. The Northern Kingdom, which in our view never willingly accepted the theology of monarchy, could do little against Solomon's manifest power, but Rehoboam was quickly rejected and, interestingly, the "men of Israel" felt no need to oppose him by one of the Davidic family (I Kings 12). "What portion have we in David?" (v. 16). Nor did Jeroboam crown himself. He is acclaimed by "all Israel" in the old manner (v. 20).

David taught the future heads of Israel the economics of royal authority, but Israel itself was always restive under the royal figure. Judah, however, was not. It is important to underscore the different forms that the institution of monarchy took in the Northern Kingdom and in the South. Hereditary sovereignty, based on a sacrosanct royal family, was a conceit unique to the Southern Kingdom. There David's house was elementally established. There were ten dynasties in Israel's brief history, one in Judah's longer chronicle. Moreover, Israel's dynasties ranged among the several tribes and legitimacy of lineage seems to have roused little or no concern. It was not felt necessary—to cite only one important example—to join Omri to any family tree (I Kings 16:15 ff.). Hierarchical forms seem to have been further developed in Judah than in Israel. The dowager queen certainly played an official role in the South, one unparalleled in the North where the citing of the dowager upon the royal ascension is entirely absent. Similarly, it is only of Judean kings that we find reference to the adoption of a royal name upon ascension. David established in Judah a royal city, part of his personal domain, "The City of David." In Israel, the kings continued to live in tribal centers until Omri purchased the Hill of Schechem about a century later, and this establishment does not seem to have won universal assent (I Kings 16:24).

How shall we account for Judah's acceptance of what Israel rejected? We do not know. Judah's partnership in the Mosaic experience is historically suspect. Could it be that Judah never felt itself an integral part of the tribal confederation and that it had evolved some differing form of authority? Could it be that whatever scruples were felt at this radical political departure were silenced by its obvious success? The answers are open. The questions are intriguing. What is clear is that David innovated a new and successful basis of power and that this power was legitimatized in the Southern Kingdom, and that it was never similarly accepted, though it was in force, in the North, Israel remained restive under the royal figure. Hosea, a Northerner, was unhappy with "the burden of kings and princes" (Hosea 8:10). He was the only prophet to denounce the whole royal institution:

> "It is thy destruction, O Israel
> That thou art against Me, against thy help.
> Ho, now, thy king,
> That he may save thee in all thy cities!
> And thy judges, of whom thou saidst:
> 'Give me a king and princes!'

I give thee a king in Mine anger,
And take him away in My wrath"

(Hosea 13:9–11).

In the North Elijah and Miciah refused to be agreeable to the royal
will or to be silent before royal excess. Ahijah, the Shilonite, played
an important role in catalyzing Israel's rebellion against the house
of David and did not feel it incumbent to choose one of royal seed.
Amos was no kinder than Hosea to the royal incumbent (Amos
3:10 ff. The future promise of Amos 9:1 ff. must be taken as a later
textual addition).

What is true of prophecy is true of the Law. Except for the
Deuteronomic stipulation of late Judean origin (17:14 ff.), the Law
is silent on the subject of monarchy. The covenant as Israel knew it
made no mention of monarchy.

What is true of prophecy and the Law is true of history. Not a
single Israelite escaped the condemnation of the editors of the Book
of Kings, though, to be sure, these were Judean.

This Northern uncertainty with monarchy reflects, in our opinion, the authentic Hebrew tradition, a tradition which could not be
discounted even in royalist Judah. Despite fanfare and paraphernalia,
Judean kings were by and large judged quite harshly by their biog-
raphers, Isaiah was no gentler than Hosea. Jeremiah was quite explicit
as to Jehoiakim's and Zedekiah's faults. The editor of the Book of
Kings was almost as harsh with many of the Southern incumbents as
he was with the Israelite rulers. The Southern kings do not establish
fundamental law of their own. Josiah, after finding the sacred scroll,
had it read aloud and confirmed by all the people. The conceit of an
enforceable covenant between king and God was conceived, to use the
legal term, without prejudice—the subject could be reopened upon
the inattention of the king to his obligations. Nor was the dream of
return as it expressed itself in Judea a purely royalist one. Deutero-
Isaiah's vision is naked of monarchic presuppositions.

Monarchy represented a departure from traditional Hebrew
norms. It was an imposed, not a home-born, idea. Monarchy came
into being out of practical, not theologic, necessity. The Mosaic tradition centered on the kingdom of God and contained an instinctive
prejudice against power and privilege. " 'I will not rule over you,
neither shall my son rule over you; the Lord shall rule over you' "
(Judges 8:23).

Governmental minimalists fared no better three thousand years
ago than they do today; however, their philosophy tempered the
organization of power. Monarchy in Israel was never sanctified. The

king remained a man and was judged as a man. The king remained bound by a strict covenant with God. There was at least the conceit that his rights were limited by certain contracts with the people. The Mosaic philosophy of the kingdom of God made its peace with monarchy, but it was at best a marriage of convenience. The faith wept no tears when after the exile monarchy was not reestablished. Monarchy lived on in Jewish life mostly as a messianic pipe dream while the realities of Jewish life struggled to establish a government of law rather than of men.

On Some Obscure Passages in the Book of Psalms I-XXXV

NAPHTALI H. TUR-SINAI

*

THROUGHOUT THE COURSE of my work in Biblical research, begun more than half a century ago, I have been concerned with the problems of the book of Psalms. I have dealt with the structure of the entire book and its arrangement, with various individual psalms and their obscure passages. My findings are largely collected in the three volumes of *The Language and the Book—*הלשון והספר (1948–1956); in the new edition of my translation of the Bible (1954–1959); and in my many notes included in Ben Yehuda's Thesaurus. Some of my more recent findings are presented in a series of articles *In the Footsteps of the Language and the Book* בעקבות הלשון והספר appearing in the quarterly *Leshonenu*, published by the Hebrew Language Academy, as well as in a lecture on the plan for a Historic Dictionary of the Hebrew Bible recently published in the Annals of the above Academy.

However, there remain many unanswered problems in connection with this difficult and important book, and there are still many obscurities in the Psalms. We still do not know the precise explanation of words and of combinations of words; but the reason for most of these obscurities is due to the textual changes in chapters and verses. Not all the extant psalms appear in their original and full text. One has only to compare, for example, those chapters which appear twice, in two different places in the book, such as Ps. 14 on the one hand and Ps. 53 on the other. It is clear that we have before us, in both places, substantially the same Psalm, with the same verses and the same order. Nevertheless, in one version it is written: "The fool hath said in his heart: 'There is no God'; They have dealt corruptly, *they have done abominably* (התעיבו עלילה); There is none that doeth good." And in the other version it states: "The fool hath said in his heart: 'There is no God'; They have dealt corruptly, *and have done abominable iniquity* (והתעיבו עול); there is none that doeth good." One Psalm has it: *"They are all corrupt;* (הכל סר), they are together become impure; there is none that doeth good, no, not one;" and the other Psalm states: *"Every one of them is unclean* (כלו סג), they are together become impure; There is none that doeth good, no, not one." In one version we find: "There are they in great fear; For God is *with the righteous generation. Ye would put to shame the counsel of the poor* (כדור צדיק עצת עני תבישו); But the Lord is his refuge" (די מחסהו); and in the other: "There are they in great fear, *where no fear was* (לא היה פחד); For God hath *scattered the bones of him that encampeth against thee; Thou has put them to shame* (פזר עצמות חנך הבישותה), because God *hath rejected them"* (מאסם). And if such be the case with verses where we have evidence of two different versions of the original text, how much more difficult is it for us in other places, where we have only one version, without any indication of another possibility or text which would perhaps be more exact than the extant one. Proof of the actual changes which occurred in the transmission of the text is also to be found, for example, in the psalms whose verses are alphabetically arranged, but lack verses for the full alphabet. Thus, in chapters 9 and 10 there have remained only a few of the 22 or even 44 possible verse headings, which are required by the alphabetical order. If in the book of Job, which is considered the most difficult in the Bible by virtue of its language and content, we can determine the main trend of thought from our knowledge of the fate of the righteous Job and the attitude of his friends toward him and his suffering, here each and every psalm is an entity in itself. Despite the meager and obscure illusions in the titles of the psalms, one can hardly know the intent of the psalmist. It is, therefore, very difficult to establish the meaning of verses and fragments of verses such as: "Serve the Lord with fear, And *rejoice with trembling* (וגילו ברעדה); *Do homage* (?) *in purity* (נשקו בר), lest He be angry (2:11–12);" "Commune (literally: *speak* אמרו), with your own heart upon your bed, *and be still* (ודמו). Selah (4:5);" "He croucheth, he boweth down, And *the helpless fall into his mighty claws* ([?] in Hebrew: בעצומיו חלכאים) 10:10);" "The wicked walk on every side, *when vileness is exalted* ([?] כרם זלת) among the sons of men (12:9);" "Let the idols of them be multiplied *that make suit* (?) *unto another* (אחר מהרו) (16:4);" and many more such as these. We do not know the exact meaning of the examples which I have mentioned here, and even of various verses which we use in our prayers.

I want to call attention to an additional factor which makes our understanding of the book of Psalms difficult, a factor which I discussed in my commentary on Job. Frequently the speeches and poetical portions repeat in similar language what had already been said elsewhere; and in such instances the copyists recorded only selected verses from the section. These verses indicated to them that here was a section similar to one that had already appeared elsewhere. To my mind, a similar process was followed in the book of Psalms; and if we recognize this, we can explain obscure passages, for which as yet no plausible interpretations have been found.

Thus, we find, for example, in Ps. 109:4–5, the following text: "In return for my love they are my adversaries; *But I (am) prayer* (ואני תפלה). And they have laid upon me evil for good, and hatred for my love." Although some commentators, such as Ibn Ezra, grasped the essential meaning of the expression "But I (am) prayer," it is nevertheless linguistically difficult; and even Ibn Ezra finds it necessary to interpret it as "But I am *a man* of prayer.[1] Rashi, on the other hand, offers the interpretation: "But I pray unto Thee always," which is not true to the sense of the passage. The modern commentators have difficulty with these words, so much so that Kittel's edition of the Bible lists Gunkel's senseless emendation ואין תפלה "and there is no folly." But the two words ואני תפלה are merely an abbreviated allusion to what is fully stated in Psalm 35:12–13: "They repay me evil for good; Bereavement (But this word שכול should be understood in the sense of putting one thing in the place of another, שכול here, substituting evil for good, as שכל את ידיו in Genesis 48:14 means putting the right in the place of the left hand) is come to my soul. *But as for me* (ואני), when they were sick, my clothing was sackcloth, I afflicted my soul with fasting; *and my prayer* (ותפלתי) may it return into my own bosom." In my opinion, the phrase ואני תפלה alludes to such complete verses as in Psalm 35.

And indeed, for many of the obscure passages, various scholars as well as I have already suggested emendations, part of which, in my opinion, offer reliable solutions. On the other hand, various other suggestions can only be regarded as experimental in nature. Solutions for obscure passages frequently should be sought by deeply penetrating into the context of the whole chapter and even of the entire book. Most of the suggestions found in the various commentaries try to shed light on one single obscure word in a given passage or chapter; but even after the particular detail seems to be clarified, the passage or chapter as a whole remains obscure.

What appears to me as tenable now, following persistent investi-

---

1 Evidently based upon the verse: "But as for me, let my prayer be unto Thee, O Lord, in an acceptable time" (Psalm 69:14).

gation, using the studies of others and mine, I am presently incor-
porating in a book on the text and its meaning in the entire Hebrew
Bible. Elsewhere, I discussed the outline of this book, and its first
volume, which deals with the Pentateuch, is finished and in print and
will appear shortly in Hebrew (under the title פשוטו של מקרה) and
some months later in English. Meanwhile I am preparing the other
volumes on the Former and Latter Prophets and on the Hagiographa.

Here, by lack of space limited to Chapter 1–35 of the Psalms, I
shall offer only a number of new suggestions which, to my knowledge,
are not mentioned in any other books. I have, however, included here
a number of suggestions culled from my more recent studies, not
collected so far in books, which enabled me to supplement and correct
here a number of points in them. Actually, these are only "gleanings,"
after the main body of my work over the years. I plan to present all
the material, including conclusions of others in my before-mentioned
book, when I deal with the Hagiographa, including the book of Psalms.

*

I shall start with the first Psalm, that didactive poem which serves as
an introduction to the entire book and which is apparently quite clear.
Nevertheless, the extant text is not fully understandable, and additional investigation casts new light on its meaning. As it seems, the
text of the Psalm was incorrectly copied, as is borne out by those
instances in which one word in the parallelism is repeated in both
stichs, whereas the author, undoubtedly, must have used two different words. Thus, we find in verse 2: "But his delight is *in the law*
(בתורת) of the Lord; And *in His law* (ובתורתו) doth he meditate day
and night." Again, in verse 6: "For the Lord regardeth the *way* (דרך)
of the righteous; but the *way* (ודרך) of the wicked shall perish."
Such instances are illustrated by the parallels in the Song of David
in II Samuel 22, and in Psalm 18. In II Samuel 22:7 it is written:
"In my distress *I called* (אקרא) upon the Lord, Yea, *I called* (אקרא)
unto my God," whereas, in Psalm 18:7 the more reliable text reads:
"In my distress *I called* (אקרא) upon the Lord, And *cried* (אשוע) unto
my God." In the same Psalm there occur additional instances of variations in both copies. In our instance, too, the repetition of the same
word in the parallelism indicates the lack of accuracy in the work of
the copyists. On this basis we can discern the same lack of accuracy
even in v. 1: "Happy is the man that hath not *walked in the counsel*
(הלך בעצת) of the wicked, nor *stood* (עמד) *in the way* (ובדרך) of
sinners, nor sat in the seat of the scornful." It does not seem natural
to say that the man "stood in the way," unless the verb "walked" is

used in the parallelism. It seems to me that the order of the verse should properly be: "Happy is the man that hath not *walked in the way* (הלך בדרך) of the wicked, Nor *stood* (עמד) in the company (במעמד [read, incorrectly: בעצת]) of sinners, Nor sat in the seat of the fools (לצים)." In v. 2, the reading could be: "But his delight is in the *word* (בדבר, [or: in the commandment–במצות]) of the Lord, And in His Law doth he meditate day and night."

In v. 5 it says: "therefore the wicked shall not stand up in the judgment, Nor sinners *in the congregation of the righteous* (בעדת צדיקים)." But is the phrase "in the congregation of the righteous" a fitting parallel to "the judgment," which means God's sitting in judgment on man? It appears that the term, "the righteous," is but an addition, influenced by the next verse, which reads, "For the Lord regardeth the *way of the righteous*." But in v. 5 the meaning is: "Therefore the wicked shall not stand up in the judgment, Nor sinners *in testimony*" (בעדת). Hence what is expressly referred to here is *the testimony of* those standing before God in His judgment. On this basis, we must revise our understanding of the last stich.

V. 6 reads: "For the Lord *regardeth* (יודע) *the way of* (דרך) the righteous; *but the way* (ודרך) of the wicked shall perish." It has always been difficult for the commentators to explain the relation of the term "regardeth" to "way." Why is regarding the way of the righteous contrasted to "but the way of the wicked *shall perish* (תאבד)?" But if what is referred to here is *the testimony* of the righteous and the wicked, then surely the sense is: "For the Lord regardeth the *word* (דבר) of the righteous," that is, God knows that the word of the righteous in testimony is right and true while in the continuation, "but the way of the wicked shall perish," the repetition of the phrase, "but the way," is not appropriate. What is required here is another word characterizing the false testimony of the wicked which shall not be sustained but "shall perish." It is possible that the original read: "*And the slander* (ודבת) of the wicked shall not last." This slanderous testimony of theirs shall not be sustained.

In Psalm 2:1, it is written: "Why are the nations in an *uproar* (if this were the meaning of רגשו) And why do the peoples mutter vain words?" Many unsatisfactory explanations have been suggested for "רגשו," but if we observe that the first part of the verse is parallel to: "And why do the peoples mutter vain words (ריק)?" we recognize that the last two letters of the word רגשו are used here in the sense of שו, in keeping with the spelling that appears also in other places for שוא, a fact which was not always recognized by tradition. The reading should, therefore, perhaps be, "why have the nations mur-

mured falseness (רגנו שו), and why do the peoples mutter vain words (ריק)?" After the letters נו had been omitted, perhaps because they were considered a variant of שו, the remaining letters, *word* רגשו, were taken as the verb in the verse. (This point was discussed in *Leshonenu* Vol. 23, p. 27.)

In Psalm 3:4, the poet, in reply to his many adversaries who rise up against him and who claim that "There is no salvation for him in God" says that God is his salvation in war; "But Thou, O Lord, art a shield about me; *My glory* (כבודי), and the lifter up of my head." This text, which is so familiar to us, may even be smoother than what appears to me to be the correct text, intended by the poet. He certainly did not intend to juxtapose in his war imagery "*a shield* (מגן) about me" with "*my glory*" (כבודי); also, "the lifter up of my head" does not follow properly from "my glory." Suffice it to compare this with such verses as Ez. 27:10: "Persia and Lud and Put were in thine army, Thy men of war; They hanged *the shield and helmet* (מגן וכובע) in thee" with Ezekiel 38:5: "Persia, Cush and Put with them, all of them with *shield and helmet*" (מגן וכובע); and, in another instance, with Ezekiel 23:24: ". . . with buckler *and shield and helmet* . . . (ומגן וקובע)." In my opinion, the poet here, too, intended to present an image of a man of war, exclaiming: "But Thou, O Lord, art a shield about me; *a helmet* (כובע), and the lifter up of my head." For, as is well known, the war helmet was decorated with various ornaments, thus lifting up the head of the warrior. Compare the shift in imagery from the concrete description of a human being in I Samuel 17:5: "And he had a helmet of *brass* (נחושת) upon his head," with the metaphoric description of God in Isaiah 59:17: "And he put on righteousness as a coat of mail, And a helmet of *salvation* (ישועה) upon his head."

In Psalm 4:5 it is apparently written: "Tremble, and sin not; Speak (אמרו) in your heart upon your bed, and be still." "Speak in your heart?" What we should speak in our heart is not mentioned; if speaking is intended here, how are we to harmonize this with the continuation "and be still. Selah," which implies silence rather than speech. Indeed, various emendations have been proposed, but they do not obviate the difficulties. The reading should perhaps be: "Tremble and sin not if revolt (אם מרי) be in your heart upon your bed, and be still. Selah," that is, if a rebellious thought comes to you upon your bed, tremble, that is, be fearful and sin not and be still. Only one מ was written instead of two, as a haplography, similar to many other instances in the Bible, such as, Jeremiah 15:1: "*Cast them* (שלח) out of my sight, and let them go forth," instead of (שלחם) with the pronominal suffix מ.

In the same Psalm, v. 7, it is written: "Many there are that say: 'Oh that we could see some good!' Lord, . . . (נסה) the light of Thy countenance upon us." Instead of נסה, which is linguistically impossible, the following suggestions have been made: a) to read here "נשא," this is untenable, for the correct form would be ישא; b) various senseless emendations, such as "כסה," "נסה," or "נם מעלינו." But what is required here can only be נגה, "it shone, similar to: "The Lord my God doth lighten (יגיה) my darkness" (Psalm 18:29); "Upon them hath the light shined (אור נגה עליהם) (Isaiah 9:1); "And light shall shine (נגה) upon thy ways" (Job 22:28), and others.

In Psalm 5:6–8 it is written: "For Thou art not a God that hath pleasure in wickedness: Evil shall not sojourn with Thee. The boasters (?) shall not stand in Thy sight; Thou hatest all workers of iniquity. Thou destroyest (תאבד) them that speak falsehood; the Lord abhorreth the man of blood and of deceit." Most of the verbs in these verses express God's aversion to the propinquity of the wicked. An exception is v. 7: *"Thou destroyest* (תאבד) them that speak falsehood." In my opinion, it was written: "Thou treateth as enemies (תאיב) them that speak falsehood," as expressed in Exodus 23:22: "then I will be an enemy (ואיבתי) unto thine enemies, and an adversary unto thine adversaries." This concept corresponds with the parallel expression: *"Thou hatest* (שנאת) all workers of iniquity." The additional ד is due to dittography before דברי כזב.

In Chapter 6:7, it is written: "I am weary with my groaning; *every night* (בכל לילה) make I my bed to swim; I melt away my couch with my tears." One might understand the words, *"every night* (בכל לילה) make I my bed to swim," on the assumption that the reader and listener will realize from the continuation: "I melt away my couch *with my tears* (בדמעתי)," that here also the implication is one of tears. Yet it is unnatural that the writer should put off this essential explanation to the next sentence, while introducing in the beginning of the verse instead the purposeless elements of the time: "every night." And since the natural parallel to "tears" (דמעה) in the Bible is "weeping," בכי it seems clear to me that the poet's intention was: "I make my bed to swim *with tears and howling* (בכי(ו)יללה); I melt away my couch with my tears." Compare the vv. in Isaiah 15:3 and 16:9: ". . . and in their broad places, every one *howleth* (ייליל), *weeping* profusely (ירד בבכי)." "Therefore *I will weep* (אבכה) with the weeping of Jazer For the vine of Sibmah; I will water thee *with my tears* (בדמעתי), O Heshbon, and Elealeh;" and elsewhere.

It is more difficult to determine the original text in Lamentations 1:2: "She weepeth sore *in the night* (בלילה), And her *tears* are on her cheeks." But even here the implication would appear to be: "She weepeth sore *and howleth* (בִּיְלָלָה), And her tears are on her cheeks," rather than "in the night." This differs from Jeremiah 8:23: "Oh that my head were waters, And mine eyes a fountain of tears, that I might weep *day and night* (יומם ולילה) for the slain of the daughter of my people." The tears naturally are not limited to the night, but it is easy to see how a careless copyist substituted: "בכל לילה" for "בכי יללה."

In Psalm 7:4-5 it is written: "O Lord, my God, if I have done this; If there be iniquity in my hands; If I have requited him that did evil unto me, Or saved (ואחלצה) mine adversary (צוררי) emptily (ריקם)." The difficulty of the combination: "Or saved mine adversary emptily," is explained by ancient and modern commentators by substituting "ואלחצה" or "oppressed" for "ואחלצה." Compare the Syriac: אלצת, and the Aramaic Targum: ודחקית. But "emptily" (ריקם) cannot mean "without cause." [2] The word is used properly with the verb "חלץ," rather than with לחץ, and the Septuagint translation ἀποπέσοιμι ... ἀπο also indicates a reading of (מן) ואחלצה. But the words "ואחלצה ריקם" do not go together properly with צוררי. In my opinion, this reading is a result of the influence of what is said of enemies and oppressors in the continuation of vv. 6 and 7: "Let the enemy pursue my soul . . . Lift up Thyself in indignation against mine adversaries" and elsewhere. Here a word parallel to "שולמי" in the beginning of the verse is required, for example, "If I have requited evil to him that lived in peace with me or spoiled empty those who did right by me (צודקי)."

In Psalm 8:2-3 it is written: "O Lord, our Lord, How glorious is Thy name in all the earth! Whose majesty . . . (תנה) above the heavens. *Out of the mouth* ([?] Hebrew: מפי) of babes and sucklings hast Thou founded strength. Because of Thine adversaries; that Thou mightest still the enemy and the avenger."

In my *The Language and the Book*, Vol. III, p. 405, I explained that "תנה" is not derived here from the verb "נתן," "to give," but rather from the root "תנה," "to praise" as, for example, in Judges 5:11: "There shall they praise (יתנו) the righteous acts of the Lord." However, there I took "תנה" to be a noun from the same root whose meaning approximates praise and adoration.

But in the continuation in v. 3, only the essence of the verse is understood: "of babes and sucklings hast thou founded strength, because of thine adversaries; That thou mightest still the enemy and the avenger," that is, infants and babes You strengthened and founded with might and strength, so that they could withstand any enemy,

2 Psalm 25:3 may correctly read: ריקם . . . ישובו instead of יבשו.

and destroy foe and avenger. This offers a transition to v. 4: "when I behold Thy heavens, the work of Thy fingers . . . ," I then recognize and admit: "What is man, that Thou art mindful of him? And the son of man, that Thou thinkest of him?", nevertheless "of babes and sucklings Thou founded strength." Thus far, the meaning of the verse is clear enough.

However, the expression "*Out of the mouth* (מפי) of babes and sucklings hast thou founded strength," is not understood thus at all, even though this strange phrase out of the Bible has become part of human thinking. Now, if the word מפי does not fit in with the phrase "Babes and sucklings hast Thou founded with strength," which in itself is complete in its content and rhythm, then we must join the word "מפי" with the previous verse: "אשר תנה הודך על השמים," whose rhythm is deficient, when compared with its parallel: "O Lord, our Lord, How glorious is Thy name in all the earth!" Adding thus the word מפי to the beginning of v. 2, we recognize that the poet, undoubtedly, intended to state in definite parallel form: "O Lord, our Lord, *how glorious* is (telling) Thy name in all the earth, Whose majesty to praise above the heavens, *how fair* is it (מה-ייף)!" The form ייף thus occurs in Ezekiel 31:7: "Thus was it fair (וייף) in its greatness," In the ancient defective spelling, "מיף" instead of מה ייף was written, similar to the spelling מזה: for מה זה in Exodus 4:2 and other instances with which I have dealt in *Leshonenu*, Vol. 23, p. 2 ff. These letters מיף were evidently interpreted by the copyist as מפי, and finally linked together with the next verse to read: "Out of the mouth of babes and sucklings." Now, by adding מה ייף to v. 2, it is possible to read תנה as a verbal form meaning: "to praise." The whole verse is thus similar to Psalm 92:2, 5, 6: "*It is a good thing* (טוב) to give thanks unto the Lord, and to sing praise unto Thy name, O Most High; For Thou, Lord, has made me glad through Thy work: I will exult in the works of Thy hands. How great are Thy works, O Lord!" whose contents resemble that of the Psalm under consideration.

In Psalm 9:6, we find: "*Thou has rebuked* (גערת) the nations, Thou has destroyed the wicked, Thou hast blotted out their names for ever and ever." Both the context and the transitive use of the Hebrew verb require the reading גדעת, "thou hast cut off," instead of גערת—Compare Malachi 2:3: "Behold, I will rebuke (גער) the seed for you," where the correct reading is גדע, "*I will cut off*," following the Septuagint (ἀφορίζω,) and the opinion of many.

In Psalm 9:11–13, it is written: "And they that know Thy name will put their trust in Thee; For Thou, Lord, hast not forsaken them that seek Thee. *For He that avengeth blood* (דרש דמים) hath remembered *them* (אותם). He hath not forgotten the cry of the humble." It has already been recognized that in v. 13 the required reading is דרש דמם, "For He has avenged their blood," as a parallel to "He has remembered. . . ." Difficulty, however, arises with the repetition of the object form אותם. Gunkel's suggestion to read אְוֺתָם—as it were: their desire—is unacceptable, since דרש דמם expresses a demand for vengeance for the blood of the slain as retribution and revenge. Therefore, the meaning of the verse is: "For He hath avenged their blood, remembered *their death* (מותם), He hath not forgotten the cry of the humble."

In Psalm 10:15 it is written: "Break Thou the arm of the wicked; and (as for) the evil man, *search out his wickedness*, (רשעו) till none be found," where the word רשע is repeated twice. However, since רשע and רע are parallels, they should be in opposite parts of the verse, רשע in the first stich and רע in the second. Hence the phrase should read: "Break Thou the arm of the wicked; seeking the bad—he will not be found." The word רשעו should be omitted in the second stich as mistakenly repeated by the copyist.

In Psalm 14:5 it is written: "*There* (שם) were they in great fear; for God is with the righteous generation." As is known, this verse is given in a fuller version in Psalm 53:6: "There were they in great fear, *where no fear was;* For God hath scattered . . . ," and the conspicuous changes in both copies of this Psalm have already been mentioned above. In my opinion the words: "where no fear was," omitted in Psalm 14, are essential in the text of the verse, but there is a question as to the correctness of the word שם, "there." Obviously, the reading should be: "*In vain* (שוא) were they in great fear, *where no fear was,* For God is with the righteous generation (or chose . . . בחר) the righteous generation."

In Psalm 16:2–3 it states: "I have said unto the Lord: 'Thou art my Lord; I have no good but in Thee'; As for the holy *that are in the earth* (בארץ המה), and for the excellent in whom is all my delight." Are there, then, "holy ones (that is, godly beings and angels) that are in the earth?" The place of the holy ones is certainly in heaven! From the parallel in the verse, it becomes clear that the meaning, with a slight metathesis of the letters, בארץ המה is: "As for the holy *whom I desire* (ארצה בהם), and for the excellent *in whom is all my delight.*" We must, therefore, reject the emendation suggested by many: "The excellent in whom I do not (בל instead of כל) desire," thus anticipating v. 4: "Let the idols of them be multiplied (?) that make suit unto another (?): Their drink-offerings of blood *will I not* (בל) offer, nor (ובל) take their names upon my lips." Perhaps one may explain the transition of ideas in this manner: Do not approach me anymore —and instead of בל עליך לקדושים the reading should be בל עלי כל קדושים —these holy ones when I desired *previously,* and these excellent ones in whom all my delight *was* before. In order, however, to understand the meaning of this section correctly, we have to find a logical solution also to the continuation in v. 4 which, in its present form, is not comprehensible at all. I will merely comment that, in contrast to ירבו, multiply, be many in the continuation, it appears that the intent is not the word אחר, another one, with ר, but to the word אחד one, with ד ; the reading may be approximately thus: "They have made many their idols, *and changed the One,*" similar to Jeremiah 2:11: "Hath a nation changed its gods, which yet are no gods? But my people hath changed its glory, for that which doth not profit." They changed one God for many idols.

In Psalm 20:5 it states: "He shall grant thee *according to thine heart* (כלבבך), And fulfil all thy counsel." According to the parallel, it is more logical to read: "He shall grant thee כל לבבך, all thy heart's wishes, by writing two ל instead of one.

In Psalm 22:11, it is written: "Upon Thee I have been cast (השלכתי) from my birth; Thou art my God from my mother's womb." The verb should be understood as active and not as passive, as though it were written: "Upon Thee I cast (השלכתי, my hope) from my birth; Thou art my God from my mother's womb." This is similar to Psalm 55:23: "Cast thy burden upon the Lord, and He will sustain thee: He will never suffer the righteous to be moved," and also to Proverbs 16:20, apparently saying: "He that giveth heed (משכיל) unto the word shall find good: And whoso trusteth in the Lord, happy is he," the meaning is approximately: "He that casts (his hope) upon my word (משליך על דברי) shall find good; And whoso trusteth in the Lord, happy is he." A single thread of thought runs through all of these verses.

In Psalm 22:17 it is written "(כלבים) have encompassed me; A company of evil-doers have inclosed me; like a lion, they are at my hands and my feet." Here, however, כלבים is not the plural form of כלב, dogs, but the כ is a כ comparative, meaning alike (lions) parallel to "כארי," in the continuation of the verse. Therefore, ancient commentators were mistaken in asserting that for כארי we should read a verb, כארו, for which various suggestions have been offered. Moreover, the words, "ידי ורגלי" should not be connected to this verse. The two verses should be interpreted in the following form: "For they have encompassed me *as lions* (כ-לבים) (that is, as the hunters surround the lions captured in the pit): A company of evil doers surrounded me like a lion," and then: "My hands and my feet I count (אספר), all my bones."

In Psalm 25:8 it apparently states: "Good and upright is the Lord; Therefore doth He instruct *sinners* (חטאים) in the way." Is He to instruct only sinners and not all men who walk in His way? Now, others have already remarked that in Job 14:16, "But now Thou *numberest my steps*, (צעדי) Thou dost not even wait (?) for *my sin* (חטאתי)," the sense of the word חטאתי is, perhaps, according to the parallelism, not that of sin and iniquity, but as in the Arabic, where the sense is that of stepping or walking. And here, in this acrostic Psalm, which combines unrelated epigrams, each of which was expressed in its own specific idiom, perhaps the meaning is: "Therefore doth He guide the *wayfarers* who walk by the way."

In Psalm 32:1–2 it is written: "A Psalm of David. Maschil. Happy is he whose transgression is forgiven, whose sin is pardoned. Happy is the man unto whom the Lord counteth not iniquity, and in whose *spirit* (ברוחו) there is no guile." This verse, however, does not refer to a man who has not sinned, but rather to one who has sinned but has been forgiven, and "unto whom the Lord counteth not iniquity" anymore. Therefore, the end of the verse, "And in whose *spirit* there is no guile," is difficult to understand. We cannot follow those who would eliminate this phrase, since it is essential for the parallelism; nor can we agree with those who would twist the verse in such a way that the original meaning would be distorted. The phrase "unto whom the Lord counteth not iniquity" seems to allude to a *book* of accounting or a tablet (לוח) on which man's sins are recorded, as in Isaiah 30:8, 9, "Now go, write it before them on a tablet, and inscribe it in a book, that it may be for the time to come for ever and ever. For it is a rebellious people, lying children, children that refuse to hear the teaching of the Lord." Hence, it is probable that the psalmist intended this verse to read: "Happy is the man unto whom the Lord counteth not iniquity and on whose *tablet* (בלוחו) there is no guile;" that is, on the tablet on which God lists man's iniquities, is not guile counted to man's debit?

In Psalm 32:3 it seemingly states: "When *I kept silence* (החרשתי), my bones wore away through my groaning all the day long." The commentators fail to understand the meaning of this verse. For example, let us mention Gunkel's query: "How is it possible that the psalmist should be roaring (שאג) and at the same time keep silent?" His answer is: "He keeps silent from mentioning his sins but he roars and groans from the depth of his pain." On the other

hand, a Jewish scholar, Moshe Shulbaum, found it necessary to suggest emending החרשתי "I kept silent to השחרתי I became darkened" (full of gloom). In fact, it was not realized that here, too, as
elsewhere, for example, Psalm 102:6, "By reason of the voice of my
sighing *My bones* cleave to my *flesh*"; עצם (bone) is used in the sense
of the hard roof of the mouth, in contrast to בשר which refers to the
soft tongue. Just as that verse: "My bones cleave to my flesh," is to
be interpreted as "the roof of my mouth cleaveth to my tongue," and
thus "I could speak no more," here, too, the meaning of החרשתי is "I
became deaf and dumb; and "my bones wore away" should be interpreted: the roof of my mouth wore away and I could speak no more
because I groaned all day. The constant roaring caused the psalmist
to become finally deaf and dumb. Hence, verse 4 is a direct continuation of the idea expressed in the proceeding verse: "For day and night
Thy hand was heavy upon me; My sap (לשדי) was turned as in the
droughts of summer. Selah." Perhaps for the word לשדי (my sap?)
we should read: my tongue (לשני). Thus the meaning is: "My
tongue became dry (incapable of speaking) as (in) the droughts of
summer."

In Psalm 32:7, we, literally, find, "Thou art my hiding-place;
Thou wilt preserve me from the adversary; *With songs of deliverance,
Thou wilt compass me about* (רני פלט תסובבני). Selah." Many have
already recognized that the phrase רני פלט is corrupted. However,
those who think that רני is a duplication of the last three letters of
the previous word תצרני are hardly right, for the remainder of the
verse פלט תסובבני would then have no meaning. The verse begins with
"Thou art my *hiding-place*" (סתר), consequently, we expect a parallel
such as that found in Psalm 17:8, "Hide me in the shadow *of Thy
wings* בכנפיך, or Psalm 61:5, "I will take refuge *in the covert* בסתר of
Thy wings, or Psalm 91:4, "He will cover thee with His pinions, And
under His wings shalt thou take refuge." Accordingly, in my opinion,
the verse should be reconstructed to read as follows: אתה סתר לי
מצר תצרני כנף לוט, that is, with the wing which serves as a cover and
protection for me, Thou hidest me, תסובבני, סלה. The text seems to
have been corrupted by the influence of the last three letters in the
word תצרני. תסוכבני instead of תסובבני has already been suggested by
others.

In this connection, I will mention the instructive comment by
G. Waldberg in his book ספר דרכי השינויים, p. 19 on Psalm 34:7:
"This poor man cried זה עני קרא and the Lord heard, and saved him
out of all his troubles," which he compares with Psalm 107:13 (and
again in v. 19): "*They cried* ויזעקו unto the Lord in their trouble, And

he saved them out of their distresses." Waldberg suggests that the initial letters in זה עני קרא form the word זעק he cried. It would be fitting to rescue this worthwhile observation from the abyss of forgetfulness.

In Psalm 35:12–14, the poet describes his exemplary behavior at the time of the mourning and troubles of his opponents, in contrast to the behavior of his enemies toward him, as in v. 15: "But when I limp they rejoice, and *gather themselves* ונאספו together; The abjects *gather themselves together* ונאספו against me, and those whom I know not; *They tear (me)*, and cease not." The difficulties involved are well known and the efforts which I, too, made to solve them do not satisfy me. We now recognize that the repetition of the words ונאספו, נאספו was caused by the similarity in the letters of the words נאספו עלי נכים (according to many, the reading should be נכרים), which properly belong above, before v. 11: "Unrighteous witnesses rise up; They ask me of things that I know not." In all probability, the order of the verses was approximately as follows: "Strangers whom I know not gathered against me, Unrighteous witnesses whom I did not rob (read: גזלתי) question me." If we eliminate those words which have no connection with the behavior of the psalmist's opponents during his illness, then we are left here with the words ובצלעי שמחו ונאספו קרעו ולא דמו in a separate line. We can now clearly discern that the words ולא דמו, meaning "and will not be silent," require, in place of קרעו, which is no antithesis to ולא דמו, a verb expressing speech which fits in with שמחו, namely, הריעו (as has been proposed by J. Halevy). However, as a parallel to ולא דמו, we should read ולא ספו, that is, they *did not cease* from rejoicing. Accordingly, the original form of the verse was: ובצלעי שמחו ולא ספו, הריעו ולא דמו. Since ונאספו was read in place of ולא דמו, the sentence נאספו עלי נכים ולא ידעתי was interpolated here.

The Origin of the Idea of the Messiah

SOLOMON ZEITLIN

*

THERE IS A saying in the Talmud "either the sword or the book." [1] This could be interpreted that one who seeks to combat injustice and is a fighter for ideas and ideals cannot produce great scholarly works. On the other hand a true scholar cannot engage in public affairs, for his place is in an ivory tower. Dr. Abba Hillel Silver has shown that this saying refers only to the average person, not to a person of superior intellect and gifted with original ideas. Such a person combines valor in fighting for his ideas and ideals and those faculties required to produce scholarly works of permanent value.

Doctor Abba Hillel Silver, who is approaching his seventieth birthday, has devoted his life to the service of the Jews. He was the main champion in defending the Jewish rights in *Eretz Israel* (Palestine) before the United Nations. History will record the great indebtedness which the State of Israel owes to him.

While Dr. Silver was engaged in the struggle for the rights of the Jews he, at the same time, produced scholarly works in which he displayed sound learning and showed keen historical insight. He has a masterful style and exhibits great courage in expounding his views.

The first of Dr. Silver's scholarly works was *A History of Messianic Speculation in Israel,* in which he traces the messianic speculations among the Jews from the end of the first century to that of the seventeenth century. This book shows a vast knowledge of the sources and literature of this period as well as the author's acute mind in dealing with this complicated subject. Some of his other books are *Religion in a Changing World, Where Judaism Differed,* and the latest, *Moses and the Original Torah,* in which Moses is presented as a living reality, a challenge which very few scholars have been able to accomplish. All of Dr. Silver's works are of lasting value.

In the volume dedicated in honor of Doctor Abba Hillel Silver's seventieth birthday, it is fitting to have an article on the origin of the

1 Abodah Zarah 17.

idea of a messiah, since the first fruit of Dr. Silver's thought was on the messianic expectation.

I

The messianic expectation among the Jews was both a blessing and a curse. The hope for a messiah gave them strength and courage during the centuries of the Middle Ages, dark ages, in their privations and degradations. They underwent great sufferings but they hoped that this would not be prolonged. They believed that the Promised Messiah would come soon, redeem them from their misery, and bring them back to their homeland, the Land of Israel, where the kingdom of Israel would be reestablished under the scepter of a scion of the family of David. Their motto was "to hope and to suffer." The expectation of a Messiah, indeed, made their survival possible. It kept alive the hope that at a not too distant time the Messiah would come. They besought God in their prayers to hasten the coming of the promised Messiah.

On the other hand, the longing and expectation of the Messiah brought misfortune and suffering to the Jews. Many opportunists and adventurers, observing the persecution and degradation of the Jews and being aware of their hopes for a Messiah, took advantage of the situation by proclaiming themselves either messiahs or prophets of messiahs. These messianic movements were catastrophic to the Jews. One of the latest was Sabbatai Zevi's messianic movement in the seventeenth century. Almost all the Jews of that period succumbed to it, rich and poor. Even the intelligent classes—bankers, doctors, and rabbis, believed Sabbatai Zevi to be the true messiah. The propaganda for this movement was led by one Nathan, who proclaimed himself to be a prophet. He was a demagogue, adventurer, and forger. He showed great ability, we may say genius, in the organization of the movement. Sabbatai Zevi's messianic movement was calamitous to the Jews as were all the others. In fact, the Jews have not yet fully recovered from the aftereffects of the collapse of the Sabbataian movement.

True, there were men who honestly believed themselves to be messiahs. They arrived at this belief because of their ascetic way of living and through their engrossment in the studies of mysticism and Kabbala. They fasted and prayed and thus their minds became deranged—they saw visions that God destined them to be messiahs to redeem His people and lead them to the Promised Land. This type of false messiah also brought great suffering to the Jews. The messianic expectation, as stated previously, was both a blessing and a curse. It was a tower of strength for survival during the dark ages and it also brought great suffering.

II

The word *Mashiaḥ*, messiah, *christos* in Greek, has the connotation of being anointed. We learn from the Bible that Aaron, the first priest; the Tabernacle and the vessels in it were anointed with oil.[2] The anointment signified that they were divine and belonged to Yahweh. The Prophet Samuel anointed Saul, the first king, and in doing so said, "Is it not that Yahweh hath anointed thee to be a *nagid* over His inheritance."[3] Saul thus became divine and thus became *Mashiaḥ* of Yahweh.[4] Later when the Prophet Samuel anointed David to become king, the same nomenclature, *Mashiaḥ* of Yahweh, was given to him.[5] God promised David that the kingship would be an inheritance of his family and would last forever.[6]

The term *Mashiaḥ* was not only applied to the Jewish kings and high priest but also to foreign kings. Cyrus, the king of Persia, was called the *Mashiaḥ* of Yahweh.[7] The word *Mashiaḥ* was used in the Bible as an adjective, not as a noun. The term "messiah" as a noun appears only in the late apocalyptic literature and in the New Testament. On the other hand, during the Second Commonwealth neither the kings nor the priests were anointed with oil. Therefore an explanation is necessary as to how the term *Mashiaḥ*, "messiah," appears later in the Hebrew literature as a person and aroused the idea in the minds of the people that God would send a *Mashiaḥ*.

The early Church Fathers, to prove that Jesus was the true messiah, *Christos*, maintained that there were references to Jesus as the messiah in the Pentateuch and in the other books of the Bible. To combat the views of the Church Fathers the rabbis interpreted the same verses as containing prophecies of the Jewish *Mashiaḥ*. To cite a few examples: The verse in Genesis 49:10 reads, "The scepter shall not depart from Judah, Nor the ruler's staff from between his feet, As long as men come to Shiloh; And unto him shall the opinions of the people be." Origen interpreted this passage as referring to the "Christ of God," Jesus.[8] The Targum, according to Jonathan, interprets it as referring to the Jewish *Mashiaḥ*. The verse in Isaiah 11:1 reads, "And there shall come forth a shoot of the stock of Jesse and

---

2 Exodus 40:9–15.
3 I. Samuel 10:1.
4 *Ibid.*, 26:11.
5 *Ibid.*, 16:13; II Samuel 19:22.
6 *Ibid.*, 7:8–16.

7 Cf. Isaiah 45:1. "Thus said Yahweh to his *mashiah* to Cyrus."
8 *Against Celsus*, B. 1, 53. "For He came for whom these things were reserved, the Christ of God."

a twig shall grow forth out of his roots." Justin Martyr interpreted this verse as a prophecy for the coming of Jesus.[9] The rabbis interpreted it as referring to the coming of the Jewish *Mashiaḥ.* In Chapter 53 of Isaiah the suffering of the servant of Yahweh is described. The Church Fathers interpreted it as referring to the Passion of Jesus. Barnabas, one of the Apostolic Fathers, interpreted this chapter as referring partly to Israel and partly to Jesus.[10] Origen, in his treatise Against Celsus, said that the Jews believed that the prophecies in this chapter referred to the whole people of Israel regarded as one individual. He denied this contention and held that the prophecies and suffering related in this chapter referred to the sufferings and the death of Jesus Christ.[11] The Targum, according to Jonathan, interpreted this chapter as referring to *Mashiaḥ,* the Jewish Messiah.

The Church Fathers as well as the rabbis injected their ideas of the messiah into the Biblical passages. However, as we have previously stated, there is no indication anywhere in the Bible of the coming of a personal messiah, natural or supernatural. The word *Mashiaḥ* appears in the Bible several times. It has the connotation of anointed and refers to the high priest [12] or to the king, of the family of David. In the Book of Psalms the word *Mashiaḥ* is found several times. It appears in Chapter 84:10, "Look upon the face of Thine *Mashiaḥ.*" This seems to refer to the anointed high priest. In Chapter 89:39, "But Thou hast cast off and rejected, Thou hast been wroth with Thine *Mashiaḥ.*" This seems to refer to the family of David. Similarly in verse 52 the word *Mashiaḥ* refers to the family of David. Again in Chapter 105:15, "Touch not My *Mashiaḥ* and do My prophets no harm." This refers to the anointed priest. The psalmist beseeches the people not to harm the priest and the prophet. It seems that this verse is dislocated and should come at the end of the chapter. In the book of Lamentations 4:20, we read, "The breath of our nostrils, the anointed of the *Mashiaḥ* of Yahweh, was taken in their pits; of whom we said: 'Under his shadow we shall live among the nations.'" The words "*Mashiaḥ* of Yahweh" refer to King Josiah. In the book of Daniel the word *mashiaḥ* occurs twice. In one place the author designates *mashiaḥ* as *nagid,* ruler.[13] This undoubtedly is a reference to the high priest who, during the Second Commonwealth, was the spiritual as well as the secular ruler of the people.[14] In the other place the

9 Cf. *The First Apology,* 32. "A flower has sprung from the root of Jesse this Christ."

10 *The Epistle of Barnabas,* 5. "For the scripture concerning him relates partly to Israel, partly to us, and

it speaks thus: 'He was wounded for our iniquities. . . .'"

11 B. 1.55. ". . . My Jewish opponent replied that these predictions bore reference to the whole people. . . . And who is this person save Jesus

author wrote, "And after three score and two weeks shall the *mashiah* be cut off." [15] Here the author refers to the elimination of the priesthood of the Zadokite family. The book of Daniel, as we have it today, was composed after Judah Makkabee purified the Temple.[16] These passages were cited to show that in the Bible the word *mashiah* has the connotation of anointed and refers to the high priests or to the kings of the family of David. Modern theologians, Christian and Jewish, have injected the idea of the expectation of a personal, supernatural messiah into the Biblical passages. All histories of the Second Commonwealth are vitiated with the idea of messianic expectations.

True, the prophets do speak of a millennium—a period of happiness and prosperity when there will be no more wars between nations, and people will live in peace with one another. But this is not an expectation of a personal messiah. We must differentiate between a millennium and a messiah. The Prophet Isaiah, who according to tradition was of the family of David,[17] voiced a longing for a period when a descendant of Jesse, that is, of the family of David, imbued with the spirit of Yahweh, would rule. That day would be the time of the millennium, when "The wolf shall dwell with the lamb, and the leopard shall lie down with the kid; and the calf and the young lion and the fatling together; and a little child shall lead them" (11:6–10). There are messianic expectations in this passage. Isaiah hoped that a time would come when the Jews would prosper and live in peace as before at the time of King Solomon, a descendant of Jesse. Isaiah was a great patriot and nationalist. As a parallel we may cite the hope of a devotee of the Bourbon dynasty that the grandeur of France will be restored as in the time of Louis XIV.

That the Jews during the first part of the Second Commonwealth did not have the expectation of a personal messiah is evident from the literature produced during that period. The word *mashiah* does not occur in the book of Ben Sirah nor does it occur in the other apocryphal literature—Tobit, Judith, The Wisdom of Solomon, I Maccabees. In the latter it is stated that when the high priesthood was given to Simon the Hasmonean, a clause was inserted, "Until a true prophet will arrive in Israel." [18] From this we may deduce that Jews believed prophecy would be restored but there is no indication that they expected a messiah. Even in II Maccabees, wherein physical resurrection [19] and the hope that all Jews would be gathered in Judaea

Christ, by whose stripes they who believe on Him are healed."

12 Cf. Leviticus 4:3.
13 9:25.
14 Cf. also I Chronicles 9:11.
15 9:26.
16 Cf. *I Maccabees*, ed. Dropsie, p. 32.
17 Talmud Megillah 10.
18 Chap. 14:41.
19 See Chap. 7.

are given prominence, the word *mashiaḥ* does not occur—the author believed this would be accomplished through the intervention of God.

The term "messiah" occurs only in the apocalyptic literature; once in the Testament of the Twelve Patriarchs,[20] twice in the Book of Enoch,[21] and twice in the last two chapters of the Psalms of Solomon.[22] The first two books mentioned as well as the last two chapters of the Psalms of Solomon (17th–18th) were written after the time of Herod. We may even assume that "Lord Messiah" in Chapter 17 is a later Christian interpolation.[23] The word "messiah" also occurs in IV Ezra [24] and the Apocalypsis of Baruch.[25] the messiah is portrayed in this literature as being a scion of David who will rule over Israel and free the Jews from their foreign yoke. The Jews believed that the messiah would be a supernatural being and yet a son of David. In the Book of Enoch the son of David is named "the anointed of God," [26] "the Elect One," [27] "the Son of Man," [28] "the Son of God." [29]

This, then, is our paradox. The idea of a supernatural messiah is mentioned only in the apocalyptic books which were considered "outside books," profane—there had been an edict against reading them [30] —nevertheless the idea of a messiah possessing supernatural power became deeply rooted among the Jews, almost an article of faith. What were the forces which gave rise to the idea of a supernatural messiah? We have pointed out that the term *mashiaḥ* had the connotation of high priest, or King David and his son Solomon, who had been anointed with oil. What were the causes which brought about this persistent idea of a supernatural messiah? Ideas which have a profound influence and are lasting are not created in a vacuum or by the whim of a person, however important he may be.

To comprehend the origin of the idea of a supernatural messiah we must briefly review the political and spiritual conditions which prevailed at the time of the Restoration. At the head of the exiles who returned from Babylonia were two men, who represented influential political factions with diametrical ideological views. One was Joshua, the grandson of Seraiah, the high priest who had been killed by the Babylonians, representing the high priesthood. The other leader was Zerubbabel, the grandson of King Jehoiachin, representing the Davidic royal family. A clash developed between these two factions

---

20 *The Testament of Reuben*, 6:8.
21 48:10; 52:4.
22 17:6; 18:8.
23 Cf. H. E. Ryle and M. R. James, *Psalms of the Pharisees commonly called the Psalms of Solomon*, ad loc.

24 Cf. 5:29; 12:32.
25 29:3; 39:7; 40:1; 70:9. Cf. also S. Zeitlin, "The Apocrypha," *Jewish Quarterly Review*, 1947, pp. 239–248.
26 48:10.
27 49:2; 51:1.

as to how the Judaean community should be organized. The adherents of Joshua maintained that the community should be ruled by the high priest, the vicar of God. In other words that it be established as a theocracy. The followers of Zerubbabel held that the new community should be ruled by a scion of the family of David. The ideology of Joshua triumphed. Zerubbabel disappeared from the political and religious arena. The Judaean community was established as a theocracy.[31]

Although the Judaean community took the form of a theocracy, the idea that a scion of the family of David should rule over Israel was not obliterated from the minds of the people. Many Judaeans still hoped that ultimately the Judaean State would be ruled by a descendant of the family of David. This hope was cherished especially among the lower classes. It was so deeply held among the Judaeans that the author of I Maccabees, in giving the Testament of Mattathias the Hasmonean, said that David "inherited the throne of an everlasting kingdom." [32] Similarly Ben Sirah, writing in his book about Phineas, the grandson of Aaron to whom God gave the high priesthood forever, said that God made a covenant with David, the son of Jesse, to whom he gave an everlasting kingdom.[33]

The followers of Joshua were of the high priestly family of the Zadokites, the Sadducees. They were strict adherents to the written law. Although they recognized the unwritten law then in vogue, they did not hold it binding. To them only the laws of the Torah were binding. Since they strictly followed the Torah they held that Yahweh is an ethnic God, the God of the descendants of Abraham, Isaac, and Jacob, with whom He made a covenant and whose children He brought out of Egypt. Hence they still called the Temple built after the Restoration the House of Yahweh, using the same nomenclature applied to the Temple built by King Solomon. The followers of Zerubbabel maintained that the unwritten laws are on a par with the written laws, the Torah. They held that anyone who transgressed the unwritten laws would be liable to punishment as if he had transgressed the written laws.[34]

The group that held that the oral law is on a par with the Pentateuchal laws; that the new community should be established under the leadership of a scion of the Davidic family and not under the

28 62:14; 69:26.
29 69:4; 105:2.
30 M. Sanhedrin 11:1.
31 Cf. S. Zeitlin, *The Rise and Fall of the Judaean State*, 1962, pp. 6–12.

32 I Maccabees 2:57.
33 47:11.
34 Cf. S. Zeitlin, "The Pharisees," *Jewish Quarterly Review*, October, 1961, pp. 97–129; idem., op. cit.

leadership of a high priest; and that Yahweh is the God of all peoples and not an ethnic god was considered heretical by the Zadokites, the high priestly family. This group was called *Perushim*, Pharisees, separatists, by the Zadokites who maintained that they separated themselves from the Judaeans, the people of Yahweh. Down to the successful revolt under the leadership of the Hasmoneans the Pharisees had no influence over the affairs of the Judaean community but they had the confidence of the rank and file of the people.[35]

The Pharisees endeavored to solve the vexing problems of individuals—why did the righteous suffer and the wicked prosper? They taught the people that there was a future world where there would be reward and punishment—the reward for good deeds in this world and punishment for the wicked. They also impressed upon the minds of the people that the soul is immortal. The physical body dies but the soul lives forever. These theological views gave meaning and essence to the lives of the people, for they now felt that their good deeds in life were not in vain and were certain that they would be rewarded for them. That life in this world is passing while the future world is eternal became an article of faith. During the entire period of the Second Commonwealth the Pharisees stressed the views that one day leadership over the Jews would be vested in a scion of the family of David, and that there would be reward for the righteous and punishment for the wicked in the future world.

When the Hasmoneans succeeded in throwing off the yoke of the Syrians and eliminated the high priesthood of the Zadokite family, the influence of the Pharisees ascended. Daniel's words that the *mashiah* will be cut off, that is,[36] eliminated, refers to the abolishment of the high priesthood of the Zadokite family.

When the Judaean Commonwealth was established in 141 B.C.E. the Great Synagogue confirmed the high priesthood of Simon, the Hasmonean, and proclaimed him the ruler of the State. In this declaration there was a clause "until a true prophet will arise in Israel." The kingship was not given to him. With this act theocracy was abolished. But the view that Judaea should be a theocratic state was not entirely obliterated from the minds of all the people. Some of them longed for its re-creation. When the Roman general, Pompey, was in Syria, a deputation of Judaeans came to him asking that the kingship of Judaea be abolished and that the affairs of the community be placed in the hands of the high priest as in the olden days when the high priest was ecclesiastic as well as civil ruler over the people.[37]

35 *Ibid.*
36 9:26.

37 *Antiquities* 14. 3.2 (41).
38 *Ibid.*, 17. 11:2. (313–314).

In other words, they wanted Judaea to be a theocratic state. Similarly, after the death of Herod a deputation of Judaeans went to Augustus Caesar with the same petition.[38]

When Jannaeus Alexander assumed the kingship over Judaea the Pharisees bitterly opposed him. This brought about a civil war which ended tragically for the state. The Pharisees recognized that their struggle first with Jannaeus Alexander and later their participation in the civil war between John Hyrcanus and Aristobolus was catastrophic, so they abandoned political activity, devoting themselves to religion. They became quietists and legalists. However, there were groups among the Pharisees who continued to fight for the freedom of Judaea. Josephus tells that when Judaea was made a province of Rome in the year 6 C.E., Quirinus was sent by Rome to take a census of Judaea with a view to levying taxes upon the people. This aroused great opposition among the Judaeans. A man named Judas of Galilee organized a new group whose doctrines Josephus called the Fourth Philosophy.[39] This group was so named because Josephus deals with the Essenes, Sadducees, and Pharisees as philosophies, and names this group as the Fourth Philosophy. Josephus wrote about this group, "These men agree in all other things with the Pharasaic notions; but they have an inviolable attachment to liberty and say that God is to be their only ruler and Lord." He further said that Judas "incited his countrymen to revolt, upbraiding them as cowards for consenting to pay tribute to the Romans and tolerating mortal masters after having God for their Lord." [40] The followers of Judas from time to time resorted to seditious acts against the Romans. They also acted vigorously against their countrymen who submitted to the Romans. They considered as traitors such Judaeans who betrayed the freedom of their people. They held that terror must oppose terror.

Not being able to engage in open battle against the Romans and their followers, the Judaeans, the members of the Fourth Philosophy, resorted to the use of the *sica* (a short dagger) to assassinate those who favored peace with the enemy. From their use of the *sica* they received the name Sicarii [41] (not to be confused with the Zealots). Josephus referred to the Sicarii as robbers, brigands. He maintained that they were responsible for the destruction of the Judaean state and the burning of the Temple.

Of course the verdict of Josephus is a gross distortion of realities, for he himself said that hunger for freedom and liberty had motivated their actions. A speech which Josephus put in the mouth of Eleazar, son of Jairus, the last leader of the Fourth Philosophy before the fall

---

39 *Ibid.*, 18. 1.1(1–5); (23–25); *Jewish War* 2: 8.1 (107–108).

40 *Antiquities* 18. 1.6 (23–24).

41 *Ibid.*, 20. 8.10 (185–186).

of Masada, could not have come from the mouth of an ordinary robber: "Long since, my brave men, we determined neither to serve the Romans nor any other save God, for He alone is man's true and righteous Lord." He concluded his speech with the following, "For it is death which gives liberty to the soul and permits it to depart to its own pure abode, there to be free from all calamity; but so long as it is imprisoned in a mortal body tainted with all its miseries, it is in sober truth dead, for association with what is mortal ill befits that which is divine." [42] An ordinary brigand could not have uttered such noble sentiments, as Josephus would have us believe.

Josephus mentioned another group which he called wicked as were the members of the Fourth Philosophy. He gave no name to this group. In writing about these two groups he said that although their hands were purer than those of the Sicarii their intentions were more impious. "Deceivers and imposters under pretense of divine inspiration, fostering revolutionary changes," he said of them. "They persuaded the people to act like madmen, and led them out into the desert under the belief that God would there give them tokens of deliverance." [43]

This group was the Apocalyptists. Its members believed in the revelation of God and, therefore, the appelation of Apocalyptists is appropriate. The Apocalyptists as well as the members of the Fourth Philosophy, the Sicarii, were offshoots of the Pharisees. These two groups had the same objectives: to free the Judaeans from the yoke of the Romans as well as from the Herodean dynasty. They both maintained that God is the only ruler over man, but they differed in their methods of advocating this view. The members of the Fourth Philosophy held that terror must oppose terror. To free the Judaeans and destroy their adversaries, force and violence, even murder, were justified. The Apocalyptists were opposed to acts of terror and the use of violence. They preached love, their watchword was, "If one seeketh to do evil unto you, do well unto him and pray for him." [44] The Apocalyptists were God-fearing people who believed that God had not forsaken the Judaeans but only chastised them. They believed that He would reestablish Israel under His anointed *Mashiah,* that a scion of the family of David would rule in Zion and destroy the persecutors of His people as well as all the sinners. They considered *Mashiah* the anointed of Yahweh, not an ordinary human being, but

42 *Jewish War* 7. 8.6–7 (321–380).
43 *Ibid.,* 2. 13. 4 (259).
44 See *The Testament of the Twelve Patriarchs;* The Testament of

Joseph 18.2.
45 Cf. *Enoch* 51:2. "For in those days, the elect one shall arise and shall choose the righteous and the holy

one possessed of supernatural powers.[45] The Apocalyptists, aware of the might of Rome, knew that the Judaeans could not free themselves from the Romans by force. They believed that God would perform miracles to free His people. They introduced the idea of a supernatural *mashiah*, who would reveal himself in due time, vanquish the Romans, free Israel, and sit on the throne of his father David. Then the millennium would come, looked forward to by the prophets of old.

The Apocalyptists were a mystic religious group. Mysticism is belief in truths which are beyond comprehension and understanding. People whose minds are deranged by physical or mental suffering are led to join such groups, and in doing so they become fanatics. On the other hand, opportunists and adventurers join such groups out of selfish motives. Josephus refers to one, Theodas, who "persuaded a great part of the people to take their effects with them and follow him to the river Jordan, for he told them he was a prophet, and that he would by his command divide the river, and afford them an easy passage over it. Many were deluded by his words." [46] He also wrote about a man from Egypt who claimed to be a prophet. He "advised the people to come along with him to the Mount of Olives where he will perform miracles."[47] The Apocalyptists, however, in general were sincere, pious people. They believed that their revelations were given by angels and through supernatural powers, that the kingdom of God was approaching, and that the *Mashiah* of Yahweh would reveal himself in all his glory.

The normative Pharisees opposed both the Sicarii and the Apocalyptists. They may not have shared the view of Josephus that the Apocalyptists were imposters, charlatans, but they maintained that the Apocalyptists were deceiving themselves; that their views were in opposition to the true views of the Pharisees; and hence that the Judaeans would be led astray. The Pharisees believed that God would some day free His people from the Roman yoke, that the kingship would again be in the hands of *Mashiah* of Yahweh, a scion of David, but that the king would not possess supernatural power and would not perform miracles. In this view they greatly differed from the Apocalyptists.

The terms "*Mashiah* of Yahweh" and "son of David" are synonymous and interchangeable. The term *mashiah* in the Bible refers to David and his descendants. The author of Lamentations, deploring

from among them . . . and the elect one shall in those days sit on My Throne." See *Psalms of Solomon* 17:23, "Raise up unto them their king, the son of David."

46 See *Antiquities* 20. 5. 1 (97–99).

47 *Jewish War* 2. 13. 5 (261–262); Cf. also *Acts* 21:38.

the untimely death of King Josiah, calls him the *Mashiah* of Yah-weh.[48] The Talmud says that Rabbi Akiba called Bar Kokba "King *Mashiah*." One of Rabbi Akiba's colleagues said to him, "Grass will grow through thy jaws, and the time of the son of David has not come."[49] The term "son of David" and "king *mashiah*" are synony-mous.

The gospels according to both Matthew [50] and Luke [51] trace the genealogy of Jesus to David, while Mark, who does not give the gene-alogy, states that Jesus is the son of David.[52] John, who stresses the view that Jesus was the son of God, nevertheless wrote, "But some said, Shall Christ come out of Galilee? Hath not the scripture said, that Christ cometh out of the seed of David and out of the town of Bethlehem where David was?" [53] According to the gospels Jesus was greeted with the words, "Blessed be the kingdom of our father David," "Hosanna to the son of David." [54] On the cross on which Jesus was crucified the words "Jesus of Nazareth, king of the Judaeans" were inscribed in Hebrew, Greek, and Latin.[55] *Mashiah*, messiah, Christ were synonymous in their minds with "son of David" and "king of the Judaeans."

After the burning of the Temple, and particularly after the tragic collapse of the Bar Kokba revolt, the belief in a supernatural messiah who would rebuild the Temple and restore the Jewish state gained sway over the minds of the people. This was their only hope. Physical revolts ended in catastrophe and they looked for their salvation, re-demption, to a supernatural *mashiah*. Not all the sages,[56] however, shared this view and it never became an article of faith. Rabbi Judah the Prince, in codifying the Mishnah, does not refer to the belief in a *mashiah*. Reference is once made to the days of *mashiah*.[57] In the Mishnah it is stated that those who do not believe in Revelation and resurrection will not have a share in the world to come.[58] Denial of the coming of *mashiah* is not included in this category. Many Tan-naim and Amoraim, however, believed in the coming of the *Mashiah*

---

48 4:20.
49 *Yerushalmi. Taanit* 4; *Midrash R. Lamentations* 2.
50 1:1–16:
51 3:24–31.
52 12:35.
53 7:41–42.
54 *Mark* 11:10; *Matt.* 21:9.
55 *Iesus Nazarenus, Rex Iudaeorum.*
56 Cf. also Maimonides *Mishne Torah,* Hilkot Melachim. Maimonides held that Messiah would be a mortal, a king, a descendant of the house

of David, a man wiser than Solo-mon, and a prophet next in great-ness to Moses.
57 *Mishnah Berachot* 1.6. The phrase, "the footsteps of the *mashiah*" oc-curs in the *Mishnah Sotah* 9. 15. This part, however, is a later addi-tion; the name of Rabbi Phineas ben Jair is mentioned in this Mishnah which indicates that it was interpolated after the time of Rabbi Judah.
58 *Mishnah Sanhedrin* 10. 1.

and even indulged in predictions as to the time when he will reveal himself.

Belief in a supernatural *mashiah,* a scion of the family of David, was first brought forth by the Apocalyptic Pharisaic group. It did not greatly influence the Judaeans during the Second Commonwealth, but after the destruction of the Second Temple, and particularly after the revolt of Bar Kokba, it gained stimulus and shaped the life of the Jewish people throughout the centuries. The idea of a supernatural *mashiah* became the cornerstone of Jewish survival, as is admirably portrayed by Doctor Abba Hillel Silver in his book *A History of Messianic Speculation in Israel.*

THE CONTRIBUTORS

David Ben Gurion—Prime Minister, The State of Israel

Izhak Ben-Zvi—President, The State of Israel

Moshe Davis—Provost, The Jewish Theological Seminary of America

Abba Eban—President, The Weizmann Institute of Science

Morton Scott Enslin—Professor of Biblical Languages and Literature, St. Lawrence University

Walter J. Fischel—Professor of Semitic Languages and Literature, University of California

Solomon B. Freehof—Rabbi, Rodef Shalom Temple, Pittsburgh

Nelson Glueck—President, The Hebrew Union College

Robert Gordis—Rabbi, Seminary Professor of Bible, Jewish Theological Seminary of America

Miriam Leikind—Librarian, The Temple, Cleveland

Walter Clay Lowdermilk—Sometime Professor of Agricultural Engineering, The Technion

Harold P. Manson—Executive, American Friends of the Hebrew University

Jacob Rader Marcus—Adolph S. Ochs Professor of Jewish History, The Hebrew Union College

Benjamin Mazar—President Emeritus, The Hebrew University

Emanuel Neumann—Chairman, American Branch, Inc., Jewish Agency for Israel

Harry M. Orlinsky—Professor of Bible, The Hebrew Union College

Raphael Patai—Director of Research, The Theodor Herzl Institute

Oskar K. Rabinowicz—Banker and Author

Ellis Rivkin—Professor of Jewish History, The Hebrew Union College

Samuel Sandmel—Professor of Bible and Hellenistic Literature, The Hebrew Union College

Gershom Scholem—Professor of Jewish Mysticism, The Hebrew University

Moshe Sharett—Chairman, Jewish Agency for Israel

Zalman Shazar—Head, Department of Education and Culture in the Diaspora, The Jewish Agency

Daniel Jeremy Silver—Rabbi, The Temple, Cleveland

Naphtali Herz Tur-Sinai—Bialik Professor of Hebrew Philosophy, Emeritus, The Hebrew University

Solomon Zeitlin—Horace Stern Professor of Rabbinic Law and Lore, The Dropsie College